THE
UNOFFICIAL ENCYCLOPEDIA
OF THE
ROCK AND ROLL HALL OF FAME

THE
UNOFFICIAL
ENCYCLOPEDIA
OF THE
ROCK AND ROLL
HALL OF FAME

NICK TALEVSKI

GREENWOOD PRESS
Westport, Connecticut • London

Library of Congress Cataloging-in-Publication Data

Talevski, Nick, 1962–
    The unofficial encyclopedia of the Rock and Roll Hall of Fame /
Nick Talevski.
        p.   cm.
    Includes bibliographical references (p.   ) and index.
    ISBN 0–313–30032–1 (alk. paper)
    1. Rock music—Bio-bibliography.   2. Rock and Roll Hall of Fame
and Museum.   3. Rock music—History and criticism.
ML105.T3   1998
781.66′074′77132—dc21   97–41928

British Library Cataloguing in Publication Data is available.

Library of Congress Catalog Card Number: 97–41928
ISBN: 0–313–30032–1

First published in 1998

Greenwood Press, 88 Post Road West, Westport, CT 06881
An imprint of Greenwood Publishing Group, Inc.

Printed in the United States of America

The paper used in this book complies with the
Permanent Paper Standard issued by the National
Information Standards Organization (Z39.48–1984).

10 9 8 7 6 5 4 3 2 1

The Rock and Roll Hall of Fame and Museum did not participate in the
writing, editing, or publication of this book and does not endorse the
information contained herein.

Every reasonable effort has been made to trace the owners of copyright
materials in this book, but in some instances this has proven impossible.
The author and publisher will be glad to receive information leading to
more complete acknowledgments in subsequent printings of the book
and in the meantime extend their apologies for any omissions.

Contents

Preface

This book is divided into four parts: three chapters and the main biographical section. Chapter 1 explores the life of "Mr. Rock and Roll," Alan Freed, and details his essential contributions to the early development of rock music. Chapter 2 chronicles Cleveland's selection over several competing cities as the Hall of Fame site and the turbulent history of the museum's construction. Chapter 3 reviews each year's induction ceremony, from bizarre acceptance speeches to mismatched concert pairings, in an annual rite that has produced some notable moments.

Arranged in an A-to-Z format, the main portion of the book tracks the personal lives and recording careers of the Hall of Fame's first 150 inductees. The individual biographies are presented in a chronological form. Chart positions were culled from several U.S. and U.K. sources. In the case of albums, the date listed refers to the year of issue, while in the case of singles, the date indicates the year of chart entry.

In dispelling well-established rock myths, the information within this book sometimes contradicts other reference sources. Every effort has been made to corroborate the facts included within the covers of this book. In the same spirit that gave rise to rock and roll, this book celebrates the freedom of the press and is in no way authorized by the Rock and Roll Hall of Fame and Museum. Additionally, the Rock and Roll Hall of Fame and Museum is a registered trademark, and this book is in no way connected to or endorsed by that institution.

Acknowledgments

My first memory of rock music came poolside at a Holiday Inn in Columbus, Ohio, at age 3 with a sunbather's transistor radio pumping out the Supremes' magnificent "Baby Love." Little could I realize at the time that music would play such an important role throughout my life.

The following people have been of great assistance in the development of this work: Jeff Terrell, David Graves, John M. Riley, John Mascolo, Erich Schrader, Brian Siewiorek, Joe Finan, Jeff Tamarkin, Steve Petryszyn, Cheryl Peters, Chris Quinn of WRMR/Cleveland, and Gary Felsinger (whose 40-year record collection often contradicted "the facts" offered by many rock reference books). Additionally I am indebted to Professor Robert West for his unmatched musical knowledge and editing skills.

Also helpful were Kent State University library assistants Stuart Moye and Jeph Remley; the interlibrary loan department at Kent State University; Karla Steward and Mary Lyons at the Fine Arts Department at the Akron Public Library; Anna J. Horton at the Public Library of Cincinnati and Hamilton County; and curator William L. Schurk at the Bowling Green State University music library. While I am forever grateful to those who offered encouragement, to the naysayers, the last laugh is mine. Lastly, I would like to thank my editor, Alicia Merritt, who put up with my many delays.

Introduction

On Labor Day weekend 1995, 22 million viewers witnessed a seven-hour, superstar concert on HBO in celebration of the opening of the Rock and Roll Hall of Fame in Cleveland, Ohio. Surviving four decades and selling billions of records, rock and roll had finally earned some respect. Consumed in civic pride, the Cleveland populace was also celebrating its baseball team's first trip to the World Series in half a century, as well as the kickoff of the city's bicentennial.

Unlike the Grammys, the Soul Train Awards, or the American Music Awards, the Rock and Roll Hall of Fame serves to enshrine both the pioneers and giants of rock music. By 1998, a total of 150 inductees had been enshrined in the museum, these individuals encompassing all avenues of rock music, including musical artists, producers, record company founders, and deejays. Sometimes controversial, these choices are announced each autumn, with an induction ceremony staged the following January.

While Elvis Presley's Memphis mansion, Graceland, pulls 700,000 annual visitors, the $92 million rock shrine in Cleveland drew 1 million pilgrims to that city in its first year of operation. A glittering lakeside, pyramid-shaped glass-and-steel structure, the Hall of Fame has surpassed all expectations.

Its walls jammed with more than guitars and old stage props, the museum is an archive of twentieth century popular culture. Presenting a cross-section of often disparate musical styles, the Rock Hall has attempted to chronicle the story of the music that changed the world. Once considered a passing fad, rock music has survived its myriad of critics.

Opening its doors 12 years after first envisioned, the Rock Hall was erected in a stormy atmosphere, in which artistry and brilliance competed with egos and politics. Syndicated humorist Dave Barry once suggested that the Rock Hall should be "the kind of place that you absolutely forbid your children to go to, but they go there anyway. . . . It should be loud. The other businesses in Cleveland should have to call the police constantly to demand that the Rock 'n' Roll Hall of Fame be turned down.

To get inside the Rock 'n' Roll Hall of Fame, you should have to wait in a ticket line outside in the rain for two days" (p. G9).

Still, some rock stars have publicly questioned the notion of putting the rebellion of rock on public display behind a glass wall. But when the Hall of Fame inducted its first class of rock pioneers, the music industry embraced the event and granted the ceremony instant credibility.

Bibliography

Barry, Dave. (1991, February 17). Rock 'n' roll exhibits high class in Cleveland. *Atlanta Journal and Constitution*, p. G9.

PART I

General Background

CHAPTER 1

Alan Freed and a Brief History of Rock and Roll

The city of Cleveland earned the right to claim the Rock and Roll Hall of Fame and Museum because of the foresight and enthusiasm of one pioneering fan of black music, deejay Alan Freed. "At 11:15 at night, after the news and sports, after Mom and Dad turned off the lights, he hit the airwaves at WJW like a renegade evangelist, selling sin instead of salvation, barking his message over choruses of strip-show horns and crap-game crooners, pounding his palm raw on a telephone book to bring home the beat" (p. 34), writes Tom Junod in *Life* magazine.

"Hello everybody, how y'all tonight? This is Alan Freed, the old 'King of the Moondoggers,'" the golden-throated deejay would begin his Cleveland-based radio show in the early 1950s. Crosstown deejay Joe Finan recalled: "The first time I heard him, I didn't know who he was. This guy's voice made me feel like he was in the room, that this is somebody I want to know. He came across three-dimensionally. Most disc jockeys were vanilla; he wasn't." First calling the music he played "rhythm and blues," Freed was crucial to the genesis of the revolutionary musical form called "rock and roll," giving the music its name.

Born in Windber, Pennsylvania, in 1922, Alan Freed moved several times as a young child before settling in Salem, Ohio, a small industrial city located between Youngstown and Akron. While his father worked as a clothier, Alan played trombone in his high school orchestra and led a New Orleans-style jazz band called the Sultans of Swing. At home, Freed's musically proficient family would gather around their piano to play big band-style jazz.

Attending Ohio State University in 1940, he majored in mechanical engineering. Though never stepping foot in the studios of the campus radio station, he often spoke of getting his start there. Young and impatient, Freed left school in 1941 to join the army. But after training for the ski patrol, he received a medical discharge a year later.

After returning to Salem and attending broadcasting school, Freed landed his first radio job at nearby WKST in New Castle, Pennsylvania, a station he would later describe as a broom closet. But by 1943, Freed had worked his way to the area's radio powerhouse, WKBN in Youngstown, landing the job by exaggerating his experience.

Playing classical music, including his favorite composer, Wagner, Freed also provided play-by-play for local football games.

Hired as a newsman in 1945 by ABC affiliate WAKR in Akron, Freed soon landed an evening deejay position, given the job when the scheduled announcer was fired for calling off. Playing contemporary pop music for the first time, Freed was an immediate sensation, his program sponsored by the now defunct O'Neils Department Store. Dominating the local airwaves, at the station's peak of popularity, WAKR drew an amazing 60 percent share of the market.

Every Saturday night, Freed hosted WAKR's *Request Review* program, broadcasting his show in front of a live in-studio audience of about 70 dancing teenagers, spinning hot jazz and big band swing, as well as pioneering rhythm and blues discs by artists such as Louis Jordan. Hiring a local 17-year-old pianist, Erich Schrader, a high school student with a penchant for upbeat boogie-woogie music, Freed would sometimes join in with his trombone. First using the term "rock and roll" in early 1946, Alan Freed would signal his younger musical partner, "'Are you ready to *rock and roll'* or 'let's get *rockin*',"" recalled Schrader.

Adopting his first radio nickname, Knucklehead Freed, the charismatic deejay became a local celebrity who was mobbed by autograph hounds. Emceeing teen sock-hops at a rented Catholic church hall in the Firestone Park section of Akron, Freed first donned his trademark plaid sports coat and bowtie, playing records for the sons and daughters of the region's tire-factory workers.

With his star on the ascent and the tripling of his salary from $60.50 a week to a then-hefty $200, Freed signed a contract containing radio's first-ever noncompete clause in 1948, prohibiting him from working within a 75-mile radius for a year, should he quit or be fired.

After hiring Lew Platt as his personal manager, Freed was fired in 1949 for demanding another raise. Walking out of WAKR's cellar studio, in a business arcade at the base of Akron's tallest building, Freed marched across the street to the since demolished two-story structure that housed WADC and transplanted his popular request program. Taken to court by WAKR's attorney-owners, Freed was off the air the very next day, legally barred from radiowork in both Akron and nearby Cleveland. Taking the case all the way to the Ohio Supreme Court, an incredulous Freed tried to take over the questioning from his own lawyer.

Losing his court case, Freed then was hired by a new Cleveland television station, WXEL channel 9, billed as a "teejay," and playing mostly Bing Crosby and other pop schmaltz. While the station was within the forbidden 75-mile radius, his previous contract failed to mention television (at the time Freed signed his radio contract, Ohio had only two operating stations). Attempting to adapt his radio program to the small screen, Freed had the camera zoom in on the spinning record during the song. With the program bombing, Freed was then cast as the co-host of an afternoon film matinee.

Returning to radio in June 1951, at 50,000-watt WJW in Cleveland, Freed was hidden away in the late-night graveyard shift. Initially playing a fare of classical music, Freed had landed the job with the assistance of his friend, record store owner Leo Mintz.

Mintz had operated the landmark Record Rendezvous store since 1939, initially selling used jukebox records that he had purchased for a couple cents each. Relocating several times before settling in downtown Cleveland, Record Rendezvous was one of the few places in Cleveland that sold records by Muddy Waters, Big Joe Turner, Wynonie Harris, and other singers popular in the black community.

These records were manufactured by a growing network of independent labels that emerged after World War II following several technological advances which had simplified the recording process. Nurturing rhythm and blues, many of these record companies had humble beginnings, often starting as one-man operations with records sold right out of car trunks. With the unwillingness of white-owned record labels to cater to the black record buyer and jukebox operator, these renegade entrepreneurs filled a growing consumer demand. Emerging record companies like Atlantic, King-Federal, and Chess began dominating the R&B charts and later the pop charts, all the while breaking the monopoly held by six established labels: Capitol, Columbia, Decca, Mercury, MGM, and RCA.

Like other record stores of the day, Record Rendezvous sported telephone booth-like listening rooms where customers could preview a potential purchase. Beginning in 1951, Mintz noticed that white teenagers were entering the booths with R&B records in hand. Former Cleveland disc jockey and program director Robert West, now a Kent State University professor, recalled that "a lot of white kids went in there and bought R&B—I know I did; there were blacks too." Informing the skeptical Freed of the practice, Mintz convinced him to program the music on WJW. Building upon his teenage love of jazz, Freed enjoyed playing the upbeat, sax-heavy R&B discs by acts like Fats Domino and Earl Bostic.

Possessing charm and wit, Freed had a velvety-cool style that his fans wanted to identfy with. "He would march around the room, and yell and shout, and would really get enthusiastic. He was brilliant on the air. He could grab an audience. He obviously enjoyed very much what he was doing—and he loved the music," recalls Robert West. "On occasion, if Alan had to go down the hall or go out to buy a beer, his brother David Freed would cover and nobody would ever know the difference; their voices were identical." Rival deejay Joe Finan remembers: "Alan always had a beer in the studio, and Erin Brew was the number one sponsor, so the station would look the other way."

From that brief overnight slot, Freed was soon promoted to a several-hour-long evening shift, quickly owning the Cleveland and Akron black radio market and slowly attracting a white audience. Cleveland alone claimed a population of 130,000 blacks in 1950, drawn to northern industrial centers during the wartime labor shortages. Only 8,500 blacks called Cleveland their home 40 years earlier in 1910. Black populations were also settling in the northern centers of Chicago and Detroit, with Chicago becoming the breeding ground for postwar electric blues, and Detroit, later, for Motown soul.

But with the strict segregation of postwar America, black music styles had mostly been restricted within black neighborhoods, played in the jukeboxes in black bars, sold in tiny, black-owned record stores, and played by a handful of black deejays around the country. But in Cleveland, Alan Freed provided blacks with an unlikely voice. "He was accepted with open arms" by the black community, "because he was

From his yearbook the *Quaker*, young Alan Freed at Salem High School. In top photo Freed is third from the left, holding his trombone. In bottom photo Freed is in the center row, fourth from the right. (*Photos courtesy of Nick Talevski.*)

the gatekeeper to a full three or four hours a night of the music which barely got on the air," recalled Joe Finan. Robert West remembered: "That's what blacks liked: A white guy playing their music. It made their music legitimate, it made it valid, that a white disc jockey would play nothing but black music, which in Cleveland was all that he played; he wouldn't play any white artists. He played 'blues and rhythm' as he called it." The promise of "integration" was seen as a victory for black Americans, who began to believe that equality was attainable.

But Freed was not the first deejay to play R&B records, just the most famous. At WLAC in Nashville, white deejay Gene Nobles was playing jazz and some proto-R&B in the early 1940s, with his program later evolving into the popular *Randy's Record Shop Show*. On the West Coast, former jazz deejay Hunter Hancock was playing R&B on KFVD in Los Angeles, while the bookwormish Zenas "Daddy" Sears spun blues and R&B on the state-owned WGST in Atlanta. The target of racist groups, Freed and other white R&B deejays received frequent threats. Bill Lowery told author Wes Smith that deejay Zenas Sears received many phoned-in "challenges for him to step outside because somebody wanted to blow him away" (pp. 70-71).

During this period, few blacks held radio programs on prominent stations. On WDIA in Memphis, Nat D. Williams was billed as "the Mid-South's first Negro disc jockey." Because of its strong nighttime signal, WDIA had a near-monopoly of millions of black listeners across dozens of states and into Canada, becoming the most influential black radio station in the country in terms of disseminating and popularizing all forms of black music, including gospel, blues, and R&B.

Back in Cleveland, Mintz had given Freed an obscure record by an eccentric Manhattan street musician named Moondog that featured a howling dog, homemade instruments and a jungle-boogie beat. Adopting the song as his theme, Freed would then segue into the Todd Rhodes 1947 hit "Blues for the Red Boy." Freed started to call himself the Moondog, and his show evolved into *The Moondog Rhythm and Blues House Party*, with the term "rock and roll" soon incorporated into the program's name to make the music more palatable to white America.

While both Leo Mintz and Alan Freed have been individually credited with coining the term "rock and roll" to describe the new music in 1951, Freed had been using the phrase on the air since 1946, during his first year at WAKR in Akron. With its origin remaining elusive, and its definition a far more complicated matter, the word "rock" was first used in the title of a record in 1922, when a nervous, unknown blues singer named Trixie Smith entered a primitive recording studio to record "My Man Rocks Me (With a Steady Roll)." The disc was released by Black Swan, the first black-owned and -operated record company, and included blues pioneer W.C. Handy on its board of directors.

For the first half of the century, the term "rock and roll" was also a euphemism for sex. The phrase appeared in the title of a song for the first time in 1934, by an immensely popular, all-white vocal trio, the Boswell Sisters. But this typical 1930s-era showtune was far from rock and roll. By the late 1940s, pockets of southern blacks began calling rhythm and blues concerts "rock and roll parties." When Wynonie Harris scored a hit in 1948 with the Roy Brown-composed "Good Rockin' Tonight," he became the first R&B artist to feature the term in a hit song title.

But up to the late 1940s, the term "race music" was still being used to describe all nonclassical forms of black music, with "sepia" and "Harlem," as in "Harlem Hit Parade," used less frequently. But in 1949, the editors at *Billboard* magazine decided that the phrase "race music" was insulting to blacks and, as a staff project, spent much of the year debating a replacement. When a young writer, Jerry Wexler (whose fame came as a co-owner of Atlantic Records), suggested "rhythm and blues," the editors adopted it immediately, with the term becoming the industry standard. An obscure, postwar phrase, the origin of "rhythm and blues" also remains elusive. Emerging in the late 1940s, "R&B" was a combination of blues, hot jazz, and gospel, while rock and roll added a touch of country music, which itself had a mutually incestuous relationship with the blues.

R&B's first star, Louis Jordan, began as a novelty act in the jazz and vaudeville traditions. Introducing the 2/4, shuffle-boogie beat to popular music, Jordan's swinging, up-tempo, danceable, saxophone-heavy music did not have a name: it wasn't jazz, it wasn't big band, and most of Jordan's material certainly was not traditional, 12-bar blues.

But it was not adults who became enthralled with this new black-based musical style. With a booming economy and postwar babyboom, the number of high school students had doubled to 10 million in the decade ending in 1955. The rise of rock and R&B coincided with the sociological creation of this "teenage" class, which unlike any previous generation, exerted its own cultural independence and financial affluence.

Rock music was also the by-product of technological advances, as teenagers began carrying Japanese-made, solid-state, portable transistor radios, which freed youth from parental supervision of programming choices: teens could now secretly tune in to the R&B station abhorred by their parents. With the money-spending teenager in mind, in 1949 RCA introduced the microgroove, seven-inch, vinylite 45 rpm record. Wanting to popularize the inexpensive "45," RCA began selling compatible record players at below cost.

Within two years, the size of Freed's white radio audience at WJW surpassed that of his black audience. But throughout the histories of ragtime, jazz, blues, and R&B, there had always been a tradition of hip whites venturing uptown to absorb black culture. A few white musicians like Mezz Mezzrow and Johnny Otis have taken this fascination to an extreme, by publicly revoking their whiteness.

In Cleveland, adventurous whites frequented East Side black nightclubs like Gleason's Musical Bar, Leo's Casino, Chin Ballard, and The Majestic Hotel. Nicknamed "black and tans," these clubs tolerated white visitors, giving them their first glimpses of jazz, low-down blues, or jumping R&B.

Expanding into concert promotion in 1951, Alan Freed and Leo Mintz were bankrolled by a pair of Akronites, Lew Platt and Milton Kulkin. Experiencing a rocky start, Freed was banned from the prestigious Meyer's Lake Ballroom in nearby Canton after a crowd of 2,500 "negroes" caused massive damage to the venue following an R&B concert.

Considered the first modern rock concert, Freed's most notorious show took place on March 21, 1952, at the 15-year-old Cleveland Arena, a hockey venue that no one believed he could fill. Although Freed had sponsored a number of smaller concerts around northeast Ohio, the mere size of the Cleveland show, plus the fact the audience consisted of blacks and whites alike, earned it the designation as the first rock and roll concert.

Billed as "the Moondog Coronation Ball," Freed had limited advertising to his radio program. Remarkably, all 7,500 tickets were sold the same day they were available. Celebrating the success, Freed's partner, Leo Mintz, took his family to Florida for a brief vacation. But due to overeagerness and miscommunication, no one was prepared for what came next. Mintz's son, Stuart, told *Scene* magazine in 1986: "On that same Tuesday, my uncle . . . had another 7,500 tickets printed up; he thought, 'If we sold that fast, we can sell another 7,500.' But he forgot to say 'second show' on the tickets. My dad got a call . . . in Florida with a voice begging, 'Leo, come home'" (p. 9).

Arriving in a taxi directly from the airport, Mintz was overwhelmed by the sight of thousands of well-dressed youth who had immobilized the boulevard for a block in each direction. When Mintz saw what was happening, he turned around and flew back to Florida. Recalls *Life* magazine: "So they came. By foot. By bicycle. By streetcar and by bus. They came from beyond Cleveland, too, from Akron, from Canton, from all over the industrial north of Ohio, many of them the children of the great black northern migration, just a generation removed from the farm, from Mississippi and Arkansas and Louisiana and the holy hell of the rural South, gathered now for the biggest party in the history of Cleveland" (p. 36).

Coheadlined by the Dominoes and Paul Williams, whose 1949 hit "The Hucklebuck" spawned a huge dance craze of the same name, no one involved with the concert was prepared for the crowd. The concert was to conclude with a grand ceremony in which Freed was to be crowned the "King of the Moondoggers." Though sold out, Freed announced the previous night that an additional 2,000 tickets were to be made available the day of the show, thereby drawing thousands more to the scene. With the early arrivals already getting rowdy, the Arena's bar was closed at 10:30.

Unequipped for music concerts, the Arena lacked adequate security and crowd control personnel, with the suited ticket window men leaving their posts at the first sign of trouble among the young, boisterous, but not yet rioting Moondoggers. A witness later told *Life* magazine: "Oh, Lord, how they poured into the hall, and soon the crowd began to move in enormous rhythmic waves, back and forth, then in a mad swirl. And then a fight started, and another, and another" (p. 36). Paul Williams, who was onstage at the time, later told Norm N. Nite on his radio program: "We played the first number and . . . I saw the doors and they looked like they were breathing." With the music starting, and thousands still outside (many without tickets), the steel doors buckled with the weight of those trying to get in, and bang, every massive door slammed to the ground, one after the other.

Opening act Paul Williams continued to play until the raging fans overtook the stage. Telling *Life* magazine, Williams recalled that as a performer, he was used to seeing people "killed every way you can imagine; Knives, guns, hammers, baseball bats—every way a person can die, I've just about seen it. And there's only one thing you can do, and that's keep on playing" (p. 36). With the crowd spilling over, 40 police officers and 30 firemen were radioed to converge on the hall.

While the *Cleveland Plain Dealer* estimated the crowd at 16,000, a suburban newspaper put the number at 25,000, and the local black newspaper, the *Call & Post* referred to the audience as "some 20,000 rabid blues fans." The *Akron Beacon Journal* reported: "Hepcats jammed every inch of the Arena floor, took every seat, filled the aisles and packed the lobby and sidewalk, overflowing onto Euclid Ave. It was impossible to dance and the orchestra could not be heard over the din" (p. A2). The *Call & Post* provided the most sensational account, describing the event as a place where males "were wearing their hats inside a public place, guzzling liquor without restraint from pocket flasks, and, here and there, actually shooting themselves with narcotics in the midst of a crowd!" (p. 2B). With politicians and civic groups in an uproar, Freed was threatened with prosecution.

Fearing imprisonment and the loss of his job, Alan Freed was unusually somber behind his microphone the next night. In a much bootlegged recording of the broadcast, Freed apologized to his many listeners, "If you wish to lay the blame on me for what happened last night, you're certainly welcome." Begging for forgiveness, he asked his fans to telephone, and send letters and telegrams to station management to keep him on the air.

An essential part of the concert's success was Cleveland's popularity as a destination for jazz and R&B acts. The same week as the Moondog Coronation Ball, scores of touring acts were scheduled to perform in Cleveland. Lionel Hampton was playing the Towne Casino; John Lee Hooker headlined an "all star Harlem Revue" at the Circle Theater; the Orioles and Jimmy Forrest were at the Ebony Lounge; and the Coronation Ball's coheadliners, the Dominoes, were already in town, booked for a week of nightclub gigs. Cleveland radio legend Norm N. Nite told interviewer Jesse Wilder, "So many performers came here from the South or wherever because of Freed and because of the hotbed of entertainment—both East and West side: Acts like a Little Richard or a Fats Domino playing at some small club on Prospect or 55th Street or Moe's Main Street on 77th and Euclid. It was amazing, utterly amazing. It was all here" (p. 143). "That was hip stuff," recalled Chuck Young, an independent record promotor and a central figure in the rise of rock in Cleveland, in a 1990 *Scene* interview: "On Friday and Saturday nights there would be more white people in these clubs than black people. You couldn't get in. There were lines outside" (p. 9).

With Freed's concert promotions thriving, he further expanded his music empire. Launching his own record company, Champagne, he first signed the Crazy Sounds, which he renamed the Moonglows, after his radio nickname. Angering business partner Leo Mintz, Freed also opened his own record store. But most significantly, Freed's WJW radio program was being syndicated around the country and was heard in New York City via a tiny suburban station, Newark's WNJR.

But in April 1953, an overworked Freed nearly died in an automobile crash when he drove his car into a tree. Suffering massive internal and facial injuries, Freed underwent extensive plastic surgery to repair his face. Always wearing makeup to hide his facial scars, Freed's injuries would nag him the rest of his life. "My father used to say to me 'I am living on borrowed time. I shouldn't be here so I have nothing to lose.' I think he had a feeling that you should live your life as a meteorite burning fast and furiously" (pp. 165-66), son, Lance Freed, told interviewer Les Smith.

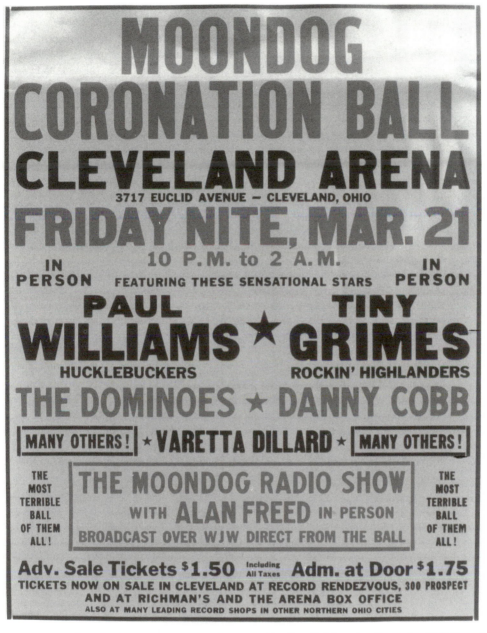

Concert poster from the first-ever rock and roll concert, Alan Freed's Moondog Coronation Ball. Staged on March 21, 1952, the oversold show ended in a riot. (*Photo courtesy of the Steve Petryszyn Rock History Archives.*)

Bandaged, but back behind the microphone at WJW within two months, Freed also returned to concert promotions. Headlined by the Dominoes and the Drifters, he launched a record-setting 30-city, all-star R&B revue, which turned away crowds at every stop, attracting its biggest audiences in Cleveland. The national press was caught off guard by Freed's success, and the music industry bible, *Billboard* magazine, began reporting his every move. Labeled the "Pied Piper" of rock and roll, Freed had become its ultimate salesman. "Alan Freed could sell tickets to the end of the world—to the first *and* second shows" (p. 11), Cleveland-born R&B pioneer Screamin' Jay Hawkins proclaimed in *Nowhere to Run*.

Thanks to Freed, Cleveland became the breakout city for new music. Deejay Joe Finan recalled that in Cleveland, a radio station could hype up a record on Monday, play it four or five times in an afternoon, and have people clamoring for the disc by Thursday. "There wasn't another city that was as fast at the retail level than Cleveland, and that's why [record companies] came here, that's why they spent their money here." Recalls Cleveland deejay and music historian Chris Quinn: "Many, many, many acts were broken out of Cleveland. Cleveland was responsible for a lot of hits, a lot of careers over the years." Chuck Young, the first music director of the 50,000-watt clear-channel outlet KYW, recalled in *Scene* that, "we were the first radio station in the country to play Bobby Darin's first hit, 'Splish Splash,' 'Chantilly Lace' by the Big Bopper, Jackie Wilson's 'Reet Petite,' Bobby Day's 'Rockin' Robin' and Freddy Cannon's 'Tallahassee Lassie.' We were playing the first four Buddy Holly records before anyone in the United States. This was almost a weekly thing, that we'd be breaking million selling records. There had to be over 200 million [sellers] that our station was responsible for. We played them all first" (p. 9).

Freed shared the Cleveland airwaves with several other powerful personalities, including Tommy Edwards, Joe Finan, Phil McLean, and Carl Reese; WJW's morning drive-time jock was a young Soupy Heinz (later known as comic Soupy Sales). But Freed's main local rival was another nationally renowned deejay, Bill Randle. Music historian Peter Guralnick wrote in *Last Train to Memphis*, "Bill Randle was a legend in radio at that time. Tall, scholarly-looking with black horn-rimmed glasses, he had just been written up in *Time*," which boasted that he "had predicted all but one of the top-five best-sellers of 1954, discovered Johnnie Ray, changed the name of the Crew-Cuts (from the Canadianaires) as well as finding them their first hit, drove a Jaguar, and made a $100,000 a year, with his Saturday-afternoon CBS network show in New York the latest in his series of unprecedented accomplishments" (pp. 176-77). Like Freed, Randle also challenged radio's prevalent color barrier. Once fired for playing a black gospel version of "Silent Night" by Sister Rosetta Tharpe, Randle was rehired when listeners clamored for his return.

Cleveland deejay Joe Finan recalled that "every artist Randle played," he called "the most exciting. He even does that today." But Randle's most important discovery came in 1955, when he predicted the stardom of a southern hillbilly singer, introducing the unknown artist on his program. When Finan was asked by Jud Phillips (brother of Sam Phillips) of Sun Records to play the Memphis-based singer, who had just landed on the country charts with his debut single "Baby Let's Play House," Finan balked: "Hearing Elvis Presley for the first time, as far as I was concerned he was a hilljack and I wasn't going to play him." But Randle did, becoming the first pop deejay north of the Mason-Dixon line to embrace the meteoric singer. Randle was leery about spinning the new Elvis Presley records on his weekend New York program but knew that Cleveland listeners would be receptive to the new artist.

"The impact of Randle's spinning of [Elvis Presley's] Sun disks in Cleveland was unforeseen and quite shattering. Teen-age listeners seemed instantly to go berserk and kept calling the station for repeat plays of 'Mystery Train,' 'I Forgot to Remember to Forget,' and 'Good Rockin' Tonight.' The word spread like a contagion from Cleveland record distributors to executive home offices in New York, Chicago, and Los Angeles that there was a 'hot' new artist on the record scene" (p. 498), recalled R&B historian Arnold Shaw in *Honkers and Shouters*.

At Presley's third Cleveland stop on October 20, 1955, as an opening act for Pat Boone, Bill Haley and the Four Lads, he asked Bill Randle to become his manager. With the busy Randle refusing, Presley instead signed with former carnival huckster Colonel Tom Parker. Three months later when Presley made his television debut on the CBS variety program, *Stage Show,* he was introduced by guest emcee Bill Randle. By next spring, Presley's first RCA single, "Heartbreak Hotel," would be perched atop the pop charts for a two month stay.

With rock and roll exploding around the country, Alan Freed was making a tremendous amount of money with his Moondog balls and creating a sensation in the national press. While blacks had constituted the majority of the audiences in 1951, the racial makeup had reversed in just a few years. Co-emceeing a concert with Freed at the since-demolished Akron Armory—which featured Roy Hamilton, the Drifters, Frankie Lymon, and Screamin' Jay Hawkins—deejay Joe Finan recalled: "I can't remember seeing any blacks" in the crowd.

Taking notice of his then-unprecedented successes, the New York music world lured Freed to the city in September 1954. While he was still based in Cleveland, Freed had created a stir with his first East Coast Moondog ball in Newark, New Jersey. Promoting the concert on his syndicated program on WNJR, Freed drew 10,000 of his listeners to the show, a fifth of whom were white.

Hired in the late-evening shift at WINS, a then-low-rated 50,000-watt station, Freed marked his Cleveland departure with a massive R&B concert. Paid a salary of $15,000 per year (the figure has been grossly exaggerated over the years), Freed also earned a percentage of his program's advertising revenue. What Freed interchangeably called "rock and roll" and "rhythm and blues" was suddenly thrust upon millions of listeners, most of whom were white. Packing several hundred 45s in the trunk of his car, Freed sent shock waves around the music world, which had settled into a pattern of banal, inoffensive, middle-of-the-road fare. (The top single of 1954 had been a light romantic ballad, "Little Things Mean a Lot" by Kitty Kallen.)

With the aid of a new business partner, the heavy-handed Morris Levy, Freed was introduced to the movers and shakers in the music industry. Levy was a notorious figure who was accused of associating with elements of organized crime. Previously operating the legendary Birdland jazz nightclub, Levy expanded into all the angles of the record industry, as he wheeled and dealed publishing houses, jukebox companies, and record labels like Rada, Gee, and Roulette.

With Freed taking WINS to the ratings forefront, he spawned scores of imitators. A national sensation, Freed hired two women to open his fan mail. Recalls a then-16-year-old Wolfman Jack in his autobiography, "As soon as he came to New York, *The Alan Freed Show* just tore up the town. Everybody went nuts, especially me" (p. 48). Singer Paul Simon told Wes Smith: "New York was a pool of sounds, but only one station was playing rock 'n' roll, the station Alan Freed was on" (p. 282).

In New York, Freed was forced to drop his Moondog moniker after street musician Louis "Moondog" Hardin took him to court. Renaming his program the *Alan Freed Rock and Roll Show*, Freed popularized the music and assumed celebrity status when his program was syndicated in two dozen cities. Losing another court fight, Freed and partner Morris Levy failed in their attempt to copyright the term "rock and roll."

While continuing his national caravan-style concert revues, Freed set up residency at the huge Paramount Theater in Brooklyn. Within two months, Freed was smashing attendance records set 25 years earlier by bobby-soxers who had jammed the Times Square auditorium to catch a glimpse of a young, rising singing idol named Frank Sinatra. "The excitement of being out in the audience was overwhelming. . . . Freed would come out in this really loud plaid jacket and blow kisses at the audience while the house band play[ed] some real down, aggressive blues vamp" (pp. 48-49), recalled Wolfman Jack in his autobiography.

Paying his acts nominal fees, Freed instead offered airplay on his radio program, ensuring consumer demand for records by LaVern Baker, Big Joe Turner, or Chuck Berry. Berry, who owed his initial stardom to Alan Freed, was summoned to New York in late 1955 for a one-week stint to promote his first hit, "Maybellene." Making his East Coast debut, Berry recalled in his autobiography: "We had five shows a day to perform, starting at one o'clock in the afternoon and continuing until one o'clock in the morning, with a one-hour movie between each show. Most shows held over seven thousand kids screaming through the live performances each of the seven days of that week"; Berry also recalled his shock in seeing that "the audience seemed to be solid white" (pp. 112-24). Within an environment of orchestrated mayhem, each act on the superstar bill was usually permitted to sing only three songs before yielding the stage to the next performer. When the preconcert filler movie was later dropped, each act was required to perform *seven* shows a day.

Meanwhile, when MGM film director Richard Brooks wanted a theme song for The *Blackboard Jungle*, he purchased the rights to Bill Haley and the Comets' "Rock around the Clock" from Decca Records for one dollar. The first-ever rock song featured in a film, "Rock around the Clock" became the first chart-topping single of the rock era in 1955, as the pudgy, spit-curled Haley became America's first rock star.

Premiering in New York City, *The Blackboard Jungle* was the first movie to expose modern urban decay. Set in a rebellious public trade school, the big-screen feature captured what America feared about rock and roll music, as teacher Glenn Ford is assaulted by rock music-inflicted delinquents who challenge all authority. Writes music historian Marc Eliot: "The film's Bronx locale helped identify New York as the capital not only of rock and roll, but of the growing problem of juvenile delinquency" (p. 54). In a metaphoric sign of the times, the unruly, defiant students destroy old jazz 78s belonging to teacher Richard Kiley, behind a musical backdrop of the seemingly outdated 1920s music of Bix Beiderbecke. Other films, like Marlon Brando's *The Wild One* and James Dean's *Rebel Without a Cause*, romanticized youth rebellion, while popularizing leather jackets, blue jeans, and motorcycles.

When violence broke out at some theaters showing *The Blackboard Jungle*, the behavior was blamed on rock and roll. Some theaters began turning off the volume during the music scenes. While the film made "Rock around the Clock" a hit and signaled the start of the rock era, it forever gave rock and roll a public relations problem.

Inspired by the success of *The Blackboard Jungle,* Alan Freed joined Bill Haley in the rock film *Rock around the Clock*. Using movies as a vehicle for defending both himself and rock music, Freed oversaw four cheapie rock flicks, including *Don't Knock the Rock*. These films contained mostly flimsy plots built around performances by established rock acts. Another film, *Mister Rock and Roll*, gave Freed his new nickname.

Expanding his media empire, in 1956 Freed launched the first-ever network radio rock music show, *The Camel Rock and Roll Party*, airing Saturday nights on CBS. Jumping on the rock and roll bandwagon, ABC television hired Freed for a television program, predating *American Bandstand*. But when a cameraman captured a black performer, 14-year-old Frankie Lymon, dancing with a white girl, the program was dropped by southern stations. Advertiser jitters forced the show's cancellation two weeks later. Soon after ABC replaced the flashy and rebellious, integration-advocate Alan Freed with the affable, soft-spoken Dick Clark and his *American Bandstand*, which instituted strict dress codes, with boys wearing suits and ties, and girls barred from wearing pants. Freed then hosted a local music program on New York's WNEW.

With the country experiencing civil rights strife, Freed and the entire rock and roll community were under constant attack from religious groups, law enforcement agencies, politicians, and, in the South, anti-integrationists. At an interview with a *New York Times* reporter, Freed mockingly drank not his usual bottle of beer but a tall glass of wholesome milk.

Also jumping on the antirock bandwagon was the powerful ASCAP, a monopolistic Tin Pan Alley-era organization of music publishers that had excluded black songwriters. ASCAP's influence and control of popular music had been undermined by the fledgling BMI service, which, unlike ASCAP, welcomed R&B and country artists. By 1955, ASCAP composers accounted for only a quarter of the charted pop songs, down from 90 percent a decade earlier. With ASCAP's members frantically looking for a scapegoat, the brash Freed was the perfect target.

Rock also came under attack over the issue of bawdy lyrics. The fight was spearheaded by *Variety* magazine, ASCAP, and by major record companies that were financially threatened by the growing market share of small, independent labels. Attacking what they sarcastically referred to as "lee-rics" (the term coined by CBS Records executive Mitch Miller), a well-funded effort tried to stamp out rock and roll.

But racy lyrics had been common long before the age of rock. In the 1920s, social crusaders successfully attacked jazz records, as they did alcoholic consumption, as causes of moral decay. The rise of big band music in the mid-1930s set those fears aside as old-style jazz and blues were again relegated to black audiences. During the rise of R&B in the late 1940s, few whites had access to the music. As long as blacks made these recordings exclusively for black consumption, there was little in the way of mainstream criticism. But when suburban white teenagers were exposed to the music, white America was outraged.

Dozens of early rock hits were targeted for their use of double entendre lyrics, which euphemistically suggested sexual behavior. A frequent source of controversial material, Cincinnati-based King-Federal Records issued sexually blatant material like "Work with Me Annie" by Hank Ballard and the Midnighters. Another King-Federal release, the Dominoes' "Sixty Minute Man," boasted of the virile prowess of Lovin' Dan; banned by some stations and considered a novelty song by others, for most Americans it was their first exposure to rock and roll. Wanting to pacify their foes, radio stations and disc jockeys launched ineffective and insincere self-policing measures. Writing in a *Variety* editorial, King-Federal Records vice president John S. Kelly promised to clean up his company's releases. Even black powerhouse WDIA promised to drop all "off-color" songs from its playlist.

But at the same time that the music industry establishment was trying to stamp out rock and roll, old-time record labels like Mercury and RCA were profiting from the music, not by signing R&B artists, but by releasing their own watered-down renditions of R&B hits. Called "cover versions," these songs usually surpassed the R&B originals in both airplay and sales. While cover versions actually helped popularize rock music in the long run, they were financially crippling to rock artists and their record companies.

Stars like LaVern Baker, Ruth Brown, and Little Richard were supplanted on radio playlists by white cover acts such as the Crew-Cuts, Georgia Gibbs, and the Diamonds. Decades before his flirtation with heavy-metal, Pat Boone's foray into cover records gave middle America sanitized versions of R&B songs that were so lame that they often bore little resemblance to the original. Scoring numerous cover hits beginning with Fats Domino's "Ain't That a Shame," Boone, an English and speech major in college, desperately wanted to retitle the song to the grammatically correct "Isn't That a Shame."

But with deejays like Alan Freed exposing the fraud and refusing to play cover versions, teenagers were demanding to hear the original versions. But to the shock of white middle America, by the late 1950s it became "increasingly difficult to separate white and black performers, largely because many black stylists ha[d] eliminated some of the coarser qualities from the blues and gospel styles, while a number of white performers ha[d] perfected their handling of black vocal accent, inflection patterns, and phrasing" (p. 282), recalled musicologist Johannes Riedel. In the end, major companies reacted by luring major rock acts with lucrative contracts and buying out pesky independent labels. With the megacorporation RCA purchasing Elvis Presley's contract for $35,000 from Sam Phillips, the label withdrew its financial and vocal support from antirock causes.

Meanwhile, the increasingly embattled Alan Freed saw his career mortally wounded following a May 1958 Boston stop of an all-star tour. In a show featuring Buddy Holly, Jerry Lee Lewis, and Chuck Berry, dozens of heavy-handed police tried to corner Freed, challenging him to a confrontation. With the fiery Jerry Lee Lewis pumping out a headlining performance of "Great Balls of Fire," "the kids jammed the aisles and converged upon the stage. In the white heat of the frenzy, the house lights went up and the crowd ceased chanting and dancing, wondering at the cause for the intrusion. Boston police [were] streaming down the aisles in pairs with flashlights and nightsticks at the ready. Alan Freed cursed and raked his hands through his hair, then charged onstage. 'Hey, kids, take a look at this,' Freed cried. 'The cops don't want you to have a good time.' Catcalls and boos spread until the house groaned its resentment. Officers in riot gear froze with muscles tensed in anticipation of an attack. . . . A sergeant signaled retreat, and the bluebellies turned and filed out to the triumphant jeers of the teenagers" (p. 175), recalled Lewis' then-14-year-old wife, Myra, in the Jerry Lee Lewis biography, *Great Balls of Fire*.

The humiliated police force quickly regrouped, wanting to make an example of Freed. After confiscating the night's receipts from the box office, they closed the show. Attacking in force, police arrested Freed, charging him with anarchy and incitement to riot. With the young crowd running through the streets, newspapers sensationalized the event, calling it a full-fledged riot.

With Freed's reported crimes becoming a national scandal, rock music had been further disgraced. Concert cancellations followed, and Freed lost hundreds of thousands of dollars in wasted advertising and already rented venues. In New Haven, Connecticut, Freed failed in his attempts to overturn a city ban of all rock concerts. "My father was definitely a victim, in the sense that he was set up," Lance Freed told writer Marc Eliot; ASCAP and the major record companies were "effective in convincing people there should be some investigation into how those 'nigger music' records could get to be hits" (p. 66). Former announcer Robert West was told by David Freed that his brother Alan "was totally innocent. They cracked down on him because he integrated the theater. He felt that was the real reason." In the racial segregation enforced by Jim Crow laws, black and white concertgoers were still segregated in theaters around the country by a rope that ran down the center of the theater from the stage to the last row.

Fired by WINS, Freed moved to New York powerhouse WABC, where he toned down his antics. Bruised by the press, Freed had difficulty maintaining his high public profile. With the tarnishing of "rock and roll," Freed began to call the music "the Big Beat."

With his Boston trial postponed for a year, Freed's concerts continued at a slower pace. Evicted from the Paramount Theater, Freed moved to the Fox, where he set new box office records. Although a horde of security guards and police stationed in the theater expected trouble, none was had. After grossing a remarkable $207,000 his first week, he mocked his critics with a full-page ad in *Billboard*.

Determined, Freed's enemies took another route: payola. In 1958, the Federal Trade Commission had begun a probe into payola, the practice whereby a record company would give a deejay money, drugs, or gifts to play, hype, or just listen to a record. The practice was also prevalent within publishing houses, distributors, and record stores and with the artists themselves. Inquiries into radio payola snowballed following the quiz show scandals of the late 1950s, when investigators discovered that popular contestants had been supplied with answers.

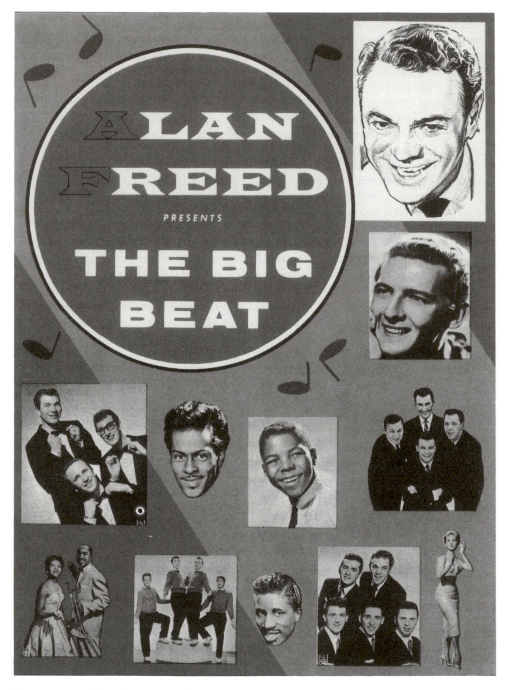

Concert program from Alan Freed's "Big Beat" show at the Brooklyn Fox Theater in 1959. (*Courtesy of John M. Riley, from private collection.*)

While music industry payola was technically not illegal, an obscure 1934 FCC code loosely forbade the practice. The vicious rivalry between ASCAP and BMI was the catalyst behind the investigation, with ASCAP charging that without the payments, no radio station would ever play rock and roll. But by the 1950s, payola became a financial necessity for most deejays, who earned little in salaries. Euphemistically called "listening fees" by deejays, payola was considered a legitimate promotional cost by record companies.

Alan Freed likened payola to lobbying in Washington, D.C., with the money never guaranteeing airplay. Deejay Joe Finan, who was also implicated in the payola scandal, defended Freed, recalling that "the records he was playing, were the records he liked." Robert West recalled that Freed "had no sense of payola. He understood favors. He didn't take money to take money; he felt they were legitimate gifts."

When Freed refused to sign a statement that he had not accepted payola, he was dismissed by WABC. Also fired from his local television show on WNEW, Freed ended his last program by staring into the camera and rubbing a record between his fingers. Firing one final volley at the powerful establishment, he said defiantly, "I know a bunch of ASCAP publishers who'll be glad I'm off the air" (p. 213), recalled music historian Wes Smith.

Alan Freed became the chief target in the series of televised payola hearings in 1960, with the proceedings resembling the McCarthy "witch-hunts," which had riveted the country only a few years earlier. Powerful music industry players were hauled before stone-faced investigators, with Freed taking the brunt of the punishment for something everyone in the industry was doing. Freed told the committee that he was paid $40,000 a year by WINS but returned $30,000 to the station to advertise his concerts. As an omnipresent figure and rock's biggest cheerleader, the downfall of Freed was seen as the key to stopping rock and roll.

The payola scandal dramatically changed the landscape of radio. While deejays had programmed their own music in the 1950s, all of that changed after 1960. Fearing FCC fines and license revocations, radio station owners took over the responsibility, which gave rise to "formula" or "top-40 radio," with the playlists determined by the record charts in *Billboard, Cashbox,* and *Record World.* The payola scandal also squelched regional artists, and the many independent labels that were now unable to land airplay. For the next decade, the deejay was little more than an announcer, a situation remedied with the rise of underground FM radio.

Meanwhile, rock was taking hits from all sides. An airplane crash outside of Clear Lake, Iowa, killed a trio of rock stars, Buddy Holly, the Big Bopper, and the headlining 17-year-old singer named Ritchie Valens. Other rock stars saw their careers end in unusual circumstances. Both the Platters and Chuck Berry were scandalized in separate incidents involving women. Jerry Lee Lewis was heckled at his concerts after marrying his 13-year-old cousin, Myra Gale Brown. Little Richard experienced a religious conversion while on tour in Australia, convinced that rock and roll was the devil's music. Most significantly, Elvis Presley entered the service, his uninhibited behavior finally tamed. With the rise of clean-cut teen idols like Paul Anka and Ricky Nelson, even Freed's former employer, WINS, had abandoned rock and roll in 1961, changing its format to a middle-of-the-road fare of Frank Sinatra and Nat King Cole.

Left without an outlet to play and popularize records, Freed was abandoned by rock artists, who saw no reason to perform at his concerts. Quietly leaving New York City in 1961, Freed was broke. An unskilled businessman who kept his money stacked in boxes in a closet, Freed had grossed several million dollars in just seven short years in New York and was now bankrupt. "Alan was very free with his money. He would give it to anybody that was broke. If a musician he knew needed money, he would give it to him. He did not spend it on the wild life at all," defended Robert West.

Few other deejays or record industry heads were prosecuted, and even fewer lost their jobs. Dick Clark, who gave an impassioned defense, denied being involved in the payola practice. Expanding into music publishing, acquiring copyrights of 162 songs, and buying shares of record companies like the Philadelphia-based Jamie label, Clark had been accused of profiting from the songs he played on *American Bandstand*. Rocker Gene Vincent's one time guitarist Jerry Merritt, recalled in a *Blue Suede News* interview: "Dick Clark's people talked to Gene about promotion and tours with strings attached. Gene Vincent told Dick Clark to take it to the moon! To this day if Dick Clark has a 25th year special or whatever you don't see Gene on it" (p. 8). Though forced to sell off some of his holdings as part of a settlement, in the end Clark emerged scot-free.

Exhausted and dispirited, Freed reluctantly pleaded guilty to bribery charges in 1962 and was given a suspended jail sentence. Left a broken man, Freed began to drink even more heavily. Drifting to the West Coast, Freed took the 22nd-ranked radio KDAY in Los Angeles to 3rd place in the ratings. Pioneering Los Angeles deejay Art Leboe, who worked with Freed at KDAY, said in *Rockonomics*, "He loved being on the air again but was frustrated because he was unable to make the impact he had in New York. Kids liked him out here, but not the way they'd loved him in New York" (p. 86). Under the pressures of legal, tax, and health problems, Freed resigned after several months. But aided by his former business partner Morris Levy, Freed was behind a microphone at WQAM in Miami. But after clashing with the station owners over his independent concert promotions and on-air music selection, Freed was fired.

Losing his properties and bank accounts to the IRS, Freed was left penniless. Returning to New York City for three months in 1963, Freed was met with cold shoulders by his former associates. When he was down and out, Freed "couldn't get his phone calls returned," recalled deejay Joe Finan.

Still hounded by the IRS, Freed was indicted by a federal grand jury in 1964 for income tax evasion, with the government claiming he owed $40,000 on unreported income of $57,000. Freed's son, Lance Freed, recalled in *Rockonomics*: "Even today, all the performance money collected on the publishing of his music goes directly to the IRS. Originally, the debt wasn't quite a hundred thousand dollars, but with all the interest accrued over the years, it's headed toward the millions. There was nothing left at the end except the house in Palm Springs, which he was able to keep through the California Homesteading Act. Without that we would have been out in the street. Right up to the day he died he continued to make plans to someday return east" (p. 86). Suffering from uremia, Freed died from cirrhosis of the liver in 1965.

Wanting to forget the scar of payola, the music industry ignored Alan Freed's legacy well into the 1970s. But when historians began looking into rock music's origins, they rediscovered Freed's essential role. Paramount Pictures chronicled a week in the life of Freed's New York period in the 1978 semifictional biographical film, *American Hot Wax,* with Tim McIntyre in the lead role. In the film, Freed's character tells the district attorney: "Look, you can close the show. You can stop me. But you can never stop rock and roll. Don't you know that?" Unhappy with the movie's inaccuracies, R&B singer Screamin' Jay Hawkins, who portrayed himself in the film, said in *Nowhere to Run:* "History done Alan Freed wrong . . . and so did Hollywood" (p. 11).

With Alan Freed's meteoric ascent synonymous with the birth of "rock and roll," Cleveland was picked as the site of the Rock and Roll Hall of Fame and Museum in 1985. Freed was voted into the Hall of Fame at its premier ceremony in 1986 in the Non-Performer category. The 40th anniversary Moondog Coronation Ball in Cleveland in 1992 included an appearance by Paul "Hucklebuck" Williams, the only act that took the stage at the original 1952 concert.

Bibliography

Belz, Carl. (1969). *The Story of Rock.* New York: Oxford University Press.

Berry, Chuck. (1987). *Chuck Berry: The Autobiography.* New York: Harmony.

Bristol, Marc & DeWitt, Dennis. (1992). Jerry Merritt interview. *Blue Suede News,* no. 20, p. 8.

Dyer, Bob. (1990, October 14). Contract clause led to Freed's fame. *Akron Beacon Journal,* p. F1.

Eliot, Marc. (1993). *Rockonomics: The Money Behind the Music.* New York: Citadel.

Finan, Joe. (1997, February 9). Interview with author.

Guralnick, Peter. (1994). *Last Train to Memphis.* Boston: Little, Brown.

Halasa, Joyce. (1990, September 13). Chuck Young, part I: Cleveland record promotions and payolas. *Scene,* p. 9.

"Hepcats bay on trail of Moondog, Freed in jam." (1952, March 22). *Akron Beacon Journal,* p. A2.

Hirshey, Gerri. (1984). *Nowhere to Run: The Story of Soul Music.* New York: Times Books.

Horowitz, Carl. (1995, March 1). Showman Alan Freed. *Investor's Business Daily,* p. A1.

Jackson, John A. (1991). *Big Beat Heat: Alan Freed and the Early Years of Rock & Roll.* New York: Schirmer.

Junod, Tom. (1992, December). Oh, what a night! *Life,* p. 32.

Lewis, Myra & Silver, Murray. (1982). *Great Balls of Fire: The Uncensored Story of Jerry Lee Lewis.* New York: St. Martin's.

Martin, Linda & Segrave, Kerry. (1988). *Anti-Rock: The Opposition to Rock'n'Roll.* New York: Da Capo.

"Moondog madness." (1952, March 29). *(Cleveland) Call & Post,* p. 2B.

Nite, Norm N. (1992, March 9). *Alan Freed Special* WMJI, Cleveland, OH.

O'Neil, Thomas. (1993). *The Grammys: For the Record.* New York: Penguin.

Passman, Arnold. (1971). *The Deejays.* New York: Macmillan.

Pratt, Ray. (1990). *Rhythm and Resistance: Explorations in the Political Uses of Popular Music.* New York: Praeger.

Quinn, Chris. (1997, February 27). Interview with author.

Rathbun, Keith. (1986, March 20). The Moondog Coronation Ball: Happy birthday, rock 'n' roll. *Scene,* p. 9.

Redd, Lawrence N. (1985, September). Rock! It's still rhythm and blues. *Black Perspectives in Music*, p. 31.

Riedel, Johannnes. (1975). *Soul Music Black and White: The Influences of Black Music on the Churches*. Minneapolis: Augsburg

Rutledge, Jeffrey L. (1985, February 1). Alan Freed: The fall from grace of a forgotten hero. *Goldmine*, p. 22.

Sangiacomo, Michael. (1996, February 3). The men of steel. *Cleveland Plain Dealer*, p. 8E.

Schrader, Erich. (1997, March 21). Interview with author.

Scott, Jane. (1982, March 14). 30 years ago, "Moon Dog" howled. *Cleveland Plain Dealer*, p. D1.

Scott, Jane. (1992, September 7). Lakewood deejay sells early film footage of Elvis. *Cleveland Plain Dealer*, p. 7D.

Scott, Jane. (1995, May 27). Light's out for Nite on radio in Cleveland. *Cleveland Plain Dealer*, p. 8E.

Shaw, Arnold. (1974). *The Rockin' '50s*. New York: Hawthorne.

Shaw, Arnold. (1978). *Honkers and Shouters*. New York: Collier.

Smith, Wes. (1989). *The Pied Pipers of Rock 'n' Roll*. Marietta, GA: Longstreet.

"Top jock." (1955, February 14). *Time*, p. 54.

Wexler, Jerry & Ritz, David. (1993). *Rhythm and the Blues: A Life in American Music*. New York: Alfred A. Knopf.

West, Robert. (1996, December 5). Interview with author.

Williams, Valena Minor. (1952, March 29). Moon Doggers "break it up." *(Cleveland) Call & Post*, p. 1A.

Wolfman Jack, & Laursen, Byron. (1995). *Have Mercy*. New York: Warner.

CHAPTER 2

Cleveland and the Building of a Rock Hall

"I thought I'd seen everything, but now we've got rock-and-roll at the Waldorf," producer Quincy Jones told the gathered audience of 1,000 rock dignitaries, who paid between $300 and $1,000, to salute the debut class of inductees at the first annual Rock and Roll Hall of Fame ceremony in 1986. Rock Hall board member and *Rolling Stone* publisher Jann Wenner added: "This is something that is long, long overdue. People are finally recognizing the fact that the music form known as rock and roll has become an integral part of 20th-century American history." Billy Joel later echoed the sentiment: "It's about time rock had a place of its own."

But at the time, the Rock and Roll Hall of Fame was still without a home, as a site selection committee had been bombarded with generous offers from several deserving cities. But several months later the Hall of Fame would land in Cleveland for the very reasons that Springfield, Massachusetts hosts the Basketball Hall of Fame, and Cooperstown, New York, the Baseball Hall of Fame. Behind an oversized microphone at 50,000-watt WJW/850-AM in Cleveland, in 1951 deejay Alan Freed popularized the term "rock and roll" and launched a musical firestorm that survived long after Freed's tragic and little-noticed death in 1965.

But in 1985, both Freed and the industrial north coast city of Cleveland experienced a renaissance. As the nation's 12th largest metropolitan area, Cleveland was enjoying a building boom as the downtown was crowded with competing construction cranes, with the Rock and Roll Hall of Fame becoming the crown jewel amid new sport complexes, a science museum, two upscale downtown malls, and a bustling waterfront entertainment district called the Flats, filled with concert venues, pleasure boats, and revelers jaunting to offshore tourist islands.

A turnaround city, Cleveland's fortunes had waned since the Depression, a period when the city forever lost its stock exchange. In the 1930s, Clevelander Bob Hope had left the city's vaudeville houses for Hollywood, while a pair of local teenagers, Jerry Siegel and Joseph Shuster, created the Man of Steel, Superman, basing the fabled Metropolis on the downtown Cleveland skyline.

A progressive populace, in the 1960s Cleveland elected the first major-city black mayor, Carl Stokes, and later gave major league sports its first black manager when Frank Robinson headed the Indians. But the city was also saddled with national embarrassments, becoming the butt of jokes when an oil slick in the polluted Cuyahoga River caught on fire in 1969. Memorialized in the Randy Newman ode "Burn on Big River," the blaze set wooden railroad trestles afire, as the rust-belt city became a symbol of urban decay. Later, Mayor Ralph Perk set his hair ablaze during a ribbon-cutting ceremony, and in 1978, the boy-wonder mayor Dennis Kucinich plunged the city into financial default. Another tragedy also divided the region when, on May 4, 1970, the Ohio National Guard fired shots at war protesters at nearby Kent State University.

Conceived in New York City, the premise of a Rock and Roll Hall of Fame was offered as an alternative to the much maligned Grammy Awards. When the Grammy Awards were hatched in 1955 in the back room of a Los Angeles landmark, the Brown Derby, the established players in the music industry were reacting to their loss of power and influence and were scheming to return to the "sanity" of the prerock world of Patti Page and Perry Como. Voting was limited to music insiders and previous Grammy winners, with music consumers shut out. Consequently, at the premier Grammy ceremony in 1958, Elvis Presley had not won a single award. (During his lifetime, Elvis won Grammys only for his religious recordings.)

Promoting highbrow snobbery, the Grammys continued to vilify rock and roll acts for the next three decades. After finally introducing a rock category in 1961, a jazz instrumental, "Alley Cat," won the award the following year, the same year that Robert Goulet was voted the Best New Artist. During the height of Beatlemania in 1965 and 1966, Frank Sinatra twice won the Album of the Year. The Beatles also lost in the Best Vocal Performance by a Vocal Group category in 1965 to the since-forgotten Anita Kerr Quartet. Maintaining an antirock bias, in the 1960s the Grammys completely passed over Jimi Hendrix, Chuck Berry, Bob Dylan, the Who, and the Supremes; during the entire decade, Motown artists won one award, at a time that the label dominated the pop charts.

Consequently, the Grammys have never achieved the impact or the prestige of the film industry's Oscars or Broadway's Tony Award contests. Instead of celebrating artistic achievement, the Grammys have always been popularity contests and have consistently discriminated against rock, especially innovative or new acts.

As a result, many rival music award shows have emerged to give rock its deserved due including *The MTV Video Music Awards*, *The People's Choice Awards*, *The Soul Train Awards*, and *The Billboard Magazine Awards*. Don Kirshner's *Rock Music Awards* faded in 1977 after three years, while the *International Rock Awards*, complete with its Elvis statuette, lasted just three years. Although also a popularity contest, the American Music Awards is the Grammy's most credible competitor, with the winners tabulated from a survey of 20,000 music consumers.

Another award ceremony was born in 1983 in the modern New York offices of Atlantic Records, a label whose inconspicuous start had come in a hotel room four decades earlier. While Ahmet Ertegun claims to have originated the idea for the Hall of Fame, Steve Pond in *GQ* magazine writes: "When it was initially proposed, the Hall of Fame was simply a money-making idea of a television producer who wanted to stage a close-circuit show entitled 'The Rock and Roll Hall of Fame.' He approached Atlantic Records Co-chairman Ahmet Ertegun and suggested that Ertegun start a nonprofit organization using that name, [and] license the title to him for a small fee" (p. 228). Ertegun liked the idea of a rock award ceremony but hated the notion of a closed-circuit television show. After litigation, the producer was awarded a cash settlement, and Ertegun ran with the idea. Ertegun later told *Rolling Stone* in 1986, "We're not going to make this a rock and roll Disneyland. We have an obligation to the world of rock & roll, the artists and the fans, to make this a dignified place" (p. 33).

Early discussions between Ahmet Ertegun and lawyer Suzan Evans envisioned a tiny hall of fame and museum honoring rock music's founders. Needing support, Ertegun corralled several of his music industry friends, including Bob Krasnow of MCA, Jann Wenner of *Rolling Stone*, Seymore Stein of Sire Records, and entertainment lawyer, Allen Grubman. Quitting her law practice, Suzan Evans became the Hall of Fame's first full-time employee.

Then with little fanfare, in 1984 the Rock and Roll Hall of Fame Foundation was officially established in New York City, with the first year's inductees nominated by a 10-member committee, which included Krasnow, Ertegun, Stein, Wenner, Robert Hilburn, Kurt Loder, John Hammond, Nile Rodgers, Jerry Wexler, and, most crucially for Cleveland, their native son, deejay and author Norm N. Nite. Then on August 5, 1985, an expanded 21-member board publicly announced the creation of a Rock and Roll Hall of Fame to preserve the music and honor its pioneers.

Meanwhile, 600 miles to the east, the like-minded K. Michael Benz, the executive vice president of the Greater Cleveland Growth Association, also came up with the notion of constructing a rock music museum in Cleveland and began soliciting radio stations and civic leaders for support. Little did he realize that a similar project had been conceived in New York. Likewise, rock impresario Bill Graham was also contemplating an identical structure in San Francisco.

But when Benz shared his proposal with Norm N. Nite (who maintains residences in both New York and Cleveland), the board member broke the news that a parallel effort was under way in the Big Apple. Benz told *Northern Ohio Live*, that "they were going to have this small hall of fame, if you will, in a brownstone [on 42nd Street] that was being donated by [Mayor Ed] Koch" (p. 74). But at a time when few in the music industry had even heard of the project, then-Cleveland mayor George Voinovich and Governor Richard Celeste rushed to New York to learn more of the proposed museum. As the first city to vie for the project, Cleveland had a head start over its competitors. While the notion of a rock museum remained hazy at best, it would mean bragging rights and tourist dollars for Cleveland and the overdue recognition of Alan Freed as father of rock and roll.

While Michael J. Fox and Joan Jett were in Cleveland shooting scenes for a film about a struggling Ohio rock band, *Light of Day*, the city was spending $250,000 in a promotional campaign to lure the rock museum. Arriving in Cleveland, the Rock Hall selection committee was greeted by energized civic leaders in an organized effort to sway the music industry bigwigs. At one point, a jubilant Ahmet Ertegun ordered the tour bus to stop, so that he and other riders could buy records as souvenirs at the legendary Record Rendezvous store, where Freed and store owner Leo Mintz had popularized the term "rock and roll" in the 1950s after watching white teenagers listen to black records.

With local support reaching rabid proportions, Clevelanders gathered 660,000 signatures in an attempt to lure the hall (the city's population stood at only 536,000). On January 21, 1986, Cleveland tallied 110,315 votes on a *USA Today* call-in poll; Memphis came in a distant second with 7,268 votes. Other vote counts included San Francisco 4,006; Nashville 2,886; New Orleans 2,500; New York 2,159; Philadelphia 1,044; and Chicago 1,030. The newspaper had unprecedentedly extended the poll a second day in a failed effort to give other cities a chance to narrow the gap.

Meanwhile, at the debut induction ceremony in January 1986 at the opulent, art deco-styled Waldorf-Astoria ballroom, the music world bestowed instant credibility to the Rock and Roll Hall of Fame. Honoring the pioneers of rock, the most powerful and influential members of the music industry had gathered. Billy Joel, Neil Young, John Fogerty, and Keith Richards were on hand to witness the honoring of Chuck Berry, James Brown, Fats Domino, and Jerry Lee Lewis. More important for Cleveland, Alan Freed became the first nonperformer inducted into the Hall of Fame.

Although planning to announce its site selection at the ceremony, the New York Foundation delayed its choice as last-minute offers began pouring in (backstage, Jann Wenner suggested that Cleveland was still the front-runner). Memphis was offering to spend $8 million on a building, while San Francisco was conducting a $60,000 museum-feasibility study. In its proposal, Philadelphia pledged to open the museum in 18 months if selected, with Mayor Wilson Good unveiling a $45.7 million financial package. Chicago, meanwhile, launched an all-out effort to grab the hall from front-leaning Cleveland. At an outdoor rally, Chicago mayor Harold Washington spoke with fervor when trying to invoke the name of the "Born to Run" rocker, mistakenly referring to him as Bruce "Springtime."

But by the end of March, the original field of eight cities was narrowed to Chicago, Cleveland, Philadelphia, and San Francisco. Dropped were Memphis, Nashville, New Orleans, and New York. The remaining cities were given a month to match Cleveland's $35 million package offer. Notable *Los Angeles Times* rock critic Robert Hilburn sided with Memphis, giving the second-place nod to both New York and Los Angeles.

In an effort to bring the Hall of Fame museum to Cleveland, a massive, citywide celebration commemorated the 34th anniversary of the original Moondog Coronation Ball, with events organized all over town. Five television and nine radio stations simultaneously aired Bill Haley's "Rock around the Clock"; and Cleveland native Eric Carmen released the single "The Rock Stops Here" as a Rock Hall anthem. But two weeks later, on April 6, the *Chicago Tribune* reported that Los Angeles had been selected as the Hall of Fame site. Nonetheless, the following day, Ohio governor Richard F. Celeste signed the state's $584 million capital construction budget for fiscal 1987-88, including $4 million for the rock museum.

Meanwhile, within the selection committee, Norm N. Nite was pushing his hometown as the only logical choice. Dick Clark told *Northern Ohio Live*, "I dare say, he was the guy standing yelling Cleveland at the top of his lungs at every free moment"

(p. 74). A native of Cleveland, Nite was a respected deejay, promoter, and music historian who authored a pioneering three-volume *Rock On*, a rock encyclopedia series.

The son of a Cleveland civil employee, Norm N. Nite was 12 years old when, in 1952, he first became absorbed by the golden throat of Alan Freed. Though fascinated with music, Nite instead pursued a degree in business administration at Ohio State. Enamored with the campus radio station, he changed his major to broadcasting and garnered a loyal listenership with his "oldies" radio program.

Entering the service, Nite moonlighted as nighttime deejay and released a pioneering oldies album, *ROCK & ROLL: EVOLUTION OR REVOLUTION.* The album was promoted by New York City deejay Pete "Big Daddy" Meyers, who, like Freed, had first established his wild radio persona in Cleveland.

Discharged from the service, Nite returned to Cleveland, at one time holding down deejay positions at three different stations. After making a name for himself as the host of *The Nite Train Show,* a popular, overnight all-oldies show at WHK, Nite moved to WGAR, where his program propelled the station in the local ratings war (WGAR also featured pioneering shock-jock Don Imus in his pre-syndication days).

A walking musical encyclopedia, "the other jocks on his station would kid [Nite] on the air, calling him Alan Freed's illegitimate son, or proclaiming him to be the lead singer of some long lost group, and ultimately out of this grew his title of 'Mr. Know-It All,' which evolved into 'Mr. Music,' as he is known today" (p. 18), recalled writer Ralph M. Newman. After syndicating his radio shows, Nite landed in New York behind a microphone at oldies powerhouse WCBS, which had just switched formats after failing with its foray into progressive rock.

Returning to Cleveland in 1978, Nite would alternate between his hometown and New York, at times flying back and forth for radio jobs in both cities. In Cleveland, Nite became instrumental in the relaunching of the annual Moondog Coronation Ball concerts, the rights granted by Alan Freed's younger brother, David Freed, to Nite's Cleveland employer, WMJI. More importantly, Nite was convinced that the Rock and Roll Hall of Fame truly belonged in Cleveland.

With rumors hitting the local press about the imminent selection of the site of the Hall of Fame, Clevelanders were uneasy about their chances of landing the hall. Then on May 5, 1986, Cleveland Mayor (later, governor) George Voinovich was met by a local rock band, Wild Horses, and hordes of media at Cleveland's downtown, Burke Lakefront Airport, and shouted, "We got it!" Joined by then-governor Dick Celeste, the usually conservatively attired elected officials were donning t-shirts that read, "Cleveland: Home of the Rock 'n' Roll Hall of Fame." With Cleveland radio blasting Ian Hunter's "Cleveland Rocks" and the state's official rock song, "Hang on Sloopy," the populace celebrated, as local television and radio stations broke away from scheduled programming for live coverage.

At a news conference announcing Cleveland's selection, Ahmet Ertegun said, "We have been swayed by the incredible community enthusiasm that has come up in Cleveland." Essential to the decision were a financial package deal and a pledge by Cuyahoga Community College to develop a popular music program. Within the music industry, the city's selection had been endorsed by Rod Stewart, Michael Jackson, Neil

Young, the Everly Brothers, the Kinks, Sting, Pat Benatar, Tina Turner, and others. The first *Rolling Stone* article announcing Cleveland's selection warned that the cost could run as high as $20 million, with construction planned for early 1987.

The following January, the New York City-based board members arrived in Cleveland to inspect prospective sites, including the spot of the demolished Cleveland Arena, where the rock and roll concert was born. The committee instead chose a compact area next to the just-opened downtown, Tower City shopping center, on land donated by the mall's developer. Plans called for the multi use building to be built atop a parking garage and linked by underground tunnels to shield against Cleveland's sometimes fierce winters, all as part of three blocks of development. Situated on a towering bluff and overlooking the industrial Cuyahoga River, the proposed museum was now estimated to cost $25 million. A separate Cleveland-based Hall of Fame board was formed to oversee the construction of the museum.

During the next several years, the Hall of Fame's pricetag spiraled, forcing Cleveland officials to raise additional moneys, twice nearly losing the Hall of Fame over the slow pace of fund-raising. After mapping a financial strategy, members of the Cleveland Founders Club were dismayed by the absence of expected corporate donations. Also a disappointment, a proposed $5 million endowment from the television rights of the induction ceremonies never materialized due to network indifference. The notion of a televised ceremony was later ruled out, with the New York board fearing that many major stars would avoid the proceedings, with cameras destroying the induction's integrity, intimacy, and inclusiveness.

Selected to design the building was the Chinese-born architect I.M. Pei. Styled in modernism, Pei's previous designs included Boston's J.F.K. Library, Washington D.C.'s National Gallery of Arts East Building, and the expansion of the Louvre Museum in France. Educated at MIT and Harvard, Ieoh Ming Pei admitted to not liking rock and roll music when first asked to design the museum. Tutored in rock history by Jann Wenner, Pei was taken on guided tours to the entertainment districts in New Orleans, and Nashville and to Elvis Presley's Graceland mansion in Memphis.

Unveiling a model of the Rock and Roll Hall of Fame in January 1988 at an informal ceremony in New York City, the price tag for the sloping, 95,000-square-foot hall had jumped to $45 million. With local business leaders rallying around Higbee Company chairman Robert Broadbent, the heads of BP America, U.S. Nestle, and East Ohio Gas Company corralled pledges and gifts of $15 million. The Rock Hall remained in the city only after officials secured the minimum $18 million interim goal demanded by the New York board. By year's end, the groundbreaking was again delayed, and the cost revised at $48 million.

Meanwhile, naysayers were multiplying both in Cleveland and in the national press. Richard Gehr charged in *Village Voice*: "The museum's planning has also been a disappointment. An architect was hired and an extravagant building designed before anyone knew what it would contain or how it would be paid for. Major collectors of rock memorabilia are turning the project a cold shoulder. Rock and roll is here to stay, but its gonna take a miracle to build this funhouse" (p. 25). With Larry R. Thompson named the director of the Hall of Fame, Rock Hall officials again delayed groundbreaking, for two years, to 1991.

In early 1989, Cleveland mayor George Voinovich unveiled a plan to give $15 million in property taxes to the hall. But tempers flared during a colorful exchange among council members, who were concerned about public tax moneys being diverted away from the city's crumbling schools. The controversial president of the Cleveland City Council, George Forbes, threatened to torpedo funding for the hall if the ceremonies weren't brought to the city. During the vote, George Forbes told the local Rock Hall board members in attendance, "I think you've been snookered by the crew in New York."

Eventually, most of the cost of the hall would be financed by the public sector, with Cleveland taxpayers especially burdened. The Cleveland/Cuyahoga County Port Authority provided the bulk of the moneys, issuing bonds totaling $38.9 million, the money to be repaid with corporate sponsorships, a 10 percent museum admission tax, and an increase in a local hotel bed tax. Additionally, Cuyahoga County pitched in $11.8 million, with the city coffers coughing up another $11.2 million. The state of Ohio granted $8 million for the Rock Hall construction and $10 million for site improvements. Lastly, tens of millions of dollars were spent rerouting utility wires, constructing streets, and a nearby rail line. (Former Cleveland Growth Association executive K. Michael Benz, later chairman of the Cleveland Rock and Roll Hall of Fame Museum Committee, had said in late 1985 that no public tax funds would be used to pay for the museum.)

But with the money at hand, the New York-based Hall of Fame Foundation in July announced its refusal to move the ceremony to Cleveland, citing "inconvenience." Former Hall of Fame board member Jeff Tamarkin admits: "All these people in New York and Los Angeles didn't want to spend the money and time to fly to Cleveland. They would rather hop in a limo and go to the Waldorf, have their steaks and champagne, and then go home."

But noted Cleveland deejay Chris Quinn insisted: "The Hall of Fame is here, the ceremony should be here. It shouldn't be Cleveland this year, somewhere else next year, then Cleveland the year after that, and somewhere else after that. No, the Hall of Fame is here. This is the city that went to bat, that showed them that we deserve it. We won it, and it should be here." Cleveland Plain Dealer rock critic Michael Norman offered the realities of the ceremony's location: "Getting the inductees to Cleveland wouldn't be the problem. Most of them would be happy to make the pilgrimage to receive such an honor. But it is unrealistic to suggest that regular Cleveland inductions would attract a crowd of other celebrities" (p. 8E).

But nearly a decade after the Hall of Fame was conceived, the only physical reminder of a museum was a billboard. Situated in a weed-infested field, the message "CLEVELAND WELCOMES . . . FUTURE HOME OF ROCK AND ROLL HALL OF FAME," took on an eyesore status, while the hall's cost was again revised, now standing at nearly $50 million. Concerned but undaunted, Norm N. Nite told *Scene*: "Granted, there have been a lot of mistakes that have been made since Cleveland got this in May of 1986. We're talking about three-and-a-half years, all we've got up is a sign" (p. 9). With Cleveland managing to reach a $40 million interim goal and then told to raise an additional $8 million, Jann Wenner told *QC* magazine, "They tried to meet their financial commitments, but we kept escalating the price on them. I mean, we set very high standards. And they swallowed and said 'Okay'" (p. 230).

Another roadblock occurred in March 1990, when the New York board demanded a site change after the opening of a Record Town music store in the adjacent Tower City Mall. While hall officials publicly bemoaned the lack of expansion space for the hall, privately there was concern over the loss in revenues for the Hall of Fame's own proposed record store.

With U.S. representative Mary Rose Oaker lobbying for the new site, museum officials relocated the Rock Hall to a lakefront location in North Coast Harbor. With a promise of a larger museum, critics complained the building would block the view of the lake. Meanwhile, a press release warned that "with the increase in size of the facility, we anticipate some increase in costs." With William N. Hulett hired as the Rock Hall's co-chairman, in January 1991, the hall construction price was upped to $60 million.

By May, the San Francisco-based Burdick Group was hired to design the museum's interior, the hall's cost again revised, now tagged at $60 to $70 million. (A rejected proposal by Malibu-based designer Barry Howard had called for moving sidewalks with visitors wearing radio-controlled headphones at all times.)

In May 1991, University of Indiana at Bloomington professor Bruce Harrah-Conforth, 40, was named director of curatorial and educational affairs at the museum. His main task was to fill the hall with rock artifacts, a difficult task in an environment where competition among collectors and commercial outlets like the Hard Rock Cafe, had made prices prohibitive. In the next several years, Harrah-Conforth convinced artists, their relatives, and other music industry professionals into donating or lending historically vital pieces, including scribbled lyric sheets, school report cards, stage clothing, and the requisite guitars. His initial budget for acquisitions was nonexistent at first, though funds were later allocated.

Using slides and drawings, architect I.M. Pei unveiled his revised plans for the Hall of Fame, featuring a main tower surrounded by separate buildings, with the Hall of Fame chamber on the top level. With local officials unhappy with the modifications, I.M. Pei offered another design in October. But critics charged that the Hall of Fame's pyramid shape closely resembled his designs of the Kennedy Library and Louvre addition. With Pei's contract finalized, his firm was paid $5.35 million.

At the seventh induction ceremony in 1992, hall officials bemoaned the absence of major corporate sponsors, fearing that autumn's planned groundbreaking might be delayed yet another year. The hall's critics were leading a separate charge. Warwick Stone, the memorabilia buyer for the Hard Rock Cafe chain, told *GQ* magazine: "The Rock and Roll Hall of Fame doesn't exist. I mean, there is no Hall of Fame. Where's the property? Where's the collection? What is it earning?" (p. 227). Noted Cleveland deejay John Lannigan told *People* magazine, "It's very embarrassing," and the late promoter Bill Graham repeated the lament, "You have to wonder why there's such a problem" (pp. 55-56). In February 1992, K. Michael Benz succeeded Larry Thompson as executive director.

In May 1993, the New York-based Hall of Fame Foundation took several legal steps to consolidate its legal authority. With the Cleveland and New York boards entering into separate operations, the New York-based Foundation retained the rights to the Rock and Roll Hall of Fame, with the name licensed to the Rock Hall in Cleveland. The joint operating agreement gave directors "the right" to move the museum to another city if funding goals were not realized. Privately, Cleveland officials were outraged by the actions but kept quiet for fear of losing the Rock Hall.

The New York Foundation also maintained its right to exclusively oversee the induction process. Meeting in a conference room at the posh Atlantic Records offices in New York City, a group of rock movers and shakers—mainly record company honchos—converged for the annual, politics-filled shoutfest over who belonged in the rock hall.

During his second and final year as a member of the selection committee, the former editor of *Goldmine* magazine, Jeff Tamarkin, recalled that the rules were changed in that "the board asked us to choose a certain number of artists before we even came to the meeting. So by the time we got there in 1993, some of the nominees had already been chosen, and it was left to us to come up with the rest at the meeting. One interesting side effect of this change was that some committee members were willing to vote for certain artists in private that they would never advocate in public. For example, some of the people on the committee were appalled that the Doors and the Grateful Dead had received enough votes in advance to make the list, yet in a discussion that took place before the meeting among five or six committee members, none of them—except me!—would admit to having voted for those artists. Had those names been bandied about at the open meeting, I'm convinced they would not have been nominated that year."

Later, the independent-minded Tamarkin lost his seat on the board, in part for criticizing the induction process in a *Billboard* magazine editorial in which he wrote: "To the vast majority of rock fans, and even to most in the industry, the makeup of this committee and its selection process are shrouded in mystery—it often appears that one would have better luck uncovering who killed J.F.K. . . . . Something is missing from that board room even as we bandy names about: the public. This is a vote by politburo, not a general election" (p. 6). Fellow board member Phil Spector had distributed copies of the article to the others in the room.

The identities of the nominating board is also a guarded secret. When a Cleveland entertainment magazine tried to obtain the list of the 15 judges they were told by the New York foundation that "they aren't allowed to give them out."

Groundbreaking for the Rock Hall finally came in June 1993, when Chuck Berry, Pete Townshend, and Billy Joel turned over inaugural shovels of dirt, to the background music of the Rolling Stones' "Satisfaction." Townshend, who had flown to Cleveland on the heels of his Tony Award win for the Broadway production of *Tommy* the night before, told the jubilant summer crowd that he hoped the hall "doesn't become a monolith to a bunch of dinosaurs." But the turning over of dirt marked the hall's reality. Although delayed many times by funding, politics, and miscalculations, nothing could stop its completion now.

In August, the controversial Dennis Barrie was named the director of the Rock Hall, replacing Bruce Harrah-Conforth. In December, James Henke was named chief curator. Making eight trips to Sam Phillips' home in Memphis, Henke later managed to do what both the Smithsonian and Hard Rock Cafe could not: convince Phillips to allow the museum to display his Sun Records historical artifacts, including the very piano used on Elvis' first hits. Other items in the museum's collection include Alice Cooper's 10-foot high guillotine prop; Jimi Hendrix's handwritten lyrics to "Purple Haze," retrieved from a waste basket; Janis Joplin's psychedelic Porsche; Jim Morrison's Cub Scout uniform; Elvis Presley's leather suit from his 1968 comeback special; and Keith Moon's report card, which shows "promise in music." The following year, fashion designer Stephen Sprouse was named costume curator, in charge of the museum's 100 mannequins. Meanwhile, Dennis Barrie voiced his dissatisfaction with the museum's emphasis on lifeless rock memorabilia, and demanded interactive, audiovisual exhibits. The resulting improvements added $8 million to the display budget of $14 million.

Reaching its target date of Labor Day weekend 1995, the Hall of Fame opening drew hundreds of thousands of visitors and a horde of 2,000 international journalists to Cleveland. Costing $92 million in the end, the museum had been tagged at $15 million nine years earlier. With board member Jann Wenner originally pegging the admission price at $2 or $3, the first year entry price instead stood at $10.90.

The highlight of the weekend-long celebration was the Concert for the Hall of Fame, which was staged at the 65-year-old, 80,000-seat Municipal Stadium, just 14 months before its hasty demolition and weeks before the announcement of the departure of the football field's sole tenant, the Cleveland Browns. Tickets ranged in price from $30 to $540, with live coverage provided by HBO on a pay-per-view basis. Hotel doormen in Elvis Presley and Little Richard masks greeted visiting rock enshrinees. With the entire city ablaze in rock and roll fever, starstruck fans tailed the bumper-to-bumper limousines that packed the downtown streets.

Emceed by local deejay Len "Boom Boom" Goldberg and former Cleveland deejay, now CBS-Sony record executive "Kid Leo" Travagliante, the $4 million dollar concert production paired musicians in never-before combinations. Kicking off just before dusk at 7:30, pioneering rocker Chuck Berry was teamed with the Boss, Bruce Springsteen, on the duck-walking, rock masterpiece "Johnny B. Goode." Other highlights in the seven-hour concert included John Fogerty performing his Creedence material, James Brown joined by his entourage on a steaming string of soul chestnuts, and local singer Chrissie Hynde, who unleashed a string of hellos to just about every city in northeast Ohio, her old stomping grounds. Closing the evening at 2:15 A.M. were Bruce Springsteen and Chuck Berry, joining on "Rock and Roll Music."

A shimmering, futuristic glass pyramid, the Rock and Roll Hall of Fame and Museum was constructed with 1,900 tons of steel, the frame built to withstand winter gale-force winds of up to 150 miles per hour. With the building's neon halo reflecting in the calm waters of the seven-acre, man-made, rectangular harbor along the Lake Erie shore, the museum became an instant landmark. The building was originally planned for 200 feet but was reduced to 167 feet because of nearby Burke Lakefront Airport. The museum is neighbored on one side by a domed, state-of-the-art science museum and on the other by the hulking, permanently docked William J. Mather-freighter-turned-museum.

In a recurring controversy, a brouhaha erupted at the 1996 induction ceremony as to whether or not Cleveland would stage the induction ceremonies the following year.

Following promises by both Ahmet Ertegun and Rock Hall CEO, William N. Hulett, Cleveland finally won the right to ceremonies in 1997, on a rotational basis, sharing the honor with Los Angeles, London, and New York.

Still, not everyone is happy with the museum. David Bowie has called it ludicrous, telling HBO: "Screw them. I'm not even remotely interested. I know my own worth. I don't need a medal. Would I turn it down? Absolutely." When reformed punk rock icons the Sex Pistols came to town, lead singer Johnny Rotten demanded to be taken out of the museum, telling an audience, "I hate it." Other critics have suggested that the museum resembles a king-sized Hard Rock Cafe, with guitars hanging on the wall. Boston Globe music critic Jim Sullivan typified the sentiment: "From an aesthetic viewpoint, there's always lurked the questionable desire to institutionalize what was never intended to be institutionalized or, especially, sanitized. When the Rolling Stones were inducted . . . some [people] wondered whether a Stones' exhibit would include Keith Richards' guitars and, maybe, a few old syringes from his days as a heroin addict?" (p. 73).

Another concern was voiced by Neil Young and others: that the Hall of Fame has inducted far too many musicians, somehow cheapening the honor. While the Baseball Hall of Fame has bestowed the honor on only a handful of players per year, former nominating committee member Jeff Tamarkin counters, "You have to weigh how many baseball players have been in the major leagues with how many people made rock and roll records."

The Hall of Fame selection committee has also been criticized for its inconsistency in choosing which group members qualify for induction and which do not. While three-dozen singers can claim membership in the Drifters, only seven members were inducted. Meanwhile, Smokey Robinson was enshrined into the hall minus his longtime backing group, the Miracles.

A number of rock historians have also bemoaned the absence of early rock pioneers such as the Dominoes and the Flamingos. "When certain semi-obscure names were mentioned, the people in charge of the Hall of Fame would start getting real nervous, and say 'how are we going to sell tickets if we don't have any name artists this year?'," recalled Jeff Tamarkin. He added: "And now that they're well into the '70s in terms of who's eligible, they'll never get to those people. . . . And it's a shame. Realistically, why are people like Crosby, Stills & Nash, Joni Mitchell, George Clinton and David Bowie being inducted before people who made this all possible? The obvious answer is money, because they have to sell tickets to the dinners, they have to get people to come to Cleveland to go their building, and they're not going to do it with the Moonglows or the Flamingos—they're going to do it with David Bowie and the people I've mentioned. I've pretty much heard things to that effect said [by the nominating committee]."

But still, the Rock Hall has thrived, adding new exhibits on a regular basis. With a break-even point at 690,000 visitors, the Rock Hall had hoped to pull 900,000 in attendance. But just short of its one-year anniversary, the museum exceeded all projections, welcoming its 1-millionth visitor. Of that number, 540,000 came from outside Ohio; 50,000 came from overseas. In contrast, the previously leading rock destination, Elvis Presley's Graceland mansion, draws 700,000 annually.

Bibliography

Barry, Dave. (1986, August 24). Rolling out the rock artifacts. *Washington Post*, p. G1.

Belardo, Carolyn. (1986, May 1). Cleveland rocks, not Philadelphia. U.P.I., n.p.

DeCurtis, Anthony. (1986, June 19). Cleveland chosen as site for Hall of Fame. *Rolling Stone*, p. 13.

Dunn, Jancee. (1995, October). Hail hail rock & roll. *Rolling Stone*, p. 35.

Farris, Mark. (1986, May 6). Rock hall of fame is Cleveland's. *Akron Beacon Journal*, p. B1.

Fricke, David. (1986, February 13). The Rock and Roll Hall of Fame: At last. *Rolling Stone*, p. 33.

Gehr, Richard. (1988, April 5). The mart of rock and roll. *Village Voice*, p. 25.

Harrington, Richard. (1988, January 27). Rock's induction production. *Washington Post*, p. D7.

Harrington, Richard. (1996, January 31). Hall of Fame director to move on. *Washington Post*, p. D7.

Hilburn, Robert. (1986, March 2). Misplacing rock's hall of fame? *Los Angeles Times*, Calendar sect., p. 58.

Holan, Mark. (1989, October 19). Norm N. Nite: The Rock Hall of Fame's unsung hero. *Scene*, p. 9.

Holan, Mark. (1991, May 2). Five years and nothing to show for it. *Scene*, p. 13.

Holan, Mark. (1996, August 29). One year after. *Scene*, p. 12.

Holan, Mark. (1998, January 8). How the Rock Hall voting process works. *Scene*, p. 18.

Johnson, Kevin C. (1994, April 24). A cool head. *Beacon Magazine*, p. 5.

Litt, Steven. (1995, August 27). Oh, for the right place. *Cleveland Plain Dealer*, p. 1J.

Litt, Steven. (1995, September 10). Architecture critics mainly approve Pei's rock museum. *Cleveland Plain Dealer*, p. 3J.

Litt, Steven. (1996, January 14). Artistic package on waterfront line an RTA letdown. *Cleveland Plain Dealer*, p. 3J.

Lubinger, Bill. (1996, April 18). Rock hall so popular it needs to expand. *Cleveland Plain Dealer*, p. 1A.

McGuire, Jack. (1990, March 12). Market profile Cleveland. *Advertising Age*, p. M22.

Montanari, Richard. (1993, July). Exile on Ninth Street. *Northern Ohio Live*, p. 72.

Newman, Ralph M. (1973). Norm N. Nite: New York welcomes "Mr. Music." *Bim Bam Boom* 2(4), p. 15.

Norman, Michael. (1995, July 28). Out of the back room and into the fore. *Cleveland Plain Dealer*, p. 22.

Norman, Michael. (1996, January 20). Why rock induction isn't here. *Cleveland Plain Dealer*, p. 8E.

Norman, Michael. (1996, January 24). Rock hall director resigns for new ventures. *Cleveland Plain Dealer*, p. 7B.

Norman, Michael. (1996, September 1). Rock Hall a huge hit. *Cleveland Plain Dealer*, p. J1.

Norman, Michael. (1996, September 19). Cleveland to host Rock Hall inductions. *Cleveland Plain Dealer*, p. A1.

O'Malley, Michael. (1985, October 4). Rock 'n' roll officials come to Cleveland. U.P.I., n.p.

O'Neil, Thomas. (1993). *The Grammys: For the Record*. New York: Penguin.

Page, Clarence. (1986, March 19). A rock hall of fame for Chicago? *Chicago Tribune*, p. B15.

Palmer, Robert. (1985, August 5). Rock music will have its own hall of fame. *New York Times*, p. C12.

Pond, Steve. (1992, September). The Rock and Roll Hall of fame, prestigious figment of the music industry's imagination. *GQ*, p. 227.

Powers, Ann. (1995, September 19). Cleveland rocks! *Village Voice,* p. 46.

Rathburn, Keith. (1986, May 8). We got it! *Scene*, p. 1.

Quinn, Chris. (1997, February 27). Interview with author.

Roldo. (1996, January 31). Barrie forced out. *Cleveland Free Times*, p. 7.

Sandstrom, Karen. (1995, August 27). What won this for Cleveland was Clevelanders. *Cleveland Plain Dealer*, p. 1A.

Sanz, Cythia & Micheli, Robin. (1991, February 4). Stars partied and played for rock's Hall of Fame. *People*, p. 55.

"Souvenir Section." (1995, August 27). Rock and Roll Hall of Fame and Museum. *Cleveland Plain Dealer*.

Sowd, David. (1981, October). Not fade away. *Northern Ohio Live*, p. 24.

Stoffel, Jennifer. (1988, January 3). What's doing in Cleveland. *New York Times*, sect. 10, p. 10.

Sullivan, Jim. (1990, January 18). A hall of fame of differences. *Boston Globe,* Living sect., p. 73.

"Suzan Evans talks about the Rock and Roll Hall of Fame." (1996, November-December). *Liner Notes*, p. 6.

Tamarkin, Jeff. (1992, February 22). Rock hall of fame: An elitist club? *Billboard*, p. 6.

Tamarkin, Jeff. (1997, March 6). Interview with author.

Van Matre, Lynn. (1986, March 23). Chicago still in the running to get Rock Hall of Fame. *Chicago Tribune*, n.p.

Walsh, Ed. (1994, August 4). The Rock Hall is here to stay. *Scene*, p. 5.

Wilder, Jesse Bryant. (1993, July). Norm N. Nite: The Rock Hall's unsung hero. *Northern Ohio Live*, p. 143.

Wise, Stuart. (1986, April 26). N.Y. is rocked and Frisco rolls. *National Law Journal*, p. 55.

CHAPTER 3

The Induction Ceremonies

Beginning in 1986, each January the Rock and Roll Hall of Fame holds its induction ceremonies. With the winners announced ahead of time, the affairs are not meant to be competitive but to reward excellence and innovation in the world of rock and roll.

The Rock and Roll Hall of Fame ceremonies have remained unscripted, informal affairs, because of the intimate nature of the untelevised events, which are free of network censors, commercial breaks, and time restraints. While television coverage was initially proposed, Cleveland officials were unable to secure a network deal in 1987. Only in 1995 did the ceremonies hit the small screen, but only in an abbreviated, tape-delay basis on MTV.

Ignoring Cleveland's demands to stage the induction ceremonies, the New York City-based foundation had remained steadfast in its decision to retain the Hall of Fame's crowning ball in New York and, for one year, in Los Angeles. Cleveland was finally granted the opportunity to host the ceremony in 1997, but only on a rotational city basis.

1986 (JANUARY 23)

"I thought I'd seen everything, but now we've got rock-and-roll at the Waldorf," producer Quincy Jones told the audience of 1,000, which paid between $300 and $1,000 at the premier Rock and Roll Hall of Fame ceremonies. Staged in New York's opulent Waldorf Astoria Hotel, the 1931-era art deco landmark has hosted Albert Einstein, Nikita Khrushchev, the shah of Iran, Winston Churchill, and Emperor Hirohito.

Opening the festivities, the house band, led by David Letterman bandleader Paul Shaffer, ran through a medley of hits by the inductees, including a brief audience sing-along of Chuck Berry classics. (Except for the 1993 ceremony in Los Angeles, Shaffer would retain the bandleader position.)

Admitting, "It's very difficult for me to talk about Chuck Berry because I lifted every lick he ever played," Keith Richards presented a trophy to the pioneering guitarist. Musing about rock music's longevity, Berry chimed that "now I look back and say, how wonderful!"

Inducted by Steve Winwood, James Brown, who was enjoying a comeback hit with, "Living in America" and was yet to commit the crime that put him in prison, said, "Hey, I'm here and I thank God I'm here. Thank God the people still want me."

Dressed in a lavender tuxedo and fresh from a recent hospitalization, inductee Jerry Lee Lewis said, "I thank God that I'm rocking and rolling from my head to my toes. Way back then, they said we were corrupting the youth of America. Of course, I was marrying them."

Attired in his pregrunge cowboy fringe, Neil Young introduced the Everly Brothers, who had recently reunited after a long, bitter feud. Phil Everly told the crowd that in the early 1960s, "everybody always used to ask us what we were going to do when this was over."

Inducting Elvis Presley were Julian Lennon and his half brother, Sean, who said: "Elvis was the thing; he is it." Julian recalled that his late father, John Lennon, admitted that he "wanted to be Elvis."

Dressed in a powder blue tuxedo, inductee Fats Domino recalled, "I sold a lot of records and I took the music to the people who bought the records and I was very happy with everything that went down. But this has made it much better." Accepting Buddy Holly's award, his widow, Maria Elena Diaz, said, "I know Buddy's here in spirit." Quincy Jones introduced Ray Charles to a standing ovation. Recovering from injuries received in a one-car crash, Little Richard was the only living inductee to miss the ceremony.

Non-Performer inductees included "Mr. Rock and Roll," deejay Alan Freed, and record producer Sam Phillips, who called the ceremony "the culmination of something I hoped I would live to see." Posthumous awards went to the rock forefathers, the yodeling country pioneer, Jimmie Rodgers, boogie-woogie pianist Jimmy Yancey, and bluesman Robert Johnson. Producer and former Rock Hall board member John Hammond was posthumously inducted with a Lifetime Achievement Award. A number of early Hall of Fame press releases erroneously claim the induction of Clarence "Pine Top" Smith.

Considered the highlight of each ceremony, the final "jam" presented various inductees and others for usually memorable performances. Opening the night, Jerry Lee Lewis and Billy Joel took to their pianos on "Roll over Beethoven" and were joined by Chuck Berry, Keith Richards, David Sanborn, John Fogerty, Neil Young, and Julian and Sean Lennon. Immediately afterward, the Everly Brothers, Fats Domino, James Brown, and Ray Charles exited the crowded stage. Berry left after the second song, "Reelin' and Rockin'." Closing the evening, John Fogerty, who had previously refused to perform his Creedence Clearwater Revival material, unleashed a rocking version of "Proud Mary."

1987 (JANUARY 26)

Served a meatloaf and mashed potatoes dinner, the audience was told that the New York Hall of Fame Foundation had narrowed down its Cleveland site selection to two locations.

The first female Hall of Fame inductee, Aretha Franklin, was this year's only living recipient to skip the ceremony. With her fear of flying, it was not meant as a sign of disrespect. Rolling Stone guitarist Keith Richards inducted Franklin, proclaiming, "You're in baby, my turn next, maybe."

Introducing his teenage singing idol Roy Orbison, Bruce Springsteen offered a touching introduction, which later appeared on the back of an Orbison album: "When I was young I wanted to grow up to make records with words like Bob Dylan and a sound like Phil Spector. But most of all I wanted to sing like Roy Orbison." A visibly moved Orbison responded, "I've spent the last 30 years trying to be cool, but now I'm nervous. You sing for many reasons, and one of them is to belong. Today I feel that I do truly belong." Springsteen then joined Orbison for a rousing duet of "Pretty Woman."

Chuck Berry inducted the late Bill Haley, recalling: "I was out for 48 days straight on the road with Bill Haley. It didn't matter about the fame, he went out and played the music because he loved it. He would play encore after encore." Haley's son, Pedro Haley, accepted the award.

Chicago bluesman Paul Butterfield inducted his former mentor, the late Muddy Waters, calling him "the greatest inspiration in the world to me." Daryl Hall and John Oates inducted Smokey Robinson, who was taken aback when the audience began singing along to the house band's musical introduction of the Miracles' "Ooo Baby Baby." Peter Wolf inducted the late Jackie Wilson, whose frenetic dance routine projected on a video screen mesmerized the audience.

Inducting a former teen idol, the late Ricky Nelson, John Fogerty recalled: "I wanted to be like Ricky Nelson." Nelson's children, actress Tracy Nelson and the future rock duo Gunnar and Matthew Nelson, accepted the award. Members of ZZ Top inducted Bo Diddley, proclaiming that "he taught us how to put fur on our guitars and drums." Overwhelmed, inductee Carl Perkins said, "What a thrill, what a night for a sharecropper's son to be standing in this building." Also inducted were the Coasters, Eddie Cochran, Marvin Gaye, B.B. King, and Clyde McPhatter.

Inducted in the Early Influence category were country singer Hank Williams and R&B pioneers Louis Jordan and T-Bone Walker. Non-Performer inductees were record company founders Ahmet Ertegun and Jerry Wexler of Atlantic Records; Leonard Chess of Chess Records; and the songwriting team of Jerry Leiber and Mike Stoller. Stoller told the crowd, "We never planned to write rock and roll, we just tried to write good rhythm and blues."

Opening the annual all-star final jam, the Isleys/Beatles hit "Twist and Shout" featured Ringo Starr on drums while Carl Perkins led "Blue Suede Shoes," with solos by Keith Richards, Mick Jones, and John Oates. Others onstage included Ben E. King, B.B. King, Smokey Robinson, Peter Wolf, and Paul Butterfield, who played his bluesy harmonica. When Ben E. King began singing "Stand by Me," R&B pioneer Ruth Brown (who had sneaked in without buying a ticket) walked out of the audience onto the stage, raising a few eyebrows.

Other highlights included Bob Dylan and George Harrison sharing lead vocals on "All along the Watchtower," Elton John's medley of "Whole Lot of Shakin' Going On" and "Hound Dog," and the Beach Boys' performance of their own "Barbara Ann." For a finale, John Fogerty headed a rendition of Wilson Pickett's "In the

Midnight Hour."

1988 (JANUARY 20)

Opening the evening, emcees Jann Wenner and Ahmet Ertegun unveiled architect I.M. Pei's preliminary building plans, with Ertegun frequently reminding the press that the museum would be more like the Smithsonian Institution than Disneyland.

Introduced by Elton John, the four surviving original members of the Beach Boys took the podium. After breaking into a snippet of "Good Vibrations," the group eulogized fallen bandmate Dennis Wilson. Mike Love was then greeted with howls and boos when he launched a barrage of insults against Paul McCartney, Bruce Springsteen, and Mick Jagger. The ceremony's stage manager, Bill Graham, eventually motioned to the house band to play loud and drown out Love's angry torrent. Elton John later commented, "Thank God he didn't mention me."

Bruce Springsteen inducted Bob Dylan, commenting, "The first time I heard Bob Dylan, his voice thrilled and scared me. It reached down and touched whatever worldliness I possessed as a 15-year-old kid in high school in New Jersey." After a long, standing ovation, the dapperly dressed Dylan thanked Little Richard and pioneering musicologist Alan Lomax.

Little Richard stole the night, returning levity to the ceremony with his introduction of the Supremes: "I love the Supremes, because they remind me of myself; they always dress like me." With Diana Ross absent, the award was accepted by Mary Wilson and a nervous Lisa Chapman, the daughter of the late Florence Ballard.

A great fan of doo-wop music, Billy Joel offered a touching introduction of the pioneering Drifters, weaving several of the group's song titles into his speech.

The final award was presented to the Beatles by their former rival Mick Jagger, who reminisced about their first meeting: "They had long hair, scruffy clothes and a record contract, and the combination made me sick." Accepting the award were George Harrison, Ringo Starr, Yoko Ono, and the late John Lennon's two sons, Sean and Julian.

McCartney, who was being sued by his former bandmates over the division of royalties, instead delivered a written statement, which read, "The Beatles still have some business differences. . . . I would feel like a complete hypocrite waving and smiling with them at a fake reunion." George Harrison said, "I don't have too much to say, because I'm the quiet Beatle. It's too bad Paul's not here, because he's the one who had the speech in his pocket."

In the Early Influence category awarded earlier in the evening, the tuxedo-less Pete Seeger read the poetry of Garcia Lorca in his induction speech of the late Leadbelly. Leadbelly's occasional singing partner, the late Woody Guthrie, was inducted with a gushing speech by Neil Young, with the award accepted by Guthrie's son, Arlo Guthrie. Guitarist Jeff Beck inducted electric-guitar pioneer Les Paul, admitting, "I've copied more licks from him than I'd like to admit." The Non-Performer inductee, Berry Gordy Jr., was introduced by Ahmet Ertegun.

After a sloppy start with "Twist and Shout," the final all-star jam quickly gelled with Mick Jagger, George Harrison and Bruce Springsteen sharing a microphone on "I Saw Her Standing There," and were backed on vocals by Bob Dylan and Billy Joel.

Julian Lennon joined Ben E. King for "Stand by Me" (a song recorded by both singers and John Lennon), while Yoko Ono sang backup for Supreme Mary Wilson on "Stop! In the Name of Love." Dylan and Jagger surprised the crowd with their tight harmonies on an anthemic sing-along of "Like a Rolling Stone," which featured a guitar solo by Les Paul. Other numbers included "Whole Lot of Shakin' Going On," "Hound Dog," "Barbara Ann," and a scorching "Born on the Bayou." With the jam appearing over, Neil Young and Jeff Beck played the opening riff to "Satisfaction," setting Jagger into his trademark prancing.

1989 (JANUARY 18)

Co-emcees Ahmet Ertegun and Jann Wenner dedicated the evening to the recently fallen Roy Orbison, the first inductee to pass away after being elected.

Wearing an uncharacteristic suit and tie, avant-garde hipster Lou Reed inducted Dion, recalling, "Dion's voice was unlike any I had heard before." Doo-wop-rocker-turned-contemporary-Christian singer, Dion replied: "I forget what all this attention was like. I've been sitting under a grapefruit tree in Miami for the last 20 years." He also commented on the financial inequities of pioneering rockers, recalling that he earned only $14,000 for his chart-topping 1962 hit, "The Wanderer."

Introduced by Paul Simon, the hall's youngest-ever inductee, Stevie Wonder, was flanked by his son and daughter. After asking the audience to close their eyes to experience what it is like to be blind, Wonder unleashed a litany of society's ills.

With the audience debating whether Mick Jagger and Keith Richards would set aside their three-year-old feud, the Rolling Stones' induction was the evening's most anticipated event. Pete Townshend's introduction was filled with charming sarcasm and with sadness for the late Brian Jones; "I miss him terribly," Townshend confessed. In a touching reunion, Jagger and Richards reconciled and were joined at the podium by Ron Wood and former Stone Mick Taylor (Charlie Watts and Bill Wyman were no-shows). Jagger mused, "Americans are funny people. First you shock them, then they put you in a museum. . . . Thanks for electing us to the waxworks of rock."

When presenters Daryl Hall and John Oates broke into an acapella version of Temptations' hit "Don't Look Back," members of the Motown group joined in as they took the podium. The only current, original member of the group, Otis Williams, was joined by former bandmates David Ruffin and the ousted Dennis Edwards, who told the crowd that he harbored "no hard feelings."

The outrageous Little Richard inducted the late Otis Redding, by singing a medley of his hits and recalling, "The first time I heard him sing 'Lucille,' I thought it was me." Redding's widow, Selma, accepted the statuette.

Introduced by Tina Turner, producer Phil Spector was inducted into the Non-Performer category. After a brief film highlighting Spector's many hits, he stumbled onto the stage and gave a rambling speech: "Tina Turner is the best. Don't believe the things they say about her because they're all true. Where is the inauguration? God bless you." Inducted as Early Influences were the Ink Spots, Bessie Smith, and the Soul Stirrers.

A madhouse, this year's all-star jam featured among others Bruce Springsteen and his band member/girlfriend Patti Scialfa, Tina Turner, Paul Simon, Little Richard, Lou

Reed, Hall and Oates, Pete Townshend, and Anita Baker. Stevie Wonder started the night with a soulful rendition of "Uptight" and later headed a lengthy Motown hit medley.

Singing their own hits, Little Richard unleashed a frenetic "Lucille," Dion jumped into the "The Wanderer," and Mick Jagger offered up the Rolling Stone classics "Honky Tonk Woman," "Start Me Up," and "Satisfaction." Other highlights included "Be My Baby," "Get Ready," "Bony Maronie," a sing-along of "My Girl" and the Otis Redding-penned, Aretha Franklin classic, "Respect." Closing the night, Tina Turner sang "River Deep—Mountain High," minus her estranged ex-husband, Ike, who had already left for the night.

1990 (JANUARY 17)

With the hall's construction delayed several times, an apologetic emcee, Jann Wenner, promised that "the shovel will hit the dirt" before year's end. He would be wrong by three years.

Returning for a second year, Phil Spector was more coherent, but still rambling, in his introduction of the Platters, during which time he denounced the U.S. invasion of Panama and insisted that Eric Carmen, Abba, and Bruce Springsteen had plagiarized his early work. Stage manager Bill Graham again came to the rescue, sending Spector back on course, though barely mentioning the Platters.

Boz Scaggs inducted Hank Ballard, the leader of the Midnighters. In a moving tribute, Ballard recalled how his manager/wife had been killed four months earlier in a hit-and-run accident; after attributing his success to her, Ballard left the podium in tears. Paul Anka introduced fellow crooner Bobby Darin, who had passed away in 1973, with the award accepted by his son, Dodd Darin (who later wrote a scathing biography of his father).

The tuxedo-clad Kinks were inducted by Graham Nash, who poked fun at the constant feuding between Ray and Dave Davies, warning that there better be four statuettes to "keep the brothers from fighting." After a mock stage fight, Ray Davies offered a biting criticism of the Rock Hall: "This is a very posh event. . . . I realize rock and roll has become respectable—what a bummer."

Following James Taylor's warm introduction of Simon & Garfunkel, Simon poked fun at his stormy relationship with Garfunkel: "We can join those other happy couples: Ike and Tina Turner, the Everly Brothers, Mick (Jagger) and Keith (Richards), Paul (McCartney) and all of the other Beatles."

Inducting the Who, the members of U2 said of the group's creative soul, Pete Townshend: "It is written in rock and roll that all you need is love. But you also need a great nose." Mandy Moon, daughter of the late Keith Moon, joined the three surviving Who members and joked about her father's legendary outbursts: "Since Father is banned from this hotel I'm here to accept on his behalf." Townshend told the crowd that the previous year's jam session inspired him to reform the Who.

Stevie Wonder introduced fellow Motown act the Four Tops adding, "We've been friends, brothers, hanging buddies. And they've all let me drive their cars at various times." The 4 Seasons were inducted by their longtime producer, Bob Crewe, who recalled paying for the session of their breakthrough hit, "Sherry," with his rent money.

Earlier in the evening, a pair of songwriting teams were inducted in the Non-Performer category: Gerry Goffin & Carole King; and Motown's star trio, Brian Holland, Lamont Dozier, and Eddie Holland. Inducted in the Early Influence category were pioneering jazz and blues artists Charlie Christian, Ma Rainey, and Louis Armstrong. A chipper Rickie Lee Jones had to improvise her induction speech for Armstrong because, "the waiter took it away with the peach cobbler."

Generating a muddied sound, almost 60 musicians packed the stage for the traditional post-ceremony jam, which even included popsters Debbie Gibson and Michael Bolton. Beginning with a lukewarm duet of "Mack the Knife" by Rickie Lee Jones and Sting (who sang in German), Bruce Springsteen joined John Fogerty for an upbeat "Long Tall Sally."

The night's reunions saw the Who run through a medley of their hits, "Substitute," "Won't Get Fooled Again," and "Pinball Wizard," while Simon and Garfunkel harmonized on "Bridge Over Troubled Waters" and "The Boxer."

Bonnie Raitt and George Benson traded guitar riffs on their electric version of the Ma Rainey blues standard "C.C. Rider," and James Taylor and Carole King performed a duet of "Will You Love Me Tomorrow." The evening's finale was the Spaniels' doo-wop classic, "Goodnite Sweetheart, Goodnite," sung by Frankie Valli, Dion, and Zola Taylor of the Platters.

1991 (JANUARY 16)

A somber mood dominated the festivities when, at 7 p.m., David Crosby (who was in a wheelchair recuperating from a motorcycle injury) announced that U.S. jets had begun their attack of Iraq, signaling the start of the Gulf War. Unlike the rock domos in attendance, the media seemed unfazed and uninterested by the revelation and continued its line of musical queries. Informed of the event, the Turkish-born co-chairman, Ahmet Ertegun was caught unprepared, telling reporters that he hoped that "not too many people die." Rock Hall board member Bob Krasnow took the stage and called for silence, and the induction ceremonies were interrupted for a televised speech by President George Bush. While no one at the ceremonies offered to sing a protest song, board member Jann Wenner recited the lyrics to Jackson Browne's "Lives in the Balance."

When the ceremonies continued, tension surfaced during the induction of the Byrds. Their first reunion in 17 years pitted the feuding Roger McGuinn, Chris Hillman and David Crosby against Michael Clarke and Gene Clark, both of whom had been sued for touring with their own, unauthorized Byrds revues.

Chaka Khan introduced LaVern Baker, recalling that her name "epitomized gospel and soul." The elegantly attired Baker provided the best philosophical message of the night: "If we can fight and die together, why can't we live in peace?" Singing her 1950s hit, "Tweedlee Dee," Baker was backed by Bonnie Raitt and Boston's Barry Marshall and Philip Hamilton.

In another feud, two members of the Impressions, Sam Gooden and Fred Cash, refused to share the stage with early members Arthur and Richard Brooks. Another onetime member, Jerry Butler, unsuccessfully tried to resolve the dispute. The longtime leader of the Impressions, Curtis Mayfield, was unable to attend the event; left a quadriplegic after a freak stage accident, he received his award via a satellite hookup from Atlanta, earning a standing ovation.

With neither Ike nor Tina Turner in attendance, Phil Spector, the producer of their hit "River Deep—Mountain High" instead accepted their award. Unhappy about Ike Turner's presence at the previous year's ceremony, Tina Turner had stayed home. An absent Ike Turner had requested but was refused early release from his incarceration at the California Men's Colony in San Luis Obispo, jailed on a misdemeanor drug offense.

Also inducted were John Lee Hooker (who sang a duet of his Grammy-winning "In the Mood" with Bonnie Raitt); the late Jimmy Reed; and Wilson Pickett, who was unable to attend.

At the start of the evening, awards went to producers Dave Bartholomew and Ralph Bass in the Non-Performer category and bluesman Howlin' Wolf in the Early Influence category. Atlantic Records jazz producer Nesuhi Ertegun was honored with a Lifetime Achievement Award.

An abbreviated, low-key, all-star jam session featured Bruce Springsteen and John Fogerty dueting on "Midnight Hour," with backing vocals by Phoebe Snow and Chaka Khan. Singing off a lyric sheet, Springsteen and Khan offered a clumsy rendition of the Impressions' gospel-soul standard "People Get Ready."

Commenting on the allied strike, Jackson Browne, Don Henley, and members of the Byrds offered the lamenting "Turn! Turn! Turn!" Following with "Mr. Tambourine Man" and "Feel a Whole Lot Better," the Byrds' Gene Clark and David Crosby ended their performances by raising their hands and signaling 1960s-style peace signs.

1992 (JANUARY 15)

Scarcely mentioning the unbuilt Rock Hall, officials blamed the recession and lack of major corporate sponsors as the causes for its delay. Launching another controversy, board member Jon Landau bemoaned the hall's scarcity of women inductees.

Introduced by a nervous Lyle Lovett, the first artist to be elected into both the country and rock halls of fame, Johnny Cash received the loudest ovation of the night. Dressed in black, Cash admitted, "It's about the last thing I thought would happen to me."

Inducting Sam & Dave, Billy Joel reminisced that his first single in 1968 (as a member of the Hassles) was a Sam & Dave number, "You Got Me Hummin'." Sam Moore hoped to put an end to the longtime public feud with his late singing partner, Dave Prater, by bringing Prater's three sons onstage, including Dave Prater Jr., who was disinvited to the ceremony by Rock Hall officials in favor of the late Prater's third wife, Rosemary Prater. An angry Moore refused to share the stage with Rosemary Prater, claiming that his former singing partner had never divorced wife number two.

Inducted as a member of the Yardbirds, guitarist Jeff Beck harbored ill feelings for his abrupt dismissal from the group at the height of their success. In a speech laced with obscenities, Beck recalled: "We paved the way for barbarism. We broke down the barriers of verse-chorus-verse and we set fire to things." Beck also brought attention to the absence of former Yardbird guitarist Eric Clapton.

Neil Young inducted the Jimi Hendrix Experience, recalling that "Hendrix threw a Molotov cocktail onto rock and roll." The award was accepted by Noel Redding, Mitch Mitchell, and Hendrix's father, Al Hendrix. Also inducted were Bobby "Blue" Bland, Booker T. & the MG's, and the Isley Brothers.

Earlier in the evening, Early Influence awards went to pioneering New Orleans pianist Professor Longhair and electric bluesman Elmore James. In the Non-Performer category, presenter Phil Spector spoke warmly of the late songwriter Doc Pomus: "I know love comes from the heart, but I have no idea where love goes when the heart dies." Inducting the electric-guitar innovator Leo Fender, Keith Richards called him "the armorer of rock 'n' roll. He gave us the weapons." Saluting fallen promoter Bill Graham, guitarist Carlos Santana played "I Love You Much Too Much" a traditional Jewish song that he learned from Graham.

This year's all-star jam was marred by technical problems, with many of the microphones not working. In an awkward moment, bandleader Paul Shaffer asked, "Is Billy Joel still here? Where's Billy Joel?" (He wasn't onstage.) Also conspicuously absent was Jeff Beck of the Yardbirds (he had joined the jam session in 1990).

With the stage full of guitarists—Jimmy Page, John Fogerty, Ernie Isley, Keith Richards, Carlos Santana, Neil Young, U2's the Edge, Steve Cropper, and Johnny Cash—Memphis soul and rock dominated the night as the band launched into Booker T. & the MG's' standard, "Green Onions."

Cash sang two of his early Sun Records releases, "Big River" and "Get Rhythm," and was backed by the searing guitar work of John Fogerty and Keith Richards. Other highlights included "Soul Man" by Sam Moore and John Fogerty; Rufus Thomas shouting "Dust My Broom," the signature piece of inductee Elmore James; and the Isley Brothers leading a sing-along of their rock standard, "Shout."

Neil Young provided the evening's standout with his rendition of Hendrix's version of "All along the Watchtower," with Jimmy Page and Keith Richards providing guitar solos. With his still extraordinarily strong vocals, Ernie Isley led a chorus of Hendrix's "Purple Haze."

Closing the night, Aaron Neville and Sam Moore joined the sons of the late Dave Prater, on Sam & Dave's "Something Is Wrong with My Baby."

1993 (JANUARY 12)

The first time the ceremony was held outside New York, the event was staged at the Los Angeles Century Plaza Hotel. While 1,400 attendees were gathered on the inside, fewer than two dozen stargazers assembled on the sidewalk outside the venue, with the local press ignoring the event.

While Paul Shaffer had led the house band in all previous ceremonies, the honor was given to bassist Don Was, who headed a group that included drummer Jim Keltner and keyboardists Roy Bittan and Benmont Tench. A mild controversy tarnished the evening when PolyGram Records boycotted the event without explanation.

The evening's most anticipated event was the reconciliation of Cream members Jack Bruce, Eric Clapton, and Ginger Baker, who had not performed together for 25 years (except briefly at Clapton's 1979 wedding). Cream's bassist Jack Bruce recalled, "It's just like it was yesterday. But now we're 100 years older. We play much slower." Added Clapton, "I've been reunited with two people I love very dearly."

Inducting the Doors, singer Eddie Vedder of Pearl Jam pondered: "It just amazes me to see all these songs . . . in the period from '67 to '71." Doors guitarist Robbie Krieger said of Doors' leader, Jim Morrison, "Jim never felt we'd made it as big as we should have." Morrison's award was accepted by his sister, Anne Churning.

Bruce Springsteen introduced CCR, remembering: "They committed the sin of being too popular when hipness was all. They weren't the hippest band in the world, just the best. To all the naysayers, ha ha, they told you so." Reuniting onstage, the three surviving CCR members—John Fogerty, Doug Clifford, and Stu Cook—appeared to have reconciled.

Reclusive Irish musical poet Van Morrison was this year's sole absentee. Calling him "the Caruso of rock and roll," presenter Robbie Robertson said that Morrison had sent a fax blaming his absence on "work commitments in Europe."

Inducting R&B pioneer Ruth Brown, presenter Bonnie Raitt described her career as "a history lesson in how exhilarating and frustrating it must have been to be a black blues singer." Brown told the crowd that songs are "not about hairdos or packaging, but whether people believe what you're singing." Celebrating her 65th birthday, Brown joined Raitt for a duet of "(Mama) He Treats Your Daughter Mean." Introduced by k.d. lang, another R&B legend, Etta James, proclaimed, "I know what I am now: I'm rock and roll."

Taking the podium, Sly and the Family Stone broke into an acapella version of "Thank You (Falettinme Be Mice Elf Agin)." Dressed in an outrageous, 1970s-era, blue leather outfit, Sly Stone joined the rest of the group near the end of their acceptance speech but said little.

Fresh from their legal victory reclaiming the rights to their compositions, the two surviving members of Frankie Lymon & the Teenagers, Jimmy Merchant and Herman Santiago, accepted the group's award. Merchant recalled that it took 26 takes to record "Why Do Fools Fall in Love;" R&B vocal group Boyz II Men followed with a soulful rendition of the song.

In the Non-Performer category, comedian Billy Crystal inducted his uncle, pioneering record producer Milt Gabler: "He's an 82-year-old man in better physical shape than Keith Richards;" while Dion inducted *American Bandstand* host, the World's Oldest Teenager, Dick Clark. In the Early Influence category, Natalie Cole inducted the late R&B crooner Dinah Washington, the award accepted by her son, Bobby Grayson.

Instead of the usual free-for-all closing jam, the finale was limited to sets by three of the inductees. Instead of the planned Creedence Clearwater Revival reunion, lead singer John Fogerty refused to perform with his former bandmates. Flanked by Bruce Springsteen, Robbie Robertson, and Don Was, Fogerty sang "Who'll Stop the Rain," "Green River," and "Born on a Bayou." Clifford and Cook stormed out of the ballroom and later filed formal complaints with the Hall of Fame protesting their exclusion.

With Eddie Vedder on vocals, the Doors launched into "Roadhouse Blues," "Break on Through," and "Light My Fire." With Vedder trying to downplay his vocal duties, the set was highlighted by Ray Manzarek's intricate keyboards.

With the crowd on its feet, a reunited Cream belted out sterling renditions of "Sunshine of Your Love," "Crossroads," and an Albert King tribute, "Born Under a Bad Sign." Backstage, the trio considered a reunion project, but Clapton later reneged.

1994 (JANUARY 19)

This year's inductees were the first to know that the hall was a certainty, with the Cleveland groundbreaking having taken place the previous June. A construction video was played on monitors to the once skeptical rock community.

The most anticipated award of the evening was that of John Lennon for his post-Beatles solo output. Inducting Lennon was his former songwriting partner, Paul McCartney, who had previously boycotted the Beatles' induction. Reading a newly written letter to Lennon, McCartney reminisced about their first meeting at age 13 and about how they would fake the lyrics while harmonizing to the Del-Vikings' doo-wop hit "Come Go with Me." After McCartney handed the award to Lennon's widow, Yoko Ono, the pair hugged warmly in a moving public reconciliation, causing many in the audience to weep. Backstage, Ono gave McCartney a demo tape of Lennon performing "Free as a Bird," which was later transformed into a full-fledged Beatles song.

British guitar legend Jeff Beck inducted his former bandmate, Rod Stewart, comically complaining: "People say we have a love-hate relationship. It's true. He loves me and I hate him." A victim of a Los Angeles earthquake, Stewart was forced to skip the event to console his four children and pregnant wife, model Rachel Hunter.

Also absent was John Fogerty, who was expected to present the award to his idol, Duane Eddy. Instead, Eddy was inducted by Foreigner's guitarist Mick Jones. The king of the twang-guitar, Eddy performed his signature, instrumental hit "Rebel-'Rouser," and was the first to enter the hall via a new rule that allows the committee to bypass the voting board if an artist has been nominated at least seven times.

Rock icon Elton John received his award from Axl Rose of Guns N' Roses. Surprising the audience with a touching speech, Rose said "For myself as well as many others, no one's been there more as an inspiration than Elton John. When I first heard 'Bennie and the Jets' I knew at the time I had to be a performer." An obviously emotional John (who was escorted to the event by RuPaul) was speechless, and handed the statuette to his longtime writing partner, Bernie Taupin.

The biggest spectacle of the evening was the sight of psychedelic kings of tie-dye, the Grateful Dead, wearing formal tuxedos. The group's guitarist, Bob Weir, joked: "I've hated tie-dye all my life." In lieu of the group's absent leader Jerry Garcia, Weir dragged out a full-color, life-size cutout. Weir then launched into a speech criticizing drug laws, which had resulted in the jailing of hundreds of "Deadheads" around the country.

Inducting the blues-rock group the Band, Eric Clapton admitted that he had always wanted to be a member: "I went to visit the Band in Woodstock and I really sort of went there to ask if I could join the Band. Only I didn't have the guts to say it." The group's drummer-vocalist Levon Helm was a no-show because of his longtime feud with former member Robbie Robertson.

Also inducted were the Animals, with Eric Burdon skipping the event, and the late reggae giant, Bob Marley, who was called "Dr. King in dreadlocks" by U2's Bono.

Earlier in the evening, the late Chicago Blues legend, Willie Dixon was inducted in the Early Influence category by Chuck Berry. Berry chimed: "Willie Dixon had the beat, man. That's what Alan Freed called it back then. The Beat. And no one had it like Willie." Inducted in the Non-Performer category by presenter Etta James, R&B songwriter, talent scout, and bandleader Johnny Otis was unknown to many in the audience.

This year's traditional all-star jam was again pre-planned. Opening with the Willie Dixon-penned "Wang Dang Doodle," his daughter, Shirli, sang lead and was backed by Bob Weir, Robbie Robertson, Bruce Hornsby, Chuck Berry, and harmonica player John Popper of Blues Traveler. Unscheduled, Chuck Berry then launched into an obligatory version of his rock standard "Roll over Beethoven." Then, Bob Marley's widow and children were joined by Bono and actress Whoopi Goldberg on "One Love."

The most unusual pairing of the night was heavy-metal shouter Axl Rose, joining Bruce Springsteen to perform the Beatles song "Come Together." A strange combination of metal and heartland vocals, their rendition later received radio airplay. (Paul McCartney, who was scheduled to perform the song with Elton John, was conspicuous by his absence.)

Closing the five-song jam session was the much anticipated Band reunion. Performing their classic, "The Weight," Robbie Robertson joined his former bandmates for the first time in 17 years, with Eric Clapton finally getting his chance to play with the group.

1995 (JANUARY 17)

Abuzz with the excitement of the hall's imminent opening later in the year, this year's ceremony became a media circus. Also a first, MTV showed highlights of the ceremony in a taped special.

The evening's most anticipated induction was that of heavy-metal pioneers Led Zeppelin. During his induction speech, Aerosmith's Steve Tyler recalled how Zep's Jimmy Page had once stolen his girlfriend. Led Zeppelin's lead vocalist, Robert Plant, was ambivalent about receiving the award: "I never wanted to do this. I thought we'd always be rebels." Taking a shot at his former bandmates, John Paul Jones was still fuming over his exclusion from a reunion album and tour the previous year: "Thank you, my friends, for finally remembering my phone number."

During his induction of the late Frank Zappa, presenter Lou Reed attacked Newt Gingrich and fondly recalled Zappa: "Whether he was writing symphonies, satiric broadsides or casting a caustic glow across the frontier of madness that makes up the American political landscape, Frank was a force for reason and honesty in a business deficient in these areas." Zappa's daughter, Moon Unit, accepted the award.

After performing an acoustic rendition of Janis Joplin's "Piece of My Heart," folk-rocker Melissa Etheridge inducted the late singer, recalling: "In 1967, Janis was strange and freaky. I think today she would be pretty hip, alternative." In his acceptance speech, Joplin's brother, Bob Gordon, inadvertently insulted Rock Hall founder Ahmet Ertegun in a bawdy anecdote involving Joplin.

Inducting Neil Young was vocalist Eddie Vedder of Pearl Jam. Vedder's grunge-style group had backed Neil Young on a concert tour the previous year. Young thanked the late Kurt Cobain for giving him "the inspiration to renew my commitment."

The Allman Brothers were inducted by Willie Nelson, who called them "rock's greatest jamming blues band." In their acceptance speech, band members recalled the group's late members Duane Allman and Berry Oakley and the late promoter Bill Graham, who frequently booked the group at his Fillmore nightclubs. Butch Trucks of the Allman Brothers added: "We don't win awards or Grammys, so we were surprised when we got nominated." The group then performed "No Way Out."

Also inducted were Martha Reeves & the Vandellas, who were inducted by the B-52's' Fred Schneider and Kate Pierson; and the Reverend Al Green, who was introduced by Natalie Cole, who said of his voice: "It bobs, it weaves, it floats, it sneaks up on you and stings."

Earlier in the evening, the doo-wop pioneers, the Orioles, were inducted by their former manager, Deborah Chessler, and Sire Records founder, Seymour Stein. The award was accepted by the group's only surviving original member, Johnny Reed. Former *Billboard* music editor Paul Ackerman was inducted posthumously in the Non-Performer category.

In the all-star jam, Willie Nelson joined Al Green on "Take Me to the River," a song popularized by the Talking Heads; the pair also sang Nelson's composition "Funny How Time Slips Away." Following were Neil Young and his longtime backing band, Crazy Horse, performing a song from their new album, "Act of Love."

With high audience expectations, Led Zeppelin regrouped. Robert Plant, Jimmy Page, and John Paul Jones were backed by drummer Jason Bonham, son of Led Zeppelin's late drummer John Bonham, and Steven Tyler and Joe Perry of Aerosmith for a 20-minute jam. Beginning with a Yardbirds' medley ("The Train Kept A-Rollin'" and "For Your Love"), they then swerved into a blues set ("Long Distance Call" and "Baby, Please Don't Go"). For an encore, Led Zeppelin was joined by Neil Young on "When the Levee Breaks" and from Young's Buffalo Springfield days, "For What It's Worth."

Closing the night were Martha and the Vandellas, who led a rendition of their hit "Dancing in the Street." Lead singer Martha Reeves was flanked on both sides by the gyrating Kate Pierson and Fred Schneider of the B-52's.

1996 (JANUARY 17)

The first ceremony since the hall's opening in Cleveland, the low-key affair paled in comparison to the festivities the previous September. A video montage of the gala opening made Cleveland look like Paris on Lake Erie. For the first time in the ceremony's history, a closed-circuit simulcast was beamed to 2,000 spectators, who each paid $50 to gather at the Cleveland Rock Hall.

A brouhaha erupted over whether or not Cleveland would hold the induction ceremonies in 1997 after both Hall of Fame board members Ahmet Ertegun and William Hulett leaked the news to the press. Surprised, executive director Suzan

Evans chided the report, calling it premature. In the end Cleveland was granted the 1997 ceremony on a rotational city basis, along with Los Angeles, London, and New York.

As usual, a number of acts skipped the ceremony. The Talking Heads' singer David Byrne inducted David Bowie, who was in Finland beginning a tour. Bowie had previously attacked the Rock Hall in the music press. Making her first hall appearance, a gushing Madonna took the podium to accept the award for Bowie, recalling her first Bowie concert at Detroit's Cobo Arena. (Madonna was a last-minute substitute for the scheduled Iggy Pop.)

Also absent was the ailing Jefferson Airplane's Grace Slick. Inducted by the Grateful Dead's Mickey Hart and Phil Lesh, the Jefferson Airplane stoically accepted their award with a long formal speech. Jorma Kaukonen plugged his home state before leaving the podium with the closing statement: "As we say in Ohio, 'with God all things are possible.'" The group then performed three songs from its early period, "Crown of Creation," "Embryonic Journey," and "Volunteers." They had been scheduled to perform only one song.

Continuing his bitter feud against his former bandmates, Roger Waters of Pink Floyd was absent (as was the once-institutionalized Syd Barrett). The remaining trio of David Gilmour, Rick Wright and Nick Mason took the stage without a single reference to the missing Waters. Billy Corgan, who presented the award, joined the band in an unplugged rendition of the Barrett tribute, "Wish You Were Here."

Introducing the Shirelles were Marianne Faithfull and 1960s singers Darlene Love and Merry Clayton (the trio were sharing a bill that week in New York). The Shirelles' leader and namesake, Shirley Alston, boisterously chastised the hall's selection committee, demanding, "I speak for all of us when I say: We deserve this. What took you so long?" The surviving members of the Shirelles then launched into a medley of their hits.

Inducting avant-garde rock group the Velvet Underground, singer Patti Smith offered a somber, acoustic version of their classic, "Pale Blue Eyes." In tribute to recently passed away Velvet bassist Sterling Morrison, VU members John Cale, Lou Reed, and Maureen Tucker performed a new composition, "Last Night I Said Goodbye to My Friend."

Stevie Wonder accepted the award for the late Little Willie John and joined John's son, Keith, in performing John's jazz-R&B chestnut "Fever" (Keith John is a backing member of Wonder's band). During her introduction of Gladys Knight & the Pips, presenter Mariah Carey took a verbal stab at Madonna, responding to insulting remarks in Spin magazine.

Earlier in the evening, folksinger Pete Seeger was inducted by Harry Belafonte and Arlo Guthrie in the Early Influence category. In accepting his award, Seeger didn't utter a single word, a Rock Hall first, to which Arlo Guthrie commented, "I think Pete said it all, frankly." Record executive Bob Krasnow inducted the late, pioneering, underground FM deejay Tom Donahue in the Non-Performer category.

This year's all-star jam was the briefest ever, lasting only three songs. Gladys Knight was absent when Joan Osborne joined Stevie Wonder and others in the Glady Knight & the Pips classic "I Heard It through the Grapevine." Wonder followed with a riveting rendition of his 1970 hit "Signed, Sealed, Delivered I'm Yours." Closing the night was an anemic version of Pete Seeger's "Goodnight Irene," a hit in 1950 for Seeger's group, the Weavers.

1997 (MAY 6)

For the first induction ceremonies held in Cleveland, organizers had initially planned to hold the proceedings under a large tent on the circular plaza in front of the museum. The event was instead staged at the posh Renaissance Hotel, the tickets sold out within a week.

Opening the evening was the induction of the George Clinton-led groups Parliament/Funkadelic. Clinton and his feather-and-sequin-attired clan were introduced by the former Prince, then known as "the Artist," who described Clinton's music as "earthy, funky and timely."

The Jackson family reunion saw the controversial, self-proclaimed King of Pop, Michael, standing apart from his brothers Marlon, Tito, Jackie, and Jermaine, and Motown records founder Berry Gordy. The beaming Gordy proclaimed that the Jacksons gave "black kids from the ghetto a license to dream." Michael accepted the award, after hugging presenter Barry Gibb. A scheduled performance by the Jacksons was scuttled due to a recent operation on Jackie's knee.

Inducted by Beach Boy Brian Wilson, the surprise hit of the night were the Bee Gees, who later in the evening brought the house down with a medley of their 1970s-era disco hits. "We are the enigma with a stigma," said Barry Gibb, describing the group's "disco" label. The Bee Gees scheduled the release of a new album to coincide with their induction.

Liver transplant recipient David Crosby of Crosby, Stills & Nash was thrilled to be onstage, remarking that "for a guy who was supposed to be dead a couple of years ago, I'm doing pretty well." Presenter James Taylor recalled that CS&N "helped an entire generation navigate themselves through very confusing times."

Stephen Stills, who was a double inductee as a member of both CS&N and Buffalo Springfield, remarked in a touching speech, "What a wonderful, beautifully strange cast of characters life has handed me." Presenter Tom Petty described Buffalo Springfield as "fringe and paisley . . . electric and absolutely new acoustic." The only controversy of the evening came with the absence of Buffalo Springfield member Neil Young. While privately angered over the Rock Hall's refusal to grant him several additional free tickets to the event, Young claimed in an open letter that he was also bitter over the ceremony's broadcast on television.

Inductee Joni Mitchell also skipped the ceremony, fearing a press assault over her recent reunion with her long-lost daughter, whom she had given up for adoption decades earlier. And the longtime feuding members of the (Young) Rascals each took a turn at the mike, setting aside their animosities for the night.

Inducted in the Early Influence category were the late gospel singer Mahalia Jackson and bluegrass founder Bill Monroe, who had passed away a few months earlier. King Records founder Sydney Nathan was inducted in the Non-Performer category.

The annual all-star jam was kicked off by Crosby, Stills & Nash. The trio was joined by James Taylor and Emmylou Harris for a rendition of "Teach Your Children." Buffalo Springfield later took the stage with guest vocalist Tom Petty, in place of the absent Neil Young. Also performing were the Bee Gees, Parliament-Funkadelic and the Rascals.

Bibliography

Onstage quotations were culled from multiple sources.

PART II

The Inductees

PAUL ACKERMAN. *(February 1908 - December 31, 1977). Inducted in the Non-Performer category in 1995.* In 1934, Columbia graduate Paul Ackerman joined the staff of *The Billboard*. Launched in 1894 in Cincinnati as *Billboard Advertising* by William H. Donaldson and James H. Hennigan, the weekly periodical originally targeted the expanding poster and billboard industry, boasting an initial circulation of 2,021. Expanding its coverage of the entertainment industry, the magazine became *The Billboard*, providing news of the theater, circus, opera, and burlesque.

With the rise of the victrola, jukebox, and, later, radio, music coverage greatly increased, eventually becoming the magazine's primary focus. A New York City native, Ackerman was hired as a reporter, later promoted to the position of radio editor.

Serving in the U.S. Coast Guard during World War II, upon his return Ackerman replaced music editor Joe Carlton. Though Ackerman's personal music tastes favored classic country like Jimmie Rodgers, Ackerman was fascinated with the emerging postwar black musical forms. In his new position, Ackerman championed the causes of emerging musical genres and was responsible for charting the rise of rhythm and blues, country music and rock and roll.

Consequently, in 1949 Ackerman ordered a change in the racially demeaning label "race records," then used in the music industry to describe all nonclassical black music forms, his staff brainstorming its replacement. When a young reporter named Jerry Wexler (later the co-owner of Atlantic Records) coined "rhythm and blues," the phrase became the industry standard. In his autobiography, Wexler describes his former boss as "bald as an egg, a tall man with smoldering brown eyes who spoke ever so thoughtfully and slowly. He was the inheritor of a genteel German-Jewish culture, his physician father having raised him on Goethe, Heine, Schiller, Mendelssohn, and Strauss" (p. 60).

As rhythm and blues became rock and roll, much of America felt threatened. With politicians, religious groups, and the press launching an attack against rock music in the mid-1950s, Ackerman and *Billboard* stood firm, siding with the upstart, independent record companies like King, Chess, and Modern.

Sun Records owner Sam Phillips had an ally in Ackerman, helping to launch the careers of Sun acts such as Johnny Cash and Jerry Lee Lewis. When Phillips delivered Elvis Presley's early discs to *Billboard* for their review, Ackerman encouraged radio stations in both the country and R&B formats to play the records. With its extensive coverage of rock music's ascent, Ackerman cemented his magazine's prominence in the record industry, beating out competing trade outlets such as *Cashbox, Radio & Records* and *Record World*.

In 1962, Ackerman briefly left his position at Billboard, joining, as executive secretary, the Association of Record Manufacturers & Dealers of America. In 1969, *Billboard's* "Rhythm & Blues" chart adopted a new name, Soul, before reverting to "R&B" in the 1990s.

Ackerman retired from *Billboard* in 1973, later becoming the executive director of the Songwriters Hall of Fame.

Bibliography
Radcliffe, Joe. (1978, January 14). Paul Ackerman's death spurs music industry tributes. *Billboard*, p. 15
Schlager, Ken. (1994, November 1). On the boards 1894-1920. *Billboard*, p. 19.
Wexler, Jerry. (1978, January 14). Jerry Wexler eulogizes long-time friend. *Billboard*, p. 15.
Wexler, Jerry & Ritz, David. (1993). *Rhythm and the Blues: A Life in American Music*. New York: Alfred A. Knopf.

THE ALLMAN BROTHERS BAND. *Duane Allman (Howard Duane Allman; November 20, 1946 - October 29, 1971); Gregg Allman (December 8, 1947); Richard "Dickie" Betts (December 12, 1943); Berry Oakley (April 4, 1948 - November 11, 1972); Butch Trucks (May 11, 1947); Jai "Jaimoe" Johanny Johanson (John Lee Johnson; July 8, 1944). Inducted in 1995.* Blending blues with country and rock, the Allman Brothers pioneered a new genre called "southern rock," spawning bands such as Lynyrd Skynyrd and .38 Special. The sons of an army sergeant who was murdered while on leave during the Korean War, Duane and Gregg Allman settled in the Daytona, Florida, area in 1958.

A self-taught Gregg Allman taught his older, 13-year-old brother, Duane, to play the guitar. Mesmerized by the instrument, Duane made it his lifelong passion, dropping out of school at age 15.

Starting in 1960, the close-knit brothers passed through a number of local bands, beginning with Kings. After Gregg graduated from high school, the pair made music their full-time careers, playing in top-40 and blues bands.

In 1965, the brothers formed a rock foursome, the Allman Joys, releasing a single on the tiny Dial Record label, but disbanding a year later. Reforming as Hourglass in 1967, the Allmans were permitted little artistic freedom, recording a pair of poorly selling albums for Liberty Records. Recording tracks at the Fame Studios at Muscle Shoals in 1968, Liberty passed on the third record.

The brothers then joined the 31st of February, which featured drummer Butch Trucks. Meanwhile, Duane was recalled by Fame Studio's owner, Rick Hall, hired as a session guitarist for the likes of Wilson Pickett and Aretha Franklin. There, Duane was befriended by Otis Redding's young manager Phil Walden.

Gregg, meanwhile, had joined a Florida band, Second Coming, which featured guitarist Dickey Betts and bassist Berry Oakley; Duane later joined the group. Soon after, Jerry Wexler of Atlantic Records bought out Duane Allman's contract for $15,000 with the hope of making a solo star. To promote Allman, a new label called Capricorn Records was formed by Wexler and Walden.

But Duane balked at solo status and assembled the Allman Brothers Band, with Oakley, Trucks, brother Gregg Allman, and percussionist, Jai Johanny Johanson. While Duane was originally the lead singer, the duties quickly shifted to his better-suited brother.

In 1969, Walden produced the group's self-titled debut album, *THE ALLMAN BROTHERS*, featuring a nude shot of the members on the inside album jacket. With bare-bones studio production and containing the heavily improvised tracks "Whipping Post," "Dreams," and "It's Not My Cross to Bear," the blues-heavy album was only a moderate success at the time, receiving most of its airplay from a few FM rock stations.

The group's double lead-guitar mixture of Duane Allman and Betts expanded the role of the instrument in rock music. Using a Les Paul guitar and then a Gibson model, Duane's blues licks and slide guitar work (using a pill bottle) were reminiscent of Elmore James.

The Allmans' fortunes improved with their follow-up release, *IDLEWILD SOUTH* (1970), featuring the tracks "Statesboro Blues," "Midnight Rider," and "In Memory of Elizabeth Reed." Immediately after the *IDLEWILD* sessions, Eric Clapton invited Duane Allman to play on his Derek & the Dominoes *LAYLA* project.

Released in 1971, the live *AT FILLMORE EAST* captured the Allmans at their peak and contained stunning, Delta-influenced versions of "Whipping Post" and "Stormy Monday."

With the group's popularity soaring, Duane Allman recorded several tracks in the fall of 1971 for their next album, *EAT A PEACH*, before tragedy struck: back home in Macon for a respite, he died in a motorcycle accident, swerving to avoid a collision with a long bed truck. A year later, bandmate Berry Oakley died less than a mile away, involved in a similar accident.

Dickey Betts assumed the reins of the group, singing lead on their highest-charting pop hit, the country-flavored "Ramblin' Man" (1973). But tensions arose with Gregg Allman and Betts fighting over the group's direction, each releasing a solo album in 1974. Following heated recording sessions, with each member recording parts separately, in 1975, the Allman Brothers released the top-10 album *WIN, LOSE OR DRAW*.

Meanwhile, Gregg married Cher at Caesars Palace in Las Vegas, later recording an album together. To the annoyance of the rest of the group, the marriage made Gregg a Hollywood celebrity, his every move reported.

A year later, the band dissolved after Gregg Allman testified against their road manager in a drug trial. After a brief Gregg Allman-less tour, the group disbanded. Betts then formed Great Southern, while the heart of the band formed a jazz-funk group, Sea Level.

With Dickey Betts and Gregg Allman setting aside their feud, the group reformed, signing with Arista Records. But with disco and then New-Wave in vogue, the group's reunion album was ignored, and by 1981 the Allmans again disbanded.

A series of solo projects ensued in the 1980s, with Gregg Allman scoring an album-rock hit in 1987 with the title track from his album *I'M NO ANGEL*.

In 1989, after Epic Records individually signed both Betts and Allman, the Allman Brothers reformed. Flanked by the other core members, Trucks and (Jaimoe) Johanson, the group was rounded out with new lead guitarist Warren Hayes, bassist Allen Woody, and percussionist Mark Quinones. In 1992, the group performed at President Clinton's inauguration party; and in 1994, they performed at Woodstock II and headlined the Horde Festival.

Bibliography

Albero, Richard. (1974). Duane Allman: Just rock on, and have a good time. In *Rock Guitarists* (pp. 4-6). Saratoga, CA: Guitar Player Productions.

Hunt, Dennis. (1989, August 6). Allman Brothers regroup for another try. *Los Angeles Times*. Calendar sect., p. 8.

Palmer, Robert. (1979, May 3). The Allman Brothers: A great Southern revival. *Rolling Stone*, p. 9.

Palmer, Robert. (1989, June 25). A band that gave an age of excess a good name. *New York Times*, sect. 1, p. 27.

Ransom, Kevin. (1994, August). Southern silver: The Allman Brothers' 25th anniversary *Guitar Player*, p. 34.

Snyder, Patrick. (1976, November 4). The sorrowful confessions of Gregg Allman. *Rolling Stone*, p. 11.

THE ANIMALS. *Eric Burdon (Eric Victor Burdon; April 5, 1941); Chas Chandler (Bryan James Chandler; December 18, 1938); Alan Price (April 19, 1942); John Steel (February 4, 1941); Hilton Valentine (May 21, 1943). Inducted in 1994.* After the Rolling Stones, the most important early British R&B group was a somber-faced, scruffy quintet called the Animals. Raised in the working-class English suburbs of Newcastle, the group's lead singer, Eric Burdon, would frequent the back-alley exits of the city's jazz nightclubs, often pestering his favorite American jazz and R&B acts. Majoring in film history, Burdon was unhappy in the university setting and instead turned to performing music. In college, he met trumpeter John Steele, whom he briefly joined in a jazz band.

In 1962 Burdon was asked to temporarily fill as vocalist for the Alan Price Combo, a jazz-blues group headed by a former government pension officer. Returning from a failed solo career in London, Burdon wowed Price with his gravelly and hoarse, genuinely black vocal style (which he attributed to heavy beer consumption). In addition to Burdon and keyboardist Price, the band featured bassist Chas Chandler, drummer John Steel, and guitarist Hilton Valentine.

Evolving into the Animals, the band earned an immediate nightclub fan base. In November 1963 the group ventured to London, where they were signed by independent producer Mickie Most, who took them to EMI and arranged a European tour with rocker Chuck Berry.

The group's debut studio album, *THE ANIMALS*, spawned the international hit "House of the Rising Sun," a song their producer and record company despised. Featuring Burdon's howling vocals and Price's frenetic, blues-styled electric keyboards, the lyrics warned of the sins of a fictional New Orleans brothel. Based on an American folk standard and inspired by Josh White's version, the song was reworked by the entire band but credited only to Price.

After the recording of "We Gotta Get Out of This Place" (1965), adopted as a theme song by GIs in Vietnam, Price left the group. Although citing a fear of flying, Price left in a dispute over royalties and was replaced by Dave Rowberry.

With the rise of the British Invasion, the Animals' persona greatly contrasted with the Beatles' early innocence. With the Rolling Stones switching to mainstream rock, the Animals stayed in the blues realm with hits such as a cover of Sam Cooke's "Bring It on Home to Me" (1965), "It's My Life" (1965), and "Don't Bring Me Down" (1966).

Unhappy with Most's pop approach, the group switched producers and left EMI records. Though landing several hit records, the band members reaped little income. Unable to support his family, Steel left in 1966, and, replaced by Barry Jenkins, the band recorded a pair of fine blues-based albums, *ANIMALIZATION* (with the cover of the blues standard "See See Rider") and *ANIMALISM*.

But after Burdon and Valentine's discovery of LSD, the group slowly disintegrated. With the departure of Chandler and Valentine in 1967, the group was renamed Eric Burdon and the Animals. Burdon moved the group to the new center of hip culture, the U.S. West Coast, recording a series of Summer of Love psychedelia-meets-blues numbers, "When I Was Young," "San Franciscan Nights," "Sky Pilot," and, inspired by the popular music festival of the same name, "Monterey." That version of the group, too, disbanded in late 1968.

Meanwhile, Price formed the Alan Price Set, landing several British hits beginning with a cover of "I Put a Spell on You" (1966). Bandmate Chandler discovered Jimi Hendrix and later managed Slade (of "Cum on Feel the Noize" fame).

In 1969, Burdon signed with MGM, fronting War, a funk-rock group. War's Latin-tinged melodies and syncopated polyrhythms were the precursors of the "world music" movement of the 1990s. Their debut release, *ERIC BURDON DECLARES WAR*, resulted in a top-10 hit, "Drink the Wine" (1970).

Leaving War after a second album, Burdon attempted a solo career but was blacklisted in the U.K. in the early 1970s following negative comments he made on the BBC following Jimi Hendrix's death.

Burdon and the Animals attempted a number of reconciliations. Brief reunions in 1968 and 1977 fared poorly due to battling egos. In 1982, a reconstituted group minus Burdon began touring as the Animals. A year later, Burdon reluctantly agreed to a reunion album and tour, which degenerated into onstage physical brawls, further exacerbating animosities.

Ignored by major labels, in 1986 Burdon released an album named after his earlier autobiography, *I USED TO BE AN ANIMAL*; he later teamed with Doors guitarist Robbie Krieger and in 1990 with former Trinity blues-rock keyboardist, Brian Auger.

Bibliography

Boehm, Mike. (1989, March 22). Road to redemption includes O.C. concert: Eric Burdon is battling the blues. *Los Angeles Times*, Calendar sect., p. 6.

Gabriel, Paul. (1994, January). The Animals: We gotta get out of this place. *Discoveries*, p. 32.

Holden, Stephen. (1983, July 22). The Animals, reunited, pay first visit since 60's. *New York Times*, p. C4.

Kiersh, Edward. (1986). *Where Are You Now, Bo Diddley?* (pp. 224-32). Garden City, NY: Doubleday.

Locey, Bill. (1991, August 29). Eric Burdon: Wry pilot. *Los Angeles Times*, p. J14.

Middlehurst, Lester. (1995, September 15). The price of fame. *Daily Mail*, p. 9.

LOUIS ARMSTRONG. *(August 4, 1901 - July 6, 1971). Inducted in the Early Influence category in 1990.* Nicknamed Satchmo, Louis Armstrong emerged from utter poverty to become one the century's greatest entertainers. Abandoned by his father and seeing little of his mother, Armstrong raised himself in a New Orleans ghetto, surviving on tips as a street performer. Receiving no formal schooling, he formed a vocal quartet at age 11, just before World War I.

In January 1913, Armstrong was sentenced to the Colored Waifs Home after firing a gun in public. There he joined the school's band on drums. Attracted to horn instruments, he switched to the trumpet. Released in 1914, Armstrong worked a series of jobs from hawking newspapers to pimping. During this time, he sold his first composition, reworked by the buyer as "I Wish I Could Shimmy like My Sister Kate."

Returning to music, Armstrong and drummer Joe Lindsey formed a short-lived jazz combo. But the closing of the famed Storeyville vice section of New Orleans in 1917 saw the scattering of the city's jazz musicians. Armstrong found lucrative work as a replacement player traveling through various Mississippi River towns.

Moving to Chicago in 1922, Armstrong landed a spot as second cornet player with King Oliver, soon marrying the group's pianist, Lil Hardin (his second of four wives). In 1923, Armstrong first appeared on record before leaving Oliver's band the following year.

Landing in New York in 1924, Armstrong joined the Fletcher Henderson Orchestra, where fellow musicians were shocked by his inability to read music. Returning to Chicago, in November 1925 Armstrong first recorded for Okeh Records with his own bands, the Hot Fives and the Hot Sevens. Considered Armstrong's finest work, these recordings define the jazz genre. "Here he changes the face of jazz on every conceivable level," writes Will Friedwald in *Jazz Singing*; "Rhythmically, he establishes the soon-to-be standard 4/4 'swing' tempo; structurally, he solidifies use of the theme-solos-theme format; conceptually, he defines the idea of jazz itself with the soloist at the center" (p. 27), with improvisational numbers such as "Hotter Than That" and "Heebie Jeebies."

Armstrong would influence jazz, blues, and rock vocalists alike. Predating rap, his scat style would later peak with the masterpiece "Basin Street Blues." Introduced to marijuana in the 1920s by white jazz musician Mezz Mezzrow, Armstrong enjoyed smoking it heavily throughout his life.

By 1929, Armstrong took a more commercial route, singing more popular tunes and replacing his combo backing with that of larger jazz orchestras. Even in this musical setting, Armstrong was more a featured soloist than a bandleader. Severely damaging his lips in 1934, Armstrong kept his playing to a minimum, preferring to sing.

Predicting the decline of the big band, in 1940 Armstrong reprised his small-combo on a part-time basis, delighting his early fans. With the rise of bebop, in 1947 Armstrong debuted with another group, a New Orleans-styled sextet, the All-Stars, with founding members Jack Teagarden and Earl Hines.

One of the country's first black superstars, Armstrong earned a new nickname at the 1949 Mardi Gras, as he was crowned the King of Zulus. Breaking the color barrier around the globe, he played at the most prestigious concert halls. Flexing his political clout, in 1954 Armstrong quit a State Department tour and called President Eisenhower a coward to protest the government's initial inaction in the desegregation of the Little Rock, Arkansas, school system.

Armstrong's success continued in the rock era, and in 1956 he landed a pair of pop hits with "Mack the Knife" and a reissue of a seven-year-old recording of "Blueberry Hill" (predating Fats Domino's version).

His sole American pop hit in the 1960s came with his chart-topping Dixieland rendition of a Broadway number, his first million-seller, "Hello, Dolly!" The follow-up release, "What a Wonderful World," initially bombed but was later popularized in the 1988 Robin Williams film *Good Morning, Vietnam*. Though severely ill in the late 1960s, Armstrong continued his heavy touring schedule, succumbing to a heart attack in 1971.

Bibliography

Edey, Mait. (1962). Young Louis Armstrong. In Martin T. Williams (Ed.), *Jazz Panorama* (pp. 111-15). New York: Cromwell-Collier.

Friedland, Will. (1990). *Jazz Singing: America's Great Voices from Bessie Smith to Bebop and Beyond*. New York: Charles Scribner's Sons.

Gleason, Ralph J. (1971, August 5). God bless Louis Armstrong. *Rolling Stone*, p. 26.

Schuller, Gunther. (1989). *The Swing Era: The Development of Jazz, 1930-1945*. New York: Oxford University Press.

Stein, Jacob A. (1990, Winter). An evening with Louis Armstrong. *American Scholar*, p. 101.

Stroff, Stephen M. (1982, March). Louis Armstrong. *Goldmine*, p. 8.

Thiele, Bob & Golden, Bob. (1995). *What a Wonderful World: A Lifetime of Recordings*. New York: Oxford University Press.

LAVERN BAKER. *(Delores LaVern Baker; November 11, 1929 - March 10, 1997). Inducted in 1991.* One of the first queens of R&B, LaVern Baker helped to shape rock and roll in the 1950s. The niece of blues songstress Memphis Minnie,

Baker was born and raised in a comfortable Chicago home. A soloist in her Baptist church choir at age 12, Baker was drawn to the city's bustling blues scene. At 17 Baker landed a long residency at the 600-seat Club DeLisa, the owners costuming her as "Little Miss Sharecropper," a backwoods, barefooted country bumpkin. There she attracted the attention of Nat "King" Cole and then Fletcher Henderson, joining his band as a featured vocalist.

Appearing at a number of Detroit clubs in the late 1940s (including the Flame, where she influenced future white R&B singer Johnnie Ray), Baker developed a wide repertoire of blues and pop, though she preferred jazz ballads. Recording unsuccessfully in 1951 as Bea Barker for CBS' Okeh subsidiary and as Little Miss Sharecropper at National, the renamed La Vern Baker landed at King Records thanks to new manager, Al Green (not the R&B singer).

Switching to Atlantic Records in 1953, Baker was the label's second female act, following R&B star Ruth Brown. After touring Europe as the featured vocalist of the Todd Rhodes Orchestra, Baker returned to the U.S. when her single, "Living My Life for You," became a hit in the South.

Taking over 50 takes to record, Baker's first major hit came with the novelty-styled "Tweedlee Dee." Penned by Winfield Scott and featuring the sax of the legendary Sam "The Man" Taylor, the single easily crossed over to the pop charts in late 1954 but was eclipsed in sales by Georgia Gibbs' bland cover version.

Possessing a playful, husky voice, Baker also sported good looks, charm, and loads of confidence. A growling, upbeat single, "Jim Dandy" (1956), became her most enduring number, and though also covered by Gibbs, Baker's version was the pop smash. Two years later, Baker scored the biggest pop hit of her career with the ballad "I Cried a Tear." In 1961, she landed an R&B hit with a Leiber & Stoller production, "You're the Boss," in a duet with the Ravens' bass singer, Jimmy Ricks.

Turning somewhat to the style of her Aunt Minnie, she scored a hit in 1962 with a soulful treatment of the blues standard "See See Rider," her last major chart entry. A phenomenally successful singer, she scored nearly two dozen R&B hits in her brief stint at Atlantic.

Leaving Atlantic for Brunswick Records on the advice of her new manager, Baker saw her career slump. In 1966, Baker scored a minor R&B hit with "Think Twice" in a duet with labelmate Jackie Wilson. It would be her last chart entry.

With her second marriage over, in 1969 Baker joined her second USO tour. Applying what she learned from her ex-husband, comedian Slappy White, she took a well-rounded stage act to Vietnam. Performing for soldiers, once only six miles from the fighting, she was stricken with bronchial pneumonia and taken to a Philippine hospital and told she would soon die.

Miraculously, Baker recovered. Deciding to stay, she landed a long-term position as a singer and entertainment manager for the on-base clubs at Subic Bay. There she had a daughter and took three other children into her home. Occasionally touring in Europe and Asia, Baker did not perform in the U.S. for nearly two decades.

After the military base closed in 1988, Baker returned stateside, performing at the Atlantic Records anniversary concert. Rediscovered, Baker took over for Ruth Brown in the lead role of the Broadway blues musical, *Black and Blue*. Returning to recording, her 1992 album, *WOKE UP THIS MORNIN'*, marked her first studio effort in three decades.

Diagnosed with diabetes in 1992, Baker suffered leg amputations. She returned to the stage the following year with the aid of a motorized wheelchair. Baker died in 1997 from heart complications in the midst of a comeback.

Bibliography

Dawson, Jim & Propes, Steve. (1992). *What Was the First Rock 'N' Roll Record?* (pp. 164-69). Boston: Faber and Faber.

Gardner, Alysa. (1995, August 26). Hall of famer returns to the spotlight. *Los Angeles Times,* p. F1.

Garvey, Dennis. (1991, July 12). LaVern Baker: The "Tweedlee-Dee" girl is back. *Goldmine,* p. 10.

McGarvey, Seamus. (1992, September). Tweedlee dee!: It's LaVern Baker. *Now Dig This,* p. 5.

Milward, Jim. (1991, April 14). Everything's just Jim Dandy. *Los Angeles Times*, Calendar sect., p. 3.

Shaw, Arnold. (1978). *Honkers and Shouters: The Golden Years of Rhythm and Blues.* New York: Collier.

HANK BALLARD. *(Henry Ballard; November 18, 1936). Inducted in 1990.* The roots of Hank Ballard and the Midnighters stretch back to 1949 when a group of teens joined forces in the halls of Detroit's Dunbar High School as the Thrillers. Built around the bass vocals of Sonny Woods and tenor Henry Booth, the doo-wop vocal group evolved into the Royals by 1950.

Patterned after the pioneering vocal group the Orioles, the Royals competed at local talent shows, where they were spotted by King-Federal talent scout Johnny Otis. Signed in late 1951, the Royals fared poorly with their initial releases, beginning with the Otis-penned "Every Beat of My Heart."

The Royals were sparked by new blood in early 1952. Drafted, baritone Lawson Smith left the group and was replaced by Hank Ballard, who assumed lead vocal duties.

Born in Detroit but raised in Alabama, Ballard worked as a Ford assembly-line worker. Chiefly influenced by gospel music and matinee cowboy singers, an unhappy Ballard ran away from home at 14, moving back to Detroit. He told writer Bruce Pollock: "[My] family was heavy into religion. They used to beat me if they caught me humming the blues in the house. They couldn't understand. I was not allowed to sing anything but gospel" (p. 107).

With Ballard at the helm, the Royals' ballad-oriented material received scant airplay. But when East Coast audiences began confusing the Royals with their more successful labelmates, the similarly named "5" Royales, Ballard and his Royals found unexpected interest.

Enamored with the Dominoes' erotic R&B smash "Sixty Minute Man," Ballard turned the group away from syrupy ballads. Landing their first hit, the Royals charged the R&B charts in 1953 with "Get It," a lyrically steamy Ballard co-composition. With

Hank Ballard. (*Courtesy of Hank Ballard.*)

the "5" Royales threatening legal action, the Royals became the Midnighters.

In 1954, the Royals/Midnighters dominated the R&B market with a series of chart-topping singles. With the low-down guitar work of the elder Alanzo Tucker, the group scored the biggest hit of its career with "Work with Me, Annie" (its original title, "Sock It to Me Annie," was rejected as too suggestive). Written by Ballard about an old girlfriend, the song was attacked by the FCC, the media, and religious leaders and was banned by many radio stations for its suggestive lyrics. In some communities, the group was arrested for performing the song.

A monster hit, "Annie" spawned plenty of answer records such as Etta James' bawdy "The Wallflower Song (Roll with Me, Henry);" white-popster Georgia Gibbs sanitized the song's lyrics scoring a pop smash with the song, retitled "Dance with

Me, Henry." (Ballard received royalties for both versions.)

After landing a smash follow-up with "Sexy Ways," the Midnighters scored major hits with a pair of "Annie" sequel hits, "Annie Had a Baby" and "Annie's Aunt Fanny." Although landing few hits in the next several years, the group remained an immensely popular concert draw.

With the original group disintegrating, Ballard assembled the renamed Hank Ballard and the Midnighters. Adopting an updated sound, the new group's first release, "Teardrops on Your Letters" (1959), signaled the start of the second phase of the group's career. Issued against the wishes of label heads, the record's B-side was a moderate R&B hit, a dance number called "The Twist."

But when "The Twist" began garnering heavy airplay in Philadelphia, *American Bandstand* host Dick Clark sensed the potential for a major hit. Clark hired a little-known former chicken-plucker turned singer, Ernest Evans, renaming him Chubby Checker, to record a note-for-note cover version of the song. Within months "The Twist" and its accompanying hip-shaking dance catapulted both Checker and Ballard to pop stardom, with Clark repaying Ballard by playing the Midnighters' records on *Bandstand*. The Midnighters' hit run continued with the country-influenced "Finger Poppin' Time" (1960) and "(Thrill on the Hill) Let's Go, Let's Go, Let's Go" (1960).

With the rise of Beatlemania, the Midnighters were pushed off the charts in the mid-1960s. After disbanding in 1965, Ballard and his backing band went to court over the Midnighters' name. Resolved in Ballard's favor in 1967, the new Midnighters were left without a record label after the sale of King-Federal later in the year.

In the late 1960s, Ballard joined James Brown's touring revue. Ironically, Ballard had befriended the struggling soul singer in the late 1950s. Recording at Brown's production company, Ballard released the funky "From the Love Side" (1972), a record that Ballard claims a jealous Brown sabotaged.

Ballard moved to Nashville to produce a few country discs and, later in the 1970s, recorded on Sylvia Robinson's Stang label. In the 1980s, Ballard reluctantly entered the oldies concert circuit. Returning to top form, Ballard released a new album in 1998.

Bibliography

Bronson, Fred. (1992). *The Billboard Book of Number One Hits*, (3rd ed.). New York: Billboard.

Dawson, Jim & Propes, Steve. (1992). *What Was the First Rock 'N' Roll Record?* (pp. 31-36). Boston: Faber and Faber.

Edelstein, Andrew. (1981, November). Hank Ballard. *Goldmine*, p. 11.

Foldberg, Marv. (1996, June). The Royals. *Discoveries*, p. 42.

Hunt, Dennis. (1988, August 19). "The Twist" and turns of Ballard's Life. *Los Angeles Times*, Calendar sect., p. 1.

McDowell, Mike. (1982, November-December). Hank Ballard: You can't keep a good man down. *Blitz*, p. 9.

Pollock, Bruce. (1981). *When Rock Was Young* (pp. 105-16). New York: Holt, Rineholt, and Winston.

Williamson, Drew. (1986-87, December-January). Hank Ballard says there really was an

"Annie" and jukebox play kept the infamous sequels coming. *Record Collector Monthly*, p. 1.

THE BAND. *Rick Danko (December 9, 1943); Levon Helm (May 26, 1942); Garth Hudson (August 2, 1937); Richard Manuel (April 3, 1944 - March 4, 1986); Robbie Robertson (Jaime Robertson; July 5, 1944). Inducted in 1994.* Although the roots of the Band reach back before the dawn of rock, the group still survives today. In 1952, Arkansas native Ronnie Hawkins formed a country group called the Hawks, later scoring a rockabilly hit with "Mary Lou" (1959). A popular touring band throughout Canada and the American Southeast, Hawkins was constantly replacing band members.

Abandoning rockabilly for blues-flavored rock, by late 1961 the Hawks had settled into its classic lineup with singer/pianist Richard Manuel, organist Garth Hudson, singer/guitarist Robbie Robertson, bassist Rick Danko, and drummer Levon Helm. All of the Hawks, except for Arkansas-born Helm, hailed from Ontario, Canada. When Danko was fired by Hawkins for bringing a girlfriend to a club, the remaining Hawks quit the group in 1964 to form Levon and the Hawks (alternatively called the Crackers and the Canadian Squires), backing the likes of blues guitarist John Hammond Jr.

The group's big break came in 1965 when Robertson and then Helm were invited to tour behind Bob Dylan. Pressured by Robertson, Dylan hired the rest of the former Hawks, though firing Helm after an argument.

The Band joined Dylan just as he was switching from acoustic to electric folk-rock. Heckled nightly during a two-year world tour, Robertson told author Edward Kiersh: "We'd pack up our equipment, go to a place, set up, play, they'd boo and throw things at us; we would tear down our equipment, go to the next place, they'd boo, and we did it all over the world, from Australia to Stockholm" (p. 6). Soon, Dylan's unnamed backing group was simply called "the Band."

After suffering a near-fatal motorcycle crash, Dylan moved into a rented pink house (nicknamed the "Big Pink") near Woodstock, New York, where he was joined by members of the Band. A recuperating Dylan and his housemates spent their days playing and recording music, many tracks bootlegged on the album *THE GREAT WHITE WONDER* and officially released in 1975 as *THE BASEMENT TAPES*. In addition, the Band began writing material for what became their first studio album.

Featuring a Dylan painting on the album jacket, the Band's debut release, *MUSIC FROM BIG PINK* (1968), included several Dylan compositions. A critical and commercial success, the album was highlighted by the group's signature hit, "The Weight," featuring the slide-guitar of guest player Duane Allman. Typical of much of the group's output, the track also featured Manuel's high-pitched lead vocals teamed with Robinson's bluesy harmony. Featured in the hippie film *Easy Rider*, the song was also a top-40 hit for Aretha Franklin the following year.

Donning western-style leather vests, earth-toned jackets, and faded jeans, the bearded, rustic-looking members of the Band approached rock from a country, blues, and folk vein. Recording at a house rented from Sammy Davis Jr., a more commercial album, *THE BAND* (1969), featured the group's highest-charting U.S. single, "Up on

Cripple Creek," and the often recorded Civil War lament, "The Night They Drove Old Dixie Down" (later a top-10 hit for Joan Baez).

With Manuel abdicated songwriting duties to Robertson, the Band continued its string of hit albums on Capitol Records, including *STAGE FREIGHT* and *ROCK OF AGES*, the latter containing their last top-40 hit, "Don't Do It" (1972), a remake of a 1964 Marvin Gaye release.

Rejoining Dylan in 1973, the Band appeared on his album *PLANET WAVES* and a subsequent live release, *BEFORE THE FLOOD*; this time they were not booed. The same year, the Band released an album of 1950s and 1960s classics, including "Ain't Got No Home," on the Alan Freed tribute, *MOONDOG MATINEE*. After recording two more studio albums, in 1976 Robertson pressured others in the group to disband.

Deciding to go out with a bang, on November 25, 1976 the Band staged a superstar show billed as "The Last Dance." Promoter Bill Graham provided an elaborate Thanksgiving dinner for the entire Winterland audience, in what turned out to be the concert of the decade. Filmed as a documentary by Martin Scorsese and released in 1978 as a triple-album, the smokey, drug-hazed stage featured "invited guests" Neil Young, Muddy Waters, Ronnie Hawkins, and at the last moment, Bob Dylan. After completing a contractually required album, the Band reluctantly disbanded.

In the 1980s, Robertson's solo career surpassed that of his former bandmates, as he spent much of his time recording movie soundtracks. With strong animonisities still lingering, Robertson refused to rejoin the Band for a brief, small-venue tour in 1986. After one of the concerts, Richard Manuel killed himself in a Winterpark, Florida, motel.

Again without Robertson, the Band reunited at the 1992 Carnegie Hall Bob Dylan tribute and at Woodstock '94. At the 1994 Rock and Roll Hall of Fame induction ceremonies, hostilities arose between Robertson and the others in the Band.

Bibliography

Bowman, Rob. (1991, July 26). The Band: Life is a carnival. *Goldmine*, p. 8.

Flanagan, Bill. (1987, September). The return of Robbie Robertson. *Musician*, p. 88.

Flanagan, Bill. (1993, December). Rick Danko on the Band. *Musician*, p. 24.

Kiersh, Edward. (1986). *Where Are You Now, Bo Diddley?* (pp. 1-13). Garden City, NY: Doubleday.

Palmer, Robert. (1978, June 1). A Portrait of the Band as young Hawks. *Rolling Stone*, p. 49.

Ransom, Kevin. (1995, May). Rolling thunder: The Band's Robertson & Danko shout across "The Great Divide." *Guitar Player*, p. 75.

DAVE BARTHOLOMEW. *(December 24, 1920). Inducted in the Non-Performer category in 1991.* An all-around musical virtuoso, Dave Bartholomew was the prime catalyst in the rise of 1950s New Orleans R&B. Born just outside New Orleans, Bartholomew was the son of a barber who moonlighted as a tuba player in a Dixieland jazz band. In his teens, Bartholomew mastered the trumpet under the schooling of Peter Davis, Louis Armstrong's music coach.

After graduating from high school, Bartholomew honed his talents during a four-year stint in Fats Pichon's band, playing jazz, swing, and even waltzes on a

Mississippi riverboat. Returning to New Orleans, he spent three months behind pioneering black bandleader Jimmie Lunceford.

Joining the service, Bartholomew played first trumpet in the 196th Army Band. Upon his discharge, he joined the Buddy Charles group, which landed a long residency at the New Orleans' famed Dew Drop Inn. Assembling his own band on the advice of a competing nightclub owner, Bartholomew quickly garnered a large following.

Hired as a producer, songwriter, and talent scout by Imperial Records head Lew Chudd, Bartholomew oversaw a satellite studio in New Orleans. Recording at the tiny, Cosimo Matassa-owned J&M studio, Bartholomew employed a strong house band that featured the talent of guitarist Walter Nelson, bassist Frank Fields, drummer Earl Palmer, and saxophonists Lee Allen, Herb Hardesty, and Red Tyler.

As a producer, arranger, and songwriter, Bartholomew was responsible for hundreds of R&B singles in his decade-long streak. "I always tried to keep things as simple as possible, and we always wanted something the kids could sing. I always kept a commercial mind and kept abreast of the market," Barthomomew told writer John Broven (p. 28).

When Bartholomew and Chudd caught a performance by a portly, teenage pianist named Fats Domino at the Hideaway club in New Orleans, they signed him on the spot. Beginning with Domino's million-selling, regional hit "The Fat Man," Bartholomew shaped New Orleans R&B in the 1950s. Pursuing a solo career on the side, Bartholomew landed his biggest hit in 1950 with "Country Boy."

After an argument with Chudd over money, and temporarily apart from Domino, Bartholomew in 1952 recorded solo material with his group for King and Specialty Records, including an early version of the bawdy, "My Ding-a-Ling" (later a hit for Chuck Berry). Discovering a teenage duo named Shirley and Lee, Bartholomew produced their breakthrough hit "I'm Gone." With Chudd relenting, Bartholomew reunited with Domino, the pair returning to top form on a series of R&B and then pop smashes, beginning in 1955 with "Ain't That a Shame" and continuing with "I'm Walkin'," "Blueberry Hill," and "Walking to New Orleans."

Bartholomew also produced hits for Texas bluesmen T-Bone Walker and Albert Collins and blues-shouters Roy Brown and Smiley Lewis. Bartholomew wrote all of Lewis' hits, including, "I Hear You Knocking" and "One Night," the latter also a hit for Elvis Presley.

In the early 1960s, Imperial Records was sold, and Domino and Bartholomew entered semi-retirement. The New Orleans' R&B tradition was continued in the 1960s by producer Allen Toussaint, who worked with acts such as Ernie K-Doe, Dr. John, and Lee Dorsey.

In the mid-1990s, Bartholomew was still involved with music as he returned to his jazz roots as the leader of a 17-piece big band.

Bibliography

Broven, John. (1978). *Rhythm & Blues in New Orleans*. Gretna, LA: Pelican.
Coleman, Rick. (1991, May 17). The New Orleans of Fats Domino and Dave Bartholomew. *Goldmine*, p. 12.
Hillburn, Robert. (1985, September 1). Bartholomew: The man behind the Fat Man. *Los Angeles Times*, Calendar sect., p. 52.

Hillburn, Robert. (1993, March 12). Some surprises in the salute to Dave Bartholomew's genius. *Los Angeles Times*, p. F28.
Joyce, Mike. (1977, November-December). Dave Bartholomew. *Living Blues*, p. 20.
Salaam, Kalamu Ya. (1990, June). Music legend Dave Bartholomew. *Offbeat*, p. 17.

RALPH BASS. *(Ralph Basso; May 1, 1911 - March 5, 1997). Inducted in the Non-Performer category in 1991.* Born in the Bronx section of New York City to European immigrants, Ralph Bass took violin lessons as a child. After attending college in the early 1930s, he moved to Los Angeles, finding work as a salesman at a bottled-water plant.

With music still an avocation, Bass opened a liquor store in 1936 before working as an engineer at Shell two years later. After suffering a severe hand injury, Bass was no longer able to play the violin. Working as a deejay, he discovered an untapped market of black record consumers.

In 1944 Bass was hired as a talent scout and record producer by Black and White Records, a small, independent jazz label. Recording in Los Angeles, Bass oversaw two of the most important records in rock's early evolution. Signing electric Texas bluesman T-Bone Walker, Bass produced the landmark single "Stormy Monday" (1946), featuring a much-copied, revolutionary, single-string guitar solo, a cornerstone of modern rock and roll. In another coup, Bass prodded black, jump-blues bandleader Jack McVea into recording a novelty song, "Open the Door Richard." A then-rare million-selling smash, McVea's record received pop airplay, demonstrating black music's mainstream potential.

After launching his own Bop label in 1948, Bass joined the expanding Savoy Records as their West Coast A&R chief, continuing his role in shaping Los Angeles' embryonic R&B scene. With the help of nightclub owner and bandleader Johnny Otis, Bass signed the Robins and Little Esther, whose pairing produced the hit "Double Crossing Blues" (1950), the first of several smashes at the label.

Leaving Savoy in 1951, Bass signed with King Records, with label-owner Syd Nathan giving Bass a new subsidiary, Federal, as well as half ownership in a lucrative publishing company. Bass' first success at Federal was an R&B vocal group, the Dominoes, who landed a massive hit with the bawdy, much banned "Sixty Minute Man."

In spite of his boss' many objections, Bass continued to release a slew of controversial records over the next several years. Moving to California to head Federal's West Coast division in 1952, Bass signed Tony Williams and the Platters, who bombed at the label (they later thrived at Mercury Records).

Returning to Cincinnati in early 1954, Bass replaced Henry Glover as the producer for an emerging vocal group, the Royals (soon renamed the Midnighters), who landed one of the most influential R&B songs of the decade with the blatantly sexual "Work with Me Annie." Written by Bass and the group's lead singer, Hank Ballard, the song spawned scores of hit answer songs.

In 1956 Bass signed soul singer James Brown and was nearly fired by Nathan, who protested Brown's guttural debut release, "Please, Please, Please." The first of many hits, Brown became the label's workhorse well into the 1960s.

A versatile producer at King-Federal, Bass also produced gospel acts such as the Violinaires and the Harold Smith Majestic Choir and blues singers such as Jimmy Witherspoon and Johnny "Guitar" Watson.

Leaving King-Federal in 1958, two years later Bass became the head of the A&R department at Chess Records, where he helped create the "Chicago Sound," producing the likes of Muddy Waters, Sonny Boy Williamson, and Howlin' Wolf. With former blues-shouter Etta James switching to jazz ballads, Bass produced her early 1960s hits, including the elegant "At Last."

With the sale of Chess in 1969, Bass' hit run at the label slowed. In 1975, the label was again sold, with the new owners instructing Bass to close the studio. A year later, Bass produced several Chicago blues albums intended for TK Records but later released on Britain's Red Lightnin' label. Working with his wife, Bass spent his last years at the Sammy Dyer School of Dance and Theater, which he owned.

Bibliography

Dance, Helen Oakley. (1987). *Stormy Monday: The T-Bone Walker Story*. Baton Rouge: Louisiana State University Press.

Dawson, Jim & Propes, Steve. (1992). *What Was the First Rock 'N' Roll Record?* (pp. 21-25). Boston: Faber and Faber.

Gart, Galen. (1986). *First Pressings: Volume One*. Milford, NH: Big Nickel.

Hess, Norbert. (1976, May-June). I didn't give a damn if whites bought it!: The story of Ralph Bass. *Blues Unlimited*, p. 17.

Pruter, Robert. (1991). *Chicago Soul*. Urbana: University of Chicago Press.

Radel, Cliff. (1994, November 6). King-sized dreams: Making former Cincinnati recording plant into museum would revive an era. *Cincinnati Enquirer*, p. G1.

Tracy, Steven C. (1993). *Going to Cincinnati: A History of the Blues in the Queen City*. Urbana: University of Illinois Press.

THE BEACH BOYS. *Alan Jardine (September 3, 1942); Mike Love (March 15, 1941); Brian Wilson (Brian Douglas Wilson; June 20, 1942); Carl Wilson (December 21, 1946 - February 6, 1998); Dennis Wilson (Dennis Carl Wilson; December 4, 1944 - December 28, 1983). Inducted in 1988.* With the promise of beaches, bikinis, surfboards, and endless sunshine, California became the center of youth culture in the 1960s. Originated by surfer-guitarist Dick Dale and helped along by the beach film genre, the Beach Boys became the leaders of the surf music craze. Ironically, Dennis Wilson was the only member who surfed.

In 1961, the Wilson brothers, Brian, Dennis, and Carl, were joined by cousin Mike Love and Brian's college friend, Ohio-born Al Jardine, in a soft, vocal harmony group, the Pendeltones (later Carl & the Passions). Patriarch Murry Wilson taught his three sons vocal harmonizations through family sing-alongs around their Hammond organ.

Though deaf in his right ear from a childhood blow by his father, college dropout Brian Wilson emerged as the group's leader. Brian (an accomplished pianist) and Carl taught themselves the guitar, while Dennis slowly learned the drums.

Auditioning as the Pendeltones for music publisher Hite Morgan at his tiny X label, the group recorded their first single, "Surfin'." After a legal scuffle with RCA over the use of the X name, Morgan took the song to Candix Records, and renamed the group the Beach Boys. A small label, Candix managed a regional hit (number one in Los Angeles) with "Surfin'," before shutting its doors.

Signing with Capitol Records, the group's first top-40 came in late 1962 with "Surfin' Safari." Assuming production duties on a new version of an earlier recording, "Surfer Girl," Brian Wilson emerged as the group's creative force. After hanging out at Phil Spector's studio, Wilson employed a similar mixing style, even hiring many of Spector's session musicians.

Unlike many of their American counterparts, the Beach Boys managed to survive the British Invasion. With their youthful vision, the Beach Boys became America's chief rival of the Beatles in the mid-1960s, with top-10 entries such as "Surfin' U.S.A." (1963); "Be True to Your School" (1963); "Fun, Fun, Fun" (1964); "I Get Around" (1964); "Dance, Dance, Dance" (1964); a remake of Bobby Freeman's "Do You Wanna Dance" (1965); "Help Me Rhonda" (1965); "California Girls" (1965); and with Jan & Dean's Dean Torrance on vocals, a cover of the Regents' "Barbara Ann" (1966).

The simplicity of Beach Boys hits belied their complex arrangements. Combining the barbershop harmonies of the Four Freshmen, and an updated variation of 1950s doo-wop, Brian Wilson assigned the various vocal roles, carefully drilling each member.

After discovering LSD and marijuana and troubled by a domineering father, Brian Wilson suffered a mental breakdown in December 1964. Though continuing with his songwriting and studio duties, the eccentric Wilson rarely joined the group onstage and was replaced by session player Glen Campbell and then Bruce Johnston.

Beginning in late 1965, Brian Wilson spent long months working on the group's critical masterpiece, *PET SOUNDS*, an experimental album later influencing the Beatles' *SGT. PEPPER* project. A departure from the uplifting, teenager-targeted material, *PET SOUNDS* failed to match earlier sales. Tackling serious subject matter, the album contained a reworking of the folk song, "Sloop B. John" (1966); featuring a 12-string guitar solo, "Wouldn't It Be Nice" (1966); and with a rare Carl Wilson lead, "God Only Knows" (1966).

Joining forces with poet/lyricist Van Dyke Parks, Brian Wilson tried to compete with the Beatles on an experimental album project called *SMILE*. Considered the Holy Grail among the group's fans, the record was scrapped, with some of the tracks destroyed by Wilson in a fit of rage. From its ashes, the group released *SMILEY SMILE* in 1967, featuring their first million-selling single, "Good Vibrations."

Overworked, Brian Wilson began sharing production and songwriting duties with the rest of the band. But with both Dennis and Carl Wilson experiencing emotional and drug problems, the group's output suffered. Becoming eccentric, Dennis Wilson began to compose music in the confines of a huge indoor sand box. Meanwhile, brother Brian befriended Charles Manson at a hippie commune, bringing a Manson composition, "Cease to Exist," to the group.

Signing with Warner/Reprise Records in 1970, the Beach Boys would continue to sell plenty of albums, while scoring few hit singles. Dropping their clean-cut personas, band members now sported long hair and bushy beards. Relegated to oldies status by the mid-1970s, the Beach Boys landed a hit single with the reissue of "Surfin' U.S.A." and topped the album charts with a compilation album of pre-1966 material, *ENDLESS SUMMER*. With Brian Wilson assuming his lead role in the band in 1976, the Beach Boys landed their only top-10 hit of the decade with a cover of Chuck Berry's "Rock and Roll Music."

After a 1977 press release prematurely announcing the group's demise, Dennis released the first solo Beach Boy album, *PACIFIC BLUE*. The Beach Boys signed with CBS-Caribou Records in 1979 for $8 million. Accomplishing little, the group strained under the weight of the dependency relationship between Brian Wilson and his psychiatrist. With Carl Wilson quitting the band for a solo career in 1981, the Beach Boys scored a pair of surprise top-20 hits with "The Beach Boys Medley" and a cover of the Del-Vikings' "Come Go with Me."

The Beach Boys' career was revived in 1983, when Secretary of the Interior James Watt tried to cancel the group's Independence Day concert in Washington, D.C., citing the group's attraction of the "wrong element." With the ensuing public outcry, the Reagan White House stepped in, reversing the decision. By year's end a drunken Dennis Wilson died in a freak diving accident.

Returning to Capitol Records in 1986, the four surviving original Beach Boys, plus longtime member Bruce Johnson, embarked on a more stable period. The group returned to the top of the pop charts with a surprise hit, "Kokomo," from the Tom Cruise film *Cocktail*. The same year, Brian Wilson released his first solo album, the critically-acclaimed, but poorly-selling, *BRIAN WILSON*, which was coproduced by Wilson's longtime psychiatrist, Dr. Eugene Lundy. In 1990, the Beach Boys' soap-opera lives were ridiculed in the made-for-television film *Summer Dreams: The Story of the Beach Boys*.

With Brian Wilson's return to the group in 1993, lawsuits flew between Wilson and Mike Love over royalties and alleged defamation in Wilson's autobiography, *Wouldn't It Be Nice?: My Own Story*. Wilson also sued Dr. Lundy over lost copyrights of the group's 1960s hits (Lundy later lost his license over the improprieties).

With Mike Love and Brian Wilson reconciling in 1995, the Beach Boys released a pair of albums the following year, including *STARS AND STRIPES*, a country music project featuring singers like Willie Nelson and Kathy Trocolli on updated duet versions of the group's classic hits. In the late 1980s, Brian Wilson's daughters, Carnie and Wendy, were joined by Chynna Phillips in the pop group Wilson Phillips.

Bibliography

Callahan, Mike. (1980, November). The Beach Boys: Both sides now, the story of stereo rock and roll. *Goldmine*, p. 16.

Crisafulli, Chuck. (1993, December). The studio heavyweights behind the Beach Boys sound. *Guitar Player*, p. 91.

Evans, Christopher. (1995, July 30). A Beach Boy's saga: Brian Wilson recounts the heady highs and lows of Los Angeles Rock. *Cleveland Plain Dealer*, p. J1.

Sharp, Ken. (1992, September 18). Love among the ruins: The controversial Beach Boy speaks his mind. *Goldmine*, p. 12.

Was, Don. (1995, September). The Beach Boy: Interview with Brian Wilson of the Beach Boys. *Interview*, p. 70.

White, Timothy. (1985, August). The king of summer comes home. *Musician*, p. 42.

White, Timothy. (1988, June 26). Back from the bottom. *New York Times*, sect. 6, p. 24.

THE BEATLES. *George Harrison (February 25, 1943); John Lennon (John Winston Lennon; October 9, 1940 - December 8, 1980); Paul McCartney (James Paul McCartney; June 18, 1942); Ringo Starr (Richard Starkey; July 7, 1940). Inducted in 1988.* The most successful group of the rock era, the Beatles reshaped and reinvigorated rock and roll, arriving in the post-Presley period just when rock music had been tamed.

Isolated from the cultural center of London, the Beatles emerged from the unlikely working-class environment of Liverpool, England, an industrial shipping-port city where residents had access to foreign goods such as American R&B and jazz records. With British radio playing few American rock records in the late 1950s, these American imports exposed aspiring musicians John Lennon and Paul McCartney to Little Richard and Fats Domino.

John Lennon's childhood was marred by exploding Nazi bombs, and an unstable home life. After the divorce of his parents, Lennon was raised by his aunt and uncle, Mimi and George Smith. After hearing Elvis Presley's "Heartbreak Hotel," Lennon pursued a career in music, abandoning the notion of being a sailor like his father. Given an inexpensive guitar by his Aunt Mimi, Lennon suffered another tragedy when she was struck and killed by a bus.

The son of a jazz bandleader, Paul McCartney grew up in a stable environment until 1956, when his mother died of cancer. While attending the prestigious Liverpool Institute, McCartney became obsessed with the guitar, finally purchasing one at age 14. A fan of rockabilly, he emulated guitarists like Gene Vincent and Eddie Cochran.

The eldest Beatle, Richard Starkey Jr. (later, Ringo Starr), was the son of a baker. A sickly child, spending two months in a coma after rupturing an appendix, Starr had a difficult life. Dropping out of school due to poor grades, he turned to music, hoping to eke out some sort of living. The first Beatle to join a band, he was drumming at the age of 16.

His father a bus driver and both parents former professional ballroom dancers, George Harrison grew up in a musical household. A scholastic disappointment, his mother gave him a guitar at age 13, hoping to discover a hidden talent.

The Beatles story began in July 1957, when Paul McCartney approached John Lennon after a performance by his skiffle/rockabilly band, the Quarry Men. The pair had first met a year earlier at a church picnic. Paul impressed John with both his rendition of "Be-Bop-a-Lula" and his ability to properly tune a guitar, and was asked to join a few weeks later.

Playing a menu of American R&B and rockabilly covers, the scruffy-looking band attracted the attention of 14-year-old guitarist George Harrison, who was hired in early 1958. Adding drummer Pete Best, the group was renamed Johnny and the Moondogs.

During this time, Lennon, a mediocre student, attended the Liverpool College of Art, where he met Stuart Sutcliffe. Sutcliffe joined the group on bass in 1960, forming (among various names) the Silver Beatles, at one time backing pop singer Johnny Gentle in a tour through Scotland. Shortening their name to the Beatles in August 1960, the group began a four-month stint in Hamburg, Germany, their musical skills and showmanship sharpened by playing grueling eight hour a night shifts in red-light district clubs.

Enamored of the band, art student Astrid Kirchherr reshaped the group's image with new outfits and updated pageboy haircuts. Deported on various charges (Harrison was only 17), the Beatles returned to Liverpool. Engaged to Kirchherr, Sutcliffe remained in Germany, where he soon died of a cerebral hemorrhage.

With McCartney switching to bass guitar in December 1960, the Beatles debuted at a dingy Liverpool teen spot, the Cavern Club, soon garnering a faithful local fan base. During a subsequent visit to Hamburg, the Beatles recorded for the first time, hired as backing musicians by pop singer Tony Sheridan. Appearing on the single, "My Bonnie," the record label attributed the song to Tony Sheridan and the Beat Brothers.

Meanwhile, a customer's request for a Beatles record at a well-stocked Liverpool record store caused the manager Brian Epstein to search out the group. After catching a performance of the Beatles at the Cavern Club, Epstein signed the rough, leather-clad foursome to a management contract.

After failing an audition with Decca Records, in June 1962 the Beatles signed with EMI's Parlophone subsidiary, impressing 36-year-old producer George Martin (a classically trained oboe player). At Martin's request, drummer Best was fired and replaced by Ringo Starr (the session drummer on "My Bonnie"). Infuriated fans protested the group's shows and vandalized Epstein's car.

Scoring their first British hit in the fall of 1962 with "Love Me Do," the song marked the first of hundreds of Lennon-McCartney compositions, the century's most successful writing team. After refusing Martin's order to record "How Do You Do It?" (instead, a hit for Gerry & the Pacemakers), the Beatles followed up with another original composition, "Please Please Me," their first number one hit in Britain.

On a roll, the Beatles toured Britain in 1963, sharing bills with Tommy Roe and Roy Orbison, topped off by a Royal Command Performance for Queen Elizabeth; at Buckingham Palace, Lennon mocked the audience, requesting they rattle their jewelry instead of applauding.

The Beatles landed their first U.S. chart entry of sorts in late 1963, when Del Shannon scored a minor hit with Lennon and McCartney's "From Me to You." While the Beatles were breaking British sales records with "She Loves You," Brian Epstein traveled to the U.S. to determine why the group was unable to break through into the American market.

With EMI's American counterpart, Capitol, refusing to issue the Beatles' early records, other labels such as Vee-Jay, Tollie, and Swan happily shared the responsibility. With Capitol Records relenting, an expensive promotional campaign imported Beatlemania to the states.

In January 1964, "I Want to Hold Your Hand" debuted on the U.S. singles charts, quickly leaping to number one. On February 7, 1964, the Beatles made their triumphal arrival at New York's Kennedy Airport, greeted by 3,000 screaming girls. Two days later, 73 million American viewers were introduced to the mop-topped Fab Four on *The Ed Sullivan Show*. As American radio stations went on Beatle binges, millions of American teenage males soon let their hair grow long.

In their banner year of 1964, the Beatles scored dozens of chart entries, turning the music industry on its ear with "She Loves You," "Please Please Me," "Twist and Shout," "Can't Buy Me Love," and, from their film of the same name, "A Hard Day's Night." In March of 1964 the group held down the top-five positions on *Billboard's* singles chart. With its haunting black and white cover, the group's debut Capitol album, *MEET THE BEATLES*, featured cheerful, upbeat material.

In 1965, the Beatles starred in their second film, *Help!*, the soundtrack album highlighted by "Yesterday," the most recorded song in rock history. Moving toward a more mature sound with their album *RUBBER SOUL*, the Beatles landed hits with the uncharacteristic "Michelle" and with Harrison on sitar, "Norwegian Wood."

In March 1966, John Lennon created a furor when he told British journalist Maureen Cleave that the Beatles were more popular than Jesus. After a series of Beatles' record burnings and record bans, Lennon apologized. Now experimenting with drugs, the Beatles brought drug use to the mainstream.

Protesting Capitol's practice of "butchering" their British album releases by substituting songs and recycling previously-issued material on the American counterparts, the Beatles delivered a controversial album cover photo for *YESTERDAY AND TODAY*, which featured the group in bloody, butcher smocks. When outraged retailers boycotted the album, the record was recalled and cover replaced. (The original cover is now a collector's item.)

Their next album, *REVOLVER*, spawned the hits "Eleanor Rigby" and "Taxman." Releasing the double-sided single, "Penny Lane"/"Strawberry Field Forever" (1967), the latter track would signal their increasing studio experimentation. Citing difficulties in re-creating their complex sound outside of the studio, the Beatles gave their last-ever concert at San Francisco's Candlestick Park on August 29, 1966.

After months of breakneck session work, in June 1967 the Beatles released their critically acclaimed psychedelic, conceptual album, *SGT. PEPPER'S LONELY HEARTS CLUB BAND*. Recorded on a four-track recorder, the album was highlighted by "Being for the Benefit of Mr. Kite," "Lucy in the Sky with Diamonds," "With a Little Help from My Friends," and the group's first song banned by the BBC, "A Day in the Life." Setting the stage for 1967's "Summer of Love," it topped the charts for months. Recorded in June 1967 before an international audience, "All You Need Is Love" was beamed to over 400 million viewers, featuring Mick Jagger and others on backup.

In August, the Beatles traveled to India to study transcendentalism under the maharishi Mahesh Yogi. A few days later, Brian Epstein died, and the shaken group (minus Ringo, who had already left due to the quality of the food) returned home. Miring the group with managerial responsibilities, Epstein's death marked the start of the Beatles' breakup.

Launching Apple Corps in January 1968, the Beatles lost millions of dollars in a series of business failures, with only Apple Records surviving. The group's debut Apple release, the double-sided hit "Hey Jude"/" Revolution," was their best-selling single ever, the former song written about Lennon's son, Julian. The group's third film, *Magical Mystery Tour*, was also a failure, while the pieced-together soundtrack album sold well.

Also released in 1968, the two-disc set *THE BEATLES (THE WHITE ALBUM)*, spawned harder-edged hits such as "Back in the U.S.S.R.," "Dear Prudence," and "Helter Skelter." With tensions increasing among band members, many of the album's tracks were essentially solo efforts. While recording the album, Ringo Starr was first to quit the band (he quickly returned); a year later, Harrison did the same.

In early 1969, Lennon divorced his wife, Cynthia Powell, and then married the Japanese-born Yoko Ono at the British consulate's office in Gibraltar; meanwhile, McCartney married photographer Linda Eastman.

With the Beatles giving an unannounced, 42-minute lunchtime show on the roof of Apple Studios on January 30, 1969, the event was captured for the film *Let It Be* and was their last-ever public performance. Joined by keyboard player Billy Preston, the group sang "Get Back," intended as the title track of their next album. The live, rooftop version of the song was included on the 1996 Beatles album *ANTHOLOGY 3*.

With their break-up inevitable, the group asked George Martin to produce their final studio album, *ABBEY ROAD*. Outselling all their previous albums, the project featured Lennon's "Come Together" and Harrison's "Here Comes the Sun" and "Something."

With Apple in near financial ruin, new manager Allen Klein reorganized the company, beginning with the release of *LET IT BE*. Combining previously released nonalbum tracks with recordings from the *GET BACK* sessions, the project was produced by Phil Spector, whose excessive use of strings angered Lennon and McCartney. The aptly titled "The Long and Winding Road" was their final single.

With McCartney the first to leave, the Beatles officially disbanded in April 1970. In December, McCartney moved to make the parting permanent, suing the rest of the band. Pursuing separate solo careers, in 1970 all four Beatles members released albums. Of the four, McCartney would have the greatest commercial success. Throughout the 1970s, rumors persisted about a Beatles reconciliation.

Murdered outside his Dakota apartment in New York City in 1980, Lennon had just returned to recording after a five-year stint as a self-described "house husband." The following year, McCartney and Starr reunited informally on the George Harrison single "All Those Years Ago," a tribute to Lennon.

Following the massive success of the 1994 album *THE BBC SESSIONS*, the Beatles released new material in a three-volume *ANTHOLOGY* series. Building upon unfinished Lennon demos, the group garnered heavy radio airplay with the singles "Free as a Bird" (1995) and "Real Love" (1996). Released in conjunction with an ABC documentary, the three double-album sets sold a combined 10 million copies. In 1996, the remaining Beatles turned down a quarter-billion-dollar offer to reunite in concert, matching a pair of earlier overtures.

Bibliography

DeYoung, Bill. (1993, November 12). They were my boys, the greatest in the world: A chat with George Martin. *Goldmine*, p. 14.

Fawcett, Anthony. (1976, December). The day John Lennon stopped believing in the Beatles. *Crawdaddy*, p. 32.

Gaar, Gillian G. (1994, November 25). Rock 'n' roll dreams: The Beatles in Hamburg. *Goldmine*, p. 14.

Harrington, Richard. (1984, February 12). The Beatles: All our yesterdays. *The Washington Post*, p. L1.

Hirshberg, Charles. (1995). Before the Fab Four, there was John, Paul, George and . . . Pete. *Life reunion special*, p. 12.

Marcus, Greil. (1976, July 15). Refried Beatles. *Rolling Stone*, p. 46.

Puckett, Jeffrey Lee. (1995, November 18). Beatlemania!: History repeats itself, and well it should with the Fab Four. *Courier-Journal*, p. 14S.

Schaffner, Nicholas. (1980). *The Boys From Liverpool: John, Paul, George, Ringo*. New York: Methuen.

White, Mark. (1985). *You Must Remember This: Popular Songwriters 1900-1980* (pp. 134-40). New York: Charles Scribner's Sons.

THE BEE GEES. *Barry Gibb (September 1, 1947); Maurice Gibb (December 22, 1949); Robin Gibb (December 22, 1949). Inducted in 1997.* Though best known for their disco run in the late 1970s, the Bee Gees first dominated the pop charts in the late 1960s with their sibling ballad harmony. Born on the Isle of Man, England, and spending several years living in Australia, the young Gibb brothers returned with their family to Manchester, England, in 1955.

Forming a youth novelty trio, nine-year-old Barry Gibb and seven-year-old fraternal twins Robin and Maurice, mimed to records during intermissions at a Manchester movie theater. But when the record player broke in midsong, the group was forced into spontaneous harmonizing, and a singing group was born. After the birth of another brother Andy in 1958, the Gibb family returned to Australia, where they continued their singing career, with their the Everly Brothers-styled delivery.

Called Rattlesnakes and then Wee Johnny Hays and the Bluecats, the trio settled on the B.G.'s (taken from Brothers Gibb), later spelled Bee Gees. With Maurice on bass and Barry on guitar, the group managed a few Australian hits, topping the charts in 1966 with "Spicks and Specks."

Encouraged, the boys' father shopped a Bee Gees' record to several British labels, attracting the attention of Cream manager Robert Stigwood, then the co-owner of a music company with Brian Epstein. Moving back to England in 1967, the group was signed to a five-year contract by Stigwood, who took over managerial duties. Dropping their suits and ties for mop-top haircuts and velvet, Victorian clothing, the Bee Gees were promoted in an expensive ad campaign as "the new Beatles."

Expanding the trio to a quintet with the addition of drummer Colin Peterson and guitarist Vince Melouney, the Bee Gees landed their first U.K./U.S. hit with "New York Mining Disaster 1941," which was actually based on a Welsh cave-in that killed 200.

With the departure of Melouney in late 1968, the group began to splinter. Robin, who had provided lead vocals on most of their hits, left for a solo career, landing a top-10 album in Britain with *SAVED BY THE BELL*. Gibb sister Leslie briefly joined the Bee Gees as a replacement. Brazenly, the departed Peterson sued to win control of the group's name.

Welcomed back by U.S. fans (not so in the U.K.), the reunited original trio returned to the charts in late 1970 with "Lonely Days" (1970); "Run to Me" (1971); and, introducing their falsetto singing, the million-selling "How Can You Mend a Broken Heart" (1971). Left without a drummer, the group instead used a mellotron drum machine.

With Atlantic refusing to release an all-ballad album in 1973, the Bee Gees left the label for Stigwood's new RSO Records. Hiring R&B producer Arif Mardin, the group reached its lowpoint with the much ignored album *MR. NATURAL*. Having fallen out of popularity, band members began abusing drugs.

Retaining Mardin and hiring a studio band, the Bee Gees returned to pop charts in 1975 with the dance-flavored album *MAIN COURSE*, which spawned a trio of hits, "Jive Talkin'," "Nights on Broadway," and the ballad "Fanny (Be Tender with My Love)." Cutting their ties with Mardin and adopting a harder-edged disco sound with Maurice Gibb's Moog synthesizer, the Bee Gees enjoyed heavy airplay with the 1976 album *CHILDREN OF THE WORLD*, which spawned the hits "You Should Be Dancing," "Love So Right," and "Boogie Child." With his flowing adonis hair and hairy chest, Barry Gibb emerged as the group's leader.

Retreating to Paris in 1977 to mix a live album and start work on their next studio album, the Bee Gees were asked by Stigwood about supplying songs for a film he was producing, *Saturday Night Fever*.

From that blockbuster film, the Bee Gees saturated the airwaves in 1978 with their disco-defining hits "Night Fever," "Staying Alive," and the ballad "How Deep Is Your Love." The Bee Gees also boasted the songwriting credits for two more of the film's hits, "Emotion" by Samantha Sang and "If I Can't Have You" by Yvonne Elliman. Besides making the Bee Gees superstars, *Fever* elevated actor John Travolta to stardom. Selling approximately 40 million copies worldwide, the heavily bootlegged soundtrack album lost approximately 10 million units in bogus copies, the most counterfeited album of all time.

As a follow-up to *Fever*, the Bee Gees starred in another Stigwood film, *Sgt. Pepper's Lonely Heart Band*. From the film, Robin Gibb landed a top-20 hit with a Beatles cover, "Oh! Darling." Meanwhile, Barry Gibb had better success writing the title track for another Stigwood film project, *Grease*, providing Frankie Valli with a number-one hit with the title track.

Recorded over a 10-month period and released with little hype, the Bee Gees' 1979 album, *SPIRITS HAVING FLOWN*, spawned a trio of chart-topping singles, "Tragedy," "Love You Inside Out," and "Too Much Heaven," the profits from the latter donated to UNICEF.

While the group never identified itself with disco music, it could never escape the label. Maurice Gibb told *People* magazine, that "disco was a rude word. I hated it! I loathed it with a passion. But all of a sudden we were the hottest disco band around. The media made it an albatross for us" (p. 38). But with antidisco sentiment peaking in the summer of 1979, the Bee Gees were banished to rock purgatory and disappeared from the charts.

After suffering through legal problems, the Bee Gees reunited with producer Arif Mardin in 1987, releasing their first U.S. album in six years, *E.S.P.* The single, "You Win Again," hit number one in England, but was ignored in the U.S. While the Bee Gees again landed international success with the 1989 single "One," they again met with resistance from U.S. radio. The group continued to release albums into the 1990s, few of which landed any U.S. airplay. The group's 1997 album, *STILL WATERS*, returned the group to its mid-1970s dance sound.

A number of Bee Gees classics became hit remakes in the mid-1990s: "Stayin' Alive" by British dance group N-Trance and "How Deep Is Your Love" by Take That.

Bibliography

Durkee, Cutler & Cooper, Jonathan. (1989, August 7). The Bee Gees search for life after disco. *People*, p. 36.

Grein, Paul. (1987, September 27). Bee Gees not taking the hype road. *Los Angeles Times*, Calendar sect., p. 82.

Jaeger, Barbara. (1989, July 21). The Bee Gees: Gibb Brothers build a new life after disco. *Record*, p. 5.

Landis, David. (1991, May 14). Bee Gees emerge from disco daze. *USA Today*, p. 4D.

Rose, Frank. (1977, July 14). How can you mend a broken group?: The Bee Gees. *Rolling Stone*, p. 42.

Scott, Barry. (1994). *We Had Joy, We Had Fun: The "Lost" Recording Artists of the Seventies* (pp. 145-59). Boston: Faber and Faber.

White, Timothy. (1979, May 17). Earthy angels. *Rolling Stone*, p. 58.

CHUCK BERRY. *(Charles Edward Anderson Berry; October 18, 1926). Inducted in 1986.* Rock music's first guitar hero, Chuck Berry was responsible for bringing the electric guitar to the forefront of popular music. Born in San Jose, but raised in a comfortable St. Louis home, Berry was influenced by an eclectic mix of country, pop crooners, and the jump blues of Louis Jordan. The son of a devout carpenter and part-time preacher, six-year-old Berry joined his family in the choir at the Antioch Baptist Church.

Musically a late bloomer, Berry was encouraged by his high school teacher. Buying an acoustic guitar at 13, Berry took lessons from a local jazz musician named Ira Harris. Frequently in trouble in the law, Berry's apprenticeship was interrupted by a three-year jail stint for armed-robbery in 1944.

Desperate to support his wife and two children, Berry augmented his hairdresser pay with nightclub work. Berry joined a blues trio led by pianist Johnny Johnson when their saxophonist called off for a New Year's Eve gig in 1952. Quickly emerging as the group's leader, Berry played jump-blues guitar, highlighting his shows at the Cosmopolitan club in East St. Louis with his crowd-pleasing, mock-country songs.

Traveling to Chicago, Berry impressed bluesman Muddy Waters with his guitar playing. Waters convinced Berry to audition for Chess Records, which was experiencing its first crossover success with rocker Bo Diddley.

Chuck Berry. (*Photo courtesy of MCA/Universal Music Group.*)

Rejecting Berry's blues material, co-owner Leonard Chess instead saw potential in a hillbilly-styled song "Maybelline," a reworked version of a country music standard called "Ida Red." Berry was forced to share the songwriter credits in return for deejay Alan Freed's promotion of the song. Scoring his first hit at age 28, Berry hoped that the record would guarantee three years of club work.

Because of the song's country-influenced rhythm, many deejays were fooled into thinking Berry was white and readily played the record, with Berry selling more records to whites than blacks. Recalled Leonard Chess' son Marshall to interviewer Joe Smith, "My father used to say, 'If Chuck Berry were white, he'd be bigger than Elvis'" (p. 114). Married with children, Berry became an unlikely teen idol. Sporting a slick pompadour haircut, Berry debuted his famous "duck walk" in 1956 at an Alan

Freed revue at New York's Paramount Theater.

Berry followed a string of rock standards which explored the themes of cars, high school, and young love, including "Roll over Beethoven" (1956), "Sweet Little Sixteen" (1957), and with its famous guitar intro, "Johnny Be Goode" (1958). His ballad releases bombed, with fans demanding upbeat material.

In 1957 Berry bought 30 acres near St. Louis for $8,000, opening an entertainment complex. Two years later, Berry was again in trouble with the law after one of his employees told authorities she was only 14 years old. Charged under the Mann Act, Berry was tried twice, found guilty both times. Serving a two-year jail stint, Berry spent the time educating himself on the legal aspects of the music industry.

Out of jail and a bitter man, Berry discovered that a new world of Beatlemania had invaded rock music. Berry returned to the pop charts in 1964 with "Nadine," "No Particular Place to Go" and with a piano on lead, "You Never Can Tell," songs he had composed while in prison.

Lured to Mercury Records with a $150,000 advance, in the late 1960s Berry released substandard material. Returning to Chess Records in 1969, Berry scored his first number-one hit in 1972 with the bawdy novelty ditty "My Ding-a-Ling," a song recorded live in Coventry, England, without Berry's knowledge. Convicted of income tax evasion in 1979, Berry was sentenced to 120 days, during which time he began writing his autobiography. While in prison, Berry was dropped by Atlantic Records.

In 1987, Berry was the subject of a musical documentary, *Hail! Hail! Rock & Roll*. Directed by Taylor Hackford and starring Keith Richards and Eric Clapton (two self-admitted Berry disciples), the film was built around a pair of 60th birthday concerts.

Bibliography

Coda, Cub. (1991, December 13). Chuck Berry: And the joint was rockin'. *Goldmine*, p. 8.

Goldberg, Michael. (1986, December 4). Sweet little sixty. *Rolling Stone*, p. 42.

Green, Michelle. (1986, November 3). Rock's Beethoven. *People*, p. 34.

Harrington, Richard. (1987, October 9). Chuck Berry's Rock of Ages. *Washington Post*, p. p. B1.

Lydon, Michael. (1969, December). Hail hail rock and roll, deliver me from the rock of old: Chuck Berry. *Ramparts*, p. 47.

McLeese, Don. (1987, October 18). The spirit of a rocker. *New York Times*, sect. 7, p. 13.

Smith, Joe. (1988). *Off the Record*. New York: Warner.

White, Timothy. (1990). *Rock Lives: Profiles and Interviews* (pp. 21-26). New York: Henry Holt.

Wolmuth, Roger. (1987, November 2). Rock's growly grandpa. *People*, p. 92.

BOBBY "BLUE" BLAND. *(Robert Calvin Barnes; January 27, 1930). Inducted in 1992*. Raised by his mother in a farming community outside Memphis, Bobby "Blue" Bland joined a gospel choir in his teens. Finishing only the third grade, Bland spent his childhood in the fields. Influenced by the country music he heard on the radio, Bland played the jew's harp and a borrowed guitar.

Wanting to escape a hard life of farming, Bland's family moved to Memphis in 1944. There Bland landed work as a mechanic and parking attendant. After a brief stint in a gospel group, the Miniatures, Bland switched to the blues. Bland was befriended by a young blues guitarist named B.B. King in 1949, and invited onto his radio program on WDIA. Landing occasional nightclub gigs, Bland later joined King in a loose-knit, R&B group called the Beale Streeters.

Bland honed his performing skills at Memphis' popular, weekly talent shows at the Palace Theater, hosted by WDIA deejays Rufus Thomas and Nat D. Williams. Bland briefly recorded for Chess and then Modern Records, whose owners suggested he return to farming.

When Beale Streeter Johnny Ace was signed by Duke Records, Bland joined his backing band. But with the Beale Streeters spawning hit solo acts with Ace, B.B. King, and Little Junior Parker, Duke Records further mined the group, signing Bland to a solo contract. After bombing with his early releases, Bland was drafted into the army in 1952, serving with crooner Eddie Fisher.

Returning to the studio in 1955, Bland was coached by Duke arranger Joe Scott, later his longtime bandleader. In 1956, Bland joined Little Junior Parker in a blues caravan tour, teamed until 1961.

Beginning a long string of R&B hits, Bland was initially considered a B.B. King imitator. Possessing a high-pitched voice, Bland's blues stylings were punctuated with a simple guitar riffs. Shifting toward ballads in the style of Charles Brown or a young Nat "King" Cole, Bland has also admitted being influenced by the pop crooners Perry Como and Andy Williams.

Bland scored his first hit in 1957 with the R&B chart-topping, blues-tinged "Farther Up the Road." Finding little crossover, pop success, Bland became a superstar in the black community. Accentuating his songs with blueslike snorts and grunts, Bland unleashed a constant stream of hits in the 1960s with "I Pity the Fool" (1961), the often recorded blues shout "Turn on Your Lovelife" (1961), "Ain't That Loving You" (1962), "That's the Way Love Is" (1963), "These Hands" (1965), and "I'm Too Far" (1966). Depending on Scott and other professional songwriters, Bland did not compose his own material.

A heavy drinker, Bland split with Scott in 1968, losing his longtime backing band. Touring with a smaller group, Bland struggled until he overcame his alcohol addiction in 1971, with the aid of his future wife.

His career in a slump, and his voice becoming strained after years of constant touring, Bland extended his career by adopted a growling, gospel-charged soulful delivery. When Duke Records was sold in 1973 to ABC Records, Bland found himself on the same label as his mentor, B.B. King. After a pair of pop-oriented albums, Bland returned to his blues roots, collaborating with King on a pair of live LPS.

After MCA Records acquired ABC, Bland released some disco-flavored material, his career slumping. Dropped by MCA in 1984, Bland was signed by the blues and gospel label Maleco Records, scoring a minor hit with the single "Members Only," from the Grammy-nominated album of same name. Returning to Delta-style blues, Bland recaptured his fan base. An international star, Bland maintained a heavy recording and touring schedule in the 1990s, frequently as the opening act for B.B. King.

Bibliography

Blau, Robert. (1986, March 27). Travelin' man Bobby "Blue" Bland hits road 40 weeks a year to sell his brand of soul. *Chicago Tribune*, Tempo sect., p. 7.

Boehm, Mike. (1988, December 30). Bland's strangled blues secure musical fame. *Los Angeles Times*, Calendar sect., p. 26.

Giddens, Gary. (1981). *Riding on a Blue Note: Jazz and American Pop* (pp. 29-47). New York: Oxford.

Guralnick, Peter. (1978, July-August). Bobby Bland: Little boy blue. *Living Blues*, p. 8.

Prudhomme, Chester. (1989, December). Bobby "Blue" Bland. *Discoveries*, p. 30.

Streissguth, Mike. (1995, July 21). From Memphis to Malaco: Bobby "Blue" Bland turns on your lovelight. *Goldmine*, p. 19.

BOOKER T. & THE MG'S. *Steve Cropper (October 21, 1941); Donald "Duck" Dunn (November 24, 1941); Al Jackson Jr. (November 27, 1935 - October 1, 1975); Booker T. Jones (November 12, 1944); Lewie Steinberg (Lewis Steinberg; September 13, 1933). Inducted in 1992.* While Motown was manufacturing glossy, crossover pop-oriented R&B, its chief competitor, Memphis-based Stax Records, was pumping out gritty soul. An integral ingredient in the Stax sound was the unmatched talent of its house band, Booker T. & the MG's.

The origins of the MG's date to the late 1950s, when high schoolers Steve Cropper and Donald "Duck" Dunn joined a rock group called the Royal Spades. The mother and uncle of the group's saxophonist, Charles Axton, operated a combination record company and record shop in a converted movie theater. Impressed with a Royal Spades' original composition, "Last Night," Estelle Axton convinced her partner, former bank teller Jim Stewart, into releasing the instrumental on their Satellite label.

Now called the Mar-Keys, "Last Night" became a smash hit in 1961, taking the teenage band across the country. With no additional hits, the Mar-Keys continued to record intermittently for several years. After Satellite became Stax Records the label entered into a lucrative distribution deal with larger Atlantic Records.

With its reputation growing, local talent began gravitating to the Stax. Hired as a session player in 1960, organist Booker T. Jones recruited his former bandmate in Willie Mitchell's group, drummer Al Jackson Jr. Two years later, at a scheduled session for rockabilly singer Billy Lee Riley (of "Red Hot" fame), Jones and Jackson were joined for the first time by a pair of white R&B musicians, Mar-Key guitarist Steve Cropper and bassist Lewie Steinberg.

Launching into a blues number, "Behave Yourself," session producer Jim Stewart smelled a hit. Needing a B-side, the group recorded an impromptu instrumental, "Green Onions," built around a riff Jones conceived on his trademark Hammond electric organ. Naming their band, Booker T. & the MG's (short for Memphis Group), the B-side became the hit. Jones, then a 16-year-old high school student, composed several more tracks for the group's debut album, *GREEN ONIONS*.

In 1964, Steinberg was replaced on bass by former Mar-Key member Donald "Duck" Dunn, the group settling into its classic lineup, the MG's becoming Stax's house band. Recording only on weekends and summers, Jones pursued a music degree at Indiana University; Cropper dropped out of Memphis State University to work as

Booker T. and the MG's: Donald Dunn, Booker T. Jones, Steve Cropper, and
Al Jackson, Jr.

a Stax engineer. Despite releasing a long string of singles, the group failed to score
another top-40 hit until 1967, co-composing dozens of hits, including "Knock on
Wood" and "(Sitting on) The Dock of the Bay."

With Isaac Hayes and David Porter overseeing MG's sessions, the band returned
to the charts in the late 1960s with instrumental hits such as "Soul Limbo" (1968);
from the Clint Eastwood film of the same name, "Hang 'Em High" (1968); "Time Is
Tight" (1969); and a cover of "Mrs. Robinson" (1969). Their 1969 soundtrack album
UPTIGHT featured a rare vocal by Jones.

Following the label's sale, Jones left in 1969, protesting the new owner's business
decisions. The band disintegrated, their last hit coming in 1971 with "Melting Pot,"

from the album of the same name. In 1973, Jackson and Dunn recorded the poorly-selling album *THE MG's*.

Pursuing solo projects, Jones produced Willie Nelson's *STARDUST* album, and Jackson joined Willie Mitchell and Al Green in composing "Let's Stay Together" and "I'm Still In Love with You." A fan of the Grand Ole Opry, Cropper turned his attention to country music.

Before a planned MG's reunion in 1975, Jackson was murdered by burglars at his home. Joined by former Bar-Kay drummer Willie Hall, the band recorded a tribute album, *UNIVERSAL LANGUAGE*. Later that year, Cropper, Dunn, and Jones joined Levon Helm's RCO All-Stars tour.

The 1980 film *The Blues Brothers* featured Cropper and Dunn backing a fictitious R&B band fronted by the duo of Jake and Elwood Blues (John Belushi and Dan Aykroyd), and featured the MG's songs "Time Is Tight" and "Green Onions." In 1982, Jones launched a solo career, scoring a hit with "Don't Stop Your Love."

The surviving members of the MG's (minus an ailing Jones), reunited in 1988 for Atlantic's 40th anniversary concert. The band worked as the house band at the Bob Dylan tribute concert; an impressed Neil Young then hired the MG's as the backing band for his next tour. The MG's were also the house band for the concert for the Rock and Roll Hall of Fame in 1995.

A long-awaited Booker T. & the MG's album, *THAT'S THE WAY IT SHOULD BE*, was released in 1994. Their first effort in 17 years, it received little attention.

Bibliography

Boehm, Mike. (1993, September 8). Booker T. and MG's gear up for Neil Young. *Los Angeles Times*, p. F8.
Dahl, Bill. (1994, July 22). Booker T. and the MG's: Still groovin'. *Goldmine*, p. 14.
Garland, Phil. (1969, April). Booker T. & MG's. *Ebony*, p. 92.
Hetfield, Walt. (1993, December). The real deal: Steve Cropper. *Guitar Player*, p. 68.
Tamarkin, Jeff. (1981, July). Booker T. Jones. *Goldmine*, p. 158.
Wenner, Jann. (1968, August 24). The Rolling Stone round table: Booker T. & the MG's. *Rolling Stone*, p. 11.

DAVID BOWIE. *(David Robert Jones; January 8, 1947). Inducted in 1996.* The chameleon of rock, David Bowie has adopted various personae in his three-decade career from Ziggy Stardust to the Thin White Duke. Bowie was born in a rough section of South London, his parents marrying after his birth. Moving to an upscale suburb at age six, Bowie was given Little Richard records by his father, and dropped his desire to become a painter. Taking saxophone lessons and singing in his school choir, Bowie later taught himself to play the guitar.

Enrolled at Bromley Tech, Bowie edited a UFO magazine, claiming to have witnessed extraterrestrial crafts. Leaving school before graduation, Bowie worked as a graphic artist at an ad agency.

With music an avocation, Bowie formed the King Bees in 1963, releasing his first single, "Liza Jane," the following year. Spending three years studying with mime Lindsey Kemp, Bowie also dabbled in painting and stage acting. After passing through several obscure bands, in 1966 Bowie dropped his real name, Davey Jones, to distinguish himself from Monkees teen throb Davy Jones.

After fronting the Lower Third, in 1967 Bowie released a poorly selling solo album (released only in Britain). Combining rock music with theatrics, Bowie created a stir in Britain with another group, Feathers. With the help of future wife Angela Barnett, Bowie landed another solo recording contract, releasing the 1969 album *MAN OF WORDS, MAN OF MUSIC*. A single, "Space Oddity" (inspired by the Stanley Kubrick-produced *2001: A Space Odyssey*), failed to dent the U.S. charts until 1973.

Pushing the limits of gender identity, the British version of Bowie's follow-up album, *THE MAN WHO SOLD THE WORLD*, pictured him in a dress. In the forefront of the glitter-rock movement, Bowie adopted an androgynous look, donning outrageous makeup and costumes and hiring a Broadway stage designer for elaborate concerts. A follow-up album, *HUNKY DORY*, spawned the pop hit "Changes."

Bowie's science-fiction interests were explored through the character of Ziggy Stardust in his 1972 thematic album *THE RISE AND FALL OF ZIGGY STARDUST AND THE SPIDERS FROM MARS*, spawning hits with "Star Man" and "Suffragette City." That same year, Bowie wrote Mott the Hoople's hit "All the Young Dudes" and produced Lou Reed's album *TRANSFORMER*, with its unlikely pop hit "Walk on the Wild Side."

Ziggy Stardust was followed by another glitter-rock character, Aladdin Sane, from an album of the same name, one of three Bowie releases in 1973. His 1974 album, *DIAMOND DOGS*, painted an Orwellian theme with the tracks "1984," "Big Brother," and "Rebel Rebel." Beginning with his 1974 American tour, Bowie dropped his elaborate stage shows and discarded his glitter and androgynous persona.

Bowie's most successful release of the decade, 1975's *YOUNG AMERICANS*, spawned a trio of hits with "Young Americans," "Golden Years," and, co-written with John Lennon and Carlos Alomar, Bowie's first U.S. chart-topper, "Fame." Bowie's next album, *STATION TO STATION*, introduced another character, the Thin White Duke, and spawned the hit "Golden Years."

Returning to an earlier vocation, Bowie landed the starring role in the much praised film *The Man Who Fell to Earth*. Exhausted and emaciated by drugs and touring, Bowie separated from his wife, Angela (made famous by the Rolling Stones 1972 hit, "Angie"). Retreating to West Berlin in 1976, Bowie joined forces with former Roxy Music co-leader Brian Eno for a trio of electronic-sounding albums, *LOW*, *HEROES*, and *LODGER*.

After making his Broadway debut in 1980 in the leading role of *The Elephant Man*, Bowie later landed several major movie roles, including an erotic vampire in *The Hunger*. Also that year, Bowie released a sequel to "Space Oddity," called "Ashes to Ashes," from the album *SCARY MONSTERS*. In 1982, Bowie joined with Queen for the hit "Under Pressure," the song later reworked by rap artist Vanilla Ice as "Ice Ice Baby."

Signing a multimillion-dollar deal in 1983 with EMI, Bowie had the best-selling album of his career with *LET'S DANCE*. Coproduced by Chic's Niles Rodgers and featuring the blistering guitar work of Stevie Ray Vaughan, Bowie straddled the dance and rock genres with the hits "Let's Dance," "Modern Love," and "China Girl," the latter spawning a banned-by-MTV video.

Flirting with heavy metal, in 1989 Bowie fronted the poorly received Tin Machine. A year later, Bowie announced his refusal to play older material in concert. In 1992, Bowie married Somali-Italian model Iman. After shedding Tin Machine, Bowie returned to solo status, in 1994 releasing the album *BLACK TIE WHITE NOISE*, featuring the track "Jump They Say."

The grandfather of alternative rock, Bowie's tie to the genre was reinforced with a Nirvana cover version of his composition, "The Man Who Sold the World," and by a much ballyhooed 1995 tour with industrial rockers Nine Inch Nails.

Reuniting with producer Brian Eno in 1995, Bowie released the concept album *OUTSIDE*. Switching directions in 1997, the 50-year-old Bowie returned to his early 1980s dance-rock style with the album *EARTHLING*.

Bibliography

Allan, Mark. (1995, April 23). Man of ch-ch-ch-ch changes. *Independent*, p. 25.

Cocks, Jay. (1983, July 18). David Bowie rockets onward: A mercurial superstar tours in triumph. *Time*, p. 54.

De Lisle, Tim. (1995, September 10). Immaculate conceptions: After 15 years, one of rock's great double acts is back. *Independent*, p. 16.

Fletcher, David. (1980, March). A decade of changes: David Bowie. *Goldmine*, p. 12.

Harrington, Richard. (1987, April 26). David Bowie, unmasked. *Washington Post*, p. G1.

Kot, Greg. (1995, October 1). David Bowie, upgraded: The latest version: Relevant '90s artist, alternative rock guru. *Chicago Tribune*, p. C1.

White, Timothy. (1990, July). Turn and face the strange: David Bowie looks back. *Musician*, p. 60.

JAMES BROWN. *(May 3, 1928)*. *Inducted in 1986*. The Godfather of Soul, James Brown revolutionized R&B, taking it from doo-wop to soul. Born in South Carolina but raised in Augusta, Georgia, as a child he shined shoes outside a radio station during the Depression. Living with an aunt after his parents' divorce, Brown taught himself to play music on a pump organ.

Dancing and singing on street corners and in amateur contests, Brown worked for tips. At age 12, he moved in with his grandmother, dropped out of school, and worked with his father at a gas station. Arrested several times during his teens on petty theft charges, Brown learned that singing for the guards often meant an early release. But after breaking into cars at age 16, Brown served a three-year jail stint.

Enamored with the entertainment industry, Brown first flirted with boxing and semi-pro baseball. After joining the Atlanta-based Gospel Starlighters, Brown jumped into R&B music in the early 1950s with the Swanees, touring around Macon and Augusta, Georgia. With Brown emerging as their leader, in 1954 the group evolved into the (Famous) Flames.

With several labels pursuing him, Brown was signed to King-Federal Records by producer Ralph Bass in 1955. Going against the grain of mid-1950s doo-wop and rock and roll, Brown's gritty, million-selling, ground breaking single "Please, Please, Please" (1956) changed the course of R&B. Label owner Syd Nathan initially refused to release the record, but was convinced by producer Ralph Bass who threatened to quit. In 1958, Brown followed up with a second million-seller, "Try Me." After scoring a series of R&B hits, Brown scored his first top-20 pop hit in 1963 with the often recorded ballad "Every Beat of My Heart" and his first million-selling album, *LIVE AT THE APOLLO*.

In 1964, Brown left King for the Mercury subsidiary Smash, with both labels issuing competing records. With a plethora of releases, Brown was constantly on the charts. Returning to King with a modified band, Brown was granted complete artistic control. Adopting a driving beat, sparse arrangements, and a funky horn section, Brown wrote most of his own material, unleashing a string of hits with the revolutionary "Papa's Got a Brand New Bag (Part 1)" (1965), "I Got You (I Feel Good)" (1965), "It's a Man's World" (1966), and the sparsely instrumented song that sparked 1970s funk, "Cold Sweat (Part 1)" (1967). During this period, Brown also recorded nearly a dozen instrumental albums.

Backed by top-notch musicians in a group nicknamed the J.B.'s, Brown earned a reputation as a consummate performer. With platform shoes, sequined shirts, a cape draped over his shoulder, and his clothes soaked in sweat, "the Hardest Working Man in Show Business" wowed crowds. Writes author Edward Kiersh: "In segregated Southern clubs and outdoor tents, Brown played the fire-breathing, sinners-be-damned preacher, whipping audiences into an orgiastic frenzy with his hip-swinging, leg-flailing contortions" (p. 281).

In the racially volatile 1960s, Brown released the black pride anthem "Say It Loud—I'm Black and I'm Proud" (1968), resulting in a loss of some pop airplay. As an influential member of the black community, Brown did much to quell rioting after Martin Luther King's death.

In the late 1960s Brown branched out, buying three radio stations and opening restaurants. A patriot who often aligned himself with Lyndon Johnson and then several Republican presidents, Brown performed for American G.I.s in Vietnam.

After forming his own record label, People, in 1971, Brown scored a hit with "Hot Pants." Joining Polydor Records, he fired most of his J.B.'s, including brothers Bootsy and Catfish Collins, who joined George Clinton.

By the mid-1970s, Brown's career was in a slump. His career was resurrected by his role as a shouting preacher in the 1980 film *The Blues Brothers*.

In the 1980s, Brown's music became the target of overzealous rappers, who frequently sampled his early records. Eventually, lawsuits halted the practice. Brown scored his last major hit with "Living in America" (1986), the Grammy-winning theme song from the film *Rocky IV*.

His fortunes waning, Brown was sentenced to six years in prison in 1989, convicted of eluding police and aggravated assault. He was later involved with domestic disputes with wife, Adrienne Brown. At a 1993 stop in Cleveland, Brown announced the creation of the James Brown Minority Internship Program at the Rock and Rock Hall of Fame.

Bibliography

Allen, Henry. (1980, January 11). Soul survivor: 44 hits later, it's still looking up for James

Brown. *Washington Post*, p. D1.

Chervokas, Jason. (1995, May 26). Make it funky? James Brown: How the Godfather of Soul became the Father of Funk. *Goldmine*, p. 18.

Haygood, Will. (1989, April 20). Inside a South Carolina prison with the King of Soul. *Boston Globe*, Living sect., p. 81.

Kiersh, Edward. (1986). *Where Are You Now, Bo Diddley?* (pp. 278-83). Garden City, NY: Doubleday.

Propes, Steve. (1993, May). James Brown: The Godfather of Soul's first decade. *Discoveries*, p. 16.

Trescott, Jacqueline. (1977, October 11). James Brown, the "King of Soul," is still cooking. *Washington Post*, p. B1.

White, Timothy. (1990). *Rock Lives: Profiles & Interviews* (pp. 56-74). New York: Henry Holt.

RUTH BROWN. *(Ruth Alston Weston; January 30, 1928)*. *Inducted in 1993*. Atlantic Records' first star, Ruth Brown dominated the R&B chart in the 1950s. Born in Portsmouth, Virginia, her father a dockworker, Brown was raised in a religious household. Singing old-time spirituals in a youth choir led by her father at the Emannuel A.M.E. Church, Brown was instead drawn to the jazz of Billie Holiday.

Without her family's knowledge, 15-year-old Brown frequented the bustling, World War II-era USO clubs, where she sang pop standards. Sneaking off to the Apollo Theater in New York City, she won first prize with her rendition of "It Could Happen to You." Turning down a week-long gig, Brown was terrified of her father's reaction.

Leaving home in 1943 for a singing career, Brown was abandoned in Washington, D.C., by bandleader Lucky Millinder. Befriended by nightclub owner Blanche Calloway (sister of jazz singer Cab Calloway), Brown was hired for a week's work at the Crystal Palace. An immediate sensation, Brown saw her engagement lasted four months. Marrying singer Jimmy Earle Brown, she toured as Brown and Brown before divorcing and going solo in 1948. After an impromptu onstage duet with Sonny Til, Brown drew the attention of Capitol Records but instead signed with Atlantic, thanks to her Calloway, now her manager.

But on her way to an Apollo Theater gig, Brown was nearly killed in a car crash. Hospitalized for 11 months, Brown never fully recovered from leg injuries. Arriving on crutches to her first recording session, the 21-year-old Brown was backed by Eddie Condon's jazz combo on a series of jazz standards, including a ballad rendition of Russ Morgan's "So Long." Intended as a practice session, Atlantic released the song as Brown's first single, giving her a top-10 R&B hit (overall, Atlantic's second chart hit).

At Herb Abramson's insistence, Brown was told to sing in an R&B style. Hesitant, Brown told writer Arnold Shaw, "I was more of a pop torch singer. I preferred the ballads" (p. 405). Written by Brown's frequent collaborator Rudy Toombs, "Teardrops from My Eyes" (1950) gave Atlantic their first million-seller and the nickname, "The House That Ruth Built." Brown was given her own nickname, "Miss Rhythm," by crooner Frankie Laine (whose own nickname was "Mr. Rhythm") onstage at a Philadelphia concert.

Touring heavily throughout the South, Brown unleashed a string of R&B hits with

"5-10-15 Hours" (1952); backed by Ray Charles' band, "(Mama) He Treats Your Daughter Mean" (1953); the Chuck Willis-penned, "Oh What a Dream (1954); and, named after the 1950s dance craze, "Mambo Baby" (1955). But like many 1950s R&B acts, Brown lost sales to the cover versions of her hits by the likes of Tony Bennett, Kay Kyser, and Georgia Gibbs.

In 1957, Brown crossed over onto the pop charts with the Leiber & Stoller-penned "Lucky Lips" and the Bobby Darin composition "This Little Girl's Gone Rockin'." After touring with her new husband, saxophonist Willis "Gatortail" Jackson, Brown semi-retired from music to start a family.

Her career waning, Brown left Atlantic in 1961 for Philips Records. Divorced, unable to find work in the music business, and receiving no royalty payments from Atlantic, Brown moved from Long Island to Boston in the mid-1960s, supporting her two sons by cleaning houses, driving a school bus, and counseling drug addicts. Too proud to perform under her true name, she took engagements as Ruth Blunt.

Recording sporadically in the 1970s, Brown sold few records. Aided by comedian Redd Foxx, who paid her way to California in 1974, Brown appeared in several plays and a pair of sitcoms, *Hello, Larry* and *Checking In*, and was cast in an all-black revue of *Guys and Dolls*.

Her career on an upswing, Brown appeared in the John Waters film *Hairspray* (1985) in the role of deejay Motormouth Mabel. The following year, she starred in the eight-month run of the Paris production of the 1920s-era jazz musical *Black and Blue*, singing bawdy songs like "If I Can't Sell It, I'm Gonna Keep Sitting on It." The show landed on Broadway in 1988, earning Brown a Tony Award.

An advocate for royalty reform in the 1980s, Brown demanded that record companies reimburse early R&B acts who had unknowingly signed away the rights to their music and was instrumental in the founding of the nonprofit Rhythm and Blues Foundation. In 1988, Atlantic Records awarded Brown and other artists back royalties. Ruth Brown's 1996 autobiography *Miss Rhythm* was made into an HBO film.

Bibliography

Brown, Ruth & Yule, Andrew. (1996). *Miss Rhythm: The Autobiography of Ruth Brown, Rhythm and Blues Legend*. New York: Donald I. Fine.

Dawson, Jim & Propes, Steve. (1992). *What Was the First Rock 'N' Roll Record?* (pp. 76-79). Boston: Faber and Faber.

Gart, Galen. (1972). Ruth Brown. *Bim Bam Boom, 2*(3), p. 11.

Grendysa, Peter. (1996, December). Ruth Brown. *Discoveries*, p. 42.

Harrington, Richard. (1987, March 28). The R&B echoes of Ruth Brown: From '50s stardom to a N.Y. musical. *Washington Post*, p. D1.

Jeske, Lee. (1990, April 19). Ruth Brown. *Rolling Stone*, p. 79.

Shaw, Arnold. (1978). *Honkers and Shouters*. New York: Collier.

Stein, Stephanie. (1990, March). Ruth Brown: The '50s queen of rhythm & blues enters the '90s on a high note. *Down Beat*, p. 51.

BUFFALO SPRINGFIELD. *Richie Furay (May 9, 1944); Dewey Martin (September 30, 1942); Bruce Palmer (1946); Stephen Stills (January 3, 1945); Neil*

Young (November 12, 1945). Inducted in 1997. A hotbed for talent, Buffalo Springfield was the launching pad for several hit acts of the 1970s. Featuring a trio of lead guitars, Neil Young, Stephen Stills, and Richie Furay, the group was taken from the nameplate of passing steamroller.

Texas-born Stephen Stills was raised in Florida, learning music in his high school marching band. Quitting college to pursue a career in rock music, he honed his guitar skills by attending dozens of Jimi Hendrix concerts. Arriving in New York City in 1964, Stills met future Monkee Peter Tork and Ohio-born guitarist Richie Furay. Furay had come to the city a year earlier in search of acting work.

While Tork headed to California, Stills and Furay formed a 10-piece folk group, the Au Go Go Singers. Recording an obscure album for Roulette, the group disbanded after six months. From the remnants of the group, Stills formed the Bay Singers, then the Company. Touring through Canada, Stills crossed paths with the Neil Young-led folk-rock band, the Squires.

With the bickering Squires disbanding in 1965, Young journeyed to New York City's Greenwich Village in search of Stills. Unable to locate Stills (who had left for Los Angeles), Young was befriended by Furay. Returning to Toronto and then moving to Detroit, Young joined a Motown group, the Mynah Birds. But with the arrest of the group's leader, future funk star Rick James, Young and a bandmate, bassist Bruce Palmer, drove to Los Angeles in 1966 in search of Stills.

Spotting Stills and Furay in a freak chance meeting during a traffic jam on Sunset Boulevard, Young and Palmer agreed to form a band. Adding drummer Dewey Martin, the group originally called itself the Herd. Renamed the Buffalo Springfield, the group garnered record company interest after opening up for the Byrds.

Signing with Atlantic Records, their debut album, *BUFFALO SPRINGFIELD*, went ignored. While Furay was the group's lead singer, both Stills and Young chose to sing their own compositions. Released as a single, which was subsequently added to their first album, the Buffalo Springfield scored their breakthrough hit with the anthemic "For What It's Worth" (1967). Featuring Young's stark lead guitar, the Stills-penned song chronicled an altercation between Los Angeles police and unruly hippies.

Buffalo Springfield's second album was personally overseen by Atlantic head Ahmet Ertegun. Released in early 1967, *BUFFALO SPRINGFIELD AGAIN* was highlighted by the Stills-penned "Rock & Roll Woman." Another single, "Bluebird," was released at 1:39, edited from its original 10-minute length.

Quitting the group for four months in mid-1967, Young had refused to appear on *The Johnny Carson Show*. For their Monterey Pop Festival appearance, Young was replaced by Doug Hastings and guest vocalist David Crosby. But when Palmer was deported to Canada on a drug charge, Young returned as the group was completing its third album.

Originally hired as a replacement for Palmer, Jim Messina produced the group's final studio album, *LAST TIME AROUND*. In the middle of a power struggle between Young and Stills, three group members were arrested on drug charges. Dispirited, the group disbanded in May 1968.

Young pursued a solo career and for a time rejoined Stills in the expanded Crosby,

Stills, Nash & Young. Furay and Messina formed Poco; Furay then formed the Souther, Hillman, Furay Band. Messina left before the first Poco album, then backed Rick Nelson, Linda Rondstadt, and the Eagles before eventually teaming with Kenny Loggins as Loggins & Messina. Palmer and Martin later released separate solo albums.

Young vetoed a Buffalo Springfield reunion in 1973. Drummer Dewey Martin briefly toured in 1988 as Buffalo Springfield Again, with former Crazy Horse guitarist Michael Curtis on lead vocals.

Bibliography
Crisafulli, Chuck. (1995, February). Stephen Stills: Still storming, still dreaming. *Guitar Player*, p. 37.
Einarson, John. (1987, January). Neil Young: A rock legend talks about his early days. *Goldmine*, p. 8.
Einarson, John. (1997, May 23). For what it's worth: Buffalo Springfield. *Goldmine*, p. 18.
Fuentes, Jerry. (1987, February 13). Buffalo Springfield: A collector's retrospective. *Goldmine*, p. 8.

THE BYRDS. *Gene Clark (Harold Eugene Clark; November 17, 1941 - May 24, 1991); Michael Clarke (June 3, 1943 - December 19, 1993); David Crosby (David Van Cortland; August 14, 1941); Chris Hillman (December 4, 1942); Jim "Roger" McGuinn (James Joseph McGuinn, III; July 13, 1942). Inducted in 1991.* A melting pot of diverse influences, the Byrds combined folk with electric psychedelia in the 1960s. A Kansas native, percussionist Gene Clark left a mainstream folk group, the New Christy Minstrels, inspired after hearing a Beatles song on the radio. Moving to Los Angeles, in 1964 Clark met Roger (Jim) McGuinn at the Troubadour nightclub, and formed a duo. McGuinn, a Chicago native, was a classically trained musician who preferred folk music. He had previously worked with Bobby Darin and Judy Collins and spent two years in the Chad Mitchell Trio.

Expanding to a trio as the Jet Set, Clark and McGuinn were joined by another folkie, guitarist and singer David Crosby, formerly with Les Baxter's Balladeers. With a friend arranging free studio time, the trio spent their nights honing their recording technique. (These tracks appeared several years later on the albums *PREFLYTE* and *EARLY L.A.*)

Later, in 1964, the trio was joined by bluegrass guitarist-turned-bassist Chris Hillman and an inexperienced drummer, former bongo player Michael Clarke. Singing in four-part harmony (Clarke did not contribute vocals), the group, now known as the Beefeaters, released a poorly selling single at Elektra.

Signed in late 1964 by CBS, guaranteed only one release, the group knew its future was on the line. Needing a hit, the Byrds recorded the then-unreleased Bob Dylan composition, "Mr. Tambourine Man." With McGuinn's exotic, Eastern, 12-string guitar, the single managed to top the pop charts. The Byrds' melodic and jangly folk-rock sound soon inspired scores of imitators. The band's de facto leader, McGuinn, had emplyed his marketing education, donning octagonal eyeglasses and embracing psychedelic imagery.

Signing with CBS, the Byrds scored with the double-sided single, another Dylan composition, "All I Really Want to Do," backed by the Clark-penned "I'll Feel a Whole Lot Better" (1965). Cher borrowed the Byrd's arrangement of the A-side, beating out the Byrds' single on the pop charts.

McGuinn brought the Byrd's next hit from his days with Judy Collins. Written by Pete Seeger, "Turn! Turn! Turn!" (1965) was taken from *The Book of Ecclesiastes*; featuring a sitar, the follow-up release, "Eight Miles High" (1966), was banned by many radio stations, fearing the song promoted drug use.

Tired of bickering with McGuinn and Crosby , the group's chief songwriter Gene Clark left the Byrds in 1966. Pursuing a groundbreaking solo career in country-rock, Clark was later joined by other Byrds members. Hillman then took over on lead vocals, with McGuinn and Crosby assuming songwriting duties.

Reduced to a three-part vocal harmony, the Byrd's third album, *FIFTH DIMENSION*, spawned a moderate hit, the McGuinn-penned "Mr. Spaceman." Their next album, the Gary Usher-produced *YOUNGER THAN YESTERDAY*, generated the singles "So You Want to Be a Rock 'n' Roll Star" and a cover of Dylan's "Back Pages." That album also saw Hillman and Crosby develop their songwriting abilities.

After Crosby's controversial appearance with Buffalo Springfield at Monterey, he was asked to leave the group. Crosby then formed the popular folk-rock trio Crosby, Stills and Nash (and later, Young). Soon after, the Byrds lost their focus, with members freely drifting through the group.

In 1967, McGuinn hired former International Submarine Band guitarist Gram Parsons. Parsons took the Byrds into a new direction with the country album *SWEETHEART OF THE RODEO*, the project missing McGuinn's trademark, chiming, 12-string guitar. With his vocals removed from the album, Parsons left the Byrds in late 1968 to form the Flying Burrito Brothers. Hillman left soon after.

Drummer Gene Parsons (not related to Gram) and a former Gasden Brothers member, guitarist Clarence White, joined the group in 1969, in time for another country-rock album, *DR. BYRDS & MR. HYDE*. The Byrds muddled along with various new members, their last successful effort coming with the 1970 album *UNTITLED*. After the departure of McGuinn, the last original Byrd, the group disbanded in 1973. By year's end, the Byrds reformed with Clark, Clarke, Crosby, Hillman, and McGuinn, releasing one final album, *THE BYRDS*. Later, Clark reunited with McGuinn and Hillman, releasing a pair of albums, and scoring a top-40 hit with "Don't You Write Her Off."

After a thwarted Byrds reunion in 1983, former Byrds, Clark and Clarke infuriated the rest of group by touring as the Firebyrds, and releasing a self-titled album that featured Byrds classics, "Tambourine Man" and "Feel a Whole Lot Better." A similar reunion billed as "20th Anniversary Tribute to the Byrds" intensified the fight over the legal control of the group's name.

A 1990 Byrds box ed set contained newly recorded material by McGuinn, Crosby, and Hillman (other Byrds members were not invited). Settling their feuds, the group appeared together at the 1991 Rock and Roll Hall of Fame induction ceremonies. In their wake, the Byrds managed to influence a host of rock groups such as R.E.M. and Tom Petty & the Heartbreakers.

Bibliography

Bronson, Fred. (1992). *The Billboard Book of Number One Singles* (3rd. ed., pp. 178, 188). New York: Billboard.

Kiersh, Edward. (1986). *Where Are You Now, Bo Diddley?* (pp. 202-11). Garden City, NY: Doubleday.

Ruhlmann, William. (1991, January 11). The Byrds: Round trip. *Goldmine*, p. 8.

Selvin, Joel. (1994). *Summer of Love: The Inside Story of LSD, Rock & Roll, Free Love and High Times in the Wild West*. New York: Dutton.

JOHNNY CASH. *(J.R. Cash; February 26, 1932). Inducted in 1992.* Spanning rock, folk, and country, Johnny Cash emerged from poverty to become a musical superstar. Raised in a backwoods shack in rural Arkansas, Cash listened to country music on a battery-powered radio. Devastated by the death of an older brother, Cash was forever affected by the incident, as he adopted an impermeable, unsmiling exterior.

Though poor, Cash took private singing lessons, with his family somehow affording a piano. Performing an original composition at age 17, Cash won five dollars at an amateur contest.

While in the air force during the Korean War, Cash honed his musical abilities. Stationed in West Germany in 1950, Cash practiced on his newly acquired guitar and wrote his future hit "Folsom City Prison" (inspired by the film *Inside the Walls of Folsom Prison*). Also experimenting with lyric writing, Cash's poetry was published in *Stars and Stripes*. After his discharge in 1954, Cash moved to Memphis, working as a salesman to support his wife.

After enrolling in a radio announcers course, Cash formed a gospel-flavored, country group, the Tennessee Three. Cash was backed by electric guitarist Luther Perkins, bassist Marshall Grant, and steel guitarist Red Kernodle. After Kernodle's departure, Cash and the renamed Tennessee Two adopted a rock-oriented approach.

Approaching Sun Records after Elvis Presley's initial success, label head Sam Phillips was intrigued by the group's sincere, musical simplicity. Straddling the line between rock and country, Cash unleashed a string of hits, beginning in 1955 with, "Hey Porter," "Cry! Cry! Cry!" "Folsom Prison Blues," and "I Walk the Line." A pair of pop-crossover hits, "Ballad of a Teenage Queen" and "Things Happen That Way," were Sun's attempts to shape the "Man in Black" into a rockabilly teen idol.

Many of Cash's lyrics were based on stories told to him by his father. Singing in a dry, restrained style, Cash's deep voice and limited vocal range were augmented by Phillips' innovative production technique of slapback tape echo. With the addition of drummer, W.S. Holland, the band expanded back into the Tennessee Three.

Unhappy with Sun's excessive studio production and heavy instrumentation on his later releases, Cash joined the larger Columbia label in 1958. Now a regular on the Grand Ole Opry, Cash moved away from rock music, his hit run continuing with "Don't Take Your Guns to Town."

After spending time in the burgeoning Greenwich Village music scene, Cash scored with folk-leaning hits "Ring of Fire" (1963) and a cover of Bob Dylan's "It Ain't Me Babe" (1964). In 1965, Cash hired rockabilly guitarist Carl Perkins for a

Johnny Cash was the first artist inducted into both the Country and Rock and Roll Halls of Fame. (*Courtesy of American Recordings.*)

10-year stint.

In 1967, Cash tackled his decade-long amphetamine dependency, reaching rock bottom after a divorce, an arrest, and a series of car crashes. Back on top, Cash hosted his own ABC variety show. He also returned to the charts with the Carl Perkins-penned, old-time country song "Daddy Sang Bass" (1968), which featured the co-vocals of his soon-to-be-wife, June Carter.

Cash followed with his best-selling single ever, the novelty tune "A Boy Named Sue" (1969), the first pop hit with an objectionable phrase bleeped out. Taken from his live *AT SAN QUENTIN* prison album, it was his first public performance of the song. The previous year, he had released his first prison album, the popular *AT*

FOLSOM PRISON. Again flirting with folk music, Cash recorded a hit cover of Tim Hardin's "If I Were a Carpenter" (1970).

In the 1970s, Cash retreated to country music, recording a prolific string of albums, including some gospel material. In 1979, Cash scored a country hit with a cover of the standard "(Ghost) Riders in the Sky," a song that the Outlaws took to the pop chart two years later.

After sharing a bill at a 1985 Christmas special, Cash formed a supergroup with Waylon Jennings, Willie Nelson, and Kris Kristofferson, scoring a smash country hit with the Jimmy Webb-penned "Highwayman." Winning a Grammy Award, the foursome regrouped in 1989 for a second album project.

After his release by CBS Records in 1986, Cash signed with Mercury, which tried to strictly limit his output to country music. Still flirting with rock music, in 1993 Cash sang "The Wanderer," a track on U2's *ZOOROPA*.

Thriving on the charts well into the 1990s, Cash signed with Rick Rubin's American Recordings label. His 1994 release, the stripped-down acoustic album *AMERICAN RECORDINGS*, landed both country and alternative-rock airplay. His follow-up album *UNCHAINED* featured the musical backing of Tom Petty & the Heartbreakers. A decade earlier, Petty and Heartbreaker Benmont Tench co-wrote "Never Be You," a number-one country hit for Rosanne Cash, Johnny's daughter.

During the middle of a tour to promote his autobiography, in 1997 Cash was diagnosed with Shy-Drager's Syndrome, a progressive disorder of the nervous system characterized by tremors.

Bibliography

Hillburn, Robert. (1973, March 1). Nothing can take the place of the human heart: A conversation with Johnny Cash. *Rolling Stone*, p. 56.

Rader, Dotson. (1995, June 11). I can sing of death, but I'm obsessed with life. *Parade*, p. 4.

Roland, Tom. (1991). *The Billboard Book of Number One Country Hits*. New York: Billboard.

Smith, John L. (comp.). (1985). *The Johnny Cash Discography*. Westport, CT: Greenwood Press.

White, Mark. (1985). *You Must Remember This: Popular Songwriters 1900-1980* (pp. 60-62). New York: Charles Scribner's Sons.

RAY CHARLES. *(Ray Charles Robinson; September 27, 1930). Inducted in 1986.* A master of soulful R&B, Ray Charles succeeded in life in spite of personal adversity. Born into poverty in rural Albany, Georgia, Charles was raised by his strict mother in nearby Greenville, Florida. Born sighted, Charles slowly lost his vision, probably from glaucoma. He was legally blind by age seven.

While still sighted, Charles received informal piano lessons from the proprietor of a combination general store and cafe, copying what he heard on a blues-filled jukebox. He also sang with the congregation at the conservative Shiloh Baptist Church and listened to the hard-luck lyrics of Grand Ole Opry singers. Placed by his mother in the segregated St. Augustine School for the Blind, he was given classical music training.

Brown stayed in school until age 15, when, in the summer of 1945, his mother died. Drifting through Florida, Charles landed occasional musical jobs. Though blind,

Charles rejected the limitations of his condition. Writing in his autobiography, he remembers that "there are three things I never wanted to own when I was a kid: a dog, a can, and a guitar. In my brain, they each meant blindness and helplessness. . . . Seems like every blind singer I'd heard about was playing the guitar" (pp. 53-54).

Joining an all-white hillbilly band on piano in 1948, Charles first donned his trademark garb of dark glasses, dark suit, and skinny tie. With the group disbanding, the restless Charles rode a bus to Seattle, where he won a talent contest his first night there.

Forming the McSon Trio, Charles was performing in the style of Charles Brown and Nat "King" Cole. Dropping his last name, Robinson, to avoid confusion with a similarly named boxer, Ray Charles made his first recordings in 1949. Backed by Oscar and Johnny Moore as the Maxine Trio, Charles landed an R&B hit with "Confession Blues."

Moving to Los Angeles in 1949, Brown bought his first electric piano and landed a touring spot with Lowell Fulson. During this period, Charles scored a pair of R&B hits on the Swingtime label with "Baby, Let Me Hold Your Hand" (1951) and "Kiss Me Baby" (1952). After leaving Fulson over money, Charles changed his vocal delivery, tiring of the constant comparisons with Brown and Cole.

In 1952, Ahmet Ertegun bought out Charles' contract from Jack Lauderdale for $2,500. Recalled Atlantic co-owner Jerry Wexler in his autobiography: "I was struck by his physical presence: strong, broad-shouldered, and barrel-chested. . . . His speaking voice, like his singing voice, was deep but ever-changing, sometimes sounding old beyond his years" (p. 104).

Using Atlantic's session musicians and songwriters, Charles had limited success at first. After hiring his own band, Charles' first big hit came with his self-penned "I Got a Woman." Combining blues with gospel stylings, Charles was criticized in some quarters for mixing the two seemingly opposite genres. Hiring away Chuck Willis' female vocal trio, the Cookies, Charles molded the renamed Raelettes into church-like shouters. A perfectionist, Charles earned a reputation as a difficult bandleader, often playing the entire concert in the preshow sound-check.

Charles' hit run continued with "A Fool for You" (1955), "Drown in My Own Tears" (1956), "Hallelujah I Love Her So" (1956), and "Lonely Avenue." His first major pop crossover entry came in 1959 with the sensuous call-and-response classic "What'd I Say." At the insistence of Atlantic producer Nesuhu Ertegun, Charles also tackled jazz, in 1959 releasing *THE GENIUS OF RAY CHARLES*, which was recorded with a large orchestra.

Switching to ABC-Paramount in 1959 after receiving a large cash advance, Charles shifted toward pop balladry, scoring hits with a cover of Hank Snow's "I'm Movin' On" and a reworking of Hoagy Carmichael's 1930 hit "Georgia on My Mind" (later named the official state song of Georgia).

In 1962 Charles shocked his black fans with the country-meets-R&B album *MODERN SOUNDS IN COUNTRY AND WESTERN MUSIC*, selling 3-million copies. Becoming a multi-format star, Charles continued with the hits "Hit the Road Jack" (1961), "Unchain My Heart" (1961), the million-selling "I Can't Stop Loving You" (1962), and "Busted" (1963).

Arrested in 1965 for heroin possession, Charles spent a year in treatment. In the late 1960s and 1970s, Charles moved away from R&B in favor of jazz and pop standards. From 1968 to 1973, Charles launched his own Tangerine label, which was marketed by ABC-Paramount. Charles operated another label, Crossover Records, beginning in 1974, before returning to Atlantic Records in 1977.

Switching to Columbia Records in 1980, he released six albums and landed on the country charts with several hit singles, including the Willie Nelson duet "Seven Spanish Eyes" (1985). Remaining active in the 1980s, he played a major role in USA for Africa's "We Are the World" (1985) and scored a minor hit in a duet with Billy Joel, "Baby Grand" (1987).

In 1990, Charles emerged as a spokesman for Diet Pepsi. Backed by a trio of scantily-clad singers known as the "Uh-huh Girls," he popularized the phrase "You've Got the Right One Baby, Uh-huh."

In 1995, Charles celebrated his 50th year of performing. After winning a Grammy in 1994 with *A SONG FOR YOU*, Charles returned in 1996, releasing, *STRONG LOVE AFFAIR*. Since 1992, Rhino Records has reissued dozens of the singer's albums spanning 1952 to 1980.

Bibliography

Charles, Ray & Ritz, David. (1978). *Brother Ray: Ray Charles' Own Story*. New York: Warner.

Grendysa, Peter. (1988, November). Ray Charles, perfectionist with perfect pitch, evolved from Nat Cole clone to jazz/blues legend. *Record Collector Monthly*, p. 1.

Wexler, Jerry & Ritz, David. (1993). *Rhythm and the Blues: A Life in American Music*. New York: Alfred A. Knopf.

Woodfin, Henry. (1962). Ray Charles. In Martin T. Williams (Ed.), *Jazz Panorama* (pp. 306-10). New York: Crowell-Collier.

LEONARD CHESS. *(Lazer Chez; March 12, 1917 - October 16, 1969). Inducted in the Non-Performer category in 1987*. During World War II, hundreds of thousands of blacks migrated to the North, filling wartime factory jobs. With the major record labels ignoring the black consumer, small independent companies like Chicago-based Chess Records thrived, selling millions of R&B, jazz and blues discs.

Escaping Soviet anti-Semitism, the Chez (Americanized as Chess) family emigrated to Chicago's predominantly black South Side in 1928. Young Leonard Chess was stricken with polio and feared he would be refused entry.

After working with their father in the scrap-metal business, Leonard and his younger brother Phil operated several liquor stores and nightclubs. Opened in 1945, their most popular club, the Macomba, offered jazz and blues entertainment. Having difficulty filling their own jukeboxes with black-oriented records, the Chess brothers launched the Aristocrat label in 1947, first recording a Macomba vocalist, Andrew Tibbs.

Aristocrat's first major success came with transplanted Delta bluesman Muddy Waters who in 1948 recorded the double-sided smash, "(I Feel Like) Going Home"/"Can't Be Satisfied" (1948). With the label taking much of Leonard's time, he abdicated the nightclub responsibilities to his brother Phil.

Buying out a partner in 1949, the Chess brothers landed their first hit a year later on their new Chess label with Gene Ammon's "My Foolish Heart." As musical novices, in 1951 Leonard Chess hired bluesman Willie Dixon as their chief producer, songwriter, and bandleader. Leonard Chess frequently traveled through the South on talent hunts, recording hundreds of performers on a primitive, wire tape recorder.

Working out of a tiny storefront studio, Chess recorded the finest in R&B and postwar blues by the likes of Dixon, Waters, Little Walter, John Lee Hooker, and Howlin' Wolf. Chess also spawned a number of subsidiaries including Checker (1952) and a jazz imprint, Argo (1955), and leased master-discs from small record labels, landing a huge hit with Jackie Brenston's "Rocket 88." Often criticized for its royalty arrangements with its acts, Chess was far more generous its competitors.

In 1955, Chess widened its scope from R&B and blues into rock and roll, as Bo Diddley and Chuck Berry recorded landmark hits such as "I'm a Man" and "Johnny B. Goode." For the first time, Chess was selling records to white consumers.

But when blues music fell out of popularity in the black community in the late 1950s, Chess Records suffered. Willie Dixon returned to Chess after a three-year absence in an attempt to save the label.

With the addition in the early 1960s of producer Ralph Bass and songwriter and A&R-man Billy Davis, Chess switched gears, entering the soul music market with its new Check-Mate subsidiary. In the decade, Chess had success with Billy Stewart, Fontella Bass, Koko Taylor, the Dells, and R&B singer turned balladeer Etta James. The Chess brothers also launched a popular and influential, low-power radio station, WVON, nicknamed "Voice of the Negro." Within months, the station outdrew all of its competitors.

In 1964, the Rolling Stones recorded their second album, *12 x 5*, at the Chess studio, the record featuring a track named after the company's address, "2120 South Michigan Avenue." Two years later, the company moved into a larger space.

By the late 1960s, Chess discovered a new market for blues music among white college students, reissuing their older material on full-length albums. Targeting the rock market, Chess also launched the Cadet Concept subsidiary in 1967.

Chess began to disintegrate in 1969 after its sale to General Recorded Tape (GRT). After Leonard Chess' death later in the year, his son Marshall was named president. Phil Chess left his vice president position in 1972, relocating to Arizona.

With artists abandoning the company, Chess limped along a few more years, with only the Dells remaining successful into the 1970s. Chess was mothballed in 1975 and resold twice, its last owners dumping thousands of records into a garbage bin. In 1985, MCA records purchased the 25,000 title Chess catalog and began reissuing the music on compact disc.

Bibliography

Golkin, Pete. (1989, September/October). Blacks whites and blues: The story of Chess Records, part one. *Living Blues*, p. 22.

Golkin, Pete. (1989, November/December). Blacks whites and blues: The story of Chess Records, part two. *Living Blues*, p. 25.

Pruter, Robert. (1991). *Chicago Soul*. Urbana: University of Illinois Press.
Shaw, Arnold. (1978). *Honkers and Shouters: The Golden Years of Rhythm and Blues*. New
     York: Collier.

CHARLIE CHRISTIAN. *(July 29, 1916 - March 2, 1942). Inducted in the Early Influence category in 1990.* A revolutionary artist, Charlie Christian brought the electric guitar into the forefront of jazz, paving the way for rock and roll. Born in rural Bonham, Texas, Christian was raised in Dallas, where his parents played Tin Pan Alley music at a Dallas silent-film theater. In 1921, his family moved to Oklahoma City, where Charlie built a primitive guitar. Though a member of his school band, he never learned to read music.

Working in a succession of bands during his teens, Christian mastered several instruments, beginning with the trumpet and moving to the guitar, bass, and piano. Christian also sang in an acapella vocal quartet.

Playing a mixture of Texas blues and southwestern jazz, Christian joined his brother's band, the Jolly Jugglers, and then Anna Mae Winburn's band. After rejecting a career in the "colored" baseball league in the mid-1930s, Christian joined a regional touring band led by Alphonso Trent. By 1937, Christian returned to Oklahoma City, forming his own quartet.

With Count Basie's Band in town, Basie's guitarist Eddie Durham discovered Christian playing guitar in a pool hall. Intrigued by his style, Durham provided his young protégé with a series of lessons, the pair regularly meeting over a pool table.

Recommended by independent producer John Hammond, Christian joined the Benny Goodman Band in August 1939. Goodman initially resisted but welcomed Christian after failing to outplay him in an impromptu, onstage contest. Usually working in Goodman's smaller sextet with players such as Cootie Williams and Count Basie, Christian was featured on "Flying Home" and, with a full orchestra, "Solo Flight" (1939).

Expanding the role of the guitar in jazz, Christian put the instrument into the forefront of the genre. His improvised solos often featured a repeating guitar riff, later a centerpiece of rock. Writes historian James Sallis: "His endless stream of ideas fueled an entire generation of players; his drive and heavy riffs shored the rafters of many drooping sessions; his phrasing, fresh use of intervals and self-dependent lines paved the way for bebop and summarily liberated the guitar from its comfortable role as accompanist" (p. 102).

Recording with the finest jazz players of the day, Christian was teamed with the likes of Lionel Hampton and Meade "Lux" Lewis. For several months in 1941, Christian frequented Minton's nightclub in Harlem, often joining the house band in legendary jam sessions.

During the middle of a tour in 1941, Christian was diagnosed with tuberculosis and confined to Bellevue Hospital in New York. He died several months later at the Seaview Sanitarium in Staten Island, with Goodman paying his medical bills. Christian's recorded output remains a mainstay of modern jazz.

Bibliography

Blesh, Rudi. (1979). *Combo USA: Eight Lives in Jazz* (pp. 161-86). NewYork: Da Capo.
Britt, Stan. (1984). *The Jazz Guitarists*. Poole, England: Blanford.
Collier, James Lincoln. (1989). *Benny Goodman and the Swing Era*. New York: Oxford
    University Press.
Friedland, Will. (1990). *Jazz Singing: America's Great Voices from Bessie Smith to Bebop and
    Beyond*. New York: Charles Scribner's Sons.
Sallis, James. (1982). *The Guitar Players*. New York: William Morrow.

DICK CLARK. *(Richard Wagstaff Clark; November 30, 1929). Inducted in Non-Performer category in 1993.* In an age before MTV, Dick Clark's *American Bandstand* was the most influential medium on television. The son of a salesman, Clark was a popular teenager, elected the class president at his high school in Bronxville, New York. After gaining some on-air experience at his uncle's radio station, Clark enrolled at Syracuse University in 1946, majoring in advertising and minoring in radio.

Graduating in 1951, Clark hosted a short-lived country-music television program as Cactus Dick. Moving to Philadelphia the following year, Clark deejayed at WFIL, drawn to the station because of its television affiliate.

Meanwhile, in September 1952, the *Bandstand* television show premiered at WFIL. Hosted by the middle-aged Bob Horn, the variety program showed video-like kinescopes of country and pop-standard performers, with comedy and interviews thrown in. But when the teens in the studio audience asked to dance, a new format was invented. Early on, a "rate-a-record" segment was introduced, with the often repeated phrase "It's got a good beat, and it's easy to dance to" coming a few years later.

Disgraced after a drunk driving charge in early 1956, Horn was fired and replaced by Tony Mammarella. But after Mammarella's voluntary departure in July 1956, the straitlaced 26-year-old Clark took over. After some initial picketing over Horn's dismissal, Clark's popularity soared.

With copycat shows proliferating around the country, the national version of Clark's program, retitled *American Bandstand*, debuted on 67 ABC stations on August 5, 1957. Broadcast daily, the program was an immediate hit, targeting teens coming home from school. The show's original theme song, "Bandstand Boogie," was recorded by Les Elgart's swing orchestra in 1953 (Barry Manilow's version of the song premiered at the show's 25th anniversary special in 1982).

Soon millions of teenagers tuned in for the music, the fashions, and the latest dance crazes. America learned to do the Pony, the Watusi, and the then-scandalous Twist.

To keep from alienating parents and sponsors (like the perennial advertiser, Clearasil), Clark instituted a dress code for its well-mannered dancers: boys wore suits with ties, and girls wore dresses. Still, *Bandstand* was daring for its time, with black and white couples dancing side by side.

Almost immediately *Bandstand* had the power to create radio airplay and consumer demand merely by featuring a record or singer on the show. Clark also discovered or popularized a number of local Philadelphia acts, including Fabian, Frankie Avalon,

Chubby Checker, and Danny and the Juniors.

During its nearly four-decade run, *Bandstand* featured 10,000 musical guests and played 65,000 records. Although the Beatles, the Rolling Stones, and Elvis never performed on the show, every other notable rocker did, including Prince, the Sex Pistols, and, in 1984, making her first national TV appearance, Madonna.

In 1960, Clark escaped prosecution during the payola hearings which ruined the likes of powerful deejay Alan Freed. Forced to divest many of his assets, he lost an estimated $8 million. Turning to concert promotion in the early 1960s, Clark launched his "Caravan of Stars" tours.

In 1963, *Bandstand* started taping its shows, that year moving to a once-a-week format on Saturday afternoons. A year later, the program relocated to a more modern studio in Hollywood, California. With the loss of his daily program, in 1965 Clark launched *Where the Action Is*, a live show featuring a regular cast of performers including Paul Revere and the Raiders.

Expanding into many aspects of the entertainment industry with his Dick Clark Productions, the affable Clark launched his perennial *Rockin' New Year* festivities in 1972 and later hosted *The $10,000 Pyramid* and *TV's Bloopers and Practical Jokes* and for a time acted in films.

By 1981 *American Bandstand* had lost its prominence with the birth of MTV, a 24-hour-a-day music cable channel. Much like the early *Bandstand*, MTV aired music videos.

In 1987 Clark refused to renew *Bandstand*, angered by ABC's frequent preempting of the program by college football games. After a six-month run on the USA Cable Network with a new host, 26-year-old Detroit-native David Hirsh, the 37-year-old show was canceled. Ironically, MTV's sister channel, VH-1, began airing *Bandstand* reruns in 1996.

Bibliography

Clark, Dick & Robinson, Richard. (1976). *Rock, Roll & Remember*. New York: Crowell.

Fong-Torres, Ben. (1973, August 16). Dick Clark: Twenty years of Clearasil rock. *Rolling Stone*, p. 1.

King, Susan. (1995, December 31). Dick Clark: Rockin' man. *Los Angeles Times*, TV Times sect., p. 4.

Miller, Holly G. (1995, July-August). Dick Clark's role after rock. *Saturday Evening Post*, p. 34.

Piccoli, Sean. (1992, May 13). Dick Clark makes us feel like dancing. *The Washington Times*, p. E1.

Schipper, Henry. (1990, April 19). Dick Clark. *Rolling Stone*, p. 67.

THE COASTERS. *Carl E. Gardner (April 19, 1928); Cornell Gunter (Cornelius Gunter; November 14, 1938 - February 26, 1990); Will "Dub" Jones; Billy "Bip" Guy (June 20, 1936). Inducted in 1987.* The comedy-inflected songs of the Coasters combined hard-edged R&B with doo-wop harmonies. The group's story began in 1948 with the A-Sharp Trio, Ty Terell and brothers Billy and Roy Richards becoming regulars at the weekly amateur night at Johnny Otis' Barrelhouse Club. At Otis' suggestion, Alabama native and former boxer Bobby Nunn was added to the group on bass vocals. Renamed the Four Bluebirds by Otis, they instead took another moniker, the Robins.

After recording for Aladdin Records, in early 1950 Otis took the group to Savoy, releasing "If It's So Baby," the first national doo-wop hit by a Los Angeles group. In an unplanned session, the Robins backed Esther Phillips, a barefoot neighborhood girl who tagged along, on a comical song from the group's repertoire, "Double Crossin' Blues." After a Los Angeles deejay played the demo, it became a smash hit, launching the 14-year-old's career.

After the Robins broke away from Otis in 1951, a pair of young, white, R&B aficionados, Jerry Leiber and Mike Stoller, convinced the group to record their composition "That's What the Good Book Says." A minor hit at Modern Records, the song was the start of a long relationship between the group and the budding record producers.

After producing several unsuccessful Robins releases at RCA Records in 1953, Leiber & Stoller started their own record label, Spark. Signing the Robins in 1954, Leiber & Stoller scored their first Spark hit with the Robins' "Riot in Cell Block #9," which featured the bass vocals of guest singer Richard Berry. A number of deejays refused to air the record, fearing the song would inspire prison violence. That year, the Robins' future manager, Lester Sill, replaced newly hired Grady Chapman with Carl Gardner. (Chapman returned by year's end.)

With the songwriting and production skills of Leiber and Stoller, the group followed up with another prison-oriented song, "Framed" (1955), which saw Nunn's bass voice return to prominence. The song was typical of the Robins' later recordings which weaved an intricate, mood-inducing tale, set in front of oddly exotic instrumentation.

But with the Spark label frustrated by their inability to promote the Robins' records outside the Los Angeles market, Leiber & Stoller sold out to the larger New York-based Atlantic Records and were hired by the label as independent producers. The Robins' last Spark release, "Smokey Joe's Cafe" (1955), was also released on Atlantic's Atco subsidiary and, with the proper promotion, did become a national hit.

Asked to join Atlantic, the Robins split into two camps, with only Bobby Nunn and lead tenor Carl Gardner making the move. The rest of the group remained in Los Angeles recording a series of unsuccessful singles for Whippit Records before disbanding in 1958.

As the Coasters, Nunn and Gardner were joined by tenor Leon Hughes (formerly with the Lamplighters), former comic-turned-singer Billy "Bip" Guy (of the duo Bip and Bob), and guitarist Adolph Jones. Recording mostly Leiber & Stoller compositions, the group would score a series of cross-over hits, beginning in 1956 with a moody, accented song similar to "Smokey Joe's Cafe" called "Down in Mexico."

Switching gears, Leiber & Stoller took the Coasters in a new direction, introducing danceable, upbeat, comical material. In 1957, the Coasters scored a double-sided smash with their new, hard-rocking brand of R&B, with million-selling "Searchin'"/"Youngblood," the record's B-side taking a farcical, near-slapstick

The Coasters.

approach to group harmony.

Homesick and tired of constant touring, Nunn and Hughes left the group in late 1958 and were replaced by bass singer Will "Dub" Jones, formerly of the Cadets, and Cornell Gunter, formerly of the Flairs and Platters.

The Coasters' hits continued with the chart-topping, "Yakety Yak" (1958); the million-selling "Charlie Brown" (1959); "Along Came Jones" (1959); and their jab at heartbreaking women, "Poison Ivy" (1959). Central to the group's sound was the legendary saxophone player King Curtis, whose solos added a lighter, carnival-like atmosphere.

The group's last pop hit came in 1961 with, "Little Egypt," a novelty song about a belly dancer. That year, former Cadillacs leader Earl "Speedo" Carroll replaced

Gunter (who in 1964 formed his own Coasters with his sister, Shirley, and former members of the Penguins). The Coasters' last Atco release came in 1966. With Ronnie Bright replacing Jones, the band recorded for CBS' Date Records in 1967, unable to repeat its earlier success.

Nunn, Gardner, and other former members later formed their own touring Coasters groups. In the 1980s, Gardner was awarded sole legal ownership of the group's name.

Bibliography

Dawson, Jim & Propes, Steve. (1992). *What Was the First Rock 'N' Roll Record?* (pp. 150-54). Boston: Faber and Faber.

Goldberg, Marv & Redmond, Mike. (1973, February). The Cornell Gunter story. *Record Exchanger*, p. 5.

Silverman, Phil. (1984, November). Coasters' founder Carl Gardner talks of successes: Handles three generations of fans—and music—with aplomb. *Record Collector's Monthly*, p. 1.

EDDIE COCHRAN. *(Edward Ray Cochrane; October 3, 1938 - April 17, 1960)*. *Inducted in 1987.* In the mid-1950s, country was melded with rock in what became known as rockabilly. Primarily a southern genre, rockabilly's stars included Gene Vincent, Buddy Holly, and Eddie Cochran.

Growing up in Albert Lea, Minnesota, Cochran, like most rockabilly performers, was reared on country-western music, buying a guitar at age 12. In 1954, at age 15, he teamed up with country guitarist and singer Hank Cochran (no relation), billed as the Cochran Brothers.

Enamored of Elvis Presley, in 1955 Eddie Cochran quit school, jumping into a rock music career. Auditioning for Sam Phillips of Sun Records the Cochran Brothers were rejected.

Moving to Los Angeles, the duo recorded some groundbreaking, but unsuccessful, rockabilly records on the Ekko label, and in 1956 landed a spot on the Stockton, California, country music television show, *The California Hayride*. Unlike his partner, Eddie Cochran became fascinated with Elvis Presley. Soon after the duo split over musical differences, with Hank preferring to stay in country music.

Launching a solo career with the assistance of Los Angeles songwriter and music publisher Jerry Capehart, Cochran launched a solo career, garnering poor sales with early releases such as "Skinny Jim." Capehart then took demos of songs that he and Cochran had co-written to Sy Waronker at fledgling Liberty Records. Signed to the label, Liberty initially rejected their original material. Instead, Cochran scored a top-20 hit with a cover version of John D. Loudermilk's "Sittin' in the Balcony."

Though not selling many records, Cochran packed concert halls with screaming fans in the U.S. and in Australia. With Waronker's help, Cochran landed a small role in the Jane Mansfield film *The Girl Can't Help It* (1956), performing "20 Flight Rock," the song featuring Cochran's intricate guitar work.

In 1958, 19-year-old Cochran released his million-selling signature tune and rock standard "Summertime Blues." With his slicked pompadour, archetypical guitar pose, and rebellious attitude, Cochran epitomized the 1950s rock and roll star. He followed up with another hit, "C'mon Everybody."

By this time, Cochran became good friends with another young rocker named Buddy Holly. Appearing in Alan Freed's low-budget rock flick *Go Johnny Go* (1959) kept Cochran out of the tragic "Winter Dance Party" tour, which saw the deaths of Holly, Ritchie Valens, and the Big Bopper. In tribute, Cochran recorded "Three Stars," with the proceeds going to the families of the fallen rockers.

With popular music tastes changing, Cochran would score his last U.S. hit in late 1959 with "Somethin' Else." In January 1960, Cochran recorded for the last time, backed in the studio by Buddy Holly's former Crickets, Jerry Allison and Sonny Curtis.

Immediately after the sessions, Cochran left for a British tour, which featured supporting acts Joe Brown, Georgie Fame, and Billy Fury. Playing to packed houses, Cochran and close friend Gene Vincent co-headlined a ten-week tour, treated by fans as though they were each Elvis. At the completion of the surprisingly successful tour, a second 10-week leg was planned. Their last performance, a last-minute addition, was at the Bristol Hippodrome.

But tragedy struck en route to the airport when their chauffeur-driven Ford blew a tire and ran into a lamppost. Cochran died within hours from massive head injuries. Vincent was seriously injured, while Cochran's girlfriend, songwriter Sharon Sheeley, suffered a broken pelvis.

Although America's taste for rockabilly had waned, British fans continued their appreciation of the music, with Cochran enjoying several posthumous British hits, including the chart-topping "Three Steps to Heaven."

Cochran's "Summertime Blues" has appeared in countless commercials and has been recorded by the likes of Blue Cheer, the Who, and Joan Jett.

Bibliography

Barrett, Frank. (1990, June 30). Rock holidays: Summertime blues on the road to heaven; Eddie
        Cochran's death is part of rock 'n' roll's legend. *Independent*, p. 43.
Bush, William J. (1983, December). Eddie Cochran: The legend lives on. *Guitar Player*, p. 71.
Eder, Bruce. (1989, September 8). Eddie Cochran: Somethin' else. *Goldmine*, p. 16.
Elson, Howard. (1982). *Early Rockers* (pp. 18-27). New York: Proteus.

SAM COOKE. *(Samuel Cook; January 22, 1935 - December 11, 1964). Inducted in 1986.* A superstar in both the gospel and pop music fields, Sam Cooke left a legacy in both worlds. Born in Clarksdale, Mississippi, but raised in Chicago, Sam Cook (no e) grew up in the hand-clapping, spirit-filled church services of his traveling preacher father, Charles Cook. At age six, Sam joined his siblings in the family gospel group, the Singing Children, often accompanying Reverend Cook on his travels.

Realizing his musical gift, young Sam would sneak out of the house to earn tip money singing for customers at a nearby tavern. Performing only gospel music as a teenager, he joined a local group, the Highway Q.C.s, while in high school. Crossing paths with the Soul Stirrers, Cook convinced member R.B. Robinson to tutor his group. Turning professional in 1948, the Highway Q.C.s took to the road, Cook's father providing them a car. The Q.C.s often substituted for the frequently-touring Soul Stirrers on their Chicago radio program.

Following the departure in 1950 of the Soul Stirrers' founder, R.H. Harris, 19-year-old Cook was hired as second tenor. At first, Cook alternated the lead vocals, before emerging into the forefront with his emotional, quivering style. A gospel sex symbol, the charismatic singer soon attracted legions of young female fans to Soul Stirrers shows as he led the group on the gospel hits "Nearer to Me" (1955) and "Touch the Hem of His Garment" (1956).

Tired of meager wages and the strict confines of the gospel road, Cook longed to sing pop material. Though fearful of alienating gospel consumers, Specialty Records owner Art Rupe permitted A&R man Robert "Bumps" Blackwell to record Cook under the pseudonym Dale Cook. With Blackwell buying out Cook's contract from Specialty, the renamed Sam Cooke was signed to Keen Records. Packing smokey nightclubs instead of church pews, many of his fans never forgave him for abandoning gospel.

Cooke's third single at Keen, the simplistic "You Send Me," was his first pop hit, selling 2 million copies. The song's success was parlayed into a spot on *The Ed Sullivan Show* and a concert at the famed Copacabana nightclub in New York City, where a disastrous outing in front of a white audience devastated the usually confident and charismatic Cooke.

Nonetheless, with his smooth and soulful, fluid tenor voice, Cooke unleashed a string of R&B/pop crossover hits with "I Love You for Sentimental Reasons" (1958); a leftover release from Specialty, "I'll Come Running Back to You" (1958); "Win Your Love for Me" (1958); "Love You Most of All" (1958); "Only Sixteen" (1959); and his final Keen hit, "Wonderful World" (1960)..

Leaving Keen over money in 1960, Cooke signed a lucrative contract with the giant RCA label. There Hugo Peretti and Luigi Creatore replaced J.W. Alexander as Cooke's producer, with Cooke now recording more of his own material. After two failed singles, Cooke continued his long string of top-10 hits with "Chain Gang" (1960); "Cupid" (1961); "Twistin' the Night Away" (1962); with Lou Rawls on backing vocals, "Bring It on Home to Me" (1962); "Send Me Some Loving" (1963); and "Another Saturday Night" (1963).

Meanwhile, in 1959 Cooke had launched his own record label, SAR Records, named for Cooke and his managers, J.W. Alexander and Roy Crain. Cooke initially signed gospel acts including the Soul Stirrers, later adding pop acts Johnnie Taylor, Mel Carter, and the Valentinos, whose "It's All Over Now" was later a hit for the Rolling Stones. A savvy businessman, Cooke hired lawyer Allen Klein in 1963 as his new manager after finding discrepancies in his RCA royalty statements.

By 1964, Cooke was returning to his soulful roots, marked by a triumphant return to the Copacabana (captured on the album *AT THE COPA)*. His lyrical themes became social consciousness, as noted in his posthumous hit "A Change Is Gonna Come." While Cooke also wanted to return to gospel music, his former fans now shunned and heckled him.

Tragedy struck Cooke in December 1964 in a bizarre incident at the three-dollar-a-night Hacienda Motel in Los Angeles. He was shot and bludgeoned to death by the motel manager, whom Cooke accused of hiding his date, Linda Boyer, after she ran out of their room with all of his clothing. Though ruled justifiable homicide, a mob conspiracy was suspected. Following Cooke's death, SAR records closed, and Bobby Womack married Cooke's widow. A film biography of Cooke's life hit theaters in 1998.

Bibliography

Bego, Mark. (1989). *Aretha Franklin: The Queen of Soul*. New York: St. Martin's Press.

Boyer, Edward J. (1994, December 23). The soulful legacy of Sam Cooke. *The Los Angeles Times*, p. A1.

Heilbut, Anthony. (1985). *The Gospel Sound: Good News and Bad Times* (rev. ed.). New York: Limelight.

Hilburn, Robert. (1986, February 16). Sam Cooke: Our father of soul. *Los Angeles Times*, Calendar sect., p. 62.

Santoro, Gene. (1995, March 13). Sam Cooke. *The Nation*, p. 357.

Wolf, Daniel & Crain, S.R. (1995). *You Send Me: The Life and Times of Sam Cooke*. New York: William Morrow.

CREAM. *Jack Bruce (John Symon Asher Bruce; May 14, 1943); Ginger Baker (Peter Baker; August 19, 1939); Eric Clapton (Eric Clapp; March 30, 1945). Inducted in 1993.* Considered rock's first supergroup, Cream set a new level of musicianship in popular music, merging blues, jazz, and progressive rock. Born out of wedlock, Eric Clapton was raised by his grandparents. Enrolled at Kingston Art School, he was dismissed for his hooliganism. Loaned money by his grandmother, Clapton bought an electric guitar, joining his first band, the Roosters, in early 1963. By year's end, he graduated to the Yardbirds and, in 1965, John Mayall's Bluesbreakers. But it was his residency with Mayall where Clapton first earned stature as a "guitar god."

London-born Peter "Ginger" Baker was raised on American jazz, playing the trumpet before discovering his drumming talent. Nicknamed Ginger for his flaming red hair, he joined a succession of New Orleans-style jazz combos, including a group led by Acker Bilk, becoming a much-sought-after player in Britain. Switching to R&B in 1962 as a member of Alexis Korner's Blues Incorporated, Baker frequently clashed with Korner's bassist, Jack Bruce. In 1963 both Baker and Bruce left Korner and joined the similarly styled R&B/blues group the Graham Bond Organization.

A classically trained musician, Scotland-born Jack Bruce mastered the cello before switching to the acoustic bass. Attracted to old-style jazz, his first break came with Jim McHarg's Scotsville Jazzband.

Bruce had joined Korner's band at about the same time as Baker. During his last months of a three-year run in Bond's group, Bruce jumped on the British Invasion bandwagon, switching to the electric bass. At the end of 1965, Bruce left Blues Incorporated to join John Mayall's Bluesbreakers, the band then featuring Clapton. Needing money, Bruce then joined a pop group, Manfred Mann, for a six-month stint, performing on their hit, "Pretty Flamingo."

In the fall of 1966, Bruce and Clapton formed Cream, lastly hiring Baker. Rock's original "supergroup," Cream provided Baker and Bruce an opportunity to rekindle their feud. After their first major concert at the National Jazz and Blues Festival in July, 1966, their manager, Robert Stigwood, signed the band to Polydor Records (distributed in the U.S. by Atco).

Released in late 1966, the group's debut album, *FRESH CREAM*, contained a pair of hit cover versions of blues classics: Skip James' "I'm So Glad" and Willie Dixon's "Spoonful." A blues-meets-psychedelia effort, Cream found an instant fan base, first in England, then the U.S. Between albums, the band released the single-only hit "I Feel Free."

Dressed in satin shirts and velvet pants, Cream assaulted audiences with volume settings at maximum. Borrowing from jazz and emphasizing long, spontaneous solos, Clapton took rock-guitar improvisation to a new level, while Bruce expanded the role of the electric bass. After a period, the shy and insecure Clapton became uncomfortable with his "guitar god" status.

At an impromptu recording session following their first American gig in New York City, Cream recorded the Felix Pappalardi-produced *DISRAELI GEARS*, the album highlighted by the tracks, "Strange Brew," "Tales of Brave Ulysses," and the million-selling "Sunshine of Your Love." Like all of Cream's output, the album received limited radio airplay at a time the group was filling large concert halls.

With Pappalardi joining as an unofficial fourth member in 1968, Cream released *WHEELS OF FIRE*, a two-disc set consisting of one live and one studio disc. The project's highlights were "White Room," the Albert King classic, "Born under a Bad Sign," and, with Clapton's impassioned lead vocals, a live, reworked version of Robert Johnson's blues gem "Crossroads."

With the Royal Albert Hall audience chanting, "God save the Cream," on November 26, 1968, Clapton announced the end of the group, citing their "lost direction." In reality, strong competing personalities and heavy drug use combined with rocketing fame to torpedo the group. Released as both a documentary and album, their final effort, *GOODBYE*, spawned the radio hit "Badge," co-written by Clapton and guest player George Harrison.

Clapton and Baker then joined another supergroup, Blind Faith, a quartet with Steve Winwood and Ric Grech. The group disbanded after releasing a chart-topping album, *BLIND FAITH* (1970).

Cream regrouped at the Rock Hall ceremonies in 1993. Though Clapton suggested a reunion, he later refused to join his former partners for a new project. With none of the expected hoopla, in 1994 Baker and Bruce formed BBM with former Thin Lizzy guitarist Gary Moore, releasing a much-ignored album *AROUND THE NEXT DREAM*.

Bibliography

Boehm, Mike. (1993, March 22). Recent reunion has people talking: Will cream rise again? *Los Angeles Times*, p. F1.

"Cream." (1974). In *Rock Guitarists* (pp. 36-37). Saratoga, CA: Guitar Player Productions.

Harrington, Richard. (1988, April 17). Eric Clapton's long and winding road: The consummate guitarist and his retrospective release. *Washington Post*, p. F1.

Robbins, Ira. (1994, October 12). It's time for Cream to rise again. *(New York) Newsday*, p. B9.

Roeser, Steve. (1993, October 15). Ginger Baker: Anyone for polo? *Goldmine*, p. 42.

Sweeting, Adam. (1994, January 17). Step forward Eric Iglesias. *Guardian*, p. 8.

Wenner, Jann. (1981). Eric Clapton. In Peter Herbst (Ed.), *Rolling Stone Interviews* (pp. 24-31). New York: St. Martin's.

CREEDENCE CLEARWATER REVIVAL. *Doug "Cosmo" Clifford (April 24, 1945); Stu Cook (April 24, 1945); John Fogerty (John Cameron Fogerty; May 28, 1945); Tom Fogerty (November 9, 1941 - September 6, 1990). Inducted in 1993.* The unlikely originators of swamp-rock, Creedence Clearwater Revival, originated not from the bayous of Louisiana but from the suburbs of San Francisco. In 1958, "Tommy" Fogerty joined his first rock group, the Playboys, at St. Mary's High School on guitar and lead vocals. His younger brother, guitarist John Fogerty , had formed the Blue Velvets in 1959 at Potola Junior High in El Cerrito, California, with bass player Stu Cook and drummer Doug Clifford. Later in the year, Tom joined the group on rhythm guitar and co-lead vocals. Renamed Tommy Fogerty and the Blue Velvets, the group recorded three obscure singles for the tiny Orchestra label.

In the early 1960s, John Fogerty landed a job as a shipping clerk at Fantasy Records, a jazz label. In 1964, he convinced the company to sign his brother, Tom, as a solo act, with the underage Blue Velvets still backing him. Renamed the Golliwogs by Fantasy, the label heads wanted a British-sounding moniker. While Tom began as the lead vocalist, the similarly styled John gradually took over the duties.

After Saul Zaentz bought Fantasy Records in late 1967, the Golliwogs became Creedence Clearwater Revival (CCR). The group garnered a local following after pioneering San Francisco radio station KMPX began playing an unreleased tape of their bluesy rendition of the Dale Hawkins' rockabilly standard "Suzie Q." The following year, the track was included on their debut album, *CREEDENCE CLEARWATER REVIVAL*, becoming their first national hit. Clad in plaid shirts and tattered jeans decades before Nirvana, CCR emerged as one of the most popular bands of the Vietnam era, bringing a West Coast version of New Orleans' rock into the mainstream.

With John Fogerty emerging as the group's leader and chief songwriter, CCR unleashed a string of top-10, million-selling hits, including their signature piece, "Proud Mary" (1969), and "Bad Moon Rising" (1969). Their fortunes improved after performing at Woodstock, the group scoring a double-sided chart hit with "Down On The Corner," backed by the war protest song, "Fortunate Son" (1969).

Their most mature album, *COSMO'S FACTORY*, contained several hits including the album-rock standard "I Heard it through the Grapevine." A double-sided hit, the Little Richard tribute "Travelin' Band"/"Who'll Stop the Rain" (1970). An angry Little Richard responded by filing a plagiarism lawsuit over the A-side. Their next two hits, the frenetic "Up around the Bend," and the Vietnam-themed "Run through the Jungle," were written by John Fogerty over a weekend before a European tour.

Resenting John's increasing control of the group, Tom Fogerty left CCR in January of 1971. His last album with the group, *PENDULUM*, was highlighted by the hit

"Have You Ever Seen The Rain" (1971), an autobiographical song describing tensions within the group.

With Cook and Clifford assuming some production and songwriting duties, the trio's *MARDI GRAS* album stalled, missing their usual R&B-inflected rock sound. CCR would limp along for another 18 months, scoring a pair of hits with "Sweet Hitch-Hiker" (1971), and "Someday Never Comes" (1972). At their last concert, hecklers in Denver pelted the group with coins.

In the 1970s, both Tom and John Fogerty recorded several solo albums, with John scoring a few country-styled hits with the Blue Ridge Rangers. Cook joined the country group Southern Pacific. After releasing a solo album in 1975, legal difficulties kept John Fogerty out of the music industry for the next decade. Except for impromptu performances at Tom Fogerty's 1980 wedding and a subsequent high school reunion, CCR never reunited.

After years of litigation with Fantasy Records, John Fogerty launched a successful comeback in 1985, playing all the instruments on his album *CENTERFIELD*. Fantasy filed another lawsuit, claiming that Fogerty was plagiarizing himself on the track "Old Man Down the Road," which Fantasy claimed was based on CCR's "Run through the Jungle." Fogerty later won that lawsuit.

In 1990, Tom Fogerty died of respiratory disease. Later, Cook and Clifford toured as Creedence Clearwater Revisited, with new vocalist John Tristao (of 1960s group People). Fogerty failed in his attempts to legally block his former bandmates from exploiting the CCR name.

Bibliography

Aikin, Jim. (1974). Stu Cook: Creedence. In *Rock Guitarists* (pp. 44-47). Saratoga, CA: Guitar Player Productions.

Blair, Iain. (1985, March 31). Creedence's Fogerty back in the big leagues with "Centerfield." *Chicago Tribune*, Tempo sect., p. 10.

Hillburn, Robert. (1985, January 6). Fogerty's nightmare is over. *Los Angeles Times*, Calendar sect., p. 54.

Hilburn, Robert. (1993, January 12). Q & A with John Fogerty: The force behind Creedence. *Los Angeles Times*, p. F1.

Matsumoto, Jon. (1985, January 6). Where did the rest of Creedence go? *Los Angeles Times*, Calendar sect., p. 55.

McDougal, Dennis. (1988, November 15). The trials of John Fogerty; Singer, executive locked in decade-old legal feud. *Los Angeles Times*, Calendar sect., p. 1.

Osborne, Jerry. (1988, November). Creedence Clearwater Revival. *Discoveries*, p. 16.

CROSBY, STILLS & NASH. *David Crosby (David Van Cortland; August 14, 1941); Graham Nash (February 2, 1942); Stephen Stills (January 3, 1945). Inducted in 1997.* A melting pot of influences, Crosby, Stills & Nash provided the most memorable performance at Woodstock. Weaving politics with folk-rock, the melodic trio found immediate success with its all-star lineup. As a guitarist and singer for the Byrds, David Crosby helped define the group's jangly folk-rock sound on hits like the exotic "Mr. Tambourine Man" and "Turn! Turn! Turn!" After the departure of Byrds

Crosby, Stills & Nash perform their anti-war anthem, "Ohio," at the annual May 4th memorial ceremony May 4, 1997 commemorating the shootings at Kent State University. (*Photo courtesy of Nick Talevski.*)

Gene Clark and Roger McGuinn, Crosby emerged as the chief songwriter.

Crosby exacerbated tensions within the Byrds when he joined Buffalo Springfield for their appearance at the Monterey Pop Festival, in place of the absent Neil Young. Angering his bandmates, Crosby was fired from the Byrds in 1967.

In the waning days of the bickering Buffalo Springfield, Crosby approached the band's co-leaders, Neil Young and Stephen Stills, about forming a trio. With Young already committed to a solo project, Crosby and Stills initially teamed as a duo.

Wanting to expand, Crosby and Stills wooed Hollies founder, Graham Nash. A native of Lancashire, England, Nash had started his musical career in his midteens, forming the Hollies in 1963 as the group's lead singer and main songwriter.

Joined by Nash, the trio released the self-titled debut album, *CROSBY, STILLS & NASH* in late 1968. The album was highlighted by the hit "Marrekesh Express," a Nash composition that the other Hollies members had refused to record because it was too experimental.

With the addition of singer and guitarist Neil Young on the heels of his poorly selling solo album, the expanded Crosby, Stills, Nash & Young appeared at Woodstock for their second-ever performance, the group wowing the audience with the Stills-composed "Suite: Judy Blue Eyes," and the Joni Mitchell-penned "Woodstock." Soon winning the Best New Artist Grammy, the group was plunged into stardom.

Meanwhile, as the group's single "Teach Your Children" was ascending the pop charts, the May 4, 1970, Kent State shootings inspired Neil Young to compose the angry lament "Ohio." Crosby told interviewer Edward Kiersh, "I remember handing Neil [Young] *Life* magazine, and he looked at the pictures of the girl kneeling over the dead guy on the pavement, looking up at him with that *why?* expression on her face. I saw the shock of it hit him. I handed him his guitar and helped him write 'Ohio.' I got him on a plane, took him to L.A., and we recorded that night" (p. 55). The song received massive airplay and invigorated the antiwar movement.

But infighting soon torpedoed the group. Young left for a hugely successful solo career, with and without Crazy Horse. And at the end of 1973, Crosby rejoined the Byrds for the album, *THE BYRDS*. Reuniting in 1974, Crosby, Stills, Nash & Young set attendance records with a massive stadium tour. But with Young demanding to travel separately, the bickering CSN&Y disbanded before recording another album.

Two years later, Young and Stills began collaborating on an album. After inviting Crosby and Nash to the recording sessions for a proposed CSN&Y reunion, Young and Stills enraged their former bandmates by erasing their vocals from the final mix of *LONG MAY YOU RUN*. Crosby and Nash instead recorded their own album, *WIND ON THE WATER*, a top-10 entry.

Occasionally regrouping, CS&N continued to enjoy a loyal fan base. From their 1977 album, *CS&N*, they landed a hit with the Nash-penned "Just a Song Before I Go." And released in 1982, *DAYLIGHT AGAIN* spawned the hits "Wasted on the Way" and "Southern Cross." A successful tour was captured on the 1983 live album, *ALLIES*. In the 1980s, Nash occasionally reformed the Hollies.

Meanwhile, with Crosby's long term drug abuse intensifying, he torched his hotel room while freebasing cocaine. Convicted of his first drug charge in 1982, he served the first of two prison terms in 1985.

A reconstituted CS&N reunited with Young in 1987. Recorded mostly at Neil Young's home studio, the million-selling *AMERICAN DREAM* was released to mixed reviews.

Launching a 25th anniversary tour in 1994, CS&N released *AFTER THE STORM*. Performing at Woodstock II, the group was put off by the exploding, muddy mosh-pit in front of the stage. A subsequent tour was interrupted by David Crosby's emergency liver transplant.

Bibliography

Crisafulli, Chuck. (1995, February). Stephen Stills: Still storming, still dreaming. *Guitar Player*, p. 37.

Crowe, Cameron. (1977, June 2). The actual honest to God reunion of Crosby, Stills & Nash. *Rolling Stone*, p. 54.

Kiersh, Edward. (1986). *Where Are You Now, Bo Diddley?* (pp. 46-68). Garden City, NY: Doubleday.

Knobler, Peter. (1977, December). Dark star: Working the vampire shift with Stephen Stills. *Crawdaddy*, p. 42.

Ruhlmann, William. (1992, January 24). Crosby, Stills and Nash: The story so far. *Goldmine*, p. 8.

BOBBY DARIN. *(Walden Robert Cassotto; May 14, 1936 - December 20, 1973)*.
Inducted in 1990. One of the few artists to freely cross the boundaries between rock
and jazz, Bobby Darin commanded respect in both fields. Born in East Harlem, Darin
was raised by his grandparents after the death of his cabinet maker father. With
Darin's heart damaged from bouts of childhood rheumatic fever, his doctors predicted
his death by age 18.

Proficient on drums, piano, and guitar, he spent his summers working in bands at
Catskill resorts. Attending Hunter College on a scholarship, in 1952 Darin dropped
out to pursue an acting career. Turning to songwriting, Darin teamed with the young
Don Kirshner, writing lyrics for radio commercials. While dating Connie Francis,
Darin recorded several poorly selling tracks for Decca Records in 1956, beginning
with a cover of Lonnie Donegan's "Rock Island Line."

Signing with R&B powerhouse Atlantic Records, Darin was the label's first white,
rock act. After releasing several pop standards, Darin was urged by Atlantic head,
Ahmet Ertegun, to change his style. Co-writing the rock ditty "Splish Splash," Darin
landed a surprise, million-selling dance record.

But anticipating his dismissal from Atlantic, Darin had recorded "Early in the
Morning" for Brunswick as the Ding-Dongs. Following legal wrangling, both labels
scored moderate hits with the song, with Brunswick's version re-recorded by Buddy
Holly. Darin followed up with more rock-oriented hits, including "Queen of the Hop"
(1958) and his own composition "Dream Lover" (1959).

A reluctant rock and roll singer, Darin was instead drawn to jazz-pop vocal
stylings. After catching a New York stage production of Kurt Weill's 1928 era
Threepenny Opera, Darin wanted to record "Mack the Knife" (friend Dick Clark
warned Darin the song would end his career). But with the backing of the Richard
Wess Orchestra, Darin recorded an album of adult standards, *THAT'S ALL*. With its
jazz-flavored feel, the Grammy-winning "Mack the Knife" was the biggest hit of
Darin's career, catapulting him to multi-generational stardom. The album spawned a
second smash, the ethereal "Beyond The Sea" (1960), originally a hit for Benny
Goodman.

Following a Caravan of Stars rock tour, Darin performed for adult audiences in Las
Vegas as the opening act for comedian George Burns. Darin's follow-up hits also
ignored the teen market: "You Must Have Been A Beautiful Baby" (1961),
"Clementime" (1960), a reworking of the 1909 hit, "Won't You Come Home Bill
Bailey" (1960), and "Lazy River" (1961).

As a performer who cut across several musical genres, Darin was cool, suave, and
extremely self-confident. Possessing a strong, warm, nimble voice, he easily could
switch from teenage rock to jazz standards. In December 1960, Darin married starlet
Sandra Dee, whom he would divorce seven years later. Darin also starred in several
films, earning an Academy Award nomination for his role in *Captain Newman, M.D.*

Following Frank Sinatra's departure from Capitol Records in 1962, Darin was
hired as his replacement. Darin's hits continued with "You're the Reason I'm Living"
(1963) and "18 Yellow Roses" (1963). Returning to Las Vegas, Darin honed his
hugely successful cabaret act.

Returning to Atlantic Records in 1966, Darin re-emerged as a socially conscious protest singer. Disillusioned with life in the Hollywood fast lane, Darin publicly atoned for his past sins, shunning materialism and selling many of his possessions. Alienating his fans with folk-rock, Darin managed only a few more hits, highlighted by a pair of Tim Hardin compositions, "If I Were a Carpenter" (1966) and "The Lady Came from Baltimore" (1967).

Leaving Atlantic, Darin launched his own record label, releasing the poorly selling, socially stinging album, *BORN WALDEN ROBERT CASSOTTO*. Drawn to politics, Darin was a friend and supporter of Martin Luther King Jr., and in the 1968 he worked on Robert Kennedy's presidential campaign.

After a disastrous return to Las Vegas in late 1969 as a protest singer, Darin was forced to trade his jeans for a tuxedo, and add his early hits to his repertoire. Signing with Motown in 1971, Darin recorded a pair of commercially disastrous albums. In 1972, Darin hosted a summer replacement variety show on NBC, which evolved into *The Bobby Darin Show*. The following year, Darin died of complications following surgery to replace a heart valve.

In 1990, Darin's son, Dodd Darin (who later wrote a tell-all book about his father), sued McDonald's restaurants for $10 million, claiming that the character in the popular Mac Tonight television commercials was based on his father's likeness.

Bibliography

Cerio, Gregory & Feeney, F.X. (1994, November 14). This boy's life; Bobby Darin and Sandra Dee's son Dodd looks back in regret—and some anger. *People*, p. 121.

Hilburn, Robert. (1995, November 24). Bobby Darin set surveys versatile singer's career. *Los Angeles Times*, p. F32.

Hochman, Steve. (1990, January 17). Bobby Darin: A reluctant rocker in hall of fame. *Los Angeles Times*, p. F1.

Klinger, Art. (1992, June). Spotlight on Bobby Darin. *Rockin '50s*, p. 8.

Lorenzo, Richard J. (1989, April 7). Bobby Darin: Doing his own thing and other things. *Goldmine*, p. 18.

Martens, Paul F. (1981, March). Bobby Darin: Reconsidered. *Goldmine*, p. 22.

Morris, Chris. (1995, October 14). Rhino surveys diverse career of Bobby Darin. *Billboard*, p. 15.

BO DIDDLEY. *(Otha Ellas Bates; December 30, 1928). Inducted in 1990.* As rhythm and blues became rock and roll in 1955, the guitar-wielding Bo Diddley became one of its first stars. Diddley was born Otha Bates in Magnolia, Mississippi, to an unmarried, 15-year-old Creole mother. Unable to support her son, Diddley's mother boarded him with her cousin, Gussie McDaniel, in nearby McComb. When McDaniel moved to Chicago in 1934, she adopted her five-year-old nephew.

Raised in a religious, extended family on Chicago's South Side, Diddley was given a $29 violin by the congregation at the Ebenezer Baptist Church. Though reared in the conservative, formal church, Diddley was drawn to the uninhibited, spirited services of a nearby sanctified church, mesmerized by the rocking, beat-heavy music.

Given an acoustic guitar by his stepsister at age 13, Diddley initially tuned it like a violin. Fighting in the boxing ring, he earned his "Bo Diddley" nickname, slang for a sly, tough opponent. Dropping out of high school at age 15, Diddley formed the Langley Avenue Jive Cats, playing covers of Louie Jordan and Muddy Waters songs. Experimenting with electronics, Diddley built an unusual, rectangular guitar with a built-in amplifier, which produced a tremolo-heavy sound.

Working as a truck driver and elevator operator, Diddley considered music a hobby. Taking a handful of his homemade demos to Vee-Jay Records, he was booted out of their offices. Walking across the street to Chess, was signed as a solo act.

Arriving at Chess during rock's infancy in 1955, Diddley and labelmate Chuck Berry found unprecedented crossover success among white teenagers. At Chess, Diddley was forced to record with the house band and the vocal backing of the Moonglows and Flamingos. His releases issued on Chess' Checker imprint, Diddley scored his first hit, a double-sided R&B entry with "I'm a Man"/"Bo Diddley" (1955). Originally titled "Uncle John," the record's B-side became Diddley's signature piece; a rock-and-roll-meets-folk nursery rhyme, the song featured a screaming slide-guitar, Jerome Green's shaking maracas, and a percussive pattern that came to be known as the "Bo Diddley Beat" (the beat pattern was borrowed from the Red Saunders Orchestra's 1952 hit "Hambone").

An imposing figure and flamboyant dresser, Diddley shocked middle America in 1955 with his appearance on *The Ed Sullivan Show*, predating Elvis Presley. With his Latin-style polyrhythms and pre-Phil Spector "wall of sound," Diddley continued scoring hits with "Pretty Thing" (1956); an impromptu, novelty, spoken-word song in which he trades insults with a jiving Jerome Green, "Say Man" (1959); and the Willie Dixon-penned "You Can't Judge a Book by the Cover" (1962).

Many of Diddley's releases like, "Who Do You Love," did poorly on the charts but later became rock standards. The song was revolutionary for its purposeful use of feedback and sound distortion, predating both the Beatles and Jimi Hendrix.

Though remaining off the U.S. charts, Diddley remained an active club performer for the next three decades. Learning to play Bo Diddley songs became a prerequisite among early British rock bands in the early 1960s. Finding a ready-made fan base in England, Diddley toured with the Everly Brothers and the Rolling Stones and charted with a pair of British hits in the mid-1960s.

In 1967, Diddley joined bluesmen Buddy Guy, Muddy Waters, and Little Walter on sessions later released as *SUPER BLUES*. Angry about his low royalty payments, Diddley left Chess Records, returning to the label in its waning days in 1970.

Diddley's profile increased in 1979 when he opened for the British punk band the Clash. Once again in demand, he appeared in George Thorogood's 1982 video, *Bad to the Bone*, and Eddie Murphy's 1983 film *Trading Places*. In 1988, Diddley co-headlined a tour with the Rolling Stones' Ron Wood, and in 1990 co-starred in Nike television ads with another "Bo," baseball and football star Bo Jackson.

In 1996, Diddley released the critically acclaimed *A MAN AMONGST MEN*, an album of new material. Diddley continued his legal fight over past royalties with the current owner of the Chess catalog, MCA.

Bibliography
Dawson, Jim & Propes, Steve. (1992). *What Was the First Rock 'N' Roll Record?* (pp. 171-

81). Boston: Faber and Faber.

DeRogatis, Jim. (1995, May 12). He's got the beat: Diddley drum roll a driving rhythm for music fans. *Chicago Sun-Times*, p. 5.

Dwyer, Bill. (1970, April). Bo Diddley. *Blues Unlimited*, p. 4.

Jancik, Wayne & Lathrop, Ted. (1995). *Cult Rockers* (pp. 96-98). New York: Fireside.

Kiersh, Edward. (1986). *Where Are You Now, Bo Diddley?* (pp. 254-62). Garden City, NY: Doubleday.

Lydon, Michael. (1971, May). The second coming of Bo Diddley. *Ramparts*, p. 21.

DION. *(Dion DiMucci; July 18, 1939). Inducted in 1989.* Nicknamed "the King of Cool," Dion competed against hundreds of aspiring teenage Italian-American doo-wop outfits on New Jersey and New York City street corners.

The son of a puppeteer, Dion DiMucci grew up in a tough Italian Bronx neighborhood, joining street gangs for protection. He was inspired to pursue a career in music after hearing the hard-luck lyrics of Hank Williams at the age of 10. Sneaking into a local nightclub with the aid of an uncle, 13-year-old Dion would perform for tip money. In his teens, Dion alternated between fighting in gangs and street-corner doo-wop. His gang friends considered singing unmanly and tried to discourage Dion from pursuing the activity.

Enlisted by Mohawk Records to record a single with the Timberlanes, a group of middle-aged session singers he had never met, Dion boasting that he knew a group of more talented singers. Returning with a trio of neighborhood friends, the Belmonts consisted of Angelo D'Aleo, Carlo Mastrangelo, and Fred Milano, and were named for a main thoroughfare in the Bronx, Belmont Street.

With Mohawk becoming Laurie Records, Dion and the Belmonts scored their debut hit with the doo-wop-styled "I Wonder Why" (1958). Respectable-looking teen idols, Dion and the Belmonts were outfitted in stylish suits and ties. In keeping with their wholesome image, Dion and the Belmonts released a series of updated pop standards including "No One Knows" (1958) and "Where or When" (1960).

Dion joined the tragic Winter Dance Party tour in the frigid winter of 1959, sharing a bill with Buddy Holly, the Big Bopper, and Ritchie Valens. Dion turned down a seat on the fateful airplane because the $35 fee seemed like a lot of money to the 19-year-old singer (it was the same amount his working-class parents scraped together for rent every month).

After a pair of top-10 hits, the Pomus/Shuman-penned "A Teenager in Love" (1959) and a cover of the Rodgers and Hart standard "Where or When" (1960), the group's career slowed, and as a result, Dion fired the Belmonts. (Minus Dion, the Belmonts later scored a pair of chart hits with "Come on Little Angel" and "Tell Me Why.")

As a solo act, Dion was backed by the uncredited Del Satins, his first hit coming with "Lonely Teenager." Extending the doo-wop era, Dion topped the charts with the swaggering "The Wanderer" (1961) and "Runaround Sue." A string of hits kept Dion solidly on the charts for the next two years. Switching to Columbia Records, Dion scored with a cover of the Drifters' R&B hit "Ruby Baby" (1963). Now billed as Dion DiMucci, he landed his final hits at the label with "Donna the Prima Donna" and the bluesy "Drip Drop."

With the rise of Beatlemania and a decade-long drug habit, Dion dropped off the charts, spending much of his time strung out on heroin and later, LSD. Briefly reuniting with the Belmonts in 1967, Dion recorded the poorly selling album *TOGETHER AGAIN*.

Following a religious conversion in April 1968, Dion quit drugs. After spending time in Greenwich Village, Dion reentered the pop charts with his lament of the assassinations of Martin Luther King Jr., John Kennedy and others, titled "Abraham, Martin and John."

After a Madison Square Garden concert with the Belmonts in 1972, a reunion album followed in 1973. Two years later, Dion recorded the poorly received, Phil Spector-produced *BORN TO BE WITH YOU*.

Hitting the coffeehouse circuit, Dion returned to stardom following Dick Clark's invitation to perform in Las Vegas. A three-year stint resurrected Dion's rock career, and in 1978 he released the album *RETURN OF THE WANDERER*.

Tired of the Vegas glitz, in 1979 Dion ventured into gospel music. Ministering God's word, he took his uplifting message across the country, performing in churches. The following year Dion recorded the first of his five religious albums for the Dayspring/Word label, including *I PUT AWAY MY IDOLS*, which was nominated for a Best Gospel Performance Grammy.

In the late 1980s, a rejuvenated Dion released a doo-wop rock album, the Dave Edmunds-produced, *YO FRANKIE*, with its minor hit, "And the Night Stood Still." Dion formed a new band in 1997, the Little Kings.

Bibliography

Dougherty, Steve. (1988, November 21). Dion: Destiny called, but the Wanderer kept his cash—and his life. *People*, p. 143.

Kiersh, Edward. (1986). *Where Are You Now, Bo Diddley?* (pp. 353-62). Garden City, NY: Doubleday.

Popson, Tom. (1987, December 4). Dion DiMucci's long, dramatic, full-circle rock 'n' roll voyage. *Chicago Tribune*, Friday sect., p. 1.

Robins, Wayne. (1992, January 10). Illustrious groups reunite tonight: A classic doo-wop reunion. *(New York) Newsday*, p. 85.

Warner, Jay. (1993, September). The Belmonts: Carlo, Angelo, Freddie and sometimes Dion. *Discoveries*, p. 46.

WILLIE DIXON. *(Willie James Dixon; July 1, 1915 - January 29, 1992). Inducted in the Early Influence category in 1996.* A prolific songwriter, producer, and performer, Willie Dixon was a central figure in the rise of Chicago blues during his reign at Chess Records. Born into a family of 14 children in Vicksburg, Mississippi, half of Dixon's siblings died young. Influenced by his mother's love of religious poetry, young Dixon wrote hundreds of poems. At age eight, Dixon was drawn to blues guitarist Little Brother Montgomery, who performed on the sidewalk near his mother's small restaurant.

Restless, at age 11 Dixon ran away from home. At 12 he spent a year in jail for stealing doorknobs from an unoccupied house. Behind bars, he was moved by the moaning cries of old-time, prison work songs. Released from prison and hopping a train for Chicago, Dixon found lodging with his married sister. After spending a year delivering ice, he returned to Mississippi. Reluctantly resuming his schooling, he also sang bass in a spiritual group called the Union Jubilee Singers, where he was taught the intricacies of harmony.

Back in Chicago for good in 1936, the large-framed Dixon became a boxer, winning a Golden Gloves championship a year later as "James Dixon." Quitting after four professional fights, he was upset that his managers were skimming his wages.

At the boxing gym, Dixon was befriended by pianist Leonard "Baby Doo" Caston. Joining Caston's group, the Five Breezes, Dixon made more money playing a primitive bass on street corners and beer joints than he did in the boxing ring. Singing in the style of the Ink Spots, the group released four singles in the early 1940s for Bluebird Records.

After disbanding the group at the start of World War II, Dixon refused to join the military and was labeled a conscientious objector. Charged with draft evasion, he was jailed.

Released from prison, Dixon returned to his music career. Switching to an upright acoustic bass, Dixon joined the Four Jumps of Jive before finding notoriety in the Big Three Trio. Joined by Caston and Bernard Dennis (later replaced by Ollie Crawford), in 1946 the group released a Dixon-composition, the much recorded "Signifying Monkey." Joining Columbia Records, the group scored its first national hit with the bluesy "You Sure Look Good To Me" (1947).

When bluesman Muddy Waters requested Dixon as a session player in late 1948, Dixon began his long association with Leonard and Phil Chess, the co-owners of the Chicago-based Aristocrat Records (renamed Chess in 1950). Possessing little knowledge of blues, the Chess Brothers eventually hired Dixon as a producer in 1951.

Reshaping and redefining modern, electric blues, Dixon cemented Chess' claim as the home of Chicago-style urban blues. At Chess, Dixon also wrote countless blues classics, his first R&B chart-topper coming with Little Walter's "My Babe" (1955). Often including southern voodoo imagery in his material, Dixon expanded the structure of the blues song form. Other Dixon hit compositions include Muddy Waters' "I'm Your Hoochie Coochie Man" (1954) and "I Just Want to Make Love to You" (1954) and Howlin' Wolf's "Backdoor Man," "Spoonful," and "The Red Rooster" (1961).

Bridging blues with rock and roll beginning in 1955, Dixon performed with Chess' first rock stars, Bo Diddley and Chuck Berry. On rare occasions, Dixon recorded solo material, landing an R&B hit in 1955 with "Walking the Blues." Leaving Chess over money in 1956, Dixon joined Cobra Records for a three-year stint in 1956.

Upon Dixon's return to Chess in 1960, blues had fallen out of popularity in the U.S. Teaming with Memphis Slim on several albums and tours, Dixon found a new fan base throughout Europe.

Meanwhile, a new generation of British rockers would soon discover blues, returning Dixon's music to the charts including "Little Red Rooster" by the Rolling Stones, "Spoonful" by Cream, and "You Shook Me" by Led Zeppelin.

In the late 1960s Dixon then formed the Chicago Blues All-Stars to bring the best Chicago players to the city's clubs. Returning to his roots and adopting a folkier blues style, he recorded for a number of labels, including Columbia and Ovation, and operated a production company and talent agency. Hiring manager Scott Cameron in 1973, Dixon won back many of his copyrights.

Though losing a leg to diabetes in 1977, Dixon remained active in the 1980s, performing on the local blues circuit. During the last several years of his life, he devoted time to his nonprofit Blues Heaven Foundation. In 1992, Dixon died of heart failure.

Bibliography

Baker, Cary. (1982, January). Willie Dixon: The blues catalyst finds peace. *Goldmine*, p. 6.
Corritore, Bob; Ferris, Bill & O'Neal, Jim. (1988, July/August). Willie Dixon, part 1. *Living Blues*, p. 16.
Flanagan, Bill. (1986). *Written in My Soul* (pp. 67-75). New York: Contemporary.
Lind, Jeff. (1995, August). From Vicksburg to blues heaven: The 77 year odyssey of Willie Dixon. *Discoveries*, p. 30.
Obrecht, Jas. (1990). Willie Dixon. In *Blues Guitar* (pp. 78-83). San Francisco: GPI.
Silverman, David. (1992, February 6). Goodbye from sweet home Chicago City wraps itself in blues for Willie Dixon. *Chicago Tribune*, p. 1.
Wolmuth, Roger. (1991, September 11). Willie Dixon: After prison farms, years of poverty and song royalties gone astray, the Bossman of Blues finally has reason to smile. *People*, p. 120.

FATS DOMINO. *(Antoine Domino Jr.; February 26, 1928). Inducted in 1986.* The classic form of New Orleans boogie-woogie piano survived into the 1950s thanks to Fats Domino. The son of a Creole violinist, Domino was taught the rudiments of piano playing by his much older brother-in-law, professional jazz musician Harrison Verrett. While working in a bed factory, Domino nearly suffered a career ending accident when he almost lost his fingers.

Discovered onstage at the Hideway club in New Orleans by Dave Bartholomew, a New Orleans A&R man for Los Angeles-based Imperial Records, Domino scored a local hit in 1949 with a play on his own name, "The Fat Man," a sanitized version of a Champion Jack Dupree hit, "Junker Blues." The million-selling single charted nationally the following year.

Of Creole descent, Domino sang with a thick New Orleans accent. Popularizing the triplet pattern of piano playing, the style became the centerpiece of 1950s-era rock and roll. Usually recording at the tiny J&M studio located behind a record shop of the same name, most of Domino's hits were co-written and produced by Bartholomew, who also provided an occasional saxophone solo.

Initially finding little crossover interest, Domino was a mainstay on the R&B charts in the early 1950s with "How Long" (1951) and his first R&B chart-topper, "Goin' Home" (1952). After a brief parting, Domino reunited with Bartholomew in 1953 beginning with his first pop chart entry "Goin' to the River."

With rock's rise in the mid-1950s, Domino unleashed a long string of crossover pop/R&B hits and was the most prolific R&B artist of the era, his style remaining unchanged during the period. Recorded against Bartholomew's wishes, "Ain't That a Shame" (1955) became Domino's first major pop smash. At five feet, five inches and weighing 220 pounds, the dapperly dressed Domino was always seen seated at his piano. Unlike the shocking Little Richard or the frenetic Chuck Berry, America was not threatened by Domino's warm charm and fuzzy singing style.

Like many 1950s R&B act Domino lost sales from cover versions of his hits. White crooner Pat Boone sold more records with his bland rendition of "Ain't That a Shame" (he wanted to change the song title to the grammatically-correct "Isn't That a Shame"). Similarly, television teen idol Ricky Nelson landed his debut hit with Domino's "I'm Walking."

Domino's hit run continued with a cover of Louis Armstrong's "Blueberry Hill" (1956), "Blue Monday" (1957), and the Bobby Charles-penned "Walking to New Orleans" (1960). Domino's career was helped along by his appearances on *The Perry Como Show* and in four quickie rock flicks including, *The Girl Can't Help It*.

Moving to ABC Records, Domino was forced to add orchestral productions to his material. After scoring his last hit with "Red Sails in the Sunset" (1963), Domino left the label. Comfortably wealthy, Domino went into semiretirement, gambling away millions in Las Vegas.

Rejoining Bartholomew in 1967, Domino launched a short-lived label, Broadmoor Records. The following year, Domino began a two year stint with Warner-Reprise Records, releasing *FATS IS BACK*. The album spawned a minor comeback hit with a cover of the Beatles' "Lady Madonna." But following the death of a band member in a car crash in 1970, Domino began a three-year touring hiatus.

Returning to the stage in 1973, Domino was in top form on his live album *LIVE AT MONTREAUX: HELLO JOSEPHINE*. Limiting his touring schedule for the next two decades, Domino kept a low profile. Returning to the studio in 1993 for first time since the 1970s, Domino released the album, *CHRISTMAS IS A SPECIAL DAY*.

Bibliography

Booth, David & Escott, Colin. (1991, May 17). Dave Bartholomew. *Goldmine*, p. 22.

Coleman, Rick. (1991, May 17). The Imperial Fats Domino. *Goldmine*, p. 8.

Coleman, Rick. (1993, December). Fats Domino and the New Orleans rock revolution. *Discoveries*, p. 22.

Cooper, B. Lee. (1984, May). The Fats Domino Decades, 1950-1969. *Record Profile Monthly*, p. 55.

Dawson, Jim & Propes, Steve. (1992). *What Was the First Rock 'N' Roll Record?* (pp. 62-65). Boston: Faber and Faber. Joyce, Mike. (1977, November-December). Intermission with Fats. *Living Blues*, p. 16.

TOM DONAHUE. *(Thomas Coman; May 21, 1928 - April 28, 1975). Inducted in the Non-Performer category in 1996.* The Federal Communications Commission (FCC) opened up the FM band after World War II. Compared to its AM counterpart, FM initially drew little interest, with programming limited to noncommercial formats such as jazz, classical, and ethnic music. But when the LP began to play an increasing role in popular music in the mid-1960s, former top-40 deejay Tom Donahue was the first to sense the change.

Born in Indiana and raised in Washington, D.C., Donahue entered radio after a two-year stint as an army intelligence agent. After deejay stints in Charleston, West Virginia and Washington, D.C., Donahue landed a long-term gig in 1950 at WIBG in Philadelphia.

WIBG went to a top-40 format in 1958, and two years later Donahue and fellow deejay Bobby Mitchell quit to escape the payola scandal that destroyed Alan Freed and others. After a brief stint as talk show host, Donahue arrived in San Francisco in 1961, joining Mitchell at top-40 AM powerhouse KYA.

In 1964, the pair started their own record label, Autumn Records, hiring a young Sly Stone as producer and scoring national pop hits by artists such as the Beau Brummels, the Mojo Men, Bobby Freeman, and later, the Great Society. The Warlocks, an early version of the Grateful Dead, had failed their audition.

Opening the city's first psychedelic nightclub, Mothers, Donahue booked acts such as the Byrds and the Lovin' Spoonful. Decorated with beads, lava lamps, and purple walls, Mothers predated the coming hippie explosion but closed after a few months. During this period, Donahue first began experimenting with LSD.

Quitting his position at KYA and shuttering Autumn Records in 1965, Donahue continued his thriving concert promotion business, filling venues like the Cow Palace. In 1966 sold out Candlestick Park for what was the final ever Beatles concert.

With the maturing of rock music by the late 1960s, Donahue lamented the fact that radio still aimed its fare toward the adolescent listener. To escape the rigid programming of top-40 radio, he wanted the deejay to select the music. Donahue told interviewer Steve Chapple: "A friend of mine . . . was talking to me . . . about stereo FM which I knew nothing about because I didn't even have an FM radio. The more he talked about it, the more fascinated I became with the idea. . . . So I started calling FM stations in town. I called KMPX and the phone was disconnected so I figured: 'Ah, now I've got one.' A drowning man doesn't care who throws him a rope" (p. 109). Donahue initially took over the 8 to midnight shift, replacing a Chinese program.

Broadcasting less than a mile from the famed Haight-Ashbury district, Donahue debuted on April 7, 1967. In his free-form format, Tom "Big Daddy" Donahue (nicknamed because of imposing 400-pound girth) was a one-man operation: he sold his own commercials, scrounged for albums, and picked his own playlist. Two months later KMPX dropped its ethnic programs and became the first underground or progressive-rock station in the country, the genesis of the Album-Oriented Rock (AOR) format. He installed a similar format at KMET in Los Angeles, for a time broadcasting nightly on both outlets.

Sending shock waves throughout the industry, KMPX cast aside previously accepted rules of radio, as nonhit album tracks were preferable to top-40 fare, and songs that did not have to conform to a three- or four-minute limit. KMPX deejays were permitted to spout antiwar, anti-establishment, and left-wing rhetoric; drug culture was openly discussed.

After a bitter employee strike, on May 21, 1968, the entire KMPX staff quit, moving to crosstown classical station KSFR. Adopting new call letters, KSAN also adopted Donahue's format. Although KSAN was popular, the station made little money until 1972. That year its new corporate owners fired Donahue. After the staff threatened to resign enmasse, as they had five years earlier, Donahue was reinstated.

When Donahue died of a heart attack in 1975, AOR and arena-rock were entering their period of dominance. Shortly before his death, he was planning to move back to KMPX. In 1981, KSAN adopted a country format. In 1991, San Francisco premiered an annual radio gala, the Donahue Awards.

Bibliography

Chapple, Steve & Garofalo, Reebee. (1977). *Rock 'n' Roll is Here to Pay*. Chicago: Nelson-Hall.

Flothow, Carl. (1975, August 2, 1975). The Tom Donahue tapes: One final interview by a student. *Billboard*, p. 20.

Fong-Torres, Ben. (1993, May 20). When KSAN broke the radio mold. *San Francisco Chronicle*, p. E1.

Krieger, Susan. (1979). *Hip Capitalism*. Beverly Hills, CA: Sage.

McDonough, Jack. (1985). *San Francisco Rock*. San Francisco: Chronicle.

Sculatti, Gene & Seay, Davin. (1985). *San Francisco Nights: The Psychedelic Music Trip, 1965-1968*. New York: St. Martin's.

Selvin, Joel. (1994). *Summer of Love*. New York: Dutton.

THE DOORS. *John Densmore (December 1, 1945); Robbie Krieger (January 8, 1946); Ray Manzarek (February 12, 1935); Jim Morrison (James Douglas Morrison; December 8, 1943 - July 3, 1971). Inducted in 1993*. Led by the mysterious and charismatic Jim Morrison, the Doors developed a cult following, their peak in popularity not arriving until the 1980s. The son of a career navy man, Morrison was born in Melbourne, Florida, his family frequently uprooted. Making few friends, Morrison was a voracious reader, writing his first poem at age 10.

Enrolled in UCLA's film school in 1964, the slightly-overweight Morrison dabbled in philosophy and poetry, and drank heavily. There he met a film student, Ray Manzarek, a classically trained musician turned blues-rock organist from Chicago. Dropping out of school shortly before graduation, Morrison spent his days at the artsy Venice Beach writing poetry.

With Morrison impressing Manzarek with his poem "Moonlight Drive," the pair decided to form a rock band. Possessing only rudimentary piano skills, Morrison saw the group as a vehicle to disseminate his written work. The unnamed group was joined by jazz-trained drummer John Densmore and former jug-band guitarist Robbie Krieger; Manzarek had met the pair in a meditation class.

Named by Morrison, the Doors earned a residency at Los Angeles' famed Whisky A-Go-Go nightclub. There they were fired for singing their oedipal mini-opera "The End" (later released on their debut album).

After initial interest from Columbia Records, the Doors were signed by Elektra, a folk-music label. At the sessions, "Jim was so strung out on acid . . . he threw a TV set through the control-room window" (p. 251), Krieger later told writer Joe Smith. From the album *THE DOORS*, their frenetic debut release "Break on Through," saw little airplay. The chart-topping follow-up single "Light My Fire" (1967) was edited down from its original seven-minute album length and featured Morrison's surly, forceful vocals and Manzarek's intricate keyboard solo (the original version become a staple on underground radio).

Their first of two album releases in 1968, *STRANGE DAYS*, contained the radio hits "People Are Strange" and "Love Me Two Times." Adding a session bass player for the album *WAITING FOR THE SUN* (featuring the hits "Touch Me" and "Hello I Love You"), the album jacket sported poetry and a drawing of a lizard, symbolizing Morrison as the self-proclaimed Lizard King. Dabbling in the occult, Morrison envisioned himself as a shaman.

Prone to erratic behavior, the sharp-witted, leather-clad Morrison was perceived as a threat to authorities. Appearing on *The Ed Sullivan Show* in July 1967, Morrison infuriated censors for reneging on his promise to change the lyrics of "Light My Fire." Later in the year, Morrison was arrested after taunting police at a concert in New Haven, Connecticut.

With Morrison's antics growing more unpredictable, the group's popularity began to slump. On March 1, 1969, while performing "Touch Me" at Miami's Dinner Key Auditorium, a verbally combative Morrison allegedly flashed his genitals. With Morrison charged with "lewd and lascivious behavior," the Doors lost concert dates around the country.

Sporting a belly and full beard, Morrison joined the Doors for the bluesy album *MORRISON HOTEL*, highlighted by "Roadhouse Blues" and "Texas Radio and the Big Beat." In September of 1970, Morrison was found guilty of profanity and indecent exposure and sentenced to a cash fine and eight months of hard labor. Free on appeal, Morrison muddled through his final album with the Doors, the group assuming production duties on, *L.A. WOMAN*. With its off-key vocals, the album's title track "L.A. Woman," became a rock standard.

Moving to Paris in March 1971, Morrison hoped to work on his poetry and escape his problems. Five months later, he was found dead in a bathtub by his common-law wife, Pam Courson. Although a heroin overdose was suspected, respiratory failure and a heart attack were ruled the cause of death. Buried at Pere Lachaise cemetery in Paris, Morrison's graffiti-scarred tomb became a tourist attraction. Courson died three years later of a heroin overdose.

The remaining Doors recorded two unfocused albums, beginning with 1971's *OTHER VOICES*, before disbanding in 1973. Krieger pursued a solo career, while Densmore and Krieger formed the Butts Band.

Sparking new interest in the Doors, the remaining members regrouped on the 1978 album, *AN AMERICAN PRAYER*, adding music to Morrison's previously recorded poetry. In 1979, the Doors' 11-minute "The End" was the musical backdrop in the dramatic opening napalm scene in *Apocalypse Now*.

With record sales surging in the early 1980s, the cover of *Rolling Stone* magazine blared the headline "He's Hot, He's Sexy and He's Dead." Sensationalist biographies such as *No One Here Gets Out Alive* also fueled Morrison's legend as a drug-crazed, out of control risk taker. In 1983, the group landed an unlikely MTV hit with the bawdy "Gloria" (banned by the network) from the live album *ALIVE SHE CRIED*.

Produced by Oliver Stone, the popular 1991 film biography *The Doors* starred Val Kilmer as Morrison and featured John Densmore in a cameo role, further fueling album sales. The surviving members of the Doors reunited in 1997 to add new backing tracks to an incomplete Jim Morrison demo "Orange County Suite," the song included on a Doors box set.

Bibliography

Fong-Torres, Ben. (1971, August 5). James Douglas Morrison, poet: Dead at 27. *Rolling Stone*, p. 1.

Garfield, Simon. (1991, April 7). Every generation needs its Doors. *Independent*, p. 10.

Gilmore, Mikal. (1991, April 4). The legacy of Jim Morrison and the Doors. *Rolling Stone*, p. 31.

Hogg, Brian. (1988, May). The Doors. *Record Collector*, p. 58.

Smith, Joe. (1988). *Off the Record* (pp. 250-52). New York: Warner.

Tamarkin, Jeff. (1985, June 21). Renew my subscription to the Doors' resurrection, part I. *Goldmine*, p. 9.

Tamarkin, Jeff. (1985, July 5). Renew my subscription to the Doors' resurrection, part II. *Goldmine*, p. 12.

Waxman, Sharon. (1993, December 9). The afterlife of Jim Morrison. *Washington Post*, p. D1.

THE DRIFTERS. *Ben E. King (Benjamin Earl Nelson; September 23, 1938); Rudy Lewis (August 23, 1936 - May 20, 1964); Clyde McPhatter (Clyde Lensley McPhatter; November 15, 1933 - June 13, 1972); Johnny Moore (1934); Bill Pinkney (August 15, 1935); Charlie Thomas (October 7, 1937); Gerhart "Gay" Thrasher. Inducted in 1988.* The most influential vocal group of the 1950s the Drifters, sported the talents of 11 different lead singers during its 18-year run. Beginning as a vehicle for the talents of Clyde McPhatter, the Drifters outlasted him. In all, nearly 40 individuals can claim membership in the Drifters.

The roots of the Drifters began in the pioneering vocal group the Dominoes. After spotting the Dominoes in New York without their talented lead tenor Clyde McPhatter, Atlantic head Ahmet Ertegun eagerly signed the unemployed singer.

Instructed to form a group, McPhatter was joined by his former bandmates from the Mount Lebanon Singers, recording a series of gospel-flavored tunes in 1953. Except for the McPhatter-penned, future B-side, "Lucille," none of the tracks were released.

Firing the entire group and hiring manager George Treadwell, McPhatter set the groundwork for the Drifters. Again searching out former gospel singers, the second lineup included bass vocalist Bill Pinkney (of the Jerusalem Stars), and Gerhart and Andrew Thrasher (of the Silvertone Singers and Thrasher Wonders). Their debut release, "Money Honey" (1953), was a smash breakthrough hit, topping the R&B charts for nearly three months. Written by their arranger, Jesse Stone, the song was later recorded by Elvis Presley.

Continuing their hit run, the Drifters were confronted with radio station bans for their bawdy "Such A Night" (1954) and the McPhatter-penned "Honey Love" (1954). Other hits included "Bip Bam" (1954) and a McPhatter/Pinkney duet of the holiday standard, their first crossover, pop entry, "White Christmas."

The Drifters.

With McPhatter drafted in late 1954, a soundalike, 15-year-old David Baughan was hired for the group's live performances. Stationed in Buffalo, McPhatter was easily able to record while on leave. But eager to launch a solo career, he soon left the group. After a year, the immature Baughan was tricked out of the group and was replaced by Johnny Moore who sang lead on "Ruby Baby" (1956) and the elegant ballad "Soldier of Fortune" (1956).

Buying the rights to the Drifters' name from McPhatter, Treadwell began exerting his authority over the group, hiring and firing at will. After dismissing both Bill Pinkney and Andrew Thrasher for asking for a raise, the Drifters faded. With replacements Tommy Evans and Charlie Hughes, the Drifters managed a minor chart entry with the Leiber & Stoller-penned, "Fools Fall in Love" (1957).

With both Johnny Moore and Charlie Hughes entering the service, Atlantic demanded that Treadwell replace the entire group. After a performance at the Apollo Theater in June 1958, the Drifters were fired, with another act on the bill, the Crowns, hired as the new Drifters. The group now consisted of Dock Green, Elbeary Hobbs, Benjamin Earl Nelson (later shortened to Ben E. King), and Charlie Thomas, who took over lead vocal duties because he sounded like Clyde McPhatter.

The replacement Drifters dropped the sparse doo-wop arrangements of the original group for a more upbeat, contemporary, pop-soul sound. The new group was assigned to Atlantic's production and songwriting team of Jerry Leiber and Mike Stoller, who augmented the group's sessions with a string section and Latin-flavored percussion.

With Ben E. King taking over lead vocal duties, the new Drifters' debut single, the King-penned, "There Goes My Baby," was detested by the Atlantic executives, who delayed its release for several months. A surprise smash, it rekindled the Drifters' reputation but created more problems. Unhappy with his meager salary, King quit touring with the Drifters, appearing only on the group's records.

Landing crossover chart success that the original Drifters could not, the new Drifters scored a string of smash R&B and pop hits including: "This Magic Moment" (1960) and a Doc Pomus/Mort Shuman composition that the Drifters members initially despised, "Save the Last Dance for Me" (1960).

With Treadwell's firing of Ben E. King in 1960, the Drifters went through a series of lead singers. After brief runs by Johnny Williams and then Charlie Thomas, Rudy Lewis (formerly with the Clara Ward Singers) assumed lead vocal duties in 1961, the group's hits continuing with "Some Kind of Wonderful" (1961), a Goffin/King composition, "Up on the Roof" (1962), and "On Broadway" (1963). The Drifters' success waned following the departure of Leiber and Stoller in 1963, when Bert Berns took over as producer.

Johnny Moore rejoined the Drifters in 1963, taking over lead vocals the following year after the drug death of Lewis. Recorded the day after Lewis' death, the Drifters scored their most enduring hit with "Under the Boardwalk." The Moore-led Drifters's hits concluded with "Saturday Night at the Movies" (1964) and "At the Club" (1965).

Amid competing lawsuits, various Drifters line-ups toured in the 1970s, with Johnny Moore's version scoring several British pop hits.

Bibliography

Allan, Tony & Treadwell, Faye. (1993). *Save the Last Dance For Me: The Musical Legacy of the Drifters, 1953-1993*. Ann Arbor, MI: Popular Culture Ink.

Daley, Steve. (1978, September 5). The Drifters, down memory lane. *Washington Post*, p. B1.

Himes, Geoffrey. (1989, May 5). Gathering up the Drifters. *Washington Post*, p. N25.

Millar, Bill. (1971). *The Drifters: The Rise and Fall of the Black Vocal Group*. New York: Macmillan.

Shaw, Arnold. (1978). *Honkers and Shouters*. New York: Macmillan.

BOB DYLAN. *(Robert Allen Zimmerman; May 24, 1941). Inducted in 1988.* In addition to jazz, blues, country, and gospel, the final ingredient in the rock and roll stew is folk music. While the Kingston Trio and the New Christy Minstrels had some popular success, Bob Dylan opened the floodgates of folk and, soon after, invented the new genre of folk-rock.

Born Robert Allen Zimmerman in Duluth, Minnesota, to middle-class Lithuanian Jewish immigrants, Dylan was a self-taught musician, buying his first guitar at age 10 and mastering the piano and the harmonica by 15. Moving to the nearby mining community of Hibbing, "Bobby" Zimmerman was attracted to the concept of the noble drifter of his hero Woody Guthrie and often ran away from home.

Briefly attending the University of Minnesota on a scholarship, he was more interested in playing folk guitar in coffeehouses. Traversing the country in 1960, he ventured to New York City to meet the bedridden Guthrie.

After returning to Minnesota and performing in a hootenanny, Dylan hitchhiked back to New York's Greenwich Village. Sleeping in doorways and subways and telling others his parents were dead, he changed his name in 1962 to Bob Dylan (after poet Dylan Thomas).

Performing in the Village's burgeoning coffeehouse circuit, Dylan became a regular at the famed Gerdes. Imitating Guthrie's vocal delivery, Dylan sang in a nasally manner. Provoking awe and respect with his biting social commentary, Dylan accompanied himself on stage with an acoustic guitar and harmonica.

Landing occasional session work, Dylan once played harmonica behind Harry Belafonte. At a session for Carolyn Hester, CBS Records producer John Hammond was taken with Dylan's charisma but not his voice or playing. Sensing potential, Hammond signed the underage singer to a recording contract.

Hammond produced Dylan's inexpensively recorded ($400) debut album, *BOB DYLAN*, which featured mostly retooled versions of traditional folk songs. With the album selling only 5,000 copies, Hammond became the brunt of company jokes, his colleagues referring to Dylan as "Hammond's folly."

But a glowing *New York Times* concert review in April 1963 sparked national interest in the folk singer. A second album, *THE FREEWHEELIN' BOB DYLAN* showcased Dylan's skills as a songwriter, and contained the masterpieces, "Don't Think Twice It's Alright," "A Hard Rain's Gonna Fall," and "Blowin' in the Wind." The latter became a hit for Peter, Paul & Mary, further garnering Dylan further exposure. His lyrics frequently controversial, Dylan was disinvited from *The Ed Sullivan Show* after threatening to perform "Talking John Birch Society Blues."

Joined by producer Tom Wilson for *THE TIMES THEY ARE A-CHANGING*, Dylan released his first true protest album. With the title track mirroring the social turbulence of the 1960s, Dylan was embraced by the counterculture movement on America's college campuses. But his follow-up release, *ANOTHER SIDE OF BOB DYLAN*, angered fans with its omission of protest songs.

In 1965 Dylan broke ranks with folk traditionalists, employing electric guitar on one side of his revolutionary folk-rock album *BRING IT ALL BACK HOME*. His first million-seller, the album featured an electric version of "Subterranean Homesick Blues" and an acoustic rendering of "Mr. Tambourine Man." Dylan took his electric persona to the Newport Folk Festival, where horrified folk purists tried to force him off the stage. Hitting the road with the Band, Dylan was heckled during a two-year world tour.

Meanwhile, the electric folk-rock group the Byrds found success with several Dylan compositions, beginning with the chart-topping "Mr. Tambourine Man." Other rock remakes followed including "It Ain't Me Babe" by the Turtles and with an arrangement pilfered from the Byrds, "All I Really Want to Do" by Cher.

Cementing Dylan's status as musical genius, his 1965 album *HIGHWAY 61 REVISITED* spawned his first pop smash, the unprecedentedly-long top-40 entry "Like a Rolling Stone." The electric, double-album *BLOND ON BLOND* continued Dylan's mainstream popularity with "Rainy Day Women #12 & 35" and "Just like a Woman." Tackling serious topics, Dylan's lyrics were forcing other artists to abandon the innocence of early rock.

After a motorcycle crash, Dylan took a long respite near Woodstock, New York, and spent his days in playing music with members of the Band. The now-legendary impromptu sessions were heavily bootlegged on *THE GREAT WHITE WONDER*, and officially released in 1975 as *THE BASEMENT TAPES*.

Dylan returned in 1968 with the religiously tinged album *JOHN WESLEY HARDING*, a pared-down acoustic work. Preaching about moral issues on "All along the Watchtower," Dylan's version received little airplay in favor of Jimi Hendrix's electric rendition.

Flirting with country music in 1969, Dylan released *NASHVILLE SKYLINE*. Singing for the first time in his natural voice, Dylan returned to the top-40 with the uncharcteristic ballad "Lay Lady Lay." Sung in a similar style, "Knockin' on Heaven's Door" was featured on the soundtrack of the 1973 film western, *Pat Garrett & Billy the Kid*, the movie featuring Dylan as an outlaw.

His CBS contract expiring, Dylan entered into a distribution deal with Asylum Records, and was rejoined by the Band on a pair of albums beginning with *PLANET WAVES*. Returning to CBS in 1975, the introspective album *BLOOD ON THE TRACKS* was highlighted by "Tangled Up in Blue." In the mid-1970s, the gruffy-bearded Dylan launched his all-star, Rolling Thunder Revue, and topped the charts with the album *DESIRE*.

Becoming a born-again Christian, Dylan released the first of three religious albums, beginning with 1979's *SLOW TRAIN COMING*. Recorded at the Fame Studio in Muscle Shoals, Alabama, with guest guitarist Mark Knopfler, the album earned Dylan his first Grammy and spawned the hit "Gotta Serve Somebody." The 1983 Knopfler-produced *INFIDELS* was Dylan's first post-Christian release, marking a period of limited commercial success.

Dylan's career was rejuvenated after teaming with Tom Petty and the Heartbreakers on a massive world tour in 1985. Dylan's association with Petty continued in the supergroup the Traveling Wilburys, where he was joined by George Harrison, Jeff Lynn, and Roy Orbison.

In 1994, Dylan performed a nonacoustic MTV, *Unplugged* segment, backed by a large band. Later in the year, an all-star tribute concert, nicknamed "Bobfest," was marred by controversy when outspoken Irish singer Sinead O'Connor was booed off the stage.

Released in 1995, the interactive CD *HIGHWAY 61* chronicled Dylan's career. Launching his own label in 1996, Egyptian Records, Dylan's first release was the various-artist tribute album *THE SONGS OF JIMMIE RODGERS.*

Bibliography

Gleason, Ralph J. (1967, December 14). The Rolling Stone interview: Bob Dylan. *Rolling Stone*, p. 12.

Hillburn, Robert (1991, May 19). Bob Dylan: A legend turns 50. *Los Angeles Times*. Calendar sect., p. 3.

Marsh, Dave. (1991, May 19). Out of the 60's, into his 50's. *New York Times*, sect. 2, p. 1.

McClure, Michael. (1974, March 14). The people's poet. *Rolling Stone*, p. 32.

McKeen, William. (1993). *Bob Dylan: A Bio-Bibliography*. Westport, CT: Greenwood Press.

Robins, Wayne. (1992, October 11). Looking back at 30 years of Bob Dylan. *Newsday*, Fanfare sect., p. 6.

THE EAGLES. *Don Henley (July 22, 1947); Don Felder (September 21, 1947); Glenn Frey (November 6, 1948); Bernie Leadon (July 19, 1947); Randy Meisner (March 8, 1946); Timothy B. Schmit (October 30, 1947); Joe Walsh (November 20, 1947). Inducted in 1998.* With their memorable lyrics and irresistibly catchy melodies, the Eagles came to dominate popular music in the 1970s. An aggregate of experienced players, guitarist Glenn Frey had worked in Detroit with Bob Seger before forming the band, Longbranch Pennywhistle, with Californian singer-songwriter J.D. Souther. Bernie Leadon had played banjo and mandolin in the pioneering country-rock group the Flying Burrito Brothers before joining the backing band of emerging star Linda Ronstadt. Bassist Randy Meisner was a founding member of Poco and also backed Rick Nelson in the Stone Canyon Band. Also coming out of the country-rock vein, drummer Don Henley had played in a group called Shiloh and was teamed with Frey in Rondstadt's band.

Signed to David Geffen's new label, Asylum Records, the group's debut, *THE EAGLES*, was recorded in London and produced by Glyn Johns, notorious for his work with the Rolling Stones. A surprise hit, the country and rock flavored album spawned a trio of hits, "Witchy Woman," "Peaceful Easy Feeling," and "Take it Easy," a song written by Frey and labelmate Jackson Browne. Henley and Frey emerged as the group's chief songwriters, with Henley frequently assuming lead vocal duties.

A concept album, their 1973 follow-up, *DESPERADO*, featured a cover shot of the group attired in western, cowboy garb. Highlighted by "Tequila Sunrise," and "Desperado," the album was characterized by the group's rich multi-layered vocal harmonies. Featuring the slide-guitar of guest musician, Don Felder, the album *ON THE BORDER* (1974) propelled the Eagles to stardom with the hits "Already Gone," "James Dean," and their first million-seller, "Best of My Love."

With the hiring of Felder in 1975, Leadon's role in the group was diminished. On a roll, the Eagles scored their first number-one album with the country-tinged *ONE OF THESE NIGHTS*, highlighted by "Take it to the Limit," and the Grammy-winning "Lyin' Eyes." Leaving the group over musical differences, Bernie Leadon was replaced by former James Gang guitarist, Joe Walsh, who added a hard-rock dimension to the group's sound.

Walsh joined just in time for the massive success of the group's opus, *HOTEL CALIFORNIA*. Taking a year to record, the Grammy-winning, multi-platinum seller spawned several hits including the chart-topper, "New Kid in Town." Completing their shift from country-rock to mainstream, West Coast rock, "Hotel California," portrayed Los Angeles and the music industry as an amoral, hedonistic asylum. Tired of touring, Randy Meisner left the group for a solo career and was replaced by fellow ex-Poco bandmate, Timothy B. Schmit.

Under great pressure to repeat their previous success, the Eagles' followup album *THE LONG RUN*, failed to meet expectations. Highlighted by "I Can't Tell You Why," and the Grammy-winning, "Heartache Tonight," the group had retreated to its country-rock leanings. A final album, the two-disc EAGLES LIVE, received mixed reviews.

Internal acrimony, most notably between founding members Frey and Henley, had torpedoed the group. Pursuing various solo ventures throughout the 1980s, Eagles members Glenn Frey and Don Henley achieved the greatest success. Turning to acting, Frey appeared on the television programs *Miami Vice* and *Wiseguy*, and landed his own CBS detective series, *South of Sunset*. He also co-starred with Robert Duvall and Gary Busey on the box-office bust, *Let's Get Harry*.

Remaining estranged from Frey, Henley often remarked that the Eagles would get back together "when hell freezes over." Frequently offered large amounts of cash to reform, the Eagles turned down $2 million to regroup for a single performance at the US Festival. But after 11 years, the group reunited for a cameo on Travis Tritt's video for "Take It Easy," a track from a 1993 Eagles tribute album, *COMMON GROUND*.

A massive media event, the Eagles regrouped in 1993, recording the aptly titled album *HELL FREEZES OVER*. The first single, "Get Over It," was a politically-incorrect anthem against victimhood. The Frey-Henley composition was inspired by the book *Nation of Victims: The Decline of the American Character.* A massive 1994-96 world tour grossed $210 million, drawing over 3.5 million paying fans.

Bibliography

Connelly, Christopher. (1991, August). Too many choices. *GQ*, p. 138.
Crowe, Cameron. (1975, September 25). Eagles. *Rolling Stone*, p. 90.
DeCurtis, Anthony. (1990, September 20). The Eagles. *Rolling Stone*, p. 89.
Flanagan, Bill. (1989, October). Don Henley: The end of the innocent. *Musician*, p. 54.
Ruhlmann, William. (1993, July 9). Seven Eagles fly. *Goldmine*, p. 14.
White, Timothy. (1990). *Rock Lives: Profiles & Interviews* (pp. 429-38). New York: Henry Holt.
Williams, Lena. (1982, June 18). At home with: Don Henley. *New York Times*, p. C1.
Willman, Chris. (1993, October 24). He's got a peaceful TV feeling. *Los Angeles Times*, Calendar sect., p. 7.

DUANE EDDY. *(April 26, 1938). Inducted in 1994.* Nicknamed the king of the twangy guitar, Duane Eddy made a career out of playing straight-forward, echo-laden instrumentals. Born in Corning, New York, but raised in Coolidge, Arizona, Eddy the was taught the rudiments of guitar playing by his father at the age of five.

Receiving his first electric guitar, a Gibson Les Paul, 13-year-old Eddy formed the duo Jimmy and Duane, a country-western outfit with guitarist Jimmy Delbridge. Catching the attention of 24-year-old Lee Hazlewood, a recently hired deejay at a Coolidge radio station, Jimmy and Duane recorded an obscure single, "Soda Fountain Girl" (1954), Hazlewood's first composition. After the duo disbanded, Eddy landed occasional work with several Phoenix country and western groups, including the Al Casey Band.

Turning to production, Hazlewood had scored a hit in 1956 with Sanford Clark's rockabilly-flavored single "The Fool." After a stint at Dot Records in Los Angeles, Hazlewood returned to Arizona and reunited with Eddy.

Recorded at Floyd Ramsey's Audio Recorders studio in Phoenix, and released on Jamie Records, Duane Eddie's first top-40 hit came with the 3-million-selling "Rebel-'Rouser." Featuring his trademark twangy guitar, the record achieved its full-toned sound with the aid of a makeshift echo chamber built from a 2,100-gallon water tank. Leaning heavily on the tremolo bar and preferring to play the melody on the bass strings, Eddy developed an easily identifiable guitar sound.

Bringing his slow-paced, twangy guitar to the forefront of rock, Duane scored over a dozen instrumental hits during his five-year chart run. Although the Rebels were credited as Eddy's backing group on his records, the band was actually an informal aggregate of session players such as saxophonists Steve Douglas and Jim Horn, pianist Larry Knechtel, and guitarist/songwriter Al Casey. A shy performer, Eddy rarely sang.

When Eddy performed a speeded-up version of "Ramrod" on Dick Clark's weekend version of *American Bandstand*, orders for the record came flooding in. Having already recorded an unfinished, slower demo of the song, panicked record execs rushed to alter the original version, giving Eddy his second hit.

Eddy's hit run continued with, "Cannonball" (1958); "Forty Miles of Road" (1959); from the film of the same name, "Because They're Young" (1960); a remake of the television theme, "Peter Gunn" (1960); and another film song, "Pepe" (1961).

Unlike his contemporaries, Eddy was more interested in making albums than singles, releasing a series of popular long-playing discs. His first album, *HAVE TWANGY GUITAR WILL TRAVEL*, was one of rock's first stereo releases.

In 1962, Eddy left Jamie for RCA records, where he was reunited with producer Lee Hazlewood on *the album TWISTIN' & TWANGIN'*; the project netted Eddy's first noninstrumental hit, the novelty-styled "(Dance with the) Guitar Man," featuring the backing vocals of the Rebelettes (actually, Darlene Love and the Blossoms). In all, Eddy recorded nine albums at RCA in three years. Signing to Colpix in 1965 and then Reprise the following year, Eddy's career would not survive the British Invasion. Semiretired from music in the late-1970s, he settled in California.

Lured back into music in 1985 by a Los Angeles club owner, Eddy was joined by Hal Blaine, Ry Cooder, and former Rebel Steve Douglas. The following year, Eddy scored an unlikely top-40/dance hit with an updated version of his "Peter Gun" theme in a collaboration with the techno-rock group the Art of Noise. The song won a Grammy in the Best Rock Instrumental category.

Attempting a comeback in 1987, Eddy releases *DUANE EDDY,* the album featured guest musicians Paul McCartney and George Harrison.

Bibliography
Caputo, Salvatore. (1993, November 21). Phoenix discs Eddyfied rock and roll. *The Arizona Republic*, p. D1.
Del Ray, Teisco. (1993, June). The twang's the thang: Inside the Duane Eddy sound. *Guitar Player*, p. 25.
Greene, Bob. (1985, September 22). Calling on a legend to brighten a day. *Chicago Tribune*, Tempo sect., p. 1.
Hoekstra, Dave. (1994, January 16). The twang of Duane Eddy. *Chicago Sun-Times*, Show sect., p. 1.
Morthland, John. (1988, May). Duane Eddy: Rebel rouser's song. *Country Music*, p. 39.
Orr, Jay. (1995, September 8). Music City: Duane Eddy and friends pull out the stops on "Ghostrider." *Nashville Banner*, p. C1.
Russell, Wayne. (1988, March 25). The Phoenix connection: Duane & Lee & Skip & Flip & more. *Goldmine*, p. 14.

AHMET ERTEGUN. *(Ahmet Munir Ertegun; July 31, 1923). Inducted in the Non-Performer category in 1987.* Thanks to technological advances, hundreds of small, independent record companies sprang up after World War II. With major labels ignoring black consumers, these burgeoning companies were filling the void. The most successful of these was the New York-based Atlantic Records, whose founder, Ahmet Ertegun, was the son of Turkey's ambassador to the United States.

With his ambassador father posted in England in the early 1930s, 10-year-old Ahmet Ertegun began his lifelong infatuation with black music, exposed to the scat-jazz of the zoot-suited Cab Calloway at the London Palladium in 1933. "I was accustomed to the sound of scratchy phonograph records, so to hear the purity and power of that orchestra in a live setting was overwhelming. I fell under the spell of black music" (p. 76), Ahmet Ertegun later told Jerry Wexler.

With his father appointed ambassador to the U.S. in 1939, Ahmet Ertegun was joined by his older brother, Nesuhi, who was forced by the war to interrupt his French schooling. Befriending jazz musicians, the Ertegun brothers brought Duke Ellington and others to the Turkish Embassy on Sundays for meals and subsequent jam sessions.

After finishing prep school in 1940, Ahmet Ertegun enrolled at St. John's College in Annapolis. With the death of their father in 1944, most of the family returned to Turkey. The brothers stayed, with Nesuhi moving to the West Coast and Ahmet enrolling at Georgetown.

After failing with the short-lived label, Quality Records, Ertegun launched Atlantic Records in 1947. With $2,500 from partner Herb Abramson and $10,000 from a Turkish dentist, Ertegun recorded jazz artists like Tiny Grimes and Joe Morris in a makeshift studio in a New York City hotel room. Eventually housing Atlantic in two floors of a small New York building, Ertegun hired classically trained session musicians, and as Atlantic's recording engineer, he enlisted physicist Tom Dowd.

In the late 1940s Ertegun became fascinated with a new, upbeat, danceable musical genre later known as rhythm and blues. Experimenting with R&B, Atlantic scored its first national hit in 1949 with Stick McGhee's R&B standard "Drinkin' Wine, Spo-Dee-O-Dee." Atlantic's first major R&B star was Ruth Brown, giving the label its nickname, "the house that Ruth built." Encouraged, the label signed the best in R&B: Clyde McPhatter and the Drifters, LaVern Baker, the Clovers, and the resurgent Big Joe Turner.

Unable to secure a steady supply of quality compositions, Ertegun wrote many of the label's early hits under the pseudonym A. Nugetre (his name spelled backwards), landing hits such as the Drifters' "Whatcha Gonna Do?" and Ruth Brown's "Wild Wild Young Men."

When Herb Abramson was drafted into the army in 1953, former *Billboard* magazine writer Jerry Wexler was brought into Atlantic as a full partner and producer. Soon after, Atlantic signed singer Ray Charles.

With Abramson returning to Atlantic in 1955, he was given his own subsidiary, Atco (he left two years later). That same year, Ahmet's brother, Nesuhi, joined Atlantic, launching a jazz division and LP line.

With white teenagers suddenly buying black R&B records, Ertegun was caught unprepared for the pop, crossover success of the Chords' "Sh-Boom." Discovering an untapped pop market, Ertegun expanded the scope of Atlantic. Sensing raw talent, Ertegun tried to purchase of Elvis Presley's contract from Sun Records in 1956, but lost in a bidding war with RCA-Victor which offered $40,000 over Atlantic's $25,000.

Experiencing a dry spell in 1957, Atlantic was near financial ruin. But the newly hired production team of Jerry Leiber and Mike Stoller brought with them a hit act, the Coasters. Also that year, Bobby Darin became Atlantic's first white, rock act, landing smash hits with "Splish Splash" and "Mack the Knife."

With soul music on the rise, Ray Charles' departure in 1959 was painful for Ertegun. But while most independent labels like Imperial, King, and Specialty were failing, Atlantic was one of the few companies to thrive. Signing few major soul acts in the mid-1960s outside of Wilson Pickett and Aretha Franklin, Atlantic instead entered into a lucrative distribution deal with Memphis-based Stax/Volt Records.

Over Ertegun's objections, Atlantic was sold to Warner Brothers/Seven-Arts in 1967 for $17.5 million. Angry at his partners, Ertegun considering the sale a giveaway.

Caught off guard by the success of the Beatles, Atlantic sought out British rock bands, with Ertegun's signing of dozens rock acts including Cream, Yes, Vanilla Fudge, and in 1968 their biggest catch, Led Zeppelin. A year later, Ertegun entered into a lucrative, long-term distribution deal with the Rolling Stones, who had just formed their own London label.

Moving into luxurious, corporate offices at Rockefeller Plaza in 1973, Atlantic thrived in the 1970s with hard-rock acts Foreigner, Genesis, and AC-DC. Continuing its mainstream-rock course in the 1980s, Atlantic was anchored by Phil Collins, Stevie Nicks, and Pete Townshend.

In 1982 Ertegun became involved in the development of a new televised music award program. In discussions with *Rolling Stone* publisher Jann Wenner, the idea was transformed into the Rock and Roll Hall of Fame and Museum.

Atlantic Records celebrated its 40th anniversary in 1988 at Madison Square Garden, with a number of reclusive acts returning to the stage, including a reformed

Led Zeppelin. Soon after, Atlantic Records increased the royalty rates for its 1950s R&B acts and donated $2 million to the establishment of the Rhythm & Blues Foundation. Still sporting his well-groomed, trademark goatee, Ertegun remains an essential part of Atlantic Records in his position of co-CEO and chairman.

Bibliography

Gillett, Charlie. (1974). *Making Tracks*. New York: E.P. Dutton.

Hilburn, Robert. (1988, May 22). A founding father of rock 'n' roll. *The Los Angeles Times*, Calendar sect., p. 60.

Pooley, Eric. (1988, June 20). Lush life: The hot and cool worlds of the Erteguns. *New York*, p. 36.

Wade, Dorothy. (1993, April 3). The godfather of rock 'n' roll. *Daily Telegraph*, p. 32.

Wade, Dorothy & Picardie, Justine. (1990). *Music Man: Ahmet Ertegun, Atlantic Records, and the Triumph of Rock'n'Roll*. New York: Norton.

Wexler, Jerry & Ritz, David. (1993). *Rhythm and the Blues: A Life in American Music*. New York: Alfred A. Knopf.

NESUHI ERTEGUN. *(November 26, 1917 - July 15, 1989). Inducted in the Lifetime Achievement category in 1991.* Born in Istanbul, Turkey, Nesuhi Ertegun spent his youth living in European capitals with his ambassador father. As a teenager, he became a fan of black music when his father took him to hear Duke Ellington at the London Palladium.

Studying at the prestigious Sorbonne University in Paris, Nesuhi Ertegun's schooling was interrupted by the start of the Second World War. Joining his family in 1939 at his father's new post in Washington, D.C., he attended American University in Washington, D.C.

At the embassy, Nesuhi and younger brother (by five years), Ahmet, amassed 20,000 jazz and blues records. Encouraged by their father in their musical appreciation, the brothers befriended a number of black jazz artists, treating them to Sunday meals at the embassy.

After the death of their father in 1944, Ahmet Ertegun stayed in Washington D.C., while Nesuhi moved to California to pursue a graduate degree. Drawn to music, Nesuhi Ertegun took a job at the Jazzman Record Shop, owned by his future wife, Marili Morden, and later edited *Record Changer*, a jazz magazine.

In 1944, actor Orson Welles asked Nesuhi Ertegun to provide a Dixieland-style jazz band for his radio show. Assembling the likes of Mutt Carey and Kid Ory, the combo was a hit. Unable to interest a record company in the group, Ertegun started Crescent Records.

At UCLA in 1951, Ertegun taught the first-ever history of jazz course. After working for another label, Contemporary Jazz, Ertegun rejoined his brother in New York City to help produce jazz trumpeter Shorty Rogers.

In 1955 Nesuhi convinced his brother, Ahmet, that a jazz subsidiary held commercial possibilities. Placed in charge of Atlantic's new line of jazz and R&B LPS, Nesuhi Ertegun recorded the finest in jazz, overseeing sessions for Herbie Mann, Charlie Mingus, Ornette Coleman, and the Modern Jazz Quartet. From 1959 to 1961

Ertegun produced 10 Coltrane LPS. In all, Ertegun worked on approximately 250 Atlantic album projects.

Ertegun also directed a number of pop projects. It was his idea to turn Ray Charles in the jazz direction, teaming him with Milt Jackson. Ertegun also worked with the Drifters and on Bobby Darin's jazz releases. In 1962, Atlantic landed a pop hit with a Nesuhi discovery: Bent Fabric's instrumental ditty, "Alley Cat."

In the late 1950s, Ertegun served as president of the National Association of Recording Arts and Sciences, which had formed to present the Grammy Awards, as a reaction to the domination of rock music.

In 1967, Nesuhi Ertegun and Atlantic copresident, Jerry Wexler, overruled Ahmet Ertegun, selling the label to Warner/Seven-Arts for $17.5 million. The new owners placed Nesuhi Ertegun in charge of Atlantic's international division in an effort to stem the flow of counterfeit records around the world. After signing Roberta Flack in 1969, the following year Ertegun retired from the production end of the label.

Returned to the studio in 1987, Ertegun produced the early Atlantic Records jazz combo the Modern Jazz Quartet. Retiring from WEA (Atlantic Records' parent), he took a position with WCI Record Group and then launched a new Atlantic jazz subsidiary, East-West Records. Ertegun died of cancer in 1989 at the age of 71.

Bibliography

Brickhouse, Keith. (1993, July 31). Atlantic remembers Nesuhi Ertegun with event at Montreux. *Billboard*, p. 11.

Gillett, Charlie. (1964). *Making Tracks*. New York: E.P. Dutton.

Harrington, Richard. (1985, December 22). The rock of Atlantic: Record czar Ahmet Ertegun, letting the music do the talking. *Washington Post*, p. H1.

Maharaj, Davan. (1989, July 16). Nesuhi Ertegun, 71: Producer, record industry leader. *Los Angeles Times*, part 1, p. 32.

Santoro, Gene. (1987, August). Atlantic at 40. *Down Beat*, p. 63.

Wade, Dorothy & Picardie, Justine. (1990). *Music Man: Ahmet Ertegun, Atlantic Records, and the Triumph of Rock'n'Roll*. New York: Norton.

West, Hollie I. (1979, October 16). Trans Atlantic jazzman: Nesuhi Ertegun. *Washington Post*, p. C1.

Wexler, Jerry & Ritz, David. (1993). *Rhythm and the Blues: A Life in American Music*. New York: Alfred A. Knopf.

THE EVERLY BROTHERS. *Don Everly (Isaac Donald Everly; February 1, 1937); Phil Everly (Philip Everly; January 19, 1939). Inducted in 1986.* Setting the standard for rock duos, the Everly Brothers spawned a host of musical progeny including the Righteous Brothers, Simon and Garfunkel, and Hall and Oates.

Don and younger brother, Phil, were the offspring of regional country stars Ike and Margaret Everly. Leaving a backbreaking coal mine job in Kentucky, guitarist Ike Everly Sr. had previously toured with two of his brothers in the 1930s, also as the Everly Brothers.

Still in grade school, Don and Phil first joined their parents on their radio show at KMA in Shenandoah, Iowa. Don was trained on guitar, while Phil played mandolin, fiddle and flute. Hitting the road, the Everly family toured in their 1946 Chevy landing radio and club work. Tiring of life on the road, the Everly family settled in Knoxville, Tennessee, in 1953, landing a two-year stint at KNOX.

After the elder Everlys retired from show business, Don and Phil were encouraged to pursue music careers by country star Chet Atkins. Arriving in Nashville in 1954, the long-haired Everlys brought songs in hand. With Atkins' help, Don Everly sold a few compositions to country singers Kitty Wells and Anita Carter. With the meager earnings, the Everlys purchased a pair of cowboy costumes.

With Wesley Rose becoming the duo's manager, the Everlys were hired as songwriters at his Acuff-Rose publishing firm. Hoping to break into the hillbilly market, Cadence Records owner Archie Bleyer signed the brothers as a country act.

Written by the husband-and-wife team of Felice and Boudleaux Bryant, the Everly Brothers debut single, "Bye Bye Love" (1957), was a hit on both the country and pop charts and was parlayed into a two-year stint on the Grand Ole Opry. Though initially touted as a country act, the duo was also embraced in the rock community.

Producing their own records, the Everly Brothers combined elements of old-style, country balladry with mainstream-rock. With tightly weaved, high-tenor harmonies, chiming folk guitars, and a clean-cut image, the Everlys became teenage heartthrobs, mobbed wherever they went. But though portraying youthful innocence, "Wake Up Little Susie" (1957) was banned by many radio stations for its subtle implications.

Close friend Chet Atkins played the guitar on many of the duo's sessions, providing the intro for their 1958 single "All I Have to Do Is Dream." The B-side, "Claudette," was written by a newcomer named Roy Orbison, penning the song about his wife.

The double-sided hit, "Bird Dog"/"Devoted to You" (1958) was followed by a Don Everly composition, "Till I Kissed You" (1959). Backed on the session by the Crickets' Jerry Allison and Sonny Curtis, the song was an asserted attempt by the group to record their own material. Leaving Bleyer after years of butting heads, the Everlys final hits at Cadence came with an Anglicized reworking of a French song, "Let It Be Me" (1959), and "When Will I Be Loved" (1960).

Moving to Warner Brothers in 1960 for a then-unheard-of $75,000 a year, 10-year guarantee, the duo continued their string of hits, beginning with the best-selling single of their career, "Cathy's Clown" (1960), which was written by Phil during an Australian tour; and a pair of double-sided entries, "So Sad"/"Lucille" (1960), and "Walk Right In"/"Ebony Eyes" (1961). But after the Everly Brothers insisted on recording a non-Acuff-Rose composition, "Temptation," an angry Acuff abandoned the Everlys and took with him the songwriting services of the Bryants. Phil later married Acuff's stepdaughter, Jacqueline.

After recording their next hit, "Crying in the Rain" (1962), both brothers served a six-month stint in the marines. Later in the year, the duo landed its final top-10 entry with "That's Old Fashioned."

Suffering the mental strains of stardom, Don Everly collapsed during a 1963 British tour. With their careers slumping, both brothers began abusing drugs. Even a reconciliation with Wesley-Rose did not help, the Everlys scoring only a single hit in 1964 with "Gone, Gone, Gone." Though eclipsed in the U.S. by the Beatles and the British Invasion, the Everlys still found appreciative audiences in Europe.

A switch to RCA Records in 1970 failed to spark the duo's career. Also that year, Don recorded his first solo album. Seemingly on the comeback trail, the Everlys landed a short-lived ABC television show with the help of Johnny Cash.

But after frequent fights, the Everly Brothers disbanded at a 1973 concert at Knott's Berry Farm, when Phil smashed his guitar and stormed off the stage. A drunken, tearful Don finished the show by himself, then announced the duo's demise. Except for their father's funeral, the brothers remained estranged for the next decade.

Reconciling in 1982, the Everlys debuted their new act at London's Royal Albert Hall, the concert aired by HBO. Releasing a new studio album, *EB 84*, the duo landed a minor chart hit, "On the Wings of a Nightingale." In the 1990s, the brothers were active in country music.

Bibliography

Escott, Colin. (1993, June 25). The Everly Brother: Brother in arms. *Goldmine*, p. 14.

Isler, Scott. (1986, July). The Everlys: Brothers in arms. *Musician*, p. 38.

Muskewitz, Jim. (1977). The Everly Brothers. *Record Exchanger*, 6(2), p. 4.

Palmer, Robert. (1984, February 29). The pop life; New record by Everlys. *New York Times*, p. C19.

Pollock, Bruce. (1981). *When Rock Was Young* (pp. 76-92). New York: Holt, Rinehart, and Winston.

Sasfy, Joe. (1984, January 26). The tender Everlys. *Washington Post*, p. B3.

LEO FENDER. *(Clarence Leo Fender; August 10, 1909 - March 21, 1991). Inducted in the Non-Performer category in 1992.* While Leo Fender didn't invent the electric guitar, he revolutionized the instrument with a series of landmark improvements. Born on a farm in Anaheim, California, Fender's teenage musical training came on the piano and saxophone; he never learned to play the guitar.

After graduating from Fullerton College, Fender worked as an accountant for the California Highway Department. After the Depression claimed his job, Fender opened a radio repair business in his garage in the mid-1930s. An uncle who made batteries first taught Fender about electricity.

But when musician Doc Kaufman came into Fender's shop in 1941, needing an electric guitar repaired, Fender was both perplexed and fascinated by its inferior design. With guitars streaming into his shop, Fender began building his own models in the mid-1940s. Becoming business partners, Kaufman and Fender started the K&F company to manufacture guitars and amps. Buying out Kaufman and changing the company's name to Fender Electrical Instruments, Fender also hired the intuitive George Fullerton as his chief engineer.

Fender's first solid-body electric guitar, the Broadcaster, hit the market in the late 1940s. First played by country guitarist Jimmy Bryant of the Little Jimmy Dickens band, the instrument created a stir among his fellow musicians.

In 1950, the Fender Broadcaster was renamed the Telecaster because that name had already been taken. Though not a perfect instrument, it was a great improvement over every other model on the market. Made to look futuristic, it was body-hugging and comfortable to play. In 1952, Gibson guitars followed Fender's lead, introducing its own solid-body electric guitar, the Les Paul model. In 1951, Fender revolutionized the electric bass with the introduction of the Precision Bass, replacing the stand-up models that most R&B bands were using at the time.

In 1954, Fender introduced his most popular model, the Stratocaster. Nicknamed the Strat, the instrument was aerodynamic, sleek, and sexy and the perfect rock and roll instrument and sold for under $100. More important, many of the Telecaster's flaws, particularly feedback, were eliminated. When rockers like Buddy Holly began using the Stratocaster, sales went through the roof.

A private, unsociable man, Fender built his company by working tirelessly and demanding perfection. After expanding his factory several times, by the mid-1960s Fender had a workforce of 600 employees.

Due to a long-term illness, Fender sold his company to CBS in January 1965 for $13 million, remaining on board as a consultant for five years. Critics have long claimed that the company's reputation for quality leveled off after the sale, making the pre-1965 instruments more valuable.

Though physically ailing, the restless Fender launched several businesses in 1970s. He launched a pair of small companies, CLF Research and G&L Guitar Company, to further improve the guitar. In 1972, he became a silent partner in Music Man, launching a new line of guitars.

Although retired in the 1980s, Fender continued to work on inventions up to his death from Parkinson's disease in 1991. Fender's last company, G&L Guitar, was bought out by BBE Sound of California in 1992. A who's who of rock that have played Fender guitars includes Eric Clapton, Stevie Ray Vaughan, Mark Knopfler, and Eddie Van Halen. Early Fender Stratocasters have become collectors items and command prices of over $15,000.

Bibliography

Flagg, Michael. (1990, July 22). The guitar man. *Los Angeles Times*, p. E1.

Flagg, Michael. (1993, August 11). Leo Fender's legacy: G&L sales on rise. *Los Angeles Times*, p. D1.

Horowitz, Carl. (1994, December 6). Guitar maker Leo Fender. *Investor's Business Daily*, p. A1.

Smith, Richard. (1990, July). The further innovations of Leo Fender. *Guitar Player*, p. 54.

Wheeler, Tom. (1991, September). Leo Fender: The late industry giant, in his own words. *Guitar Player*, p. 88.

FLEETWOOD MAC. *Lindsey Buckingham (October 3, 1947); Mick Fleetwood (June 24, 1947); Peter Green (Peter Greenbaum; October 29, 1946); Danny Kirwan (May 13, 1950); John McVie (November 26, 1945); Christine McVie (Christine Perfect; July 12, 1943); Stevie Nicks (Stephanie Nicks; May 26, 1948); Jeremy Spencer (July 4, 1948). Inducted in 1998.* After replacing Eric Clapton in John Mayall's Bluesbreakers, British guitarist Peter Green left the group in 1967, taking drummer Mick Fleetwood with him, to form Peter Green's Fleetwood Mac, a white blues band. Adding blues-freak guitarist Jeremy Spencer and short-lived bassist Bob Brunning, the group debuted at the prestigious 1967 Windsor Jazz and Blues Festival.

With the departure of Brunning, the group was joined by a third former Bluesbreaker, John McVie. A tight ensemble, in the late 1960s the group was hired to back touring blues acts such as Otis Spann and Duster Bennett.

Ignored in the U.S., the renamed Fleetwood Mac found quick success in their native England. Their blues-based debut album *FLEETWOOD MAC* (1968) was highlighted by a cover of Little Willie John's "Need Your Love So Bad" and the Green-penned "Black Magic Woman," the song later a hit for Santana.

Released later in 1968, the group's second top-10 British album *MR. WONDERFUL* (released in an altered form in the U.S. as *ENGLISH ROSE*) featured guest pianist Christine Perfect. She would later leave her own band, Chicken Shack, to join Fleetwood Mac. With the refusal of Spencer to play anything but blues, Green hired Danny Kirwan as group's third guitarist. Remaining a sensation in England, Fleetwood Mac continued its hit run with the chart topping instrumental "Albatross," "Oh Well," and the lovely ballad, "Man of the World."

After ingesting a large dose of LSD given to him by German fans, Peter Green began exhibiting erratic behavior and was sporting a messiah-like, long white robe on stage. His last hit with Fleetwood Mac, "The Green Manilishi," chronicled Green's personal demons. He later released several solo projects including the marvelous *THE END OF THE GAME*. Longtime fans predicted Fleetwood Mac's demise following Green's exit.

With Kirwan assuming greater songwriting duties, Fleetwood Mac's 1971 album *KILN HOUSE* took the group in a mainstream rock direction. Though a disappointment to British fans, the album gave Fleetwood Mac its first top-100 U.S. entry. Meanwhile, the former Christine Perfect had joined the group on a full-time basis and married John McVie.

Tragedy struck the group during a Los Angles stop of a U.S. tour when John Spencer disappeared just hours before the concert. He had been lured into a cult, the Children of God. A desperate Fleetwood convinced Green to return, if only for the conclusion of their two-month tour. After nearly disbanding, Fleetwood Mac persevered with the addition of American guitarist, singer-songwriter, Bob Welch. Supplanting its blues roots with hard rock, Fleetwood Mac further alienated its British fans with the 1971 album *FUTURE GAMES*.

Psychologically troubled and refusing to tour, Kirwan left the Fleetwood Mac after the release of their poor selling 1972 project *BARE TREES*. The group was then expanded with a pair of British, rock-based musicians, singer Dave Walker (of Savoy Brown) and guitarist Bob Weston. After the release of another bomb, *MYSTERY TO ME*, Dave Walker left the group.

But after the firing of Bob Weston over an affair with Fleetwood's wife, the group disintegrated in the middle of a U.S. tour. An opportunist, the group's manager assembled a substitute version of Fleetwood Mac built around Walker and Weston and was immediately sued. Regrouping, Fleetwood Mac recorded the disjointed album *HEROES ARE HARD TO FIND*, the group's release first to break into the U.S. top-40. The album's chief songwriter, Bob Welch, left shortly after its release for a lucrative solo career. About this time, Fleetwood Mac relocated to southern California.

While inspecting prospective studios for the group's next, Mick Fleetwood met rock duo, guitarist Lindsey Buckingham and his girlfriend Stevie Nicks, who were then recording their second album as Buckingham-Nicks. Inducing the pair to join Fleetwood Mac, the group settled into its classic lineup. Recorded in just ten days, the album *FLEETWOOD MAC* spawned a trio of hits, "Over My Head," "Rhiannon" and "Say You Love Me." Becoming the new focus of the group, the gypsy-attired, raspy-voiced Nicks was attracting legions of teenage male admirers. Meanwhile, relationships within the group disintegrated: the McVies divorced, Mick Fleetwood left his wife, and Buckingham and Nicks separated.

Despite internal strife, Fleetwood Mac jelled on their next release, *RUMOURS*, their massively successful signature album which spawned four top-ten singles, "Dreams," "Go Your Own Way," "You Make Loving Fun," and "Don't Stop." Another track, "Chains," was the only song on the record written by all five members. By 1995, *RUMOURS* had been certified as selling 16 million copies, then surpassed only by Michael Jackson's *THRILLER*. Meanwhile in England, Peter Green was placed in a psychiatric hospital after a scuffle with his accountant over a royalty check.

Under pressure to repeat their massive success, the group's next project, *TUSK*, was two years in the making, costing $1 million in studio time. A double album, it was attacked by critics. The album spawned a pair of hit singles, the Stevie Nicks sung and written ballad "Sara," and the odd "Tusk," which featured the musical backing of a college marching band.

Following the release of the disappointing live album MIRAGE in 1982, band members pursued solo ventures. Stevie Nicks' solo debut, *BELLA DONNA*, spawned a pair of top-10 duet smashes, "Stop Draggin' My Heart Around" with Tom Petty and the Heartbreakers, and "Leather and Lace" with Eagles member Don Henley. Lindsey Buckingham landed the pop hit "Trouble" from *LAW AND ORDER*, while Christine McVie charted with "Got a Hold on Me," from her release, *CHRISTINE McVIE*. Meanwhile, Mick Fleetwood's expensive solo effort, *THE VISITOR*, bombed and he soon filed for bankruptcy.

Regrouping in 1987, Fleetwood Mac enjoyed its best single album since *RUMOURS* with *TANGO IN THE NIGHT*, which featured the hit singles "Seven Words," "Little Lies," the ephemeral "Everywhere," and the strangely erotic, "Big Love." Simultaneously pursuing a solo career, Buckingham was dismissed for failing to join a Fleetwood Mac tour. He was replaced by Rick Vito and Billy Burnette, who appeared on the poor-selling *BEHIND THE MASK*.

Angered by Mick Fleetwood's scathing autobiography, Stevie Nicks and Christine McVie left Fleetwood Mac in protest. Fleetwood Mac reunited in January 1993 to perform "Don't Stop" at Bill Clinton's presidential inauguration.

Mick Fleetwood formed a new version of the group in 1993, hiring Dave Mason (a member of Mick Fleetwood's solo band, the Zoo) and Bekka Bramlett (daughter of rock duo Delaney and Bonnie) as replacements for Buckingham and Nicks. The following year, Christine McVie quit touring with the band. Released in 1995, the Fleetwood Mac album *TIME* was their worst seller ever.

Considered a media event, Fleetwood Mac reformed in its classic lineup in 1997. Releasing a live greatest-hits album, *THE DANCE*, the project was recorded before a studio audience at a Los Angeles sound stage. The event was also captured as an

MTV special. A subsequent tour coincided with the 20th anniversary of *RUMOURS*.

Bibliography

Harding, Frank. (1992, October 2). Fleetwood Mac: Macsimum rock 'n' roll. *Goldmine*, p. 12.
McLane, Daisann. (1980, February 7). Five not so easy pieces. *Rolling Stone*, p. 37.
Morse, Steve. (1990, July 19). Fleetwood Mac's long, strange trip. *Boston Globe*, Calendar
        sect., p. 11.
Robins, Wayne. (1990, July 29). As Fleetwood Mac turns: Despite its soap-opera relationships,
        the band endures. *(New York) Newsday*, part II, p. 13.
Schruers, Fred. (1997, October 30). Back on the chain gang. *Rolling Stone*, p. 32.

THE 4 SEASONS. *Tommy DeVito (June 19, 1936); Bob Gaudio (November 17, 1942); Nick Massi (Nicholas Macioci; September 19, 1935); Frankie Valli (Francis Stephen Castellucio; May 3, 1937). Inducted in 1990.* The king of falsetto singing, Frankie Valli led the 4 Seasons through two decades of hits. Emerging out of the Italian-American doo-wop tradition, the 4 Seasons outlasted all of their contemporaries.

Reared in a tough, lower-income housing project in Newark, New Jersey, seven-year-old Valli became infatuated with music business after his mother took him to a Frank Sinatra concert. Joining a neighborhood doo-wop group, Valli would impersonate female singers like Dinah Washington with his high-pitched, falsetto voice.

Aided by his mentor and future namesake, hillbilly singer Texas Jean Valley, 16-year-old Valli made a demo recording in 1953. Releasing the poorly selling "My Mother's Eyes," as by Frankie Valley, he was discouraged by his father (a toy factory worker), who urged him to seek more traditional employment.

Changing his name to Frankie Love and forming the Four Lovers, Villi and the group were signed by RCA Records in. After a minor hit with the Otis Blackwell-penned "You're the Apple of My Eye" and a subsequent pair of appearances on *The Ed Sullivan Show*, the group was dropped by RCA.

As Frankie Tyler, Valli then recorded another solo record, "I Go Ape," at Okeh Records, where he met his future producer and co-writer, Bob Crew. With Valli rejoining the Four Lovers, the group recorded under a variety of names including Frankie Valle & the Romans.

The Four Lovers—which now included Frankie Valli, Nick Massi, Tommy DeVito, and pianist Bob Gaudio of the Royal Teens (and writer of the hit "Short Shorts")—signed with Crewe in 1960, working as uncredited session players behind Bobby Darin and others. The renamed 4 Seasons (the moniker taken from a New Jersey bowling alley) later bombed during a stint at Gone Records.

When Bob Gaudio wrote "Sherry" (originally called "Jackie" for Jackie Kennedy) in 15 minutes, he suggested that Valli sing the lead in his easily identifiable falsetto voice. Smelling a hit, Crew shopped the single around, with the bidding war won by Vee-Jay Records. A chart-topping smash, many listeners assumed the group was black. The follow-up release, the near-novelty "Big Girls Don't Cry" (1962), was also a chart-topper. Although Valli had a pair of smashes under his belt, he refused to move out of the projects, fearing his success would be short-lived.

With follow-up hits such as "Walk like a Man" (1963) and "Candy Girl" (1963), the group moved to the Philips label in search of a more favorable royalty arrangement. With the strong writing team of Gaudio and Crewe, the 4 Seasons hits continued strong in 1964 with the top-10 entries "Dawn," "Ronnie," "Rag Doll," and "Save It for Me." The departure of Massi in 1964 would signal a steady flow of members through the group.

Releasing several singles under the moniker the Wonder Who? In 1965, Valli and the 4 Seasons grouped scored a hyperfalsetto-style hit with the Bob Dylan composition "Don't Think Twice." Surviving the British Invasion, the 4 Seasons' hit run continued with "Let's Hang On!" (1965), "Working My Way Back to You" (1966), and "C'Mon Marianne" (1967). In a solo venture, in 1967 Valli landed a hit with the romantic ballad "Can't Take My Eyes off You." Suffering hearing problems, 33-year-old Valli was told by a doctor that he was legally deaf.

Their career slumping in the early 1970s, the 4 Seasons entered into an unfruitful association with Motown. During this time, DeVito left, and Gaudio retired from touring, preferring to compose and perform on the group's records.

Before leaving Motown, the 4 Seasons bought back the rights to the track "My Eyes Adored You." Released by Private Stock Records in 1975 as a Valli solo effort, the song topped the charts, relaunching the 4 Seasons' fame.

Since Private Stock was interested only in signing Valli, the 4 Seasons landed at Warner Brothers, where, with Crewe's departure, Gaudio assumed production duties. The disco-flavored album *WHO LOVES YOU* spawned the best-selling hit of the group's career, "December 1963 (Oh What a Night)" (1976). Written by Gaudio and his future wife, Judy Parker, the song typified that album in which Valli had abdicated most of the lead vocal duties.

With Valli leaving the 4 Seasons at the end of 1977, the group fell apart. Meanwhile, Valli topped the pop charts in 1978 with "Grease," the title track of the immensely popular John Travolta/Olivia Newton-John film.

In 1980, Valli and Gaudio launched a new version of the 4 Seasons, recording an occasional album. A new version of "December 1963 (Oh What a Night)" reentered the pop charts in 1994. The brainchild of a pair of Dutch deejays, the updated, percussion-heavy remix was popularized in the U.S. by the syndicated, dance-music radio show *Open House Party.*

Bibliography

Bleiel, Jeff. (1990, March 9). The Four Seasons: '70s chameleons. *Goldmine*, p. 38.

Engel, Edward R. (1977, July-August). The end of an era: Frankie Valli & the Four Seasons. *Time Barrier Express*, p. 10.

Harrington, Richard. (1983, July 4). Frankie bayyy-aaa-beee! *Washington Post*, p. D1.

Ticineto, Alfred. (1992, September). Frankie Valli and the 4 Seasons: Thirty years of excellence. *Discoveries*, p. 20.

White, Timothy. (1990). *Rock Lives: Profiles & Interviews* (pp. 80-100). New York: Henry Holt.

Wloszczyna, Susan. (1994, October 27). A 1994 heat wave for "December 1963." *USA Today*,

p. 1D.
Woodard, Rex. (1981, August). The Four Seasons: A lesson in survival. *Goldmine*, p. 18.

THE FOUR TOPS. *Renaldo "Obie" Benson (1937); Abdul "Duke" Fakir (December 26, 1935); Lawrence Payton (1938 - June 20, 1997); Levi Stubbs (Levi Stubbles Jr.; June 6, 1936). Inducted in 1990.* One of Motown's top acts, the Four Tops took a different route to success than did most of their inexperienced labelmates. While Motown founder Berry Gordy Jr. built the label by shaping raw, undiscovered talent, the Four Tops spent nearly a decade together before joining their hometown label.

Singing doo-wop harmonies, Obie Benson, Abdul Fakir, Lawrence Payton, and lead singer Levi Stubbs began as the Four Aims in 1954. Renamed the Fours Tops in 1956, they briefly recorded for Chess Records. A part-time fifth member, Bill Davis, acted as songwriter and manager. Performing throughout the South's "chitlin" circuit, the group struggled for several years, all the while perfecting their dance routines.

After recording one single each for Columbia and Riverside Records in the early 1960s, the group landed on a tour with jazz crooner Billy Eckstine. Returning to Detroit, the unsigned Four Tops caught the attention of Berry Gordy Jr., whose original overtures had been rejected by the group in 1959.

Signing the Four Tops to Motown's short-lived jazz subsidiary, Workshop Jazz, Gordy's aim was to appeal to older consumers. But after recording an album's worth of material, the record was shelved.

Instead, the Four Tops were recipients of the production and songwriting talents of Holland-Dozier-Holland (H-D-H), where as a pop-soul group, they scored a huge crossover hit with their debut Motown release. Featuring a string section, "Baby I Need Your Loving" (1964) launched a fruitful association between the Four Tops and H-D-H. Competing on the charts with their labelmates the Temptations, the Four Tops scored some of Motown's best sellers, including "I Can't Help Myself" (1965), and "Reach Out I'll Be There" (1966).

As lead singer, Levi Stubbs was considered the star of the Four Tops and was frequently pressured by Berry Gordy to emerge as a solo act. On a number of releases, a female chorus replaced the Four Tops on backing vocals.

Moving toward a more mature direction, the Four Tops continued its run with "Standing in the Shadows of Love" (1966) and "Bernadette" (1967). But with the departure of H-D-H, the Four Tops saw their fortunes decline. Relegated to recording cover material, the late-1960s hits included: the Left Banke's "Walk Away Renee" (1968), Tim Hardin's "If I Were a Carpenter" (1968), and Ike & Tina Turner's "River Deep—Mountain High" (1970), the latter a duet with the Supremes. Shortly before the Four Tops' departure from Motown, Obie Benson co-wrote Marvin Gaye's hit "What's Going On?"

Lured to ABC-Dunhill Records with a pair of compositions written for them, the Four Tops adopted a smoother soul sound. After scoring a few more hits, including "Keeper of the Castle" (1972) and the million-selling "Ain't No Woman (Like the One I've Got)" (1973), the Four Tops disappeared from the pop charts in the 1970s.

Recording a pair of albums for the disco label Casablanca in 1981, the Four Tops landed a comeback hit with "When She Was My Girl." Following their appearance on Motown's televised anniversary celebration, the Four Tops returned to Motown Records in 1983. In the late 1980s, Levi Stubbs starred in the stage production of *Little Shop of Horrors* as the voice of Audrey II, the flesh-eating plant. Founding Four Tops member Abdul "Duke" Fakir died in 1997.

Bibliography

Gaul, Emily. (1995, March 3). Something about the Four Tops. *Goldmine*, p. 16.

Kiersh, Edward. (1986). *Where Are You Now, Bo Diddley?* (pp. 292-99). Garden City, NY: Doubleday.

Tamarkin, Jeff. (1981, August). The Four Tops: 28 years and still tops. *Goldmine*, p. 7.

Taraborrelli, J. Randy. (1986). *Motown: Hot Wax, City Cool & Solid Gold* (pp. 85-88). New York: Dolphin/Doubleday.

ARETHA FRANKLIN. *(March 25, 1942). Inducted in 1987.* For much of the 1950s and 1960s, the gospel choirs of America's black churches were training grounds for R&B and pop stars. As "the Queen of Soul," Aretha Franklin revitalized R&B in the late 1960s with her church-born hits. Her mother, Barbara Siggers, was a prominent gospel singer who deserted the family when Aretha was six, dying four years later; her father, Reverend C.L. (Clarence LeVaughn) Franklin was an immensely popular, flashy preacher who drove a Cadillac.

During a brief move to Buffalo, four-year-old Aretha made her first public performance, singing in the choir of her father's church. In 1946, Rev. Franklin settled his family in his new base at the New Bethel Baptist Church in Detroit, soon attracting an overflow congregation of 4,500 members.

With her father frequently on out-of-town tours, Franklin was coached by the best in the gospel field, learning piano chords from the live-in Rev. James Cleveland and vocal stylings from Mahalia Jackson and Clara Ward. Singing her first solo at age 12, two years later Franklin first appeared on record, singing spirituals. From age 13 to 16, Franklin traveled the hard gospel road with the top acts of the day. At age 15, Franklin was pregnant with her first son, the father's identity never revealed.

Taken by her father to New York City in 1960, Franklin recorded a demo, having switched to secular, non-church material. After a series of performances around New York, the five-octave mezzo-soprano voice of 18-year-old Franklin attracted the attention of a Columbia Records producer, John Hammond, who signed the singer to a six-year contract. While members of her church were critical of the move into pop music, the powerful Rev. Franklin quieted their criticisms.

While former gospel singer Ray Bryant was assigned as her musical director, producer Hammond tried to mold Franklin into the new Barbra Streisand. Scoring a top-10 R&B hit with "Today I Sing the Blues" (1960), Franklin had limited success at the label with her pop-oriented standards. Assigned to various producers, including Clyde Otis, Franklin's nine Columbia albums failed to spark much interest.

Advised by her manager and husband, Ted White, to leave Columbia, Franklin signed with Atlantic in 1966, coming under the wing of legendary producer Jerry Wexler. Recording at the Muscle Shoals Fame studio, Franklin was finally permitted to sing in the church style in which she had been raised.

With her passionate, Clara Ward-like gospel delivery, Franklin's first major pop hit came with the sultry and erotic "I Never Loved a Man (The Way I Love You)" (1967). The first of her seven million-sellers in the next two years, Franklin came to dominate soul music. Usually backed by her sisters Erma and Caroline (as the Sweet Inspirations), Franklin's soulful wails garnered her much press. Earning the nickname "the Queen of Soul," she won the Grammy for "Best R&B Performance, Female" every year from 1967 until 1974. But with her success at Atlantic, Columbia continued to pump out album releases of older material.

After a derriere-pinching incident at the Muscle Shoals studio that infuriated Franklin's husband, Wexler took Aretha Franklin to New York, where she recorded her most notable works, including her only number-one pop hit, the Otis Redding-penned "Respect" (1967), "(You Make Me Feel like a) Natural Woman," and "Chain of Fools."

In the early 1970s, Franklin scored several cover-hits including "Eleanor Rigby," "Bridge over Troubled Water," and "Spanish Harlem." Her album *ARETHA LIVE AT THE FILLMORE WEST*, recorded over three days at the famed club, enlarged her base among rock fans. A homecoming of sorts occurred in 1972, when she recorded a live church album, her first since her pre-Atlantic days.

Franklin's 1975 album *YOU* was her last produced by Wexler, who entered semiretirement in Florida. Working with a series of producers, including Curtis Mayfield, Franklin saw her career in a decline during the second half of the 1970s. Meanwhile when burglars shot Franklin's father and left him in a coma, Aretha Franklin became his nursemaid until his death.

After garnering favorable press for her acting role in *The Blues Brothers*, Franklin signed with Arista and returned to the charts in 1982 with the Luther Vandross-produced "Jump to It." Enjoying a comeback in the mid-1980s, Franklin's hit run continued with "Freeway of Love" (1985), "Who's Zoomin' Who" (1985), and the chart-topping duet with George Michael "I Knew You Were Waiting (For Me)" (1987).

Returning to her gospel springwell in 1988, Franklin released the album *ONE LORD, ONE FAITH, ONE BAPTISM*. But, developing a fear of flying, Franklin's concert touring came to a near halt. In 1987, Franklin became the first woman inducted into the Rock and Roll Hall of Fame. In 1994, she received a lifetime Grammy Award and became the youngest person to earn Kennedy Center Honors.

Bibliography

Bego, Mark. (1989). *Aretha Franklin: The Queen of Soul*. New York: St. Martin's Press.

Geracimos, Ann. (1994, November 29). Aretha Franklin: Queen of Soul getting respect for her many achievements in music world. *Washington Times*, p. C10.

Harrington, Richard. (1994, December 4). Aretha Franklin: Baring her soul. *Washington Post*, p. G6.

Hodenfield, Chris. (1974, May 23). Reassessing Aretha. *Rolling Stone*, p. 63.

Nathan, David. (1994, July 8). Aretha Franklin: The Columbia years (1960-1965). *Goldmine*, p. 47.

White, Timothy. (1990). *Rock Lives: Profiles and Interviews* (pp. 194-98). New York: Henry Holt.

ALAN FREED. *(Aldon James Freed; December 15, 1922 - January 20, 1965). Inducted in the Non-Performer category in 1986*. Initially referring to the music he played as "rhythm and blues," Alan Freed was crucial to the genesis of a revolutionary genre called rock and roll, giving the music its name.

Born in Windber, Pennsylvania, Alan Freed was raised in nearby Salem, Ohio, where his father worked as a clothier. Playing trombone in the school orchestra, Freed also led a New Orleans-style jazz band called the Sultans of Swing. At home, Freed's musically proficient family would gather around their piano to play big band-style jazz.

Attending Ohio State University in 1940, Freed majored in mechanical engineering. Fascinated with the campus radio station, he later spoke of getting his start there, though he never stepped foot in the studio. Young and impatient, Freed left school in 1941 to join the army, receiving a medical discharge the next year.

After attending broadcasting school in Youngstown, he worked his way to the area's radio powerhouse, WKBN, landing the job by exaggerating his experience. Playing classical music and announcing local football games, Freed left after two years.

Hired in 1945 by ABC affiliate WAKR in Akron Freed quickly ascended from a news announcer to a popular deejay. Adopting the radio moniker Knucklehead Freed, he was an immediate sensation, becoming a local celebrity. Dozens of angry fans once picketed the station when management fired Freed for insubordination.

With his star on the ascent and a tripling of his salary, in 1948 he renegotiated a contract that included the radio's first-ever noncompete clause, prohibiting him from working within a 75-mile radius for a year, should he leave the station. But taking the advice of his new manager Lew Platt, Freed was fired for good in 1949 for demanding a raise. Since his previous contract did not mention television, Freed tried took a position at Cleveland television station WXEL channel 9 as a self-described "teejay," playing records on a shortlived music program. A stint as an afternoon movie host also proved unpopular.

Returning to radio in June 1951 at WJW in Cleveland, Freed initially played classical music in the overnight graveyard shift. Wanting to advertise the R&B records he sold to blacks and whites alike, Record Rendezvous owner Leo Mintz convinced Freed to play records by black artists such as Wynonie Harris and Big Joe Turner.

Within months, Freed owned the local black market and attracted a growing white audience. Calling himself the Moondog, Freed had borrowed the moniker from an obscure Manhattan street musician. Possessing charm and wit, Freed had a velvety-cool style that his fans wanted to identify with. While drinking bottles of the local Erin Brew beer that sponsored his show, Freed would howl and beat a phone book to the R&B records he played. "He would march around the room, and yell and shout, and would really get enthusiastic. He was brilliant on the air. He could grab an audience,"

Alan Freed attired in his trademark plaid jacket and bowtie. (*Photo courtesy of John M. Riley, from private collection.*)

recalled former radio executive Robert West.

Naming the music "rock and roll," Freed made it palatable to white America during an era of strict segregation. While both Mintz and Freed have been credited with coining the term, "rock and roll," Freed had first used the term on the air in late 1945 in Akron. Refusing to play the watered-down, white pop, cover versions of black songs on his "Moondog" show, Freed loyally stuck with the R&B originals.

Turning to concert promotion, Freed and Mintz staged what was considered the first-ever rock and roll concert on March 21, 1952. An all-star revue at the Cleveland Arena, the Moondog Coronation Ball attracted 25,000 mostly black fans in spite of sparse advertising. Coheadlined by the Dominoes and Paul Williams, the event erupted into a full-scale riot. Nearly fired from his radio position and arrested by police, Freed was later cleared of all charges.

Nearly dying in an automobile crash in April 1953, an overworked Freed suffered massive internal injuries. For a time he broadcast his radio program from his bedside. After a miraculous recovery Freed returned to concert promotion, launching a record-setting 30-city R&B tour, turning away crowds at every stop. Expanding his music empire, Freed operated his own Champagne record label and managed a doo-wop group, the Moonglows.

But when Freed's radio program was broadcast on Newark's WNJR, he made waves in nearby New York City. Lured to the Big Apple in September 1954, he landed the late-evening shift at WINS, then a 50,000-watt station with few listeners. What Freed interchangeably called rock and roll and rhythm and blues was suddenly thrust upon millions of listeners, many of whom were white. Freed took WINS to the ratings forefront and within months spawned scores of imitators.

Immediately upon his arrival, Freed and the entire rock and roll community came under attack from religious groups, law enforcement agencies, politicians, and especially ASCAP, a powerful music publishing agency that was losing millions of dollars to rock artists. Freed was also targeted by blacks who were angry that a white man was making money speaking in a black dialect while playing R&B records. But unlike his contemporaries, Freed was a champion of civil rights, breaking down negative racial stereotypes.

In New York, Freed and partner Morris Levy failed in their attempt to copyright the term "rock and roll." Freed was also forced to drop his Moondog moniker after street musician Louis "Moondog" Hardin took him to court. Renaming his program the *Alan Freed Rock and Roll Show*, Freed became a national celebrity, with his program syndicated in two dozen cities. In 1956 Freed launched the first nationally broadcast rock radio show, *The Camel Rock and Roll Party* (CBS) and predated *American Bandstand* with his own ABC rock music program.

Continuing his thriving concert promotion business, Freed set up residency at Brooklyn's Paramount Theater, setting attendance records with his seven-shows-a-day schedule. Inspired by the film *Blackboard Jungle*, Freed also produced and starred in several pioneering, cheapie rock and roll flicks, including *Don't Knock the Rock* and *Mister Rock and Roll*.

With rock music under attack, the brash Freed became an easy target. After riots erupted at his concerts in both Boston and New York, Freed was fired by WINS.

But after taking a position with crosstown station WABC, Freed's troubles intensified when he charged with accepting payola, a then-legal practice of playing records in exchange for cash payments. The chief target in a series of televised hearings in 1960, Freed and rock and roll were forever muddied. When Freed failed to sign a waiver that he had never taken payola, he was fired by WABC. Many of rock's critics were hoping that the music would perish along with Freed.

Forced to cancel concert tours, Freed went bankrupt. After pleading guilty to bribery charges in 1962, a complacent Freed was fined and given a suspended sentence. A broken man, Freed began to drink more heavily.

Drifting to Los Angeles in 1962, Freed took 22nd-ranked KDAY to third place in the ratings. But under pressures of legal, tax, and health problems, he quickly resigned. Landing a position at WQAM in Miami, Freed quit, unhappy that he was unable to program his own music.

After the IRS seized his properties in 1964, Freed was left with only a home in Palm Springs. Returning to New York City for three months, the once most powerful man on radio was unable to find a job. Recalls deejay Joe Finan, "Alan couldn't get his phone calls returned." Still hounded by the IRS, Freed was indicted by a federal grand jury in 1964 for income tax evasion. Suffering from uremia, he died from cirrhosis of the liver, and escaped trial. His death went unnoticed in the music industry, which wanted to forget the scar of payola. Remaining a forgotten part of rock music until the 1970s, Paramount celebrated Freed in the 1978 film *American Hot Wax*.

With Alan Freed synonymous with the origin of "rock and roll," Cleveland was picked as the site of the Rock and Roll Hall of Fame and Museum in 1985. Freed was voted into the Hall of Fame in its premier year, 1986, in the Non-Performer category.

On March 21, 1992, Cleveland radio station WMJI sponsored a 40th anniversary Moondog Coronation Ball, featuring an appearance by Paul "Hucklebuck" Williams, the only artist who performed at the original 1952 concert.

Bibliography

Dyer, Bob. (1990, October 14). Contract clause led to Freed's fame. *Akron Beacon Journal*,
        p. F1.
Finan, Joe. (1997, February 9). Interview with author.
"Hepcats bay on trail of Moondog, Freed in jam." (1952, March 22). *Akron Beacon Journal*,
        p. A2.
Horowitz, Carl. (1995, March 1). Showman Alan Freed. *Investor's Business Daily*, p. A1.
Jackson, John A. (1991). *Big Beat Heat: Alan Freed and the Early Years of Rock & Roll*. New
        York: Schirmer.
Junod, Tom. (1992, December). Oh, what a night! *Life*, p. 32.
"Moondog Madness." (1952, March 29). *(Cleveland) Call & Post*, p. 2B.
Nite, Norm N. (1992, March 9). *Alan Freed Special*, WMJI, Cleveland, Ohio.
Passman, Arnold. (1971). *The Deejays*. New York: Macmillan.
Rutledge, Jeffrey L. (1985, February 1). Alan Freed: The fall from grace of a forgotten hero.
        Goldmine, p. 22.
Scott, Jane. (1982, March 14). 30 years ago, "Moon Dog" howled. *Cleveland Plain Dealer*,
        p. D1.
Shaw, Arnold. (1978). *Honkers and Shouters*. New York: Collier.
Smith, Wes. (1989). *The Pied Pipers of Rock 'n' Roll*. Marietta, GA: Longstreet.
West, Robert. (1996, December 5). Interview with author.

MILT GABLER. *(Milton Gabler; May 20, 1911). Inducted in the Non-Performer category in 1993.* During his six-decade-long involvement in the music industry, Milt Gabler played an integral part in the birth of bebop jazz, rhythm and blues, and rock and roll.

In 1926 Julius Gabler opened the Commodore radio store in New York City. An Austrian immigrant who took an American wife, in 1927 he hired the eldest of his three sons, 16-year-old Milt Gabler, who had just finished high school. At Milt Gabler's insistence, jazz records were stocked a year later after walk-by customers began requesting the songs heard on the store's sidewalk speaker.

Promoted by his father to manager in 1931, Milt Gabler built the renamed Commodore Record Shop into the city's best-stocked jazz outlet. A hangout for jazz collectors and musicians, the store regularly drew the future giants of the record industry including Columbia producer John Hammond and Atlantic heads Jerry Wexler and brothers Nesuhi and Ahmet Ertegun.

Unable to fill his customer's requests for out-of-print jazz 78s, Gabler began leasing the masters from record companies in 1934 for pressing on his own Commodore label, the first "oldie" reissue company. But when record companies began reissuing their own oldies, Gabler was deprived of music product. "I had to finally begin making records when Columbia started putting out reissues at a cheaper price than what the Commodore music shop was selling them at. I realized it was no good unless you made your own masters" (p. 23), Gabler told interviewer Joe Smith.

Recording the best in jazz in the late 1930s, Commodore emerged as the first, major independent label in the post-Depression era. Working with the likes of Lester Young, Eddie Condon, and the Kansas City Six, Gabler's most notable session produced the Billie Holiday classics "Fine and Mellow, and Commodore's best-seller, the racially-charged protest song "Strange Fruit."

Recording what was later termed bebop jazz, Gabler pioneered the practice of listing session musicians and recording dates on the record label. Gabler also formed an organization of jazz enthusiasts, the United Hot Clubs of America, and launched a series of legendary, all-star, Sunday jam sessions.

Though hired by Decca Records in 1941, Gabler kept his own Commodore label active into the 1950s. At Decca, Gabler assumed the position of reissuer, in charge of their old Brunswick-Vocalion catalog. Also working as a producer he supervised the recording sessions of Decca's pop superstars Guy Lombardo and Bing Crosby before switching to jazz acts Ella Fitzgerald, Woody Herman, and Lionel Hampton. Gabler also oversaw the pre-doo-wop harmony groups, the Mills Brothers and the Ink Spots.

But Gabler's most enduring Decca assignment was Louis Jordan, the father of R&B. Beginning in 1942 with "Outskirts of Town," Gabler guided all of Jordan's revolutionary, crossover hits, including "Five Guys Named Moe" (1943), "Caledonia" (1945), and the Gabler co-composition "Choo Choo Ch'Boogie" (1946). Appointed the head of Decca's A&R department, Gabler also was in charge of Decca's new Coral division in 1948.

Signing the politically active folk quartet, the Weavers, Gabler produced their 1950 smash "Goodnight Irene." When the group was later charged with Communist activity, Gabler offered to resign from the label.

After Decca announced it would not re-sign Jordan in late 1953, Gabler signed Jordan's unlikely successor, Bill Haley. Taken aback by the former hillbilly singer; "the odd 'Bill Haley' sound was new to him. It seemed raw, erotic and powerful and it wasn't like anything he heard before" (p. 91), wrote Bill Haley's biographers. Updating the formula used in dozens of Jordan's hits, Gabler's production work gave Haley a national hit with a sanitized version of Big Joe Turner's bawdy "Shake, Rattle and Roll." (Later, Gabler even had Haley record Jordan's "Choo Choo Ch'Boogie.")

But Haley's greatest moment was yet to come. Recording at the cavernous Pythian Temple studio in Manhattan (converted from a former ballroom), Gabler spliced together both takes of "Rock around the Clock." Released in 1954, the song was only a moderate hit.

But the following year, Gabler sold the rights to the song for one dollar to MGM, which splashed it in the opening credits of the film *The Blackboard Jungle*. Re-released, "Rock Around the Clock" became rock's first chart-topper and launched the rock and roll era.

Becoming Decca's vice president, in the 1960s Gabler produced artists such as Brenda Lee, for whom he was the uncredited co-writer of her hit "I'm Sorry" (1960). Later in the decade, Gabler was a key figure in the promotion of the rock musical *Jesus Christ Superstar*.

In 1971 Gabler was fired by Decca when the company's new parent firm, MCA, wanted a youthful staff. During his 30 years with Decca/MCA, Gabler was responsible for over 40 individual million sellers.

Reactivating Commodore Records, Gabler's old masters were re-released first by Atlantic (which especially wanted the rights to his Billie Holiday masters), then Columbia and Mosaic.

Bibliography
Erskine, Gilbert. M. (1977, Winter). Milt Gabler of Commodore. *The Second Line*, p. 9.
Fox, Ted. (1988, February). Milt Gabler: Commodore music's steady captain. *Audio*, p. 66.
Frazier, George. (1950, November). Platter paradise. *Cosmopolitan*, p. 64.
Gabler, Milt. (1984, September 29). Things used to be different. *Billboard*, p. 10.
Gleason, Ralph J. (1971, December 9). Perspectives: The revival of a pioneer label. *Rolling Stone*, p. 14.
Haley, John W. & von Hoelle, John. (1990). *Sound and Glory*. Wilmington, DE: Dyne-American.
Obrecht, Jas. (1981, August). Q/A: Milt Gabler. *Guitar Player*, p. 16.
Smith, Joe. (1988). *Off the Record* (pp. 23-25). New York: Warner.

MARVIN GAYE. *(Marvin Pentz Gay Jr.; April 2, 1939 - April 1, 1984). Inducted in 1987*. Dubbed "the Prince of Soul," Marvin Gaye endured lifelong turmoil, never grasping the genius of his own talent. Gaye was reared in Washington, D.C., first singing as a young child at his Apostolic church. Writes biographer David Ritz, "In his early life, Marvin had access to the keyboard, which he learned totally by ear. Even as a pre-teen, he had developed into a fine two-fisted country-church pianist. He could also play heartfelt blues" (p. 10).

Quarreling with his strict and abusive father much of his life, Gaye experienced little success in the boxing ring and on the football field. At Cardoza High School in 1959, the painfully shy Gaye joined a fledgling R&B group the D.C. Tones on piano. (During this period, he is often miscredited as being a member of the Rainbows.)

Dropping out of high school to join the air force, Gaye resented the authoritarian atmosphere. Honorably discharged, he then joined a doo-wop vocal group the Marquees as second tenor. Befriending the group, Bo Diddley tutored the band members and produced their first of two singles, "Hey Little School Girl."

After the Marquees shared a bill with Harvey and the Moonglows at the legendary Howard Theater in Washington, D.C., Moonglows leader Harvey Fuqua fired his backing group, and enlisted the Marquees as his new group. Taken to Chicago's Chess Records, Gaye recorded his first solo lead vocal on "Mama Loocie," a song he co-wrote with Fuqua.

After disbanding the Moonglows, Fuqua brought along Gaye to Detroit and launched a pair of labels, Harvey and Tri-Phi. With Fuqua selling both companies to Berry Gordy, Gaye was hired under the pretense as a session drummer. A quick learner, Gaye drummed on recordings for the Miracles and the Marvelettes and worked as the Miracles' road drummer. The Miracles' lead singer, Smokey Robinson, befriended the young Gaye, encouraging him to write songs. Gaye's first Motown songwriting credit came with the Marvelettes' hit "Beechwood 45789." At age 20, Gaye started dating Berry Gordy's older sister, 37-year-old Anna.

Yearning to be the black Sinatra, Gaye bombed with his debut album, *THE SOULFUL MOODS OF MARVIN GAYE*, which consisted of old standards. All of Gaye's early records were for naught, with Motown unable to promote that kind of music.

Switching to a soulful style, Gaye's first success came with a song he co-wrote, "Hitch Hike" (1963). A crossover, pop hit, it spawned a dance craze of the same name, landing him on *American Bandstand.*

Launching his stardom, Gaye landed his first top-10 hit in 1963 with "Pride and Joy." Marrying Anna Gordy later in the year, Gaye would forever enjoy special consideration by his new brother-in-law. But Gaye continued to suffer through bouts of insecurity. In his autobiography, Smokey Robinson recalled that Gaye confided in him that "women expect so much of me . . . they've made me into this sex symbol thing until sometimes it just messes with my head" (p. 139).

One of Motown's top acts, Gaye's hit run continued in the mid-1960s with, "I'll Be Doggone" and "Ain't That Peculiar." Gaye also had fruitful stints with several duet partners, including Mary Wells, Kim Weston, and Diana Ross. Gaye's most prolific pairing came with his confidant Tammi Terrell on "Ain't No Mountain High Enough" (1967), "Ain't Nothing like the Real Thing" (1968), and "You're All I Need to Get By" (1968). At a 1967 concert, the terminally ill Terrell collapsed in Gaye's arms.

Scoring the biggest hit of his career in 1968 with "I Heard It through the Grapevine," Gaye had actually recorded the song before the earlier hit version by Gladys Knight & the Pips.

Returning to the studio after a deep depression over the death of Tammi Terrell, Gaye broke from Motown's assembly-line tradition, writing and producing his next album, *WHAT'S GOING ON.* A departure from Motown's usual, lighthearted fare, the ideological album promoted messages of peace and conservation and was expected to bomb. Featuring Gaye's rich, multi-tracked vocals, the album was reluctantly released by Motown in 1971 and spawned the surprise hits "What's Going On" and "Mercy Mercy Me." Gaye was devastated when the project failed to win a Grammy.

Spending two years on his next effort, the erotic and bawdy, *LET'S GET IT ON*, Gaye again shocked Motown execs. The album's hit title track propagated Gaye's virile image. After renegotiating a lucrative contract with Motown in 1973, Gaye's subsequent hits were less frequent.

Gaye's life was in shambles by the late 1970s: his marriage to his second wife, Janis Hunter, ended; he owed the I.R.S. millions in back taxes; and Motown was constantly pressuring him for new material. Suicidal and abusing cocaine, he became unreliable for concert appearances. Forced to flee the country, Gaye landed in London in 1980. After touring throughout Europe, Gaye recorded tracks for the album *IN OUR LIFETIME*. Released without his permission, an incensed Gaye left Motown.

Joining CBS Records in 1982, Gaye scored a comeback hit with the Grammy-winning, "Sexual Healing," from an album produced by old friend, Harvey Fuqua. Seemingly back on top, Gaye's life took a tragic turn. At the Los Angeles home he had bought for his parents, Gaye's lifelong antagonism with his father came to a head in a shooting which left the 44-year-old singer dead.

Bibliography

Dahl, Bill. (1989, June 16). Marvin Gaye: Troubled man. *Goldmine*, p. 8.
Fong-Torres, Ben. (1972, April 27). A visit with Marvin Gaye. *Rolling Stone*, p. 32.
Randolph, Laura B. (1994, June). Ten years after the Marvin Gaye tragedy. *Ebony*, p. 90.
Ritz, David. (1985). *Divided Soul: The Life of Marvin Gaye*. New York: McGraw-Hill.
Robinson, Smokey & Ritz, David. (1989). *Smokey: Inside My Life*. New York: McGraw-Hill.
Salwicz, Chris. (1994, March 24). Last of a troubled man. *Evening Standard*, p. 28.

GERRY GOFFIN AND CAROLE KING. *Carole King (Carole Klein; February 9, 1942); Gerry Goffin (February 11, 1939). Inducted in the Non-Performer category in 1990.* In the first decades of the twentieth century, Tin Pan Alley songwriters dominated popular music, laboring in small offices on Manhattan's 28th Street. With the rise of R&B, country, and rock and roll, in the mid-1950s a new wave of professional songwriters assembled on New York's Broadway Avenue in the vicinity of the Brill Building. Here, teams of professional songwriters huddled in cubicles pumping out hundreds of rock and R&B hits in what became known as the Brill Building Sound.

Notable Brill songwriters included Neil Sedaka, Howard Greenfield, Bobby Darin, and the teams of Barry Mann and Cynthia Weil, Jeff Barry and Ellie Greenwich, and Doc Pomus and Mort Shuman. But the youngest and most prolific team consisted of Gerry Goffin and Carole King.

Born and raised in Brooklyn, King had studied acting at New York's High School for the Performing Arts before enrolling at Queens College in New York. There she met the musically oriented Gerry Goffin, who was studying chemistry. Marrying, Goffin and King signed with publisher Donny (later Don) Kirshner as songwriters and were given an office at the crowded Brill Building.

King usually composed the music, while Goffin wrote the lyrics, a skill he had learned in his childhood. Targeting the teen market, Goffin and King wrote a long string of hit compositions beginning with the Shirelles' "Will You Love Me Tomorrow?" (1960). Unhappy with the session drummer, an uncredited King played the kettle drum on the record.

Attempting her own singing career, King recorded an obscure single "Oh, Neil!"(1959) as an answer song to Neil Sedaka's hit "Oh! Carol." Finally scoring her first hit in 1962 with "It Might as Well Rain until September," the song was released on the new Goffin/King label, Dimension Records. The label's biggest hit came with another of their compositions, the often recorded rock standard "Locomotion," sung by their teenage baby-sitter, Little Eva.

Other Goffin and King compositions include "One Fine Day" by the Chiffons, "Take Good Care of My Baby" by Bobby Vee, "Up on the Roof" by the Drifters, "Oh No, Not My Baby" by Maxine Brown, and the debut hit for Herman's Hermits, "I'm into Something Good." Apart from King, Goffin teamed with Barry Mann on "Who Put the Bomp."

With Goffin and King's compositions becoming more adult-oriented and mature by the mid-1960s, the Animals landed a hit with "Don't Bring Me Down," and the Monkees scored an uncharacteristic hit with the socially relevant "Pleasant Valley Sunday." Written several years earlier, Goffin and King's sensual paean to femininity, "(You Make Me Feel like a) Natural Woman," was Aretha Franklin's breakthrough hit in 1967.

With the rise of the self-sufficient, singer-songwriter in the mid-1960s, there was a diminished need for professional composers. The sophistication of Bob Dylan and the Beatles' Lennon and McCartney signaled the demise of the Brill Building's usually light fare. Divorcing by 1968, Goffin and King also dissolved their songwriting partnership. King formed a rock band, the City, with her new husband, bassist Charles Larkey, releasing a poorly-received album.

Taking a singer-songwriter route, King moved to the West Coast. Her second solo album, *TAPESTRY*, sold ten-million copies in two years and spent six years on the album chart. One of the album's tracks, the King-penned "You've Got a Friend," was recorded by James Taylor, giving him his only number-one hit.

Meanwhile, Goffin's lyrics turned more political, as he tried to follow in the Bob Dylan vein. Teaming with Barry Goldberg, Goffin wrote Gladys Knight & the Pips' "I've Got to Use My Imagination" (1974). With Michael Masser, he wrote Diana Ross' "Theme from Mahogany" (1975) and Whitney Houston's "Saving All My Love for You" (1985).

Goffin and King later reunited for occasional sessions. Their eldest daughter, Louise Goffin, had a moderately successful recording career in the late 1970s. King's recorded output slowed in the 1980s as she turned to film and stage acting and engaged in environmental activism.

Bibliography

Gehman, Pleasant. (1993, November 29). Music News: Brill Building makes music as landmark. *Daily Variety*, p. 8.

Greene, Bob. (1989, August 1). Carole King: She read our minds. *Chicago Tribune*, Tempo sect., p. 1.

Smith, Joe. (1988). *Off the Record* (pp. 128-29). New York: Warner.

White, Mark. (1985). *You Must Remember This: Popular Songwriters 1900-1980* (pp. 123-26). New York: Charles Scribner's Sons.

BERRY GORDY JR. *(November 28, 1929). Inducted in the Non-Performer category in 1988.* The most successful black-owned American business ever, Motown Records was the brainchild of Berry Gordy Jr. A native of Detroit, Gordy was influenced by his hardworking, entrepreneurial parents, his mother selling insurance and his father operating a grocery store.

Standing at five feet six inches Gordy followed the lead of his hometown idol, the boxer Joe Louis, quitting high school and winning 12 of his 15 boxing matches. Joining the army in 1950, he fought in Korea and earned his high school equivalency diploma.

Returning to Detroit in 1953, Gordy opened a jazz record shop, the 3-D Mart, which failed, Gordy refusing to stock the R&B and blues disks his customers preferred. Working on a Ford assembly line in 1955, Gordy alleviated the boredom by writing songs.

Teaming with former boxer and ex-Dominoes lead singer Jackie Wilson, Gordy co-penned "Reet Petite," "To Be Loved," and "Lonely Teardrops." After reaping little profit as a songwriter, Gordy formed his own production company, where he recorded singles by Eddie Holland, the Miracles, and Marv Johnson, which he leased to other labels.

Buying out the fledgling Harvey Fuqua-owned Harvey Record Company, Gordy merged the label with his sister, Gwen Gordy's Anna label. Anna had just landed a hit with the Gordy-penned, Barrett Strong single "Money."

Naming the company Motown (a contraction of Motor-Town) and the studio Hitsville U.S.A., Gordy set up shop in the basement of his $25,000 home and enlisted the services of his family members. Motown's first major hit came in late 1960 with "Shop Around" by the Miracles. Remembers Smokey Robinson in his autobiography, "Damn if that sucker didn't hit all over the country! Problem, though, is that we still weren't set up for national distribution" (p. 80).

Hiring dozens of Detroit singers, many from out of the projects, Motown expanded, scoring its first number-one hit in 1961 with the Marvelettes' "Please Mr. Postman." The song was recorded on just only tracks using a 1939 Western Electric radio station console.

Taking his stable of acts on the road with his first "Motor Town" revue in October 1962, Gordy showcased the Miracles, the Supremes, and other young acts around the country on a bus. But with most of the acts lacking stage experience, the concerts were disasters.

Out of necessity, Gordy set up an artist development department to groom and educate Motown acts. Headed by former Moonglows leader Harvey Fuqua, performers were schooled in an assembly line fashion. While Cholly Atkins taught the acts their synchronized dance routines, Maxine Powell provided lessons in etiquette, poise and social skills, and elegantly attired the performers in sequined evening gowns or matching tuxedos.

Though celebrating its second chart-topper in late 1963 with (Little) Stevie Wonder's "Fingertips—Part 2," Motown was on the brink of closing. But by the end of 1964, the Temptations, the Miracles, the Four Tops, Marvin Gaye, and Mary Wells were landing top-10 singles, with the Supremes especially dominating the charts. With Gordy targeting the pop market, Motown adopted the slogan "The Sound of Young America."

Crucial to the label's turnaround was the songwriting trio of Eddie and Brian

Holland and Lamont Dozier. Dozier told writer Joe Smith, "We punched a clock, literally punched a clock, nine o'clock in the morning. That was the procedure at Motown. Berry Gordy had worked at Ford, so he ran Motown like a factory" (p. 169). Hiring experienced jazz players as the house band, most of Motown's 1960s hits were characterized by a pulsing heartbeatlike dance beat.

But trouble began brewing at Motown when acts began complaining about their financial arrangements. Beginning with Mary Wells' departure in 1964, a steady stream of acts left, punctuated by the crippling departure of Holland-Dozier-Holland in 1968.

Mothballing the Hitsville studio in 1972 Gordy moved the Motown headquarters to Los Angeles. Though losing the majority of its stars, the label signed only a few new acts. Veterans Stevie Wonder and Marvin Gaye were joined by Rick James, the Commodores, and the Jackson 5.

Turning his energy away from music, Gordy launched a film division. With his reported paramour, Diana Ross, in the starring roles, Gordy shot the Billie Holiday biography *Lady Sings the Blues* (1972) and the rags-to-riches saga *Mohogany* (1975).

The 1983 NBC television tribute to Gordy, *Motown 25: Yesterday, Today, and Forever*, received nine Emmy nominations. With Motown existing primarily as a reissue company, in 1988 Gordy sold the label to MCA/Boston Ventures for $61 million. But with the resounding success of the vocal group Boys II Men, Motown was revived. In 1996, Motown relocated from Los Angeles to New York. Today the Hitsville studio operates as a museum.

Bibliography

Fitzgerald, Jon. (1995). Motown crossover hits 1963-1966 and the creative process. *Popular Music, 14*(1), p. 1.
Harrington, Richard. (1994, December 6). Maestro of Motown. *Washington Post*, p. E1.
Robinson, Smokey & Ritz, David. (1989). *Smokey: Inside My Life*. New York: McGraw-Hill.
Smith, Joe. (1988). *Off the Record* (pp. 169-70). New York: Warner.
Snook, Debbi. (1995, July 16). That Motown magic. *The Cleveland Plain Dealer*, p. 1J.
Taraborrelli, Randy J. (1986). *Motown: Hot Wax, City Cool & Solid Gold* (pp. 36-43). Garden City, NY: Dolphin/Doubleday.
White, Adam. (1994, November 5). Gordy speaks: The Billboard Interview. *Billboard*, p. 63.

BILL GRAHAM. *(Wolfgang Wolodia Grajonca; January 8, 1931 - October 25, 1991). Inducted in the Non-Performer category in 1992*. A legendary figure who brought underground rock to masses, Bill Graham transformed rock promotion into a multi-million dollar industry.

Graham's early life was marred by tragedy. His Polish-Jewish family fled the anti-Semitism of 1920s Russia, joining a booming Jewish community in Berlin. Two days after Graham's birth, his architect father was killed in a construction accident. After the horrors of Kristallnacht, in 1939 Graham and his youngest sister were hidden in Jewish orphanages, first in Berlin, then near Paris.

Whisked away from France during the Nazi invasions, 11-year-old Graham survived a grueling trek to Portugal that killed most of the other orphans in his group,

Concert promotor Bill Graham. (*Copyright Bill Graham Presents. Photo credit: Chris Scott.*)

including one of his sisters. Permitted passage on a freighter, the emaciated, 44-pound Graham landed in the Bronx, where he was adopted. Graham's mother and another sister had perished in a German concentration camp.

Not yet a U.S. citizen, Graham fought in Korea and was awarded both the Bronze Star and the Purple Heart. Working as a waiter at resorts in the Catskill Mountains, Graham was exposed to the world of entertainment. Returning to New York, Graham drove a taxi while pursuing a degree in business administration from City College.

Falling in love with acting, Graham traveled back and forth between New York and San Francisco in search of stage work. Unable to support himself, he returned to California, landing a white-collar, managerial position at a manufacturing firm.

Quitting his secure job, Graham took a huge pay cut to manage a guerrilla-style, theatrical ensemble, the San Francisco Mime Troupe. With the troupe arrested in 1965 on obscenity charges, Graham staged a benefit concert for their legal bills. Hiring Allen Ginsberg and Jefferson Airplane to perform, Graham later told writer Joe Smith, "It was the first time I saw the undercurrent of San Francisco—long hair, short hair, pants, no pants, signs, tattoos" (p. 231).

Renting out the Fillmore Auditorium, Graham stumbled upon a career in concert promotion. Entertainer Johnny Otis described the nightclub in his autobiography: "It came spectacularly back to life in 1966 when an enterprising young man began promoting psychedelic dances in the ballroom. With fantastic shapes and colors, old-time movies, stroboscopic and ultraviolet effects projected on walls, and white rock and roll bombarding the youthful, costumed audience with a blasting cacophony of hard rockabilly twangs, East-Indianisms, and pseudo blues, attendance skyrocketed" (p. 204). Initially, police harassed the concertgoers outside of the club, trying to discourage them from entering the high crime neighborhood. But Graham continued to sell out the 1,500-seat venue, notoriously filling it past its capacity. As a gimmick, Graham offered free apples to customers.

Outgrowing his original location, in 1968 Graham moved to the 4,000-capacity former Carousel Ballroom, which he renamed the Fillmore West, and also operated a second venue, a former skating rink called Winterland. At these clubs, Graham was crucial to the development of the San Francisco Sound, instrumental in the careers of Santana, the Grateful Dead, and Steve Miller.

Expanding in 1968, Graham and partner Albert Grossman opened the 2,400-seat Fillmore East in New York City, where Led Zeppelin made their American debut as the opening act for Iron Butterfly. But wanting to pursue other interests, at the end of 1969 Graham sold the Fillmore West, closing the Fillmore East 18 months later. Documenting the Fillmore West's last days, the film *Fillmore* was released in 1972.

Turning to larger-scale concert promotion, the astute Graham turned rock music into a megabusiness. With his company Bill Graham Presents, he oversaw national tours by the Who, Led Zeppelin, Bob Dylan, and the Grateful Dead. Earning a reputation as brash, unyielding and confrontational, Graham wielded an incredible amount of power, able to dictate even what songs were to be played.

In 1976, Graham charged 5,400 patrons a then-exorbitant $25 admission to the legendary farewell performance of the Band, billed as "the Last Dance." Later turned into a film and album, the all-star Thanksgiving Day show was staged at the Winterland and included an elaborate, catered turkey dinner. Two years later, Graham closed that venue as well.

His concert promotion business booming, by 1990 Graham was grossing over $100 million annually. Though considered a shrewd businessman, Graham silenced his critics by raising millions for charity. He promoted the New York half of Live Aid and staged fund-raising concerts for multiple sclerosis, drug abuse, and Jewish causes.

Returning to his first love, Graham co-produced and had a small role in the film *The Doors* and played a mobster, Charles "Lucky" Luciano, in *Bugsy*.

Graham was killed in a helicopter crash in 1991, which also took the life of his longtime companion Melisa Gold. Staged at Golden Gate Park, a free memorial concert billed as "Laughter, Love and Music" was attended by 300,000 and featured performers who owed their success to Graham, including the Grateful Dead, John Fogerty, Santana, Journey, and Crosby, Stills, Nash and Young.

Graham's promotion company, Bill Graham Presents, continues to thrive. In 1993, the San Francisco Civic Auditorium was renamed after Graham. Graham's record label, Wolfgang Records, was reactivated in 1995, signing Eddie Money.

Bibliography
Cahill, Tim. (1972, April 27). Bill Graham drives his Chevve [sic] to the levee. *Rolling Stone*,
        p. 1.
Goldberg, Michael. (1991, December 12/26). Rock's greatest showman. *Rolling Stone*, p. 97.
Otis, Johnny. (1968). *Listen to the Lambs*. New York: W.W. Norton.
Smith, Joe. (1988). *Off the Record* (pp. 231-33). New York: Warner.

THE GRATEFUL DEAD. *Tom Constanten (March 19, 1944); Jerry Garcia (Jerome John Garcia; August 1, 1942 - August 9, 1995); Keith Godchaux (July 14, 1948 - July 23, 1980); Donna Godchaux (August 22, 1947); Mickey Hart (September 11, 1943); Robert Hunter (June 23, 1941); Bill Kreutzmann (William Kreutzmann Jr.; April 7, 1946); Phil Lesh (Philip Chapman Lesh; March 15, 1940); Ron "Pig Pen" McKernan (August 8, 1946 - March 8, 1973); Brent Mydland (October 21, 1952 - July 26, 1990); Bob Weir (Robert Hall Weir; October 16, 1947); Vince Welnick (February 22, 1952). Inducted in 1994.* One of the originators of the San Francisco Sound, the Grateful Dead outlasted its many contemporaries, surviving until the death of Jerry Garcia in 1995. Building a legion of devout fans called "Deadheads," the group spawned a cottage industry by the 1980s.

A product of the postbeatnik folk era, the group jelled in San Francisco in the early 1960s. Keyboard player Ron "Pig Pen" McKernan met drummer Bill Kreutzmann at an instrument store, the two forming a blues-based group, the Zodiacs. The Zodiacs often crossed paths on the coffeehouse circuit with the Wildwood Boys, a group led by guitarist Jerry Garcia.

Garcia's Spanish immigrant father was a former musician turned bar owner. After his father's death, five-year-old Jerry lived with his maternal grandparents, whose penchant for the Grand Ole Opry rubbed off on their grandson. Receiving an accordion for his 15th birthday, Garcia exchanged it for an electric guitar. Joining the army at age 17 in 1959, Garcia was court-martialed a year later for going AWOL.

Back in California, Garcia joined a jug band, Mother McCree's Uptown Jug Champions. With McKernan on lead vocals, and the financially affluent Bob Weir on rhythm guitar, the group struggled with its rustic, acoustic, folk material.

Switching to electric music in 1965, the renamed Warlocks added bassist Phil Lesh and McKernan's earlier bandmate, Bill Kreutzmann. Settling into a communelike existence in the Haight-Ashbury section of San Francisco, the band celebrated hippiedom, flower power, and the emerging drug culture.

Becoming the house band for Ken Kesey and his Merry Pranksters' "acid tests" parties, the Warlocks joined others in experimenting with the then-legal hallucinogenic drug LSD. Embracing drug culture Garcia nicknamed called Captain Trips. Staging a series of free, massive outdoor concerts during San Francisco's "Summer of Love," the Dead built a large fan base.

Signing with Warner Brothers in 1967, their moderately selling debut album, *GRATEFUL DEAD*, was recorded in three days. With Weir on lead vocals and an occasional number by McKernan, the group blended blues-rock with jazzlike improvisation. Their performance at the Monterey Pop Festival in 1967 was their catalyst for national recognition.

Expanding with a second drummer, Mickey Hart, a classically trained keyboardist Tom Constanten, and lyricist Robert Hunter, in 1968 the group followed up with the album *ANTHEM OF THE SUN*. Recorded over a six-month period well over budget, the experimental project indebted the group to Warner until the early 1970s. Performing at both Woodstock and Altamont in 1969, that year the group released the psychedelic album *AOXOMOXOA*, using an early 16-track mixer. Constanten left the group in 1970, disillusioned by the end of the flower power era.

Releasing several commercially oriented albums in 1970, including *AMERICAN BEAUTY*, the Dead scored their first radio hit with "Truckin'." Internal strife mired the Dead in 1971 when manager Lenny Hart (the father of Mickey Hart) was arrested for embezzling $70,000 from the group.

Suffering from liver damage and close to death, McKernan left the group in 1972, replaced by Merle Saunders and then Keith Godchaux and his vocalist wife, Donna. Without McKernan, Garcia emerged as the group's leader, with Weir assuming more lead-vocal duties.

Their popularity waning by the mid-1970s, the Dead launched their own label, Grateful Dead Records, releasing several substandard albums, including *BLUES FOR ALLAH*. Throughout the 1970s, band members pursued various solo ventures, including Bob Weir's side band, Kingfish.

After signing with Arista Records in 1977, the Dead garnered plenty of press for their performance near the Great Pyramid in Egypt. Selling few records during this period, the group considered recording secondary to touring.

In April 1979, the Godchauxs were forced to leave the band, and were replaced by German-born keyboardist Brent Mydland, formerly of Weir's side group, Bobby and the Midnighters. Their popularity on the rise, the Dead's 1980 album, *GO TO HEAVEN*, spawned the hit "Alabama Getaway."

By the 1980s the Grateful Dead had become an institution. Achieving cult status, the parking lots outside their concerts became New Age marketplaces with tie-dyed-clad Deadheads following the group all around the country.

After completing a package tour with Tom Petty & the Heartbreakers and Bob Dylan, in 1986 Garcia collapsed, his health damaged by decades of substance abuse. The following year, *BUILT TO LAST* became the Grateful Dead's best-selling album, spawning their first bona fide pop-hit with "Touch of Grey."

In 1990, Brent Mydland became the group's third keyboardist to perish. Replaced by former Tubes member Vince Welnick, the band continued its grueling road schedule, in 1994 grossing over $50 million in gate receipts.

Suffering from ill health and in and out of drug treatment centers, Jerry Garcia died in 1995 of a heart attack at the age of 53. With the Grateful Dead disbanding, former members occasionally regrouped.

Bibliography

Carlsen, Clifford. (1995, August 4). What a long, strange—and profitable—trip it's been. *San*

Francisco Business Times, p. A4.

Flaum, Eric. (1987, July 17). The Grateful Dead, part 1: Sunshine dream. *Goldmine*, p. 10.

Fong-Torres, Ben. (1995, September-October). A Grateful man: Jerry Garcia was glad to have taken that long, strange trip. *People*, p. 26.

Gilmore, Mikal. (1995, September 21). Jerry Gracia (1942-1995). *Rolling Stone*, p. 44.

Pareles, Jon. (1995, August 10). Jerry Garcia of Grateful Dead, icon of 60's spirit, dies at 53. *New York Times*, p. A1.

Reid, Dixie. (1995, August 10). Grateful blues. *Sacramento Bee*, p. F1.

Stuckey, Fred. (1974). Jerry Garcia. In *Rock Guitarists* (pp. 71-76). Saratoga, CA: Guitar Player Productions.

Wenner, Jann & Reich, Charles. (1981). *The Rolling Stone Interviews* (pp. 180-201). New York: St. Martin's Press.

AL GREEN. *(Albert Greene; April 13, 1946). Inducted in 1995.* A soul legend whose pop career spanned just seven years, Al Green dominated soul music with romantic ballads. Born in Forrest City, Arkansas, Green was raised in a sharecropping family. At nine, he joined four of his eight siblings in a family gospel quartet, the Greene Brothers. After moving to Grand Rapids, Michigan, Green was fired for listening to non-religious music— a Jackie Wilson record.

Assembling a soul group in 1964, Al Greene and the Creations, he spent three years touring through the South and Midwest. Forming Al Greene and the Soul Mates in late 1967 with brother Robert Greene and Lee Virgins, the group scored a national R&B hit with "Back Up Train" (1968). The trio toured for two years on the strength of their one hit.

Launching a solo career, Green (now no e) was signed by Willie Mitchell, bandleader and the vice president of Hi Records, after the two shared a nightclub bill in Midland, Texas. Recording with Hi's strong house band (brothers Charles, Leroy, and Mabon "Teenie" Hodges and Booker T. & the MG's' drummer, Al Jackson), Green unleashed a string of soul ballad hits, beginning with a slowed-down rendition of the Temptations' "I Can't Get Next to You."

Writing "Tired of Being Alone" (1971) about his live-in girlfriend who was rarely home, Green landed his first million-seller. A skinny, 140-pound man, the 25-year-old Green became a sex symbol, donning knee-high boots, gold chains, and frilly, unbuttoned shirts.

Aided by Willie Mitchell and Al Jackson's superb production and composing skills, Green dominated 1970s soul with his intimate singing style. Green's string of million-selling hits include his sensual signature piece which was released against his wishes, "Let's Stay Together" (1971); "Look What You Done for Me" (1972); "I'm Still in Love with You" (1972); "You Ought to Be with Me" (1972); "Here I Am" (1973); and a song he would later re-record with Lyle Lovett, "Call on Me" (1973).

From the album *AL GREEN EXPLORES YOUR MIND* the chestnut, "Take Me to the River" (1974) was covered for an R&B hit by Syl Johnson and was later the breakthrough record for the Talking Heads. Green had written the religiously-tinged song after witnessing a river baptism.

The usually cited catalyst for Green's religious conversion came in 1974, when he was scalded by a jilted girlfriend who doused him with a boiling pot of grits and then killed herself. In later interviews, Green claims he had already converted, receiving a revelation in his hotel room following a concert.

Working religious themes into later hits such as "L-O-V-E" (1975) and "Full of Fire" (1975), Green began spreading the gospel on stage. After fulfilling all of his contractual obligations, Green redirected his energies to God. Ordained in December 1976, the Reverend Al Green opened the Full Gospel Tabernacle Church in Memphis.

Parting with producer Willie Mitchell, Green's *THE BELLE ALBUM* (1977) consisted mostly of religious material. From the album, his dramatic recording "Belle" (1977) was an autobiographical account of his personal struggles between God and earthly temptation.

Severely injuring himself in a fall from a Cincinnati stage in 1979, Green spent 15 days in a hospital. Reading it as a sign from God, he stopped straddling the world of pop and gospel music and no longer performed his R&B hits.

Returning to the studio in 1980, Green recorded the first of several gospel albums, beginning with *THE LORD WILL MAKE A WAY*. Though failing to win any Grammys for his earlier R&B material, Green earned a number of awards for his gospel releases.

In 1982, Green joined Patti LaBelle in a Broadway production of *Your Arm's Too Short to Box With God*. But Green continued to disappoint some fans, refusing to incorporate some of his sensual R&B classics. Compromising, Green eventually worked in a medley of his hits.

From the film soundtrack *SCROOGED*, Green scored a surprise pop hit with his cover of the Jackie DeShannon's "Put a Little Love in Your Heart" (1988) in a duet with Annie Lennox. From the album *RHYTHM, COUNTRY & BLUES*, in 1995 Green won a Grammy for "Funny How Time Slips Away," a duet with country singer Lyle Lovett. Just short of his 50th birthday, Green recorded his first pop album in 18 years, *YOUR HEART'S IN GOOD HANDS*.

Bibliography

Hill, Dave. (1993, October 9). Portrait: Minister for love. *Guardian*, Weekend sect., p. 16.

Hoerburger, Rob. (1986, March 27). The gospel according to Al. *Rolling Stone*, p. 27.

Light, Alan. (1996, June-July). Love and happiness. *Vibe*, p. 96.

Nager, Larry. (1995, November 4). With his whole soul now. *(Memphis) Commercial Appeal*, p. 1C.

Palmer, Robert. (1983, July 27). Al Green at his peak with gospels. *New York Times*, p. C18.

Schoemer, Karen. (1995, November 13). Praise be to Al Green. *Newsweek*, p. 82.

Willman, Chris. (1995, December 1). Al Green: 18 years after going gospel, the reverend is singing "baby" again; Can he get an amen? *Entertainment Weekly*, p. 32.

WOODY GUTHRIE. *(Woodrow Wilson Guthrie; July 14, 1912 - October 3, 1967). Inducted in the Early Influence category in 1988*. The father of American folk music, Woody Guthrie inspired Pete Seeger, Bob Dylan, Joan Baez, and others to embrace the power of protest songs.

Born into a middle class family in the oil-boom community of Okeman, Oklahoma, two years after the territory was opened to settlers, Guthrie suffered much personal tragedy in his youth: his father lost his business; his sister burned to death; and his mother was committed to an insane asylum.

After passing through the homes of relatives, Guthrie quit high school, traveling through the Dust Bowl region in empty railcars. Working odd jobs and earning tips by playing a harmonica, Guthrie witnessed the hardships of America's unemployed.

Moving to Pampa, Texas, at age 17, Guthrie rejoined his father who was running a rooming house. Working at a general store, Guthrie found an old guitar in the back room and was taught to play by an uncle.

After marrying the first of his three wives, a restless Guthrie preferred the vagabond's life and drifted around the region. In awe of the ravages of the Depression, in 1935 Guthrie was inspired to write his first of many "Dust Bowl" ballads, "Talkin' Dust Bowl."

With California holding promise for shelter from cold winters, in 1936 Guthrie left his family to join his cousin, Jack Guthrie. Drawn to the migrant camps, Guthrie became a political balladeer, attracting the attention of left-wing radio station KFVD in Los Angeles. Landing a daily program, *The Woody and Lefty Lou Show*, Guthrie pitched his mimeographed songbook, selling thousands of copies. Discovered by Communist writer Mike Quinn, Guthrie was introduced to actor Will Geer, who became his financial backer.

In an era when capitalism was seen by some as a failed system, Guthrie was viewed as a populist hero. In reaction to Irving Berlin's patriotic "God Bless America," in 1940 Guthrie composed his best-known song, the then-radical "This Land is Your Land."

Rejecting governmental laws and regulations, Guthrie often refused to copyright his material. An amateur musicologist, Guthrie collected hundreds of American folk songs, reworking them as his own with new lyrics.

Moving to New York City in 1940 with Geer's aid, Guthrie landed a well-paying local radio show (sponsored by a tobacco company), quitting after he was barred from performing his more political material. Also in 1940, Guthrie was recorded by John A. Lomax for the Library of Congress and by Victor Records, which released the 12-record set *DUST BOWL BALLADS*, highlighted by the track, "Tom Joad." Commissioned in 1941 by the Bonneville Power Administration to write songs about a pair of dams, Guthrie composed "Roll on Columbia" and his last Dust Bowl ballad, "Pastures of Plenty" (which borrowed the melody of Leadbelly's "Goodnight Irene").

In the spring of 1941, Guthrie joined his protégé, Pete Seeger, and Millard Lampell in the Almanac Singers. With Guthrie's guitar emblazoned with the message "this machine kills fascists," the group performed at Communist meetings and folk-music concerts called "hootenannies." Funded by unions, the Almanac Singers took their protest songs to worker rallies, with Guthrie commissioned to write labor rally songs like "Union Maid" and "Which Side Are You On?" The Almanac Singers best-known songs are the Guthrie-penned "Reuben James," "Pretty Boy Floyd," and "So Long, It's Been Good to Know You." Guthrie also spread his politics in Communist newspapers such as The *Daily Worker*. Calling it his "autobiographical novel," he wrote *Bound for Glory*.

Joining the U.S. Merchant Marine in 1943, he was nearly killed in battle. But displaying signs of Huntington's chorea, a neurological disease he inherited from his mother, Guthrie's behavior become erratic.

After the war, Guthrie moved to Brooklyn and recorded extensively for Folkways Records, his last releases targeted toward school children. Leaving his second wife in 1952, Guthrie left his second wife, hitchhiking back to California. With his mental state worsening, he was institutionalized in 1956.

In the early 1960s, Bob Dylan moved to New York to be close to the bedridden Guthrie. Adopting Guthrie's nasally singing style, Dylan rarely sang in his natural voice.

Guthrie died in 1967, leaving a treasure of folk standards. According to Pete Seeger, Guthrie wrote over a thousand songs in his lifetime. The 1976 Guthrie film biography, *Bound for Glory*, starred David Carradine in the title role. Guthrie's eldest child, Arlo Guthrie, followed his father into music, scoring his biggest hits with "Alice's Restaurant" and a cover of the Steve Goodman standard, "City of New Orleans."

Bibliography

Alvarez, Rafael. (1995, May 3). Preserving Woody's legacy. *The Baltimore Sun*, p. 19A.

Bishop, Stephen. (1996). *Songs in the Rough*. New York: St. Martin's.

Gardner, Fred. (1975, December). Woody approve? *Crawdaddy*, p. 77.

Grissim, John. (1975, November 20). Woody Guthrie on film: Bound for glory again. *Rolling Stone*, p. 20.

Hampton, Wayne. (1986). *Guerrilla Minstrels* (pp. 93-148). Knoxville: The University of Tennessee Press.

Perrusquia, Marc. (1991, July 11). Red menace?: Woody Guthrie's Communist ties still cause friction in his hometown. *Chicago Tribune*, p. 10D.

Settle, Mary Lee. (1980, December 7). This land was his land. *New York Times*, sect. 7, p. 3.

BILL HALEY. *(William John Clifton Haley Jr.; July 6, 1925 - February 9, 1981). Inducted in 1986.* Called the father of rock and roll, Bill Haley successfully merged country and western with rhythm and blues to create rock and roll. Born in Highland Park, Michigan, Haley was raised in a musical atmosphere, given piano lessons by his British-born mother. Blinded in one eye after a botched operation, Bill Haley became painfully introverted.

Moving to Chester, Pennsylvania, young Haley was drawn to singing matinee-cowboys. Receiving a used guitar at age 13, Haley was taught to play by his Kentucky-born father.

After dropping out of school, 17-year-old Haley landed a singing job at a large, local farmer's market. Outfitted in a frilly cowboy suit, he drew large crowds with Gene Autry imitations. Taking the moniker Silver Yodeling Bill, he then joined evangelist-turned-hillbilly music bandleader Cousin Lee.

His star on the ascent, in 1943 Haley temporarily filled as the yodeler in the Downhomers, a popular hillbilly group with their own national radio program. Rejoining the Downhomers in 1945, Haley appeared on a pair of their records the following year.

Bill Haley and His Comets. (*Photo courtesy of MCA/Universal Music Group.*)

Forming his own all-string band, the Range Drifters, Haley landed a spot on WLS/Chicago's *National Barn Dance* touring company. Discovering jazz and blues at stops in St. Louis and New Orleans, Haley fell in love with black musical styles.

Disbanding his group, in 1947 Haley worked as a radio deejay. Appointed music director at a new station WPWA in Chester, Pennsylvania, Haley talked the owner into adopting an unconventional mix of formats, including a jazz and R&B program.

Performing on the air with his new group, the Four Aces of Western Swing, Haley's nontraditional country-western band occasionally featured an electric guitarist. Recording several singles for Cowboy Records in 1948, the group sold few records. After breaking his playing hand in a juke joint, Haley disbanded the group.

Forming the Saddlemen in 1950, Haley recorded for several labels, including

Atlantic and Keystone. Performing in a self-described "cowboy jive" style, the Saddlemen secured a long residency at a New Jersey nightclub, playing a hybrid of black and country styles. Breaking ranks with his country contemporaries, Haley added a saxophone player and drummer, with younger audiences responding to the hard, fast, danceable beat.

Bill Haley and the Saddlemen's first rock-styled record came in 1951 with a cover of Jackie Brenston's "Rocket 88." A regional hit, the renamed Bill Haley & the Comets subsequently dropped their cowboy attire and hillbilly sound. Signing with Essex Records, the group scored a string of national hits, including "Crazy, Man, Crazy" (1953), "Fractured" (1953), and "Live It Up" (1953).

Aided by songwriter/publisher Jim Meyers, Haley signed a lucrative contract with Decca Records in 1954. Landing the talented Milt Gabler as his producer, Haley recording the Meyers-penned "(We're Gonna) Rock Around the Clock," the song was patterned by Gabler after the saxophone-heavy, pre-R&B sound of jump-blues legend Louis Jordan. With "Rock around the Clock" only a moderate hit, Haley followed up with a lyrically sanitized cover version hit of Big Joe Turner's, "Shake, Rattle And Roll" (1954).

But with the prominent placement of "Rock around the Clock" in the opening credits of the film *The Blackboard Jungle*, the single was re-released. As the first rock and roll single to top the pop charts, the song launched the rock era. Starring Glenn Ford, *The Blackboard Jungle* captured the social flux and urban decay of postwar America, while blaming juvenile delinquents and their rock music. With the success of *The Blackboard Jungle*, Haley starred in his own film, the appropriately titled, *Rock around the Clock*.

Overnight, rock and roll got a black eye, and Bill Haley became its first superstar. But with a cowlick curl dangling over his forehead, Haley possessed little of the rebelliousness or raw sexuality of rockers like Elvis Presley. In late 1955, three of the seven Comets quit over a salary dispute, leaving to form the Jodimars.

Haley scored a string of rockabilly-inflected hits in the 1950s, including "Razzle-Dazzle" (1955); "Burn That Candle" (1955); "See You Later Alligator" (1956); "R-O-C-K" (1956); a cover of Little Richard's "Rip It Up" (1956); and featuring the blistering sax of Rudy Pompilli, "Rudy's Rock" (1956). Haley's last top-40 hit came in 1958 with "Skinny Minny."

Like many early American rock acts, Haley had greater success in England, where at a 1957 concert overzealous fans went berserk in a melee of mass destruction. With the event captured on film, Haley received much negative press.

Desperate for cash after a series of poor investments, Haley signed with Warner Brothers in 1959. In trouble with the I.R.S., Haley moved to Mexico, occasionally sneaking into the U.S. for an occasional concert date. Recording in Mexico, Germany and Sweden, little of his new material reached the U.S.

After paying his I.R.S. bill in 1971, Haley became a regular on the oldies circuit. Returning to the U.S. in 1973, Haley settled in Harlington, Texas.

In 1973, Haley's "Rock Around The Clock" was used as the theme song for a sitcom set in the 1950s, *Happy Days*. Re-released the following year, the song landed in the top-20, relaunching Haley's career.

Devastated by death in 1976 of his longtime saxophone player Rudy Pompilli, Haley left music for some time. Recording his last album in 1979, Haley's final performance came a year later in South America. Suffering from a reported brain tumor, in 1981 Haley died of a heart attack.

Bibliography

Scott, Colin, (1991, April 19). Bill Haley: Indisputably—the first. *Goldmine*, p. 12.

Flippo, Chet. (1981, March 19). Bill Haley. *Rolling Stone*, p. 76.

Haertel, Joe. (1995, March 19). Rock's "Clock" turns 40: On a spring day in 1955, *Blackboard Jungle* changed the times. *Washington Post*, p. C5.

Haley, John W. & von Hoelle, John. (1990). *Sound and Glory*. Wilmington, DE: Dyne-American.

Mennie, Don. (1986, February-March). "Rock around the Clock" composer recalls Bill Haley's early days. *Record Collector's Monthly*, p. 5.

JOHN HAMMOND. *(John Henry Hammond Sr.; December 15, 1910 - July 10, 1987). Inducted in the Non-Performer category in 1996.* The son of a wealthy lawyer father and a deeply religious and far richer Vanderbilt-heir mother, John Hammond was raised in a New York City mansion. Receiving piano lessons at age four, he later switched to the viola. But Hammond was more interested in "lowbrow" entertainment, first sneaking into a bawdy "Negro review" at age 11.

Discovering the world of live jazz, Hammond recalled in his autobiography, "I went to every theater and club in Harlem and was usually the only white person there. I would order lemonade while I listened, and I'm sure that people thought I was crazy, for these were Prohibition years and in Harlem, as everywhere else, lemonade was legal and therefore unfit to drink" (p. 46). While Hammond's parents owned a large music library of classical and opera records, he preferred the jazz records played on the phonographs in the black servant quarters.

At age 18 in 1929, Hammond donned his lifelong trademark crewcut (then quite unpopular), and landed a summer job at a liberal Maine newspaper. Later a music journalist, he wrote for *The Gramophone*, *Melody Maker* and became *Downbeat's* first columnist.

Dropping out of Yale after two years, 21-year-old Hammond moved to Greenwich Village, living off a $12,000 trust fund. After sponsoring the Columbia recordings of jazz pianist Garland Wilson during the Depression, two years later he was hired by the British arm of the label as an independent producer.

Discovering a number of acts during East Coast excursions, Hammond produced the finest in jazz, recording Billie Holiday, Teddy Wilson, Lionel Hampton, and Benny Goodman. When CBS bought Columbia, new president Ted Wallerstein assigned Hammond to the popular-music division.

Hammond's notoriety increased with a pair of concerts held in 1938 and 1939. Staged at Carnegie Hall, the "From Spirituals to Swing" revues marked the first time the prominent venue permitted integrated black and white audiences. The concerts introduced to white America a wide spectrum of performers already popular in the black community Big Bill Broonzy, Sonny Terry, Big Joe Turner, Pete Johnson, and

Sister Rosetta Tharpe to white America. The only white act, Benny Goodman (the first white bandleader to hire a black musician), appeared at the second concert.

A social outcast all his life, Hammond was ostracized for defending the causes of Blacks and Jews. Fighting for civil rights, he joined the NAACP board of Directors in 1935, helping the organization raise money for the legal defense of the Scottsboro Boys (which he also covered as a reporter for *The Nation*). Writes author Alan Pomerance, "Along the dark streets and alleys, the word had gone out, silently, casually, but with the same mysterious thoroughness of jungle drumming—'Don't touch this kid. Don't lean on him. Maybe keep an eye out to see he's OK. Tell the brothers he's cool. . . . Let him stay in one piece. He's got a lot of soul'" (p. 19). In the early 1940s, Hammond pressured both CBS and NBC radio networks to hire black musicians.

Drafted in 1943, Hammond was stationed at Fort Belvoir in Virginia. Learning the camp offered no entertainment, he convinced his commanders to permit concerts as a means of maintaining morale. Hammond brought Count Basic, who was forced to play two shows: one for blacks, the other for whites. Transferred to Camp Blanche in New Orleans, Hammond was appointed the liaison for the black troops and managed to break the color barrier at concerts and intramural sporting events.

Discharged in 1945, Hammond worked for Keynote, Majestic, and then Mercury Records, where he hired Mitch Miller as the A&R chief. Returning to CBS in 1959, Hammond quickly made a name for himself with a generation of rock fans.

Discovering Aretha Franklin, Hammond was unhappy with the label's decision to overproduce her recording sessions. Hammond's signing of blacklisted folksinger Pete Seeger in 1959, brought his protégé Bob Dylan to the label two years later.

Losing Franklin to Atlantic Records, in 1965 Hammond signed George Benson, and in 1972, Bruce Springsteen. Retiring from CBS in 1975 Hammond turned to independent production. He was later instrumental in the career of Stevie Ray Vaughan, whom he brought to CBS/Epic in 1983.

Hammond died of natural causes in 1987 while listening to a Billie Holiday record. Hammond's son, John Paul Hammond, is a blues guitarist.

Bibliography

Goldberg, Michael. (1987, August 27). John Hammond 1910-1987. *Rolling Stone*, p. 23.

Hammond, John & Townsend, Irving. (1977). *John Hammond on Record: An Autobiography*. New York: Ridge/Summit.

Pomerance, Alan. (1988). *Repeal of the Blues: How Black Entertainers Influenced Civil Rights*. Secaucus, NJ: Citadel.

Skelly, Richard. (1990, September 7). John Hammond: An American original. *Goldmine*, p. 11.

Tiegel, Eliot. (1978, January 7). Hammond: Still seeking talent. *Billboard*, p. 6.

West, Hollie I. (1977, November 14). A life in jazz, John Hammond. *The Washington Post*, p. C1.

W.C. HANDY. *(William Christopher Handy; November 16, 1873 - March 29, 1938). Inducted in the Early Influence category in 1996.* Called "the Father of the Blues," W.C. Handy was instrumental in taking blues music into the mainstream. Born in Florence, Alabama, Handy was raised in a log cabin with a dirt floor. Both of Handy's parents were freed slaves, his father a pastor.

As a child, Handy was impressed by the trumpet player at his Baptist church. Too poor to buy a musical instrument, Handy built himself a primitive guitar.

Saving his meager earnings from selling fruit, nuts, and home-made soap, Handy bought a guitar. Forced by his horrified parents to return the "devil's instrument," Handy traded the guitar for a dictionary. When his parents insisted he learn to play "sacred" music, Handy instead took organ lessons.

Inspired by a local bandleader named Jim Turner, Handy secretly purchased a cornet, later joining the group. Assembling a vocal quartet at age 15, Handy enlisted with a small minstrel troupe. With the troupe going bankrupt, Handy was abandoned far from home.

After graduating from Huntsville Teachers Agricultural and Mechanical College in 1892, Handy refused to accept a low-paying teaching job. After a taking a steel mill job, he quit to form a vocal group, the Lauzetta Quartet. The group disbanded after reaching St. Louis, then a hub for such groups. Handy's original destination had been the 1892 Columbian Exposition in Chicago, which had been delayed a year. Destitute and without employment, Handy nearly starved.

Moving to Kentucky, Handy took menial jobs before returning to his career in music. As a janitor of a German singing society, he received informal musical training from the director, an accomplished music professor.

Now playing trumpet, Handy joined the popular, all-black touring revue, the W.A. Mahara's Minstrels. Emerging as the bandleader and music director, Handy toured with the company from 1896 to 1900 and from 1902 to 1903. In the interim, he taught college music courses at his alma mater.

Turning down an offer to lead an all-white band in Michigan, Handy instead formed a nine-piece orchestra in the Delta town of Clarksdale, Mississippi. Performing in a variety of styles, Handy would play jazz, classical, and popular tunes.

But an experience in a Mississippi town in 1903 altered Handy's destiny. Startled by the wailings of a solitary blues musician at a train station, Handy wrote in his autobiography: "His face had on it some of the sadness of the ages. As he played, he pressed a knife on the strings of the guitar in a manner popularized by Hawaiian guitarists who used steel bars. The effect was unforgettable. His song, too, struck me instantly" (p. 74). Exposed to blues, Handy gave the music its name.

Though Handy did not invent the blues, he was instrumental in its popularity, by adding respectability to what had previously been a marginal folk genre. Offering a more commercial version of the blues, Handy incorporated Tin Pan Alley and ragtime styles within a 12-bar framework in a traditional, notational form.

Handy first performed the blues in the Beale Street taverns in Memphis (later immortalized in his composition, "Beale Street Blues"). Writing "Boss Crump's Blues" as the campaign theme for Memphis mayoral candidate Edward H. "Boss" Crump in 1909, Handy was surprised when the song became a popular hit. Cheated out of the composition for only $50, the song was renamed by the buyer as "Memphis Blues." In response, Handy formed his own music publishing company, Pace & Handy, with friend Harry A. Pace.

Reminiscing about his earlier hardships, in 1914 Handy wrote his best-known piece, the haunting "St. Louis Blues." A hit in 1921 for the Dixieland Jazz Band and for Handy's own orchestra two years later, the song is the third most recorded American song of all time. Other notable Handy compositions include "Livery Stable Blues," "Jogo Blues" (1913), "Joe Turner Blues" (1915), and "Beale Street Blues" (1917).

Tiring of the racial tensions in the South, Handy moved his publishing company to Manhattan in 1918. A thriving business, in 1920 it was renamed the Handy Brothers Music Company. Widely respected, Handy performed a classical concert at New York's Carnegie Hall in 1928. He also edited the pioneering reference book *Blues: An Anthology*, and in 1940, he published his autobiography, *Father of the Blues*.

Fracturing his skill in a subway accident in 1943, Handy was left blind and wheelchair-bound. After witnessing the rise of blues during his lifetime, Handy died in 1958 of bronchial pneumonia. That year, Nat King Cole portrayed the role of the Handy in the film biography, *St. Louis Blues*. Inaugurated in 1980, the annual Handy Blues Awards honor the best performers in the field.

Bibliography
Ewen, David. (1970). *Great Men of American Popular Song* (pp. 116-22). Englewood Cliffs, NJ: Prentice-Hall.
Handy, W.C. (1941). *Father of the Blues*. New York: Macmillan.
Niese, Jay. (1995, January 24). The music goes 'round and 'round. *St. Louis Post-Dispatch*, p. 1D.

THE JIMI HENDRIX EXPERIENCE. *Jimi Hendrix (Johnny Allen Hendrix; later, James Albert Hendrix; November 27, 1942 - September 18, 1970); Mitch Mitchell (John Mitchell; July 9, 1946); Noel Redding (December 25, 1945). Inducted in 1992.* Innovative heavy metal guitarist who expanded rock music's limits, Jimi Hendrix forever fused the relationship between rock music and the electric guitar.

Born in Seattle, Hendrix was raised by his authoritarian, hard working father. After toying with a ukulele and harmonica, Hendrix was given a five-dollar acoustic guitar. Left-handed, Hendrix learned to play restringed right-handed guitars, upside down. Listening to Muddy Waters and other blues masters, Hendrix was self-taught, never learning to read music.

Switching to an electric guitar, Hendrix formed the Rocking Kings in 1959, playing teen dances and fairs throughout Washington. Quitting high school the following year, Hendrix emerged as the lead guitarist for the renamed Thomas and the Tomcats.

With his father's written permission, the underage Hendrix enlisted in the army. Stationed at Fort Campbell, Kentucky, as part of the 101st Airborne Division, he was discharged 26 months later after a parachuting accident. Joining a fellow soldier, bassist Billy Cox, Hendrix formed the King Kasuals, performing in the Memphis blues circuit. Under the tutelage of promoter "Gorgeous" George Odell, Hendrix spent the next several years touring as a backing guitarist for Solomon Burke, Sam Cooke, and Jackie Wilson.

Moving to New York City in 1964, Hendrix found session work behind the Isley Brothers, providing guitar work on their single "Testify" (1964). Returning to Memphis and calling himself Maurice James, Hendrix hooked up with Little Richard but was fired by his boss for stealing some of the limelight with his guitar prowess.

Returning to New York in late 1965, Hendrix joined the Knights, an R&B group led by Jimmy Knight. When the group made its first recordings, Hendrix signed an unfavorable contract that would forever haunt him. Hired away by bandleader King Curtis, Hendrix became the second guitarist for the Kingpins.

Forming his own R&B group Jimmy James & the Blue Flames, Hendrix drew rock's royalty at performances at the Club Wha? in Greenwich Village in 1966. Signing a management deal with former Animals bassist, Chas Chandler, Hendrix was taken to London. There Chandler assembled the Jimi Hendrix Experience, the trio rounded out by guitarist-turned-bassist Noel Redding and former child actor, drummer Mitch Mitchell. Hendrix would be paid 50-percent of the group's profits, with Redding and Mitchell splitting the rest.

But while Hendrix attacked the British charts in 1966 with "Purple Haze," "The Wind Cries Mary," and the Billy Roberts' arrangement of the folk standard "Hey Joe," he remained unknown back in the U.S.

At Paul McCartney's insistence, Hendrix performed at the Monterey Pop Festival in June 1967, his first significant American exposure. Dominating the show, Hendrix shocked the audience when he dropped to his knees and set his guitar on fire with lighter fluid.

With his wild, gypsy clothing, long, free-flowing hair, and an uninhibited persona, Hendrix was the definitive psychedelic rocker. An outrageous performer, Hendrix could play guitar with his tongue and behind his back. Expanding the boundaries of the electric guitar, Hendrix was innovative in his manipulation of the instrument's strings, of maximizing reverb, and employing feedback.

A strange pairing, in July 1967 Hendrix was hired by fan Mickey Dolenz of the Monkees as their opening act. A genuine farce, the disgusted Hendrix quit after the tour's seventh stop.

Releasing a pair of timeless albums in 1967, *ARE YOU EXPERIENCED?* and *AXIS BOLD AS LOVE*, the standard for rock guitarists with classics such as "Are You Experienced," "Fire," and "Foxey Lady." Like its predecessors, the 1968 compilation album *SMASH HITS* landed in the top-10.

From the 1968 double-album *ELECTRIC LADYLAND*, Hendrix landed his highest-charting U.S. pop hit with an electrified cover of Bob Dylan's "All along the Watch Tower." The controversial album jacket pictured nude women. Tiring of record company politics, Chandler left his managerial post, abdicating the duties to Michael Jeffries.

After quitting in late 1968, Mitchell and Redding rejoined Hendrix in the studio in early 1969, with many of the tracks appearing on the 1970 albums *CRY OF LOVE* and *RAINBROW BRIDGE*. But when Hendrix was arrested for heroin possession during a Canadian tour in 1969, the incident tainted his reputation.

As Woodstock's highest-paid act, Hendrix awed the crowd with his distorted rendition of "The Star-Spangled Banner." Backed at the festival by Electric Sky

Church, the group included Mitchell and Cox but not Redding, who had formed his own group, Fat Mattress.

Buckling under pressure from his black critics, Hendrix hired an all-black group, the Band of Gypsys. Debuting at the Fillmore East in January 1970, the performance was captured on the album *BAND OF GYPSYS*. Featuring drummer Buddy Miles and Billy Cox, the trio lacked cohesion and was disbanded after two shows.

In July of that year, Hendrix completed his new, state-of-the-art Electric Ladyland studio. Weeks later, Hendrix died from asphyxiation following an accidental barbiturate overdose at the London apartment of girlfriend Monika Dannemann. Within hours Hendrix's New York apartment was broken into and looted.

Released in 1971, *CRY OF LOVE* was the last Hendrix-approved album. But with producer Alan Douglass controlled hundreds of hours of raw recordings, "new" Hendrix albums regularly hit store shelves throughout the 1970s, beginning with *WAR HEROES* which featured added instrumental backing by musicians who had never even met Hendrix.

Hendrix's father launched a legal battle in 1993 against his own attorney and Alan Douglass over the rights to his son's recorded output. A settlement was reached in 1995, with Hendrix regaining legal control.

Hendrix won a Lifetime Achievement Award at the 1993 Grammys. The Experience Music Project, a $50 million Seattle popular music museum centered primarily on Hendrix's career, is set to open in 1999.

Bibliography

Kiersh, Edward. (1986). *Where Are You Now, Bo Diddley?* (pp. 324-32). Garden City, NY: Doubleday.

Leiby, Richard. (1993, December 19). Who owns Jimi Hendrix? *Washington Post*, p. G1.

MacDonald, Patrick. (1990, September 18). Jimi remembered: 20 years after his death, the legendary guitarist is more popular than ever. *Seattle Times*, p. D1.

Mettler, Mike. (1995, September). Will I live tomorrow?: The Hendrix experience continues to unfold. *Guitar Player*, p. 62.

Morris, Chris. (1993, May 1). Al Hendrix suit lays claim to son Jimi's legacy. *Billboard*, p. 10.

Obrecht, Jas. (1995, September). Billy Cox: "Jimi was a blues master." *Guitar Player*, p. 79.

Redding, Noel & Appleby, Carol. (1986, September). Bad Trips: The end of the Jimi Hendrix Experience. *Musician*, p. 88.

Sexton, Paul. (1992, November 28), Jimi at 50: Gone but still a star. *Billboard*, p. 1.

Shapiro, Harry & Glebbeek, Caesar. (1990). *Jimi Hendrix: Electric Gypsy*. New York: St. Martin's.

HOLLAND-DOZIER-HOLLAND. *Brian Holland (February 15, 1941); Lamont Dozier (June 16, 1941); Eddie Holland (October 30, 1939). Inducted in the Non-Performer category in 1990.* A trio of Detroit natives, the songwriting team of Holland-Dozier-Holland (H-D-H) was an integral cog in Berry Gordy's Motown hit factory in the 1960s.

A former member of the Romeos, Lamont Dozier sang with future Temptations member David Ruffin in the Voice Masters, joining Motown's predecessor, Anna

Records, in 1959. Recording as Lamont Anthony at Motown in the early 1960s, he had little success.

Similarly, Eddie Holland had recorded for Mercury in 1958, before joining Motown a year later. After a stint with United Artists, Holland returned to Motown, scoring a minor hit in 1962 with the Gordy composition, "Jamie." But suffering from stagefright, Holland switched to songwriting, a more lucrative and less grueling vocation.

Eddie's younger brother, Brian Holland, was a teenage friend of Gordy, originally hired by Motown as a sound engineer. Turning to songwriting in 1961, Holland co-wrote the Marvelettes' hits "Please Mr. Postman," "Twistin' Postman," and "Playboy." Teaming with Lamont Dozier, the pair composed the Marvelettes' hit "Someday, Someway" (1962).

Discouraged by his stalled singing career, Eddie Holland joined his brother in the trio that was dubbed Holland-Dozier-Holland. Recorded by Dozier, the trio's first composition, "Dearest One" (1962), bombed.

With Lamont Dozier emerging as the leader, the trio scored several collaborative hits in 1963, beginning with the Marvelettes' "Locking Up My Heart." Writing the Miracles' smash hit "Mickey's Monkey," the song also spawned a huge dance craze. Also that year, the Supremes landed their first hit with a H-D-H composition "When the Lovelight Starts Shining Through."

Following a successful formula, a song idea usually began with Lamont Dozier and Brian Holland. After Lamont toyed at the piano to come up with a riff, Brian wrote the arrangements and chord patterns. Eddie then added the final touches, writing most of the lyrics; he also recorded the final product, singing the demo versions for the artists and musicians to learn. Under constant pressure from Gordy to deliver hits, the trio was granted an autonomy not given to other Motown employees.

Barely in their 20s, the team of H-D-H, "with their well-coifed processed hair, their Blye knits . . . had a real insight into the taste of the buying public. They may not have been versed in Miles [Davis] and [Thelonious] Monk or very proficient instrumentalists, but they did possess an innate gift for melody, a feel for story song lyrics, and an ability to create the recurring vocal and instrumental lines known as 'hooks'" (p. 116), writes Nelson George in his history of Motown. Still, the trio was limited by their lack of musical training and received a good deal of assistance from the skilled Motown house band.

Wanting hits, Motown acts fought over H-D-H compositions. Most H-D-H songs went to the Supremes and the Four Tops, with the latter receiving the more complex material, including, "Reach Out I'll Be There" and "I Can't Help Myself." After reluctantly recording "Where Did Our Love Go?" the Supremes learned their lesson, burning up the charts in the mid-1960s with the H-D-H numbers "Baby Love," "You Can't Hurry Love," "You Keep Me Hanging On," and others. For Martha & the Vandellas, H-D-H wrote "Heat Wave" and "Jimmy Mack."

H-D-H found many sources for their compositions. Recalls Motown historian Sharon Davis: "The Four Tops' 'Bernadette' was born from Dozier's teenage love for a girl; The Supremes 'Stop! In the Name of Love' was an expression used by another girlfriend, and Martha and the Vandellas' 'Jimmy Mack'" was about a songwriter who had died after writing a hit song (p. 191).

Unhappy with his salary, Dozier demanded a share of the publishing royalties from Motown. With the trio's contract set to expire, in 1968 Motown sued H-D-H for several million dollars, with the trio countersuing for $22 million. Without H-D-H material, many Motown acts suffered, with the Four Tops especially wounded.

With their lawsuits unresolved, H-D-H were barred from working with other labels. They instead launched their own record companies, Invictus and Hot Wax, landing hits with "Band of Gold" by Freda Payne and "Want Ads" by the Honey Cone. Dozier also scored a solo R&B hit with "Why Can't We Be Lovers" (1972), and recorded a few singles with Brian Holland in 1973. Wanting to break their legal partnership in 1972, Dozier was unsuccessfully sued by the Holland Brothers.

In 1987, the trio received an overdue Lifetime Achievement Award from the American National Academy of Songwriters. The following year, Dozier co-wrote the Grammy-winning single "Two Hearts" with Phil Collins and penned material for Eric Clapton in 1997. Remarkably, H-D-H never won a Grammy during their period with Motown. The trio's lawsuit against Motown has lingered into the late 1990s.

Bibliography

Davis, Sharon. (1988). *Motown: The History*. London: Guinness.

George, Nelson. (1985). *Where Did Our Love Go?: The Rise & Fall of the Motown Sound*. New York: St. Martin's Press.

Grein, Paul. (1987, November 20). Motown songwriting trio will be honored for cranking out the hits. *Los Angeles Times*, Calendar sect., p. 1.

Snook, Debbi. (1995, July 16). That Motown magic: The people, hits that launched a revolution in black music. *Cleveland Plain Dealer*, p. 1J.

Taraborrelli, J. Randy. (1986). *Motown: Hot Wax, City Cool & Solid Gold*. New York: Dolphin/Doubleday.

White, Mark. (1985). *You Must Remember This: Popular Songwriters 1900-1980* (pp. 111-13). New York: Charles Scribner's Sons.

BUDDY HOLLY. *(Charles Hardin Holley; September 7, 1936 - February 3, 1959)*. *Inducted in 1986*. Inspiring thousands of budding guitarists to jump into rock and roll, Buddy Holly democratized the music, proving that nerdy guys could become rock stars. Holly also pioneered the self-contained rock band with the rhythm guitar, lead guitar bass and drums combination.

Raised in Lubbock, Texas, Holly took piano lessons at age 11 before switching to the guitar. Drawn to country music, Holly's first musical influence was the Grand Ole Opry.

In junior high, Holly teamed with guitarist Bob Montgomery in the country and bluegrass duo Buddy & Bob. Regulars on a local radio talent show on KDAV in 1953, the duo began adding elements of rockabilly. Adding a bassist, the popular trio began performing around western Texas. During this period, Holly learned to play both the rhythm and lead parts on the same guitar.

When Bill Haley's backing band failed to show for a KDAV-sponsored concert, Holly and his group were last-minute substitutes. Spotted by Nashville music agent Eddie Crandall, he contacted talent scout Jim Denny, who signed Holly and his then-

Buddy Holly and the Crickets. (*Courtesy of John M. Riley, from private collection.*)

backing group, the Three Tunes, to Haley's label, Decca Records. After recording a pair of unsuccessful singles at Decca's Nashville studios in 1956, Holly was temporarily dropped from the Decca roster.

Returning to Texas, Holly formed his more famous backing band, the Crickets, retaining drummer Jerry Allison and adding Niki Sullivan on rhythm guitar and Joe B. Maudlin on bass. Traveling to Clovis, New Mexico, in early 1957, Holly began a rewarding relationship with independent producer Norman Petty. Petty had built the small recording studio in his home after scoring two national hits with his own trio.

Pioneering the notion of the recording artist as his own producer, Holly was freed from the strict demands that had shackled him at his Decca sessions. Issuing a new version of "That'll Be the Day" on Brunswick Records (ironically, a subsidiary of

Decca), the single far surpassed the overly produced, earlier Decca record. Topping the pop charts, the million-seller propelled Holly into the national spotlight.

Hiring Petty as their manager, the group set out on an East Coast tour, booked unseen, as a rhythm and blues group at the Apollo Theater in Harlem. At first heckled by the all-black audience, Holly's Crickets were warmly received after adding Bo Diddley material to their set.

In an effort to increase the group's exposure, a number of Crickets records were marketed as Holly solo releases on another Decca subsidiary, Coral. A second hit, "Peggy Sue" (originally titled "Cindy Lou" after Holly's niece but renamed after Jerry Allison's girlfriend, Peggy Sue Gerron), landed Holly and the Crickets on *The Ed Sullivan Show*. A follow-up release, "Oh, Boy," featured "Not Fade Away" on the flip side, a Holly composition that was intended for the Everly Brothers (on the latter song, Jerry Allison played percussion on a cardboard box). Niki Sullivan left the Crickets at the end of 1957.

Along with the pioneering rock guitarists Bo Diddley and Chuck Berry, Holly altered the role of the guitar in rock music, moving the instrument to the forefront. With his black-rimmed glasses, skinny tie, and contorted, hiccuping vocals, Holly was an unlikely rock star. Lacking the guttural sexuality of an Elvis Presley, Holly thrived on charm and an unyielding confidence.

In mid-1958, Holly met his future wife, Puerto Rican-born Maria Elena Santiago, at a New York publishing house. In a socially conservative America, the marriage caused Holly personal and career strains. At the urging of his wife, Holly moved to New York, severing his relationship with Petty and abdicating his rights to the Crickets name.

As a solo act, Holly had limited solo success, scoring hits with "Early in the Morning" (1958) and the posthumously released, "True Love Ways" (1959). On his last few sessions, Holly was forced by his New York producer, Dick Jacobs, to employ a large string section.

Holly's career, like those of many rockabilly artists, had nose-dived in the late 1950s. Financially strapped, he agreed to join the Winter Dance Party, joining the Big Bopper and headliner Ritchie Valens. Although the Crickets were yearning to rejoin their former leader, Holly put together a new band with Tommy Allsup on guitar, Carl Bunch on drums, and a young Waylon Jennings on bass.

Wanting to escape a freezing tour bus, Holly chartered an airplane. All aboard were killed when 21-year-old newlywed pilot Roger Peterson experienced vertigo and flew the craft into the ground during a blinding snowstorm, crashing at the edge of a cornfield near Mason City, Iowa.

Though soon forgotten in the U.S., Holly continued with a remarkable string of top-40 hits in England. Influencing rock music well after his death, Holly spawned imitators like Tommy Roe and Bobby Vee, while Roy Orbison and Elvis Costello adopted Holly-like black-rimmed glasses. Meanwhile, Norman Petty reworked Holly's early apartment tapes, adding new backing tracks by the Fireballs, posthumously releasing the material on several albums.

In a tribute to Holly, Don McLean's 1971 smash hit "American Pie," lamented the day the music died. A biographical film *The Buddy Holly Story* (1978) featured Gary

Busey in the title role.

A 1995 tribute album, *NOTFADEAWAY: REMEMBERING BUDDY HOLLY*, was highlighted by a simulated duet of "Peggy Sue Got Married" by Buddy Holly and the Hollies.

Bibliography

Aquila, Richard. (1982, Spring). "Not Fade Away": Buddy Holly and the making of an American legend. *Journal of Popular Culture*, p. 75.
Cartwright, Gary. (1995, October). Ravin on. *Texas Monthly*, p. 112.
Doggett, Peter. (1984, April). Buddy Holly. *Record Collector*, p. 3.
Doggett, Peter. (1989, February). Buddy Holly: 1936-1959. *Record Collector*, p. 37.
Draper, Robert. (1995, October). The real Buddy Holly. *Texas Monthly*, p. 108.
Flippo, Chet. (1978, September 21). The Buddy Holly story. *Rolling Stone*, p. 49.
Griggs, Bill. (1984, August 31). Niki Sullivan: The forgotten Cricket remembers. *Goldmine*, p. 6.

JOHN LEE HOOKER. *(August 22, 1917)*. *Inducted in 1991*. A legendary figure in the old-school, Delta-styled blues, John Lee Hooker was the genre's last star. Raised in a sharecropping family in Clarksdale, Mississippi, Hooker was enthralled with his new stepfather's guitar work. In an interview with Craig Harris, Hooker later described what he heard as "a very sad music—very lonesome, deep, and blue" (p. 81). After trying to copy his stepfather on a crude, homemade instrument, Hooker was given a mail-order guitar.

Hating farm life and drawn to the city, Hooker left home at age 14, entering the army by lying about his age. Stationed in Detroit, he was discharged after three months. Landing in Memphis in 1931, Hooker spent two years playing with Robert Nighthawk and others. Moving to Cincinnati in 1933, Hooker worked as a theater usher, and joined several gospel groups, including the Fairfield Four.

Returning to Detroit in 1943, Hooker worked as a janitor at a Ford plant. With the help a record store owner, Hooker spent months working on a marketable demo disc, hoping to land a recording contract.

Attracting the interest of record distributor Bernie Besman, the unknown, 30-year-old Hooker became an unlikely blues star. Near the end of an unproductive session, Besman suggested that Hooker substitute an electrically amplified guitar for his acoustic model. Recording without a backing band, Hooker stomped on a board for percussion. Unable to record an acceptable take of the intended A-side, "Sally Mae," the producer asked Hooker to sing something else as a diversion. With the B-Side garnering radio airplay, the improvised "Boogie Chillen" gave Hooker his first hit, becoming one of the most influential modern blues songs of all time. The song was a link between the old, country-blues style of Delta field-workers and the modern, electrified music of northern, citified blacks. Hooker's nimble, fast-paced playing style contrasted with his drowsy, smokey, and distant persona.

Forming his own band, Hooker unleashed a string of blues hits including "Hobo Blues" (1949), "Crawling King Snake Blues" (1949), and an unlikely million-selling, pop-crossover hit, "I'm in the Mood" (1950). Unhappy with the terms of his Modern

Records contract, Hooker recorded at various labels under dozens of pseudonyms, including Texas Slim, Johnny Williams, and John Lee Booker.

Moving to Vee-Jay Records in 1955, Hooker performed with a full band, which included guitarist Eddie Taylor. With the waning popularity of blues in the U.S. in the late 1950s, Hooker retreated to Europe, which was just discovering Delta-style blues.

Adopting a pared-down sound upon his return to the U.S., in 1962 Hooker scored his second crossover hit with the retro-styled "Boom Boom." Performing at the Newport Folk Festival that same year, Hooker's stature in the blues world was solidified.

Hooker recorded his last album for Vee-Jay in 1964, just as the Animals landed a blues-rock hit cover of "Boom Boom." With the rise of the British Invasion, Hooker was rediscovered by white, college-aged audiences. Moving to San Francisco, in 1971 Hooker collaborated with the white, blues-rock band Canned Heat on the album *HOOKER 'N' HEAT*.

Hooker spent the next two decades touring the U.S. and Europe. His 1989 album, *THE HEALER*, featured duet recordings with many of his musical progeny, including Robert Cray, George Thorogood, and Bonnie Raitt, whose rendition of "I'm in the Mood" earned a Grammy.

With his newly-recorded version of "Boom Boom," in 1992 Hooker was the oldest person to score a British pop hit. Still performing in his 70s, in 1995 Hooker recorded the album *CHILL OUT*. Hooker opened a blues club in San Francisco in 1997.

Bibliography

Dawson, Jim & Propes, Steve. (1992). *What Was the First Rock 'N' Roll Record?* (pp. 42-45). Boston: Faber and Faber.

Dougherty, Steven & Mathison, Dirk. (1990, October 29). John Lee Hooker, whose boogie blues hooked a generation, is lionized by his rock admirers. *People*, p. 113.

Escott, Colin. (1992, March 20). John Lee Hooker: King of the one-chord boogie. *Goldmine*, p. 10.

Harris, Craig. (1991). *The New Folk Music*. Crown Point, IN: White Cliffs Media.

Marine, Craig. (1995, September 10). Hook shots. *San Francisco Examiner*, p. M12.

Obrecht, Jas. (1990). John Lee Hooker. In Jas Obrecht (Ed.), *Blues Guitar* (pp. 92-101). San Francisco: GPI.

Woodard, Josef. (1990, February). John Lee Hooker: Continuing saga of the boogie king. *Down Beat*, p. 20.

HOWLIN' WOLF. *(Chester Arthur Burnett; June 10, 1910 - January 10, 1976). Inducted in the Early Influence category in 1991.* Born near West Point, Mississippi, and raised on a plantation near Ruleville, Arkansas, Howlin' Wolf was reared on the blues of Charlie Patton. Just short of his 18th birthday in 1928, Howlin' Wolf was given a guitar by his father. Rarely venturing far from home, Wolf played guitar and harmonica in informal settings like street corners, fairs, and small juke joints.

Moving to Parkin, Arkansas, in 1933, Howlin' Wolf received harmonica lessons from his future brother-in-law, Sonny Boy (Rice Miller) Williamson. Introduced to blues master Robert Johnson, Howlin' Wolf acquired a large repertoire of blues songs.

Still working as a full-time farmer, Howlin' Wolf's interest in music was never more than a serious hobby. Drafted into the U.S. Army in 1941, he was stationed in Seattle, never seeing action. Discharged, he returned to farming.

Moving to West Memphis in search of better wages, he discovered a burgeoning music scene. Deciding upon a career change, he borrowed an electric guitar, formed his own group, working up an explosive stage show. Unlike most of his contemporaries, he preferred up-tempo, danceable, electric blues.

A slow-fingered guitarist and lively harmonica player, Howlin' Wolf possessed a moaning, guttural, gruff voice likened to that of a wolf. Though a large man at six feet three inches and 320 pounds, he was not an intimidating figure.

Building up a popular radio program at WKEM in the late 1940s, Howlin' Wolf attracted the attention of independent producer Sam Phillips. Recording Howlin' Wolf at his Memphis Recording Studio, Phillips would sell the masters to either RPM or Chess Records. With Howlin' Wolf sometimes recording slightly different versions of the same song, with Chess would get "Moanin' at Midnight," while RPM received the similar "Morning at Midnight."

While Chess Records threatened to sue Phillips over the practice, the label instead signed Howlin' Wolf to an exclusive contract. An infuriated Phillips soon started his own label, Sun Records. Howlin' Wolf's last recording in Memphis, "House Rockers," was named after his first band.

Selling his farm and moving to Chicago in 1952, Howlin' Wolf recorded full-time for Chess. There he was often the beneficiary of the label's workhorse, Willie Dixon, who supplied both compositions and production skills. Though wanting to record his own material, many of Howlin' Wolf's biggest hits were Dixon compositions: "Smokestack Lightning" (1956), "I Asked for Water" (1956), "Spoonful" (1960), and a double-sided entry, "Wang Dang Doodle"/"Back Door Man" (1960).

Dropping his moaning singing style and no longer playing the harmonica, Howlin' Wolf's records became more polished in the 1960s, even employing an occasional horn section. Parting with Dixon in 1964, Howlin' Wolf began recording his own compositions, including the blues standard "Killing Floor."

In 1965, Howlin' Wolf landed an unlikely teenage audience when the Rolling Stones refused to appear on the ABC music program *Shindig!* program unless their mentor was added to the bill. Wearing a dark, dapper suit and singing "How Many More Years," it was Howlin' Wolf's network television debut.

Scores of rock acts have covered Howlin' Wolf in the 1960s, including "Smokestack Lightning" by the Yardbirds; "The Red Rooster" by the Rolling Stones; and "Back Door Man" by the Doors. With the blues explosion in the late 1960s, Howlin' Wolf emerged as a superstar among college-aged fans. With Chess Records targeting the youth market, in 1969 Howlin' Wolf scored an unlikely hit with a psychedelic, blues-rock updating of "Evil." While in London in 1970, he recorded *THE LONDON HOWLIN' WOLF SESSIONS*, collaborating with Ringo Starr, Steve Winwood, Eric Clapton and others.

Believing he was cheated, in the early 1970s Howlin' Wolf sued his former record and publishing companies. Severely injuring his kidneys in a 1973 auto accident, three years later he died from heart and kidney disease. The Blues Heaven Foundation of

Chicago awards the annual "Howlin' Wolf—Keepin' the Blues Alive" prize to the blues artist of the year.

Bibliography
Koda, Cub. (1993, April 16). Howlin' Wolf: The Wolf is at the door. *Goldmine*, p. 10.
Morris, Chris. (1992, April). *Howlin' Wolf. Discoveries*, p. 32.
Shurman, Dick. (1992, April). *Howlin' Wolf. Discoveries*, p. 33.

THE IMPRESSIONS. *Arthur "Pops" Brooks Sr.; Richard A. Brooks; Jerry Butler (December 8, 1939); Fred Cash (October 8, 1940); Sam Gooden (September 2, 1939); Curtis Mayfield (Curtis Lee Mayfield; June 3, 1942). Inducted in 1991.* By 1960, doo-wop and blues had been replaced in popularity in the black community by soul, an expressive, emotion-laden music born in gospel music and black pride. A pioneering Chicago soul group, the Impressions sported two future solo stars, Curtis Mayfield and Jerry Butler.

Raised by his mother in Chicago, Curtis Mayfield worked odd jobs to help support his struggling family. Moving frequently, Mayfield settled in the rough Cabrini-Green housing project on the city's North Side. With prodding from his grandmother, Rev. A.B. Mayfield, the younger Mayfield sang in her Traveling Souls Spiritualist storefront church.

A transplanted Mississippian, Jerry Butler came to Chicago at age three. While training to be a cook at a high school vocational program, he sang in a doo-wop group called the Quails.

Mayfield and Butler first met as members of the Northern Jubilees, a gospel group that included three of Mayfield's cousins. Several years later, in 1956, Butler joined the Roosters, a Chattanooga, Tennessee-based vocal group, after three of its five members moved to Chicago. At Butler's suggestion, Mayfield was hired, originally as their guitarist.

Signing with Vee-Jay Records, the renamed Jerry Butler and the Impressions took their sound right out of the church. Featuring Butler's lead vocal, the gospel-styled ballad "For Your Precious Love" substituted romance for spirituality and was based on a poem Butler had written in high school. A major hit, the song made a star out of Butler.

With Vee-Jay looking to shape Butler into a solo act, he left the Impressions in 1958 and was replaced by former Rooster Fred Cash. With Butler's lead baritone replaced by Mayfield's near-falsetto tenor, the Impressions struggled until disbanding a year later.

After taking a job in a tobacco shop to pay an I.R.S. debt, Mayfield reformed the Impressions in 1961. Moving the group to New York City, Mayfield landed a contract with ABC-Paramount, which had just signed Ray Charles. After scoring a hit with "Gypsy Woman," the Brook Brothers quit the group, with the remaining trio of Mayfield, Cash, and Gooden returning to Chicago.

As a solo act, Butler had become a soul powerhouse in the 1960s, often aided by Mayfield's guitar work and songwriting assistance on hits such as "He Will Break

Your Heart" (1960), "Find Another Girl" (1961), and "I'm Telling You" (1961). Mayfield also wrote and produced records for Gene Chandler and his former high school buddy Major Lance.

In 1963, the Impressions scored their biggest hit with "It's All Right." Writes music historian Robert Pruter, "The vocal style of the three was now fully developed, the lead switching off from among the three and the two others singing in harmony with the lead on the end phrases" (p. 140). The group followed up with an amazing five top-40 hits in 1964, including "Amen" and the civil rights-themed "Keep On Pushing." With its religious overtones, the spiritual-like "People Get Ready" (1965) was an unlikely crossover hit.

In 1968, Curtis Mayfield and Eddie Thomas formed Curtom Records. Inking a distribution deal with Buddah Records, the label thrived, signing acts such as the Five Stairsteps, Linda Clifford, and the pop-gospel group the Staple Singers.

Meanwhile, the Impressions lost radio airplay in the late 1960s with political songs like "We're a Winner." Leaving the Impressions in 1970 Mayfield was replaced by Leroy Hutson (who left in 1972), and then by Reggie Torian, and Ralph Johnson. Mayfield continued to steer the group as a writer and producer.

Adopting a funkier, harder-soul style as a solo act, Mayfield's initial releases failed to cross over onto the pop charts. But providing the soundtrack for the low-budget, blaxploitation film *Superfly* (1972), Mayfield landed a pair of million-selling hits, "Superfly" and "Freddie's Dead," the latter preaching an antidrug message.

Mayfield's last top-40 hit came in 1974 with "Kung Fu." Also that year, the Staples Singers scored a number-one hit with the Mayfield-penned "Let's Do It Again," and the Mayfield-less Impressions scored their final major hit with "Finally Got Myself Together."

Closing Curtom Records in 1980, Mayfield moved to Atlanta. Reuniting with Butler and two former Impressions for reunion tour in 1982, the group enjoyed rave reviews. An encouraged Mayfield reactivated Curtom Records in 1987. But his soundtrack album for the 1990 sequel, *Return of Superfly*, bombed as did the film.

Tragedy struck Mayfield in 1990 at a free outdoor concert at Brooklyn's Wingate Field. Minutes after taking the stage, a wind gust dropped a lighting scaffold atop Mayfield, paralyzing him from the neck down. In 1994, Mayfield received the Grammy Legend Award; two years later the bedridden Mayfield released his long-awaited solo album, *NEW WORLD ORDER*, highlighted by the track "Get on the Bus."

Bibliography

Mills, David. (1990, September 23). Curtis Mayfield, back with a "Superfly" sound. *The Washington Post*, p. G8.
Mills, David. (1992, August 2). Curtis Mayfield, pushing on. *Washington Post*, p. G1.
Pruter, Robert. (1991). *Chicago Soul*. Urbana: University of Illinois Press.
Pruter, Robert. (1996, March 1). Only the strong survive: The Jerry Butler story. *Goldmine*, p. 40.
Tamarkin, Jeff. (1983, June). Curtis Mayfield and Jerry Butler talk about the Impressions. *Goldmine*, p. 30.
Tancredi, L. Carl. (1979, May). Jerry Butler: Callin' out with the "Ice Man." *Goldmine*, p. 28.

THE INK SPOTS. *Bill Kenny (1915 - March 23, 1978); Charlie Fuqua (1911 - December 1971); Orville "Hoppy" Jones (February 17, 1905 - October 18, 1944); "Ivory" Deek Watson (1913 - November 1969). Inducted in the Early Influence category in 1989.* Emerging in the mid-1800s, barbershop-harmony singing thrived well into the twentieth century. A precursor of doo-wop, the acapella-style music regained its popularity during the post-Depression years as all-black groups like the Ink Spots and the Mills Brothers found crossover success.

The origins of the Ink Spots stretch back to the late 1920s, when "Ivory" Deek Watson performed on Indianapolis street corners in a quartet called the Percolating Puppies, with the group featuring three "teapot" players. Arrested for stopping traffic with their impromptu sidewalk shows, the charges were dropped after a spirited performance for the judge. The group soon parlayed the press coverage into a nightly radio program. Watson then formed the Four Riff Brothers, landing a program at WLW in Cincinnati as replacements for the departing Fats Waller.

Moving to Cleveland, Watson formed a new group with Indianapolis natives Charlie Fuqua and Jerry Daniels, who had previously performed as "Charlie and Jerry." Billed as the King, Jack and the Jesters, the group soon added Orville "Hoppy" Jones, a cello-playing bass singer. The quartet landed a brief slot on Cleveland radio station WHK.

After a two-year stint back at WLW in Cincinnati, the group made its first trek to New York. After a slow start, the renamed Ink Spots landed a three-times-a-week gig on WJZ, the flagship station of the NBC-Red radio network. Recording for RCA, the Ink Spots landed their first hit in early 1935 with "Your Feet's Too Big."

Touring England for six months in the summer of 1935 at the invitation of leading British bandleader and promoter, Jack Hilton, the group took England by storm. To the Ink Spots' astonishment, their ship was greeted by thousands of fans. Besides touring with Hilton's "All Night Revue," the Ink Spots provided a command performance at the coronation of the Prince of Wales, and landed a twice-a-week radio show on the BBC.

Returning to New York in January 1936, the Ink Spots' popularity soared. Tired of receiving a paltry salary, Daniels left the group and was replaced by a Baltimore-native, tenor Bill Kenny, who was initially relegated to backing vocals. A past winner of the Apollo Theater's famed amateur night, Kenny did not play an instrument. After dropping most of their instrumental backing, the Ink Spots experienced a drop in popularity.

Leaving RCA over money, the revamped Ink Spots signed with Decca in 1936, landing several moderate sellers, including a vocal version of "Stompin' at the Savoy" (1936), "Let's Call the Whole Thing Off" (1937), and "When the Sun Goes Down" (1938). With their record sales waning, the Ink Spots nearly disbanded in early 1939.

Turning to ballads, the Ink Spots landed a career-making hit with the Jack Lawrence-penned "If I Didn't Care." With Kenny switching to lead vocals and the debut of Jones' famous "talking solos," the group hit on a successful formula. Writes Deek Watson in his autobiography, "We were sure glad to finish it, and all of us thought we had done a very bad job. Then [producer Dave Kapp] and his assistant rushed out telling us what a fine record we had made. They played it back for us, but we still thought it was the worst record we had ever made" (p. 32). Aided by a gushing concert review by columnist Walter Winchell, the Ink Spots became international stars.

The song's success led to an opening slot for the group at New York's Paramount Theater for the Glenn Miller Orchestra. A huge success, the Ink Spots were retained for a long headlining residency.

After appearing in the film, *The Great American Broadcast of 1941*, the Ink Spots headed their own touring revues with Ella Fitzgerald, Pearl Bailey, and proto-R&B bandleader Lucky Millinder. During this period, the Ink Spots' chief competitors were equally popular Mills Brothers, whose records lacked the Ink Spots' lush orchestration.

A pioneering crossover act, the Ink Spots scored a series of ballad hits in the 1940s including "We Three" (1940), "Don't Get Around Much Anymore" (1942), and "Into Each Life Some Rain Must Fall" (1944).

Still angry at losing his lead-singer role to Kenny, in 1944 Watson left to form his own short-lived version of the Ink Spots. By year's end, Jones passed away, his health devastated by constant touring. Jones was replaced on bass vocals by Bill Kenny's brother, Herb. Meanwhile, Fuqua returned to the group in 1945 after a three-year stint in the service.

With lawsuits flying over the ownership of the group's name, by 1945 Watson was touring with an Ink Spots sound-alike group called the Brown Dots. (When Watson's new group abandoned him in 1946, they formed the 4 Tunes.) Retaining the Ink Spots name, Fuqua, the Kenny Brothers, and replacement Billy Bowen scored a smash hit in 1946 with "The Gypsy."

Various incarnations of the Ink Spots competed against one another in the early 1950s, with the last Decca sessions coming in 1953. That year, Kenny lost the legal control of the group's name to Fuqua, who later recorded several Ink Spots records for King Records.

Meanwhile, a number of pioneering doo-wop groups like the Ravens and the Orioles were successfully modernizing the Ink Spots sound, reinventing vocal quartet harmony singing. Another group, the Moonglows, was founded by the nephew of Charlie Fuqua, Harvey Fuqua. The last member of the Ink Spots classic line-up, Bill Kenny, died in 1978.

Bibliography
Abbott, Lynn. (1992, Fall). "Play that barber shop chord": A case for the African-American origin of barbershop harmony. *American Music*, p. 289.

Friedwald, Will. (1990). *Jazz Singing*. New York: Charles Scribner's Sons.

Goldberg, Marv. (1989, February). The Brown Dots and the 4 Tunes. *Discoveries*, p. 46.

Grendysa, Peter. (1984, August 31). The Ink Spots: Harold Jackson & the King Ink Spots. *Goldmine*, p. 26.

Grendysa, Peter; Moonoogian, George; Whitesell, Rick & Goldberg, Marv. (1978). The Ink Spots. *Yesterday's Memories*, 3(1), p. 4.

Heckman, Don. (1989, July 29). New Ink Spots seek to take old name back to top again. *The Los Angeles Times*, Calendar sect., p. 10.

Watson, Deek & Stephenson, Lee. (1967). *Story of the Ink Spots*. New York: Vantage.

THE ISLEY BROTHERS. *Ernie Isley (March 7, 1952); Kelly Isley (O'Kelly Isley Jr.; December 25, 1937 - March 31, 1986); Marvin Isley (August 18, 1953); Ronald Isley (May 21, 1941); Rudolph Isley (April 1, 1939); Chris Jasper (1951). Inducted in 1992.* Had the Isley Brothers disbanded after their first two hits, "Shout" and "Twist and Shout," their stature in rock and roll would had been guaranteed. Instead, the veteran group has survived four decades of stylistic and personnel changes, having explored doo-wop, soul, funk, and even hard rock.

Natives of Cincinnati, the four oldest Isley brothers—Ronald, Rudolph, Kelly, and (the eldest) Vernon—got their musical start at the Mt. Moriah Church, forming a gospel quartet in the early 1950s. With the tragic bicycle death of Vernon Isley, the group disbanded for a year.

Convinced by their parents to reform, the Isley Brothers switched to R&B, with Ronald Isley taking over on lead vocals. Securing a recording contract with record mogul George Goldner, the group's early efforts received scant airplay.

Signing with RCA, the Isleys scored their first hit in 1959 with "Shout (Pts. 1 & 2)," a rollicking, spirit-filled, call-and-response, gospel-based send-up, which celebrated not the love of God but the love of a woman. Featuring their church organist Professor Herman Stephens, the Ronald Isley-penned song was inspired by a live rendition of Jackie Wilson's "Lonely Teardrops." Produced by the team of Hugo Peritti and Luigi Creator, "Shout" sold a million copies but failed to land on either the pop or R&B charts. Unable to follow up with another hit, the Isleys were dropped by RCA and suffered a similar fate at Atlantic.

Moving to Wand Records in 1961, the Isleys scored their first chart-hit with a 3 million-selling smash, "Twist and Shout" (1962). An often recorded rock standard, the Beatles rendition was a bigger hit on the pop charts. Another Wand release, "Nobody but Me," was later a hit for the Human Beinz. Signing with United Artists in 1963, here the Isleys recorded the slow, original version of "Who's That Lady?"

Launching their own T-Neck record label in 1964, the name was taken from the Isleys' adopted home of Teaneck, New Jersey. Featuring their newly hired guitarist, Jimmy (later Jimi) Hendrix, the Isleys flopped with their first T-Neck release, "Testify."

After a brief return to Atlantic, the Isleys landed at Motown in 1965. Though teamed with Motown's star tunesmiths, Holland-Dozier-Holland, the Isleys' only crossover success came with, "This Old Heart of Mine" (1966).

Leaving Motown, in 1969 the Isleys reactivated T-Neck Records, as O'Kelly Isley dropped the "O" from his name. Moving in a funk-rock direction, the Isleys expanded to a sextet. Hiring the two youngest Isley brothers, Ernie and Marvin, along with a brother-in-law, Chris Jasper, the new members provided a tight rhythm section, with Ernie on guitar, Marvin on bass, and Jasper on keyboard. The younger trio attended college during the weekdays and entered the studio on the weekends.

The revamped Isley Brothers unleashed a decade-long string of R&B hits, beginning with the crossover entries "It's Your Thing" (1969) and "I Turned You On" (1969). A subsequent million-selling album, *IT'S OUR THING*, was followed by a concert film captured at Yankee Stadium performance, *It's Your Thing*.

Experimenting with harder-rock styles, the Isleys expanded the bounds of R&B.

Recording an entire album of rock cover songs, the Isleys' 1971 release *GIVING IT BACK* featured Stephen Stills' "Love the One You're With" and Bob Dylan's "Lay Lady Lay."

After earning their music degrees, the younger members joined the group on a full-time basis in 1973, beginning with the landmark funk album *3 + 3*. Updating their sound and embracing electronics, the expanded Isley Brothers utilized phase shifters and a Moog synthesizer. Continuing their funk-rock approach, the Isleys scored their biggest hit of the decade with a newly recorded, upbeat version of their earlier ballad, "That Lady."

Becoming more album-oriented, the Isleys enjoyed a string of gold- and platinum-certified releases, including LIVE IT UP, the chart-topping *THE HEAT IS ON,* and *SHOWDOWN.* Their hit singles during this period include the anthem-like "Fight the Power—Part 1" (1975); "For the Love of You—Part 1 & 2" (1975); and "Livin' in the Life" (1977).

Meanwhile the Isleys' classic, "Shout," had a second life following Otis Day & the Nights' version from the John Belushi, college frat film *National Lampoon's Animal House* (1978).

In 1984 the Isleys splintered into two groups, a rift developing after CBS Records requested a separate album featuring only the younger members. The younger trio formed their own group as Isley, Jasper, Isley . Signing with CBS, they landed several R&B hits beginning with "Caravan of Love" (1985).

Meanwhile, the pared-down Isley Brothers of Ronald, Rudolph and Kelly switched to Warner Brothers. Becoming a ballad-oriented group, the Isleys debuted with the poorly-selling album *MASTERPIECE.*

The death of Kelly Isley of a heart attack and the departure of Rudolph Isley for the ministry in 1987 necessitated the return of Ernie and Marvin Isley in 1990. Their 1993 release *ISLEY BROTHERS LIVE!*, captured the intensity of their stage shows. With Ronald marrying R&B singer Angela Winbush, the two acts often toured together. Returning to the charts in 1996, the Isleys landed a top-10 R&B album, *MISSION TO PLEASE*, landing duet hits with Angela Winbush and Babyface; meanwhile Ronald Isley scored a top-10 duet hit with R. Kelly, "Down Low."

Reaching a new generation of fans, the Isleys enjoyed several hit remakes by top rap acts, including "It's Your Thing" reworked as "Shake Your Thing" by Salt-N-Pepa; a redesigned "Fight the Power" by Public Enemy; and "At Your Best" by Aaliyah.

Bibliography

Baker, Cary. (1981, August). The Isley Brothers: Entering their third decade of soul. *Goldmine*, p. 16.

Hunt, Dennis. (1987, July 3). Isley Brothers' "Sailing" back on the charts. *Los Angeles Times*, Calendar sect., p. 21.

Nager, Larry. (1994, September 9). Rock that thang! *(Memphis) Commercial Appeal*, p. 14E.

Peck, Abe. (August 10, 1978). The Isley Brothers are ready for the next phase. *Rolling Stone*, p. 8.

Popson, Tom. (1986, March 28). Vocal variety makes Isley spinoff distinctive. *Chicago Tribune*, Friday sect., p. 6.

Roeser, Steve. (1991, November 29). The Isley Brothers: Rock 'n' roll survivors. *Goldmine*, p. 10.

Zibart, Eve. (1978, June 19). Isleys: Brothers with a midas touch. *The Washington Post*, p. B 1.

THE JACKSON 5. *Jackie Jackson (Sigmund Esco Jackson; May 4, 1951); Jermaine Jackson (Jermaine LaJaune Jackson; March 12, 1957); Marlon Jackson (Marlon David Jackson; March 12, 1957); Michael Jackson (Michael Joseph Jackson; August 29, 1958); Tito Jackson (Toriano Adaryll Jackson; October 15, 1953). Inducted in 1997.* Motown's last golden age soul group, the Jackson 5, dominated top-40 radio in the early 1970s. Pushed hard by their authoritarian working-class father, Joe Jackson, the Jackson clan was shaped into singing stars.

The first lineup of the Jacksons consisted of the eldest three Jackson boys, Tito, Jackie and lead singer Jermaine. Expanding in 1962 with the addition of Marlon and five-year-old Michael, the group took their act around Gary, Indiana. Following a pattern set by Frankie Lymon & the Teenagers, the renamed Jackson 5 was fronted by the energetic boy wonder Michael, who was borrowing dance routines from James Brown and Jackie Wilson.

Not permitted to participate in normal childhood activities by their father, the young Jacksons were forced to constantly practice. Winning their first talent show in 1965 with a rendition of the Temptation's "My Girl," the group was approached by Gordon Keith, the owner of a tiny record company. Releasing a pair of singles on the Steeltown label, their first single, "Big Boy" (1967), received only local airplay. (The Steeltown sessions would be released in 1996 on the album *PRE-HISTORY: THE LOST STEELTOWN RECORDINGS.*) Constantly on the road for a series of one-nighters, the Jackson 5 won a grueling talent contest at the famed Apollo Theater in July 1967.

Auditioning for Barry Gordy Jr. of Motown Records, the Jackson 5 signed an unfavorable five-year contract. Befriended by their new mentor, Motown star Diana Ross, the group was introduced to a national audience in late 1969 on the ABC variety program *The Hollywood Palace*. The Jacksons marked this relationship with their debut album, *DIANA ROSS PRESENTS THE JACKSON FIVE*.

An impressed Gordy relocated the group to California, taking personal interest in their recordings. Featuring Michael's dynamic, soaring soprano lead, the Jackson 5's first four Motown singles all topped the charts in 1970: "I Want You Back," the Grammy-winning "ABC," "The Love You Save, and "I'll Be There." When the athletic Jackie Jackson was drafted by the Chicago White Sox, he passed on the offer.

Continuing their hit run in 1972, the Jackson 5 landed a trio of top-10 "bubble-gum soul" hits with "Mama's Pearl," "Sugar Daddy," and, composed by actor Clifton Davis, "Never Can Say Goodbye." Often compared at the time to the Osmonds, the Jackson 5 were featured on lunch boxes and starred in their own ABC Saturday morning cartoon show, with the five brothers providing the voices.

With Motown wanting to capitalize on their success, three of the five Jackson brothers pursued solo side projects in 1972. Outselling albums by Jackie and

Jermaine, little Michael emerged the star in the group. From his solo album *GOT TO BE THERE*, Michael scored a trio of hits with "Got to Be There," "I Wanna Be Where You Are," and a cover of Bobby Day's "Rockin' Robin." Later in the year, Jackson scored a million-selling hit with "Ben," a paean to a rat from the film *Ben*.

With Michael Jackson's high soprano voice beginning to change, a concerned Motown ordered the Jackson 5 to record about 100 songs, few of which were ever released. With their fortunes waning, the group tried targeting targeted the adult market with their 1975 Holland-Dozier-Holland-produced album *MOVING VIOLATION*.

Frustrated that they were not permitted to write their own songs nor play any instruments, the Jackson brothers left Motown for a lucrative contract with CBS/Epic. Suing the group, Motown won $600,000 in damages and retained the "Jackson 5" name.

Teaming with producers Kenny Gamble and Leon Huff, the renamed Jacksons returned to the top-10 with the 2-million-selling dance hit "Enjoy Yourself" (1976). In 1976, the Jacksons hosted a short-lived CBS variety program with their manager father as executive producer.

Finally permitted to produce their own records, the 1978 album *DESTINY* showcased Michael Jackson's developing talent on the chart-topping disco record "Shake Your Body (Down to the Ground)" (1979). Making his acting debut in the role of the Scarecrow in the film *The Wiz* (1978), Jackson played opposite Diana Ross. From the film, Jackson and Ross scored a Quincy Jones-produced hit, "Ease on Down the Road."

Retaining Jones as the producer for his next album, the 10 million-selling *OFF THE WALL*, Jackson cemented his solo stardom with the dance-flavored hits "Don't Stop 'Til You Get Enough," "Rock with You," and the touching ballad "She's Out of My Life." Meanwhile, the Jacksons released their fourth CBS album, *TRIUMPH*, which spawned the hits "Lovely One" and "Heartbreak Hotel."

After firing his father as manager, Michael reunited with his brothers on 1983's Motown's 25th anniversary television special. He subsequently joined them for an album, *VICTORY* (1984), and a $70 million-grossing tour. During this period, the Jackson sisters, Janet, LaToya, and Rebbie Jackson, each pursued solo careers.

Returning to his prolific solo career, Michael Jackson emerged as a superstar in the 1980s. Releasing the massive sellers *THRILLER* and *BAD*, the self-described "King of Pop" garnered a record-setting string of hits, with the former album winning eight Grammys. Embracing music video production, Jackson earned critical acclaim for the high-priced projects "Billie Jean" and "Thriller."

But after a series of controversies—plastic surgeries, legal problems, molestation charges, and a short marriage to Lisa Marie Presley—Jackson's career was irrevocably harmed.. A myriad of Jackson family secrets were aired in a 1992 ABC television mini-series, *The Jacksons: An American Dream*, and in LaToya Jackson's stinging autobiography, *Growing Up in the Jackson Family*. The Jackson legacy has continued with 3T, the vocal group consisting of Jermaine Jackson's three sons, Taj, Taryll, and TJ. The Jacksons reunited in 1997 for an album and international tour. Michael Jackson later remarried.

Bibliography

Fong-Torres, Ben. (1971, April 29). The Jackson 5: The men don't know but the little girls understand. *Rolling Stone*, p. 24.

Gaar, Gillian G. (1995, October 13). It's a family affair: The triumphs and tribulations of the Jacksons. Goldmine, p. 18.

Goldberg, Michael. (1992, January 9). Michael Jackson: The making of the King of pop. *Rolling Stone*, p. 32.

Jones, James T. IV. (1992, November 12). Jacksons tell their side of the story. *USA Today*, p. 3D.

Katz, Larry. (1995, June 7). Ancient HIStory; A Long Island record firm re-releases Jackson 5's first single before Michael unveils newest CD. *Boston Globe*, Arts & Life sect., p. 49.

Taraborrelli, J. Randy. (1986). *Motown: Hot Wax, City Cool & Solid Gold* (pp. 141-48). Garden City, NY: Dolphin/Doubleday.

MAHALIA JACKSON. *(October 26, 1911 - January 27, 1972). Inducted in the Early Influence category in 1997.* With her booming contralto voice, Mahalia emerged as the Queen of Gospel in the 1940s. Born into poverty in New Orleans, the daughter of a lay Baptist preacher, Mahalia was raised by her extended family after the death of her mother. Quitting school after eighth grade, Jackson spent her teen years working as a laundress and nursemaid. Secretly listening to blues records against her family's wishes, her favorite artist was Bessie Smith.

Leaving home at age 17 with $100 in her pocket, Jackson moved to Chicago, where she first found employment as hotel maid. Arriving in the city during gospel's formative period, Jackson embraced the new genre. After landing a soloist spot at the Greater Salem Baptist Church, Jackson formed the John Gospel Singers with the pastor's son and a boogie-woogie-style piano player. Combining secular, blueslike strains with old-time spirituals, Jackson "put blue notes in gospel, she moaned and growled and *shouted.* . . . She was also known for her habit of 'dancing to the glory of the Lord'—skipping, strutting, and hiking up the long gospel robe when she felt like it" (p. 71), wrote gospel historian Hettie Jones.

Initially considered sinful, gospel music was banned in most black churches and black college campuses in the 1930s. "The more gospel singing took hold in Chicago and around the country, the more some of the colored ministers objected to it. They were cold to it. They didn't like the hand-clapping and the stomping and they said we were bringing jazz into the church and it wasn't dignified" (p. 63) Jackson recalled in her autobiography.

Signing with Decca Records, Jackson landed her first hit with "God's Gonna Separate the Wheat from the Tares" (1937). Teaming with the Father of Gospel, pianist and songwriter Thomas A. Dorsey, throughout the 1940s, Jackson took her passionate spirituals to tent revival shows and churches, often shouting, "Lord have mercy on me."

Moving to Apollo Records in 1946, Jackson frequently rammed heads with producer Bess Berman over inconsistent royalty payments. Her third Apollo single, the 2 million-selling "Move On Up a Little Higher" (1948) was the centerpiece of her concerts, the performance of the highly-charged song sometimes lasting 25 minutes. Reworking the standard hymn "Amazing Grace" (written in 1732 by slave-ship captain John Newton, who quit his job in disgust), Jackson delivered the authoritative version of the song. Another signature Jackson piece, "Go Tell It on the Mountain," was released in 1950.

Finding mainstream success at Columbia Records, Jackson was soon attacked by gospel purists for taking a pop-oriented turn. When asked to record secular material, she told gospel historian Anthony Heilbut: "I can't get with this commercial stuff. I'm used to singing in church till the spirit comes. Here they want everything done in two or three minutes" (p. 68). During her career Jackson rejected numerous offers to sing R&B, and in a 1957 television interview with Dinah Shore, Jackson angrily denied that she sang the blues. But at Columbia, Jackson once teamed with the Percy Faith Orchestra, singing romantic ballads.

Always a favorite of jazz aficionados for her Bessie Smith-like vocals, Jackson performed at the 1958 Newport Jazz Festival. She also teamed with Duke Ellington on the album *BLACK, BROWN AND BEIGE*. Pursuing a film career, Jackson was cast in the W.C. Handy film biography *St. Louis Blues* (1958) and in *Imitation of Life* (1959), with the sensual Lana Turner.

With black spirituals embraced by the civil rights movement, Jackson sang at the St. John A.M.E. in Birmingham, Alabama, at a ceremony honoring Rosa Parks, who had refused to give up her bus seat to a white passenger. At the second civil rights march in Washington, D.C., in 1963, Jackson was asked by Martin Luther King Jr. to sing an acapella version of "I've Been 'Buked and I've Been Scorned" to the 200,000 blacks and whites in attendance. Minutes later, King unleashed his passionate "I Have a Dream" speech.

By the 1960s, Jackson limited her performances to mostly large concert halls, singing a more polished style of gospel music. Sometimes a hard woman, Jackson fired her piano accompanist of 20 years for asking for an increase in her $100 a week salary.

After suffering several heart attacks, Jackson died of heart failure in Chicago in 1972. Jackson's life was celebrated in the Broadway production *Truly Blessed: A Musical Celebration of Mahalia Jackson*.

Bibliography
Heilbut, Anthony. (1985). *The Gospel Sound* (rev. ed.). New York: Limelight.
Jackson, Mahalia & Wylie, Evan McLeod. (1966). *Movin' On Up*. New York: Hawthorn.
Jones, Hettie. (1995). *Big Star Fallin' Mama* (rev. ed., pp. 57-77). New York: Viking.

ELMORE JAMES. *(Elmore Brooks; January 27, 1918 - May 24, 1963); Inducted in the Early Influence category in 1992*. The last, great, postwar, Delta-born, electric slide-guitarist, bluesman Elmore James influenced the likes of Jimi Hendrix, Eric Clapton, Duane Allman, and Stevie Ray Vaughan and served as the originator of blues-rock.

Born to an unmarried sharecropper in Ridgeland, Mississippi, Elmore Brooks became Elmore James, taking the last name of his mother's common-law husband, Joe Willie James. As dirt-poor migratory farmworkers, the entire James family was forced to work the fields. As a child, Elmore James built a number of homemade instruments, including a primitive guitar.

After moving 50 miles south to Belzoni, Mississippi, in the late 1930s, James left farm work, attracted to the musical scene of nearby Jackson. With his store-bought guitar, James hit the Southern blues circuit. A contemporary of Sonny Boy Williamson (#2) and Robert Johnson, James adopted many of their techniques. A key song in James' repertoire was Johnson's "Dust My Broom" (originally titled, "Dust My Room"). Although James neither wrote nor was the first to record the tune, it become his signature piece.

After touring with Williamson in the early 1940s, James landed a radio show at KFFA in Helena, Arkansas. His career interrupted by World War II, James fought in Guam, returning to Mississippi in 1945.

Settling down with his wife in Canton, Mississippi, James seemingly abandoned his musical career. Working in his half brother's radio shop, he was introduced to the world of amplified, electric guitars.

When Sonny Boy Williamson landed a series of radio gigs including his legendary *King Biscuit Time* radio show, James was hired as his sidekick. Playing his electric guitar bottleneck style, James received considerable airtime and exposure, his popularity parlayed into much session work. Combining a loud, distorted guitar with his impassioned, almost-screaming tenor voice, James spawned many imitators.

But with the opportunity to record some solo records, the unexpected occurred: James was unable to sing and became terrified by the sight of the studio microphone. Tricked by Williamson and the other musicians, James recorded "Dust My Broom" in 1951, believing it was a rehearsal. Released the following year on Trumpet Records under the name Elmo James, it became his first hit.

Recovering from his fear of recording, James appeared on a series of labels throughout the 1950s. Now billed as Elmore James and adopting a more R&B-flavored sound, his hits continued with "I Believe" (1953); "Dust My Blues" (1955); and Tampa Red's "It Hurts Me Too" (1957). Recycling "Dust My Broom," James released many variations of the song. Fronting the Broomdusters, an electric band that included cousin Homesick James, Elmore James became a popular Chicago attraction. By the late 1950s, James' career had slowed. Leaving Chicago, James returned to Jackson, Mississippi, in 1958, where he found deejay work.

Back in Chicago at the end of 1959, James was sought out by Fire/Fury Records owner Bobby Robinson. A hastily set-up and hurried session launched the second part of James' career. Considered his finest recordings, James released the instrumental "Bobby's Rock"; still another rendition of "Dust My Broom"; and the impromptu-written "The Sky Is Crying" (1960). The latter became a blues standard, later recorded by Stevie Ray Vaughn. Follow-up Robinson-produced singles include the double-sided hit "Look on Yonder Wall"/"Shake Your Moneymaker" (1961) and an updated, posthumously released "It Hurts Me Too" (1965).

Returning to the South in ill health, James had left Chicago over a disagreement with the musician's union over back dues. Dying of a heart attack shortly after his return to Chicago in 1963, James did not live to see the mid-1960s blues revival.

Bibliography

Obrecht, Jas. (1993, September). Rollin' and tumblin': The ballad of Elmore & Homesick
    James. *Guitar Player*, p. 68.
Weinstock, Ron. (1994, Spring). Elmore James. *Blues Revue Quarterly*, p. 24.
White, Timothy. (1992, July 25). Elmore James: The slide is crying. *Billboard*, p. 3.
Whiteis, David. (1992, March 20). Elmore James: The sky is crying. *Goldmine*, p. 18.

ETTA JAMES. *(Jamesetta Hawkins; January 25, 1938). Inducted in 1993.* With her grasp of jazz, blues, and R&B, Etta James predated 1960s soul singers like Tammi Terrell and Aretha Franklin. Enduring a lifetime of tragedy, James fought a host of personal demons. Born Jamesetta Hawkins in Los Angeles, her mother was a 14-year-old sometimes-call girl, and her father was allegedly the pool shark Minnesota Fats. Biracial, young Jamesetta lived with an aunt before being adopted. Passed off as a younger sister, Jamesetta referred to her birth mother as "Dorothy."

In her childhood, James received formal lessons in ballet, piano, and even acting. Drawn to gospel music, James was considered a child prodigy at St. Paul Baptist Church, where she was featured as a soloist in the choir. Writing in her autobiography, James recalled: "I don't know if the Bible lessons took hold of me, but the music sure did. The music was thunder and joy, lightning bolts of happiness and praise, foot-stomping, dance-shouting, good-feeling singing from the soul. Reverend Branham's sermons were so fiery and the choir so hot that white folks would come all the way from Hollywood, sit in the back, and just groove" (p. 17). With Jamesetta's stepfather attempting to profit from her singing, he forced her to switch to a larger, distant church. There the 10-year-old girl stopped singing altogether.

With West Coast R&B in its bustling infancy, James discovered the music on jaunts into the city's nightclubs, led by the hustling "Dorothy." After the death of her elderly stepmother, at age 12 James was taken to San Francisco by her birth mother.

Trapped in an abusive, unpredictable home life, young Etta James saw a music career as her escape from the projects. Forming the Creolettes at age 14, James sang at teen dances and talent shows. In the jazz and R&B vocal trio, James emerged as the lead singer.

With answer songs common in R&B, the group wrote a reply to Hank Ballard and the Midnighters' bawdy hit "Work with Me Annie." Told of the song, an intrigued Ballard went to hear the group. With the aid of Ballard, the group was signed by R&B bandleader Johnny Otis after a midnight audition. Just short of her 15th birthday, James joined Otis' touring revue.

Forging a note from her mother, Jamesetta signed with Modern Records. Recording "The Wallflower (Work with Me Henry)" as an answer record to the Midnighters' "Work with Me Annie," the "Henry" in the title was, of course, Hank Ballard. Renamed by Otis, Jamesetta Hawkins became Etta James, while the Creolettes were now the Peaches. Meanwhile, white singer Georgia Gibbs stole most of the pop airplay with her sanitized cover version, reworking the song as "Dance with Me

Henry."

Possessing a feisty, yet innocent singing voice, James followed up with the Richard Berry-penned "Good Rockin' Daddy." Soon after, James left Otis, upset with her minuscule salary and lack of royalty payments.

Bleaching her hair blond in 1955, James popularized the style. Very light-skinned, James' hair color caused her problems in the South, police harassing her for cavorting with blacks!

With Chess Records buying her contract from Modern, James recorded tearjerker ballads like "All I Could Do Was Cry." At the label, she also appeared on a series of hit duets with real-life boyfriend Harvey Fuqua (formerly of the Moonglows), as Betty and Dupree, until Fuqua's departure from the label in 1960. Switching to the melancholy style of jazz diva Billie Holiday, James found immense success with hits such as "At Last" (originally a hit in 1942 for Glenn Miller) and "Don't Cry Baby" (1961).

In the 1960s and 1970s, James' career became erratic as she divided her time between touring, heroin addiction, and jail time. In Los Angles, she briefly joined the Black Muslims after attending a mosque headed by a young Louis Farrakhan. With her drug use intensifying, she nearly died after contracting tetanus from a dirty needle.

Recording at the Muscle Shoals Fame studio, James returned to the charts in the late 1960s with the soul nugget "Tell Mama" (1967) and the Otis Redding-penned "Security" (1968).

After a 1972 drug bust, James moved to New York, where she entered a detox program and worked in the promotions department of the relocated Chess Records. In 1973, she beat drugs for a time after a 17-month stint at the Tarzana Psychiatric Hospital.

Occasionally recording in the 1970s, James was assisted by legendary producers Jerry Wexler and Allen Toussaint. In the late 1970s, James toured with the Rolling Stones and sang backup for Bonnie Raitt.

Addicted to cocaine, then codeine, in the 1980s James entered the Betty Ford Clinic, quitting drugs for good in 1988. Returning to a full-time music career in the late 1980s, James recorded a pair of albums with sax player, Eddie "Cleanhead" Vinson and in 1989 even tackled a rap song.

Performing jazz and pop standards in the 1990s, James won her first Grammy with her 1994 album *MYSTERY LADY: THE SONGS OF BILLIE HOLIDAY*. In 1996, James landed a surprise British top-10 hit with a cover of the blues classic "I Just Want to Make Love to You."

Bibliography
Cromelin, Richard. (1992, November 1). Rollin' with Etta. *Los Angeles Times*, Calendar sect., p. 8.
James, Etta & Ritz, David. (1995). *The Etta James Story: Rage to Survive*. New York: Villard.
Kohlhaase, Bill. (1994, March 17). Inspired by the jazz legend, Etta James crafts a revealing collection of Lady Day's music. *Los Angeles Times*, Calendar sect., p. 2.
"Living Blues Interview: Etta James." (1982, Autumn-Winter). *Living Blues*, p. 12.
Schoemer, Karen. (1994, November 21). Lady sings ballads, too. *Newsweek*, p. 98.

JEFFERSON AIRPLANE. *Marty Balin (Martyn Jerel Buchwald; January 30, 1943); Jack Casady (April 13, 1944); Spencer Dryden (April 7, 1938); Paul Kantner (March 12, 1941); Jorma Kaukonen (December 23, 1941); Grace Slick (Grace Barnett Wing; October 30, 1939). Inducted in 1996.* A pioneering, psychedelic-era, San Francisco group, the Jefferson Airplane was musically more sophisticated than its peers. Although experiencing constant personnel and name changes, the band survived well into the 1990s.

Assembling a house band for his new Fillmore Avenue nightclub, the Matrix, former folksinger Marty Balin hired guitarist Paul Kantner in what became known as Jefferson Airplane. After some fine-tuning, the group included Kantner, bassist Jack Casady, drummer Skip Spence, and the band's political voice, guitarist Jorma Kaukonen; Balin shared lead vocal duties with Signe Anderson.

After building a large fan base, the Jefferson Airplane signed with RCA Records in late 1965, staying with the label throughout its various incarnations. In October 1965 the Jefferson Airplane first crossed paths with a group called the Great Society at a concert organized by a commune/promotion company called the Family Dog. Kantner was very impressed the Great Society's lead singer, Grace Slick, a former department store model.

Releasing several poorly-selling singles and a subsequent debut album, *JEFFERSON AIRPLANE TAKES OFF*, the Jefferson Airplane had limited success. Garnering little radio airplay, much of the group's early material was banned for its controversial lyrics.

On the eve of the Great Society's major-label signing, Casady asked Grace Slick to join the Jefferson Airplane as a replacement for the pregnant Anderson. Enticed to switch bands by a salary increase, Grace advanced the group's fortunes, bringing along her stunning good looks, mezzo-soprano voice, and penchant for lyric writing. Though sharing lead vocal duties with Balin, Slick emerged as the focal point of the group, becoming a major rock personality. Soon after, Spence left to form Moby Grape and was replaced by jazz drummer Spencer Dryden.

The Jefferson Airplane's second album, the million-selling *SURREALISTIC PILLOW*, included two songs that Slick brought from the Great Society: the million-selling "Somebody to Love" (written by Slick's brother-in-law, Darby Slick) and the Slick-penned, drug-culture tune "White Rabbit," which was inspired by "Alice in Wonderland" and Ravel's "Bolero." With both singles huge hits, the group was crucial in the development of the San Francisco Sound.

In 1968, the group released a pair of hit albums, *AFTER BATHING AT BAXTER'S* and *CROWN OF CREATION*, neither of which received much airplay. By year's end Casady and Kaukonen had formed an acoustic blues-based, offshoot band, Hot Tuna. The group's most political album to date, *VOLUNTEERS*, spawned a minor hit with the title track, "Volunteers."

Touring heavily in 1969, the Jefferson Airplane played Woodstock, then the disaster at Altamont, where Balin was assaulted by a member of the Hell's Angels security crew. With the death of the 1960s, Jefferson Airplane experienced a myriad of personnel changes. Dryden in 1970 left to form the New Riders of the Purple Sage, while Kaukonen and Casady split to continue Hot Tuna, now an electric trio; Balin left in 1971, forming his own group, Bodacious D.F.; and Slick and Kantner paired up for an album project. Meanwhile, from Hot Tuna, the elderly Papa John Creach joined the Jefferson Airplane on electric fiddle. Greeted with little fanfare, the original Jefferson Airplane's final studio album *LONG JOHN SILVER,* was released in 1972.

Moving in a mainstream-rock direction, the renamed Jefferson Starship was launched in 1974 by Kantner, Slick, Creach, and two new members, their debut album coming with *DRAGONFLY.* Also that year, a moonlighting Slick released her first solo album, *MANHOLE.*

With Balin returning in 1975, the album *RED OCTOPUS* gave the group its biggest hit to date with the pop-flavored "Miracles." Soon after, Creach left the band. On a roll, the reinvigorated Jefferson Starship released back-to-back number-one albums with *SPITFIRE,* featuring the hit "With Your Love" (1976), and *EARTH,* highlighted by , "Count on Me" (1978) and "Runaway" (1978).

After rioters in Germany destroyed the band's equipment in 1978, Slick quit the group. She also left her second husband, Paul Kantner, for the group's roadie, Skip Johnson.

When Balin was replaced in 1979 by new lead vocalist Mickey Thomas (who had previously sung with Elvin Bishop), the group flirted with heavy metal. In 1980, a solo Balin hit, "Hearts," competed with the Jefferson Airplane chart entry, "Jane." With Slick's return in 1981, she shared the lead vocals with Thomas on the hits "Find Your Way Back" (1981) and "Winds of Change" (1983).

But when both Slick and Kantner left the group in 1984, all of the original members were gone. Unhappy with the band's new direction, Kantner claimed ownership of the Jefferson Airplane name, suing the remaining members. With the subsequent group now known as Starship, a trio of former members of the band, Kantner, Balin, and Casady, formed the KBC Band in 1985, releasing a poorly received album the following year.

With Slick again rejoining on lead vocals, Starship landed a hit with "Nothing's Gonna Stop Us Now" (1987) from the comedy film *Mannequin.* A year later, Slick quit again.

Amid lawsuits over legal ownership of the group's name, in 1988 a touring Kantner, Casady, and Kaukonen were joined onstage by Slick. With Balin reluctantly reuniting with his former bandmates, the new Jefferson Airplane signed with Epic Records in 1989. Missing from the group's classic lineup was Dryden who was not invited to join. Together for a brief tour and album, *JEFFERSON AIRPLANE,* the group was poorly received.

In 1991, Kantner, Casady, Creach, and singer Darby Gould formed Jefferson Starship: The Next Generation. Both Grace Slick and Signe Anderson guested on a number of dates. Creach passed away in 1994. In the mid-1990s, the group continued its musical-chairs lineup.

Bibliography

Campbell, Mary. (1993, January 1). The bus may be different but it's the same trip. *Los Angeles Times,* Calendar sect., p. 20.

Fong-Torres, Ben. (1971, September 30). Jefferson Airplane grunts: Gotta evolution. *Rolling*

Stone, p. 1.

Hogg, Brian. (1990, January). The Great Society. *Record Collector*, p. 68.

Leimbacher, Ed. (1970, January). The crash of the Jefferson Airplane. *Ramparts*, p. 14.

Pareles, Jon. (1989, August 29). On-again off-again Jefferson Airplane is on again. *New York Times*, p. C11.

Ruhlmann, William. (1992, October 30). Tryin' to revolutionize tomorrow: The flight of Jefferson Airplane. *Goldmine*, p. 12.

Sculatti, Gene & Seay, Davin. (1985). *San Francisco Nights: The Psychedelic Music Trip, 1965-1968*. New York: St. Martin's.

Seigal, Buddy. (1995, July 6). Starship: The next generation. *The Los Angeles Times*, p. F2.

ELTON JOHN. *(Reginald Kenneth Dwight; March 25, 1947). Inducted in 1994.* Rock's Liberace, Elton John dominated popular music in the 1970s, bringing extravagance to rock and roll. A loner and an only child, John was born into a working-class family in Pinner, England. His authoritarian father was a former trumpeter in the Royal Air Force.

Teaching himself to play the piano at age four, the shy Elton later entertained adults by lip-synching to records. After studying classical music for five years on a scholarship at the Royal Academy of Music, he quit, yearning for the excitement of rock music.

Drawn to 1950s piano fireballs like Little Richard and Jerry Lee Lewis, John had formed his own group, Corvette, at age 14. In 1965, that band evolved into Bluesology, with John backing a number of London R&B acts, including John Baldry.

Taking the stage name Elton Hercules John, the singer failed an audition at Liberty Records in 1968. But when Liberty executive Ray Williams introduced John to lyricist Bernie Taupin, a partnership and life-long friendship were born. Originally a poet, Taupin left school to apprentice as a newspaper printer and had also been rejected by Liberty.

Composing music in a style contrary to most songwriting teams, Taupin's lyrics were followed by John's melodies and arrangements. Williams took John/Taupin compositions to music publisher Dick James (of Beatles fame). Although rejecting their early works, James signed the pair as songwriters and demo musicians.

With Elton John creating a mild stir in England with a Taupin/John composition, "Lady Samantha" (1969), James authorized a subsequent solo album on his DJM label, *EMPTY SKY*. Joined by former Spencer Davis members Dee Murray and Nigel Olsson, John's second album, *ELTON JOHN*, spawned a breakthrough hit the romantic ballad "Your Song." In the U.S., the song was first popularized by Three Dog Night.

An incredibly shy performer, John made his first appearance in the U.S. at the Troubadour nightclub in Los Angeles in August 1970. Coheadlining the bill with folkie David Ackles, the crowd was expecting another folk musician. With the room filled with record executives and music critics, John shocked the audience with his hot-pants and winged boots. Garnering superlative press reviews and newfound radio airplay, John's stardom was on the ascent.

Abandoning his softer, light-rock style, John dominated the pop charts in the first half of the 1970s. Along with Billy Joel and Gerry Rafferty, John brought the piano back to the forefront of rock. With his outlandish feather and silk outfits, outrageous glasses, and exaggerated platform shoes (once wearing see-through heels holding live goldfish), John brought theatrical showmanship to rock music.

Adding guitarist Davey Johnstone to his band, John's million-selling hits included "Rocket Man" (1972); "Crocodile Rock" (1972); "Goodbye Yellow Brick Road" (1973); "Bennie and the Jets" (1974); "Don't Let the Sun Go Down on Me" (1974); a cover of the Beatles' "Lucy in the Sky with Diamonds" (1974); and "Philadelphia Freedom" (1975).

His hit albums include *TUMBLEWEED CONNECTION* (1971); *MADMAN ACROSS THE WATER* (1972); *HONKY CHATEAU* (1972); *DON'T SHOOT ME, I'M ONLY THE PIANO PLAYER* (1973); his biggest seller, *GOODBYE YELLOW BRICK ROAD* (1973); and *CARIBOU* (1974). In 1973, John started his own label, Rocket Records, signing Kiki Dee and the resurgent Neil Sedaka.

Murray and Olsson were fired in April 1975, shortly before the release of John's album *CAPTAIN FANTASTIC AND THE BROWN DIRT COWBOY*, the title borrowed from John and Taupin's nicknames. Soon after, John and Taupin parted amicably. Making his film debut in the Who's *Tommy*, John scored a radio hit with a cover of "Pinball Wizard."

After two more top-10 studio albums, *ROCK OF THE WESTIES* and *BLUES MOVES* and a duet hit with Kiki Dee, "Don't Go Breaking My Heart," Elton John's fortune's nose-dived in 1976. Also harming his career was the disclosure of his bisexuality.

Emotionally and physically exhausted from the rigors of the road, suffering from bulimia, and fighting alcohol and cocaine addictions, John quit touring. Taking a long respite in his Surrey, England, home, John took spent much of his time overseeing a professional soccer team.

Dropping his outlandish costumes fro his stage act, the balding performer made a low-key return to music. Teaming with new lyricist Gary Osbourne in 1978 for the album *A SINGLE MAN*, John would land his last million-seller in several years. Touring the USSR in 1978, the following year John scored an unexpected hit with the disco-flavored, two-year-old track "Mama Can't Buy You Love."

Experiencing a major comeback in the 1980s, John reunited with Murray and Olsson. His new run of hits included "Little Jeannie," "I Guess That's Why They Call It the Blues," "Sad Songs," "Nikita," and a John Lennon tribute, "Empty Garden." John scored a surprise top-10 hit in 1987 with a live version of his Marilyn Monroe tribute, "Candle in the Wind."

Finally beating his personal demons, in 1990 John moved to Atlanta. Joining Alcoholics Anonymous, he also entered rehab for drug and eating disorders. After regaining his health, a hair transplant took years off his appearance. In 1993, John's longtime bassist Dee Murray died of skin cancer.

Collaborating with lyricist Tim Rice, John won a Grammy and Oscar for "Can You Feel the Love Tonight?" (1995), from the 10 million-selling soundtrack album *THE LION KING*. Also in 1995, John toured with another piano man, Billy Joel.

Elton John's tribute to Princess Diana "Candle in the Wind 1997," set sales records around the globe, surpassing the all-time sales champ "White Christmas" by Bing Crosby. John donated all the profits to the Princess of Wales Memorial Fund, and was subsequently knighted by Queen Elizabeth.

Bibliography

Bernardin, Claude & Stanton, Tom. (1995). *Rocket Man: The Encyclopedia of Elton John.* Westport, CT: Greenwood Press.

Carr, Rick. (1992, May). Elton John. *Discoveries*, p. 22.

DeCaro, Frank. (1992, March 11). Uncovering surprises about Elton John. *(New York) Newsday*, part II, p. 55.

Dollar, Steve. (1992, August 9). Peachtree's pop icon British rocker Elton John pursuing laid-back life in adopted hometown. *Atlanta Journal and Constitution*, p. A1.

Grossberger, Lewis. (1979, November 4). The new Elton John: A brief dossier. *Washington Post*, p. L1.

Jahr, Cliff. (1976, October 7). Elton John: It's lonely at the top. *Rolling Stone*, p. 11.

John, Elton. (1991). *Two Rooms: Elton John & Bernie Taupin In Their Own Words.* London: Boxtree.

Norman, Philip. (1994, November 26). The night timid Reg of Pinner transformed himself into Elton John and rocked the world. *Daily Mail*, p. 32.

Salewicz, Chris. (1987, March). Elton John: Without the glitz. *Musician*, p. 72.

LITTLE WILLIE JOHN. *(William Edward John; November 15, 1937 - May 26, 1968). Inducted in 1996.* Emerging in the 1950s, R&B balladeer Little Willie John combined the smooth character of jazz with the emotional wails of church-based gospel music. Born near Camden, Arkansas, John moved to Detroit before his 10th birthday. Encouraged by his factory worker father, John and siblings formed a family gospel group, the United Five, which was led by his oldest sister, Mabel.

Against the wishes of his religious parents, John secretly sang doo-wop on street corners. When 14-year-old John performed at the Detroit stop of Johnny Otis' traveling amateur show in 1951, an impressed Otis tried to sign John to King Records. Though rejected by King, John landed touring stints with Paul Williams (of "The Hucklebuck" fame), and the Count Basie Orchestra. John's shocked parents learned of his foray into nonreligious music when Williams requested their permission to take their underage son on the road.

With Williams' assistance, John re-auditioned at King Records in 1955 and was signed by producer Henry Glover. Earning the nickname "Little" Willie John due to his height (he stood five feet four inches). Insecure and short-tempered, John always carried a loaded gun.

His career quick to take off, John landed R&B hits with "All around the World" (1955) and a double-sided entry, the emotion-laden "Need Your Love So Bad"/"Home at Last" (1956). Wanting crossover success, the innocent-looking 18-year-old "John came across as a kind of black Bing Crosby, even down to the pipe. In his homburgs and tailored, wide-shouldered suits, he looked like a boy who had just stepped out of his father's closet" (p. 22), wrote rock critic Kim Field.

John's signature piece came in late 1956 with "Fever," an R&B smash and breakthrough pop crossover hit. Combining jazz with R&B elements, the song also revealed John's gospel-spirited past. Though claiming to have penned the song, John did not receive writer's credit. The cover version of "Fever" was a bigger pop hit for Peggy Lee in 1958.

During this period, John hired a young labelmate named James Brown as his regular opening act. Released in 1958, John's second rock standard came with "Talk to Me, Talk to Me" (1958). Written by actor Joe Seneca, the haunting tune was later a hit for Sunny & the Sunglows.

John's hits continued with "Tell It like It Is" (1958); "Leave My Kitten Alone" (1959); "Heartbreak" (1960); and a cover of Fred Waring's 1924 release "Sleep" (1960). John's last hit came in 1961 with "Take My Love (I Want to Give It All to You)." His career petering out, John began drinking heavily. Having squandered all of his money, he was dropped by King Records in 1963.

After jumping bail on an assault charge in Miami in 1964, John headed to the West Coast. Then in August 1964, John got into a career-ending fight in an illegal after-hours bar, killing Kendall Roundtree, who had taken someone's seat at John's table. After again jumping bail, a lengthy trial ensued.

Convicted of manslaughter, Little Willie John was sentenced to 8 to 20 years. Jailed at the Washington State Penitentiary in the city of Walla Walla, John died two years later from a heart attack. In tribute, James Brown recorded "Thinking about Little Willie John" in 1968. John's sister, Mable John, recorded for Motown and Stax-Volt and sang backup for Ray Charles in the Raelettes.

Singer Madonna had a minor hit with "Fever" in 1993. The rock standard has also been recorded by the McCoys, Tom Waits, and Joe Cocker. The Beatles recorded a reworked version of John's "Leave My Kitten Alone."

Bibliography

Grendysa, Peter. (1987, September-October). Little Willie John rides rough road of R&B to fame but dies in prison a forgotten pioneer. *Record Collector's Monthly*, p. 1.

Field, Kim. (1990, March 27). The strange story of Little Willie John: Fever and fate. *Village Voice*, p. S20.

"Little Willie John: In BIG trouble this time." (1965, January). *Sepia*, p. 60.

Propes, Steve. (1987, February 13). Little Willie John: King of Detroit soul music. *Goldmine*, p. 22.

Williams, Richard. (1993, July 18). Strictly for the grown-ups; Lives of the great songs: "Fever." *Independent*, p. 22.

ROBERT JOHNSON. *(Robert Leroy Dodds; May 8, 1911 - August 16, 1938). Inducted in the Early Influence category in 1986.* A mythical figure in blues, Robert Johnson died just before gaining national notoriety. Rediscovered in the early 1960s, Johnson's popularity has grown with each decade.

The illegitimate son of a field laborer, Johnson was born in Hazelhurst, Mississippi, relocating with his migratory mother from farm to farm. When Johnson was nine, his mother put down roots in the Delta town of Robinsonville. After teaching himself to play the harmonica, the teenage Johnson would sneak into blues joints, pestering the older bluesmen into showing him how to play the guitar. Tiring of a sharecropper's existence, as soon as Johnson was able, he left home. Taking his birth father's surname at age 17, Robert Johnson married a year later, his wife dying during labor.

After disappearing for about a year, Johnson became a proficient guitar player. Building upon the styles of Delta bluesmen like Charlie Patton, Son House, and Skip James, Johnson was said to have been able to play any song after just one listen. Johnson's legend was solidified by the notion that he sold his soul to the devil in exchange for musical prowess. This theme of meeting the devil at "the crossroads" was central in his song "Cross Road Blues."

Bending the notes with a bottle neck of his acoustic guitar, Johnson's style was as revolutionary as it was intriguing. Not fond of sharing his technique, Johnson often played with his back to other musicians. A much better guitarist than singer, Johnson's voice was high and shrill, with his metaphor-laden lyrics sometimes garbled. With his pained wails, he could conjure up images of Satan, lust, and sexual conquest.

Discovered by talent scout H.C. Speir, Johnson managed only two recording sessions. Sent to San Antonio in 1936 by the American Record Corporation for release on their Vocalian label, Johnson recorded in a makeshift studio at the Gunter Hotel. Unaccompanied, he performed "I Believe I'll Dust My Broom," "Cross Road Blues," "Sweet Home Chicago," and his best selling-record, named after an automobile he desired, "Terraplane Blues." Recording a year later at Dallas warehouse, Johnson's second session produced "Love in Vain," "Hellhound on My Trail," "Me and the Devil Blues," and "Traveling Riverside Blues." In all Johnson recorded only 29 songs.

Shortly after the second session, Johnson toured the country with blues guitarist Johnny Shines. To earn better tips, the pair would play everything from polka to jazz and even gospel. After a year together, the pair disbanded, and Johnson was soon dead.

A hard-drinking womanizer, Johnson had scores of lovers. He was likely poisoned by a jealous husband after playing at a house party in the town of Three Forks near Greenwood, Mississippi. Drinking from a bottle of tainted whiskey, the convulsing Johnson died three days later.

With the news of Johnson's death slow to emerge, in the late 1930s both Vocalion Records and a pair Library of Congress musicologists tried to the locate the blues player. Promoter John Hammond was also looking to hire Johnson for his first Spirituals to Swing concert at Carnegie Hall in 1938 (Hammond instead settled for Big Bill Broonzy).

With Columbia Records reissuing Johnson's material in 1961 on the album *KING OF THE DELTA BLUES SINGERS*, British blues-rock bands began to emulate the long-dead musician. Considered the first rock-style guitarist, Johnson spawned dozens of cover versions, including Cream's "Crossroads," the Rolling Stones' "Stop Breaking Down," and Led Zeppelin's "Traveling Riverside Blues." Johnson is sometimes credited for compositions he did not record, such as "Ramblin' on My Mind," and "Mr. Downchild."

Little was known about Johnson until the 1970s when, independently, two blues researchers located his surviving kin and, for the first time, published the only two known photographs of the singer. In exchange for marketing Robert Johnson's music, blues researcher Stephen LaVere legally acquired half the rights to his estate from Johnson's half sister. But with Johnson's music selling at a steady pace in the 1980s, a number of heirs became embroiled in court battle over Johnson's earnings. Johnson's stepson and protégé, Robert Jr. Lockwood, still performs in his home base of Cleveland. CBS records donated $10,000 in 1990 to fund a gravesite marker next to Mt. Zion Missionary Baptist Church near Morgan City, Mississippi.

A "lost" Johnson song is the plot of the 1986 film *Crossroads*, the soundtrack featuring the music of Ry Cooder and Sonny Terry. The film reprised the notion of the devil and the crossroads. Capturing Johnson's entire recorded output, the boxed set *ROBERT JOHNSON: THE COMPLETE RECORDINGS* earned a Grammy in 1991.

Bibliography

Charters, Samuel. (1991, June 23). King of the blues. *Atlanta Journal and Constitution*, p. M1.

Guralnick, Peter. (1989). *Searching for Robert Johnson*. New York: Obelisk-Dutton.

Hamilton, Denise. (1995, October 8). A bluesman's tangled legacy. *Los Angeles Times*, Calendar sect., p. 5.

Hammond, John & Townsend, Irving. (1977). *John Hammond on Record: An* Autobiography. New York: Ridge/Summit.

Obrecht, Jas. (1990). Robert Johnson. In Jas Obrecht (Ed.), *Blues Guitar* (pp. 2-13). San Francisco: GPI.

Scherman, Tony. (1991, January). The hellhound's trail: Following Robert Johnson. *Musician*, p. 31.

JANIS JOPLIN. *(Janis Lyn Joplin; January 19, 1943 - October 3, 1970). Inducted in 1995.* Following in the tradition of Bessie Smith, Janis Joplin was a vocal dynamo. The queen mother of blues-rock, a lethal combination of insecurity and hard-living led to Joplin's demise at the height of her career.

Born into a middle-class family in Port Arthur, Texas, Joplin was a social outcast who was taunted by her classmates. Schooled in the arts, Joplin took dancing lessons, volunteered in a local theater troupe, and was taught to play piano by her mother.

An accomplished painter, Joplin hoped to earn an art degree. After attending Lamar College for a semester, Joplin returned home, taking a business course in keypunch operation. Restless, Joplin moved to Los Angeles, discovering the artsy Venice Beach conclave. Drawn to San Francisco's embryonic folk scene, Joplin was befriended by like-minded beatniks.

Returning to Texas in 1962, she re-enrolled at Lamar before transferring to the University of Texas in Austin. Finding a thriving folk club circuit, Joplin joined a country/folk trio, the Waller Creek Boys. Embracing counterculture art and politics, Joplin began experimenting with drugs and hard liquor.

With failed marriage plans and the embarrassment of being nominated the "ugliest *man* on campus," Joplin hitchhiked to New York City, briefly performing in the folk clubs of Greenwich Village. Tagging along with college classmate Chet Helms, Joplin returned to San Francisco in 1964, where her drug use intensified.

Near death, an emaciated, 88-pound Joplin returned to Port Arthur in May 1965. But returning to Lamar College, she was unable to stay sober. Back at Austin in 1966,

Joplin became an overnight singing sensation, and turned down an invitation to join the psychedelic rock group the 13th Floor Elevators.

Joplin instead took Helms' offer to return to San Francisco to front a six-month-old band he managed, Big Brother & the Holding Company. In spite of her mediocre backing group, Joplin garnered a huge local following. Shortchanged by a Chicago club owner and needing money to get home, the group reluctantly signed with the small Mainstream Records, and were paid a small advance.

Wowing the audience at the Monterey Pop Festival in 1967, Joplin became an instant star. Though shy offstage, with the help of drugs and an always-present bottle of Southern Comfort whiskey, Joplin was transformed into an uninhibited, growling, blues powerhouse. Outrageously dressed in a sea of psychedelia—bell-bottoms, floppy hats, and ropes of beads—Joplin overflowed with charisma. With her Texas drawl and self-described "full-tilt" singing style, Joplin was often compared to blues greats like Bessie Smith and Big Mama Thorton.

Rush-released to capitalize on Joplin's fame, the uneven album *BIG BROTHER & THE HOLDING COMPANY* was a strong seller, highlighted by a cover of Big Mama Thorton's "Ball and Chain."

With new manager Albert Goldman arranging a contract with Columbia Records in early 1968, Joplin saw some substantial royalties. Topping the album charts for two months, *CHEAP THRILLS* featured Joplin's powerful performances of "Down On Me," a cover of Erma Franklin's "Piece of My Heart," and a reworking of George Gershwin's "Summertime."

Convinced by Goldman to hire a new backing band, at the end of 1968 Joplin assembled the Kozmic Blues Band, retaining Big Brother guitarist Sam Andrew. Big Brother & the Holding Company limped along with new lead singer, Nick Gravenites.

Now shooting heroin, Joplin began to buckle from the stresses of rock stardom. At a November 1969 performance in Tampa, Joplin was arrested for using "vulgar and obscene" language. Subsequently losing bookings, some promoters refused to hire Joplin.

Backed by her new group, in late 1969 Joplin released *I GOT DEM OL' KOZMIC BLUES AGAIN MAMA!*, which highlighted by the singles "Kozmic Blues" (1969) and "Try (Just a Little Bit Harder)" (1970). In April 1970, Joplin reunited with Big Brother & the Holding Company for a pair of live appearances in San Francisco. Soon after, the Kozmic Blues Band was expanded into the Full Tilt Boogie Band, Joplin's most proficient backing group.

Engaged to be married and her career on an upswing, Joplin was back on heroin after a brief respite. While recording a new album, on October 4, 1970 Joplin was found dead at the Landmark Hotel in Hollywood, California, with a needle in her arm, the victim of an accidental overdose. Joplin's final sessions were captured on the album *PEARL*, which spawned the posthumous number-one single "Me and Bobby McGee." In 1971, Joplin was nominated for three Grammys.

Although Joplin felt estranged from her hometown of Port Arthur, Texas, the city honored the singer with a bronze bust and exhibit in 1988. The 1980 Bette Midler film *The Rose* was loosely based on Joplin's career.

Surfacing in 1993 were alleged Janis Joplin tapes, reportedly found in a dumpster in the early 1970s. Two separate Joplin film biographies began production in 1997, one starring Melissa Etheridge, and the other Lili Taylor. The latter project was made with the cooperation of the singer's family.

Bibliography

Bronson, Fred. (1992). *The Billboard Book of Number One Singles* (3rd ed.). New York: Billboard.

Draper, Robert. (1992, October). O Janis. *Texas Monthly*, p. 120.

Eberwein, Eric. (1985, July 19). Big Brother and the Holding Company: An updated legacy. *Goldmine*, p. 8.

Johnson, Jon E. (1988, May/June). Port Arthur honors Janis Joplin. *Discoveries*, p. 14.

Joplin, Laura. (1992). *Love, Janis*. New York: Villard.

Lupoff, Richard. (1972, July). Janis Joplin: Death watch. *Ramparts*, p. 51.

Willis, Ellen. (1976, November 18). Janis Joplin. *Rolling Stone*, p. 60.

LOUIS JORDAN. *(Louis Thomas Jordan; July 8, 1908 - February 4, 1975).* *Inducted in the Early Influence category in 1987.* The father of R&B, Louis Jordan was a product of the jazz and vaudeville traditions. Born in Brinkley, Arkansas, Jordan was taught to play the clarinet by his father, a former big-band leader turned music teacher.

Buying an alto saxophone with his own money, Jordan spent his teenage summers on the stage. After a stint with Ma and Pa Rainey's Rabbit Foot Minstrels as a singer, dancer, and occasional musician, Jordan joined Rudy Williams' Belvedere Orchestra.

Moving 60 miles east to Little Rock, in the late 1920s Jordan studied music at Arkansas Bible College. Playing jazz on weekends, Jordan joined several combos, including Jimmy Pryor's Imperial Serenaders.

Moving to the East Coast in 1929, Jordan landed in Philadelphia, briefly joining the Chick Webb Orchestra. Landing in a jazz orchestra led by Charlie Gaines, Jordan appeared on several records, making his vocal debut in 1934 on "I Can't Dance, I Got Ants in My Pants."

Rejoining Chick Webb's Harlem-based 13-piece orchestra in 1936, Jordan played the alto saxophone in the horn section, backing the band's new featured vocalist, Ella Fitzgerald. Emerging as the group's emcee, Jordan assumed additional duties, providing vocals on Webb's 1937 release "Gee, But You're Swell." Angered by Webb's refusal to let him sing onstage, Jordan quit in early 1938.

Forming his own band, Jordan assumed control of a group led by Jesse Stone (later, the writer of "Shake, Rattle and Roll"). Adopting the stage name Bert Williams, Jordan and his new 9-piece orchestra landed a residency at a Harlem jazz club, the Elk's Rendezvous. Recording for Decca in 1939, the renamed Elk's Rendezvous Band became a New York sensation.

Though usually sporting six to eight musicians, Jordan renamed his group the Tympany Five later. Embracing novelty-style material and adding comedic showmanship to his stage act, Jordan began to pack concert halls, his first big seller coming in 1942 with "The Outskirts of Town." Adopting a danceable, shuffle-boogie beat, Jordan's percussion-heavy music was the precursor of 1950s R&B. Bringing the tenor sax into the forefront of popular music as a lead rhythm instrument, Jordan spawned hundreds of imitators.

An early crossover star, Jordan played for black and white audiences alike, becoming the first act to draw mixed racial audiences. Criticized by some in the black community, Jordan was accused of perpetuating racial stereotypes with his vaudeville-style humor. Touring heavily, Jordan auditioned potential record releases in concert, guaranteeing a string of hits, including "Five Guys Named Moe" (1942); the often recorded "Is You Is or Is You Ain't My Baby" (1944); and "Caledonia" (1945), a blistering, upbeat R&B number, predating Little Richard with its near-shrieking vocals.

Adding an electric guitarist to his group, Jordan released his signature piece, "Choo Choo Ch'Boogie" in 1946, the first million-seller by a black artist in modern times. During the 1940s, Jordan also recorded with Bing Crosby, Louis Armstrong and Ella Fitzgerald and appeared in dozens of feature films and music shorts. Jordan's career was harmed in the late 1940s by the Petrillo ban on recording. Released in 1949, Jordan's last number-one hit came with, "Saturday Night Fish Fry."

Wanting to follow in the tradition of Count Basie, in early 1951 Jordan acquired a 15-piece big band, two years later recording with the Nelson Riddle Orchestra. Experiencing a number of well-publicized personal problems, Jordan's hits came to a halt at the end of 1951. Disbanding after a 15 year-run, Jordan and the Tympany Five's last session for Decca came in early 1954, resulting in a minor hit with the appropriately titled, "Nobody Knows You When You Are Down and Out."

With the birth of rock, a whole new crop of imitators had replaced the 46-year-old bandleader. Borrowing Jordan's shuffle-boogie and sax-heavy sound, Jordan's longtime producer, Milt Gabler, turned former hillbilly singer Bill Haley into a star.

Following a brief hiatus, Jordan came out of retirement in 1956, recording an album at Mercury Records with the help of a young arranger named Quincy Jones.

Touring England in 1962, Jordan shared a bill with legendary British jazz bandleader, Chris Barber. Reinvigorated, Jordan settled in Los Angeles, assembling a new Tympany Five. Recording mostly new versions of his older hits throughout the 1960s and 1970s, Jordan was unable to rekindle his career. Jordan's last public performance came in October 1974 in Sparks, Nevada, where he suffered a heart attack. He died four months later.

Rock singer Joe Jackson recorded several of Jordan's classics on the 1940s-inspired album *JUMPIN' JIVE* (1981). Documented Jordan's career, the touring stage musical *Five Guys Named Moe* debuted in 1990.

Bibliography

Burke, Tony & Rye, Howard. (1992, August). Louis Jordan on film. *Blues & Rhythm*, p. 4.

Chilton, John. (1994). *Let the Good Times Roll: The Story of Louis Jordan*. Ann Arbor: University of Michigan Press.

Gelinas, J.P. (1983, June). Louis Jordan: The entertainer. *Goldmine*, p. 38.

Seroff, Doug. (1976). Louis Jordan. *Record Exchanger*, 4(6), p. 20.

Shaw, Arnold. (1978). *Honkers and Shouters*. New York: Collier.

Tosches, Nick. (1992, August 18). The hep cosmogony: Louis Jordan, forefather of rock 'n' roll. *Village Voice*, p. 65.

B.B. KING. *(Riley B. King; September 26, 1925). Inducted in 1987.* Born near Indianola, Mississippi on a plantation, B.B. King had little time for music during his youth. With his parents divorcing, King joined his mother in the cotton fields.

King's blues-hating, religious mother insisted that her son attend church and sing in the choir. "A few of the spiritual people *liked* blues, but they would play *their* blues after 12:00, when they were in their room and nobody could hear them" (p. 113), King told interviewer Tom Wheeler. Following his mother's death, nine-year-old King quit school, working on a tenement farm to keep from starving.

Buying his first guitar at age 12, King borrowed $15 from his employer for a used Stella. Ordering sheet music of country hits from a Sears Roebuck catalog, King taught himself to play. Rejoining his father two years later, King gained some stability in his life.

Running away, King returned to Indianola, joining a gospel quartet, the Elkhorn Singers. Paid compliments and food but no money, King saw little future in gospel music. Turning to blues, he could at least earn a free drink or two, if not tip money.

Discovering a world of like-minded blues musicians in the army during World War II, King contemplated a career in music. Returning home, a tractor accident soured King's appetite for farmwork. Inspired by Sonny Boy Williamson's blues radio show, King landed radio work in Greenwood, Mississippi, before migrating to Memphis in 1946. Living with a distant cousin, blues singer Bukka White, King initially found employment in a factory.

Hired on the spot by WDIA in 1948, King began with a 10-minute program. Calling himself "the Beale Street Blues Boy," King later shortened his moniker to "Blues Boy" and finally, "B.B." A popular local draw, King worked as both a solo act and as a member of the Beale Streeters, a loose-knit group that featured future stars Johnny Ace and Bobby Bland.

After releasing a few obscure singles for Bullet Records, in 1951 King signed with the larger, Los Angeles-based Modern Records. With his debut Modern release, King topped the R&B charts for two months with a remake of Lowell Fulson's "Three O'Clock Blues." Often on the road, King reluctantly quit his radio program in 1953.

Although rooted in the gruff, earthy, Delta tradition, King's version of the blues was more sophisticated and melodic. Playing single-string guitar solos and employing a trademark vibrato, King patterned his technique after the pioneering urban-blues guitarist T-Bone Walker. But with his polished, nimble-fingered style, King was derided by blues purists for being too mainstream. Naming his guitar Lucille, King had once risked his life to retrieve the instrument in a barroom blaze started during a brawl over a woman by that name.

On the road for up to 300 dates a year, King scored a long string of hits, including "You Know I Love You" (1952); "Please Leave Me" (1953); "You Upset Me Baby" (1954); his signature tune, the Memphis Slim-penned "Every Day I Have the Blues" (1955); "Bad Luck" (1956); and "Please Accept My Love" (1958). Nearly leaving his label in 1958 over an unfavorable royalty arrangement, King renegotiated the terms, staying for another three years.

Unlike his contemporaries, King's career did not suffer during the blues slump of the early 1960s. Signing with ABC Records in 1961, King continued his run of hits with the label well into the 1970s.

With white, college-age students discovering blues in the late 1960s, ABC promoted King in the pop markets. After crossing over with the hit "Paying the Cost to Be the Boss" (1968), King received additional exposure as the opening act for the Rolling Stones in 1969.

Featuring a small string section, King's biggest pop hit, "The Thrill Is Gone" (1972), earned him his first Grammy. Garnering celebrity status, King became a regular at Las Vegas and was the first blues act to perform on *The Johnny Carson Show*. Touring the Soviet Union in 1979, King played to packed houses.

Recording a duet with U2 in 1989, "When Love Comes to Town," King was introduced to younger audiences via an MTV video. In 1989, King further expanded blues when he employed synthesizers on his album *KING OF THE BLUES*. King returned to the pop charts in 1996 when the vocals from his song "How Blue Can You Get?" were prominently sampled by the alternative rock band, Primitive Radio Gods, on their hit "Standing outside of a Broken Phone Booth with Money in My Hand."

Still touring up to 250 dates a year, King maintained his popularity well into the 1990s. By 1994, King was up to Lucille number 16.

Bibliography
Cantor, Louis. (1992). *Wheelin' on the Beale* (pp. 78-87). New York: Pharos.

Escott, Colin. (1994, April 29). An appreciation of B.B. King: The fortunate son. *Goldmine*, p. 14.

Kofsky, Frank. (1969, October). T-Bone Walker & B.B. King interview. *Jazz & Pop*, p. 15.

Obrecht, Jas. (1993, September). B.B. the boogie man. *Guitar Player*, p. 30.

Richardson, Jerry & Bowman, Rob. (1989). Conversation with B.B. King: King of the blues. *Black Perspectives in Music, 17*(1,2), p. 135.

Tamarkin, Jeff. (1983, June). B.B. King: A chat with royalty. *Goldmine*, p. 5.

Wheeler, Tom. (1990). B.B. King. In Jas Abrecht (Ed.), *Blues Guitar*, (pp. 110-25). San Francisco: GPI.

THE KINKS. *Mick Avery (Michael Charles Avery; February 15, 1944); Dave Davies (David Russell Gordon Davies; February 3, 1947); Ray Davies (Raymond Douglas Davies; June 21, 1944); Pete Quaife (December 27, 1943). Inducted in 1990.* One of the last surviving British Invasion groups, the Kinks have thrived in spite of their frequent internal squabbles. Born out of the London R&B explosion, the Kinks group predated heavy metal with their crunching guitar chords.

Their father a gardener, Ray and his younger brother Dave Davies were born into a large, working-class family. Though given a guitar on his 13th birthday, Ray Davies planned on becoming a professional soccer player.

Joined by a pair of classmates, including future Kinks bassist Pete Quaife, the Davies brothers formed their first rock band in 1960, featuring three guitarists and one drummer.

While Ray Davies enrolled at Hornsey Art College in 1962, brother Dave was expelled from high school after getting caught with a girl, and was forced into menial jobs. Experimenting with drugs and dropping out of college, Ray rejoined his brother and Pete Quaife in an R&B-flavored rock band, the Ravens (the name inspired by their favorite horror film, *The Raven*). Bankrolled by a pair of young bluebloods, the Ravens performed around London. Firing their drummer, the Ravens hired the jazz-trained Mick Avery, who had responded to a newspaper ad.

Sporting long hair and attired in red hunting jackets and frilly yellow shirts, the Kinks were originally billed as a mod group. Signing with Pye Records (their records released in the U.S. by Warner/Reprise), the renamed Kinks scored a British Invasion hit with their third release, "You Really Got Me" (1964). Written by the group's chief songwriter, Ray Davies, the song featured Ray Davies' stripped-down, three-chord guitar work (contrary to most accounts, Led Zeppelin's Jimmy Page did not play on the record). Recycling the same three guitar chords, the Kinks' hits continued with "All Day and All the Night" (1965) and a pair of ballads, "Tired of Waiting for You" (1965) and "Set Me Free" (1965).

Frequently quarreling among themselves, the Kinks nearly disbanded after an onstage brawl between Mick Avery and Ray Davies during their first British tour in 1965. The following year, the boisterous Kinks were banned from performing in the U.S. by the musician's union after suing a concert promoter.

With Ray Davies' social commentary, in 1966 the Kinks lampooned the upper class on "A Well Respected Man" and mocked trendy youth on "Dedicated Follower of Fashion." Dropping out of the band for a time, an emotionally exhausted Ray Davies wrote the group's next hit, "Sunny Afternoon," during his respite. Also that year, Herman's Hermits scored a top-10 hit with the Davies' composition "Dandy."

By the late 1960s the Kinks hits were drying up, first in the U.S., then England, where they were unable to land decent-paying bookings. After the release of "Days" in 1968, a dejected Peter Quaife quit the band and was replaced by John Dalton. Pursuing a simultaneous solo career, Dave Davies scored a pair of British hits, including "Death of a Clown."

Finally allowed back in the U.S. after Ray Davies signed a letter of apology, the Kinks were relegated to opening-act status, instead of headliners. Landing airplay with "Victoria," the single was from their rock-opera, concept album, *ARTHUR*, the project compared to the Who's *TOMMY*. With the albums ignored and their British television production of *ARTHUR* scrapped, the group nearly disbanded from lack of income.

Expanding the group with keyboardist John Gosling in 1970, the rested Kinks adopted a more mature sound, returning to the top-10 with the smash "Lola." Written by Ray Davies, the song was an autobiographical account of his misadventure with a transvestite at a Paris nightclub. The song was banned on British radio not over its lyrical content but because it mentioned a commercial product, Coca-Cola.

Signing with RCA in 1971, the Kinks turned introspective on the moderately successful album *MUSWELL HILLBILLIES* (the title inspired by the *Beverly Hillbillies* program). Adding a brass section and theatrics to their stage show, the Kinks fared poorly with their subsequent, concept-styled albums such as *PRESERVATION ACTS 1 & 2*. A dejected Ray Davies also experimented with film making.

After signing with Arista in 1976, the Kinks moved away from pop, adopting a harder-rock sound. Releasing their best-selling album in a decade, *SLEEPWALKER* was highlighted by the hit "Life on the Road."

The Kinks enjoyed a pair of cover versions in the late 1970s, with Van Halen scoring their breakthrough hit with "You Really Got Me" (1978) and the Pretenders landing a British chart-entry with "Stop Your Sobbing" (1979).

Earning their first gold album in over a decade, the Kinks' *LOW BUDGET* spawned a comeback hit single, "(I Wish I Could Fly Like) Superman" (1979). Follow-up albums include the live *ONE FOR THE ROAD*, spawning the radio hits "Lola" and "You Really Got Me"; and *GIVE THE PEOPLE WHAT THEY WANT*, with the angry punk-flavored "Destroyer" (1981), the track considered a sequel to "Lola." Ray Davies and girlfriend Chrissie Hynde of the Pretenders celebrated the birth of a daughter in 1983. A year later, Hynde left Davies for Jim Kerr of the Simple Minds.

The Kinks' success began to fade after the release of the album *STATE OF CONFUSION* (1984); the quirky project was highlighted by the melancholy ballad "Don't Forget to Dance" and "Come Dancing," a big band-styled song written by Ray Davies about his older sister. Following an altercation with Dave Davies, Avery was fired from the Kinks in 1984.

After their final Arista album, *WORD OF MOUTH*, the band reduced its output in favor of side projects. In 1985, Davies wrote and directed the film, *Waterloo*. Switching to RCA records, the Kinks fared poorly with their label debut, *THINK VISUAL*. Their 1993 release, *PHOBIA*, was highlighted by "Hatred (A Duet)," which poked fun at the nasty, competitive relationship between Ray and Dave Davies. Both Davies brothers penned autobiographies in 1990s. In his book, Dave Davies details his encounters with supernatural beings.

Bibliography
Forte, Dan. (1977, September). Dave Davies of 'The Kinks.' *Guitar Player*, p. 24.
Mitchell, Greg. (1976, March). Self preservation: A multi-media production starring Raymond
        Douglas Davies as (himself). *Crawdaddy*, p. 27.
Ruhlmann, William. (1993, March 19). Working the Kinks out. *Goldmine*, p. 10.
Savage, Jon. (1984). *The Kinks*. London: Faber and Faber.
Schruers, Fred. (1978, November 2). The once and future Kinks. *Rolling Stone*, p. 1.
Sharp, Ken. (1996, March 1). He's not like everybody else: God save Ray Davies. *Goldmine*,
        p. 23.

GLADYS KNIGHT AND THE PIPS. *William Guest (June 2, 1941); Gladys Knight (Gladys Maria Knight; May 28, 1944); Merald "Bubba" Knight (September 4, 1942); Edward Patten (August 2, 1939). Inducted in 1996.* A veteran R&B outfit formed a decade before their successful run at Motown, Gladys Knight and the Pips began as an informal family singing group. Knight had been a member of the Morris Brown gospel choir at Atlanta's Mount Moriah Baptist Church since the age of four, as a child standing on a chair to be seen. Winning a national talent competition on *The Ted Mack Amateur Hour* with her rendition of Nat King Cole's "Too Young," Knight earned $2,000 and a year-long touring spot with Mack. Homesick, Knight quit the tour after several months.

Knight first sang with the future Pips at her brother, Bubba's, 10th birthday party in 1952, prodded to perform after their record player broke. Impressing cousin James "Pip" Wood, he became their manager, finding them nightclub gigs as the Pips and gospel engagements as the Fountaineers. In the family act, Gladys Knight was joined by her brother, Merald "Bubba" Knight, sister Brenda, and cousins William and Eleanor Guest.

One of their regular bookings was at a tiny Atlanta nightclub called Builders. After touring with Jackie Wilson and Sam Cooke, the Pips released an obscure single in 1958 on Brunswick Records. With both Brenda Knight and Eleanor Guest leaving in 1959 to get married, Gladys Knight was the last remaining female member. The Pips lineup was then expanded with cousins Edward Patten and Langston George.

When the owner of the Builders nightclub launched Huntom Records, he released the Pips' rendition of the Royals "Every Beat of My Heart." Catching the interest of the larger Fury Records, Gladys Knight and the Pips recorded a second version of the song. With the original master sold to Vee-Jay, both versions landed on the R&B charts, with the Vee-Jay version (as the Pips) outselling the Fury release. After a few follow-up Fury releases, Langston George quit the group, with a pregnant Gladys Knight leaving soon after.

Though adding a dance routine, the remaining Pips struggled as a stage act, instead surviving as session singers. After having two children, Knight returned to the group in 1964. Signing with Van McCoy's Maxx label, the group managed a pair of minor R&B chart entries, including the McCoy-penned and produced "Giving Up."

Against Gladys Knight's wishes, the group voted to sign with Motown in 1965. Capitalizing on Motown's hit factory, the group's first hit came with the Eddie Holland/Norman Whitfield-penned "Everybody Needs Love" (1967). The follow-up release, "I Heard It Through the Grapevine," gave the group their first major pop hit, predating Marvin Gaye's better-selling version by a year. Subsequent Motown hits included "The End of Our Road" (1968); a cover of Shirley Ellis' "Nitty Gritty" (1969); "If I Were Your Woman" (1970); and their only self-penned Motown hit, "I Don't Want to Do Wrong" (1971).

Unhappy with their treatment at the label, the Pips left Motown when their contract expired in 1972. Lured to Buddah Records with a lucrative contract, Gladys Knight and the Pips continued their string of hits, beginning with the Grammy-winning, "Midnight Train to Georgia" (1973). But when Motown scored a surprise hit with a Pips' leftover track "Neither One of Us," the group sued their former label, alleging unpaid royalties.

The Pips Buddah hits continued with "The Best Thing That Ever Happened to Me" (1974), "On and On" (1974), and the medley "The Way We Were/Try to Remember" (1975). Red-hot, the group landed its own NBC variety show, and Knight starred in the film *Pipe Dreams*.

After receiving a bad check for $100,000 from Buddah, Gladys Knight and the Pips tried to join Columbia Records. But with lawsuits flying, Knight and the Pips were unable to record together, each forced into releasing separate albums.

Reuniting in 1980 at CBS, Gladys Knight and the Pips recorded the Ashford and Simpson-produced album *ABOUT LOVE*. Slow to reignite their career, the group landed little crossover airplay. Moving to MCA in 1987, their album *ALL OUR LOVE* spawned a pair of R&B hits, "Love Overboard" and "Lovin' on Next to Nothin'."

In the 1985-86 television season, Knight co-starred with comedian Flip Wilson on the sitcom *Charlie & Company*. That year she also joined Dionne Warwick, Elton John, and Stevie Wonder under the moniker Dionne & Friends for the top-10 million-seller "That's What Friends Are For."

Knight left the Pips for a solo career in the late 1980s, releasing the albums *GOOD WOMAN* (1991) and *JUST FOR YOU* (1994). As separate acts, both Gladys Knight and the Pips fared poorly in the 1990s. As part of a supergroup quartet of Chaka Khan, Brandy and Tamia, Knight returned to the R&B charts in 1996 with, "Missing" from the soundtrack of the film *Set It Off*.

Bibliography

Fong-Torres, Ben. (1974, July 6). Gladys Knight & the Pips. *Rolling Stone*, p. 52.
Holden, Stephen. (1980, August 7). Gladys Knight: The end of a nightmare. *Rolling Stone*, p. 16.
Little, Benilde. (1991, October). Just Gladys. *Essence*, p. 52.
Taraborrelli, Randy J. (1986). *Motown: Hot Wax, City Cool & Solid Gold* (pp. 80-85). New York: Dolphin/Doubleday.
Warner, Jay. (1994, January). 35 years later and still going strong: Gladys Knight & the Pips. *Discoveries*, p. 18.
Whitaker, Charles. (1988, September). Gladys Knight & the Pips mark 36 years of making music. *Ebony*, p. 72.

LEADBELLY. *(Huddie William Ledbetter; January 15, 1888 - December 6, 1949). Inducted in the Early Influence category in 1988.* Combining folk and blues, Leadbelly helped popularize both genres of American music. Born near Shreveport, Louisiana, and growing up in Texas, Leadbelly tended to the livestock and crops, while his parents cleared the 68 acres of their newly acquired land. Taught Cajun-style accordion at age six by an uncle, Leadbelly later played the organ at the local Shiloh Baptist Church.

Quitting school after finishing the eighth grade, the muscular Leadbelly was attracted to the vices of women and liquor and the shanty bars that housed them. A father by age 15, Leadbelly worked as a transient farm laborer during the weekdays, and played a 12-string "Mexican" guitar on Saturday nights. Convicted of assault at age 18 and sentenced to 30 days of hard labor, he escaped after three days.

Settling in New Orleans under an assumed name, Walter Boyd, Leadbelly's violent nature again emerged in 1918. After serving 7 years of a 30-year murder sentence, he was pardoned after writing an impassioned song for governor of Texas. After killing a man in self-defense in 1928, two years later Leadbelly was convicted of attempted murder for slashing a white man at a street corner Salvation Army concert. Back in prison in 1930, Leadbelly was sentenced to six to eight-years at the notorious Angola Prison.

Meanwhile, while searching southern prisons for "Negro" work songs, in 1933 musicologist John A. Lomax landed at Angola Prison, and recorded Leadbelly for the

Library of Congress, the sessions highlighted by his signature piece, "Irene" (later known as "Goodnight Irene"). Benefitting from another pardon, in 1934 Leadbelly joined Lomax, first working as his chauffeur and butler.

With Lomax's assistance, Leadbelly was recorded by ARC Records, his old-time folk songs then considered out of fashion. Taking Leadbelly on tour, Lomax marketed him as a prison musician, costuming him as a barefoot savage in prison garb or overalls. Though garnering much positive press with songs like "Mr. Tom Hughs" and "Midnight Special," Leadbelly never achieved mass stardom.

Moving to New York City in 1935, Leadbelly performed his politically oriented material at folk-clubs, union rallies, and college campuses. Embraced by America's left-wing intellectuals, he shared their philosophies.

Parting with Lomax, Leadbelly had resented working as his servant. But Lomax further profited from the association with the release of the 1936 book *Negro Folk Songs as Sung by Lead Belly*, for which Leadbelly was paid only five dollars. Leadbelly was also angered by the book's demeaning drawings of blacks.

Recording additional songs for the Library of Congress, Leadbelly performed a string of classics, including "Rock Island Line," "Mama, Did You Bring Me Any Silver," and, challenging racial injustice, "Scottsboro Boys." Much like his frequent partner Woody Guthrie, Leadbelly derived much of his material from the southern and Appalachian-style hillbilly ballads common to both poor blacks and whites.

Again jailed, Leadbelly served a year's time at Rikers Island for assault. Upon his release, he recorded several tracks with a pioneering gospel group the Golden Gate Quartet. Peppering his songs with spoken narratives, Leadbelly later recorded for Stinson, Capitol, and most often for Moses Asch's Folkway Records.

Hoping to break into film, Leadbelly traveled to the West Coast in the mid-1940s. Unsuccessful, he instead sang to dwindling nightclub audiences in Los Angeles and San Francisco. Returning to New York he died of Lou Gehrig's disease in 1949. Several months later, his composition, "Goodnight Irene" was a million-selling hit for the Weavers.

During the folk explosion of the 1960s, Leadbelly was discovered by millions of college-aged fans. Directed by Gordon Parks, the 1976 film biography *Leadbelly* emphasized the performer's early life.

Bibliography

Cowley, John. (1991, March). Take a whiff on me. *Blues & Rhythm*, p. 59.
Filene, Benjamin. (1991). "Our singing country": John and Alan Lomax, Leadbelly, and the construction of American past. *American Quarterly, 43*(4), p. 602.
Obrecht, Jas. (1996, August). Lead Belly: King of the 12-string guitar. *Guitar Player*, p. 55.
Ward, Geoffrey C. (1993, October). Leadbelly: The great Louisiana bluesman made his first recordings inside the Angola Penitentiary. *American Heritage*, p. 10.

LED ZEPPELIN. *John Bonham (John Henry Bonham; May 31, 1948 - September 25, 1980); John Paul Jones (John Baldwin; January 3, 1946); Jimmy Page (James Patrick Page; January 9, 1944); Robert Plant (Robert Anthony Plant; August 20,*

1948). Inducted in 1995. The pioneers of British heavy metal, Led Zeppelin dominated rock music in the 1970s. By combining R&B-styled vocals with updated, electrified Chicago blues, the group became the Beatles of hard rock.

Born out of the ashes of the Yardbirds, Led Zeppelin was assembled by Jimmy Page to fulfill contractual obligations. A popular session player, Page had joined the Yardbirds in 1966, sharing rhythm guitar duties with Jeff Beck. Forced to recruit a substitute group called the New Yardbirds after all of his bandmates quit, Page first hired session bassist, John Paul Jones. Rejected by his first choice for drummer, B.J. Wilson of Procol Harem, Page instead added the former leader of Band of Joy, John "Bonzo" Bonham. At Bonham's suggestion, the group was completed by singer Robert Plant, a former accountant apprentice who had fronted a series of blues-rock bands. After a brief Scandinavian tour, the group adopted a new moniker, Led Zeppelin.

Managed by Peter Grant (a former professional wrestler), Led Zeppelin hit the U.S. in December 1968 as the opening act for MC5 and Iron Butterfly. Following a bidding war, Led Zeppelin signed a lucrative deal with Atlantic Records, receiving a then unheard of $200,000 advance for their first album.

Demonstrating their blues influences on their debut, self-titled release, *LED ZEPPELIN*, the band recorded a pair of Willie Dixon songs, "I Can't Quit You Baby" and "You Shook Me." Receiving a poor review in *Rolling Stone* magazine, the top-10 album also featured the soon-to-be rock standards "Good Times Bad Times," "Dazed and Confused," and "Communication Breakdown."

Heavily borrowing from early blues songwriters (often without crediting their sources), Led Zeppelin updated the genre with crunching guitars and sophisticated studio technique. With Page and Plant dabbling in the occult, the pair infused mysticism and Celtic mythology into their lyrics. (Page even bought Aleister Crowley's home.)

Though initially ignored by the rock press and top-40 radio in the U.S., Led Zeppelin regularly broke attendance records and sold tens of millions of albums. The band never matched the same level of success in their native England. Fronted by Robert Plant, a powerful, versatile singer with flowing blond hair and good looks, Led Zeppelin invented arena-rock, employing the now standard fare of smoke machines, explosions, and laser beams.

Written and recorded during an 18-month tour, their second album, *LED ZEPPELIN 2*, was an international smash, highlighted by "Ramble On" and Bonham's 15-minute drum solo on "Moby Dick." Another track, the group's only top-10 pop hit, "Whole Lotta Love," spawned a lawsuit over its similarity to Willie Dixon's "You Need Love." Releasing their third album in two years, *LED ZEPPELIN 3* included the top-20 hit "Immigrant Song" (1971).

Their landmark, untitled fourth album (alternatively known as *LED ZEPPELIN IV*, *RUNES*, and *ZOSO*) was highlighted by their signature piece, "Stairway to Heaven," which was suspected of harboring a satanic message. Even without the benefit of a single-release or top-40 airplay (in England, the group released no commercial 45s), the song became a cornerstone of album-rock radio. The album also featured a cover of Memphis Minnie's "When the Levee Breaks"; a guitar-grinding, "Rock and Roll";

Led Zeppelin.

with Page on acoustic guitar, "Going to California"; and the pop hit "Black Dog" (1972). While on tour to promote their keyboard-heavy, follow-up album *HOUSES OF THE HOLY*, a thief escaped with $180,000 in gate receipts at a Madison Square Garden concert in 1973.

Signing a new lucrative contract with Atlantic Records in 1974, Led Zeppelin was given its own subsidiary label, Swansong, whose roster later included Bad Company, Dave Edmunds, and Maggie Bell. Led Zeppelin's first Swansong album, the two-disc *PHYSICAL GRAFFITI*, included outtakes from previous sessions and was highlighted by "Trampled Underfoot" and the exotic, Eastern-influenced "Kashmir."

Trouble beset the group in 1975 when Robert Plant and his wife were involved in a serious car crash in Greece. Recorded with Plant on crutches, the uneven album *PRESENCE* was released the following year. Also in 1976, Led Zeppelin released its only live recording, the soundtrack to their concert/fantasy film *The Song Remains the Same*.

Led Zeppelin's misfortunes continued into 1977 when John Bonham was convicted of assault after attacking an employee of promoter Bill Graham at an Oakland concert; later in the year, Bonham broke three ribs in an automobile accident. With the sudden death of Plant's son, Karac, Plant withdrew from the public arena leaving the group in limbo. After 1977, Led Zeppelin would never again perform in the U.S.

After a long hiatus, Led Zeppelin returned in 1979 with, *IN THROUGH THE OUT DOOR*, scoring pop and album-rock hits with "All of My Love" (1979) and "Fool in the Rain" (1980). Welcomed back by fans, remarkably all eight of the group's previous albums recharted.

Following a European tour, which had been cut short due to Bonham's reported "physical exhaustion," the group readied itself for a North American leg. But on the eve of their departure, tragedy again struck the group. After consuming a reported 40 shots of vodka, John Bonham died in his sleep on September 25, 1980. In December, the group formally announced its breakup. Produced by Jimmy Page, a collection of Zeppelin outtakes was released on the 1982 album *CODA*. But even without new material, Led Zeppelin remained a staple of rock radio in the 1980s.

All three surviving members of the group pursued solo careers. Robert Plant was the most successful, releasing solo albums and forming a roots-rock group the Honeydrippers, landing a pair of cover hits with the rock standards "Sea of Love" and "Rockin' at Midnight." Jimmy Page released a series of soundtrack albums and had fruitful pairings with vocalist Paul Rodgers in the Firm, and with former Whitesnake frontman David Coverdale in the duo Coverdale/Page. John Paul Jones experimented with classical music, later teaming with avant-garde rocker Diamanda Galas.

Only rarely reuniting in concert, the surviving members of Led Zeppelin were joined by drummers Phil Collins and Tony Thompson for the 1985 charity concert Live Aid, a hoarse Robert Plant struggling to reach the high notes on "Rock and Roll." But an announced reunion album never materialized. The band also performed at Atlantic Records' 40th anniversary concert in 1989 with drummer Jason Bonham filling in for his deceased father.

When MTV offered Robert Plant an *Unplugged* segment, he decided to regroup with Jimmy Page for an "Unledded" special. Reuniting on the 1994 album *NO QUARTER*, the pair re-recorded updated versions of Led Zeppelin classics, and followed with a sold-out "Unledded" concert tour. A miffed John Paul Jones was not asked to participate. The trio later reunited at the Rock & Roll Hall of Fame ceremony in January 1995.

A series of redundant Led Zeppelin compilation albums were released by Atlantic in the 1990s. A 1990 boxed set, *LED ZEPPELIN*, was highlighted by the previously unreleased track "Traveling Riverside Blues." Released in 1997, the two-disc set *THE BBC SESSIONS*, spawned the radio hit "The Girl I Love."

Bibliography

Considine, J.D. (1994, December). In through the out door. *Musician*, p. 56.
Crowe, Cameron. (1975. March 13). The durable Led Zeppelin: A conversation with Jimmy

Page and Robert Plant. *Rolling Stone*, p. 32.

Davis, Stephen. (1986). *Hammer of the Gods*. New York: Ballantine. Goldwin, Robert. (1990, August 24). Led Zeppelin: Alchemists of the '70s. *Goldmine*, p. 12.

Humphries, Patrick. (1994, December). The second coming. *Vox*, p. 42.

Jerome, Jim. (1982, August 9). With the crash of Led Zep behind him, lead singer Robert Plant is flying solo. *People*, p. 54.

Ruhlmann, William. (1990, August 24). Does anybody remember laughter: Led Zeppelin now and then. *Goldmine*, p. 8.

LEIBER & STOLLER. *Jerry Leiber (Jerome Leiber; April 25, 1933); Mike Stoller (March 13, 1933). Inducted in the Non-Performer category in 1987.* Born just six weeks apart, the unlikely team of Jerry Leiber and Mike Stoller combined to write and produce some of the best R&B of the 1950s. The son of Polish Jews, Jerry Leiber received piano lessons from an uncle. While delivering groceries to a mostly black clientele, he discovered jazz and blues.

At age 12, Leiber moved with his widowed mother moved to Los Angeles, settling just two blocks from the RKO-Paramount studio. Frequenting the studio, Leiber once asked Cecil B. DeMille to make him a actor. Securing a job in a record store at age 16, Leiber began writing song lyrics. Needing a collaborator to write the music, a classmate suggested fellow student Mike Stoller.

Born on Long Island, the introverted Stoller was first exposed to R&B at summer camp, where older black teenagers belted the music on the piano. At age 10, Stoller received music lessons from legendary stride pianist James P. Johnson. While Stoller's father worked as an engineer, his model/actress mother took him to Broadway shows. Though underage, Stoller later frequented New York City's legendary jazz clubs.

Moving to a Mexican section of Los Angeles at age 16, Stoller was drawn to the music of a neighborhood Spanish social club, briefly joining the house band. After injuring himself at his father's machine shop, Stoller quit to pursue a career in music.

Meeting Leiber, Stoller was initially hesitant about a collaborative relationship. Gravitating toward the emerging Los Angeles R&B scene, the like-minded teens soon found much in common, with both youths dating black women.

As songwriters, their first successes came with "Hard Times," a hit for Charles Brown, and the often recorded "Kansas City," first reworked as "K.C. Loving" by Little Willie Littlefield. Then at the request of bandleader Johnny Otis, the pair composed "Hound Dog," a smash hit for blues shouter Big Mama Thorton.

Aided by Lester Sill of Modern Records, in 1953 Leiber & Stoller opened their own label Spark Records. Their first success came with the Robins, landing regional hits with "Riot in Cell Block #9," "Framed," and "Smokey Joe's Cafe." Unable to promote their releases outside southern California, Leiber & Stoller signed a deal with Atlantic Records. With half of the Robins refusing to join Leiber & Stoller in New York City, the group splintering into two camps, with Carl Gardner and Bobby Nunn opting to join a new Leiber & Stoller-produced group, the Coasters.

Hired by Atlantic in 1956 as independent producers (then an unheard of practice), Leiber & Stoller also delivered the Coasters. The talented duo wrote and produced most of the Coasters' hits, including, "Yakety Yak," "Poison Ivy," and a double-sided entry, "Searchin'"/"Youngblood." Writes Atlantic's Jerry Wexler in his autobiography, "Leiber had a flair for theatrics. In fact, in another era, he could have made some fantastic white-boy rhythm and blues on his own. The demos, on which he sang lead, were terrific. He had a great growl of a voice, and it's clear that [Coaster] Billy Guy, his black surrogate, was his musical alter ego" (p. 135).

Leiber & Stoller's other major Atlantic success came with the Drifters, highlighted by the pair's pioneering use of a string section on their 1961 hit, "There Goes My Baby." After Drifters lead singer Ben E. King quit the band for a solo career, he landed his signature hit with the Leiber & Stoller-composed "Stand by Me."

Recorded without their knowledge, Leiber & Stoller's biggest hit came with Elvis Presley's reworked version of "Hound Dog." Consequently, the duo supplied Presley with several film hits, including "Jailhouse Rock," "King Creole," and "Treat Me Nice." Their relationship with Presley was severed after a financial disagreement with the King's manager, Colonel Tom Parker.

Leaving Atlantic in 1963, Leiber & Stoller were unhappy with their royalty arrangements and with the loss of the Drifters to another producer. Moving to United Artists Records, they veered toward mainstream pop, producing hits for the Exciters and Jay & the Americans. But tired of making others rich, Leiber & Stoller launched a pair of short-lived record companies, Daisy and Tiger.

Starting another label, Red Bird Records, Leiber & Stoller employed a number of Brill Building songwriters, including Shadow Morton and Ellie Greenwich. Primarily a girl-group label, Red Bird's successes included the Dixie Cups' "Going to the Chapel" and the Shangri-Las' "Leader of the Pack." Tiring of the rigors of the record industry, Leiber & Stoller sold out to their partner, George Goldner, in 1966.

After writing the apocalyptic Peggy Lee hit "Is That All There Is," Leiber & Stoller slowed their output. In the 1970s, the team produced albums for Procol Harem and Stealers Wheel (also writing their hit "Stuck in the Middle With You"). In the 1980s, Leiber & Stoller wrote Michael McDonald's 1982 hit "I Keep Forgettin'" and saw their old production of Ben E. King's "Stand By Me," return to the charts. The Broadway production *Smokey Joe's Cafe* showcases 42 Leiber & Stoller hits.

Bibliography

Booth, Dave & Escott, Colin. (1984, October 26). Jerry Leiber & Mike Stoller: What is the secret of your success? *Goldmine*, p. 14.

Fox, Ted. (1986, December). Jerry Leiber & Mike Stoller: The first independent producers: Part II. *Audio*, p. 54.

Fricke, David. (1990, April 19). Leiber & Stoller. *Rolling Stone*, p. 97.

Kubernik, Harvey R. (1995, April 28). Yakety yak with Leiber and Stoller. *Goldmine*, p. 60.

Metcalf, Steve. (1996, September 30). Leiber, Stoller exemplify musical melting pot. *The Hartford Courant*, p. 4J.

Palmer, Robert. (1978). *Baby, That Was Rock & Roll: The Legendary Leiber & Stoller*. New York: Harcourt Brace Jovanovich.

Wexler, Jerry & Ritz, David. (1993). *Rhythm and the Blues: A Life in American Music*. New York: Alfred A. Knopf.

White, Mark. (1985). *You Must Remember This: Popular Songwriters 1900-1980* (pp. 129-33). New York: Charles Scribner's Sons.

JOHN LENNON. *John Winston Lennon; October 9, 1940 - December 8, 1980).*
Inducted in 1994. The co-leader of the Beatles, John Lennon emerged as a prolific
solo artist after the Fab Four's demise in 1970. Born in Liverpool, England, in 1940
to Julia and Alfred Lennon, John Lennon rarely saw his father after his parents
divorced. Considering herself an unfit mother, Julia Lennon gave up John to her sister.

Raised in a middle-class Liverpool suburb by Mimi (Mary) and her husband, dairy
farmer George Smith, Lennon planned to work at sea (like his birth father who was a
ship's steward). Inspired by Elvis Presley's "Heartbreak Hotel," Lennon instead
turned to music.

Forming the Beatles with Paul McCartney, Lennon reinvented popular music in the
1960s. Shortly before the group landed their first British hit with "Love Me Do" on
August 23, 1962, Lennon married Cynthia Powell.

Not content with his status as pop star, Lennon published two books, *In His Own
Write* (1964) and *A Spaniard in the Works* (1965). Written in a stream-of-
consciousness style, neither of the volumes sold well at the time. Apart from several
Beatles films, Lennon attempted acting, co-starring in the Richard Lester-directed film
How I Won The War (1966); Lennon played the role of Private Gripweed,
necessitating the cutting of his then-long hair.

Leaving his wife, Cynthia, Lennon began dating avant-garde artist Yoko Ono in
1968. Seven years his senior, the Tokyo-raised Ono had first met Lennon at a London
art exhibition of her works two years earlier. Often blamed for the Beatles' breakup,
Ono was constantly at Lennon's side during the group's recording sessions, even
providing backing vocals on a pair of songs, "Birthday" and "The Continuing
Adventures of Bungalow Bill."

Coinciding with the release of the Beatles album, *THE BEATLES (THE WHITE
ALBUM)* in November 1968, Lennon teamed with Ono on the album *UNFINISHED
MUSIC NO. 1: TWO VIRGINS.* Featuring a nude photograph of Lennon and Ono on
the cover, *TWO VIRGINS* was sold in record stores packaged in a brown paper
wrapper. Following a New Jersey judge's order, 30,000 copies of the album were
confiscated in that state.

Dressed in white, Lennon and Ono married at the British consulate's office at
Gibraltar on March 20, 1969, with Lennon changing his middle name to Ono.
Honeymooning at the Amsterdam Hilton, Lennon and Ono held a protest for world
peace at their infamous "bed-in" press conference.

Meanwhile, with its controversial lyrics, Lennon's Beatles-related single "The
Ballad of John and Yoko" stirred much negative press. Forming the Plastic Ono Band,
Lennon's first single apart from the Beatles, the anthemic "Give Peace a Chance"
(1969) was recorded at a Montreal hotel during the honeymooning couple's second
bed-in.

Following a secretive agreement in April 1969 to disband the Beatles, Lennon
began pursuing a career apart from the Fab Four. The Plastic Ono Band released a
pair of albums in 1969. Featuring rock classics such as "Money" and "Blue Suede
Shoes," the uneven *THE PLASTIC ONO BAND: LIVE PEACE IN TORONTO 1969*
was recorded at an all-star oldies concert with Carl Perkins, Jerry Lee Lewis and
others. Released as by "John and Yoko," a two-disc album, *THE WEDDING ALBUM,*

consisted of electronic test signals and other experimental material.

A month before the May 1970 release of the Beatles' final album, *LET IT BE*, McCartney publicly announced the group's breakup. Fresh from his work on *LET IT BE*, Phil Spector produced Lennon's psychedelic-styled single "Instant Karma."

Issued in 1971, the album *JOHN LENNON: PLASTIC ONO BAND* was inspired by primal-scream therapy and was highlighted by the tracks "Mother" and "Working Class Hero." More commercially oriented, *IMAGINE* spawned a pop hit with "Imagine" and included a personal attack against Paul McCartney, "How Do You Sleep?"

Making New York City their home, John and Yoko moved into the Dakota Building in 1971. Taking far-left stances on a myriad of causes, Lennon became the frequent target of authorities. At the orders of President Nixon and congressional investigators, Lennon was placed under surveillance by the FBI. Citing a previous drug conviction, the U.S. Immigration Department prevented Lennon from obtaining permanent resident status.

Releasing the politically tinged double-album *SOME TIME IN NEW YORK CITY*, one disc teamed Lennon with Elephant Memory, while the other captured Lennon in concert performances with Frank Zappa and the Mothers of Invention. In April 1972, Lennon headlined his only true solo concert at Madison Square Garden. (The concert was captured on the 1986 album and video *LIVE IN NEW YORK CITY*.) Released at year's end, the holiday classic, "Happy Xmas (War Is Over)" (1972) initially flopped in the U.S.

In March 1973, Lennon was ordered to leave the U.S. by the Immigration Department, after a long legal struggle for a green card. Fighting deportation, he was finally granted residency status in 1976.

Separating from Ono in 1973, Lennon began his famed 18-month lost weekend with a new flame, his former secretary May Pang. Spending much of 1974 carousing with Harry Nilsson in Los Angeles, Lennon also produced Nilsson's album *PUSSYCATS*.

Now crafting commercially accessible music, in late 1973 Lennon released *MIND GAMES*, highlighted by the ephemeral top-10, title track, "Mind Games." Teaming with Elton John on the hit "Whatever Gets You thru the Night" (1974), the song was from Lennon's number-one album *WALLS AND BRIDGES*. A follow-up single, "#9 Dream," also hit the top-10. Joining Elton John at a concert in November 1974, Lennon made his last-ever stage appearance. Releasing a long awaited album of early rock classics, *ROCK 'N' ROLL*, Lennon scored his last hit of the decade in 1975 with a remake of Ben E. King's "Stand by Me." That year, Lennon reconciled with Ono and co-wrote David Bowie's chart-topper "Fame."

With the birth of Sean Taro Ono Lennon on October 9, 1975, John Lennon quit music to become a self-described "house-husband" and Sean's full-time caretaker. Except for a brief collaboration with Ringo Starr, Lennon spent the next five years away from the music business.

Inspired to record after hearing the B-52s on the radio (he thought it was Yoko Ono) while in Bermuda, in 1980 Lennon signed with Geffen Records. With the November release of Lennon/Ono comeback album *DOUBLE FANTASY*, Lennon was gratified to see the doo-wop-styled first single, "(Just Like) Starting Over," zooming up the charts.

But tragedy befell Lennon upon returning home with his wife. Shot seven times shortly before 11 p.m. on December 8, 1980, outside his New York City apartment building by a deranged, 25-year-old publicity hound, Lennon bled to death in a police cruiser en route to Roosevelt Hospital. Gathering by the thousands, mournful fans sang Lennon's songs at a candlelight vigil at the scene.

After Lennon's death, 12 of his solo and Beatles albums re-entered the best-seller charts. From *DOUBLE FANTASY*, Lennon scored a pair of posthumous top-10 hits with "Woman" and "Watching the Wheels." Earning four Grammy nominations in 1981, Lennon and Ono won for Best Album. Lennon tributes included George Harrison's "All Those Years Ago" (1981), Yoko Ono's "My Man" (1982), and Elton John's "Empty Garden" (1982).

Ono kept Lennon's memory alive by occasionally issuing previously unreleased material. Containing primarily *DOUBLE FANTASY* outtakes, the platinum certified *MILK AND HONEY: A HEART PLAY* spawned the top-10 hit "Nobody Told Me" (1984). Ono and Mayor Ed Koch dedicated the two-and-a-half-acre, tear-shaped Strawberry Fields garden in New York's Central Park on Lennon's 45th birthday in 1985. A syndicated weekly radio program, *The Lost Lennon Tapes*, debuted in 1988, featuring studio conversations, alternate takes, and unreleased material.

Ono also oversaw a pair of biographical film projects. A 1985 made-for-television NBC film, *John and Yoko: A Love Story*, starred Mark McGann as John and Kim Miyori as Yoko (the two actors later married in real life). The 1988 documentary *Imagine: John Lennon* (1988) was a box-office success, as was the soundtrack album.

Lennon's musical legacy continued as his widow, Yoko Ono, and sons Sean and Julian both pursued recording careers. With an uncanny vocal resemblance to his father, Julian Lennon in 1984 released the hit album *VALOTTE*.

On the 10th anniversary of Lennon's death in 1990, thousands of radio stations around the world joined a simulcast of the antiwar theme "Imagine." In 1991, Lennon was awarded a Lifetime Achievement Grammy. The surviving members of the Beatles reunited in 1995 for an ABC documentary and recording sessions, adding new backing instrumentation and vocals on the Lennon demos "Free as a Bird" and "Real Love."

Bibliography

Cott, Jonathan & Doudna, Christine (Eds.). (1982). *The Ballad of John and Yoko*. Garden City, NY: Rolling Stone.

Fawcett, Anthony. (1976, December). The Day John Lennon Stopped Believing in the Beatles. *Crawdaddy*, p. 32.

Hampton, Wayne. (1986). *Guerrilla Minstrels* (pp. 1-41). Knoxville: The University of Tennessee Press.

Isler, Scott. (1988, April). John Lennon: Lost in sound. *Musician*, p. 48.

Wenner, Jann. (1981). John Lennon. In Peter Herbst (Ed.), *The Rolling Stone Interviews* (pp. 128-55).

New York: Rolling Stone Press. White, Mark. (1985). *You Must Remember This: Popular Songwriters 1900-1980* (pp. 134-40). New York: Charles Scribner's Sons.

Wiener, Allen J. (1988, June 3). John Lennon: The solo years. *Goldmine*, p. 8.

JERRY LEE LEWIS. *(September 29, 1935). Inducted in 1986.* Born on a farm near the Mississippi River town of Ferriday, Louisiana, Jerry Lee Lewis was reared in a strict, evangelical family. Joining his cousins and close chums Jimmy Swaggert and Mickey Gilley, Lewis converted to the Assembly of God Church, where "speaking in tongues" was a common practice among parishioners.

Discovering Lewis' natural talent for the piano, his dirt-poor family mortgaged their home to buy a secondhand instrument. Straddling the fiery, "tent revival" gospel music with whiskey-joint R&B, Lewis angered his overbearing father. But when Lewis earned $13 in tip money playing Stick McGhee's R&B party song "Drinking Wine, Spo-Dee-O-Dee" at a Ford dealership, his father relented.

Landing a local 20-minute radio program, Lewis was often joined by Swaggert and Gilley. While Lewis was still performing "the sort of music that most folks had only heard in conjunction with the Holy Ghost . . . the boy wasn't singing about any Holy Ghost" (p. 65), writes Lewis biographer Nick Tosches.

At his parents insistence' Lewis returned to his religious roots, enrolling at the Southwestern Bible Institute in Waxahachie, Texas. But after a rollicking, boogie-woogie, chapel performance of the hymn "My God Is Real," Lewis was expelled.

Joining Johnny Littlejohn's band in 1954, Lewis played a mixture of R&B and country songs. Signing with Sun Records in 1956, Lewis first scored a regional hit with the country-flavored "Crazy Arms" (1956). Urged by Sun owner Sam Phillips to update his style, Lewis emerged as a rockabilly fireball.

The impromptu-recorded follow-up single "Whole Lotta Shakin' Goin' On" (1957) was initially banned by most radio stations for its sexual innuendo-filled lyrics. But following Lewis' performance of the song on *The Steve Allen Show*, the record went on to sell millions. Frightening middle America, Lewis pounded and kicked his piano with his fists, head, and feet, his wavy hair flying around his face. Convinced by Sam Phillips into recording the bawdy "Great Balls of Fire" (1957), Lewis landed back-to-back million-sellers. Written by Otis Blackwell, the song had been earlier rejected by Carl Perkins.

Before leaving for a British tour in 1957, Lewis scored another hit with "Breathless." He also secretly married his 13-year-old cousin, Myra Gale Brown, his third wife. Posing with his bride for British press, Lewis claimed she was 16. But when reporters discovered Brown's true age, Lewis was heckled at concerts, his tour cut short.

Returning home, Lewis' American fans were equally appalled. His career destroyed, Lewis was blackballed by radio and barred from concert halls. "His records started coming back by the carload. The older generation was looking for something it could use to squelch rock and roll, and it seized on this. Jerry was the nation's whipping boy" (p. 31), Sam Phillips told interviewer John Pugh. Lewis still managed a moderate hit with "High School Confidential" (1958), from the film of the same name. Trying to improve his fortunes, Lewis tried secretly recording as the Hawk, with a single released on the Sun Records' subsidiary, Phillips International. Finally returning to the charts after a three-year hiatus, Lewis landed a top-40 hit with a cover of Ray Charles' "What'd I Say" (1961).

Nicknamed "The Killer" since high school, Lewis' life was rife with tragedy.

Jerry Lee Lewis bowing to the crowd after performing at the topping-off ceremony, which marked the placement of the final beam of the Rock and Roll Hall of Fame in Cleveland. (*Photo courtesy of Nick Talevski.*)

Following the untimely death of a brother a decade earlier, Lewis' three-year-old son died in 1962. Believing his misfortunes were a sign from God, Lewis has frequently expressed the notion that he expects to burn in hell for playing rock and roll.

His contract with Sun expiring, Lewis signed with the Mercury Records subsidiary Smash in 1963. Re-recording his earlier Sun material, Lewis sold few records. Abusing drugs and drinking heavily, Lewis toured up to 300 dates a year, relegated to playing fairs and small venues.

Switching to country music in 1967 at the insistence of his new producer, Eddie Kilroy, Lewis unleashed a string of hits with, "Another Place, Another Time" (1968), "To Make Sweeter Love For You" (1969), and "There Must Be More to Love than This" (1970). Capturing some pop-crossover airplay, Lewis recorded several rock covers, including "Me and Bobby McGee" (1971) and "Chantilly Lace" (1972). Limiting himself to large venues, Lewis believed that performing in bars and nightclubs conflicted with his Pentecostal faith.

But tragedy continuing to dog Lewis: his wife left him in 1970, and another son, Jerry Lee Lewis Jr., was killed in a tow-truck crash. Lewis himself was injured in an accident in 1976 that demolished his Rolls Royce. Shortly thereafter, he shot his bassist, Butch Owens.

Leaving Mercury/Smash after the label tried to add orchestration to his music, Lewis returned to his rock roots, releasing several disastrous albums at Elektra Records. Then in 1979, the IRS confiscated much of Lewis' wealth, with agents also finding drugs at his home. Suffering a string of calamities that year, Lewis wrecked another car, canceled an Australian tour after breaking ribs in an onstage brawl with a fan, and sued wife, Jaren, for divorce (she died soon after).

While hospitalized in 1981 with a severe stomach ailment, Lewis was sued by Elektra in an effort to break his contract. A recuperated Lewis rejoined former Sun artists Carl Perkins and Johnny Cash in 1981 for a German television performance, the concert captured on the album *THE SURVIVORS*. That year, Lewis scored his last chart hit with "Thirty-Nine and Holding." Curtailing his musical career, Lewis turned down a request in 1983 by the Rolling Stones to play on their album *UNDERCOVER*. That year, Lewis's fifth wife died, under mysterious circumstances. Suffering with poor health throughout the 1980s, Lewis entered the Betty Ford Clinic in 1986 for substance abuse.

Starring Dennis Quaid in the role of Lewis, the 1989 film biography, *Great Balls of Fire*, rekindled interest in the singer. Still indebted to the IRS, Lewis opened his Mississippi home in 1994 to tourists, charging five dollars admission. Returning to the studio the following year, he recorded the album *YOUNG BLOOD* for Sire Records.

Bibliography

Hubner, John. (1981, July). The Killer at 45: Jerry Lee Lewis. *Goldmine*, p. 23.

Palmer, Robert. (1979, December 13). The devil and Jerry Lee Lewis. *Rolling Stone*, p. 57.

Pugh, John. (1973, November). The rise and fall of Sun Records. *Country Music*, p. 26.

Roland, Tom. (1991). *The Billboard Book of Number One Country Hits*. New York: Billboard.

Smith, Joe. (1988). *Off the Record* (pp. 97-99). New York: Warner.

Swaggert, Jimmy & Lamb, Robert Paul. (1977). *To Cross a River*. Plainfield, NJ: Logos International.

Tosches, Nick. (1982). *Hellfire: The Jerry Lee Lewis Story*. New York: Delacorte.

Tosches, Nick. (1984, November 9). Jerry Lee Lewis: The Smash/Mercury years. *Goldmine*, p. 6.

LITTLE RICHARD. *(Richard Wayne Penniman; December 5, 1932). Inducted in 1986*. Calling himself "the architect of rock and roll" and "the Georgia Peach," Little Richard personified the rebellion and spirit of early rock and roll. Raised in Macon, Georgia, Richard vacillated between the gospel sounds of a family singing group, the Penniman Singers, and the sinful world of rock and roll. Intending to be a preacher, his earliest influences were the gospel/pop of Marion Williams and Sister Rosetta Tharpe.

Often running away from home, Little Richard was a mischievous child. Dropping out of the ninth-grade and joining several traveling minstrel troupes, he dressed as a woman in the chorus line of the Sugarfoot Sam from Alabam minstrel group.

His enraged father disowning him, Richard found shelter with the owners of the Tick Tock Club, who sent him to school during the day and allowed him onstage at

The Bethel S. D. A. Concert Committee
PRESENTS

LITTLE RICHARD
(RICHARD PENNIMAN)
CENTRAL HIGH SCHOOL AUDITORIUM
102 UNION STREET   **AKRON, OHIO**
Sunday, December 14, 1958   -   7:30 P. M.
JAMES A. WASHINGTON, PASTOR

Church program of a concert and sermon by the "Reverend"
Little Richard shortly after his religious conversion. (*Photo
courtesy of Gary Felsinger.*)

night. Adopting the effeminate extravagances of a little-known pianist named Esquirita
and the frenetic piano pounding and urgent, high-pitched vocals of R&B singer Billy
Wright, Little Richard was a hit in gay bars.

Attracting the attention of legendary Atlanta deejay Zenas Sears, Little Richard won
a radio station talent contest in 1951, his prize an RCA-Victor record contract.
Dropping his real name, Richard Penniman, Little Richard was concerned about
shaming his family. Releasing four blues-oriented singles, the records bombed.
Returning to Macon after the sudden death of his father, Richard was forced to take a
dishwashing job in a Greyhound bus station.

Recording a pair of obscure singles for Peacock Records as the leader of the Tempo
Toppers, Richard flirted with gospel music. After touring heavily throughout the South

as a solo act, he recruited a backing band, the Upsetters.

Taking the advice of R&B singer Lloyd Price, Little Richard sent a demo tape to Specialty Records in 1954. With his Peacock contract bought out by Specialty in 1955, he was taken to legendary J&M studio in New Orleans.

After initially performing several blues number, Little Richard unleashed an unplanned, sizzling, bawdy version of what would become "Tutti Frutti." Smelling a hit record, producer Bumps Blackwell was concerned about its lewd, barroom lyrics. With new lyrics provided by songwriter Dorothy La Bostrie, "Tutti Frutti" was a rock smash, capturing the attention of America's youth. But when white crooner Pat Boone recorded a straitlaced rendition of the song, his cover eclipsed the original in airplay.

Dressed in a shimmering loose suit, sporting an exaggerated pompadour, wearing thick mascara and a pencil-thin mustache, the uninhibited Little Richard shocked *American Bandstand* viewers. Terrifying middle-America, his well-placed, shrieking falsetto "oohs" convinced many they were watching the devil himself. Touring with his choreographed backing band, the Upsetters, Richard forced them to wear makeup.

Frenetically pounding his piano, Little Richard unleashed a string of hits, most of which he wrote, including "Long Tall Sally" (1956), "Rip It Up" (1956), "Lucille" (1956), "Jenny, Jenny" (1957), and his only release featuring the Upsetters, "Keep a Knockin'" (1957).

His musical career coming to an end, Little Richard was convinced by R&B-singer-turned-preacher Joe Lutcher that rock and roll was the devil's music. After spotting the Sputnik satellite in the sky during an Australian tour, Little Richard took it as a sign from God and dropped out of rock and roll after an incredible two-year run.

Enrolling at the Oakwood College seminary, Richard would sing only gospel material. Meanwhile, Specialty continued to issue the singer's studio outtakes, landing a top-10 hit with "Good Golly, Miss Molly" (1958). Ordained as a minister, Richard married at the urging of church elders (he divorced after two years).

During a 1962 tour of England, Little Richard reverted back his rock persona, angry at being shown up by Sam Cooke. Also befriending the then-obscure Rolling Stones and Beatles, Little Richard gave a starstruck Paul McCartney singing lessons. But throughout the 1960s and 1970s, Little Richard would move back and forth between secular and religious music.

Returning to the U.S. and now abusing drugs, Little Richard was unable to land airplay with his first new rock release in several years, "Bama Lama Bama Loo" (1964). Riding an oldies revival in the late 1960s, he reunited with producer Bumps Blackwell, in 1972 releasing the album *THE SECOND COMING.*

Shaken by the death of his brother, Little Richard quit drugs and left rock and roll in 1975. Taking an evangelical route, in 1979 he released the gospel album *GOD'S BEAUTIFUL CITY.*

After a long recording sabbatical, Little Richard returned to the pop airwaves in 1986 with "Great Gosh A'Mighty" from the film *Down and Out in Beverly Hills.* Suffering an automobile accident, his comeback screeched to a halt. Little Richard experienced a new wave if religious vigor following a hospital visit by Bob Dylan, a born-again Christian.

Returning to the oldies concert circuit, Little Richard meshed his shows with rock, country, and spiritual material. Naive in his youth about the legalities of the music industry, he spent much of his career trying to wrangle royalties from his early hits.

Bibliography

Dalton, Dave. (1970). Little Richard: Child of God. *Rolling Stone*, p. 28.

Little Richard & White, Charles. (1984). *The Life and Times of Little Richard*. New York: Harmony.

Puterbaugh, Parke. (1990, April 19). Little Richard. *Rolling Stone*, p. 51.

Tamarkin, Jeff. (1987, April 10). Little Richard: Leaves a message. *Goldmine*, p. 10.

White, Timothy. (1990). *Rock Lives: Profiles & Interviews*. New York: Henry Holt.

FRANKIE LYMON & THE TEENAGERS. *Sherman Garnes (June 8, 1940 - February 26, 1977); Frankie Lymon (September 30, 1942 - February 28, 1968); Jimmy Merchant (February 10, 1940); Joe Negroni (September 9, 1940 - September 5, 1978); Herman Santiago (February 18, 1941). Inducted in 1993.* Frankie Lymon & the Teenagers set the standard for future singing acts such the Jackson Five, the Osmonds, and New Edition. While 1950s child singers Little Jimmy Dickens and Sugar Chile Robinson found some pop success, none matched Lymon's short-lived superstardom.

Raised in a large, extended family, Lymon shared his grandmother's apartment in the Washington Heights section of Harlem. Joining a family gospel trio, Lymon was instead drawn to doo-wop music.

Intimately knowledgeable about women and drugs during his youth, Lymon was paid by local prostitutes to flag down customers. "I learned everything there was to know about women before I was 12 years old" (Peters, p. 42), Lymon recalled in a 1967 *Ebony* interview.

Meanwhile at nearby Stitt Jr. High, 14-year-old Sherman Garnes convinced Jimmy Merchant to join two Puerto Ricans, Joe Negroni and Herman Santiago, in forming a vocal quartet. Calling themselves the Coupe De Villes, the Ermines, and then the Premieres, the group crossed paths with Lymon at a school talent show in 1954. Several months later, Lymon joined the Premieres as a backing vocalist.

Discovered by talent scout Richard Barrett, the renamed Teenagers signed with the George Goldner-owned Gee Records in 1955. Although Santiago was the group's lead singer, Goldner replaced him with Lymon. Possessing charm, good looks, and an innocent, boyish smile, 13-year-old Frankie Lymon became the recipient of Barrett's dance and vocal coaching.

Impressing Goldner with their doo-wop-styled "Why Do Birds Sing So Gay," the Teenagers were told to retitle the song "Why Do Fools Fall in Love." Though a Garnes/Santiago composition, the songwriting credits were assigned to Lymon, Santiago, and Goldner and later to record mogul Morris Levy. Not paid royalties, Lymon and the Teenagers were instead promised a trust fund payment at age 21.

A million-selling smash hit, "Why Do Fools Fall in Love" contrasted Lymon's soprano voice with Garnes' deep-bass backing and featured Jimmy Wright's searing sax. But within months, Gale Storm and the Diamonds both landed top-10 cover versions of the song.

Frankie Lymon. (*Courtesy of John M. Riley, from private collection.*)

Wearing white sweaters emblazoned with a large "T," the renamed Frankie Lymon and the Teenagers were an international sensation. Their quick run of hits included "I Want You to Be My Girl" (1956); a song written by Lymon's classmate, understudy, and future R&B star, Jimmy Castor, "I Promise to Remember" (1956); and "The ABC's of Love" (1956). Appearing in the Alan Freed quickie rock-film *Rock, Rock, Rock* (1956), the group performed "I'm Not a Juvenile Delinquent." Dropping out of school to go on a worldwide tour, the group was on the road for the next year.

While Gee Records chiefs worried about Lymon's childlike voice maturing, something else torpedoed the group. During the British leg of the tour, Lymon was convinced by his record label to pursue a solo career. Recorded in London, the group's last hit came with "Out in the Cold Again" (1957). After shooting a second Alan Freed film, *Mister Rock and Roll*, the group disbanded.

As separate acts, Lymon and the Teenagers both faded from the charts. Backed by an orchestra and session singers, Lymon scored his first of only two solo hits with "Goody Goody" (1957). Lymon's career was further harmed when he was spotted dancing with a white girl on Alan Freed's pre-*American Bandstand* music television program. Lymon's final chart entry came in 1960 with the release of a two-year-old track, "Little Bitty Pretty One." Also faring poorly, the Teenagers hired several replacement lead singers, beginning with Bill Lobrano.

When Lymon and the Teenagers later reached 21, their promised trust fund payments amounted to a paltry $1,000 each. "That's all we ever got. Everything else, the company kept it—all those guys got the mansions . . . " (p. 7), a bitter Herman Santiago later told interviewer Seamus McGarvey.

On a downward spiral, Lymon was arrested several times for narcotics possession. Joining the army in 1966, he was hoping to avoid jail time. Stationed at Fort Gordon, Georgia, he was dishonorably discharged for repeated AWOL violations.

Marrying schoolteacher Elmira Eagle and landing a new recording contract, Lymon returned to New York in 1968. But before he could enter a studio, Lymon was found dead of a heroin overdose in the bathroom of his grandmother's apartment. He died penniless.

Regrouping in 1971, the Teenagers hired new lead singer Pearl McKinnon (of the Kodaks). Returning to the oldies circuit in 1980, Santiago and Merchant led a new version of the Teenagers. A year later, "Why Do Fools Fall in Love" was reprised by Diana Ross, with the original version appearing in a number of television commercials.

With royalty moneys accumulating, Lymon's three alleged widows fought for control of his estate. At stake were over $750,000 in past payments and one-half of future proceeds. While Lymon's last wife, Elmira Eagle, was challenging Zola Taylor (of the Platters) and Elizabeth Waters, Morris Levy claimed to have acquired the rights from Lymon in 1968 for $1,500. While Waters emerged the victor in 1988, a New York appellate court later sided with Eagle, awarding her half of the song's royalties.

But in a 1992 ruling, the song's actual writers, Herman Santiago and Jimmy Merchant, were declared by the court as "the true and rightful authors" and stood to gain several million dollars. But an appeals court reversed the decision in 1996, citing the statute of limitations. The duo had argued before the court that publisher Morris Levy had threatened them with physical harm had they pursued any legal claims, and they kept quiet until after his death.

Bibliography

Goldblatt, David. (1991, April 15). The Teenagers after 25 years: Boys of rock 'n' roll. *Village Voice*, p. 68.

Goldberg, Marv. (1995, June). Frankie Lymon and the Teenagers. *Discoveries*, p. 45.

Groia, Phil. (1972). The Teenagers. *Bim Bam Boom*, 2(5), p. 9.

Jones, Wayne. (1982, March). Wayne Jones talks with Jimmy Merchant of the Teenagers. *Goldmine*, p. 17.

McGarvey, Seamus. (1991, July). Why do fools fall in love? *Now Dig This*, p. 6.

Peters, Art. (1967, January). Comeback of an ex-star. *Ebony*, p. 42.

THE MAMAS AND THE PAPAS. *John Phillips (August 30, 1935); Denny Doherty (Dennis Doherty; November 29, 1941); "Mama" Cass Elliot (Ellen Naomi Cohen; September 19, 1941 - July 29, 1974); Michelle Phillips (Holly Michelle Gilliam; April 6, 1944); Inducted in 1998.* Instrumental in the rise of 1960s folk-rock, the Mamas and the Papas offered brilliant upbeat pop songs and harmonies in an era rooted in social upheaval and protest. Considered the group's leader, singer-guitarist John Phillips had emerged from a popular early 1960s, Greenwich Village folk group, the Journeymen, which featured future singing star Scott McKenzie. In all, the Journeymen released three albums on Capitol Records. In 1962, Phillips divorced his wife and married 17-year-old, Michelle Phillips.

Meanwhile, struggling actress Cassandra "Cass" Elliot dropped out of American University and moved to Greenwich village in 1960. Finding work in folk clubs, she sang lead in the acoustic folk trio the Big Three, before joining the John Sebastian-led electric trio, the Mugwumps. Signing with Warner Brothers, the Mugwumps provided music for the film *Freak Out.* (Sebastian and Mugwumps member Zalman Yanovski later emerged in the Lovin' Spoonful.)

After forming the New Journeymen, John and Michelle Phillips and Denny Doherty vacationed in the Virgin Islands, where the trio bumped into a friend from New York City, Cass Elliott. Setting up camp on the beach, the quartet sang early versions of songs that would appear on their first album. Refusing an invitation to join the group, Elliott moved to California. But reuniting in San Francisco, the foursome was hired to provide backing vocals on Barry McGuire's album *PRECIOUS TIME*, a project released on producer Lou Adler's new Dunhill label.

After impressing label heads with their repertoire of original songs, the renamed the Mamas and the Papas were signed by Dunhill. Produced by Lou Adler, their debut hit, "California Dreamin'," was a melding of folk and rock influences and featured the group's distinctive four-part vocal harmony. The John Phillips-penned track had originally appeared on McGuire's album. A smash hit, the Mamas and the Papas became instant media darlings. Riding a crest of popularity, the group stuck with its successful formula of post-Dylan commercial folk-rock.

Portraying a bohemian image, the group donned psychedelic costumes complete with Russian hats and thigh-high boots. As the leader of the group John Phillips did not permit the female members to wear make-up on stage. Nicknamed "Mama Cass" because of her hefty girth, Cass Elliot emerged as the visual focus of the group.

Their hit run lasting only two years, the group's million-selling singles included "Monday, Monday" (1966); a song inspired by an adulterous affair, "I Saw Her Again Last Night" (1966); a remake of the Shirelles/5 Royales' "Dedicated To The One I Love" (1967); and the autobiographical "Creeque Alley" (1967). The group's chief songwriter, John Phillips, also penned Scott McKenzie's flower-power anthem "San Francisco (Be Sure to Wear Some Flowers in Your Hair)."

Embracing the Summer of Love, Michelle and John Phillips were joined by Lou Adler and Beatles publicist Derek Taylor in coordinating the three-day Monterey Pop Festival. But internal strife soon torpedoed the Mamas and Papas when John Phillips dismissed his wife from the band for several months. The group was further shaken by the sale of Dunhill to ABC Records.

Pursuing a solo career on the side, Mama Cass scored a hit with a cover of Wayne King's 1931 hit, "Dream A Little Dream." Shortly thereafter, Dunhill sued the group members for not fulfilling their contractual obligations. They disbanded after reuniting to record their fourth album, *THE PAPAS & THE MAMAS*. Following their divorce, Michelle Phillips pursued an acting career, while John Phillips turned to film production, financing the Robert Altman-produced comedy *Brewster McLoud*.

Overweight all her life, Elliot went on a crash diet in 1968, losing 110 pounds in a three month period by eating just one meal a week. Scheduled for an extended Las Vegas stint, she became violently ill on stage during opening night and canceled her engagement. Teaming with former Traffic guitarist Dave Mason in 1971, the pair released the album *DAVE MASON AND MAMA CASS*. Reuniting in 1971 to record a final album, the Mamas and the Papas found only moderate success with *PEOPLE LIKE US*. Her heart weakened by a series of crash diets, Mama Cass died in bed at a friend's London apartment in 1974.

John Phillips spent the 1970s wasting his $150,000 a year royalty checks on hard drugs. In 1980, Phillips, his daughter, MacKenzie (star of 1970s sitcom, *One Day at a Time*, and former bandmate, Denny Doherty (who was abusing alcohol), all entered chemical treatment programs.

A new version of the Mamas and the Papas was assembled in 1982 with MacKenzie Phillips replacing Cass Elliot. By 1986, the group included Elaine "Spanky" McFarlane (former leader of Spanky & Our Gang) and Scott McKenzie as the replacement for Denny Doherty. In the 1980s, Denny Doherty was the host of a Canadian Children's television show, while Michelle Phillips portrayed the role of vixen Anne Winston Matheson on television's *Knots Landing* (on an 1987 episode Phillips sang "Dedicated to the One I Love").

As a songwriter, John Phillips wrote the often recorded "Me and My Uncle" and the Beach Boys smash hit "Kokomo" (1988). Two years earlier, the Beach Boys landed a hit single with a remake of the Mamas and the Papas' "California Dreamin'." And in another Beach Boys connection, John and Michelle Phillips' daughter, Chynna, joined the daughters of Beach Boy Brian Wilson, Carnie and Wendy, to form the pop harmony group Wilson Phillips. (Cass Elliot's out-of-wedlock daughter, Owen Elliot, was nearly a member as well.)

A pair of Mamas and Papas autobiographies, *California Dreamin': The True Story of The Mamas and the Papas* by Michelle Phillips and *Papa John* by John Phillips, frequently contradict each other.

Bibliography

Fuss, Charles J. (1991, September 6). Cass Elliot: Don't call her Mama. *Goldmine*, p. 22.

Johnson, Jon E. (1991, April). The Mamas & the Papas. *Discoveries*, p. 26.

Phillips, John & Jerome, Jim. (1986). *Papa John*. Garden City, NY: Dolphin.

Phillips, Michelle. (1986). *California Dreamin': The True Story of The Mamas and the Papas*. New York: Warner.

Scoppa, Bud. (1971, May). Cass & Dave . . . pros at work. *Circus*, p. 24.

Toombs, Mikel. (1990, January 11). Mamas and the Papas' Phillips never really stopped dreamin'. *San Diego Union-Tribune*, p. D9.

BOB MARLEY. *(Robert Nesta Marley; April 6, 1945 - May 11, 1981). Inducted in 1994*. Emerging as a mythical figure, Bob Marley brought reggae to the mainstream. A product of the slums of Jamaica, a country whose wealth is controlled by a very tiny minority, Marley became an outspoken advocate for the world's downtrodden.

Marley's father, Norval Sinclair Marley, was a white, 50-year-old, decorated British veteran of World War I. After marrying a pregnant 19-year-old Jamaican girl, Cedela Malcolm, Marley's father quickly abandoned the family. (In thousands of published interviews, Bob Marley never mentioned his father.)

Moving with his mother to the Trenchtown ghetto of Kingston, 10-year-old Marley learned to play a homemade banjo. Leaving school at 14, Marley immersed himself in the local ska musical scene. A welder during the day , at 16 Marley recorded his first single. Then forming the Teenagers in 1962, Marley was joined by Peter Tosh, Neville "Bunny" Livingston (later called Bunny Wailer), and two others. Recording for the local Kong label, the renamed Wailers scored their first of many Jamaican hits with "Simmer Down" (1963).

Disbanding the Wailers in 1966, Marley moved to Wilmington, Delaware, to join his mother who had emigrated three years earlier. Finding work in a Chrysler plant, Marley returned to Jamaica in 1967 to avoid the Vietnam War draft.

Before reforming the Wailers, Marley studied the Rastafarian faith, a Bible-based religion. Believers, called Rastas, view 1930s Ethiopian emperor Haile Selassie as God or "Jah." Rastas grow their hair in long dreadlocks and wear clothing in the colors of the Ethiopian flag: red, yellow, and green. Considered a sacrament, marijuana is called herb or ganja. The pope is seen as the Anti-Christ, while capitalistic whites are viewed as evil exploiters of the black race. At first Marley's conversion upset his deeply religious, Christian mother. Infusing Rastafarians into his reggae music, Marley forever intertwined the two. Other common themes of Marley's music include unemployment, tyrannical government, and freedom for the oppressed.

Befriended in 1969 by producer and pioneering reggae artist Lee "Scratch" Perry, the Wailers' lineup was expanded with brothers Aston and Carlton "Family Man" Barrett. Now billed as Bob Marley & the Wailers, their breakthrough albums, *SOUL REBELS* and *SOUL REVOLUTION*, sold well only in Jamaica and the U.K. During this period, Marley emerged as a talented guitarist. Instead, Marley's first international success came as a songwriter, penning Johnny Nash's hits, "Guava Jelly" and "Stir It Up."

After launching their own label, Tuff Gong, the Wailers signed with Island Records in 1972. The following year, the Wailers released the heavily promoted albums *CATCH A FIRE* and *BURNIN'*, the latter featuring "Get Up, Stand Up" and "I Shot the Sheriff." With Eric Clapton taking "I Shot the Sheriff" to the top of the U.S. charts in 1974, music fans searched out the original version. But concerned about the marketing of his music, Marley kept the word "reggae" out of his lyrics and off record covers because of its mixed connotations. To mask the revolutionary aspect of his music, most of Marley's album covers featured friendly, smiling photographs

With Marley emerging as the Wailers' leader, the disgruntled Peter Tosh and Bunny Livingston left the group in 1974 for solo careers. Adding a female backing trio, the I-Threes, the group featured Marley's Cuban-born wife, Rita. (With Rastafarianism permitting polygamy, Marley sired 11 children by seven wives, including four by Rita.)

Attacking the government on *NATTY DREAD* with songs like "Them Belly Full (But We Hungry)," Marley became a powerful political force in Jamaica. The album was Marley's belated first U.S. chart entry. Seen as a threat by Jamaican authorities, in 1976 Marley was almost killed by an alleged government gunman. Moving to Miami for the next 18 months, the injured Marley recorded EXODUS, the album highlighted by his signature song, "Jamming" (1977).

Returning to Jamaica in 1978, Marley created a sensation by peacefully uniting longtime political rivals Edward Seaga and Prime Minister Michael Manley. But later in the year, Marley was wounded in another assassination attempt.

Diagnosed with cancer after a fluid buildup in one of his toes, Marley refused amputation on religious grounds. Eventually the cancer spread to his brain. Preparing for a tour, Marley collapsed in New York City's Central Park in October 1980, dying seven months later.

Though persecuted during his life, Marley was embraced by the Jamaican government and given a state funeral. He was buried with a guitar in one hand and a Bible in the other, and is considered a prophet of Jah by Rastafarians who await his resurrection (Marley's mother later became a convert). With Marley leaving no will, court battles were waged over his estate.

Marley's greatest-hits album, *LEGEND*, remains a strong seller, reaching the 9 million mark by 1997. Following in his father's footsteps, Marley's son, David "Ziggy" Marley, joined several siblings in the Melody Makers, scoring a top-10 hit in 1989 with "Tomorrow People."

Two other Wailers members have died untimely deaths as both Carlie Barrett and Peter Tosh were shot to death in Jamaica in separate incidents.

Bibliography

Doole, Kerry. (1991, May). Rastaman vibrations. *Music Express*, p. 45.

Fergusson, Isaac. (1982, May 18). So much things to say: The journey of Bob Marley. *Village Voice*, p. 39.

Goldman, Vivian. (1981). *Bob Marley: Soul Rebel/Natural Mystic*. New York: St. Martin's.

Jacobson, Mark. (1995, November). Bob Marley live. *Natural History*, p. 48.

McCormack, Ed. (1976, August 12). Bob Marley with a bullet. *Rolling Stone*, p. 37.

McCulloch, Art. (1993, January 3). How Bob Marley hid his white father from the world. *Daily Mail*, p. 48.

Palmer, Robert. (1994, February 24). One love. *Rolling Stone*, p. 38.

Santelli, Robert. (1983, October). Reggae: Life after Marley. *Music and Sound Output*, p. 54.

Taylor, Don & Henry, Mike. (1995). *Marley and Me: The Real Bob Marley Story*. New York: Barricade.

MARTHA & THE VANDELLAS. *Rosalind Ashford (September 2, 1943); Betty Kelly (September 16, 1944); Lois Reeves; Martha Reeves (July 18, 1941); Annette Sterling. Inducted in 1995.* One of Motown's leading girl-groups, Martha & the

Vandellas churned out a string of soul chestnuts in the 1960s. Born in Eufaula, Alabama, Martha Reeves was the eldest daughter in a family of 11 children. Moving to Detroit, she won a church talent contest at the age of three at her minister grandfather's Methodist church. With both of her parents playing guitars at family sing-alongs, little Martha yearned to become a jazz singer in the tradition of Billie Holiday.

After graduating from high school (where she acted in plays and studied voice), Reeves performed in talent contests and nightclubs. After joining a pair of local vocal groups, the Fascinations and the Mellowtones, Reeves recorded an obscure single for the Chess subsidiary, Check-Mate, as a member of the Del-Phis.

While singing in a Detroit jazz club under the stage name Martha Lavaille, Reeves was approached by a Motown executive, Mickey Stevenson. Later rejected at an audition by Motown-head Berry Gordy Jr., because of an overabundance of female acts at the label, Reeves was instead hired as a secretary. Earning Gordy's confidence, Reeves became his executive assistant.

With Gordy utilizing all of his employees during the recording process, Reeves also sang backup and provided hand-claps on demo and commercial discs. But unlike most of her Motown cohorts, Reeves could boast formal musical training.

After substituting for an ailing Mary Wells in 1962, an impressed Berry Gordy and Smokey Robinson instructed Reeves to form her own group. Reforming the Del-Phis, Reeves was joined by Annette Beard, Rosalind Ashford, and lead singer Gloria Williams. Renamed the Vels, their debut single "There He Is at My Door" (1962) flopped. With Williams leaving the group, and Reeves assuming lead vocal duties, the Vels first label success came as backup singers on Marvin Gaye's early hits, including "Hitch Hike" and "Pride and Joy."

Now known as Martha & the Vandellas, they landed a trio of hits in 1963 with "Come and Get These Memories," the Grammy-nominated million-seller, "Heat Wave," and "Quicksand." All three hits were penned by Motown's new songwriting team Holland-Dozier-Holland.

Joining Motown's first "Motor Town Revue," the Vandellas toured with Marvin Gaye, the Miracles, and the then-unknown Supremes. Soon after, Sterling left the Vandellas to marry and was replaced by Betty Kelly of the Velvelettes (of "Really Saying Something" fame).

With Kim Weston and Mary Wells both rejecting the Marvin Gaye co-penned "Dancing in the Streets," in 1964 Martha & the Vandellas recorded the song for a million-selling smash; creating an unlikely controversy, the song was accused of promoting social disorder.

The group's hits continued with "Nowhere to Run" (1965), "I'm Ready for Love" (1966), and, recorded three years earlier, "Jimmy Mack" (1967). Following a final top-40 hit with "Honey Chile" (1967), Betty Kelly and Annette Beard would leave the group, now billed as Martha Reeves & the Vandellas.

But bound by her contract to pay the rest of the group out of her own salary, the outspoken Reeves enraged Gordy by demanding an accounting of the group's royalties. Also creating tensions was a bitter rivalry between Reeves and labelmate Diana Ross. Abusing drugs and suffering the first of three mental breakdowns, an exhausted Reeves was institutionalized in 1970.

Reforming the Vandellas in 1971, Reeves landed a few R&B hits. Dissolving the group at the end of 1972, Reeves pursued a solo career. Leaving Motown in an ugly separation, Reeves lost the legal use of the Vandellas name.

Signing with MCA, Reeves joined J.J. Johnson on the soundtrack of the blaxploitation film *Willie Dynamite* (1973). Released the following year, Reeves' first solo album, *MARTHA REEVES*, was produced by Richard Perry and featured an all-star backing band that included George Harrison and Billy Preston.

A born-again Christian, Reeves signed with Arista Records in 1975 and then Fantasy in 1978, where she released the disco album *WE MEET AGAIN*. After reuniting with the Vandellas in July 1978 at a benefit for actor Will Geer, Reeves retired from music.

Settling her lawsuit against Motown, Reeves reconciled with Gordy and appeared in a number of Motown television specials. In the 1990s, Reeves rejoined original Vandellas, Annette Beard and Rosalind Ashford, on the oldies circuit.

Bibliography
Jones, James T. IV. (1994, August 26). Reeves revs up her Motown memories. *USA Today*, p. 10D.

Jones, Wayne. (1981, June). Martha Reeves. *Goldmine*, p. 162.

Moore, Clarence A. (1989, June 16). Martha & the Vandellas: Come and get these memories. *Goldmine*, p. 26.

Rosen, Steven. (1994, September 20). Confessions of a Motown diva. *The Denver Post*, p. E8.

Skelly, Richard. (1995, March 3). Martha Reeves and the Vandellas: The Motown Years. *Goldmine*, p. 34.

Taraborrelli, Randy J. (1986). *Motown: Hot Wax, City Cool & Solid Gold* (pp. 73-77). Garden City, NY: Dolphin/Doubleday.

CLYDE McPHATTER. *(Clyde Lensey McPhatter; November 15, 1932 - June 13, 1972). Inducted in 1987.* With his velvety, fluid tenor voice, Clyde McPhatter anchored two of the top R&B vocal groups of the 1950s, the Dominoes and the Drifters, before launching a solo career. The most copied singer of the decade, McPhatter influenced scores of soul greats including Jackie Wilson and Sam Cooke.

Born in Durham, North Carolina, McPhatter joined his siblings in the choir at Mount Cavalry Baptist Church. With his father the preacher, and his mother the church organist, at the of age 10 Clyde was the featured soprano soloist.

After moving to Teaneck, New Jersey, at the end of World War II, 14-year-old McPhatter joined several classmates in 1947 to form a gospel group, the Mount Lebanon Singers. A strong high-tenor, McPhatter was the popular group's lead singer. Sneaking off to Harlem nightclubs, McPhatter also sang pop music with various partners.

Meanwhile in 1950 the classically trained Billy Ward organized an all-black vocal group, hoping to capitalize on the new doo-wop craze. Catching McPhatter, a shipping clerk, at an Apollo Theater amateur night performance, Ward was convinced he had found his lead singer.

Clyde McPhatter.

Originally naming his group the Ques, Ward wrote most of their material, played the piano, and occasionally sang backup. Winning Arthur Godfrey's *Talent Scouts* contest, McPhatter and the renamed Dominoes landed a recording contract with King-Federal.

An immediate sensation in R&B, McPhatter provided the lead vocal on their first release, the ballad hit, "Do Something for Me" (1950). Initially, many record buyers believed McPhatter was Ward's brother or that Ward was actually the lead singer.

Featuring Bill Brown's booming bass vocals, the Dominoes' best-seller came with the racy and boastful "Sixty Minute Man" (1951). Banned by some stations and considered a novelty song by others, the song was for many whites their first exposure to rhythm and blues.

With McPhatter's impassioned, gospel-based stylings, the Dominoes' R&B hits continued with "That's What Your Love Is Doing to Me" (1952); the bluesy "Have Mercy, Baby" (1952); "I'd Be Satisfied" (1952); and, with a sobbing vocal lead, "The Bells" (1953). After recording a cover of Billie Holiday's "These Foolish Things Remind Me of You," McPhatter was fired by Ward for requesting an increase in his meager $100 a week salary. He was replaced by his protégé Jackie Wilson.

When Atlantic Records chief Ahmet Ertegun discovered that McPhatter had been fired, he went through the New York City phone book and called everyone with that last name. Signed to Atlantic and instructed to form a group, McPhatter was joined by his former bandmates from the Mount Lebanon Singers, recording a series of gospel-flavored tunes in 1953. Except for the McPhatter-penned, future B-side, "Lucille," none of the tracks were released.

Firing the entire group and hiring manager George Treadwell, McPhatter set the groundwork for the Drifters. The group's debut release, "Money Honey" (1953), was a million-selling, R&B smash. "The singing was like nothing I'd ever heard. The three- and four-part harmony was pitch-perfect, with Clyde [directing] the various parts. The gospel feel was real" (p. 89), recalled Atlantic producer Jerry Wexler.

The Drifters' next hit, the double-sided entry "Such a Night"/"Lucille" (1954), was banned by radio for its suggestive lyrics. Penned by McPhatter, the bawdy "Honey Love" (1954) also caused problems at radio. A McPhatter/Bill Pinkney duet of the holiday standard "White Christmas" was the Drifters first crossover, pop entry.

Drafted in late 1954, McPhatter was replaced in concerts by soundalike, 15-year-old David Baughan. Stationed in Buffalo, McPhatter was able to rejoin the group on weekends but was soon permanently replaced by Johnny Moore. McPhatter landed his final Drifters hit in 1955 with the Ahmet Ertegun-penned "What'cha Gonna Do."

Scoring his first hit apart from the Drifters, McPhatter teamed with Ruth Brown on "Love Has Joined Us Together" (1955). Officially leaving the Drifters upon his discharge in April 1956, McPhatter sold the rights to the group's name to their manager, George Treadwell.

Now backed with the syrupy, pop-flavored Ray Ellis Orchestra, McPhatter's hit run continued slowed with "Treasure of Love" (1956); "Without Love (There Is Nothing)" (1957); "Long Lonely Nights" (1957); "Come What May" (1957); and his biggest pop effort, "A Lover's Question." Signing with MGM Records in 1959, McPhatter retained Ray Ellis. Given a $40,000 advance, McPhatter's only MGM success came with "Let's Try Again" (1959).

Switching to Mercury in 1960, McPhatter was teamed with veteran R&B producer Clyde Otis. His material still over-orchestrated, McPhatter landed a pop hit with "Ta Ta," which he co-wrote with Drifters guitarist Jimmy Oliver. But with Otis leaving Mercury Records, McPhatter was produced by Shelby Singleton, who convinced him to record "Lover Please." Featuring King Curtis solo sax break, the top-10 hit eclipsed several competing versions. His career nearly finished, McPhatter's last pop hit came in 1964 with a cover of Thurston Harris' "Little Bitty Pretty One."

Recording eight poorly-selling albums at Mercury, a desperate McPhatter even recorded the Drifters hits, "Up on the Roof" and "On Broadway." Dropped by Mercury in 1965, McPhatter had just scored a minor R&B hit with the appropriately titled "Crying Won't Help You Now."

After releasing five ignored singles at Amy Records, a dejected McPhatter moved to England in 1968, where he was met with dwindling crowds. Charged by authorities with "loitering with intent" and with his work permit expiring, McPhatter returned to the U.S. in 1970.

Depressed, broke, and rejected by his former label, Atlantic, McPhatter abused alcohol and drugs. Befriended by Clyde Otis, McPhatter signed with Decca Records in 1971. Recording one final album, *WELCOME HOME* included a cover of Tom Jones' "Without Love."

Passing away in his sleep in 1972, probably of a heart attack, McPhatter's tragic death went unnoticed. Though the defining voice of 1950s R&B, he died a broken and disillusioned man, with little to show for his success.

McPhatter became the first artist to be elected into the Rock and Roll Hall of Fame twice: as a solo performer in 1987 and as a member of the Drifters in 1988. McPhatter's son, Billy McPhatter, later joined a revival version of the Moonglows.

Bibliography

Allan, Tony & Treadwell, Faye. (1993). *Save the Last Dance for Me: The Musical Legacy of the Drifters, 1953-1993*. Ann Arbor, MI: Popular Culture Ink.

Garbutt, Bob. (1983, June). Clyde McPhatter: The forgotten hero. *Goldmine*, p. 22.

Goldberg, Marv. (1995, October). The Dominoes. *Discoveries*, p. 26.

Grendysa, Peter A. (1993, May). The Dominoes. *Discoveries*, p. 23.

Millar, Bill. (1971). *The Drifters: The Rise and Fall of the Black Vocal Group*. New York: Macmillan.

Watson, Tony. (1998, May-June). Deep in the heart of Harlem. *Blues & Rhythm*, p. 16.

Wexler, Jerry & Ritz, David. (1993). *Rhythm and the Blues: A Life in American Music*. New York: Alfred A. Knopf.

JONI MITCHELL. *(Roberta Joan Anderson; November 7, 1943). Inducted in 1997.* A leader of the Woodstock generation, singer-songwriter Joni Mitchell built a career upon the political folk traditions of Bob Dylan and Joan Baez. Born an only child to a grocery store manager father and ex-school teacher mother in mountainous Fort McLoud, Alberta, Canada, Mitchell grew up listening to her mother recite Shakespeare.

After moving to Saskatoon, Saskatchewan, Mitchell received a piano. Refusing to take lessons because they conflicted with airings of *The Wild Bill Hickok* show, she instead taught herself to play with a Pete Seeger instruction book. Suffering a bout of polio at age nine, Mitchell was not expected to walk again.

While studying commercial art at Saskatoon and then Alberta College in Calgary, Mitchell was drawn to folk coffeehouses. Learning to play the guitar and ukulele, she dropped out of school after a stunning performance at the Mariposa Folk Festival in Ontario. Having an out-of-wedlock child, she gave her daughter up for adoption.

Moving to Toronto and immersing herself in the city's burgeoning folk scene, she married folk musician Chuck Mitchell, occasionally hitting the stage as a duo. Her career on the ascent, she moved to Detroit in 1965, divorcing her husband the following year. Relocating to New York and embracing the Greenwich Village folk scene, she gained a wider audience by infusing rock into her melodic folk stylings.

Moving to Los Angeles and signing with Reprise Records in 1967, Mitchell was assisted by folk-rocker David Crosby. While her debut album, *JONI MITCHELL*, went ignored, Mitchell gained notoriety as a songwriter, penning Judy Collins' hit "Both Sides Now" and Tom Rush's "Circle Game." Now attracting attention, Mitchell's 1969 Grammy-winning album *CLOUDS* won accolades for tracks like "Chelsea Morning" and her own version of "Both Sides Now." The album cover featured a self-portrait by Mitchell. While Mitchell did not attend Woodstock, the Crosby, Stills & Nash acoustic rendition of her composition "Woodstock" was one of festival's most memorable highlights.

Inspired by the beauty of the Laurel Canyon near her home, Mitchell released *LADIES OF THE CANYON*, highlighted by her signature piece, "Big Yellow Taxi" (1970), and a version of "Woodstock." Chronicling her relationships with celebrity paramours and her discomfort with fame, Mitchell's final Reprise album, *BLUE*, was her most rock-oriented effort to date.

Leaving the music industry for nearly two years, Mitchell took a country turn on her Asylum Records debut, *FOR THE ROSES*. The album spawned her first top-40 pop hit, "You Turn Me On, I'm a Radio." Teaming with jazz arranger Tom Scott and backed by the Crusaders, Mitchell achieved her artistic and commercial high point in 1974 with *COURT AND SPARK*, which included, "Free Man in Paris" and her only top-10 hit, "Help Me." The following year, Mitchell scored her final top-40 hit with a live version of "Big Yellow Taxi," taken from the album *MILES OF AISLES*.

Leaving folk-rock to experiment with jazz and international folk music, Mitchell dropped out of the mainstream music scene for several years. Mitchell told *Rolling Stone* interviewer David Wild, "I paid a big price for doing what I've done. I started working in a genre that was neither this nor that. People didn't know where I fit in anymore, so they didn't play me at all. And so I disappeared" (p. 64). Collaborating with jazz legend Charlie Mingus in 1979, the jazz album *MINGUS* (1979) was very poorly received by jazz and folk fans alike.

Marrying bassist Larry Klein and moving to Geffen Records in 1982, Mitchell abandoned jazz. Exploring romantic themes on her 1982 album, *WILD THINGS RUN FAST*, she was aided by guest musicians Lionel Richie and James Taylor. With its startling cover shot, Mitchell's 1985 album, *DOG EAT DOG*, employed a synthesizer, and was aided by several producers including computer-music whiz Thomas Dolby. The album retraced Mitchell's political roots, exploring leftist political themes and attacking the church and censorship.

Returning to Reprise Records in 1994 with the album *TURBULENT INDIGO*, Mitchell won her first Grammy in 23 years. Amy Grant reprised Mitchell's "Big Yellow Taxi" in 1996, landing a top-40 hit; the following year Janet Jackson employed a sample of the same song into her hit, "Got 'Til It's Gone."

Bibliography
Blair, Iain. (1985, December 1). Joni Mitchell takes high-tech turn onto a political path. *Chicago Tribune*, Arts sect., p. 7.

Hall, Carla. (1979, August 25). The new Joni Mitchell; The Songbird of Woodstock soars into
    jazz. *Washington Post*, p. B1.
Newman, Melinda (1996, August 24). Joni Mitchell offers "Hits" and "Misses." *Billboard*, p.
    1.
Stern, Perry. (1986, February). Joni Mitchell: A benign dictator. *Canadian Musician*, p. 32.
White, Timothy. (1990). *Rock Lives: Profiles & Interviews* (pp. 328-39). New York: Henry
    Holt.
Wild, David. (1991, May 30). A conversation with Joni Mitchell. *Rolling Stone*, p. 61.

BILL MONROE. *(William Smith Monroe; September 13, 1911 - September 9, 1996). Inducted in the Early Influence category in 1997.* Fusing folk, country and old-style, southern gospel to invent a new musical genre, Bill Monroe emerged as the Father of Bluegrass. The youngest of eight children, Monroe was reared in a musical Kentucky farm family, reluctantly choosing to play the mandolin at age eight, because his older siblings had already selected the guitar and fiddle. Painfully shy and suffering from poor vision, Monroe dropped out of school, never learning to read music.

Orphaned after the deaths of his mother and then father, 11-year-old Monroe was taken in by an uncle, Pendleton Vandiver, a professional square-dance fiddler who was later immortalized in Monroe's "Uncle Pen." During this period, Monroe was also influenced by an older, black guitarist and fiddler named Arnold Schultz, who taught the youngster to play blues.

Following his brothers Charlie and Birch to suburban Chicago, 18-year-old Monroe found a job cleaning 50-gallon oil barrels. Joining his sibling in a trio, Monroe performed in area country bars and landed a touring spot in the popular WLS *National Barn Dance* troupe.

With Charlie Monroe offered his own radio program in 1944, he hired Bill as his partner. Billed as the Monroe Brothers, the duo's sound was characterized by tightly woven vocal harmonies and guitar-mandolin interplay. The frequently feuding brothers recorded the first of 60 tracks for RCA Victor-Bluebird Records in 1936, highlighted by the shape-note gospel standard "What Would You Give in Exchange (For Your Soul)?"

With the duo disbanding in 1938, Bill Monroe moved to Little Rock and formed the Kentuckians. Relocating to Atlanta, the quartet evolved into the Blue Grass Boys, giving the new musical genre its name.

Joining the Grand Ole Opry in 1939, Monroe brought his mandolin-centered bluegrass to mainstream America. Performing his first hit on the program, a cover of Jimmie Rodgers' "Mule Skinner Blues," Monroe set the standard for bluegrass singing with his "high, lonesome" voice. Monroe created waves not only with his music but with his attire, introducing formal white shirts and neckties to the Opry stage.

But it would be another two years before Monroe would achieve his classic sound, finally adding a banjo player in 1941. With a constant stream of young musicians earning their dues playing behind Monroe, the Blue Grass Boys achieved its classic lineup in 1946, with guitarist Lester Flatt, banjo player Earl Scruggs, fiddler Chubby Wise, and Howard Watts on bass. Borrowing from jazz, Monroe encouraged his musicians to take solos.

Becoming a country superstar in the 1940s, Monroe headlined his own traveling tent show. Moving to Columbia Records, his hits continued with "Kentucky Waltz" (1946), "Footprints in the Snow" (1946), "Blue Moon of Kentucky" (1947), and "Wicked Path of Sin" (1948). Flatt and Scruggs left Monroe in 1948, forming their own popular duo. To Monroe's frustration, his proteges had achieved mainstream popularity before him, scoring crossover-pop hits with "The Ballad of Jed Clampett," and "Foggy Mountain Breakdown.".

Signing with Decca Records in 1950, Monroe remained a popular concert draw. Experimented with his sound in the 1950s, Monroe briefly added drums, accordion, and electric guitar. But with the rise of rock and the honky-tonk brand of country music, Monroe faded from the charts, his last hits coming with "Scotland" (1958) and "Gotta Travel On" (1959).

Meanwhile a host of rockabilly acts like Roy Orbison, Johnny Cash, and Eddie Cochran were soon building upon Monroe's legacy. On his debut 1955 release, Elvis Presley recorded a country-R&B hybrid version of Monroe's "Blue Moon of Kentucky." Presley later apologized to an understanding Monroe for "taking liberties" with the song.

After playing his first folk festival in 1963, Monroe saw his career reinvigorated. Three years later he launched the annual, weeklong Bill Monroe Festival in Beanblossom, Indiana. Elected to the Country Hall of Fame in 1970, Monroe received a string of accolades and awards in the next two decades. Monroe's 1988 album, *SOUTHERN FLAVOR*, earned the first-ever bluegrass Grammy. His career was chronicled in the 1994 documentary *High Lonesome: The Story of Bluegrass Music*. The following year, he was presented a National Medal of the Arts.

Monroe died four days short of his 85th birthday in September 1996; he had suffered a stroke a few months earlier. His last Opry appearance came in March of that year. Meanwhile, a new generation of musicians led by Ricky Skaggs and the Osborne Brothers, have kept bluegrass vital.

Bibliography
Bruce, Dix. (1987). In Judie Eremo (Ed.), *Country Musicians*. Cupertino, CA: GPI.
Harrington, Richard. (1981, June 7). Bill Monroe: The original blue-grass boy. *Washington Post*, p. K1.
Smith, Richard D. (1995). *Bluegrass: An Informal Guide*. Chicago: A Capella.
Smith, Richard D. (1996, October). William Smith Monroe 1911-1996. *Bluegrass Unlimited*, p. 30.
Webb, Steve. (1996, December 6). Bill Monroe: An American genius. *Goldmine*, p. 54.

VAN MORRISON. *(George Ivan Morrison; August 31, 1945). Inducted in 1993*. Nicknamed "Van the Man" and "the Belfast Cowboy," Van Morrison has remained a cult figure in music, his output melding Celtic culture with folk and rock. Born into a blue-collar, Protestant family in the strife-torn community of Belfast, Northern Ireland, Morrison was an only child.

Exposed to music at home, Morrison listened to his father's extensive jazz and blues record collection. Trained on harmonica and guitar, the teenage Morrison joined a series of skiffle, pop, and R&B groups. Leaving school at 15 to take a window-cleaning job, Morrison later wrote "Cleaning Windows" about the ordeal.

Playing the saxophone, Morrison joined the Monarchs in 1960. A big-band/pop-flavored show band, the group performed in West Germany in 1962, playing for German students and black American servicemen. With the rise of the Beatles, the Monarchs added R&B and Merseybeat rock to their set.

Back in Northern Ireland, in 1964 Morrison became fascinated with a London pub band, the Downliner Sect, which played R&B and blues covers. Answering a newspaper advertisement, Morrison joined the Gamblers, originally as their sax player. Hired as the house band of the new Maritime R&B club, the renamed Them (named after a horror flick) played to sold-out houses for several months. Adding former members of the Monarchs, Them built up a loyal following, their shows highlighted by a 20-minute version of Bobby Bland's "Turn on Your Love Light." Creating a stir, the group attracted the attention of Decca Records.

Recording several blues standards at their first session in July 1964, Them also tackled a few originals. Overlooking the Morrison-penned "Gloria" as a potential hit single, Decca instead released the Slim Harpo number "Don't Start Crying Now."

Featuring Jimmy Page on guitar, Them's second session provided the group's first British hit with a cover of Big Joe Williams' "Baby Please Don't Go" (1964). Ironically, "Gloria" was the record's B-side. Touring across the U.K., the label forced the scruffy-haired members of Them to wear suits.

Teamed in 1965 with American producer Bert Berns (writer of "Shout" and "Hang on Sloopy"), Them scored their first U.S. hit with the Berns-penned "Here Comes the Night" (Lulu's earlier version had failed to chart). Leaving the group in 1966 after the release of Them's second album, Morrison rejoined upon learning of an American tour. Arriving in the U.S., Them found that their earlier release, "Gloria," was earning airplay on the heels of the Shadows of Knight's top-10 remake. Disbanding the group, Morrison returned to Ireland.

Paying his own way to New York, Morrison signed with the Bert Berns-owned Bang Records. The Berns-produced "Brown Eyed Girl" gave Morrison his first solo hit. But unhappy at the pop-oriented Bang label, Morrison switched to Warner Brothers after Bern's sudden death from a heart attack.

Homesick, Morrison returned to his Irish home in 1969, composing the tracks for his autobiographical, *ASTRAL WEEKS*. Recorded in two days, sales were initially slow, building over the years. Elevating Morrison's stature to a poet and philosopher, the critically acclaimed acoustic album combined Celtic folk, gospel, and jazz within the structure of rock music. Exploring Celtic mythology and spiritualism, Morrison became Northern Ireland's unofficial spokesman.

Taking a commercial pop-jazz turn, Morrison garnered a large fan base in the early 1970s with a trio of hit albums. Taking over production duties, Morrison landed a hit with the alluring and moody "Moondance" (1970), from the upbeat album of the same name. Released in 1970, *HIS BAND & STREET CHOIR* spawned the hits "Domino" and "Blue Money." Written for his wife and backup singer Janet Planet, the album *TUPELO HONEY* was highlighted by the upbeat, "Wild Night."

Forming the 11-piece Caledonia Soul Orchestra, Morrison earned a reputation as a temperamental, stage-fright prone performer. But after divorcing his wife in 1973 and moving back to Belfast, a dejected Morrison worked little in the next three years.

Returning to music in 1977 with the uneven *A PERIOD OF TRANSITION*, Morrison was joined on the album by New Orleans pianist Dr. John. Though sales improved with the 1978's rock-oriented *WAVELINK* and the gospel-tinged *INTO THE MUSIC*, Morrison was dropped by his record label.

Signing with PolyGram/Mercury, Morrison sold few discs in the U.S. during the 1980s (his U.K. record sales remained healthy). Flirting with Scientology and further exploring his Celtic roots, Morrison's albums became more personal.

Morrison in 1978 teamed with the veteran Irish act, the Chieftains, on the well-received album *IRISH HEARTBEAT*, which featured updated versions of seven traditional Irish songs. In a duet with born-again Christian Cliff Richard, Morrison scored a top-20 British hit with "Whenever God Shines His Light on Me."

Enjoying renewed popularity in the 1990s, Morrison landed his first U.S. hit album in a decade with 1993's *TOO LONG IN EXILE*, which included a duet with bluesman John Lee Hooker. The same year, Rod Stewart scored a top-10 hit with the Morrison-penned "Have I Told You Lately That I Love You." Returning to his childhood love of R&B and jazz, in 1996 Morrison released the Georgie Fame co-produced, Verve album, *HOW LONG HAS THIS BEEN GOING ON*, followed with *THE HEALING GAME*.

Fearful of fame, Morrison sued to keep a plaque from being placed at his childhood home; he also offered to buy all the copies of an unauthorized biography.

Bibliography

Davis, Clive. (1996, May). Van Morrison: Jazz revisited. *Down Beat*, p. 26.

DeWitt, Howard A. (1994, January). Van Morrison and the incredible Them. *Discoveries*, p. 27.

Doggett, Peter. (1992, January). Them. *Record Collector*, p. 112.

Grissim, John, Jr. (1972, June 20). Van Morrison: Blue money & tupelo honey. *Rolling Stone*, p. 36.

McIntyre, Ken. (1990, September 5). The gospel according to Van Morrison. *The Washington Times*, p. E1.

Ruhlmann, William. (1987, October 23). Van Morrison: A look at the mystic's career so far. *Goldmine*, p. 8.

Turner, Steve. (1993). *Van Morrison: Too Late to Stop Now*. New York: Viking.

Turner, Steve. (1995, June 11). Off the beaten record track. *Daily Mail*, p. 68.

JELLY ROLL MORTON. *(Ferdinand Joseph Lamothe; October 20, 1890 [possibly 1885] - July 10, 1941). Inducted in the Early Influence category in 1998.* Emerging from the French Creole community in New Orleans, Jelly Roll Morton was an underappreciated pioneer who was crucial in the development of early jazz. A light-skinned mulatto, Morton often denied his black roots. A self-taught player, Morton combined the various influences of cosmopolitan New Orleans, creating a sound that was an amalgamation of ragtime, Creole, French opera and the spirited jazz of coronet-player Buddy Bolden.

Earning hundreds of dollars a week during his teens performing in the brothels and gambling houses of the city's famed Storeyville vice district, Morton was booted from his home by his religious grandmother. Adopting the name "Jelly Roll," a black sexual slang term, the Morton joined traveling vaudeville troupes and tent shows. A flashy dresser and a braggart, Morton wore a diamond in his front tooth, and earned a reputation as a pool hustler, card shark, and pimp.

Settling in Chicago and then on the West Coast, Morton led several small jazz combos in Los Angeles between 1917 and 1922. Back in Chicago in 1923, Morton performed on recording sessions for Gennett Records behind an all-white group, the New Orleans Rhythm Kings, passing himself off as a Spaniard.

Jazz's first great composer, Morton shaped the direction of jazz with standards such as "The Pearls," "Jungle Blues," "The Wolverine Blues," and "King Porter Stomp," the latter written for fellow pianist, Porter King. A prolific songwriter Morton penned over 1,000 songs and, for a time, joined the Melrose Publishing House as an arranger.

Entering his classic period in the late 1920s, Morton formed the Hot Red Peppers. Recording for Victor Records, he was backed by jazz greats such as Kid Ory and the Dodds Brothers on innovative works that brought improvisation to the forefront of jazz.

With the onset of the Depression and the collapse of the record industry, Morton was dropped by Victor in 1930. Relocating to New York City, Morton lost much of his fortune on a failed cosmetics company. Though Morton faded into obscurity in the 1930s, his "King Porter Stomp" became a swing-era standard, with the most popular rendition by Benny Goodman.

Moving to Washington D.C., Morton was reduced to managing a Washington D.C. nightclub, The Jungle Inn, reportedly the city's first racially integrated tavern. Rediscovered by Alan Lomax in 1938 for his Library of Congress folk series, Morton was interviewed and recorded over an eight-week period. Providing his own slanted history of twentieth century music, Morton claimed that he invented jazz in 1902.

With his career reinvigorated, Morton landed in New York City in the late 1930s. But his musical activity was soon limited by failing health. Returning to California, the 50-year-old Morton died penniless in 1941 in the colored wing of the Los Angeles County Hospital. He was convinced his illness was the result of a voodoo curse. Superstitious all of his life, he once burned all of his fancy suits at a fortune teller's urging.

Premiering in 1992, the biographical Broadway musical *Jelly's Last Jam* won three Tonys, including the best actor award for Gregory Hines in the title role. Computer-enhanced recordings of early piano roll music by Jelly Roll Morton were released on the 1997 album, *JELLY ROLL MORTON: THE PIANO ROLLS*.

Bibliography

Charters, Samuel. (1984). *Jelly Roll Morton's Last Night at the Jungle*. New York: Marion.
De Toledano, Ralph. (1991, April 1). The Jelly Roll Morton centennial. *National Review*, p. 49.
Rule, Sheila. (1992, June 30). Reconstructing Jelly through his music. *The New York Times*,

p. C11.

Russell, William. (1959). Jelly Roll Morton. In Martin T. Williams (Ed.), *The Art of Jazz* (pp. 33-42). New York: Oxford University Press.

Wilson, Gerald. (1991, April 16). Getting Jelly out of his latest jam. *Los Angeles Times*, p. F4.

SYD NATHAN. *(Sydney Nathan; April 27, 1904 - March 5, 1968). Inducted in the Non-Performer category in 1997.* Crucial to the rise of rhythm and blues in the late 1940s was the Cincinnati-based King Record Company. The label was the brainchild of a legally blind, guitar-chomping asthmatic named Syd Nathan. A native of Cincinnati, Nathan returned to the city in 1939 after his Florida photo-finishing business went bankrupt.

After learning the retail business at his brother's pawnshop, Nathan opened his own record store. Initially selling used jukebox records that he had purchased for two-cents each, Nathan was overwhelmed by the demand. With wartime industry bringing blacks and whites to the city, Nathan serviced the previously ignored market for blues and hillbilly records.

Realizing the potential profit in manufacturing his own records, Nathan first hired acts from Dayton and Cincinnati radio programs. Recording Merle Travis and Grandpa Jones in 1943 as the Sheppard Brothers, Nathan was unhappy with the poor quality of the pressed discs.

Opening his own record plant in a former ice warehouse, Nathan and five investors poured $25,000 into the venture. Buying his own record presses and manufacturing his own discs, Nathan somehow managed to obtain shellac and other rare material during the height of the wartime shortages.

Initially targeting the country-western market King Records found early success with releases by the Delmore Brothers, Cowboy Copas, and Hawkshaw Hawkins. But, in 1946, King split into two divisions, with the King label continuing its output of "hillbilly" records, and Queen introducing a line of jazz and "race" records. Queen's first race star was Cleveland native Bull Moose Jackson who enjoyed a string of hits beginning with "I Know Who Threw the Whiskey in the Well" (1946).

By 1947, Nathan supplemented the King-Queen roster by purchasing master discs from competitors. He also expanded into the exploding gospel market with acts such as the Wings Over Jordan Choir. Merging the Queen subsidiary back into King Records, Nathan enjoyed R&B chart action with pioneering hits like Wynonie Harris' "Good Rockin' Tonight" (1948).

Enjoying a booming R&B market, Nathan began buying out several competitors, including DeLuxe, Miracle, Bethlehem, Rockin', and Glory Records. Overwhelmed by the success of King's R&B roster, Nathan launched another subsidiary, Federal Records, placing producer Ralph Bass in charge. Bass' first success at Federal came with the bawdy, much-banned single, "Sixty Minute Man" by the Dominoes, the best-selling R&B records of 1951. In spite of Nathan's objections, Bass continued to produce controversial, but popular, hits. Besides Bass, Nathan surrounded himself with a host of talented managers: Henry Stone, Seymore Stein, and pioneering black record executive Henry Glover.

King-Federal sported many of the biggest R&B acts of the 1950s including the Dominoes, Hank Ballard and the Midnighters, Charles Brown, Earl Bostic, Little Willie John, Freddy King, Roy Brown, and the "5" Royales. Also recording pop and jazz, Nathan enjoyed success with Nina Simone, Mel Torme, Jonah Jones, Erroll Garner, and Duke Ellington.

King enjoyed crossover success in 1956 with the debut disc of newcomer James Brown, "Please, Please, Please." Hating the song, Nathan released the record only after producer Ralph Bass threatened to quit. Other noteworthy releases during this period include "Honky Tonk (Parts 1 & 2)" by Bill Doggett and the original version of "The Twist" by Hank Ballard & the Midnighters.

An extremely frugal entrepreneur, Nathan refused to outsource any of the work involved in the making of a record, manufacturing everything except the inner LP sleeves. Establishing a massive distribution network, Nathan managed to thrive at a time other independent labels were selling out to the majors.

Accused of making payola payments to deejays, Nathan and King Records were devastated by the charges. Except for the skyrocketing James Brown, King had little success in the 1960s.

Out of economic necessity, Nathan merged King with Starday Records in 1967. Following Nathan's death the following year, King was sold to Starday, which shuttered the studio in 1970.

When Gusto Records began reissuing King material in 1970s, the tracks were altered with added instrumental backing in an attempt to update the music. Consequently when Rhino Records began releasing classic King material in the 1980s, it had great difficulty in locating the original unaltered master recordings.

Released in 1996, *THE KING R&B BOX SET* collects the best of the label's output and includes Nathan's speeches to his employees. Today the former King building houses the maintenance department of a convenience store chain.

Bibliography

Grendysa. Peter. (1990, September 7). King/Federal. *Goldmine*, p. 29.

Radel, Cliff. (1994, November 6). King-sized dreams: Making former Cincinnati recording plant into museum would revive an era. *Cincinnati Enquirer*, p. G1.

Rumble, John W. (1992). Roots of rock & roll: Henry Glover at King Records. *Journal of Country Music, 14*(2), p. 30.

Tracy, Steven C. (1993). *Going to Cincinnati: A History of the Blues in the Queen City*. Urbana: University of Illinois Press.

RICK NELSON. *(Eric Hilliard Nelson; May 8, 1940 - December 31, 1985). Inducted 1987*. Parlaying his teen heartthrob role on the sitcom, *Ozzie and Harriet* into rock stardom, Rick Nelson discovered the power of television. Born in Teaneck, New Jersey, into a showbiz family, Rick Nelson was the son of popular 1940s bandleader Ozzie Nelson and singer Harriet Hilliard. In 1944 the Nelsons transferred their act to radio on *The Adventures of Ozzie and Harriet*.

Joining their parents on the show in 1949, eight-year-old Ricky and his brother David replaced the child actors who had previously portrayed them. After a successful spinoff film, *Here Come the Nelsons*, the Nelson family launched a television program in October 1952. (The radio version continued for another two years.)

Drawing millions of adolescent female viewers, the clean-cut and wholesome Ricky Nelson became a teenage idol. Wanting to impress a girlfriend, on one episode Nelson sang Fats Domino's "I'm Walking." With fans clamoring for the record, Nelson rushed to record the single, landing a surprise million-selling, top-10 hit.

Signing with Imperial Records (the same label as Fats Domino), Nelson was backed by a talented rockabilly band, featuring a former *Louisiana Hayride* guitarist, 16-year-old James Burton. Nelson, himself an accomplished guitar player, also played the clarinet, piano, and drums. Receiving 50,000 fan letters a week, Nelson was pictured on the cover of *Life* magazine in December 1958.

With the opportunity to promote his songs, weekly on his television show, Nelson scored three dozen hits, including "A Teenager's Romance" (1957); "Stood Up" (1957); the Sharon Sheeley-penned "Poor Little Fool" (1958); "Nobody Else but You" (1959); "It's Late" (1959); and the double-sided entry "Travelin' Man"/"Hello Mary Lou" (1961), the latter written by Gene Pitney. In 1961, 21-year-old Ricky Nelson became Rick Nelson, his crewcut now grown out.

Moving to Decca Records in 1963, Nelson's very lucrative contract was negotiated by his lawyer father. His singing career eclipsed by the rise of Beatlemania, Nelson managed only a few hits at the label. Turning to film acting, Nelson co-starred with John Wayne and Dean Martin in the western *Rio Bravo* (1959). Nelson's other films included *The Wackiest Ship in the Army* (1960) and *Love and Kisses* (1965).

By the mid-1960s, Nelson's real-life wife, Kristin Harmon (sister of actor Mark Harmon), joined the cast of *Ozzie and Harriet*. But in September 1966, the show was canceled.

Ignored by rock fans in the late 1960s, Nelson switched to country music. Influenced by the emerging folk music boom, Nelson's 1968 album, *ANOTHER SIDE OF RICK*, contained three Tim Hardin compositions, including "Reason to Believe." Forming the Stone Canyon Band, Nelson scored his next-to-last hit with the Bob Dylan composition "She Belongs to Me." (Nelson's bassist Randy Meisner later cofounded the Eagles.)

Wanting to shed his image as an oldies artist, Nelson was met with resistance. "Backed by his souped-up band, his hair still long, Rick came to New York's Madison Square Garden in the fall of 1971. The crowd expected him to be the old Ricky, the squeaky-clean teenager who was eons removed from the torn America of the Vietnam War era. But since this strange-looking Rick was wired into the rebellious seventies, the crowd mercilessly booed him" (p. 385), recalled music critic Edward Kiersh. Disheartened, Nelson chronicled the incident in his last top-40 hit, "Garden Party" (1972).

After releasing the poorly-selling 1974 album *WINDFALL*, Nelson left MCA Records and parted with the Stone Canyon Band. Becoming musically adventurous, Nelson played in a jazz combo in the late 1970s.

Following a painful divorce in 1977, Nelson adopted a low profile. He released his last charting album in 1981 with *PLAYING TO WIN*. Returning to acting, Nelson guested on several television shows including *McCloud*. Starring in the 1983 television film *High School U.S.A.* (NBC), Nelson was joined by his mother, who played his secretary.

En route from Guttersville, Alabama, to Dallas for the half-time festivities at the Cotton Bowl, tragedy struck Nelson's DC-3 airplane (previously owned by Jerry Lee Lewis). Killed were Nelson, his fiancee Helen Blair, and several members of the Stone Canyon Band when a malfunctioning gas heater exploded and started a fire. Initially attributing the fire to the freebasing of cocaine, investigators found no traces of drugs.

Nelson's daughter, Tracy, became a television actress, co-starring in the ABC series *Father Dowling Mysteries.* Nelson's twin sons, Matthew and Gunner, formed a rock duo called Nelson. Their 1990 debut album, *AFTER THE RAIN*, spawned the top-10 hit "(Can't Live without Your) Love and Affection."

Bibliography

Brennan, Patricia. (1987, November 15). Rick Nelson; An affectionate recollection by his brother. *Washington Post*, p. Y11.

Callihan, Mike; Buschardt, Bud & Goddard, Steve. (1990, August). Both sides now: Rick Nelson. *Goldmine*, p. 17.

Demaret, Kent. (1986, January 20). Rick Nelson 1940-1985. *People*, p. 28.

Kiersh, Edward. (1986). *Where Are You Now, Bo Diddley?* (pp. 380-87). Garden City, NY: Doubleday.

Obrecht, Jas. (1987). In Judie Eremo (Ed.), *Country Musicians* (pp. 82-84). New York: Grove Press.

Osborne, Jerry. (1988, October). Rick. *Discoveries*, p. 16.

ROY ORBISON. *(Roy Kelton Orbison; April 23, 1936 - December 6, 1988); Inducted in 1987.* Singing of broken hearts and unrequited love, Roy Orbison bridged rockabilly with pop balladry. Born in Vernon, Texas, Orbison was taught to play guitar at age six by an adult neighbor, after playing along with country songs on the radio.

After a move to Fort Worth, little Roy was sent back to Vernon to escape a polio outbreak. After landing a radio program at KVWC at age eight, he later hosted an amateur hour. After moving to the desert town of Wink, Texas, at the end of World War II, the teenage Orbison formed the Wink Westerners and performed throughout western Texas

Expected by his family to take a job in a local oil company after college, Orbison studied geology at North Texas State University near Fort Worth. There in 1954 he was first exposed to rockabilly. After hearing a rockabilly group's original composition, "Ooby Dooby," Orbison and the renamed Teen Kings retooled their country and western repertoire. Transferring to another college in Odessa, Orbison was encouraged by classmate Pat Boone to make a record. In Odessa, the Teen Kings landed their own television program.

Drawn to Norman Petty's small studio in Clovis, New Mexico, Orbison and the Teen Kings made their first recordings. With the master of the rockabilly-inflected "Ooby Dooby" leased to Jewel Records, Orbison landed a regional hit in early 1956.

Then with Johnny Cash's assistance, Orbison signed with Sun Records. A newly recorded, polished version of "Ooby Dooby" would be Orbison's only hit at the label. Dropping the Teen Kings in mid-1957, Orbison began relying on session players. Not permitted to sing ballads at Sun Records, Orbison was angry that label-owner Sam Phillips made him sing novelty-styled songs like, "Chicken Hearted." Receiving a minuscule royalty rate, Orbison was forced by economics to leave Sun.

After opening for the Everly Brothers in Indiana, Orbison was asked if they would record his song "Claudette" (named after Orbison's wife). A B-side hit for the Everlys in 1957, the song was parlayed into a songwriting position for Orbison at the Acuff-Rose publishing company. The grateful Everlys also aided Orbison in signing with RCA Records.

Now managed by Wesley Rose (co-owner of Acuff-Rose), Orbison signed with the new Monument Record label. After a series of flops, Orbison's moody "Only the Lonely" (1960) became his first top-40 hit. Possessing a lonely, quivering, three-octave voice, Orbison was well suited to songs of heartbreak and loss.

Composing autobiographical material, Orbison scored a string of top-10 hits, including "Blue Angel" (1960); "Running Scared" (1961); "Crying" (1961); "Dream Baby" (1961); "In Dreams" (1961); and "It's Over." His best-known hit, the out-of-character, up-tempo hit, "Pretty Woman" (1964), gave Roy Orbison and the Candymen their first million-seller.

Forgetting his regular glasses, Orbison first donned his trademark, dark sunglasses, at an Alabama concert in 1963. Becoming part of his image, his Buddy Holly-like Ray Ban Wayfarer specs were popularized during a spring 1963 British tour with the then-upstart Beatles. Switching to MGM Records in 1965, Orbison's career lost its momentum. With MGM also in the movie business, Orbison starred in *The Fastest Guitar Alive* (1966).

After buying an 11,000-acre Texas ranch, Orbison was struck by tragedy. After the death of his wife in a 1966 motorcycle accident, Orbison lost two of his three sons in a house fire. Disappearing from the pop charts in 1967, he would remain forgotten until the 1980s. Marrying German-born Barbara Wellhonen in 1969, Orbison moved to Germany, limiting his touring to Europe and Australia.

During the 1970s, Orbison began to include Sun material in his concert. Returning to the U.S. unnoticed, in 1977 Orbison hit an American concert stage for the first time in a decade. Then following open-heart surgery, Orbison released an ignored album in 1979.

Returning to the charts in 1980 in a duet with Emmylou Harris, Orbison won his first Grammy with "That Loving You Feeling Again." During this period, Orbison reappeared on the pop charts via several hit remakes, including Linda Ronstadt's "Blue Bayou" (1977); Don McLean's "Crying" (1981); and Van Halen's "Pretty Woman" (1982). Suing his former manager, Wesley Rose, in 1982 for $50 million, Orbison claimed mismanagement and "under-reported" royalties.

Signing with Virgin Records, Orbison recorded a new version of "In Dreams" for the album *IN DREAMS: THE GREATEST HITS*. The song was prominently featured in the David Lynch film *Blue Velvet*.

Adopting the pseudonym, Lefty Wilbury (after Lefty Frizzell), Orbison joined the rock supergroup the Traveling Wilburys. With the surprise success of *THE*

TRAVELING WILBURYS, VOLUME I and the lead-off single "Handle with Care," Orbison's career was on a major upswing. But tragedy struck and halted any comeback plans. After a concert in Cleveland in December 1988, Orbison flew to his mother's Tennessee home, where he died of a heart attack. The video for the Traveling Wilburys' second single, "End of the Line" featured a simple photograph of Orbison. The group's plans for a tour and film project were scrapped. A followup Wilburys album contained the Orbison tribute "You Take My Breath Away."

Completed shortly before his death, Orbison's solo album *MYSTERY GIRL* spawned a top-10 posthumous hit with the upbeat "You Got It" (1989). Orbison's earlier hit "Pretty Woman" received heavy airplay after being featured in the 1990 Julia Roberts film of the same name. But when the shock-rap group, 2 Live Crew, recorded an unauthorized parody of the song, Acuff-Rose launched a highly publicized, but unsuccessful lawsuit against the group's leader Luther Campbell.

Featuring Bob Dylan and B.B. King, the star-studded "Roy Orbison Tribute" was staged on February 24, 1990. An Orbison monument was erected in his hometown of Wink, Texas, in 1991. Considered Orbison's stylistic progeny, singer-songwriter Chris Isaak recorded Orbison's "Only the Lonely" in 1996.

Bibliography

Barnes, Harper. (1990, June 24). Rock's ugly duckling: Retracing Roy Orbison's torturous road to stardom. *St. Louis Post-Dispatch*, p. 3C.
Harrington, Richard. (1986, July 17). Roy Orbison, soaring again. *The Washington Post*, p. B1.
Jerome, Jim. (1988, December 19). Bard of the lonely; Roy Orbison, rock original, dies at 52. *People*, p. 60.
Tamarkin, Jeff. (1979, October). A candid conversation with Roy Orbison. *Goldmine*, p. 5.

THE ORIOLES. *Tommy Gaither (Lloyd Gaither Jr.; c. 1920 - November 5, 1950); George P. Nelson (c. 1923 - 1959); Johnny Reed (1924); Alexander Sharp (1930 - 1969); Sonny Til (Earlington Carl Tilghman; August 8, 1925 - December 9, 1981). Inducted in 1995.* In the tradition of doo-wop pioneers the Ravens, scores of early, black vocal groups named themselves after birds. The most famous of these bird groups was the Orioles.

Led by Sonny Til, a World War II-era USO singer, the group met and formed in 1947 at a Baltimore talent contest, originally calling themselves the Vibranairs. An emotionally-charge, high tenor whose favorite singer was Nat King Cole, Til projected a virile sexuality which stirred the passions of screaming female fans.

Consisting of Til, George Nelson, Alexander Sharp and Johnny Reed, the Orioles were directly patterned after the Ravens, who transformed the 1940s styles of the Ink Spots and Mills Brothers into modern, street-corner, doo-wop balladry. Employing four-part harmony and the standup bass of Johnny Reed, the group later added a classically-trained guitarist Tommy Gaither.

In an odd pairing, a young, white, Jewish sales clerk and struggling songwriter named Deborah (Shirley) Chessler talked her way into managing the Orioles. After receiving vocal and stage instruction from Chessler, the group landed a spot on Arthur

Godfrey's *Talent Scouts* radio show in 1948. Though losing to pianist George Shearing, the group was asked by Godfrey to perform on his more popular daytime program. There they met and were signed by Jerry Blaine of Natural Records, who renamed the group the Orioles, after the Maryland state bird.

Recording the Chessler-penned "It's Too Soon to Know" (1948), the Orioles landed on both R&B and pop charts. On Blaine's renamed Jubilee label, the Orioles launched a string of groundbreaking, top-10 R&B hits, including another Chessler composition, "Tell Me So" (1949); and the doubled sided entry "What Are You Doing New Year's Eve"/"Lonely Christmas" (1949). Defining the doo-wop genre, the Orioles spawned scores of imitators including the Dominoes, the Drifters, as well as a number of "bird" groups like the Robins, the Crows, and the Flamingos.

But after a car crash killed Tommy Gaither and seriously injured two other members, the Orioles became apprehensive about traveling. The cutback of touring kept the group from achieving greater success. Hiring guitarist Ralph Williams and pianist Charlie Harris, the battered Orioles returned to the R&B charts in 1952 with "Baby, Please Don't Go."

Following the alcoholism-related departure of George Nelson in 1953 (replaced by Gregory Carroll), the Orioles landed a crossover, pop smash with the sensual and emotionally charged cover version of Darrell Glenn's gospel classic "Crying in the Chapel." Eager to repeat their success, the group's subsequent gospel-styled releases with the exception of "In the Mission of St. Augustine," all bombed. After Johnny Reed's departure in 1955, the group disintegrated, their last release coming with "If You Believe." Reed and Sharp later joined a revival version of the Ink Spots.

Til then hired the Regals (whom he saw at the Apollo) as the new Orioles. Adopting an updated style of harmony, the new group scored a minor R&B hit with "Happy Till the Letter" (1956). After switching to Vee-Jay Records, Sonny Til and the Orioles disbanded in 1958.

Returning to Jubilee as a solo act, Til recorded several tracks, including an updated rendition of "Crying in the Chapel." A new version of the Orioles led by Til recorded for Charlie Parker Records in 1961. Forming new versions of the Orioles in the 1960s and 1970s, Til frequented the oldies circuit, and in 1978 recorded the album *SONNY TIL AND THE ORIOLES TODAY*. Til performed until his death in 1981. The Orioles persevered into the 1990s, a new version led by Orioles/Regals members Albert "Diz" Russell and Jerry Holeman. Johnny Reed is the only surviving member of the original group.

Bibliography

Considine, J.D. (1995, January 12). Baltimore group from birth of rock will be enshrined: Early birds. *Baltimore Sun*, p. 1E.

Goldberg, Marv. (1995, May). Odds and ends on the Orioles. *Discoveries*, p. 44.

Hamlin, Jesse. (1993, December 21). Soulful sounds in Sebastopol: R&B legend Johnny Otis turns a produce market into a hot venue. *San Francisco Chronicle*, p. E1.

Jones, Wayne. (1982, February). Wayne Jones talks with Sonny Til of the Orioles. *Goldmine*, p. 21.

Joyce, Mike. (1995, April 5). The legendary Orioles, still flying. *Washington Post*, p. B7.

Marcus, Greil. (1993, June 24). The Deborah Chessler story. *Rolling Stone*, p. 41.

JOHNNY OTIS. *(John Veliotis; December 28, 1921). Inducted in the Non-Performer category in 1994.* A crucial figure in the genesis of Los Angeles R&B, Johnny Otis was instrumental in bringing the music to the attention of mainstream America. Born in Vallejo, California, but raised in nearby Berkeley, Otis lived in a racially mixed neighborhood where his Greek-immigrant father operated a small grocery store. Though white, Otis became immersed in black music and culture.

First learning to play the tuba, Otis switched to drums, teaching himself by watching others at school. During the Depression, the teenage Otis earned money salvaging parts from junked roadside autos.

Mesmerized by the sight of the Count Basie and Duke Ellington orchestras, Otis forged his father's name at a music store to buy a drum kit. In 1940 he joined a local band led by Delta-born, barrelhouse style pianist Count Otis Matthews.

Performing in black nightclubs, Otis had to feign being black to skirt strict segregation laws. "I lived under constant pressure to abandon my social direction and become 'white.' I got this at school from my teachers and counselors, from my white friends, and especially my mother" (p. 13), Otis recalled in his autobiography. Against his mother's strong objections, Otis married a black woman, eloping to Las Vegas in 1941.

Joining a series of jazz and proto-R&B bands, Otis toured the country's midsection, in 1942 joining the Serenaders. The group featured saxophonist Preston Love, with whom Otis formed a short-lived group the following year. The Otis-Love Band disbanded in 1943 at an Omaha stop, after Nat King Cole convinced Otis to audition for Harlan Leonard's Kansas City Rockets, the house band at the Club Alabam cabaret in Los Angeles.

In 1945, the owner of the Club Alabam instructed Otis to assemble his own group as the new house band. Hiring a series of lead vocalists beginning with Bing Williams and pianist Bill Doggett, the Johnny Otis Orchestra also backed the top acts of the day Wynonie Harris and Pearl Bailey, the nightclub drawing flocks of servicemen on leave.

After playing drums on the Three Blazers/Charles Brown smash hit "Driftin' Blues," Otis recorded his own material initially with Jimmy Rushin on vocals. Backed by his mostly black orchestra, Otis' first hit came with a gritty, jazz-flavored cover of the standard "Harlem Nocturn" (1946). A year later, Otis and his orchestra were hired as the touring band for the Ink Spots. But with the death of the swing era, Otis soon fired his orchestra. Influenced by Louis Jordan, Otis formed a small combo and gravitated toward a modern R&B sound.

Investing a total of $400 in 1948, Otis and three partners opened the Barrelhouse Club in a rough part of Los Angeles. Leading the house band and running a popular Thursday night amateur show, Otis discovered many early R&B and blues acts including the Robins, Mel Walker, and Marie Adams. By year's end, Otis took an R&B revue on the road, predating the all-star caravans of both Alan Freed and Dick Clark.

Also operating a chicken and egg farm, Otis advertised his products on a black radio program. But after seriously injuring his hand while constructing a chicken coop, Otis was forced to end his drumming career. Now playing his trademark vibraharp,

Otis closed his chicken farm and sold his interest in the Barrelhouse Club to concentrate on recording and touring.

Recording a barefoot, 13-year-old, neighborhood girl named "Little" Esther Phillips as a lark, Otis stumbled upon a hit R&B record. Signing with Savoy Records, Otis and Phillips scored several collaborative R&B hits beginning with "Double Crossing Blues." Signed by King-Federal Records as a talent scout, Otis later discovered Little Willie John, Jackie Wilson, and the Royals (Midnighters). Another Otis find, Ray Charles, was rejected by label chief Syd Nathan for sounding too much like R&B balladeer Charles Brown.

Entering into a longterm relationship with the Don Robey-owned Duke-Peacock Records, in 1953 Otis produced and played drums on Big Mama Thorton's blues smash "Hound Dog" (Otis can be heard howling at the end of the song). Otis also backed R&B balladeer Johnny Ace on several hits, including a posthumous smash, "Pledging My Love" (1955).

Discovering R&B singer Etta James, Otis collaborated on her huge R&B hit, "The Wallflower" (1955), an answer record to the Midnighters' "Roll With Me Henry." James later recalled, that "from his phone voice, I figured he was black. For years many people believed Johnny 'was' black, not only because of his swarthy skin tone but because he talked, walked, acted, played, and pushed black music so hard" (p. 45).

After landing his own radio program in 1953 at KFOX in Long Beach and a television program two years later, Otis was shocked to see whites displacing blacks at his concerts.

Signing a lucrative contract with Capitol Records in 1957, Otis scored his biggest pop hit with a cover of the standard "Willie and the Hand Jive," his band billed as the Johnny Otis Show. The song employed a rhythm Otis had first heard while with Count Matthews in 1940, but which was later known as the "Bo Diddley beat." Leaving Capitol, Otis launched another label, Eldo, before becoming King-Federal's West Coast A&R chief.

Becoming politically active in the 1960s, Otis started a black-empowerment organization, picketing racially segregated businesses. Running for the California state assembly, he was unsuccessful.

Returning to the R&B charts in 1969 with "Country Girl," Otis was accompanied by his son, Shuggie Otis, on guitar. After performing at the 1970 Monterey Jazz Festival, Otis joined an R&B oldies revue. Ordained a minister in 1975, Otis spent the next decade preaching in front of a predominantly black congregation.

Forming a new version of the Johnny Otis Show in 1981, Otis signed with Alligator Records. Releasing a self-titled album, Otis garnered his first Grammy nomination. In the late 1980s, Otis operated a pair of blues clubs: the Johnny Otis Market and the larger Rhythm and Brews.

Though an experienced musician with impressive credentials, Otis was nominated into the Rock and Roll Hall of Fame in 1994 in the Non-Performer category. Also an artist, Otis's multimedia and ink pieces are collected in the book *Chords and Colors*.

Bibliography
Hansen, Terry. (1994, April 1). Otisology: The spirit of Johnny Otis. *Goldmine*, p. 14.

Hildebrand, Lee & Lovelace O'Neal, Mary. (1995). *Colors and Chords: The Art of Johnny Otis*. San Francisco: Pomegranate Art Books.
Hite, Richard James. (1990, February). Johnny Otis in his own words. *Discoveries*, p. 24.
James, Etta & Ritz, David. (1995). *The Etta James Story: Rage to Survive*. New York: Villard.
Otis, Johnny. (1968). *Listen to the Lambs*. New York: W.W. Norton.
Welding, Pete. (1971, December 9). Johnny Otis. *Rolling Stone*, p. 48.

PARLIAMENT-FUNKADELIC. *Jerome "Bigfoot" Brailey; George Clinton (George Edward Clinton; July 22, 1940); Bootsy Collins (William Collins; October 26, 1951); Ray Davis (Raymond Davis); Glen Goins (Glen Lamont Goins; 1953); Ramon "Tiki" Fulwood; Michael "Mickey" Hampton (1957); Clarence "Fuzzy" Haskins; Eddie Hazel (April 19, 1950 - December 23, 1992); Walter "Junie" Morrison; Cordell "Boogie" Mosson (Cordell Mosson, Jr.); Billy "Bass" Nelson (William Nelson, Jr.; 1949); Garry M. Shider (1952); Calvin Simon; Grady Thomas (Gene Grady Thomas); Bernie Worrell (April 19, 1944). Inducted in 1997.* Merging psychedelic rock, hard-driving funk and theatrical antics, the various incarnations of Parliament-Funkadelic have flourished over four decades. The brainchild of North Carolina native George Clinton, the roots of the musical regiment originated in 1955 in a New Jersey doo-wop quartet called the Parliaments. Hair stylists by day, the Parliaments were frequent Apollo Theater talent show winners. Recording for variety of record companies beginning in 1959, the group sold few records.

Hired as a staff songwriter at the Motown-owned Jobete publishing company, Clinton failed in his attempts to impress the label with several demo records. Signing with a new label, Rivelot Records, Clinton and the Parliaments signed landed their debut hit in 1967 with the Clinton-penned, top-20 pop-soul nugget "(I Wanna) Testify."

Embracing the emerging hippie culture in Boston and New York, Clinton and the group were spending their barber salaries on studio time, hoping to score a followup hit. After sharing a concert bill with progressive rock band Vanilla Fudge, Clinton was inspired to form a side band, an experimental psychedelic soul group called Funkadelic. Employing top musicians, Funkadelic featured the talents of guitar wizard Eddie Hazel and classically trained keyboardist Bernie Worrell.

Temporarily losing the legal right to use the Parliaments name, Clinton signed with Westbound Records under his Funkadelic moniker. After regaining control of the Parliaments name, he dropped the "s" from the group's name and maintained two overlapping groups.

While Parliament and Funkadelic recorded on separate labels, the entire assemblage toured together as Parliament-Funkadelic. Nicknamed Dr. Funkenstein, Clinton headed the troupe's chaotic stage show, employing macabre stage props and a cacophony of performers wearing everything from wedding dresses and diapers.

Employing dozens of musicians in at any given time (including up to 10 guitarists), Clinton hired top R&B session men, including Walter "Junie" Morrison on keyboards, Ramon "Tiki" Fulwood on drums, and the team of Maceo Parker and Fred Wesley on horns. In 1972, Clinton hired the former James Brown sidemen, drummer Frankie

Waddy, guitarist Catfish Collins, and his brother, bassist William "Bootsy" Collins. Playing a futuristic-looking, star-shaped bass, and sporting a glittering space-age suit and star-shaped sunglasses, Bootsy Collins emerged as a star in his own right.

Although sharing much of the same personnel, Parliament and Funkadelic took different musical directions. Funkadelic employed components of hard soul and guitar-rock, in 1970 releasing the including the LSD-inspired *album FREE YOUR MIND AND YOUR ASS WILL FOLLOW*. Intended as a commentary on the Vietnam War, the 1971 album, *MAGGOT BRAIN*, captured the attention of rock fans with its title track, "Maggot Brain," which featured a searing, 10-minute, Hendrix-like guitar solo by Eddie Hazel. But with Hazel jailed on drug charges, guitarist Michael Hampton was hired as his replacement.

Becoming a trademark of the group's mid-1970s period, Bootsy Collins' electronically synthesized vocals were introduced on the Funkadelic album *LET'S TAKE IT TO THE STAGE*. Released in 1978, *ONE NATION UNDER A GROOVE* (1978) featured the million-selling "One Nation under a Groove (Part 1)." Revolting against disco, the hard-funk album *UNCLE JAM WANTS YOU* (1979) spawning the R&B chart-topper "(not just) Knee Deep—Part 1" (1979), a track highlighted by the blazing guitar work of Michael Hampton.

While Funkadelic was embracing hard-rock influences, Parliament's R&B and soul flavored sound was augmented with a horn section. Recording for a separate record label, Parliament had its own strong hit run including a pair of million-sellers, "Tear the Roof Off the Sucker" (1976) and "Flash Light" (1978).

Throughout the 1970s, Parliament-Funkadelic spun off various side groups, including the Brides of Funkenstein, the Horny Horns, Parlet, and solo projects by Worrell, Morrison, and Bootsy Collins. In the late 1970s, Clinton took his massive "Mothership Connection" on the concert road, the stage set built around a massive, hovering flying saucer.

But by the early 1980s, Clinton's empire collapsed under the massive costs of paying dozens of performers and dancers. Adding to Clinton's problems were IRS troubles and confrontations between his two record companies. After announcing the end of Parliament-Funkaledic, Clinton launched Uncle Jam Records, releasing an album by Funkadelic member and former Spinners lead singer Phillippe Wynne. Clinton also produced the Red Hot Chili Peppers' 1982 album, *FREAKY STYLEY*.

After returning to the stage with a streamlined group, renamed the P-Funk All-Stars, Clinton also pursued a separate solo career. Signing with Capitol, Clinton scored a massive dance-club hit with the gritty, funk-flavored "Atomic Dog" (1983), taken from the album *COMPUTER GAMES*. Clinton followed up in 1986 with another solo hit, "Do Fries Go with That Shake," from the album *R&B SKELETONS*. Meanwhile, his releases with the P-Funk All-Stars fared poorly.

After influencing a generation of funk rockers, Clinton signed with Paisley Park Records, the label owned by one of his protégés, Prince. While Clinton's hit run had slowed by the late-1980s, his older material emerged as a favorite of rap samplers, appearing on hits by De La Soul, Digital Under Ground, and (M.C.) Hammer.

Rejoining Clinton's P-Punk All-Stars in 1992, an ailing Eddie Hazel left midtour. He died later in the year from liver failure. The group's classic 1970s lineup was reassembled in 1996 for the album *T.A.P.O.A.F.O.M.* (short for The Awesome Power of a Fully Operational Mothership).

Bibliography

Corbett, John. (1993, July-August). Un-funkin'-believable: George Clinton's P-Funk legacy. *Option*, p. 74.

Fricke, David. (1990, September 20). George Clinton. *Rolling Stone*, p. 75.

Green, Tony. (1996, April). Up for the Downstroke. *Guitar Player*, p. 70.

Mulhern, Tom. (1979, April). Bootsy Collins: Funk's premier bassist. *Guitar Player*, p. 32.

Pareles, Jon. (1984, January 1). George Clinton builds fun empire. *New York Times*, sect. 2, p. 15.

Rosen, Steve. (1977, December). Sci-fi funkiness. *Guitar Player*, p. 28.

Seiler, Andy. (1996, June 16). George Clinton and crew launch '90s mothership. *USA Today*, p. 4D.

LES PAUL. *(Lester William Polfus; June 19, 1915). Inducted in the Early Influence category in 1988.* While Les Paul was instrumental in the development of the solid-body electric guitar, it was his multitrack recording process that was truly revolutionary. With the invention, a single musician was able to play every instrument on a record and to provide his own backing vocals.

Born and raised in Waukesha, Wisconsin, Paul became fascinated with music when a ditchdigger gave him a harmonica. Graduating to the guitar and piano, Paul was more interested in how the instruments worked.

Enamored with electronics, nine-year-old Les Paul electrically amplified his parent's player piano in 1924. He also constructed a radio broadcasting unit and built a primitive recording device from a Cadillac flywheel.

Reasoning that his acoustic guitar needed a boost to be heard in public, in 1928 Les Paul rigged the sound mechanism from a Victrola arm, creating a primitive electric guitar. Astounding audiences with the instrument, Paul was a local sensation. Befriended by singing cowboy Gene Autry, 13-year-old Paul was invited backstage after a concert and taught guitar chords.

Dropping out of high school and taking the name Red Hot Red, the red-haired Paul joined an established local country group. Changing his moniker to Rhubarb Red, he then formed an acoustic country duo, touring throughout the midwest.

Settling in Chicago at age 19, Paul became enthralled with the city's burgeoning jazz scene. Abandoning country music for jazz, he landed his own radio show. Adopting the name Les Paul, he recorded for a Montgomery Ward-owned label.

Forming a jazz trio with Ernie Newton and Jim Atkins (Chet Atkins' brother), Paul moved to New York in 1937, landing a spot on Fred Waring's NBC radio show. But Paul's electric guitar drew complaints from listeners who were perplexed by its unorthodox sound. Spending his nights in uptown Harlem, Paul performed with jazz greats like Art Tatum. Leaving Waring in 1940, Paul returned to Chicago.

With the Gibson Guitar Company refusing Paul's request in 1941 to manufacture a solid-body electric guitar, he built his own instrument. "They thought I was crazy, so I took a two-by-four and put two wings on the side of it so it would look like a guitar. Everybody laughed at me" (p. 84), Paul told writer Joe Smith. Attaching an electric pickup to the instrument, he nicknamed it "the log."

Moving to Los Angeles in 1941, Paul regularly appeared on Bing Crosby's radio show, frequently playing behind singer Judy Garland. Drafted in 1942, Paul entertained the troops in the special forces. Aided by Crosby, Paul was hired by Decca Records the following year as a session player. Upon his discharge in 1945, Paul turned his garage into a recording studio, the facility used by Kay Starr, Jo Stafford, and W.C. Fields. Teamed with the popular singing group the Andrews Sisters, Les Paul scored a duet hit in 1946 with "Rumors Are Flying."

On a suggestion by Eddie Dean (brother of Jimmy Dean), Paul teamed in 1945 with 21-year-old country singer Iris Colleen Summers, a regular on Gene Autry's radio program. Giving her the stage name Mary Lou, and then Mary Ford, Paul married his musical partner four years later.

Still experimenting with electronics, Les Paul rigged together an eight-foot-tall stack of tape recorders, and recorded six, separately taped guitar tracks. Though rudimentary, he had built the world's first multitrack recorder. Fearing the device would put musicians out of work, the musicians union grudgingly gave Paul special permission to use the recorder. A double-sided smash, Paul's first multitrack hits came with the instrumentals "Lover"/"Brazil" (1948).

While trying to protect Ford from injury in a car crash, Paul permanently damaged his arm in 1948. Setting the bones in a fixed position, his arm bent at the elbow, Paul was still able to play guitar. Combining Paul's love of jazz and Ford's love of hillbilly music, the pair landed a radio program in 1949, taping the daily radio show while on tour. Billed as "Les Paul and Mary Ford," the duo scored a string of pop hits beginning with a cover of "Tennessee Waltz" (1950), which featured the groundbreaking use of Ford's double-tracked vocals in which she provided her own two-part harmony.

Les Paul and Mary Ford's hits continued with a pair of million-selling smashes, "Mockin' Bird Hill" (1951) and "How High the Moon" (1951). Their cover version of Anita O'Day's "Vaya con Dios" spent over two months atop the pop charts in 1952. Continuing to release solo records, Paul landed hits with "Josephine" (1951), which utilized a tape-delayed guitar; and "Carioca" (1952), which featured rich, multitracked, orchestra-like backing. In 1952, Paul and Ford transferred their popular radio show to television.

By the early 1950s, Paul's electronic inventions finally hit the market. With the Fender solid-body guitar enjoying brisk sales, the Gibson Guitar Company began mass-producing the Les Paul model in 1952. First rejected by the Westrix company, Ampex began marketing the Paul-designed, eight-channel tape recorder, with Atlantic Records the first label to buy a system.

Switching to Columbia Records in 1956, the pair released their last album, *TIME TO DREAM*. With the rise of rock in the mid-1950s, Paul and Ford faded from the charts. By 1960, their television program was canceled.

When Les Paul and Mary Ford announced their divorce in 1964, their radio spots for the Robert Hall clothing chain were pulled. Marrying her high school sweetheart, Ford retired from music. Damaging his eardrum and needing several surgeries, in 1965 Les Paul Paul also retired from the stage.

By the early 1960s the Gibson Company had stopped manufacturing Les Paul guitars. But when rockers Duane Allman, Jeff Beck, and Eric Clapton began playing vintage Les Paul instruments, Gibson reintroduced an updated model in 1968.

Returning to the music industry in 1974, Paul was hired as the musical director for television's *Happy Days*. Recording a pair of albums in the 1970s with Chet Atkins, *CHESTER AND LESTER* and *GUITAR MONSTERS*, Paul earned two Grammy Awards. In 1977, Mary Ford died from pneumonia.

Undergoing a heart operation in 1979, Paul was sidelined for five years. Despite suffering crippling arthritis, Paul formed a new version of the Les Paul Trio and continued to perform well into his 80s.

Bibliography

Dodson, Reynolds. (1993, July). The boy who heard the future. *Reader's Digest*, p. 38.
Flipo, Chet. (1975, February 13). I sing the solid body electric. *Rolling Stone*, p. 44.
Sirota, Warren. (1989, January). Les Paul: A celebration of genius. *Guitar Player*, p. 40.
Smith, Joe. (1988). *Off the Record*. New York: Warner.
Smotroff, Mark. (1991, October). Les Paul: Edison would have been proud. *Discoveries*, p. 22.
Varga, George. (1995, June 18). Les Paul is no guitar legend: He IS the guitar. *San Diego Union-Tribune*, p. E8.
Walker, Michael. (1991, November 24). Solid-body legend. *Los Angeles Times*, Calendar sect., p. 68.

CARL PERKINS. *(Carl Lee Perkings; April 9, 1932 - January 19, 1998). Inducted in 1987.* A pioneering rockabilly singer, Carl Perkins was a contemporary of Elvis Presley at Sun Records. Born on a sharecropping farm in the Mississippi River town of Tiptonville, Tennessee, Perkins picked cotton from age four. Working in the fields Perkins was exposed to the gospel and blues strains of bellowing black field laborers.

Moving into a house with electricity at age 14, Perkins considered radio a luxury. Scrimping to save three dollars, Perkins' parents bought him a guitar from an elderly black neighbor who taught the youngster the only three chords he knew.

With his father bedridden with tuberculosis, Carl Perkins quit school to support the family. In 1950, Carl joined brothers Jay and Clayton, who were working in a mattress factory, in forming the Perkins Brothers. Adding drummer W.S. "Fluke" Holland, the group's country-hybrid sound was accentuated by an R&B-styled rhythm. Featuring Carl Perkins' prominent electric-guitar leads, the group's demos were rejected by record companies because the music did not conform to any existing format.

Inspired by the success of Elvis Presley's updated, rockabilly-flavored rendition of Bill Monroe's "Blue Moon of Kentucky," the Perkins Brothers auditioned at Sun Records in 1954. Signed as a solo act, Carl Perkins bombed with his first release, "Movie Magg," a song he had written at age 13. Perkins and his band were instead sent to tour with Presley and another newcomer, labelmate Johnny Cash.

After selling Presley's contract to RCA, Sun Records owner Sam Phillips was intent on shaping Perkins into the next Elvis. But the lanky, side-burned singer had neither Elvis' irresistible charisma nor his unbridled sensuality. Perkins later told interviewer Dave McGhee, "Let's face it, Elvis had sex appeal . . . he was young, single, handsome; I was married and looked like Mr. Ed" (p. 75).

Lunging into rock, Perkins scored his career-defining hit with the rockabilly-styled "Blue Suede Shoes" (1956). Writing the song at 3 a.m., Perkins scribbled the words on an emptied potato bag. Recorded with only one microphone, it was the first record to simultaneously hit the top-10 pop, R&B, and country charts. Also a hit, the record's flip side, "Honey, Don't!"

But with tragedy striking Perkins and his group, their dramatic ascent came to an abrupt end. Driving to New York for appearances on a pair of nationally televised programs, *The Perry Como Show* and *The Ed Sullivan Show*, their driver fell asleep, crashing their car into a truck. While Jay Perkins was mortally wounded, Carl suffered a fractured skull and neck.

With his breakthrough record becoming Sun's first million-seller, "Perkins was put in traction, and from his hospital bed he saw Elvis Presley debut on *The Ed Sullivan Show*—singing 'Blue Suede Shoes'" (pp. 5-6), recalled writer Gary Theroux. Presley, who scored his own hit with the song, sent Perkins a telegrammed apology.

Returning to the studio, the recuperated Perkins scored a quick trio of top-10 country hits, "Boppin' the Blues," "Your True Love," and "Dixie Fried." Landing only spotty top-40 airplay, Perkins was relegated to the country market for the rest of his career. Unhappy at Sun Records, both Perkins and Johnny Cash joined Columbia Records in 1958.

But with his popularity waning, a depressed Perkins turned to liquor. Nearly losing three fingers in a fan accident in 1962, his career was seemingly over. But with his wife begging the doctor not to amputate his fingers, Perkins experienced a miraculous healing.

While sharing the bill with Chuck Berry through Britain in 1964, Perkins was met by the admiring Beatles, with Ringo Starr asking if the group could record his songs. Giving his blessing, Perkins' career was revitalized by the Fab Four's recordings of "Honey, Don't!" "Everybody's Trying to Be My Baby," and "Matchbox."

Joining Johnny Cash's band in 1967 (originally for a two-day stint), Carl Perkins replaced guitarist Luther Perkins (no relation), who had died in a tragic house fire. Appearing as both an opening act and as Cash's backing guitarist, Perkins also joined Cash's television program from 1969 to 1971. Cash landed a chart-topping country hit in 1969 with a Perkins composition, "Daddy Sang Bass." Haunted by personal demons, Perkins continued abusing alcohol. But after an embarrassing, inebriated performance at the Los Angeles Shrine Auditorium in 1971, he quit the habit for good.

Leaving Cash amicably in 1975, Perkins formed a band, hiring his sons, Stan, Greg, and Steve. Incorporating Christian songs into his rock and roll repertoire, Perkins built a loyal fan base.

Attempting a comeback with the album *OLD BLUE SUEDE'S BACK,* Perkins remained active throughout the 1980s. During this period he would work individually with all three surviving Beatles, as well as Sun Records alumni Johnny Cash and Roy Orbison. In 1989, Perkins co-wrote and played guitar on the Judds' number-one country hit "Let Me Tell You about Love."

After losing several relatives to cancer, Perkins was himself diagnosed with a throat tumor in 1991, beating the disease three years later. Recorded at the Sun studio, the

1996 tribute album *GO CAT GO!* teamed Perkins with a number of superstars, including Paul Simon and Tom Petty & the Heartbreakers. After suffering several strokes, Perkins passed away in 1998.

Bibliography

Bleiel, Jeff. (1990, June 15). Carl Perkins: Rockin' into the '90s (part 1). *Goldmine*, p 16.

Jancik, Wayne. (1990). *The Billboard Book of One Hit Wonders*. New York: Billboard.

Locey, Bill. (1995, March 30). "Blue Suede Shoes" and other feats. *The Los Angeles Times*, p. J25.

McGhee, Dave. (1990, April 19). Carl Perkins. *Rolling Stone*, p. 73.

Perkins, Carl: & Rendleman, Ron. (1978). *Disciple in Blue Suede Shoes*. Grand Rapids, MI: Zondervan.

Sievert, Jon. (1989, June). Carl Perkins: A rock and roll pioneer heads into the '90s. *Guitar Player*, p. 75.

Theroux, Gary. (1986, September 26). Carl Perkins: A legend in blue suede shoes. *Goldmine*, p. 5.

SAM PHILLIPS. *(Samuel Cornelius Phillips; January 5, 1923). Inducted in the Non-Performer category in 1986.* Playing an integral role in the genesis of rock and roll, Sam Phillips operated a small, independent label called Sun Records, launching the careers of Jerry Lee Lewis, Johnny Cash, and a shy, former truck driver named Elvis Presley.

A native of Florence, Alabama, Phillips barely survived a childhood bout of pneumonia. Exposed to blues music on his father's cotton farm, Phillips was fascinated by the impassioned wailings of the black migrant workers. Following his father's death, Phillips quit high school to support his family.

Yearning to be a lawyer but unable to afford law school tuition, Phillips instead took a short course in broadcasting at a local technical college. After deejaying in Muscle Shoals, Decatur and Nashville, he settled in Memphis in 1945, landing a four-year stint as a radio announcer and sound engineer at WREC.

Frustrated by the departure of local blues talent for Chicago, Phillips constructed a recording studio out of a converted radio repair shop. Opening in 1949, the Memphis Recording Service initially survived by letting amateurs cut their own vanity records at $1.99 per song.

Drawing the area's finest blues talent to his tiny, rudimentary studio, Phillips was the first to record Howlin' Wolf, B.B. King, and Junior Parker. Working as an independent producer, Phillips sold the master discs to large, independent, R&B record companies like Chess in Chicago and Modern/RPM in Los Angeles. At a groundbreaking session in 1951, Phillips produced Jackie Brenston's hit "Rocket 88," which is considered the first rock and roll song ever recorded. With its danceable 2/4 beat and prominent lead guitar, the song inspired Bill Haley and others.

Angered by Chess' signing of Howlin' Wolf, Phillips launched the Sun Record Company in March 1952, financially aided by another record label owner, Jim Bulleit. Sun's early roster included Billy Lee Riley, Harmonica Frank, and Rufus Thomas Jr., who in 1953 gave the Phillips his first hit with "Bear Cat," a note-for-note sequel to

Big Mama Thorton's "Hound Dog."

Sun also had gained early notoriety with the Prisonaires, a vocal sextet from the Tennessee State Penitentiary. Integral in the success of Sun Records were Phillips' brother, Jud, office manager Marion Keisker, and producers Bill Justis and Jack Clement.

When white teenagers discovered R&B in 1954, and called it rock and roll, many record companies were caught unprepared. "I had the feeling all along that if I could ever find a white man who could sing this black music I could open up a whole new market" (p. 27), Phillips recalled in a 1973 interview. But he realized this goal in 1954 when an insistent young guitarist named Elvis Presley was permitted an audition.

With Presley recording several hillbilly and gospel standards, Phillips was not overly impressed. But with the tape machine turned off during a break, the trio of Elvis, guitarist Scotty Moore and bassist Bill Black launched into a rousing, impromptu version of Arthur Crudup's R&B hit "That's All Right (Mama)." With the tape recorder turned back on, Presley and his new backing duo of "Scotty and Bill" recorded his first of five rockabilly-styled Sun singles.

On the heels of Presley's meteoric rise, hundreds of budding rockabilly singers like Jerry Lee Lewis and Carl Perkins were drawn to Sun. Other Sun rockers like Charlie Rich, Johnny Cash, and Conway Twitty emerged as country superstars after leaving the label. Another Sun act, Roy Orbison, bombed before finding success elsewhere. Busy with his stable of rock acts, Phillips soon found little time to record R&B or blues.

After a bidding war, Phillips sold Presley's contract to RCA Records in 1956 for a paltry $35,000. Immersed in his many business activities, Phillips had lost most of his hit musical acts by the late 1950s. Investing his profits from the sale of Presley's contract, Phillips became an original shareholder of the Holiday Inn motel chain, and earned millions.

Although moving his studio to a larger building in 1960 and opening a satellite studio in Nashville the following year, Phillips permitted Sun Records to decline. Also operating several radio stations, Phillips rarely recorded by the mid-1960s.

Shuttering Sun Records in 1968, Phillips sold the label's catalog to Shelby S. Singleton Jr. the following year. Within months, Singleton released dozens of Sun reissue compilations, while leasing additional tracks to England's Charly Records. The label was criticized in 1978 for overdubbing early instrumental tracks with an Elvis soundalike.

In 1987 the Sun studio was sold to musician Gary Hardy, who operated the building as a tourist attraction. In 1988, U2 entered the studio, recording three tracks for their album *RATTLE AND HUM*. In 1994, Phillips lent the original Sun studio equipment to the Rock and Roll Hall of Fame. He continues to operate the rarely used Sam Phillips Recording Studio.

Bibliography

Davis, Hank & Escott, Colin. (1987, July 31). Sam Phillips: America's other Uncle Sam. *Goldmine*, p. 12.

DeWitt, Howard A. (1993). *Elvis, the Sun Years: The Story of Elvis Presley in the Fifties*. Ann

Arbor, MI: Popular Culture Ink.
Jackson, Joe. (1993, January 22). Sun of Sam. *Irish Times*, p. 11.
Pugh, John. (1973, November). The rise and fall of Sun Records. *Country*, p. 26.
Shaw, Arnold. (1978). *Honkers and Shouters*. New York: Collier.

WILSON PICKETT. *(March 18, 1941). Inducted in 1991.* With his pioneering brand of gritty soul, Wilson Pickett dominated the pop and R&B charts in the 1960s. Born into a family of 10 children, he was raised on a sharecropping farm in Prattville, Alabama. His parents divorcing, 16-year-old Pickett moved to Detroit to live with his father. Dropping out of high school, Pickett formed a gospel group called the Violinaires, regularly performing in the city's many black churches.

Hearing Pickett sing on his front porch, Willie Schofield asked him to join the Falcons (of "So Fine" fame)." Bringing his gospel-styled vocal delivery to the group, Pickett was criticized by his religious mother for switching to "the devil's music." (During this period, the Falcons were frequently backed on stage by the Ohio Untouchables, the group later evolving into the Ohio Players.)

Receiving financial backing from Atlantic Records co-head Jerry Wexler, the Falcons recorded at Detroit's LuPine Records. With Pickett's frenetic lead vocal on "I Found a Love" (1962), the Falcons landed in R&B top-10. But angry over his paltry salary, Pickett quit the group.

After failing an audition at Atlantic Records as a solo act, Pickett managed to sell the label his composition "If You Need Me." Undaunted, Pickett himself recorded the same song at Double-L Records (co-owned by Lloyd Price), which competed on the charts with a version by Atlantic's Solomon Burke. Ironically, the two singers began touring together, taking turns who performed the song.

After landing his first top-10 R&B hit in 1963 with "It's Too Late," Pickett was signed by relenting Atlantic executives. With his initial Atlantic releases ignored by radio, Pickett was sent to the Stax studios in Memphis. Befriended by guitarist Steve Cropper of Stax's talented session band, Pickett impressed Atlantic with the soulful "In the Midnight Hour." Employing a strong, danceable, 2/4 beat, the gritty Pickett/Cropper-penned song set the pattern for Pickett's future hits.

A soaring star, Pickett crisscrossed the country, continuing his hit run with "Don't Fight It" (1965) and "634-5789" (1966), the latter featuring the backing vocals of Patti LaBelle and the Bluebelles. With Stax wanting a greater share of the profits, Pickett was sent to Rick Hall's Muscle Shoals Fame studio in Alabama. Recording several cover songs, "Wicked" Wilson Pickett continued his string of gritty, soul classics with "Land of a 1000 Dances" (1966), "Mustang Sally" (1966), a remake of his Falcons' hit, "I Found Love (Part 1)" (1967), "Everybody Needs Somebody to Love" (1967), and a remake of Dyke and the Blazer's "Funky Broadway" (1968), which eclipsed the competing original version on the charts. Pickett also recorded a number of Bobby Womack compositions, including "I'm in Love" (1967) and "I'm a Midnight Mover" (1968). In 1969, a then-unknown, Muscle Shoals' studio guitarist named Duane Allman, convinced Pickett to record the Beatles "Hey Jude," an unlikely soul ballad hit.

Teaming with an upstart production company led by Philadelphia's "Gamble and

Huff," Pickett's hits continued with "Engine Number Nine" (1970) and "Don't Let the Green Grass Fool You" (1971). Returning to Muscle Shoal, Pickett landed a million-selling hit, with the impromptu-composed "Don't Knock My Love—Pt. 1" (1972).

Leaving Atlantic over low royalties, Pickett signed with RCA records in 1973. Moving in a pop direction, Pickett managed only a few more R&B hits, such as "Take a Closer Look at the Woman You're With" (1973) and "Soft Soul Boogie Woogie" (1973).

His career nosediving in the 1970s, Pickett launched the shortlived Wicked Records, and then jumped from label to label. Then after criticizing disco music, Pickett released a pair of poorly received disco albums in the late 1970s. Signed to Motown, Pickett's overlooked 1987 album, *AMERICAN SOUL MAN*, contained a new version of "In the Midnight Hour."

Pickett experienced a surprise comeback in 1991 as the result of the hit film *The Commitments,* which centered around an all white, Irish soul group that idolized the soul singer. A subsequent top-10 soundtrack album was highlighted by "In the Midnight Hour" and "Mustang Sally."

Reputed for his temper, Pickett garnered much negative press in bouts with the law, including a 1975 incident when he fired shots at the Isley Brothers. Regularly arrested for assault and drunk driving, Pickett was sentenced to a year in prison in 1993. Pickett's brushes with the law continued into the mid-1990s; he was sentenced to a year in prison in 1996 for cocaine possession.

Bibliography

Emerson, Ken. (1979, February 8). Wilson Pickett: Soul man on ice. *Rolling Stone*, p. 18.

Landau, Jon. (1968, February). Wilson Pickett. *Crawdaddy*, p. 30.

Matsumoto, Jon. (1995, September 22). Wilson Pickett plans to pick up where he left off. *Los Angeles Times*, p. F28.

Nooger, Dan. (1987, June 5). Wilson Pickett: The golden years. *Goldmine*, p. 79.

White, Adam & Bronson, Fred. (1993). *The Billboard Book of Number One Rhythm & Blues Hits*. New York: Billboard.

PINK FLOYD. *Syd Barrett (Roger Keith Barrett; January 6, 1946); David Gilmour (March 6, 1944); Nick Mason (Nicholas Berkeley Mason; January 27, 1945); Roger Waters (George Roger Waters; September 6, 1944); Richard Wright (Richard William Wright; July 28, 1945). Inducted in 1996.* Emerging out of the British psychedelic scene of the mid-1960s, Pink Floyd changed their musical course and destiny after the departure of their first leader, Syd Barrett. Avoiding the media spotlight, the group's members remain unrecognizable to many of their fans.

While attending London's Regent Street Polytechnic school, bassist Roger Waters formed an R&B/blues-rock group in 1965 with a pair of architecture students, drummer Nick Mason and keyboardist Rick Wright. The group expanded into a quartet with the addition of Waters' classmate, art student Syd Barrett on guitar and lead vocals. Named after two little-known Georgia bluesmen, Pink Anderson and Floyd Council, Pink Floyd earned a Sunday afternoon residency at London's famed

Marquee Club.

With flower power thriving in San Francisco, Pink Floyd dropped their R&B base for psychedelia. Signing with EMI, the group landed a pair of British hits, "Arnold Layne," which escaped strict BBC censors with its theme of a thieving transvestite, and the pop-flavored "See Emily Play."

Emerging as the group's leader, Barrett also served as chief songwriter. Ingesting large doses of mind-altering LSD, Barrett soon became undependable, with his behavior and onstage musicianship becoming bizarre. During a lip-synched taping of *American Bandstand* in 1967, Barrett refused to mouth the words.

In the middle of the recording sessions for the album *THE PIPER AT THE GATES OF DAWN* in January 1968, self-taught guitarist and singer David Gilmour joined Pink Floyd as their fifth member, substituting for the usually incapacitated Barrett. Suffering from drug-related permanent brain damage, Barrett was booted from the band nine months later.

While Gilmour emerged as the new lead singer, Waters became the group's chief songwriter and de facto leader. Infusing his troubled childhood memories into his lyrics, Waters took Pink Floyd in a moody and introspective direction.

With guest trumpeter Ron Geesin, Pink Floyd's 1970 album *ATOM HEART MOTHER* topped the British charts, highlighted by the 23-minute track "Atom Heart Mother Suite." Touring in support of the album, Pink Floyd hired a supporting choir and a 10-piece orchestra. Though churning out a series of masterful albums such as *A SAUCERFUL OF SECRETS*, Pink Floyd remained an underground favorite in the U.S., garnering little radio play.

Combining Gilmour's slide-guitar with Waters' anguished lyrics, Pink Floyd achieved its signature sound on their 1971 album, *MEDDLE*. The follow-up release, *OBSCURED BY THE CLOUDS*, garnered the band some overdue mainstream U.S. success.

Building upon the rock theater framework popularized by *Jesus Christ Superstar* and the Who's *Tommy*, Pink Floyd revolutionized the rock concert through elaborate stage props, light shows, and gigantic, hovering, animal-shaped balloons. Introducing a massive, state-of-the-art, "360-degree" quadraphonic sound system that enveloped concertgoers, Pink Floyd left their audiences awestruck.

One of the first rock albums to employ the Dolby system and utilize modern synthesizers, *DARK SIDE OF THE MOON* was recorded on a new 24-track mixer over a nine-month period at London's Abbey Road Studio. Primarily written by Waters, the concept project explored themes of alienation, insanity, and death. The album's continuity was interrupted by the hit "Money," a sarcastic jab at rock's commercial nature. A surprise monster hit, the album was sparsely promoted by Capitol/Harvest Records, with the group scheduled to join Columbia Records later in the year. Spending 15 years on the best-seller charts and selling an excess of 26 million copies worldwide, *DARK SIDE* revolutionized the album-rock genre.

Intended as a tribute to Barrett, Pink Floyd's 1975 album, *WISH YOU WERE HERE*, was highlighted by the anti-record industry themed, "Have a Cigar" (with guest vocals by Roy Harper) and a retreat to their blues roots, "Shine on You Crazy Diamond." Although refused membership back into the group, Barrett was permitted in the studio during the recording sessions.

Marking the release of their 1977 album, *ANIMALS*, Pink Floyd introduced their classic prop, a hovering, anatomically correct, inflated pig. The album's lyrics personified human sins through the bodies of farm creatures. Pursuing side projects, both Wright and Gilmour released their first solo albums in 1978.

Their commercial opus, Pink Floyd's 1979 double-album, *THE WALL*, garnered heavy AOR and pop airplay. With its themes of alienation and abandonment, Waters had intended *THE WALL* as a solo album. Featuring a children's choir, the chart-topping lead-off single, "Another Brick in the Wall (Part II)," was banned by the BBC and dozens of American school systems for its attack of educators.

Constructing an expensive and labor-intensive, 30-foot-tall, onstage brick wall for *THE WALL* concert tour, Pink Floyd was limited by logistics to stadium dates in Los Angeles, New York, and London. Preferring to play smaller venues, Waters infuriated his bandmates by turning down a million-dollar offer to stage a concert in Philadelphia. A partially animated companion film, *The Wall*, starred Boomtown Rats' singer Bob Geldof in the lead role of Pink.

Experiencing internal strife in the early 1980s, Pink Floyd fired Nick Mason. The final Pink Floyd album with the Gilmour-Waters nucleus was appropriately titled *THE FINAL CUT*. Essentially a Waters solo project augmented by session players, the album captured Waters' anger over the World War II death of his father in Anzio, Italy. Highlighted by the tracks "Your Possible Pasts" and "Not Now John," the album's political messages angered Gilmour. After canceling a scheduled concert tour, Waters disbanded Pink Floyd; he could not conceive of the group being able to continue without him.

Pursuing solo careers in 1984, Gilmour and Waters both experienced limited records sales and partially filled concerts halls. During this period, Gilmour launched a legal challenge against Mason over the Pink Floyd name. But when Gilmour's next solo project emerged as a Pink Floyd album, Waters entered into the fray, suing for control of the group's name and expensive stage props. Entering into a bitter conflict, Gilmour and Waters traded nasty barbs in the press.

With Mason rejoining Gilmour, the pair was granted the right to use the Pink Floyd name and were rejoined by Wright in 1987. Although selling 3 million copies, the album *A MOMENTARY LAPSE OF REASON* was considered a commercial disappointment. Releasing the competing solo album, *RADIO K.A.O.S.*, Waters hit the concert road, also performing Pink Floyd classics. Waters celebrated the fall of the Berlin Wall in 1990, headlining an all-star "The Wall" concert.

With the 1994 release of Pink Floyd's 15th studio album, *THE DIVISION BELL*, fans finally accepted the abbreviated lineup. Their best seller in a decade, the album spawned the AOR hits "Keep Talking" and "Take It Back." In their first world tour in seven years, Pink Floyd attracted multiple generations of fans. A bitter Roger Waters boycotted Pink Floyd's induction into the Rock and Roll Hall of Fame in 1996.

Bibliography

Harrington, Richard. (1987, August 30). Roger Waters, up against the wall. *Washington Post*, p. G1.

Harrington, Richard. (1993, April 28). 20 years ago, "Dark Side of the Moon" began its cosmic
    trip. *Washington Post*, p. C1.
Paytress, Mark. (1988, April). Pink Floyd and Syd Barrett. *Record Collector*, p. 3.
Robbins, Ira. (1994, June 10). Pink Floyd hides in plain sight. *(New York) Newsday*, p. B5.
Ruhlmann, William. (1993, January 8). Pink Floyd: Variations on a theme of absence.
    Goldmine, p. 12.
Schaffner, Nicholas. (1991, February). The dark side of Pink Floyd. *Musician*, p. 38.
White, Timothy. (1990). *Rock Lives: Profiles & Interviews* (pp. 506-23). New York: Henry
    Holt.

THE PLATTERS. *David Lynch (1929 - January 2, 1981); Herbert Reed (1931);
Paul Robi (1932 - February 1, 1989); Zola Taylor (1934); Tony Williams (April 5,
1928 - August 14, 1992). Inducted in 1990.* The most popular vocal group of the late
1950s, the Platters dominated the charts with their sweet, romantic ballads, their
success a result of talent, good material, and capable management.

Following the decline of the big band era after the Second World War, lawyer
Samuel "Buck" Ram moved to Los Angeles to formulate a new approach to pop
music. Having worked with a number of acts, including Count Basie, Duke Ellington,
and the Dorsey Brothers, Ram decided to enter the business side of music. A
demanding manager, producer, and songwriter, Ram worked with a who's who of Los
Angeles R&B and doo-wop talent in the 1950s, including the Flairs, Joe Houston,
Obedieah "Young" Jessie, and Shirley Gunter.

Another of Ram's discoveries, the doo-wop-styled Platters had been formed in a
Los Angeles high school by David Lynch, Joe Jefferson, brothers Alex and Gaynel
Hodge, and lead singer Cornell Gunter. Sensing the group was going nowhere, Gunter
quit and was replaced by tenor Tony Williams. Raised on the East Coast, Williams got
his singing start in a Baptist church and later studied classical voice. Soon after, Hodge
and Jefferson were replaced by David Lynch and Herb Reed. But after Hodge was
imprisoned for selling marijuana to police, baritone Paul Robi was brought in as his
replacement. Completing the group was female vocalist Zola Taylor, who was added
more for her beauty than for her competent singing ability.

Now in its classic lineup of Tony Williams, Paul Robi, David Lynch, Herbert Reed,
and Zola Taylor, the Platters R&B-flavored recordings for Federal Records went
unnoticed. But with Mercury Records eager to sign another Ram-managed group, the
Penguins, who had just landed a smash hit with "Earth Angel," Ram demanded that
Mercury also take the Platters.

With Mercury reluctantly agreeing, the Platters recorded a new, polished, pop-
flavored version of their earlier Federal release, "Only You" (1955). With Ram a last-
minute substitute on piano, the ballad crossed over into the pop top-10 and soon
competed with a white cover version by the Hilltoppers. Criticizing Ram over his
selection of material, Mercury wanted the Platters to sing teenage, rock-oriented
material. Even the Platters protested, initially unhappy with songs that Ram had
originally written in the 1940s.

Staying the course, the impeccably attired Platters emerged as the kings of 1950s
romantic ballad hits. Emerging as the star of the group, Williams joined Ram in

co-writing several of the Platters' releases. With his elegant, yet powerful, tenor voice, Williams displayed dramatic vocal dynamics on songs like "My Prayer." Featuring Tony Williams' soaring lead vocals, "The Great Pretender" (1955) was the first rock ballad to top the pop singles charts. Their other hits included: "(You've Got) The Magic Touch" (1956); "My Prayer" (1956); and, taken from the 1933 stage musical, *Roberta*, and their best-known song, "Smoke Gets in Your Eyes" (1958). Their 1958 hit, "Twilight Time," was one of the first songs in the rock era to feature a string section.

But scandal struck the Platters on August 10, 1959, when the four male members of the group were arrested in a Cincinnati motel on soliciting charges. Although acquitted of the charges, the group never recovered. Their last top-10 hit came with a cover of "Harbor Lights," originally a hit for Frances Langford in 1937.

Now billed as the Platters featuring Tony Williams, the group landed a minor hit in 1960 with "Red Sails in the Sunset." Leaving soon after, Williams was tired of clashing with back-up singer Herb Reed. Williams was replaced by Johnny Barnes and then by Charles "Sonny" Turner. An angry Mercury Records unsuccessfully sued Ram and the Platters over the loss of Williams.

Remaining a popular draw, especially overseas, Williams continued to tour. Signing with Frank Sinatra's Reprise label and then with Philips, Williams failed to match his previous success, his biggest solo effort coming with "Sleepless Nights" (1961).

With only Herbert Reed remaining from the classic lineup, the Platters returned to the pop charts in the late 1960s with a pair of pop-flavored hits, "I Love You a Thousand Times" (1966) and "With This Ring" (1967). Reed left the group in 1969. The following year, Turner was replaced on lead vocals by Monroe Powell.

Joined by his wife, Helen, Tony Williams formed a competing Platters group in 1967. After touring for the next 15 years as Tony Williams as the Platters, Williams was barred in 1982 by the New York Supreme Court from using "the Platters" name; he later joined an "authentic" Platters group. The legal ownership of the group's name was finally resolved in 1990, when an appeals court upheld a $3.5 million judgment against Buck Ram, canceling his trademark registration of the Platters name. Suffering with diabetes, Williams died of emphysema in 1992.

Bibliography

Beachley, Chris. (1979). The Platters: Their magic touch remains. *It Will Stand*, *2* (issue 17/18), p. 4.
Bronson, Fred. (1992). *The Billboard Book of Number One Hits*. New York: Billboard.
Stierle, Wayne. (1989, February). They all copied the Tony Williams style! *Discoveries*, p. 110.
Stierle, Wayne. (1989, December). The Tony Williams interview. *Discoveries*, p. 22.
"The Platters." (1976, December). *Ebony*, p. 109.
Wasserman, Steve. (1972, July). Buck Ram and the Platters. *Bim Bam Boom*, p. 4.
Weinger, Harry. (1992, February 12). The Platters' glory days. *Goldmine*, p. 10.

DOC POMUS. *(Jerome Solon Felder; June 27, 1925 - March 14, 1991). Inducted in the Non-Performer category in 1992*. A prolific rock songwriter, Doc Pomus composed dozens of rock, blues, and R&B hits in the 1950s and 1960s. The son of a blue-collar lawyer, the Brooklyn-born Pomus was disabled from polio at age six and was home-schooled by a tutor.

A huge fan of bluesman Big Joe Turner, Pomus taught himself to play the saxophone. Sneaking into George's Tavern, a Greenwich Village blues club, 18-year-old Pomus was confronted by the owner. Claiming to be a blues singer, Pomus was forced onstage by the doubting proprietor. Nervously singing Big Joe Turner's "Piney Brown," Pomus wowed the audience and landed a long-term gig. Wanting to shield his family's name, the former Jerome Felder performed as Doc Pomus.

After studying political science at Brooklyn College during the day, Pomus hit the stage in his leg braces and his crutches. "I wore a dark stubble to make myself look older. . . . I was an 18-year-old cool wonder trying to convince the world and myself that I had been doing this forever" (p. 10), Pomus later told writer Peter Guralnick.

Befriended by his idol, Big Joe Turner, Pomus penned a number of songs in the 1950s for the popular R&B shouter, including "Still in Love" (1950); "Boogie Woogie Country Girl" (1956); and "I Need a Girl" (1957).

Releasing about a dozen singles himself, Pomus was backed by star players such as King Curtis and Mickey Baker. Devastated when his last record, "Heartlessly," was sabotaged by a major record company, Pomus turned to full-time songwriting. Pomus landed his first top-10 R&B hit in 1956 with Ray Charles' "Lonely Avenue." The following year, Pomus scored his first top-10 pop hit with the Coasters' "Youngblood."

Teaming with a much younger (by 13 years) songwriter named Mort Shuman in 1956, Pomus paid him out of his own salary. A fellow Brooklyn native, Shuman had studied philosophy at New York City College. Co-writing "Love Roller Coaster" with Big Joe Turner, Pomus and Shuman landed their first collaborative R&B hit in 1957. During this period, Pomus also wrote magazine fiction and briefly operated a record label.

Signing with the Hill & Range Publishing Company and moving into the famous Brill Building, the duo's first pop success came in early 1959 with "Plain Jane" by Bobby Darin. On a roll, Pomus and Shuman provided Fabian with several smash hits: "I'm a Man"; the title track of the film *Hound Dog Man*; and, featuring Shuman on piano, a song rejected by Elvis Presley, "Turn Me Loose." Inspired by Frankie Lymon's "Why Do Fools Fall in Love," Pomus and Shuman wrote Dion & the Belmonts' biggest hit, "Teenager in Love."

Other Pomus and Shuman hit compositions include "This Magic Moment" (Drifters; Jay & the Americans); "Hushabye" (Mystics); "Suspicion" (Terry Stafford); and "Sweets for my Sweet" (Drifters). Writing the autobiographical "Save the Last Dance For Me" in just 30 minutes, Pomus had based the song on dates with his attractive wife.

Apart or together, Pomus and Shuman wrote 16 songs for Elvis Presley in his post-army days, including "A Mess of Blues," "(Marie's the Name of) His Latest Flame," "Kiss Me Quick," "Viva Las Vegas," "Little Sister," and based on an Italian melody, "Surrender." Later in their partnership, Pomus wrote more of the lyrics, while Shuman tackled the melodies.

A prolific songwriter who wrote hundreds of compositions, Pomus nearly always stayed away from the studio side of the recording process, telling interviewer Martin Porter: "When I finish a song, it's over with. In fact, sometimes when I listen to a song on the radio and it sounds familiar, I never know if it's just familiar or one of mine" (p. 94).

Pomus was struck by multiple tragedies in 1965. After suffering a severe fall, he further injured his legs; both of his parents were hurt in car accidents; he was divorced by his wife; and he lost his writing partner, Mort Shuman, who left the country upset with the U.S. political climate. A devastated Pomus left music, working the next decade as a professional gambler.

Pomus hesitantly returned to music in the mid-1970s at the invitation of New Orleans piano player Dr. John on the albums *CITY LIGHTS* and *TANGO PALACE*. Pomus was also instrumental in assembling the Blues Brothers band for John Belushi and Dan Aykroyd. Then reuniting with Big Joe Turner, Pomus produced his Grammy-winning album, *BLUES TRAIN*. Pomus' final project was the musical score for the 1990 Warren Beatty film *Dick Tracy*.

Diagnosed with lung cancer, Pomus died in 1991 at a Manhattan hospital. A 1995 tribute album, *TILL THE NIGHT IS GONE*, featured artists Bob Dylan, Lou Reed, Dion, and Los Lobos.

Bibliography

Bratton, William. (1993, Autumn). A note on Doc Pomus. *Antaeus*, p. 149.
Guralnick, Peter. (1988, Summer). Call the doctor. *(Village) Voice Rock & Roll Quarterly*, p. 9.
Palmer, Robert. (1986, July 25). Doc Pomus still writes, rocks and rambles. *New York Times*, p. C23.
Pollock, Bruce. (1975). *In Their Own Words* (pp. 14-23). New York: Macmillan.
Porter, Martin. (1981, November). Interview: Doc Pomus. *Music and Sound Output*, p. 93.
Sapia, Joseph. (1982, November). What's up doc?: The Doc Pomus interview. *Goldmine*, p. 7.

ELVIS PRESLEY. *(Elvis Aaron Presley; January 8, 1935 - August 16, 1977). Inducted in 1986.* The first musical artist to combine all of the ingredients of rock and roll—gospel, country and western, R&B, and, to a lesser extent, blues and jazz—Elvis Aaron Presley emerged as the King of Rock and Roll. Born at 4:35 a.m. on January 8, 1935, in East Tupelo, Mississippi, he was named after his father, Vernon Elvis Presley; Elvis' twin brother, Jesse Garon, died at birth.

Grounded in poverty, Elvis was reared in a religious home by an overprotective mother and a Depression-scarred father. Working odd jobs, including moonshining, the elder Presley struggled to feed his family. First singing at the Tupelo Pentecostal First Assembly of God Church at age two, Elvis was later exposed to the emotional gospel outbursts of interracial tent revivals.

At 12, Elvis was given a guitar by his mother, in lieu of a more expensive bicycle, which the family could not afford. Initially a fan of country and western singers like Jimmie Rodgers and Bob Wills, the teenage Elvis was rebuked by his mother for listening to "sinful" music on Memphis radio station WDIA by pioneering, black R&B artists like Arthur "Big Boy" Crudup and Stick McGhee.

Hoping for a better life, Vernon Presley moved the family 90 miles north to Memphis, settling into the new Lauderdale public housing complex. Attending L.C. Humes High School, Elvis was considered an outcast with his wild thrift store clothes, slicked, piled hair, and ever-present guitar. Embracing black music, Elvis regularly attended gospel concerts at Memphis' Ellis Auditorium. Just 15, Presley frequented a black nightclub to catch the Thursday night performance of a jazz-blues group, the Pineas Orchestra.

After graduating from high school, Presley landed a series of menial jobs, including as an usher at a Loew's Theater and a truck driver for Crown Electric. Too poor to live on his own, Elvis continued to share his parents' home.

Walking into the Sam Phillips-owned Sun Studio in 1953, Presley paid $3.98 to make a 78 rpm record as a birthday present for his mother, singing, "My Happiness" and "That's When Your Heartaches Begin." Taking notice of the talented, shy young man was Phillips' business manager, Marion Keisker. When Presley returned in January 1954, to cut another disc, Keisker took down his name and address. During this period, Presley was hired as an intermission act for a local country group, Doug Poindexter and the Starlite Wranglers.

At Keisker's suggestion, Sam Phillips brought Presley into the Sun studios for an informal session in April 1954. Returning on July 5, Elvis was backed by a pair of session players, guitarist Scotty Moore and stand-up bass player, Bill Black (both members of the Starlight Wranglers). With the trio launching into an impromptu, countrified version of the R&B song "That's All Right," Phillips had finally found the sound he was looking for: a white man singing the blues. While Moore and Black offered concern that Southerners might be offended by the musical mixture of country and R&B, Phillips sensed commercial potential. Needing a B-side, the following day, Presley recorded an R&B-inflected, rockabilly rendition of Bill Monroe's hillbilly waltz "Blue Moon over Kentucky."

With Memphis disc jockey Dewey Phillips playing an acetate of "That's All Right Mama" on his WHBQ R&B radio show, the switchboard lit up with requests for repeat spins. Landing a local hit with the first of his five Sun releases, the single propelled Presley and his new backing duo, "Scotty & Bill," onto the country-music touring circuit, including an opening spot for crooner Slim Whitman.

After notching a second regional hit with a driving rockabilly-flavored cover of Roy Brown's R&B hit "Good Rockin' Tonight," Presley was invited onto the Grand Ole Opry. Then billed as "The Hillbilly Cat," Presley sang, "Blue Moon of Kentucky." After receiving only a polite reception, stage manager Jim Denny advised Presley to go back to driving a truck.

Landing his first national hit in the summer of 1955, Presley landed on the country charts with a cover of Arthur Gunter's recent R&B entry "Baby Let's Play House," attributed on the label to Elvis, Scotty, and Bill. Presley's final Sun single, the double-sided country hit "I Forgot to Remember To Forget"/"Mystery Train" also failed to cross over onto the pop charts.

Spotting raw talent, former carnival-huckster Colonel Tom Parker pursued Presley,

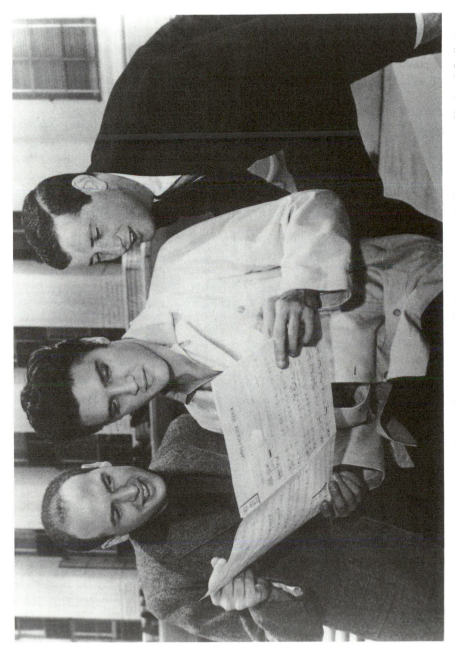

Mike Stoller, Elvis Presley, Jerry Leiber, MGM Studios, Culver City, California. Spring, 1957. (*Photo courtesy of Leiber & Stoller.*)

with contract in hand. Giving in to Parker's high-pressure tactics, Presley signed a management deal, first getting written permission from his parents. Overbearing and brash but profit minded, Parker cut himself in for 50-percent of Elvis' profits.

With a bidding war erupting over Presley's recording contract, Sam Phillips earned a then-unheard-of sum of $35,000 from RCA (just beating out a bid by Atlantic Records). Receiving a $5,000 signing bonus, Elvis in 1955 bought his first of many Cadillacs.

At RCA, Presley's formerly equally billed backing group saw its position diminish. While Elvis earned millions, Black, Moore, and the newly hired drummer D.J. Fontana basically received union scale.

Released on January 27, 1956, Presley's debut RCA single, "Heartbreak Hotel," was inspired by the suicide of a heartbroken lover. Making his television debut the next day, Presley sang a trio of songs on the CBS variety program *Stage Show*. With "Heartbreak Hotel" perched at the top of the pop charts for a two-month stay, Elvis Presley become an overnight superstar.

Creating a furor on the *Milton Berle Show*, Presley shocked viewers with his sexually charged, hip-gyrating performance of "Hound Dog." Subsequently humiliated on *The Steve Allen Show*, the tuxedo-clad Presley was barred from dancing and forced to serenade a real "Hound Dog," a live but very docile canine. Pushing his own agenda, Allen was determined to rein in Elvis and all of rock and roll.

Allen, like much of America, was alarmed by the sight of a white singer acting like a black man. With his surly, curled lip and twitching leg, Presley initially enjoyed a mostly adolescent female fan base. To counter his critics during hostile press interviews, Elvis answered with the polite manners of a southern gentleman, and addressed journalists as sir or ma'am.

Dominating pop music in 1956, Presley scored a series of number one hits, including the Hank Williams-influenced "I Want You, I Need You, I Love You" and the title track of his first film, the romantic ballad "Love Me Tender." The biggest hit of Presley's career, the double-sided chart-topper "Don't Be Cruel"/"Hound Dog" was the first to feature his longtime, Southern-gospel backing group, the Jordanaires.

With Presley setting sales records on a monthly basis, RCA was unable to keep up with the demand and was forced to press records at rival plants. Turning Elvis into a multimillion-dollar commodity, RCA feared oversaturating the market. During this time, Presley had nose-narrowing plastic surgery.

Making his third and final *Ed Sullivan Show* appearance, on January 6, 1957, Presley was captured on camera only from the waist up. With his silky, hiccuping voice, dyed black hair, and confident smile, Elvis made the best of the situation.

Buying the Graceland mansion in March 1957 for $102,500, the Memphis estate had been named by its previous owners. On a roll, Presley's 1957 hits included "Love Me"; All Shook Up"; from the Presley film *Loving You*, "(Let Me Be Your) Teddy Bear"; and from the film of the same name, "Jailhouse Rock." On the set of *Jailhouse Rock*, Presley was permitted to choreograph his own dance routines.

Parting with Elvis after a pay dispute, Scotty and Bill left in March 1958. Receiving $100 per week, plus another $100 if they were on the road, the pair's request for an additional $50 was refused.

Also in March, Presley was drafted following a two-month delay to finish shooting the black-and-white film *Kid Creole*. A patriot who was concerned about his image, Presley refused to ask for special treatment to stay out the service. Recording "Wear My Ring around Your Neck," it would be his last session before entering the army. With his hair cut, Elvis Aaron Presley was sworn in on March 24, 1958, as U.S. private 53310761. Within the year, Presley would be granted special leave to fly to his dying mother's side. Her death in August would break Presley's spirit.

Stationed near Frankfurt, West Germany, Elvis occasionally recorded while on leave. While living off-base in a house with his father, grandmother, and friends, he met his future wife, 14-year-old Priscilla Ann Beaulieu. Promoted to sergeant in January 1960, Presley was discharged two months later.

Thanks to his diligent record company, Elvis had maintained his chart-run during his army stint with several hits including "Hard Headed Woman" (1958) and the double-sided chart entry "One Night"/"I Got Stung" (1958).

His career taking a pop-flavored turn, the post-army Presley first returned to the studio in March 1960. His string of top-10 hits continued with "Stuck on You" (1960); "Surrender" (1961); and "I Feel So Bad" (1961). A double-sided hit, Presley scored with a pair of Doc Pomus-Mort Shuman compositions, "Little Sister" and "(Marie's the Name Of) His Latest Flame."

A deeply religious person, Presley released his first spiritual album in 1960, *HIS HAND IN MINE*. During his lifetime, Presley's only Grammy wins came for his spiritual material.

His film career restarted, Presley first co-starred with Juliet Prowse in the appropriately titled *G.I. Blues*, which was set in West Germany. Following a strict formula, Presley would appear in a series of lighthearted, Hal Wallis-produced pictures. Though critical failures, the films were box office successes that spawned hit soundtrack albums and singles. One of Presley's better films *Blue Hawaii*, co-starred Angela Lansbury (of *Murder, She Wrote* fame) and produced the top-10 ballad hit, "Can't Help Falling in Love" (1961).

Other film hits include "Follow That Dream" (1962) from the film of the same name; "Return to Sender" from *Girls! Girls! Girls!* (1962); "Bossa Nova Baby" from, *Fun in Acapulco* (1963); the double-sided entry "What'd I Say"/"Viva Las Vegas" from *Viva Las Vegas* (1964); and "Puppet on a String" from *Girl Happy* (1965).

With the arrival of the British Invasion in the mid-1960s, Presley's career slowed. Meeting the Beatles, Presley was hurt by John Lennon's suggestion that he should "return" to making rock and roll records. Insecure, Presley had already quit touring.

Following a lengthy romance and engagement, Presley married Priscilla on May 1, 1967. After a civil ceremony in Las Vegas, the honeymooners flew to Palm Springs. Exactly nine months after their wedding date, the Presleys celebrated the birth of their only child, daughter Lisa Marie.

With MGM refusing to renew his expiring film contract, Presley returned to television in December 1968, starring in the NBC special *Elvis*. Dressed in black leather, still thin, and now sporting sideburns, Presley was a rousing smash. An accompanying soundtrack gave Presley his first gold-certified album in three years and spawned the top-40 hit "Memories."

Regaining his confidence, Presley entered the lounge singer portion of his career, opening at Las Vegas' International Hotel in August 1969. He hesitantly signed a lucrative deal with the Las Vegas Hilton, where he had bombed in the 1950s. A huge draw, Presley raked in millions performing for tourists.

His career reignited, a mature-sounding Presley returned to the top-10 with "In the Ghetto" (1969); "Suspicious Minds" (1969); "Don't Cry Daddy" (1969); Kentucky Rain" (1970); a live version of "The Wonder Of You" (1970); "The Next Step Is Love" (1970); and "Rags to Riches" (1971).

Delighting his older fans, Presley released the retro-rocker "Burning Love" in 1972. Reminiscent of his 1950s rockabilly numbers, it was his last top-10 hit. Suffering from drug abuse, Elvis legally separated from Priscilla in February 1972, divorcing 20 months later.

Becoming a parody of himself by the mid-1970s, an overweight, sweaty, side-burned Elvis squeezed into sequined jumpsuits in a ritualistic spectacle for mostly older crowds. Regardless of their quality, Elvis' records kept selling, his mid-1970s hits including the James Taylor-penned "Steamroller Blues" (1973), "Hurt" (1976), and his last top-40 hit released before his death, the million-selling "Way Down" (1977).

Written by former Presley employees, the biography *Elvis: What Happened?* was published less than a month before his death. Portending his downfall and detailing the dark side of the King's life, the book was the first of many tell-all tomes.

Wearing his pajamas, Presley was found dead on August 16, 1977, in his personal bathroom at his Graceland mansion by his fiancee, Ginger Alden. On the day of his death, he was to have begun a two-week East Coast tour, the first stop coming at Portland, Maine (tickets were $15).

Rex Humbard, who gave the funeral eulogy, claimed that Elvis had premonitions of his death. A large, hulking man at the time of his death, Elvis had gorged himself on the junkfood and those treats he was too poor to afford as a child. Traces of dozens of drugs such as codeine and percodan were found in Presley's bloodstream, prescribed by his personal physician, George "Dr. Nick" Nichopoulos.

Worth over $15 million by 1995, the Elvis Presley estate continues earning money from album releases, record royalties, and product licensing. Opened to tourists on June 7, 1982, the Graceland mansion is visited by 700,000 pilgrims a year who, in turn, spend over $12 million on admission fees and concessions. A 1992 Elvis stamp earned $36 million in profit for the U.S. Postal Service.

Elvis' life and death continue to fascinate fans and historians alike. A crucial figure in American popular culture, Elvis has spawned hundreds of books and films.

Bibliography

Flippo, Chet. (1977, September 22). Love me tender: Funeral in Memphis. *Rolling Stone*, p. 38.

Ford, Kevin. (1979, July-August), Elvis: The Sun years. *Time Barrier Express*, p. 18.

Guralnick, Peter. (1994, September 11). The hillbilly cat: Elvis Presley on the brink of stardom. *The Los Angeles Times*, Magazine sect., p. 32.

Haertel, Joe. (1990, August 10). Retracing Elvis's Memphis and Tupelo footsteps. *Goldmine*, p. 29.

Hopkins, Jerry. (1971). *Elvis*. New York: Simon & Schuster.

Hopkins, Jerry. (1977, August 22). Fame and fortune: The life and times of Col. Tom Parker. *Rolling Stone*, p. 44.

Mikelbank, Peter. (1987, August 14). D.J. Fontana: Elvis' drummer capsulizes the King's career. *Goldmine*, p. 12.

Miller, Jim. (1987, August 3). Forever Elvis. *Newsweek*, p. 48.

Presley, Priscilla. (1985). *Elvis and Me*. New York: Putman.

Thompson, Dave. (1996, September). The boy who hogged the ham: A tale of early Elvis. *Discoveries*, p. 26.

Umphred, Neal. (1996, January 19). A hundred years from now: Elvis's studio recordings of the '70s. *Goldmine*, p. 20.

LLOYD PRICE. *(March 9, 1934). Inducted in 1998*. One of New Orleans' first R&B stars, Lloyd Price was reared in the suburban community of Kenner, Louisiana. It was there that his gospel singer mother insisted he join a church choir. Mastering the trumpet, Price formed a popular teenage quintet, the Blueboys, which appeared on local radio station WBOK.

Following a rejection by Imperial Records, Price was signed in 1952 by Specialty Records based on the popularity of one of his radio jingles. Aided by legendary New Orleans producer Dave Bartholomew and featuring the backing piano of Fats Domino, Price released the single "Lawdy, Miss Clawdy," a reworked version of a Maxwell House Coffee jingle he had written. The song title was taken from an expression used by James "Okie Dokie" Smith, a deejay at WBOK. A massive hit, the song topped the R&B chart for nearly two months, and was followed by a string of R&B hits, including "Oooh, Oooh, Oooh"/"Restless Heart" (1952), "Tell Me Pretty Baby" (1953), and "Ain't It a Shame" (1953).

Price's hit run was interrupted when he was drafted in 1953. Joining a military band, he performed for personnel in Korea and Japan. Price attempted a comeback upon his discharge but had been supplanted at Specialty Records by a singer he had recommended to the label, Little Richard.

Moving to Washington D.C. in 1956, Price formed the Kent Record Company with partner Harold Logan. Leasing the masters to ABC-Paramount, he returned to top form with "Just Because," his first crossover pop hit. Price followed with an updated, rollicking reworking of a blues-folk standard, "Stack-O-Lee," which he recorded as "Stagger Lee." A crossover smash, the song chronicled the exploits of two gamblers. A much recorded tune, the song was reprised by Wilson Pickett and Tommy Roe, and appeared on Elvis Presley's first album. Price's hit run continued into the early 1960s with "Where Were You (On Our Wedding Day)?" (1959), "Personality" (1959), "I'm Gonna Get Married" (1959), "Lady Luck" (1960), and his last at ABC Paramount, "Question" (1960).

Veering from his New Orleans' R&B-based style, Price landed his final pop hit in 1963 with a cover of the standard "Misty." Launching another record company, Double-L, Price signed former Falcons singer Wilson Pickett as a solo act. Within a year, Pickett's contract was sold to the larger Atlantic Records.

Leaving the stage in the late 1960s, Price did not appear in concert for nearly a decade. Purchasing a New York City nightclub (the building once housing the 1920s legendary jazz hot spot, the Birdland), Price renamed it the Turntable. From that location, he also operated a record company, recording studio, and publishing business.

Teaming with Don King in 1974, Price organized the Zaire '74 music festival which was held in conjunction with the Muhammad Ali/George Foreman "Rumble in the Jungle" heavyweight-championship match. The concert featured a host of black stars including James Brown, B.B. King, and the Spinners. Inspired by their success, King and Price launched a shortlived label, LPG.

In addition to returning to the oldies circuit, Price has spent much of his time on non-musical ventures including minority scholarship fundraising and the construction of low-income housing in Harlem.

Bibliography
Bronson, Fred. (1992). *The Billboard Book of Number One Hits* (3rd ed.). New York: Billboard.

Dawson, Jim & Propes, Steve. (1992). *What Was the First Rock 'N' Roll Record* (pp. 108-11). Boston: Faber and Faber.

Henican, Ellis. (1994, March 13). Sad songs sometimes have happy endings. *(New York) Newsday*, p. 4.

PROFESSOR LONGHAIR. *(Henry Roeland Byrd; December 19, 1918 - January 30, 1980). Inducted in the Early Influence category in 1992.* Called the grandfather of rock and roll, Professor Longhair was the conduit between early jazz-based, boogie-woogie piano and the frenetic rock of Little Richard. Remaining relatively obscure outside of New Orleans until 1970s, Professor Longhair was rediscovered after appearing at a jazz festival.

Born Henry Byrd in Bogalusa, Louisiana, he was raised in a New Orleans tenement, where his mother taught him to play guitar. Drawn to tap dancing, he performed for tips on street corners during his teens.

Trying to learn to play an abandoned piano he had found, 15-year-old Byrd would smear on a charcoal mustache and sneak into nightclubs to watch the piano players. Befriended by stride-style pianist Tuts Washington, the teenage Byrd lacked his mentor's dexterity.

Instead developing his own primitive, unorthodox style, Byrd dispensed with the expected trappings of the day. Influenced by barrelhouse and boogie-woogie-style players, Byrd's energetic piano pounding predated that of rock pioneer Jerry Lee Lewis.

During a stint in the Civilian Conservation Corps in the late 1930s, Byrd was exposed to Mexican mariachi bands, and incorporated the structure and percussion into his own music. Byrd's musical career was interrupted during World War II; although rejected as a volunteer in 1940, he was drafted in 1942.

Returning to New Orleans in the mid-1940s, Byrd became a barbecue chef . Drawn back to music, he joined a local R&B group, the Mid-Drifs, from 1947 to 1949. Shaving his head in 1948, he was given his Professor Longhair nickname by the proprietor of the Caladonia Inn in New Orleans.

Employing a blended backdrop of Caribbean, Spanish, and African polyrhythms, Byrd became a legend in New Orleans. Recording at Star Talent Records as Professor Longhair and the Shuffling Hungarians, he released "She Ain't Got No Hair" (1949) and an early version of his signature piece, "Mardi Gras in New Orleans" (1950), which became the theme song of the city's annual festival. He recorded a less popular version of the latter song for Atlantic Records in 1950.

Byrd's earlier release "She Ain't Got No Hair" was reworked at Mercury Records as "Bald Head" (1950). Now billed as Roy Byrd & His Blues Jumpers, it was his first national R&B hit. Recording at Federal in 1951 (as Roy Byrd), Wasco in 1952 (as Robert Boyd), and Atlantic again in 1953 (as Professor Longhair and his Blue Scholars), Byrd had fallen out of popularity. Meanwhile, fellow New Orleans pianists were building upon Byrd's style: his former gambling buddy Fats Domino was recording "Mardi Gras in New Orleans," and Huey "Piano" Smith borrowed Byrd's rumba rhythm on the hit "Rockin' Pneumonia."

Just 36 years old in 1954, Byrd suffered a debilitating stroke and was hospitalized for a year. Returning to music in the late 1950s, Byrd recorded for a series of labels. His last chart entry, Professor Longhair landed a minor R&B hit at Watch Records in 1964 with "Big Chief," featuring Earl King on vocals.

With fans believing him dead, an ailing Byrd was financially destitute by the mid-1960s. A poor businessman, he made little from his recordings, usually working on a flat-fee, no royalty arrangement.

But at the 2nd annual New Orleans Jazz and Heritage Festival in 1971, the undernourished and toothless performer was rediscovered, as offers of work soon poured in. "When he started playing that upright [piano] . . . everything else stopped dead on the other stages. There were four acts playing simultaneously, and the crowd just gathered and gaped. They had never heard anything like him. It was truly a magic moment" (White, p. 32), promoter Quint Davis told *Rolling Stone* magazine. A year later, Atlantic reissued a collection of Byrd's 1950s tracks on the album *NEW ORLEANS PIANO*.

Paying homage to the rock music pioneer, Paul McCartney hired Byrd in 1976 to perform, capturing the concert on the British-only release *LIVE ON THE QUEEN MARY*. In the 1970s Byrd performed at large festivals and enjoyed a long residency at Tipitina's, a nightclub he co-owned and was named after one of his early compositions. Byrd died in his sleep of natural causes in 1980 at his home in New Orleans.

Bibliography

Dahl, Bill. (1982, June). Roy Byrd, Professor Longhair: He taught them all how. *Goldmine*, p. 7.

Giddens, Gary. (1979, June 4). Professor Longhair woogies. *Village Voice*, p. 74.

Greensmith, Bill & Turner, Bez. (1978, May-August). Fess. *Blues Unlimited*, p. 4.

Scott, Liz. (1996, April). The remaking of Professor Longhair. *New Orleans*, p. 86.

White, Timothy. (1980, March 20). The Professor Longhair story: Lessons of a rock & roll legend. *Rolling Stone*, p. 12.

MA RAINEY. *(Gertrude Melissa Nix Pridgett; April 26, 1886 - December 22, 1939). Inducted in the Early Influence category in 1990.* After a decade of rejections from record companies, New York City songwriter Perry Bradford convinced Okeh Records in 1920 to venture into blues music. Mamie Smith shocked the record industry when her 78 rpm recording of "Crazy Blues" sold several hundred thousand copies, affirming a market for "race" music. Purchased by blacks and whites alike, Smith's record signaled a recording boom, with every major label signing its own jazz or blues singer. The most successful of these newly signed blues singers was Ma Rainey.

Born in Columbus, Georgia, in 1886 to former vaudeville actors, Gertrude Pridgett left home at 14. With vaudeville entering its golden age in the 1890s, Pridgett was drawn to the traveling and glitz of show business. Spotted at a talent show by manager William Rainey of the Rabbit Foot Minstrels at a talent show, he added her to their touring revue. With Pridgett marrying Rainey, the couple was billed as "Ma and Pa Rainey, Assassinators of the Blues."

A year before W.C. Handy's often cited discovery of blues music at a Mississippi train station in 1903, Rainey heard the mournful, brokenhearted wailings of a young Missouri woman who was lamenting the loss of her man. Taken with the unfamiliar style, Rainey was the first professional singer to put the music on the stage, creating a new art form of vaudeville blues. Touring through the South, Rainey was soon joined in the troupe by rising blues singer, Bessie Smith. Separating from her husband in 1917, the renamed "Madame" Rainey formed the Georgia Jazz Band.

Developing a bawdy, boisterous stage act, Rainey was a popular draw. Glittering with sleek costumes, jewelry, and a necklace of 20 gold coins, Rainey flirted with an oversized ostrich feather fan. "Dubbed 'the ugliest woman in show business,' with her bulging eyes and gold teeth, Rainey was still a tough, self-possessed ironist, captivating audiences with the direct folksy purity of her music. She was the blueswoman as mother and preacher" (p. 9), recalled author Lucy O'Brien. Within the black community, Rainey was soon called "the Mother of the Blues."

Belting out double-entendre lyrics with her towering contralto, 38-year-old Rainey was "discovered" in 1923 by Paramount Records her first big hit coming in 1924 with "Ma Rainey's Mystery Record," retitled by a public contest as "Lawd, I'm Down wid de Blues." Flanked by the finest musicians of the day—Fletcher Henderson, Coleman Hawkins, and "Georgia" Tom Dorsey—Rainey was backed by a young cornet player named Louis Armstrong on her best-known hit, the often recorded "See See Rider Blues." Her other hits include "Bo-Weavil Blues" and "Ma Rainey's Black Bottom."

With the rise of jazz in the late 1920s, blues music was falling out of fashion. Her repertoire of deep Delta blues increasing, Rainey was dropped by Paramount in 1928.

Returning to Columbus, Georgia, in 1935 after the death of a sister, Rainey turned her back on her blues past. Joining a Baptist church, she spent her last years singing gospel. Unlike many of her peers who had squandered their earnings, Rainey had accumulated a nest egg, purchasing, among other things, two movie theaters.

Bibliography
Jones, Hettie. (1995). *Big Star Fallin' Mama*, (rev. ed., pp. 17-31). New York: Viking.

O'Brien, Lucy. (1995). *She Bop: The Definitive History of Women in Rock, Pop and Soul.* New York: Penguin.

Palmer, Robert. (1984, October 28). The real Ma Rainey had a certain way with the blues. *New York Times*, sect. 2, p. 6.

Richards, David. (1984, November 18). Look! Ma! "Rainey" brings life to tired Broadway. *Washington Post*, p. H1.

OTIS REDDING. *(Otis Redding Jr.; September 9, 1941 - December 10, 1967). Inducted in 1989*. In the forefront of gritty-styled soul, Otis Redding had reached his goal of crossing over into the pop market shortly before his tragic demise. Born in Dawson, Georgia, but raised in the Tindall Heights housing projects in nearby Macon, Redding was passionate about breaking free of his childhood poverty.

Displaying initiative as a child, Redding formed his own youth gospel choir at the age of 8, performing in his preacher father's small Mount Ivy Baptist Church. Not able to afford formal lessons, Redding taught himself the drums, piano, and guitar by playing along with his stack of 45s.

After discovering the frenetic rock and roll of fellow Macon resident Little Richard, Redding formed an R&B band. Against the wishes of his deeply religious father, Redding took nightclub work. Maintaining his church ties, Redding continued to play drums for a local gospel group on a Sunday morning radio program. With his father falling ill, Redding dropped out of school to support his family.

After crossing paths with guitarist Johnny Jenkins at a talent show in 1958, Redding joined Jenkins' group, the Pinetoppers, as lead singer. Hiring an 18-year-old, white, R&B enthusiast and college-student named Phil Walden as their manager, the Pinetoppers secured bookings throughout the region.

Leaving the Pinetoppers to pursue a solo career, Redding moved to Los Angeles in late 1959. Frustrated by his lack of progress and tired of working at a car wash, he returned to Macon. Continuing with his Little Richard-like vocals, Redding recorded in nearby Athens, landing scattered airplay with "Shout Bamalama."

Performing on and off with the Pinetoppers until 1962, Redding rejoined the group for a session at the Stax-Volt studio in Memphis. But at the end of a Pinetoppers session, Redding sang a pair of solo tracks with the musical backing of the label's talented studio band built around Booker T. & the MG's. Emerging as Redding's first Volt single, "Hey Hey Baby" was paired with a B-side that was uncharacteristic of Redding's early style. Performing a gospel-like ballad, "These Arms of Mine," Redding had finally dropped his Little Richard-like delivery. A slow chart climber, the B-side became Redding's first hit.

Though garnering limited success in the pop market, Redding became an instant R&B superstar with his grotty, low-down, southern soul, his sound contrasting with the smooth, glossy sound of Motown. Co-writing much of his material with MG's guitarist Steve Cropper and utilizing the label's Mar-Keys horn section, Redding took R&B in a funkier direction.

Completed in just 24 hours, the album *OTIS BLUE* featured Redding's first pop hit, the Jerry Butler co-penned "I've Been Loving Too Long" (1965); and the Redding-composed "Respect," which became Aretha Franklin's defining hit two years

Otis Redding.

later. From the album *DICTIONARY OF SOUL*, Redding's finest vocal work came on the crescendoing ballad "Try a Little Tenderness" (1966), the song originally a hit for Ted Lewis in 1933.

Teaming with balladeer Carla Thomas in 1967, and billed as "the King and Queen" of soul, the pair's hits included "Tramp" and "Knock on Wood." A savvy businessman, Redding joined partner Phil Walden in launching Jotis Records, scoring a hit with Arthur Conley's "Sweet Soul Music." Meanwhile, Redding's backing band, the Bar-Kays, landed an instrumental hit with "Soul Finger" (1967).

Redding's crowning achievement came at the Monterey Pop Festival in June 1967. In a calculated and successful career move to win over rock fans, Redding overwhelmed the predominantly white crowd. Backed by the festival's house band,

Booker T. & MG's, and performing in a chilly drizzle, Redding dazzled the psychedelically-attired audience and emerged as a surprise hit.

Yearning for mainstream acceptance, Redding recorded "(Sittin' On) the Dock of the Bay," the song despised by his producer Steve Cropper for its pop-flavored turn. After rushing the session, Redding flew to Cleveland for an appearance on the syndicated *Up Beat* music show, sharing the bill with Mitch Ryder. But wanting to reach his next gig on time, Redding ignored weather warnings.

En route to Madison, Redding's $20,000 Beechcraft airplane lost power and went into a spin, dropping into the icy waters of Lake Monoma, just three miles short of Madison Municipal Airport. With the exception of Bar-Kay Ben Cauley, everyone on board perished.

With Cropper rushing the release of "(Sittin' On) The Dock of the Bay," complete with the sounds of splashing waves, Redding became the first recording artist to score a posthumous number-one single. The song won two Grammy Awards in 1968, for R&B vocal performance and for R&B song. With his record label continuing to release material, Otis remained on the charts for the next several years.

Redding's sons, Otis III and Dexter, joined cousin Kirk Locket in 1980 to form the Reddings. The group landed a minor hit in 1982 with their cover of "Dock on the Bay."

A fictitious Irish soul group, the Commitments, was born in 1991 via a successful film of the same name. Highlighted by several Redding covers, including "Try a Little Tenderness," the soundtrack was nominated for a Grammy.

Bibliography

Bowman, Rob. (1990, June 15). Otis Redding: R-E-S-P-E-C-T. *Goldmine*, p. 8.
"Death of a soul man." (1968, February). *Sepia*, p. 8.
Schiesel, Jane. (1973). *The Otis Redding Story*. Garden City, NY: Doubleday.
Thomas, Keith L. (1991, September 9). Otis Redding: His 50th birthday reprises loss for family
        in Macon. *Atlanta Journal and Constitution*, p. D1.

JIMMY REED. *(September 6, 1925 - August 29, 1976). Inducted in 1991.* Reared in a Mississippi sharecropping family, Jimmy Reed never attended school. After joining a gospel singing group, he acquired the rudiments of guitar playing with the aid of future blues star Eddie Taylor. After a two-year navy stint Reed returned to farming.

Tired of working the land, Reed resettled in the Chicago area in 1947, taking a steel mill job. Landing only an occasional stage gig, Reed would accompany himself on the guitar and harmonica.

Buying an inexpensive, tabletop record-making machine, Reed made his own amateur recordings beginning in 1950. Taking his homemade records to Chess Records in 1953, Reed was turned away by owner Leonard Chess who claimed he had enough blues acts on his roster. Taking the advice of a young Albert King, Reed auditioned for deejay Vivian Carter and her boyfriend Jimmy Bracken at their new Vee-Jay label.

Reunited in the studio with childhood friend Eddie Taylor, Reed landed a local hit with "Found My Baby" (1953). Several follow-up singles garnered little attention. Earning little royalties, Reed continued to work as a butcher for Armour meats, only occasionally performing in nightclubs. But with the release of a nearly two-year-old track, "You Don't Have to Go," Reed scored his first national hit, allowing him to quit his day job.

One of the last great Delta-based players, Reed possessed a greater proficiency on harmonica than guitar. Contrasting with the more polished sounds of modern blues-men like B.B. King, Reed played in an earthy, backwoods style. A fixture on the R&B charts in the second half of the 1950s, Reed unleashed a string of hits with, "Ain't That Lovin' You Baby" (1956), "Can't Stand to See You Go" (1956), "You've Got Me Dizzy" (1956), and a crossover pop hit, "Honest I Do" (1957).

Entering into a rocky management deal in 1958 with Al Smith, Reed continued his hit run with "I'm Gonna Get My Baby" (1958), "Baby What Do You Want Me to Do" (1960), and "Big Boss Man" (1961). With the popularity of blues waning in the early 1960s, Reed's career slowed, his last major hit coming in 1961 with his self-penned and often recorded standard "Bright Lights Big City."

Abusing alcohol since navy days, Reed began missing concerts, his health failing. Following Vee Jay's bankruptcy in 1965, Reed recorded for a series of labels begin-ing with Exodus. His best sessions behind him, Reed's later output was poorly received.

Suffering a severe epileptic seizure in 1969, Reed spent three years convalescing. Finally overcoming his drinking problem in 1975, Reed died a year later.

In debt at the time of his death, Reed was receiving no songwriting or performing royalties. Regaining control of his compositions in 1990, Reed's widow had filed lawsuits against several record companies.

Bibliography

Forte, Dan. (1990). Jimmy Reed. One of the last interviews with the big boss man of the blues. *Guitar Player*, p. 16.

Leishman, David. (1976, October 7). Jimmy Reed, "Big Boss Man," dead at 50. *Rolling Stone*, p. 15.

Phillips, Chuck. (1991, January 16). Fame, no fortune for rock pioneers: Jimmy Reed will be honored tonight, yet the industry abandoned him and others. *Los Angeles Times*, p. F1.

Whiteis, David. (1993, October 1). Ain't that lovin' you baby: The blues life of Jimmy Reed. *Goldmine*, p. 26.

SMOKEY ROBINSON. *(William Robinson Jr.; February 19, 1940). Inducted in 1987.* As the leader of the Miracles and vice president of Motown Records, William "Smokey" Robinson was a chief architect in the development of the Motown Sound. The grandson of slaves, Robinson was born in urban Detroit, his parents divorcing when he was just three. Raised by his self-educated, strong-willed mother, Robinson was taught to be independent. Following the death of his mother, 10-year-old Robinson came under the care of his eldest sister, Gerry, and his returning father.

Robinson's fascination with singing cowboys like Roy Rogers earned the youngster his "Smokey" nickname. A frequent childhood playmate of neighbor Aretha Franklin, young Robinson was also exposed to gospel music. Taking a series of jobs out of economic necessity, Robinson was styling hair by age 16. Enjoying school, he excelled in writing, jotting down what would later emerge as song lyrics.

Joining a succession of vocal groups, Robinson recalled in his autobiography, "I was raised in a dazzling din of doo-wop, seduced by the silver sounds of Harvey and the Moonglows—me and my pals would memorize their background blends—the Dells, Flamingos, Spaniels, Sonny Til and the Orioles, Lee Andrews and the Hearts. Heavenly harmony—five different parts merged like magic" (p. 50).

Forming the Five Chimes at Northern High School, the quintet included future Miracles members Ronnie White and Warren "Pete" Moore. With his silky, high-pitched voice, Robinson emerged as the lead singer. With the addition of Bobby Rogers and his sister, Claudette (soon to be Robinson's wife), the renamed Matadors auditioned for Jackie Wilson's manager, Nat Tarnapol, and songwriter Berry Gordy Jr.

Impressed with Robinson's original compositions, Gordy became manager of the renamed Miracles. After charting with their debut single, "Got a Job" (an answer song to the Silhouettes' hit "Get a Job"), Robinson dropped out of Highland Park Junior College. With Emerson Rogers entering the army, Claudette Rogers became a full-time member of the group, which now included Robinson, Ronnie White, Bobby Rogers, and Warren "Pete" Moore. Bombing at their Apollo Theater debut, the Miracles were unprepared for show business.

With Gordy landing a hit with Barrett Strong's "Money (That's What I Want)," Robinson wrote "Shop Around" intended as Strong's followup release. But Gordy insisted that the Miracles record the song instead. A week after the record was released and getting airplay, Gordy reassembled the group for a middle-of-the night session to record a new, faster, upbeat version of the song. Rush-released, the updated "Shop Around" gave the Gordy and the Miracles their first number one hit, ushering in the Motown era.

Appointed vice president of Motown in the early 1960s, Robinson was given the authority to sign new acts. Also a talented producer, Robinson worked with Motown's first female star, Mary Wells, also writing most of her hits, including "Two Lovers" and "My Guy." As a sequel to "My Guy," Robinson co-wrote "My Girl" for the Temptations.

Motown's first superstar act, the Miracles unleashed a string of usually romantic hits, including "You've Really Got a Hold on Me" (1963); "Mickey's Monkey" (1963); a song written onstage during a concert, "Ooh Baby Baby" (1965); and "Going to a Go-Go" (1966). Renamed Smokey Robinson and the Miracles in late 1966, their hits continued with "More Love" (1967) and "I Second That Emotion" (1967). The group briefly disbanded in 1968.

Tired of squabbling with bandmate Ronnie White, Robinson announced his retirement from the Miracles in 1969. But with his "departure" delayed for several years, the Miracles' hits continued with "Tears of a Clown" (1970) and "I Don't Blame You at All" (1971).

With Robinson finally leaving the group in June 1972, the Miracles managed only two more top-40 hits, including the chart-topping "Love Machine (Part 1)." The Robinson-less Miracles left Motown for CBS, releasing two poor-selling albums before disbanding in 1978.

Joining Gordy at Los Angeles' new Motown home in the 1970s, Robinson wasted his talent signing payroll checks and performing other executive duties. Eager to return to recording, Robinson launched a solo career in 1973 with the album *SMOKEY*.

Releasing *A QUIET STORM* in 1975, Robinson predated the adult urban-contemporary format of the 1990s, targeting adults instead of teens. Experimenting with longer, six to seven-minute songs, Robinson flirted with jazz and utilized backing female vocalists.

After a four-year lull, Robinson returned to the top-10 in late 1979 with the elegant "Cruisin'." Released against Berry Gordy's wishes, the song was first played by deejays as an album-track. In 1981, Robinson landed a million-seller with "Being with You."

With his cocaine habit intensifying in the 1980s, Robinson disappeared from the public eye. His body emaciated and near death, Robinson quit drugs cold turkey following a religious experience.

Experiencing a comeback in the late 1980s, Robinson returned to the charts with "One Heartbeat" and his first Grammy winner, "Just to See Her." He was also celebrated in the hit tribute by British rock group ABC "When Smokey Sings." A prolific songwriter, Robinson has composed over 1,500 songs in his lifetime.

Bibliography

Dahl, Bill. (1993, December 10). Smokey Robinson and the Miracles: Ooh baby baby. *Goldmine*, p. 14.

Harrington, Richard. (1988, August 2). Smokey Robinson: Tracks of his years; The singer at 48, in harmony and still in love with song. *Washington Post*, p. E1.

Lydon, Michael. (1968, September 28). Smokey Robinson. *Rolling Stone*, p. 20.

Lydon, Michael. (1971). *Folk Rock* (pp. 69-83). New York: Citadel.

Robinson, Smokey & Ritz, David. (1989). *Smokey: Inside My Life*. New York: McGraw-Hill.

Taraborrelli, J. Randy. (1986). *Motown: Hot Wax, City Cool & Solid Gold* (pp. 44-50). New York: Dolphin/Doubleday.

JIMMIE RODGERS. *(James Charles Rodgers; September 8, 1897 - May 26, 1933). Inducted in the Early Influence category in 1986.* Combining western folk songs with Delta blues, Jimmie Rodgers emerged as "the Father of Country Music." Popular among blacks and whites alike, many of his record buyers believed he was black.

Born near Meridian, Mississippi, of Scotch-Irish origins, Rodgers followed his widower father into railroad work at age 14. Starting as a waterboy, Rodgers was soon traveling the tracks throughout the South from Georgia to Texas, often entertaining his co-workers with his guitar or banjo. Exposed to the blues by black porters and mechanics, Rodgers infused the music into his own songs.

Losing his railroad job shortly after getting married, Rodgers spent the rest of his life changing jobs and towns. Entering show business, he wore blackface in a series of medicine shows. Following the destruction of his carnival show in 1925, the sickly Rodgers ignored the advice of his doctor and returned to railroad work.

Responding to a newspaper ad, Rodgers auditioned for independent talent scout Ralph Peer, who had taken his mobile recording unit to the hills of Bristol, Tennessee, in August 1927. The previous day, Peer had discovered a hillbilly trio the Carter Family.

Abandoned by his backing band before the scheduled audition, Rodgers accompanied himself on guitar, impressing Peer with his renditions of "The Soldier's Sweetheart" and "Sleep, Baby, Sleep." The latter song was highlighted by Rodgers' trademark quivering blue yodel and was influenced by Riley Puckett's original 1924 version.

Combining hillbilly music with blues, Rodgers released the million-selling "T for Texas" (1928), an original 12 bar blues-style composition that he had performed with his former backing band, the Entertainers. "T for Texas" was later renamed "Blue Yodel #1," the first of his 13 blue yodels, songs which shared a similar melody but featured different lyrics. The first white performer to record the music of Delta blacks, Rodgers incorporated blues phrasing and octave leaps. Singing in an unpretentious, down-to-earth style, Rodgers incorporated a southern drawl, targeting his records at the often ignored rural "common folk" in Appalachia. Embracing sentimentality and nostalgia, Rodgers laid the cornerstone of country music.

Dressed in railroad attire and nicknamed the "Singing Brakeman," Rodgers released several train-themed songs like, "Hobo Bill's Last Ride," often incorporating train whistle sounds. Employing western imagery in songs such as "Yodeling Cowboy," Rodgers influenced future matinee singing cowboys like Gene Autry.

Though suffering from advanced tuberculosis, Rodgers maintained a grueling touring schedule, also working a twice-a-week radio gig at San Antonio's WMAC. Predicting his demise, Rodgers lamented his fate in "T.B. Blues" (1931) and "My Time Ain't Long" (1932).

Traveling by train to New York City with a nurse at his side, Rodgers died at the age of 36 in a hotel room in 1933, days after his last studio session. For his last recording, "Fifteen Years Ago Today," Rodgers dismissed the backing band, preferring to accompany himself on guitar.

Remaining popular decades after his death, Rodgers continued to sell records. Influencing the next stage of country music, Rodgers' hits "Land of My Boyhood Dreams" and "Yodeling Cowboy" were instrumental in the development of the western-swing movement of the 1930s and 1940s.

Rodgers' often recorded 1928 composition "In the Jailhouse Now" gave Webb Pierce the biggest hit of his career, topping the country charts in 1955. Rodgers' 1930 sequel, "In the Jailhouse Now No. 2," was overdubbed with new instrumentation in the 1950s by Chet Atkins and Hank Snow, giving the dead singer his first actual country hit (the first country music chart debuted in 1944).

In 1961, Rodgers became the first inductee into the Country Music Hall of Fame. Organized by Bob Dylan, a 1997 Rodgers tribute album featured Cheap Trick, Steve Earle, Keith Richards, and Ronnie Wood.

Bibliography
Collins, Ace. (1996). *The Stories Behind Country Music's All-Time Greatest 100 Songs* (pp. 11-16).
New York: Boulevard. Paris, Mike & Comber, Chris. (1981). *Jimmie the Kid: The Life of Jimmie Rodgers*. New York: Da Capo.
Santoro, Gene. (1991, April 8). Country comforts. *The Nation*, p. 456.

THE ROLLING STONES. *Mick Jagger (Michael Phillip Jagger; July 26, 1943); Brian Jones (Lewis Brian Hopkins-Jones; February 28, 1942 - July 3, 1969); Keith Richards (December 18, 1943); Ian Stewart (1938 - December 12, 1985); Mick Taylor (Michael Taylor; January 17, 1948); Charlie Watts (Charles Roberts Watts; June 2, 1941); Ron Wood (June 1, 1947); Bill Wyman (William Perks; October 24, 1936). Inducted in 1989.* The scruffy, "bad boy" counterparts to the Beatles, the Rolling Stones brought Anglicized blues to the British Invasion. Rebellious and unkempt, the Stones promoted an anti-establishment image, with the dynamic, poutty-lipped Mick Jagger the antithesis of 1950s teen idols.

The son of a gym teacher, Jagger was attracted to American blues singers like Muddy Waters and Bo Diddley. Earning a scholarship, Jagger attended the London School of Economics. Joining Dick Taylor's London-based R&B group, Little Boy Blue and the Blue Boys in 1960, Jagger was soon joined by a childhood friend, guitarist Keith Richards.

Meanwhile, British blues guitarist Brian Jones was inspired to form his own blues group after sitting in with a pioneering British blues band, Alexis Korner's Blues Incorporated. Placing an advertisement in *Melody Maker*, pianist Ian Stewart was the first hired. Following were Jagger, Richards, bassist/saxophonist Taylor, and future Kinks drummer Mick Avory (soon replaced by Tony Chapman).

After EMI's rejection of the group's demo tape, Taylor left for art school (later forming a mid-1960s rock group, the Pretty Things) and was replaced by bassist Bill Wyman. With the addition of drummer Charlie Watts in early 1963, the Rolling Stones (named after a Muddy Waters song) were rounded out by Jagger, Richards, Wyman, Stewart, and Jones.

Riding on the coattails of Blues Incorporated, the Rolling Stones regularly substituted for the group at London's famed Marquee nightclub. Discovered by Giorgio Gomelsky, owner of the Crawdaddy Club, the Stones were signed to an eight-month residency.

Fresh from his publicist role for the Beatles, the brash 19-year-old Andrew Loog Oldham was hired in 1963 as the Rolling Stones' manager and initial session producer. Giving the group a tough-guy veneer, Oldham also removed the homely, straitlaced Stewart from the group, relegating him to background duties.

Performing their first British hit, "Come On" (an obscure Chuck Berry song), Mick Jagger and the Stones were perceived by BBC television audiences as primal and uncouth. Becoming media darlings, the Stones shocked the press with their flippant remarks and lack of manners, and were the group parents loved to hate. Adding to their bad-boy mystique, the long-haired group broke with tradition by refusing to wear stage uniforms.

Landing their first U.S. hit in early 1964 with a cover of Buddy Holly's "Not Fade Away," the Rolling Stones were at the forefront of the British Invasion. With Brian Jones pushed aside from his leadership role, the strutting Mick Jagger assumed the group's reins.

Initially considered a blues cover-group, the Rolling Stones realized the need to write their own material. Beginning with "Tell Me (You're Coming Back)," Jagger and Richards (nicknamed the Glimmer Twins) emerged as the group's chief songwriters. Songs written by the entire group were credited to Nanker Phelge.

Following in the Beatles' wake, the Rolling Stones dominated the American pop charts in the 1960s. The Rolling Stones' debut U.S. album, *ENGLAND'S NEWEST HIT MAKERS*, showcased their blues roots on "I'm a King Bee" and "I Just Want to Make Love to You." Creating a stir on their *Ed Sullivan Show* debut in October 1964, the group was blamed for the rioting audience. Later in the year Jones overdosed on barbiturates, the group's first of many drug-related misadventures.

Continuing their dependence on cover songs, the Rolling Stones charted with the Valentinos' "It's All Over Now" (1964) and from their second U.S. album, *12 x 5*, a blues-rock rendition of Irma Thomas' R&B hit "Time Is on My Side" (1965).

Recorded as an album filler track, "(I Can't Get No) Satisfaction" was released as a single over Keith Richards' objections. Their signature piece and first U.S. million-seller, it was banned by many radio stations for its alleged sexual innuendo. In 1965, the group recorded the album *OUT OF OUR HEADS*, their first in stereo.

On a roll, the Rolling Stones unleashed a string of hits in the mid-1960s with "Get off of My Cloud" (1965); a Jagger-Richards composition that was a hit the previous year for Jagger's girlfriend, Marianne Faithfull, "As Tears Go By" (1966); "19th Nervous Breakdown" (1966); the psychedelic "Paint It Black" (1966); and a lament about Valium abuse among suburban housewives, "Mother's Little Helper" (1966).

Returning to *The Ed Sullivan Show* in 1967, the Rolling Stones were forced by CBS to change the lyrics of their song "Let's Spend the Night Together," with Jagger instead mumbling, "Let's Spend Some Time Together." Scoring their first of only two hits in 1967 with "Dandelion," the group was shaken by negative publicity after the drug convictions of Jones, Jagger, and Richards and rioting at their European concerts.

As a response to the Beatles' groundbreaking *SGT. PEPPER* album, Jones pushed the group to record the drug-oriented album project *THEIR SATANIC MAJESTIES REQUEST*, complete with an expensive 3-D cover. Bombing, the album's only hit came with "She's a Rainbow" (1968). Later in 1968, Jones was jailed for a second time, for another drug conviction.

Returning to top form, the Rolling Stones hit number-one with the million-selling, single-only release "Jumpin' Jack Flash" (1968). Adopting a hard-rock sound, *BEGGAR'S BANQUET* (its release delayed by its controversial cover) was highlighted by a salute to Lucifer, "Sympathy for the Devil." Featuring Richards' forceful acoustic guitar, another track, "Street Fighting Man," was banned by radio, fearing the song would incite rioting.

Leaving the Rolling Stones on June 9, 1969, over artistic differences, the emotionally fatigued Brian Jones was unhappy with the group's pop-rock direction.

He was replaced by Mick Taylor. A month later, Jones was found dead in his own swimming pool after a taking a midnight dip. Two days later, a quarter million spectators gathered for a free, open-air, previously planned Rolling Stones concert at London's Hyde Park, with the local Hell's Angels assigned security duties. Releasing the country-rock flavored "Honky-Tonk Woman" days later, the Rolling Stones returned to the top of the charts.

Released as a commentary of the Beatles' album *LET IT BE*, the Rolling Stones' *LET IT BLEED* explored dark, urban themes on tracks such as "Gimme Shelter" and "Midnight Rambler." Meanwhile, Jagger also pursued a film career, starring in *Ned Kelly* (1969) and *Performance* (1970).

Wanting to stage a West Coast version of Woodstock, the Rolling Stones sponsored a free rock festival on December 6, 1969, at the Altamont racetrack in Livermore, California. With the local Hell's Angels paid $500 in beer to provide security, the concert was a violent finale to the most turbulent decade in American history. After attacking the Jefferson Airplane's Marty Balin, the Hell's Angels murdered an 18-year-old spectator, Merideth Hunter. Shaken by the incident, the Rolling Stones rushed through their set and nervously exited via a helicopter. The entire fiasco was captured on the documentary *Gimme Shelter*. (With witnesses refusing the testify the Hell's Angels were acquitted in court.)

Launching their own label, Rolling Stones Records, the group signed a distribution deal with Atlantic Records and adopted an Andy Warhol-designed cartoon emblem of Jagger's protruding lips. In 1971, Jagger married longtime girlfriend Bianca (his first of two wives), the daughter of Nicaraguan merchants.

Taking a turn toward mainstream rock with *STICKY FINGERS* and its lusty single "Brown Sugar," the Rolling Stones enjoyed continued stardom in the 1970s. Beginning with *EXILE ON MAIN STREET* in 1972, the Rolling Stones limited their U.S. tours to every three years. After completing the album *IT'S ONLY ROCK AND ROLL*, Mick Taylor left the group in 1974 and was replaced the following year by ex-Faces guitarist Ron Wood.

Their best-selling album of the decade, the Rolling Stones' *SOME GIRLS*, was highlighted by the disco-flavored "Miss You," Jagger's favorite song. A return to basic rock and roll, the album also featured "When the Whip Comes Down," "Shattered," and "Beast of Burden." On a roll, the group topped the charts with the albums *EMOTIONAL RESCUE* (1980) and *TATTOO YOU* (1981), the latter aided by several popular MTV videos.

Their output becoming less inventive, *UNDERCOVER* (1983) and *DIRTY WORK* (1984) were only moderate sellers. With tensions arising between Jagger and Richards, the Rolling Stones did not tour for eight years. With Jagger releasing a pair of solo albums beginning with *SHE'S THE BOSS*, Richard responded with his own effort, *TALK IS CHEAP*.

Setting aside their animosities, Richard and Jagger reconciled to write tracks for the 1989 album *STEEL WHEELS*. That year, Wyman married 18-year-old Mandy Smith (they divorced in 1992). Following suit in 1990, Jagger married his longtime paramour, model Jerry Hall.

In a strange twist, *Rolling Stone* publisher Jann Wenner presented the Rolling

Stones with a lifetime achievement award at the 1994 MTV Video Music Awards. That year, the group released the Grammy-winning album *VOODOO LOUNGE*. Promised a minimum of $100 million to tour (plus $15 million from a corporate sponsor, Budweiser), the Rolling Stones hit the road in 1992 with bass player Darryl Jones replacing the retiring Bill Wyman.

Released in 1995, the poorly selling album *STRIPPED* contained live acoustic versions of the group's classic hits. Released as the leadoff single was a cover of Bob Dylan's "Like a Rolling Stone." Also that year, Bill Gates paid several million dollars for the rights to the group's hit "Start Me Up" for use in his Windows-95 ads.

The long-shelved project *The Rolling Stones Rock and Roll Circus* was released in 1996 as a video and soundtrack album. The film sported a superstar rock cast and captured Brian Jones' last Rolling Stones performance. The Stones' 39th album, *BRIDGES TO BABYLON*, was released to mixed reviews in 1997.

Bibliography
Cohen, Rich. (1994, August 25). It's show time! *Rolling Stone*, p. 54.

Cott, Jonathan. (1981). In Peter Herbst (Ed.), *The Rolling Stone Interviews* (pp. 44-51, 328-39). New York: St. Martin's Press.

Eder, Bruce. Brian Jones. *Goldmine*, p. 10.

Flanagan, Bill. (1986, May). Stones at the crossroads. *Musician*, p. 40.

Fricke, David. (1989, September 7). Satisfaction. *Rolling Stone*, p. 36.

Greenfield, Robert. (1971, August 19). Keith Richards. *Rolling Stone*, p. 58.

Kent, Nick. (1979, October). Brian we hardly knew ye. *Trouser Press*, p. 26.

Norman, Philip. (1984). *The Stones*. New York: Simon & Schuster.

Ruhlmann, William. (1995, November 24). The Rolling Stones in America: 1964-1970 the London Records years. *Goldmine*, p. 18.

Wheeler, Tom. (1983, April). Keith Richards. *Guitar Player*, p. 68.

DIANA ROSS & THE SUPREMES. *Florence Ballard (June 30, 1943 - February 21, 1976); Diana Ross (Diane Ross; March 26, 1944); Mary Wilson (March 6, 1944). Inducted in 1988.* The most popular female act of the 1960s, Diana Ross & the Supremes were crucial to Motown's success. As students at Detroit's Northwestern High School, Florence Ballard, Betty Travis, and Mary Wilson formed the Primettes in 1959 as the backing group for an all-male vocal group called the Primes (who later evolved into the Temptations). All the members of the Primettes resided in the Brewster housing project, located near the small Hitsville U.S.A. studios, where Berry Gordy Jr. would build his Motown empire.

The Primettes expanded into a quartet when Paul Williams of the Primes suggested the addition of another Brewster resident, Diana Ross. But when Ballard and Travis were forced by their mothers to leave the group to concentrate on their schoolwork, the Primettes disbanded for several months.

The reformed quartet of Ballard, Ross, Wilson, and newcomer Barbara Martin staged a basement audition in late 1960 for William "Smokey" Robinson, then Gordy's right-hand man. Rejected by Motown, the Primettes recorded an obscure single for the Detroit-based LuPine Records. Undaunted, the Primettes loitered around the Motown studios, volunteering for whatever needed done. Taking notice of the eager young quartet, Gordy eventually signed the group but demanded a name change.

Beginning with the release of "I Want a Guy" in 1961, the renamed Supremes' early singles sold poorly. Although Ballard had the strongest voice in the group, Gordy insisted that Ross assume lead vocal duties. During this period, Ballard moonlighted as a touring member of the Marvelettes in 1962, while Ross attended cosmetology school on a loan from Smokey Robinson. With the departure of Martin (who had once wrecked Gordy's Cadillac) to marry, the Supremes were pared down to a trio.

Garnering massive exposure as part of the Motown Revue and Dick Clark rock caravan, the Supremes toured extensively throughout the U.S. and Britain from 1962 to 1964. Often mistaken for a Freedom Fighters group in the South, their Motown bus was once fired upon.

Managed personally by Gordy, the Supremes received much of Motown's resources. Aided by Motown's new songwriting team of Holland-Dozier-Holland, the Supremes landed their first top-40 hit in late 1963 with "When the Lovelight Starts Shining through His Eyes." The recipients of H-D-H's best material, the Supremes became overnight superstars, scoring a string of Motown-defining number-one pop and soul hits with "Where Did Our Love Go" (1964), "Baby Love" (1964), "Stop! In the Name of Love" (1965), "I Hear a Symphony" (1965), "You Can't Hurry Love" (1966), and "You Keep Me Hangin' On" (1966).

While the group's three members began on equal footing, Ross soon emerged as the leader. "Diana's remarkable abilities as an entertainer kicked her up into another category. She demanded that attention; she earned it. She had the charisma to fill football stadiums full of fans all over the world" (p. 153), recalled Smokey Robinson in his autobiography. But with Ross attracting most of the attention, tensions grew within the group.

Gaining weight and abusing alcohol and pills, Ballard was fired in April 1967, right before a major concert at the Hollywood Bowl (she briefly returned to the group). Although Ross has been blamed for the dismissal, the undependable Ballard was equally at fault.

Joined by newcomer Cindy Birdsong (of Patti LaBelle and the Blue Bells), the renamed Diana Ross & the Supremes continued their string of hits with "Reflections" (1967) and "In and Out of Love" (1967). But after losing the songwriting services of Holland-Dozier-Holland, who had left Motown over monetary issues, the Supremes' hit run stalled.

Now depending on a variety of Motown songwriters, including Smokey Robinson and R. Dean Taylor, the Supremes' hit streak slowed. With tensions continuing within the group, Ross used session singers instead of the Supremes for vocal backing on "Love Child," a controversial chart-topping lament about illegitimacy. Hoping to improve their fortunes, the Supremes duetted with both the Four Tops and the Temptations.

After scoring their last chart-topping single with the melancholy "Someday We'll Be Together" (1969), Ross left the group in January 1970. Ross' final performance with the Supremes was captured on the album *FAREWELL*.

Emerging as a solo star beginning with the chart-topping hit "Ain't No Mountain

High Enough" (1970), Ross remained prolific into the 1990s. With the nurturing of Berry Gordy (her reported paramour), Ross starred in a pair of blockbuster films, the Billie Holiday biography *Lady Sings the Blues* and, mirroring her own rags-to-riches life story, *Mahogany*.

With Jean Terrell taking over lead vocal duties, the new Supremes debuted on *The Ed Sullivan Show*, enjoying a brief run of hits in the early 1970s with "Nathan Jones" and "Floy Joy." Following Terrell's departure in 1973, the Supremes rambled along before disbanding in 1977. The following year, Mary Wilson formed a new, short-lived version of the Supremes, and then pursued a solo career.

Meanwhile, Ballard had married Motown employee Tom Chapman, who managed her brief solo career. Claiming that Motown had cheated her of millions, Ballard ran out of money before she ran out of litigation. Losing her confidence to perform, the financially destitute former star was forced to go on welfare to feed her three daughters. Ballard died from a heart attack in 1976.

Opening at New York's Imperial Theater in 1981, the perennial Broadway musical *Dreamgirls* was based on the Supremes' story. Mary Wilson unsuccessfully sued Motown in the 1980s over the ownership of the Supremes name and master recordings.

Bibliography

Robinson, Smokey & Ritz, David. (1989). *Smokey: Inside My Life*. New York: McGraw-Hill.

Taraborrelli, J. Randy. (1986). *Motown: Hot Wax, City Cool & Solid Gold* (pp. 134-40). New York: Dolphin/Doubleday.

Thomas, Michael. (1973, February 1). Diana Ross goes from riches to rags. *Rolling Stone*, p. 8.

Warner, Jay. (1994, January). First ladies of Motown: The Supremes. *Discoveries*, p. 10.

Wilson, Randall. (1983, September). The Supremes: You control my destiny, forever faithful: The story of Florence Ballard. *Goldmine*, p. 10.

SAM & DAVE. *Dave Prater (David Prater Sr.; May 9, 1937 - April 9, 1988); Sam Moore (Samuel David Moore; October 12, 1935). Inducted in 1992.* Nicknamed "Double Dynamite," Sam & Dave brought gritty, sweaty soul to the forefront of popular music in the mid-1960s. The son of a deacon and grandson of a Baptist minister, Miami-native Sam Moore was secretly performing in nightclubs during his teen years. After a stint singing religious material in the Melonaires, he turned down a coveted spot in the Soul Stirrers gospel group. Unable to support himself as a singer, Moore took a day job as a construction worker.

Dave Prater also received his musical education in the church. Born in Ocilla, Georgia, the son of a laborer, Prater moved to Miami after graduating from high school, hoping to land a singing job. While working as a grill cook and cashier at a restaurant in 1959, Prater first met Moore, a frequent customer.

Recalling his first onstage pairing with Prater in 1960, Moore told interviewer Mike McDowell: "We were in a talent contest at a local nightclub, where I sang 'Danny Boy' and Dave sang Sam Cooke's 'Wonderful World.' The club owner was so impressed with our styles, that he came up with the idea of having Dave and I perform together" (pp. 8-9). With the crowd roaring its approval, the team of "Sam & Dave" was born.

Signed by Morris Levy of Roulette Records, Sam & Dave released several unsuccessful R&B-styled singles beginning with "I Need Love" (1962). These tracks were complied on the 1963 album *SAM & DAVE.*

Switching to Atlantic Records in 1965, there label chief Jerry Wexler arranged for Sam & Dave to record at the Stax studios in Memphis. Teamed with the songwriting team of Isaac Hayes and David Porter and the musical backing of Booker T. & the MG's and the Memphis Horns, Sam & Dave dropped their old-style R&B sound, pumping out a string of gospel-inspired, gritty soul hits, beginning with the debut chart entry "You Don't Know Like I Know" (1966).

In the studio, Prater's funkier, rough-edged vocals complemented Moore's cool, smooth delivery on their soul chestnut "Hold On, I'm Coming" (1966); their Grammy-winning, million-selling signature piece, "Soul Man" (1967); "I Thank You" (1968); and "Wrap It Up" (1968). During this period their hit albums included *HOLD ON, I'M COMING* (1966), *DOUBLE DYNAMITE* (1967), and *SOUL MEN* (1967).

Hardworking performers, Sam & Dave possessed a close-knit onstage interplay, choreographing their high-energy dance moves. With Stax's arrangement with Atlantic Records expiring in 1968, Sam & Dave reverted back to Atlantic. That year, Prater escaped prosecution for shooting his wife in a domestic incident.

With Atlantic now recording Sam & Dave in Miami and then Muscle Shoals, Alabama, and employing a new group of songwriters and backing musicians, the duo's output suffered. Additionally their former songwriter, Isaac Hayes, left to pursue a solo career. Except for the million-selling single "Soul Sister, Brown Sugar" (1968), the duo would never again appear on the top-40 chart.

After a bitter separation in 1970, Prater and Moore both pursued solo careers. While Moore remained at Atlantic, Prater signed with Alston Records. Though still feuding, Sam & Dave periodically regrouped in the 1970s. After a brief stint at United Artists in 1971, the pair recorded a poorly received album, *BACK AT 'CHA* (1975), for the Steve Cropper-owned TMI label. The following year, the duo were guest vocalists on the debut album of jazz-fusion great Jaco Pastorius. A collaboration in 1977 resulted in minor hit with a cover of the Beatles' "We Can Work It Out."

With the Blues Brothers reprising "Soul Man" in 1979, Sam & Dave enjoyed a revival. Touring extensively, Sam & Dave were hired as the opening act for the Clash and were featured in the 1980 Paul Simon film *One Trick Pony.* Spending most of his earnings in the 1970s on cocaine and heroin, Moore often hit the stage during this period in bad shape, if he showed up at all.

With their clashes intensifying, Sam & Dave disbanded for good in 1982. But when Dave Prater teamed with Sam Daniels as the new Sam & Dave, Sam Moore sued his former partner. In an unlikely duet, Moore teamed with art-rocker Lou Reed in 1986 for a new version of "Soul Man," from the film of the same name.

Prater was killed in 1988 on Interstate-75 near Sycamore, Georgia, when his car veered off the road, landing in a tree. The previous month, he had been convicted of selling crack cocaine.

At the Atlantic Records 40th anniversary concert at Madison Square Garden in 1988, a drug-free Moore teamed up with Blues Brother Dan Aykroyd. Atlantic was later sued by Moore and Prater's estate over royalties for the period from 1970 to 1990.

Bibliography
Jancik, Wayne. (1987, January 2). Sam & Dave: Hold on, they're comin' . . . maybe. *Goldmine*, p. 16.
Landau, Jon. (1968, January 20). Soul men. *Rolling Stone*, p. 18.
McDowell, Mike. (1978). Sam & Dave: Double Dynamite. *Blitz*, no. 27, p. 8.
Moore, Sam. (1984, March 26). Heroin and the soul man: A cautionary tale of degradation and redemption. *People*, p. 84.
Sperrazza, Gary. (1979, September-October). Looka here!: It's Sam & Dave. *Time Barrier Express*, p. 18.

SANTANA. *Jose Chepito Areas (July 25, 1946); David Brown (February 15, 1947); Mike Carabello (November 18, 1947); Coke Escovedo (Thomas Escovedo; April 30, 1941); Gregg Rolie (June 17, 1947); Carlos Santana (July 20, 1947); Neil Schon (February 27, 1954); Michael Shrieve (July 6, 1949). Inducted in 1998.* Born in the Mexican state of Jalisco, Carlos Santana was reared on traditional Mexican music. His father a professional musician, Santana was taught to play the violin. Moving to Tijuana where he discovered blues music, Santana switched to the guitar, teaching himself by playing along to records by B.B. King and T-Bone Walker. At the age of 13, he landed a year-long gig in the house band of a Tijuana strip-joint.

Joining his family in San Francisco in 1963, Santana immersed himself in the city's burgeoning psychedelic-rock scene. While peeling potatoes at a fast-food restaurant, he was inspired to pursue a musical career after seeing Jerry Garcia and the Grateful Dead pull up in a limousine.

Bridging traditional Latin-American music with blues, Carlos Santana formed the Santana Blues Band in 1968 with high school friend, keyboard player Gregg Rolie. In a *Boston Globe* interview, Santana recalled: "I remember playing in Golden Gate park at a peace and freedom festival. When I took a solo, I closed my eyes, then opened them and saw [Jerry Garcia] grinning in front of me, cheering me on. He taught me a lot . . . [and] spent a long time showing me things on guitar. He'd say, 'That should hold you awhile.'"

Santana's group was also nurtured by the owner of the Fillmore Auditorium, Bill Graham, who became their co-manager and frequently booked the band alongside Janis Joplin and the Grateful Dead. During this period, Carlos Santana made his recording debut on the blues album *LIVE ADVENTURES OF MIKE BLOOMFIELD AND AL KOOPER*.

Signed to CBS Records as Santana, the group garnered star status after performing at Woodstock, where they delivered a blistering rendition of "Soul Sacrifice." Their debut album, *SANTANA*, was a critical success, and was highlighted by "Jingo" and the top-10 hit "Evil Ways." The followup release, *ABRAXAS*, topped the album charts and featured a cover of Tito Puente's "Oye Como Va" and a bluesy, definitive version of the Fleetwood Mac classic "Black Magic Woman." Espousing American Indian and Eastern philosophies, Carlos Santana weaved those themes into much of his lyrics.

Experiencing frequent personnel changes, Santana was joined by percussionist Coke Escovedo and guitarist Neil Schon in time for their 1971 release, *SANTANA III*. Schon and Gregg Rolie left the following year to form Journey.

During the next several years, Santana explored the limits of jazz-rock fusion, collaborating on records with the likes of Mahavishnu John McLaughlin and Turiya Alice Coltrane. Aside from his group, Carlos Santana teamed with jazz great Buddy Miles.

Santana remained a fixture on album-rock radio in the 1970s. The 1976 release, *AMIGOS*, marked a return to mainstream rock, while the mostly live release, *MOONFLOWER*, was highlighted by a bluesy, top-40 rendition of the Zombies' "She's Not There." The group's popularity waning somewhat, Santana continued to release a prolific string of albums into the early 1980s, their hits continuing with "Winning" (1981) and "Hold On" (1982). A solo Carlos Santana project, *HAVANNA MOON*, featured guest appearances by Willie Nelson, the Fabulous Thunderbirds, and Booker T. Jones.

Nearly a solo effort, the next Santana album, 1985's *BEYOND APPEARANCES*, featured only two group members, Carlos Santana and percussionist Orestes Vilato. A reformed Santana emerged in 1987 for the album, *FREEDOM*, the album signaling a decline in record sales. Leaving their longtime record company, Sony-CBS, Santana passed through several labels in the 1990s.

Carlos Santana teamed with brother, Jorge, and nephew, Carlos Hernandez, in 1994 as the Santana Brothers, releasing the album *BROTHERS*. And in 1997, Columbia issued the raw, *LIVE AT THE FILLMORE '68* with material previously available only on bootlegs. Though Carlos Santana's latter work has received little radio airplay, he remains a strong concert draw. In 1993, Carlos Santana launched a reissue label, Guts & Grace, to promote classic jazz and blues.

Bibliography

"The man behind the music." (1996, March). *Hispanic*, p. 19.

Morse, Steve. (1995, August 11). Carlos Santana: A life inspired by the Dead. *Boston Globe*, arts & film sect., p. 57.

Obrecht, Jas. (1988, January). Carlos Santana. *Guitar Player*, p. 46.

Washburn, Jim. (1992, August 15). Santana: Blues, beliefs and beyond. *Los Angeles Times*, p. F1.

White, Timothy. (1996, December 7). A portrait of the artist. *Billboard*, p. 14.

PETE SEEGER. *(Peter R. Seeger; May 3, 1919). Inducted in the Early Influence category in 1996.* A folk music pioneer, Pete Seeger was instrumental in the folk-rock boom of the 1960s. The son of the chairman of the music theory department at Juilliard, who had lost his previous job over his Marxist politics, Pete Seeger was reared in New York City. First given a ukulele at age eight by his violist mother, Seeger taught himself to play a series of instruments, including his trademark five-string banjo.

Initially preferring jazz, 15-year-old Pete Seeger discovered folk music in 1936 after accompanying his father to a square dance festival in Asheville, North Carolina. Meeting musicologist John Lomax and folk-blues singer Leadbelly two years later, Seeger was set on his life course.

After studying sociology for two years, Seeger dropped out of Harvard in 1939. Unable to land work in journalism, Seeger joined the Young Communist League, touring in a political puppet show for the purpose of unionizing striking New York dairy farmers.

Befriended by Library of Congress musicologist Alan Lomax (son of John Lomax), Seeger moved to Washington D.C., and was paid $15 per week as his assistant. Quitting his post, Seeger spent much of 1940 drifting through the country on railroad cars, and stopping at migrant labor camps.

Brought to New York City by left-wing activist, actor Will Geer, Seeger joined his new mentor, Woody Guthrie, and Millard Lampell in founding the Almanac Singers. Funded by the labor unions, the Almanac Singers took their protest music to union rallies, Communist meetings, and folk music concerts called "hootenannies." But with the wartime rise of anti-Red sentiment, the press turned against the group, labeling them Communists. Drafted in 1942, Seeger served in the special services.

Discharged at the end of 1945, Seeger returned to New York. Wanting to promote political folk music, Seeger played a central role in the formation in 1946 of the People's Songs, an organization of over 3,000 like-minded leftist musicians. Two years later, Seeger published his perennial best-selling instructional guide *How to Play Five-String Banjo*.

With the end of People's Songs in 1949, Seeger formed its successor, People's Artists, in 1950. The organization's monthly publication, *Sing Out!*, continues today. Seeger regularly wrote for the magazine, once serving as associate editor.

Teaming with Lee Hays, Ronnie Gilbert, and Fred Hellerman, Seeger formed a folk quartet, the Weavers. Signed by Decca, the Weavers were the first folk act in the modern era to land pop acceptance; their biggest hits came with "Tzena, Tzena" (1950) and a cover of Leadbelly's "Goodnight Irene" (1950), both featuring orchestral backing. The group's other Decca releases include a Seeger-Hays composition, "Rock Island Line," "The Hammer Song" (1949) (later known as "If I Had a Hammer"), and a cover of a South African pop song, "Wimoweh" (1952), later updated by the Tokens as "The Lion Sleeps Tonight."

With America experiencing a Communist scare during its Cold War with the Soviet Union, the Weavers' political views were considered dangerous. Losing bookings and unable to land airplay, the group disbanded in 1952.

Blacklisted by mainstream record companies, Seeger recorded on the Moe Asch-owned folk label Folkways Records. Touring college campuses as a solo act, at one stop he befriended 12-year-old Joan Baez. Drawing on various sources, Seeger continued to compose new material: "Where Have All the Flowers Gone?" was inspired by the poetry of Russian Yevgeny Yevtushenko; "Guantanamera" is based on a poem by Cuban revolutionary, Jose Marti; and "Turn, Turn, Turn" borrowed from *The Book of Ecclesiastes*.

Refusing to answer investigators' questions about his politics for the House Un-American Activities Committee in 1955, Seeger was charged with contempt. Reforming the Weavers later in the year, Seeger left in 1957 when the other members wanted to record a cigarette jingle. In the next few years, Seeger played a key role in the inauguration of the Newport Folk Festival.

With the rise of the Greenwich Village folk scene, a new wave of folkies led by Bob Dylan were embraced on college campuses. Suddenly, Seeger's material was recorded by a host of mainstream artists. While the Kingston Trio's "Where Have All the Flowers Gone" (1962), and Peter Paul and Mary's, "If I Had a Hammer" (1962) were true to the original versions, the Byrds topped the pop charts with an electric rendition of Seeger's "Turn! Turn! Turn!" (1966). Seeger himself scored a folk hit in 1964 with a redefining version of the Malvina Reynolds' folk classic, "Little Boxes."

Though back in vogue, the blacklisted Seeger was banned from the ABC folk music show *Hootenanny*. Seeger's blacklisting from television ended in 1967 as the country began a gradual shift to the Left. Appearing on *The Smothers Brothers Comedy Hour*, Seeger sang the antiwar tirade "Waist Deep in the Big Muddy" (which was cut by CBS censors during his first visit).

Remaining politically outspoken during the Vietnam conflict, Guthrie supported North Vietnam's leader, Ho Chi Minh, calling him a "hero." But Guthrie turned away from communist Russia after Soviet tanks attacked Prague, Czechoslovakia, in 1968.

Distancing himself from the trappings of stardom, Seeger built a log cabin along the Hudson River near Peekskill, New York. In 1972, Seeger was described by *Rolling Stone* music critic Gene Marine as "wearing work clothes that sometimes looked as though they were hand-me-downs from someone two sizes smaller; he might have been a gas attendant in middle America. . . . His shirt [is] full and flowered but relatively subdued; his black denim pants flare just at the bottom, above heavy, high work shoes" (p. 41).

Signing with Warner Brothers in the late 1970s, Seeger teamed with Guthrie's son, Arlo, on the album *PETE SEEGER AND ARLO GUTHRIE TOGETHER IN CONCERT*. Reuniting with the Weavers in 1980, Seeger sold out two concerts at Carnegie Hall.

Bibliography

Fisher, Marc. (1994, December 4). America's best-loved Commie: Even a radical can become a national treasure; just ask Pete Seeger. *Washington Post*, p. G1.

Isler, Scott. (1979, October 18). Pete Seeger: Still fighting the good fight. *Rolling Stone*, p. 20.

Marine, Gene. (1972, April 13). Guerrilla minstrel. *Rolling Stone*, p. 40.

Outerbridge, Laura. (1994, November 28). Pete Seeger: Despite his best efforts, this radical is finding honors are being added to his fame. *The Washington Times*, p. C10.

Plant, Sarah; Lusk, Bob & Bluestone, Mimi. (1980). Folk music, what's that? *Sing Out!*, 78(2), p. 2.

Shipp, Randy. (1980, January 24). Pete Seeger: His answers are in his songs. *The Christian Science Monitor*, p. B10.

Smith, Joe. (1988). *Off the Record* (pp. 154-56). New York: Warner.

Vranish, Jane. (1995, November 19). Pete Seeger and granddaughter give the PBT a sense of family values. *The Pittsburgh Post-Gazette*, p. G1.

SHIRELLES. *Doris Kenner (August 2, 1941); Beverly Lee (August 3, 1941); Addi "Micki" Harris (Michelle Harris; January 22, 1940 - June 10, 1982); Shirley Alston Reeves (June 10, 1941). Inducted in 1996.* A pioneering girl-group, the Shirelles bridged pop and soul in the late 1950s with their sweet harmonies. Originally called the Poquellos (Spanish for "birds"), the group formed in 1956 at Passaic High School in New Jersey. When Shirley Owens and classmates Beverly Lee, Doris Kenner, and Addi "Micki" Harris were overheard singing by their gym teacher, he forced them to enter a school talent contest.

Singing their own composition, "I Met Him on a Sunday," the girls wowed the audience with their acapella rendition. An impressed classmate, 16-year-old Mary Jane Greenberg, hounded the girls into auditioning for her mother, Florence Greenberg, who operated the tiny Tiara Records as a hobby.

With Greenberg insisting on a more commercial moniker, the group was renamed the Shirelles (after Shirley Alston). After landing local airplay with "I Met Him on a Sunday" (1958), Greenberg leased the master disc to Decca Records in 1958 for $4,000. A minor hit nationally, the Shirelles were unable to repeat the feat and were dropped by Decca.

Undaunted, Greenberg and songwriter Luther Dixon (of "16 Candles Fame") formed Scepter Records. Signing the Shirelles, Greenberg became their manager and Dixon their producer and arranger. Projecting a simple innocence with their full skirts and bouffant wigs, the Shirelles landed pop airplay with their warm, sincere harmonies.

The Shirelles' first Sceptor release, a cover of the 5 Royales doo-wop hit, "Dedicated to the One I Love" (1959), went unnoticed outside New York City. With many fans believing the all-black group was white, the Shirelles landed the first chart-topping single by a black female group, the Gerry Goffin/Carole King-penned "Will You Love Me Tomorrow" (1960). Re-releasing "Dedicated to the One I Love" in 1961, the Shirelles hit the top-ten.

Defining the girl-group sound, the Shirelles were soon copied by several Motown acts. But unlike their contemporaries, the Shirelles wrote some of their own material. The Shirelles hit run continued with "Mama Said" (1961); the Burt Bacharach/Hal David-penned "Baby It's You" (1962); recorded in only one take, a cover of the Four Fellows doo-wop classic, "Soldier Boy" (1962); "Welcome Home Baby" (1963); and "Foolish Little Girl" (1963). For a time, labelmate Dionne Warwick substituted for a pregnant Owens.

After the Shirelles turned down the opportunity to record "He's a Rebel" (their manager claimed they would be unable to perform the song in the South), it became a hit for the Crystals. Instead, the Shirelles reluctantly recorded the theme song for the comedy film *It's a Mad, Mad, Mad, Mad World*. The group's final top-40 hit came in 1963 with "Don't Say Goodnight When You Mean Goodbye." The arrival of the British Invasion had marked the end of the Shirelles' success.

The Shirelles left Scepter when the label refused to pay the members a promised lump sum payment when they turned 21. While the Shirelles were unable to sign with another label due to contractual restrictions, Scepter continued releasing previously recorded tracks. Returning to Scepter to close out their contract, the Shirelles managed their last chart entry in 1967 with "Last Minute Miracle" (1967). A year later, Kenner left the group.

After brief, unfruitful stints at Blue Rock, Bell, and United Artists, the Shirelles released a pair of albums on RCA Records, their last coming in 1976 with *LET'S GIVE EACH OTHER LOVE*. With Alston leaving the group to have a baby, she convinced Kenner to return. Alston later pursued a solo career as Lady Rose.

The Shirelles remained a popular draw on the oldie circuit into the early 1980s. But after the death of Harris from a heart attack in 1982, the group disbanded. Lee and Kenner later formed separate Shirelles revues. In 1983, Lee and Kenner were joined by Alston to back Dionne Warwick on her recording of "Will You Love Me Tomorrow."

Launching a lawsuit in 1987 to recover past royalties from a pair of reissue companies that controlled the Sceptor master recordings, the Shirelles emerged victorious with each member awarded $119,537 plus interest.

Bibliography

Jones, Wayne. (1980, September). The Shirelles. *Goldmine*, p. 10.
Pollock, Bruce. (1981). *When Rock Was Young* (pp. 117-30). New York: Holt, Rinehart, and Winston.
Tortelli, Joseph A. (1987-88, December-January). Shirelles' lead Shirley Reeves recalls girl group sound. *Record Collector's Monthly*, p. 1.
Trescott, Jacqueline. (1978, July 8). The pop power of the girl groups: The Shirelles. *Washington Post*, p. E1.
Warner, Jay. (1994, March). Will you still remember tomorrow: The Shirelles. *Discoveries*, p. 109.

SIMON & GARFUNKEL. *Art Garfunkel (Arthur Garfunkel; November 5, 1941); Paul Simon (October 13, 1941). Inducted in 1990*. Combining intricate folk melodies with rock-oriented instrumentation, Simon & Garfunkel were the most successful duo in the second half of the 1960s. Raised in the Forest Hills section of Queens, New York, the son of educators, Paul Simon enjoyed a middle-class existence. Living nearby was the tall, blond, bushy-haired Art Garfunkel, his father in the packaging business.

Meeting in their sixth grade production of *Alice in Wonderland*, the pair solidified a friendship over their love of R&B music. Teaming at a school assembly at New York's P.S. 164 in 1955, Simon & Garfunkel sang the Chords' doo-wop classic "Sh-Boom." Now playing an acoustic guitar, Simon had earlier failed in his attempt to master the piano.

Both very bright, Simon & Garfunkel attended a gifted student program at Parsons Junior High. Adopting the stage names of Tom Graph and Jerry Landis, the 16-year-olds signed with Big Records. Influenced by the Everly Brothers, the duo tried to imitate their tight harmonies. With Simon switching to an electric guitar, the pair released a moderate-selling single, "Hey Schoolgirl" (1957), as by Tom and Jerry. Appearing on *American Bandstand*, they shared the bill with Jerry Lee Lewis.

With their follow-up singles fizzling, the duo disbanded. While pursuing an architecture degree at Columbia, Garfunkel occasionally performed as Art Garr. While studying English literature at Queens College, Simon also pursued a musical avocation, releasing several singles under a variety of pseudonyms and singing demo records for publishing companies.

Dropping out of law school after one semester in 1962, Simon regrouped with Garfunkel. Drawn to Greenwich Village, the duo frequented the area's many folk coffeehouses.

Signed to CBS records in 1964 by Tom Wilson, the duo was forced by the label to use their real names. Setting a career-long pattern, Simon wrote nearly all of their material, with Garfunkel providing most of the lead vocals.

Containing mostly folk standards, Simon & Garfunkel's debut album, *WEDNESDAY MORNING 3 A.M.*, sold few copies. With their short hair and clean-cut images separating them from other folkies, the duo did not appeal to folk music record buyers. A dejected Simon drifted through Europe, playing in folk clubs.

But when "Sounds of Silence" landed heavy airplay in Miami, CBS decided to salvage the album. Without the duo's knowledge, the previously acoustic song was remixed, with producer Tom Wilson adding drums and electric, rock-styled guitar. Released as a single, the reworked folk-rock tune topped the charts, their first of several million-sellers. Returning to the U.S., Simon planned on staying only six months.

The remixed single appeared on the duo's second album, *SOUNDS OF SILENCE*, which also featured material taken from Simon's solo British album *THE PAUL SIMON SONGBOOK*. A surprise hit, the album also contained "Homeward Bound" (1966) and the stark, despairing "I Am a Rock" (1966). On a roll, their next album, *PARSLEY, SAGE, ROSEMARY AND THYME* was highlighted by the hits "A Hazy Shade of Winter" (1966), "At the Zoo" (1967); "The 59th Street Bridge Song (Feelin' Groovy)" (1967), and "Scarborough Fair" (1968). Continuing to attend Columbia, Garfunkel completed a master's degree in mathematics education in 1967.

Commissioned to provide music for the Dustin Hoffman film *The Graduate* (1967), Simon & Garfunkel supplied five songs, including one new track, the chart-topping, Grammy-winning salute to older women, "Mrs. Robinson." With their music heavily promoted throughout the box office smash, Simon & Garfunkel emerged as folk-rock superstars. Their follow-up album, *BOOKENDS*, contained some previously released tracks and an updated version of "Mrs. Robinson."

Recorded over a two-year period on an early 16-track mixer, Simon & Garfunkel's final studio album, *BRIDGE OVER TROUBLED WATER* (1970), sold 9 million copies. The album was highlighted by "The Boxer," "Cecilia," "El Condor Pasa," and the Grammy-winning, spiritual-like, title-track, "Bridge over Troubled Waters" (Aretha Franklin's 1971 remake of the song also earned a Grammy).

During the recording of the album, Garfunkel launched an acting career, portraying Captain Nately in the film version of, *Catch-22*. With both Simon and Garfunkel pursuing individual projects, the bickering duo disbanded after a brief 1971 tour.

Remaining cold toward one another, the duo occasionally reunited in the 1970s, including an appearance in 1972 at a McGovern rally. In 1975, the pair landed a duet hit with "My Little Town" (1975), a song that Simon wrote for Garfunkel but appeared on both of their solo albums. Three years later, the duo teamed with James Taylor on a cover of the Sam Cooke standard "Wonderful World."

Thriving at CBS, Simon enjoyed a fruitful solo career, his music infused with gospel, reggae, and African elements. Garfunkel continued his acting career in the controversial film *Carnal Knowledge* and he briefly taught math at a private school in Connecticut. While Garfunkel also attempted a solo singing career, his low-key approach contrasted with Simon's high-profile persona.

After experiencing a box-office bust with the musical film, *One-Trick Pony*, Simon decided to rejoin his former partner. Reuniting in 1981 at New York's Central Park for a free concert attended by 400,000, the event was televised by HBO. From the album *LIVE AT CENTRAL PARK*, the duo landed a top-40 hit with "Wake Up Little Suzie." Launching a world tour in 1982, Simon & Garfunkel were met with packed venues.

Feeling betrayed upon learning that Simon had recorded a solo album, Garfunkel disbanded the duo in 1983. Simon returned to a successful solo career, highlighted by 1986's *GRACELAND*. Ending their feud in 1990, Simon & Garfunkel reunited for several charity performances and subsequent concert tours.

Bibliography

Alterman, Loraine. (1970, May 28). Paul Simon. *Rolling Stone*, p. 37.
Connelly, Christopher. (1981, October 29). Simon & Garfunkel: After all these years. *Rolling Stone*, p. 9.
Holden, Stephen. (1982, March 18). Class reunion: It looks like a lasting thing. *Rolling Stone*, p. 26.
Marsh, Dave. (1980, October 30). What do you do when you're not a kid anymore and you still want to rock & roll? *Rolling Stone*, p. 42.
Sweeting, Adam. (1993, September 18). Brill on the old turf: Paul Simon's talent for mix'n'match began in Queens, New York. *The Guardian*, p. 29.
Varga, George. (1993, June 14). Singularly Garfunkel: He'd rather be known for his own work. *San Diego Union-Tribune*, p. E1.
White, Timothy. (1984, March). The luminous heart of a dark horse: Paul Simon. *Musician*, p. 60.

SLY & THE FAMILY STONE. *Sly Stone (Sylvester Stewart; March 15, 1944); Jerry Martini (October 1, 1943); Greg Errico (September 1, 1946); Larry Graham (Larry Graham, Jr.; August 14, 1946); Freddie Stone (Fred Stewart; June 5, 1946); Rosie Stone (Rosemary Stewart; March 21, 1945); Cynthia Robinson (January 12, 1946). Inducted in 1993.* Blending psychedelic rock with funky soul, the Sly Stewart-led Sly & the Family Stone ignored rigid radio formats. The son of a former musician and sometime preacher, Sylvester Stewart was born and raised in Dallas. Joining his family's gospel group, the Stewart Four, he sang harmony with future Family Stone members, sister Rose and brother Freddie. Teaching himself the guitar and organ, Stewart was soon drawn to doo-wop music.

After moving to San Francisco in the late 1950s with his family, Stewart teamed with brother Freddie as the Stewart Brothers, releasing a pair of obscure singles in

1959. Attending Vallejo Junior College, Stewart studied music theory.

After releasing several solo singles, Stewart joined a doo-wop group, the Viscaines. With the addition of future Family Stone member Jerry Martini in 1961, the group landed some local airplay.

Hired by deejays Tom Donahue and Bobby Mitchell in 1963, 19-year-old Sylvester Stewart joined their new Autumn label. After a brief stab at a solo career under the name Sly Stewart, he turned his efforts to production, working with Beau Brummels and the Grace Slick-fronted Great Society, overseeing the original version of "Somebody to Love" (later a hit for Slick's new group the Jefferson Airplane).

With Autumn Records closing in 1965, Stewart enrolled in a broadcasting course. After deejaying at a San Francisco R&B radio station, the renamed "Sly Stone" moved to KDIA in Oakland, where he added progressive rock to his soul playlist. Stone's surprise success with the format inspired him to launch a short-lived soul-flavored, psychedelic-rock group, the Stoners.

With the Stoners disbanding in 1966, Sly Stone retained trumpet player Cynthia Robinson and formed the Family Stone. The racially mixed group was augmented by his brother, Freddie on guitar, cousin Larry Graham on bass, and a pair of old friends, guitarist Jerry Martini and drummer Greg Errico.

Signing with CBS Records in 1967 as a "black hippie" band, Sly & the Family Stone shocked label-heads with their gypsy clothes and hybrid rock sound. CBS released, but refused to promote their first album, *A WHOLE NEW THING*, calling the project uncommercial. The group was soon completed with the addition of Stone's sister, Rose, on piano.

As the group's producer and chief songwriter, Sly Stone was determined to deliver a single acceptable to CBS. Released in 1968, their top-10 breakthrough single "Dance to the Music" was followed by a hit album of the same name. A follow-up album, *LIFE*, spawned the chart-topping smash hit "Everyday People" (1969). Embraced by soul and rock fans alike, the group made a triumphant appearance at Woodstock in 1969.

Enjoying rock airplay alongside other black rockers like Jimi Hendrix and War, Sly & the Family Stone continued their hit run with "Hot Fun in the Summertime" (1969) and the double-sided entry "Thank You (Falettinme Be Mice Elf Agin)"/"Everybody Is a Star" (1970).

But with Sly Stone's increasing drug use, the group began to disintegrate. With Stone canceling or missing a third of their shows in 1971, promoters stopped booking the group. His troubles increasing, Stone experienced the first of many drug-related arrests in 1972. With two full years passing before the release of the group's next studio album, CBS issued a million-selling greatest-hits package.

A chart-topping "comeback" album, the heavily-produced *THERE'S A RIOT GOING ON*, featured the group's best-selling single of its career, "Family Affair." The song was one of the first pop hits to employ an electronic drum machine, which was necessitated by Greg Errico's departure. Leaving soon after, Larry Graham formed Graham Central Station, later landing a solo hit with "One in a Million You" (1980).

With politics and drugs in the way of the group's success, Sly & the Family Stone's last hit came in 1973 with "If You Want Me to Stay." As a publicity stunt, Stone was married onstage at Madison Square Garden in 1974, with his uncle officiating (he was divorced five months later).

With concert attendances dropping, Sly & the Family Stone disbanded in 1975. Emerging as a solo act, Stone recorded a poorly-selling album later in the year. After filing for bankruptcy in 1976, Stone reformed the Family Stone, releasing a pair of ignored albums. Meanwhile, newcomers like Prince and Rick James soon built upon Stone's groundbreaking style.

After a brief reunion with the Family Stone in 1982, Sly Stone landed session work behind George Clinton, Bobby Womack, and others. Dueting with the Time's Jessie Johnson in 1986, Stone landed his last hit with "Crazay." Parlaying the hit into a brief recording contract, Stone found little success at A&M Records.

Continuing his battle against drugs, Stone was jailed for cocaine possession in 1987. Still dressing in his outrageous 1970s-style costumes, Stone continues to make occasional appearances.

Bibliography

Corcoran, Michael. (1994, March 17). The Stone age: Few talents ever outshone Sly, but at 50 he's just a faded memory. *The Dallas Morning News*, p. 5C.
Crouse, Timothy. (1971, October 14). The struggle for Sly's soul at the Garden. *Rolling Stone*, p. 1.
Font-Torres, Ben. (1970, March 19). Everybody is a star: The travels of Sylvester Stewart. *Rolling Stone*, p. 28.
Heibutzki, Ralph, (1994, February 18). Lookin' at the devil: The energy and exile of Sly and the Family Stone. *Goldmine*, p. 14.
White, Timothy. (1990). *Rock Lives: Profiles & Interviews* (pp. 280-85). New York: Henry Holt.

BESSIE SMITH. *(April 15, 1894 - September 26, 1937); Inducted in the Early Influence category in 1989.* While Ma Rainey moaned through her records, Bessie Smith offered a more refined and better orchestrated interpretation of vaudeville blues. Her father a Baptist preacher who ran a mission, Smith was orphaned at a young age in the slums of Chattanooga, Tennessee. Barely surviving, she earned money performing on street corners.

Round-faced, with a booming contralto voice, Smith first hit the black vaudeville stage in 1912, encouraged by her performer brother. Joining the popular Rabbit Foot Minstrels touring revue later in the year, Smith impressed the troupe's star singer, Ma Rainey. Initially a dancer, Smith soon added singing and comedy to her routine.

Landing a long-term gig at Charles Bailey's 81 Theater in Atlanta in 1913, Smith was paid $10 per week (but earned much more in tips). Building a strong fan base on her tours throughout the South, Smith headed her own troupe by 1920. Journeying north to Atlantic City, Smith was welcomed into the bustling jazz community.

Smith was signed to Columbia Records in 1923 by Frank Walker, the head of the label's new black division. Walker had caught Smith's performance at an Alabama nightclub several years earlier. Nonetheless, Columbia's owners echoed the apprehension of previous labels that had rejected Smith, fearing that her old-style, vaudeville blues were too uncommercial to sell records.

Recording her debut disc in 1923, Smith was backed by pianist Clarence Williams on her rendition of Alberta Hunter's "Down Hearted Blues." The first of Smith's 14 releases that year, the record sold a then-remarkable 780,000 copies in six months, saving Columbia from impending bankruptcy. Landing a million-seller with her self-penned "Tain't Nobody's Bizzness If I Do," Smith emerged as a superstar in the black community. Marrying Jack Gee in 1923, it was the start of a stormy relationship.

Earning the nickname "The Empress of the Blues," Smith appeared onstage in full regalia, with beads, long gowns, and elaborate feather hats. Confident and commanding, standing at five feet nine inches and weighing 210 pounds, the full-figured Smith was more attractive than Ma Rainey. But her determination not to target a crossover, mainstream audience kept her from becoming a bigger success. (Historians claim that Smith's darker complexion also kept her from attaining crossover success.)

Backed by cornet player Louis Armstrong, Smith scored a trio of hits in 1925 with a cover of the W.C. Handy standard "St. Louis Blues," "Careless Love Blues," and "I Ain't Gonna Play No Second Fiddle." Constantly on the road, Smith continued her hit run with "I Ain't Got Nobody" (1926); with Buster Bailey on clarinet, "After You've Gone" (1927); and "A Good Man Is Hard to Find" (1928).

Earning no more than $200 per record, Smith instead made her money at nightclub appearances, demanding up to $2,000 per week. Drinking heavily, squandering her earnings, and suffering marital problems, Smith became more eccentric.

Originally limiting her bawdy material to her Southern audiences, many of Smith's later recordings employed double-entendre lyrics, including "Empty Bed Blues" (1928) and "Need a Little Sugar in My Bowl" (1930). This sexual playfulness on and offstage furthered her legend.

Recording the self-penned "Nobody Knows You When You're Down and Out" in 1929, the record signaled the end of her career. That year Smith appeared in her only film, *St. Louis Blues*, singing the title track. With old-style country blues falling out of popularity, and the country experiencing the ravages of the Depression, Smith was dropped by Columbia in 1931.

After a two-year recording hiatus, jazz producer John Hammond coaxed Smith back into the recording studio. Backed by Benny Goodman on the track "Gimme a Pigfoot," Smith scored her final hit in 1933.

With her career on an upswing, Smith died in 1937 from severe injuries suffered when her wooden-frame Packard struck a truck near Clarksdale, Mississippi. A passing doctor who arrived at the scene two minutes after the crash was unable to treat Smith's mortal wounds. A heavily circulated myth propagated by *Downbeat* magazine suggested that Smith died after she was refused treatment by a white-only hospital.

Influencing generations of singers, Smith was celebrated by LaVern Baker on her tribute album, *SINGS BESSIE SMITH*. Smith's stepson, Jack Gee Jr., sued Columbia Records in 1977 over past royalties.

Bibliography
Balliett, Whitney. (1971, November 6). Jazz records: Miss Bessie. *New Yorker*, p. 160.

Dixon, Robert M.W. & Godrich, John. (1970). *Recording the Blues*. New York: Stein and
   Day.
"Empress of the Blues dead 21 years ago beside dark highway, north of Clarksdale. (1959,
   July-August). *Second Line*, p. 9.
Jones, Hettie. (1995). *Big Star Fallin' Mama*, (rev. ed., 33-54). New York: Viking.
Lear, Len. (1977, September). A lawsuit for what's owed Bessie Smith. *Sepia*, p. 65.
Oliver, Paul. (1959). *Bessie Smith*. New York: Perpetua. Provizer, Norman. (1992, April-
   May). Empress of the blues. *Jazziz*, p. 39.

THE SOUL STIRRERS. *S.R. Crain (Silas Roy Crain; 1911 - September 14, 1996);
J.J. Farley (Jessie J. Farley; 1915 - October 11, 1988); R.H. Harris (Rebert H.
Harris; March 23, 1916); E.A. Rundless (Edward A. Rundless; c. 1914); Inducted
in the Early Influence category in 1989*. Years after *Billboard* magazine adopted
Jerry Wexler's proposal in 1949 to change the name of their "race music" chart to
"rhythm and blues," he admitted to erring, wishing he had called it "rhythm and
gospel," since nearly all major soul and R&B artists received their musical training in
the black church.

Pioneering modern gospel harmony, the Soul Stirrers spawned hundreds of
imitators, in gospel and pop music alike. Writes Sam Cooke biographer Daniel Wolf,
"The [Soul] Stirrers had begun as a teenage gospel group back in 1922 at Mount
Pilgrim Baptist Church in Trinity, Texas. When a choir trainer described the eleven-
year-old boys as soul-stirring, their leader, Senior Roy Crain, had latched onto the
name" (p. 44). But by the late 1920s, the original group had disbanded.

Taking a job in Houston in 1931, Crain joined the New Pleasant Green Gospel
Singers (formed four years earlier by W.L. La Beaux) and convinced them to change
their moniker to the (Five) Soul Stirrers. Discovered by musicologist John Lomax, the
group made a series of Library of Congress recordings in 1936.

The Soul Stirrers experienced several personnel changes in 1937, beginning with
the additions of M.L. Franklin, and Texas native Rebert H. Harris. Emerging as the
group's leader, R.H. Harris began writing songs at age 8 and was raised on the blues
of Blind Lemon Jefferson. Forming a gospel singing group at age 10 with several
family members at the Harris Christian Methodist Church in Trinity Texas, Harris later
attended the Mary Allen Seminary in Crockett, Texas, quitting in 1936. With Crain
lastly adding his childhood friends, A.L. Johnson and J.J. Farley, the Soul Stirrers were
in their classic lineup.

Leaving Houston for Chicago, the Soul Stirrers were drawn to the Windy City's
bustling gospel scene. Befriended by the "Father of Gospel Music," Thomas A.
Dorsey, the Soul Stirrers landed a radio program in 1939 at WIND. During the World
War, the group joined several USO tours.

Revolutionizing gospel music, the Soul Stirrers had added a second tenor, allowing
the first tenor to step forward as a lead singer, a device later copied by 1950s doo-wop
groups. R.H. Harris also introduced several other innovations to gospel, including
improvised lyrics, the falsetto, and the "delayed-time" lead vocal, which added a
jazzlike tension to their acapella sound. Preferring newer songs over old spirituals, the
Soul Stirrers landed fame with the Dorsey gospel standard "Precious Lord" and their

own compositions, such as "He's My Rock, My Sword, My Shield."

Recording for Aladdin Records in 1948, the Soul Stirrers scored a hit with "Lord I've Tried," a blues-inspired, 16-bar gospel song penned by the prolific songwriter Rev. William Herbert Brewster. In 1949, Franklin was replaced on second tenor by Hall Foster.

Signing with Los Angles-based Specialty Records in 1950, the Soul Stirrers began to add instrumental backing, pioneering the electric bass in gospel music. Their early Specialty hits included the standard "By and By" and "How Long."

Disheartened by the worldly temptations of the gospel road, R.H. Harris announced his departure from the group in September 1950. With Leroy Taylor refusing to join the group on a full-time basis, Harris handpicked Sam Cooke as his successor. The other members, all in their 40s, were initially apprehensive about a singer not yet 20. Previously the leader of the Highway QCs, Cooke had earlier crossed paths with the Soul Stirrers at a Chicago church concert. Also leaving the group was James Medlock, who was replaced by former Houstonaire member Paul Foster.

Initially alternating vocals with the gruffy-styled Foster, the velvety-voiced Cooke emerged as the group's lead singer by 1952. While Harris possessed a greater vocal range, Cooke displayed a sensual, fiery delivery that drew a much younger, mostly female audience. But when the revamped Soul Stirrers showed up at a recording session with Cooke in Harris' place, Specialty owner Art Rupe was not pleased.

But with Cooke at the helm, the Soul Stirrers landed their biggest seller to date with the Cooke-penned, "Until Jesus Calls Me Home." Adding instrumentalists Faidest Wagoner and Bob King in 1953, the Soul Stirrers emerged as gospel superstars rivaling the stature of their R&B counterparts. Their hit run continued with "Nearer to Me" (1955), and featuring Cooke's soaring, emotional vocal and pop-styled orchestration, "Touch the Hem of His Garment" (1956).

Earning little money singing gospel, Cooke switched to pop music in 1957. Hired as Cooke's replacement, 19-year-old Johnnie Taylor had earlier replaced Cooke in the Highway QCs. S.R. Crain also left the group, joining Cooke as his road manager and business partner. Unable to survive the losses of both Harris and Cooke, the Soul Stirrers saw their popularity decline.

Dropped by Specialty Records in 1959, the Soul Stirrers signed with Cooke's new SAR Records, recording the label's inaugural single, "Stand by Me Father." Two years later, Johnnie Taylor followed Cooke's lead into pop music and was replaced in the Soul Stirrers by new lead singer Jimmy Outler. After Jimmy Outler was killed, Willie Rogers took over as lead tenor. Recording at the Chess subsidiary, Checker Records, in the late 1960s, Rogers shared lead vocal duties with tenor Martin Jacox on the album *THE BEST OF THE SOUL STIRRERS* (1966).

From the group's classic lineup, J.J. Farley maintained a version of the Soul Stirrers until his death in 1988. With 80-year-old founding member R.H. Harris in attendance, a new lineup of the Soul Stirrers recorded a live album at a Chicago church in 1997.

Bibliography

Boyer, Horace Clarence. (1995). *How Sweet the Sound: The Golden Age of Gospel.*

Washington, DC: Elliott & Clark.

Broughton, Viv. (1985). *Black Gospel: An Illustrated History of the Gospel Sound.* Poole, England. Blandford.

Hart, Hugh. (1992, November 2). Doing it right Soul Stirrers have been shaking up gospel for 6 decades. *Chicago Tribune*, Tempo sect., p. 3.

Heilbut, Anthony. (1985). *The Gospel Sound: Good News and Bad Times*, (rev. ed.). New York: Limelight.

Hilburn, Robert. (1986, February 16). Sam Cooke: Our father of soul. *Los Angeles Times*, Calendar sect., p. 62.

Wolf, Daniel & Crain, S.R. (1995). *You Send Me: The Life and Times of Sam Cooke.* New York: William Morrow.

PHIL SPECTOR. *(Harvey Phillip Spector; December 26, 1940). Inducted in the Non-Performer category in 1989.* The most influential producer of the 1960s, Phil Spector revolutionized popular music with his "wall of sound" recording technique. Born into a working-class family in the Bronx, Spector was devastated by the suicide of his ironworker father.

Moving to Los Angeles with his family in 1953, Spector received a guitar for his bar mitzvah. Discovering a local, burgeoning doo-wop scene, Spector tracked down the R&B production team of Jerry Leiber and Mike Stoller, dropping by their studio to watch them work.

While attending Fairfax High School, 17-year-old Spector assembled a trio, the Teddy Bears, writing, producing, and singing backup on their wry ballad "To Know Him, Is to Love Him" (the title taken from his father's tombstone). Featuring the lead vocals of Annette Kleinbard, the song was a surprise chart-topper for the small Dore Records. After suffering a humiliating assault in a public bathroom during a tour, Spector developed a lifelong obsession with personal security.

After graduating to the larger Imperial Records, the Teddy Bears disbanded when Kleinbard was injured in a serious auto accident. Taken under the wing of record promoter Lester Sill, Spector moved to Phoenix and produced the Spectors 3 (the group included Spector's soon-to-be first wife, Annette Merar).

After attending UCLA for a year, Spector moved to New York City and was hired by Atlantic Records as the assistant to production team of Leiber & Stoller. "Wry, short, relentlessly intense, Spector was convinced he knew as much as—or more than—anybody at Atlantic" (p. 141), recalled Atlantic chief Jerry Wexler in his autobiography.

Moonlighting at Dunes Records, Spector produced Ray Peterson's "Corinna, Corinna" and Curtis Lee's doo-wop throwback "Pretty Little Angel Eyes." Claiming he was underage when he signed his contract, Spector left Atlantic and began working with Gene Pitney and Connie Francis.

Reuniting with Lester Sills in Los Angeles, Spector produced the million-selling single "I Love How You Love Me" for the Paris Sisters. Wanting to record a new discovery, the Crystals, Spector and Sills launched Philles Records. Hearing Vicki Carr's demo of the Gene Pitney-penned "He's a Rebel," Spector was determined to release the song first. But with the Crystals touring on the East Coast, Spector instead recorded Darlene Love and the Blossoms, releasing the song as by the Crystals. (The real, touring Crystals had to learn "their" new hit in between concert dates.)

Buying out his partner, Spector took control of Philles in 1962. Recording on a three-track mixer at Gold Star Studios, he released nearly all of his records in mono. An overbearing producer, Spector assembled rock symphonies of dozens of session players and formulated a complex system of microphones and tape recorders to achieve his trademark "wall of sound." Wanting to ensure that deejays played only the A-sides of his records, Spector learned to issue substandard B-sides.

Employing the team of Jeff Barry and Ellie Greenwich as his chief songwriters and Jack Nitzchie as arranger, Spector landed a string of mostly girl-group hits, with the Crystals, Bobb B. Soxx, and the Ronettes. Receiving much of Spector's attention, the Ronettes, which were headed by former go-go dancer Veronica (Ronnie) Bennett, recorded the label's biggest records, beginning with the pop masterpiece "Be My Baby" (1963).

When the Ronettes shared a concert bill in 1964 with "blue-eyed soul" duo, the Righteous Brothers, an impressed Spector bought out their contract from Moonglow Records. Deviating from his normal pop formula, Spector employed mixed tempos on their chart-topping ballad "You've Lost That Loving Feeling," the duo's first of several similarly styled hits.

Losing most of his hit acts by 1966, Spector was determined to salvage Philles Records. Investing a great deal of time on Ike and Tina Turner's "River Deep—Mountain High," Spector considered the song to be his creative apex. Although a hit in England, the song was sabotaged by U.S. deejays who had tired of Spector's egotism. Devastated by the song's failure, Spector closed Philles and became a near hermit.

Marrying his longtime paramour Ronnie Bennett, Spector divorced his first wife in 1968. Spector kept his new wife cloistered in his mansion, her recording career ended.

Returning to music production in 1969, Spector worked on Ike and Tina Turner's album *RIVER DEEP—MOUNTAIN HIGH*. Remixing the Beatles album, *LET IT BE*, and adding new backing orchestrations, Spector angered the group's regular producer, George Martin. After the Beatles' break-up, Spector produced several solo albums for John Lennon and George Harrison.

Signed by Warner Brothers, Spector produced less than stellar discs for Cher, Dion, and avant-garde rocker Leonard Cohen. In the late 1970s, Spector began remixing his Philles-era hits for reissue on his own label, Phil Spector International. His last significant work coming in 1980, Spector produced the Ramones *END OF THE CENTURY* (during one point holding a gun Joey Ramone's head), the album highlighted by the tracks "Rock 'n' Roll High School" and "Do You Remember Rock 'n' Roll Radio?"

Making a rare public appearance at the 1989 Rock Hall ceremonies, Spector gave a rambling speech. Also that year, he filed a defamation suit against biographer Mark Ribowsky over his tome *He's a Rebel*.

Returning to the studio in 1996, Spector was angered when Celine Dion deleted a Spector-produced track from her album. Also that year, the members of the Teddy

Bears unsuccessfully sued Spector and several labels over past royalties. Former Ronettes lead singer Ronnie Spector filed her own lawsuit against her ex-husband in 1997.

Bibliography
Beach, Keith A. (1980, December). Phil Spector. *Goldmine*, p. 11.
Hoerburger, Rob. (1993, June 20). The power of love. *New York Times*, sect. 6, p. 20.
Hubbard, Kim; Belfour, Victoria & Lustig, David. (1989, February 6). Phil Spector. *People*, p. 84.
Wenner, Jan. (1969, November 1). The Rolling Stone interview: Phil Spector. *Rolling Stone*, p. 23.
Wexler, Jerry & Ritz, David. (1993). *Rhythm and the Blues: A Life in American Music.* New York: Alfred A. Knopf.
Williams, Richard. (1972). *Out of His Head: The Sound of Phil Spector.* New York: Outbridge and Lazard.

ROD STEWART. *(Roderick David Stewart; January 10, 1945). Inducted in 1994.* A rock chameleon, Rod Stewart has weathered three decades of musical fads. Born of Scottish descent in North London, Stewart enjoyed a happy childhood listening to records by Al Jolson and Sam Cooke. Unexpectedly receiving a guitar from his construction worker father, the disappointed 14-year-old was hoping for an addition to his train set.

Pursuing a career in professional soccer, Stewart left school, augmenting his income as a grave digger, among other odd jobs. Leaving home at age 17, he performed in a folk duo on the sidewalks of continental Europe. After adding blues to his repertoire, Stewart joined Jimmy Powell and the Five Dimensions, the group frequently backing rocker Chuck Berry on British tours. The group parlayed its association with Berry into a residency at London's famed Crawdaddy Club in 1963.

Days before his 19th birthday in 1964, Stewart joined Long John Baldry's band, the Hootchie Coochie Men, providing backing vocals on the live album *LONG JOHNS BLUES*. Baldry soon gave the fashion-conscious singer his "Rod the Mod" nickname.

Simultaneously pursuing a solo career, Stewart recorded "Good Morning Little Schoolgirl" in 1964 (later a hit for the Yardbirds). Also a popular session musician, Stewart provided the harmonica solo on Millie Small's novelty hit "My Boy Lollipop."

With Baldry's band disbanding in 1965, Stewart joined Baldry to form Steampacket. With the departure of keyboardist Brian Auger, the innovative group disbanded a year later. Then teaming with Peter Green and Mick Fleetwood (later with Fleetwood Mac), Stewart formed the short-lived group Shotgun Express.

Joining a band led by former Yardbirds guitarist Jeff Beck, Rod Stewart took over lead vocal duties beginning with the breakthrough album *BECK-OLA*.. Touring through the U.S., the painfully shy Stewart initially hid behind the amplifiers or speakers when performing onstage.

But with Beck firing his backing band, Stewart and bandmate Ron Wood joined the Small Faces in 1969 as the replacements for Steve Marriott. Featuring Stewart's sandpaper tenor vocals, the renamed Faces landed a pair of hits: a cover of the Temptations, "(I Know) I'm Losing You" (1971) and the hard-rocking "Stay with Me" (1972). Recording and touring intermittently, the Faces fared poorly after Stewart's departure in 1975.

During the same period, Stewart enjoyed a more successful solo career. Signed by Mercury, he scored a career-making, chart-topping single with "Maggie May" (1971), from the album *EVERY PICTURE TELLS A STORY*. Though the B-side of "Reason to Believe" (a Tim Hardin composition), "Maggie May," became a hit after a Cleveland deejay flipped the record over. Employing a mandolin as the lead instrument, the song was a true life account of Stewart's brief tryst with an older woman. Stewart's hit run continued with "You Wear it Well" (1972) from the album, *NEVER A DULL MOMENT*.

Settling in Los Angeles in 1975 to escape Britain's confiscatory tax laws, Stewart signed with Warner Brothers. His first album recorded in the U.S., *ATLANTIC CROSSING*, found Stewart backed by the core of Booker T. & the MG's. Enjoying a jet-setter's life, Stewart also began dating starlet Britt Ekland.

Taking a pop-rock turn, Stewart unleashed a string of hits, including "Tonight's the Night" (1976), the Cat Stevens-penned "The First Cut Is the Deepest" (1977), "You're in My Heart" (1977) and the bawdy "Hot Legs" (1978). Stewart's parting with Britt Ekland resulted in a $15 million palimony suit. He subsequently married Alana Hamilton in 1979.

Sporting long, spiky hair and spandex outfits, Stewart jumped on the disco bandwagon in the late 1970s. From the album *BLONDES HAVE MORE FUN*, Stewart landed a monster hit with "Do Ya Think I'm Sexy" (1979), borrowing the song's melody from a South American pop hit. Profits from the record were donated to a United Nations children's charity.

Rebounding in the early 1980s with a pared-down sound, Stewart landed a string of upbeat, dance-style hits, including "Passion" (1980), "Young Turks" (1980), and, with Jeff Beck on lead guitar, "Infatuation" (1984) and "Some Guys Have All the Luck" (1984). Stewart reciprocated by guesting Beck's album *FLASH*, the pair landing rock-radio hit with a sizzling blues cover of the Impressions' "People Get Ready." His music a staple of top-40 radio, Stewart's hit run continued with "Lost in You" (1988), "Downtown Train" (1989), a duet with Ronald Isley, "This Old Heart of Mine" (1990), and the Scottish-flavored "Rhythm of My Heart" (1991). In 1990, Stewart married 21-year-old swimsuit model Rachel Hunter.

After improving his health regimen and receiving vocal coaching, Stewart's voice became less hoarse in the 1990s. Reuniting with former Faces-bandmate Ron Wood on the 1993 acoustic project *UNPLUGGED . . . AND SEATED*, Stewart scored a surprise smash hit, the album highlighted by the Van Morrison-penned "Have I Told You Lately," Tim Hardin's "Reason to Believe," and Sam Cooke's "We're Having a Party." Also that year, Stewart reunited with members of the Faces for a performance on the Brit Awards.

In April 1995, Stewart announced, then denied, his retirement from music. Returning to his R&B roots, Stewart landed a hit in 1996 with "If We Fall in Love Tonight."

Bibliography

Nelson, Paul. (1978, April 6). Rod Stewart under siege. *Rolling Stone*, p. 46.

Palmer, Robert. (1982, March 18). Rod Stewart say's he's sorry. *Rolling Stone*, p. 50.

Ross, Deborah. (1995, April 14). Do ya think I'm sexy? *Daily Mail*, p. 6.

Sweeting, Adam. (1995, April 17). Jack the lad rocks on: Rumours that Rod Stewart is retiring are premature. *Guardian*, p. T6.

Thompson, Dave. (1992, May 15). Rod Stewart's early years: The story that every picture tells. *Goldmine*, p. 8.

White, Timothy. (1990). *Rock Lives: Profiles & Interviews* (pp. 317-27). New York: Henry Holt.

THE TEMPTATIONS. *Dennis Edwards Jr. (February 3, 1943); Melvin Franklin (David English; October 12, 1942 - February 23, 1995) Eddie Kendricks (Edward James Kendricks; December 17, 1939 - October 5, 1992); David Ruffin (Davis Eli Ruffin; January 18, 1941 - June 1, 1991); Otis Williams (Otis Miles; October 30, 1949); Paul Williams (July 2, 1939 - August 17, 1973); Inducted in 1989.* With their soulful harmonies and tight stage choreography, the Temptations were Motown's most prolific male group. Moving to Detroit in the late 1950s, Birmingham native Eddie Kendricks joined former high school classmate, guitarist Paul Williams, in a Milton Jenkins-managed doo-wop group, the Primes.

Meanwhile, Elbridge Bryant and Texas-native Otis Williams (no relation to Paul) and had formed the Elegants in Detroit in 1957. Joined in 1959 by former Wayne State student Melvin Franklin, his cousin Richard Street, and Albert Harrell, the group was became the Questions. Renamed the Distants, the group first recorded for Northern Records.

After Milton Jenkins signed the Distants to a management deal, he combined the group with the Primes. Following the departure of member Richard Street, the Primes signed a recording contract with 20-year-old Berry Gordy Jr.'s fledgling label, Motown Records. Renamed the Temptations in 1961, the group landed a moderate R&B hit the following year with "Dream Come Home." The headlining act of grueling tours called Motown Revues, the Temptations struggled for three years to achieve stardom. With Bryant quitting the group in 1963, Gordy replaced him with Motown session drummer David Ruffin.

Beginning their long collaboration with songwriter and producer Smokey Robinson, the Temptations' efforts paid off in 1964 with "The Way You Do the Things You Do." Their first crossover pop hit, the song featured Kendricks' mild-falsetto-styled tenor vocal.

With the Temptations moving away from a doo-wop sound, Ruffin assumed most of the lead vocal duties, taking the group in a soul direction, beginning with the Robinson-penned "My Girl" (which was initially intended for the Miracles). Opening with James Jamerson's memorable bass line, the song came to define the Motown sound.

Groomed by the Motown hit factory, the choreographed Temptations scored a string of top-10 Robinson-produced hits with "Ain't Too Proud to Beg" (1966), "Beauty Is Only Skin Deep" (1966), "(I Know) I'm Losing You" (1966), "All I Need"

(1967), "You're My Everything" (1967), and "I Wish It Would Rain" (1968). Featuring Kendricks on lead vocals, the Temptations scored a collaborative hit with Diana Ross and the Supremes in 1968 with "I'm Going to Make You Love Me."

Following the firing of the headstrong David Ruffin in 1968, new lead singer Dennis Edwards took the group in a rock direction. With their updated approach, the Temptations' top-10 hit run continued with "Cloud Nine" (1968), "Run Away Child, Running Wild" (1969), "I Can't Get Next to You" (1969), "Psychedelic Shack" (1970), and "Ball of Confusion" (1970).

Again switching gears, the Temptations returned to their soul roots in the early 1970s with the ballad "Just My Imagination." But by year's end both Paul Williams and Eddie Kendricks would leave the group, Kendricks to pursue a moderately successful solo career ("Keep on Truckin'"), and Williams due to an alcohol problem (he died two years later). Mirroring Motown's decline, the Temptations scored their last major hits in 1973 with the socially conscious, urban lament "Papa Was a Rollin' Stone" and an edited version of a 14-minute album-track "Masterpiece."

After hiring a series of replacement lead singers, the Temptations faded from the charts. After Gordy tried unsuccessfully to claim legal ownership of the group's name, the Temptations (minus Edwards, who left for a solo career) joined Atlantic Records in 1977). Poorly received with their disco-styled material, the Temptations were dropped by Atlantic in 1980.

With Edwards returning, the Temptations rejoined Motown in 1980 with little fanfare. Two years later, Kendricks and Ruffin returned for the *REUNION* album and a subsequent oldies tour. With the box office success of the 1983 film, *The Big Chill*, the Temptations enjoyed renewed interest. With Ollie Woodson replacing Edwards on lead vocals, the Temptations landed a comeback hit in 1984 with "Treat Her like a Lady" (1984), taken from the album *TRULY FOR YOU.*

Leaving the Temptations, Ruffin and Kendrick (now no s) teamed with blue-eyed soul duo Daryl Hall and John Oates in 1985 on the surprise hit album *LIVE AT THE APOLLO*. Parlaying the success into a record contract, Ruffin and Kendrick were signed by RCA. Unable to sustain a comeback, Ruffin died in 1991; Kendrick passed away a year later.

Meanwhile, Otis Williams and Melvin Franklin continued to operate a touring version of the Temptations. But with Franklin's death in 1995, Williams remained the last living original member of the group. In 1998 Williams was awarded the sole legal right to perform as the Temptations in a lawsuit against Dennis Edwards.

Bibliography

Aletti, Vince. (1992, December). The Temptations: The early years (1960-1973). *Goldmine*, p. 106.

Kiersh, Edward. (1986). *Where Are You Now, Bo Diddley?* (pp. 380-87). Garden City, NY: Doubleday.

Robinson, Louie. (1975, July). The Temptations: Singing group sets new goals. *Ebony*, p. 114.

Sbarbori, Jack. (1980, October). The way they do the things they do: The story of the Temptations. *Goldmine*, p. 11.

Taraborrelli, J. Randy. (1986). *Motown: Hot Wax, City Cool & Solid Gold* (pp. 89-95). New York: Dolphin/Doubleday.

ALLEN TOUSSAINT. *(Allen R. Toussaint; January 14, 1938). Inducted in the Non-Performer category in 1998.* A prolific songwriter and producer, Allen Toussaint shaped New Orleans R&B in the 1960s on hundreds of singles and albums. Influenced by his father, a railroad worker and weekend trumpet player, Toussaint became fascinated with music after his sister was given a piano by their aunt. But Toussaint quit piano lessons after two months, preferring to learn by watching his sister play classical music. By the age of ten Toussaint began composing jazz flavored instrumentals.

Influenced by New Orleans' legendary boogie-woogie pianist Professor Longhair, the 13-year-old Toussaint joined several neighborhood friends in forming a jazz combo, the Flamingos (not the popular doo-wop group). Landing a pair of lucky breaks, Toussaint toured in a band backing teenage R&B duo Shirley and Lee, and as a replacement for an ailing Huey Smith in a popular group led by Earl King. Frequenting the city's many nightclubs, the teenage Toussaint joined the house band at New Orleans' famed Dew Drop Inn as a result of his ability to mimic the popular R&B hits of the day.

Hired as a session player under the tutelage of legendary producer and bandleader Dave Bartholomew, Toussaint honed his abilities, appearing on the records of Smiley Lewis, Lloyd Price, and Fats Domino. Attempting a solo career, Toussaint recorded for RCA-Victor in 1958 under the moniker Al Tousan. An all-instrumental album, *WILD SOUNDS OF NEW ORLEANS*, sold poorly but was highlighted by a Toussaint co-composition "Java," a career-making hit for trumpeter Al Hirt in 1964.

Hired in 1960 as the music director of the new Minit Records, Toussaint adapted skillfully to his new roles of producer, songwriter, and session pianist. Employing his trademark funky, danceable, piano-based sound, Toussaint landed his first number-one hit with Ernie K-Doe's "Mother-in-Law" (1961). Other success followed, including, Jessie Hill's "Ooh Poo Pah Doo," Chris Kenner's "I Like It Like That," Benny Spellman's "Lipstick Traces," Aaron's Neville's "Over You," and several hits for his favorite singer, Irma Thomas.

As a songwriter, Toussaint was responsible for a host of R&B classics including "Mother-In-Law," "Ruler of My Heart" and Herb Alpert's "Whipped Cream" (also known as *The Dating Game* theme song). Many of Toussaint's compositions were credited to his mother, Naomi Neville.

After returning from a two year stint in the Army, Toussaint left Minit Records and teamed with record industry veteran Marshall Sehorn, to form Sansu Enterprises. Toussaint's first move was to sign the Meters as the label's house band. Minit's greatest success came with auto mechanic-turned-singer Lee Dorsey who landed a string Toussaint-composed hits, including "Ride Your Pony" and "Working in a Coal Mine." Solo artist Aaron Neville (the brother of the Meters' keyboardist Arthur Neville) landed in the top-10 with the Toussaint-produced "Tell It Like It Is" (1966). Toussaint subsequently opened the now famed New Orleans studio, Sea-Saint, the popular facility used by Paul McCartney, Joe Cocker, Paul Simon, Sandy Denny, Patti LaBelle, and Ramsey Lewis.

Continuing his hit run into the 1970s, Toussaint produced a pair of breakthrough albums for New Orleans veteran Dr. John, including the top-10 seller, *RIGHT*

PLACE, WRONG TIME. Toussaint subsequently joined Dr. John on his 1973 tour as backing keyboardist. Two years later, Toussaint landed another chart-topper when he produced LaBelle's disco smash, "Lady Marmalade."

Although he had the ability to make stars of others, the soft-spoken Toussaint fared poorly in his own solo ventures. Signing with Reprise Records, his much-ignored 1972 album, *LIFE, LOVE AND FAITH*, featured the musical backing of the Meters and was highlighted by the dance-club hit "Soul Sister." A follow-up album entitled *SOUTHERN NIGHTS* (1975) sold poorly but spawned a cover hit for Glen Campbell. Given a country-tinged treatment, Campbell's rendition of "Southern Nights" was voted the Country Music Association's song of the year.

Turning to stage musicals, Toussaint provided the score for the 1987 off-Broadway production *Staggerlee*. Starring in the popular 1992 Broadway revue *The High Rollers Social and Pleasure Club*, Toussaint showcased the musical heritage of New Orleans.

Launching a new label NYNO (short for New York/New Orleans) to promote New Orleans talent, Toussaint's first releases were by Wallace Johnson and Amadee Castenell. He also released his first solo album in nearly two decades, *CONNECTED* (1996).

Bibliography

Christensen, Thor. (1996, May 23). The patience of Toussaint; Modest artist is New Orleans' best-kept secret. *Dallas Morning News*, p. 5C.
Gaul, Emily. (1997, November 21). Allen Toussaint: A chat with the New Orleans piano master. *Goldmine*, p. 32.
Himes, Geoffrey. (1996, August 7). Bounty of blue notes: Toussaint puts the big easy in the spotlight. *Washington Post*, p. C7.
Lipp, Marty. (1996, July 26). Spreading around that Bayou beat. *(New York) Newsday*, p. B23.
Wallach, Allan. (1992, April 21). Bourbon Street meets Broadway. *(New York) Newsday*, part II, p. 47.

IKE & TINA TURNER. *Ike Turner (Izear Luster Turner; November 5, 1931); Tina Turner (Anna Mae Bullock; November 26, 1939). Inducted in 1991.* While Ike and Tina Turner each enjoyed successful solo runs, their tumultuous two-decade relationship was legendary for its creative output. Unlike Tina Turner, Ike spent his formative years pursuing working in bands. Raised in the Delta town of Clarksdale, Mississippi, Ike Turner possessed a natural musical talent. Encouraged by his mother, who scrimped to pay for formal lessons, Turner studied under legendary pianist Pinetop Perkins. By 1947, the teenage Turner was spinning blues records on WROX in Clarksdale.

Born out of the ashes of his high school jazz group, the Tophatters, Turner formed a popular regional jump-blues group, the Kings of Rhythm. Recording at the Sam Phillips-owned Memphis Recording Service (soon renamed Sun Records), Turner led his band on piano on a groundbreaking record "Rocket 88" (1951), with the master sold to Chess Records. Often considered the first rock and roll song, the chart-topping R&B single featured Willie Kizart's prominent electric guitar. Enraging Turner, Chess instead chose to credit the record to the vocalist Jackie Brenston.

Hired in 1952 as a talent scout for the Los Angeles-based Modern Records, Turner traveled through the South recording a number of undiscovered R&B and blues acts. Returning to Memphis in 1953, Turner assumed a similar role for Sam Phillips and his new Sun Records.

Relocating to St. Louis in 1954, Ike Turner and his Kings of Rhythm were soon the city's top drawing band, competing with a rival band led by Chuck Berry. Performing at the Club Manhattan in East St. Louis, there Turner met his future wife, 18-year-old Anna Mae Bullock.

A native of Nutbush, Tennessee, Bullock spent her summers picking cotton with her sharecropper family. Following her parent's divorce, Bullock joined her mother in St. Louis. Frequenting the Club Manhattan, Bullock was angered by Turner's repeated refusals to let her sing. Finally grabbing the microphone one night during an intermission without the band's permission, the church-trained Bullock impressed Ike Turner. Occasionally singing with Turner's band for the next two years as "Little Anna," Bullock dated a backing band member before hooking up with Turner.

Marrying Bullock, Ike Turner gave her a new stage name, Tina, and a new, glitzy stage persona. The renamed Ike & Tina Turner scored a million-selling hit at Sue Records in 1960 with "A Fool in Love." A huge draw in the black community, the Turners churned out sweaty soul hits with, "I Idolize You" (1960), "It's Gonna Work Out Fine" (1961), "Poor Fool" (1961), and "Tra La La La La" (1962). While Ike was content to stay in the background and direct his gritty R&B-styled band, the long-legged Tina Turner would steal the show, strutting across the stage in her outrageous, form-fitting outfits.

Signed by producer Phil Spector for his Philles Record label, Ike & Tina Turner recorded what was intended as Spector's crowning achievement, the dramatic "River Deep—Mountain High." While Ike Turner's name appeared on the record, he was not present at the recording sessions. Although a hit in England, the song was sabotaged by U.S. deejays who had tired of Spector's egotism. "River Deep" was ignored by R&B stations for being too pop-oriented.

Opening for the Rolling Stones in 1969, Ike & Tina Turner gained a new fanbase, recording soul-oriented versions of rock songs. Their 1971 updating of CCR's "Proud Mary" won the duo their first Grammy. Emerging as a star apart from Ike, Tina Turner pursued a separate solo career, releasing the autobiographical *NUTBUSH CITY LIMITS* and *THE ACID QUEEN*, the latter album named for her character in the rock film *Tommy*.

But with Ike allegedly abusing Tina, tensions between the couple grew unbearable. After walking out on Ike onstage in Dallas in 1976, Tina traded all her future royalty rights in exchange for the right to use her stage name. Returning to nightclub work a year later, Tina Turner initially drew small audiences.

But aided by new manager Roger Davies, Turner scored a British duet hit with synthesizer band, Heaven 17. Experiencing a major comeback in 1984, Turner scored a series of rock-flavored smashes from her major-label debut, *PRIVATE DANCER*, the album selling 11 million copies worldwide. Topping the charts with "What's Love Got to Do with It?" Turner became the oldest woman to land a number-one single.

Still strutting across stages in a frilled microdress, Turner continued to proudly display her remarkably shapely legs.

Co-starring with Mel Gibson in the futuristic film *Mad Max beyond Thunderdome*, Turner also landed a top-10 hit with the film's theme, "We Don't Need Another Hero" (1985). Embraced by rock fans, Turner recorded hit duets with rockers Bryan Adams and Eric Clapton.

Meanwhile, Ike Turner faded from prominence, experiencing numerous brushes with the law. Freed from jail in 1991 after a two-year stint for cocaine possession, Turner had finally beaten his three-decade long drug addiction. The film *What's Love Got to Do with It* (1993) was based on Tina Turner's scathing autobiography, *I, Tina*. Starring Angela Bassett as Tina and Laurence Fishburne as Ike, the project portrayed ex-husband Ike (who claims to have never viewed the film) as a manipulative, crazed wife beater.

Bibliography

Collier, Aldore. (1993, July). What's love got to do with it. *Ebony*, p. 110.

Fong-Tores, Ben. (1971, October 14). The world's greatest heartbreaker. *Rolling Stone*, p. 37.

Hoerburger, Rob. (1993, June 20). The power of love. *The New York Times*, sect. 6, p. 20.

Norment, Lynn. (1996, September), Living my wildest dream: Tina. *Ebony*, p. 38.

Palmer, Robert. (1993, June 27). Commentary: What Ike had to do with it. *Los Angeles Times*, Calendar sect., p. 3.

Propes, Steve. (1989, November 3). I like Ike: The Ike Turner interview. *Goldmine*, p. 22.

BIG JOE TURNER. *(Joseph Vernon Turner; May 18, 1911 - November 24, 1985). Inducted in 1987.* "He could sing over an entire brass section without a microphone" (p. 73), Atlantic Records founder Ahmet Ertegun told writer Joe Smith. With his spirited, upbeat, shouting baritone voice, Big Joe Turner pioneered rhythm and blues in the 1930s before shifting to rock and roll in the 1950s. Born in Kansas City, Missouri, Turner grew up listening to his mother's blues records. He acquired his musical skills during his childhood while assisting a pair of blind street singers in collecting their tip money, and later accompanying one of them on vocals.

Breaking both of his legs at 12 while escaping a burning building, Turner was told he would never walk again. Miraculously, he quickly recovered. After his father's sudden death, Turner dropped out of school, taking restaurant jobs to support his family.

Sneaking into Kansas City music clubs at age 16, the tall and skinny Turner would pester boogie-woogie pianist Pete Johnson in letting him sing a few songs. Later working as a bartender, Turner would alternate between pouring drinks and shouting blues from behind the bar. The team of Johnson and Turner soon became a fixture in the city's thriving jazz circuit. With his sensuality and good looks, 20-year-old Turner would win the hearts of female patrons on tours through the Midwest and East Coast.

Returning to Kansas City, Turner and Johnson worked a long residency at the Sunset Club. Spotted by record producer John Hammond in 1938, Turner headed to New York City to appear in the landmark "From Spirituals To Swing" concert at

Carnegie Hall.

A huge draw during the war years, Turner often recorded and performed with Johnson and other boogie-woogie-style pianists Albert Ammons and Meade "Lux" Lewis. With his powerful jump-blues vocals, Turner scored hits with "Roll 'Em Pete" (1938), "Cherry Red" (1939), and "Wee Baby Blues" (1941). Later in 1941, Turner joined Duke Ellington Orchestra's "Jump for Joy" revue. After providing music for a pair of film shorts in 1944, the following year Turner earned a three-year contract with National Records, his hits continuing with "My Gal's a Jockey" and "Mad Blues."

Turner and Johnson stayed in New York, riding out the boogie-woogie craze until its end in the mid-1940s. Moving to Los Angeles, the pair opened the Blue Room Club, before parting in the late 1940s.

During R&B's infancy, Turner recorded for a variety of small labels, enjoying a revival hit in 1950 with "Still in the Dark." At Imperial, Turner was teamed with a little-known pianist named Fats Domino. After a mismatched stint as a singer in Count Basie's Orchestra, Turner was signed by longtime fan Ahmet Ertegun to Atlantic Records.

Adding a strong, danceable beat to his 1930s boogie-woogie, up-tempo, jump blues, Turner emerged as a ready-made rock star. A sharp dresser and confident performer, the 50-year-old singer became an unlikely teen favorite. At Atlantic, Turner unleashed a string of hits with the million-selling "Chains Of Love" (1951); with its Dixieland groove, "Honey Hush" (1953); with its bawdy double-entendre lyrics, "Shake, Rattle, and Roll" (1954); "Flip, Flop and Fly" (1955); and an updated version of his 1941 Decca recording, "Corrine Corrina" (1956).

A frequent victim of the cover record phenomenon, Turner watched as white acts landed on the pop charts with his material. While Pat Boone recorded a sappy rendition of "Chains of Love," Bill Haley tried to sanitize Turner's "Shake, Rattle, and Roll" by removing the sexual references.

A strong draw in the mid-1950s, Turner appeared in the 1956 quickie rock film named after his hit, *Shake, Rattle, and Roll*, and joined several Alan Freed revues. Teaming with his ailing former partner in 1956, Turner and Johnson recorded an album of their old hits, *BOSS OF THE BLUES: JOE TURNER SINGS KANSAS CITY JAZZ*.

Enjoying another revival during the blues boom in the late 1960s, Turner toured internationally and recorded several albums on Pablo Records. While Turner's voice remained powerful, his vocalizations were getting harder to understand. Turner experienced renewed interest in 1978 when the Blues Brothers recorded "Flip, Flop and Fly."

Outliving all of his contemporaries, Turner was still working until two months before his death in 1985. A 300-pound diabetic who liked to drink, he succumbed to a stroke and kidney failure.

Bibliography
"Big Joe Turner." (1986, January 16). *Rolling Stone*, p. 14.
"Boss of the blues." (1954, March). *Ebony*, p. 102.

Harrington, Richard. (1985, December 1). His shouts were heard: Big Joe Turner's rock foundation. *Washington Post*, p. G1.

Smith, Joe. (1988). *Off the Record* (pp. 73-75). New York: Warner.

VELVET UNDERGROUND. *John Cale (December 4, 1940); Sterling Morrison (August 29, 1942 - August 30, 1995); Lou Reed (Louis Firbank; March 2, 1943); Moe Tucker (Maureen Tucker; 1945). Inducted in 1996.* In spite of their lack of commercial success, the Velvet Underground influenced an entire generation of rockers, at the same time providing the basis for the rise of punk-rock in the 1970s.

A trained trumpeter, Sterling Morrison attended Syracuse University for two semesters, where in 1964 he met literature major and poet, Lou Reed. After graduating, Reed worked as a songwriter for Pickwick Records, and brought in multi-instrumentalist John Cale, a classically trained viola player from Wales. Reed, Cale, and two others were also delegated by Pickwick to tour as a manufactured top-40 group called the Primitives.

After leaving Pickwick, guitarists Reed and Morrison formed their own band. Hiring Cale on bass and electric viola and Angus MacLise on drums, the group played its first paid concert for shocked students at a high school dance. MacLise soon quit and was replaced in the summer of 1965 by a friend of Reed's, the androgynous New Jersey-born Maureen "Moe" Tucker, hired because she owned an amplifier. Supplementing her $50 J.C. Penney drum kit, Tucker beat on garbage can lids and other unorthodox percussion instruments.

Going through a series of name changes, the group finally settled on Velvet Underground, taken from a book about New York's S&M scene, *The Velvet Underground* by Michael Leigh. But early audiences were hostile toward the group. Recalls Morrison in the punk-rock tome, *From the Velvets to the Voidoids*: "The murmur of surprise that greeted our appearance as the curtain went up increased to a roar of disbelief once we started to play 'Venus,' and swelled to a mighty howl of outrage and bewilderment by the end of 'Heroin'" (Clinton, p. 13).

Performing at Greenwich Village's Cafe Bizarre, the Velvet Underground (VU) impressed Pittsburgh-born artist Andy Warhol. Hired as their manager, he financed a new sound system and gave them rehearsal space. He also directed the group in a series of controversial multimedia shows called the Exploding Plastic Inevitable. In spite of Reed's objections, Warhol expanded the group with the addition of Nico, an attractive, German-born fashion model whose claim to fame was a bit part in the Fellini film *La Dolce Vita*.

Signing with MGM/Verve Records in 1966, the group's debut album, *THE VELVET UNDERGROUND AND NICO*, was a critical success but a commercial failure. Reed wrote most of the songs, including, specifically for Nico, the ballads "Femme Fatale" and "I'll Be Your Mirror." Other tracks were shocking for the time: "All Tomorrow's Parties" and rock's first blatantly drug-oriented song, "Heroin."

In 1968, Reed fired Warhol, with the rest of the group dismissing Nico. After the September 1968 release of VU's second album, *WHITE LIGHT/WHITE HEAT*, Cale also left, tired of feuding with Reed, and was replaced by bassist Doug Yule. VU took a slight commercial turn with their follow-up, *THE VELVET UNDERGROUND*, the album highlighted by "Pale Blue Eyes."

After MGM/Verve dropped the group in 1969, a pregnant Tucker quit and was replaced by Yule's brother, Billy. Moving to Atlantic Records, which demanded a more commercial project, the group released *LOADED* (1970), the album highlighted by the original versions of later Lou Reed solo hits "Sweet Jane" and "Rock Roll." Reed soon left the band, and was followed by Morrison. After Moe Tucker's return in 1972, VU recorded the album, *SQUEEZE*, before disbanding the following year.

VU members had various levels of success. Cale and Reed made a series of critically acclaimed albums, with Reed garnering the greatest acclaim with hits such as the heavily censored, David Bowie-produced "Walk on the Wild Side" (1972) and a live, bluesy version of "Sweet Jane" (1974). The struggling Nico was usually produced by Cale and frequently teamed with Brian Eno. Morrison, who returned to academe to earn a Ph.D., recorded a single solo album. Tucker became a housewife, and once worked at Wal-Mart, before returning to music in the 1980s. Both Nico and Warhol died in 1988.

Lou Reed and John Cale performed at a Warhol tribute in 1989, the songs captured on the album *SONGS FOR 'DRELLA*. But after performing "Heroin" at a second Warhol tribute, Velvet Underground regrouped in 1993 for a reunion tour and subsequent live album, *LIVE MCMXCIII*. But with Reed and Cale bickering over the group's direction, a scheduled studio album never materialized. Tucker and Morrison subsequently teamed for an album and tour.

Morrison died in 1995 and was eulogized by the surviving members at their induction into the Rock and Roll Hall of Fame. Neither Nico nor Andy Warhol were inducted as part of the group. Tucker guested on Cale's computer-driven 1996 album *WALKING ON LOCUSTS*, which was highlighted by the Morrison tribute "Some Friends."

Bibliography

Davis, Francis. (1990, April). Infamous: Lou Reed and John Cale, still the antithesis of good vibes. *The Atlantic*, p. 89.

Flanagan, Bill. (1989, April). White light white heat. *Musician*, p. 74.

Fricke, David. (1989, May 4). Lou Reed: The Rolling Stone interview *Rolling Stone*, p. 5.

Gore, Joe. (1994, February). The Velvet Underground. *Guitar Player*, p. 19.

Heylin, Clinton. (1993). *From the Velvets to the Voidoids: A Pre-Punk History for a Post-Punk World*. New York: Penguin.

Roberts, Chris. (1988, July 30). Femme Fatale. *Melody Maker*, p. 36.

GENE VINCENT. *(Eugene Vincent Craddock; February 11, 1935 - October, 12, 1971). Inducted in 1998.* Cool and confident, pioneering rockabilly idol, Gene Vincent, spawned a host of imitators in the late 1950s. A native of Norfolk, Virginia, Vincent dropped out of high school and enlisted in the Navy during the Korean War by lying about his age. In the service he entertained fellow troops by playing country songs on his guitar.

After nearly losing a leg in a motorcycle accident, Vincent was discharged from the service. During a six-month hospital stay, he paid fellow patient Donald Graves $25 for the rights to a composition "Be-Bop-A-Lula," the song based on the Little Lulu comic strip.

Occasionally sitting in with the house band at Norfolk radio station WCMS, Vincent impressed deejay Bill "Sheriff Tex" Davis, with his Elvis Presley imitation. Davis sent a demo of Vincent's act to Capitol records, which was desperately searching for a challenge to Elvis. Poised for stardom, Vincent possessed good looks, sharp clothes, and a James Dean persona.

Released as the A-side of his debut single, "Woman Love" (1956) was banned by the BBC and some U.S. radio stations for its sexual content. But the B-side, "Be-Bop-a-Lula," was an instant smash, with its frenetic vocals, prominent guitarwork and grinding beat. Vincent's backing band, the Blue Caps, sported early guitar wizard Cliff Gallup and, later, Johnny Meeks. Though still on crutches and wearing a cast, Vincent maintained a heavy concert schedule.

Vincent's followup hits included "Blue Jean Bop" (1956) and "Lotta Lovin'" (1957). With his cast painted to match his pant leg, Vincent garnered exposure in a pair of rock films, *The Girl Can't Help It* (1956) starring Jane Mansfield and *Hot Rod Gang* (1958).

On the concert road for two solid years, Vincent did not allow his injured leg time to heal. To combat the pain, he developed a two-bottle a day aspirin habit. Eventually the cast was replaced by a life-long brace.

With the decline in the popularity of rockabilly music, Vincent's last U.S. hit came in 1958 with "Dance to the Bop." Additionally, Capitol's inexperience with rock music hastened his downfall. A victim of sloppy management, Vincent had realized little profit during this period. Penniless, and his house confiscated by the I.R.S., Vincent was also unable to pay his musicians. Temporarily losing his union card, he was left with a band.

Remaining popular overseas, reformed his band with new guitarist Jerry Merritt, Vincent and the Blue Caps were greeted by 10,000 screaming fans at a Japanese airport. But midway through the tour, a homesick Vincent returned to the U.S., leaving Merritt (who physically resembled Vincent) to complete the sold-out tour.

Vincent and singer Eddie Cochran had similar success in their sold-out tour of England in 1960. But tragedy struck the pair on April 17, 1960 when their chauffeur-driven car crashed, killing Cochran and reinjuring Vincent's leg. Emotionally distraught over the death of his close friend, Vincent blamed himself for the incident.

While America's taste for rockabilly music had waned, Britain remained a sanctuary for many of the artists. Moving to England, Vincent gradually adopted a British accent. Recording at London's EMI studio, Vincent scored several British chart hits beginning with "Pistol Packin' Mama."

Returning to the U.S. in 1965, Vincent began to drink more heavily. Admitted to a veteran's hospital in 1966, Vincent refused his doctor's advice to amputate his troubled leg. Enjoying renewed interest during the early rock revival in the late 1960s, Vincent performed at Toronto Rock & Roll Festival, sharing the bill with Chuck Berry, Little Richard, the Plastic Ono Band, and the Doors. Onstage Vincent was backed by Alice Cooper and his band.

Poised for a comeback, Vincent assembled a top-notch studio group for the recording *I'M BACK AND I'M PROUD*. But the album bombed, as did a pair of followup releases. After completing two tours through England in 1971, the despondent Vincent died from a burst ulcer at his California home. Commenting on Vincent's demise, former Blue Cap drummer Dickie Harrell told the *Los Angeles Times*, "Changes in management, changes in the band, trouble with record labels, promoters, [and] women messed him up. All that drinking he did—it all takes its toll. I've heard people say he got pretty rowdy toward the end."

Vincent's "Be-Bop-A-Lula" became a rock standard and has been recorded by countless acts including Elvis Presley, John Lennon, Jerry Lee Lewis, and was the highlight of Paul McCartney's *MTV Unplugged* concert. With the rise of the Stray Cats and other neo-rockabilly artists, Vincent's music experienced a revival in the 1980s. British guitarist Jeff Beck released *CRAZY LEGS*, an entire album of Vincent material in 1993.

Bibliography

Davis, Hank. (1989, September 8). Gene Vincent: Race with the devil *Goldmine*, p. 8.
DeWitt, Dennis. (1992, Fall). Gene Vincent never stopped rockin'. *Blue Suede News*, p. 6.
Seigal, Buddy. (1996, August 17). Propagating the rockabilly gene. *Los Angeles Times*, p. F2.
Shapiro, Craig. (1997, January 21). Vindicating Vincent. *The (Norfolk) Virginian-Pilot*, p. E1.
Smallwood, Sue. (1993, November 26). Gene Vincent's crazy times. *Goldmine*, p. 14.

T-BONE WALKER. *(Aaron Thibeaux Walker; May 28, 1910 - March 16, 1975). Inducted in the Early Influence category in 1987.* Bluesman extraordinaire T-Bone Walker has been called the first guitar hero. The son of a lumberyard worker, Walker was born in Linden, Texas. When Walker's father announced his intentions to become a farmer, his mother left for Dallas, taking two-year-old Walker with her. At age 8, Walker was picking up tips on sidewalks for bluesman Blind Lemon Jefferson, a close family friend. Though exposed to gospel music at a Holiness Church, at age 10 Walker regularly joined his stepfather's blues group as a singer and dancer.

Taught the ukulele and then guitar by his mother, Walker began his professional musical career in 1925. At 14, he joined a traveling medicine show; at 17, he was hired in a revue led by blues singer Ida Cox, as a dancer and banjo player. Returning to Dallas, he joined the 16-piece Lawson Brooks Band as a banjo player, on his travels meeting future jazz guitar legend Charlie Christian.

Winning a talent contest sponsored by Cab Calloway in 1929, Walker briefly performed around Dallas with the bandleader. A week-long stint with Calloway was followed by a one-time recording session at Columbia Records. Backed by pianist Douglas Fernell, Walker recorded "Trinity River Blues" in 1929 under the name Oak Cliff T-Bone.

Receiving lessons from the same instructor in Oklahoma City, Walker teamed up with Charlie Christian for occasional performances around the city. At the time, both were still playing unamplified, acoustic instruments.

Moving to California in 1936 to please his wife, Walker was hired by bandleader Big Jim Wynn. Though initially playing an acoustic guitar, Walker bought a Gibson electric guitar in order to be heard over boisterous crowds. (Meanwhile, Charlie Christian soon popularized the electric guitar in the jazz field.) Walker's exposure to Christian and Calloway enabled him to incorporate jazz styles into his upbeat blues, playing hornlike riffs on his guitar.

Walker was hired away from Wynn's band in 1939 by orchestra leader Les Hite. Backed by Hite's group and now recording as T-Bone Walker, he scored his first hit in 1940 with "T-Bone Blues," which featured the electric guitar of Frank Pasley. Walker's stint with Les Hite's jazz orchestra exposed him to the possibilities of blues backed by a full rhythm section.

Joining a band headed by former Will Bradley pianist Freddie Slack at Capitol Records, Walker appeared on a double-sided hit in 1942 with "I Got a Break Baby"/"Mean Old World." But more significantly, Slack's 1943 instrumental hit "Riffette," introduced Walker's soon-to-be-legendary single-string guitar riff.

After the war, Walker made his first recordings under his own name on a series of poorly selling discs for the Chicago-based Rhumboogie label. Instead, Walker's first success came at the Black & White record company, beginning with a song aimed at the burgeoning teenage market, "Bobby Sox Blues" (1947).

Walker's follow-up hit, the groundbreaking "Call It Stormy Monday," was released in 1947. With his trademark single-string guitar solo, Walker emerged as the country's leading blues guitarist. Becoming his signature tune, the blues classic contained one of the most copied guitar riffs in all of R&B and rock history. With the song, Walker established the guitar as the lead instrument in popular music.

Signing Walker in 1950, Capitol also acquired his master recordings from Black & White Records. Walker's polished, blues-guitar playing style soon inspired and influenced a new set of guitarists including Chuck Berry, B.B. King, and Bobby "Blue" Bland.

Enjoying a long string of European tours, Walker traveled to France in 1965 where he was backed by John Mayall's blues group. Returning to the U.S. concert trail in the late 1960s, Walker frequented blues festivals. He won his first Grammy in 1970 for the album *GOOD FEELIN'*.

The Allman Brothers Band's 1971 blues-rock recording of "Call It Stormy Monday" introduced Walker's music to a new generation of rock fans. Suffering a stroke in late 1974, Walker later died of pneumonia in a Los Angeles nursing home.

Bibliography

Burke, Tony & Penny, Dave. (1985, July). Stand up and shout the blues: Big Joe Turner. *Blues & Rhythm*, p. 4.

Gill, Chris. (1995, August). T-Bone Walker: electrifying the blues; electric guitarist. *Guitar Player*, p. 72.

Kofsky, Frank. (1969, October). T-Bone Walker & B.B. King Interview. *Jazz & Pop*, p. 15.

Morthland, John. (1991, April). Jump starter. *Texas Monthly*, p. 68.

Shaw, Arnold. (1978). *Honker and Shouters*. New York: Collier.

"Talented T-Bone Walker." (1953, October). *Ebony*, p. 59.

DINAH WASHINGTON. *(Ruth Lee Jones; August 29, 1924 - December 14, 1963).* *Inducted in the Early Influence category in 1993.* A remarkably versatile singer, Dinah Washington could easily glide from pop and jazz to blues and R&B. Born in Tuscaloosa, Alabama, as Ruth Lee Jones, her mother was a maid, and her father a poker player. Moving north with her family at age five, she was raised on the Chicago's South Side.

While accompanying her music teacher and church pianist mother, Washington learned to play the piano. A fiery singer in her church choir, Washington formed a mother-daughter singing duo, performing throughout Chicago's gospel circuit. At 16, Washington joined the pioneering all-girl, touring gospel group, the Sallie Martin Colored Ladies Quartet.

Without her mother's knowledge, the underage Washington entered and won an amateur talent contest at Chicago's Regal Theater, performing a song she would later record, "I Can't Face the Music." Still in high school, Jones was hired as a coat-check girl at a Chicago nightclub, the Three Deuces. Impressing the club owner with her singing, she first performed with visiting bands. Hired in 1943 by Lionel Hampton for a three-year stint as the lead vocalist of his orchestra, the former Ruth Jones was rechristened Dinah Washington. Abandoning gospel music, Washington devastated her deeply religious mother.

With Decca Records barring Hampton from recording with Washington, music critic Leonard Feather helped her sign with the tiny Keynote Record Company. Backed by a sextet from Hampton's orchestra, Washington landed a pair of blues hits in 1944 with the Leonard Feather-penned "Salty Papa Blues" and "Evil Gal Blues." Parting with Hampton in 1946, Washington's last collaborative hit with his group came the following year with the pop-crossover entry "Blow Top Blues."

Signing with a pair of fledgling independent record companies, Apollo and then Mercury, Washington enjoyed a remarkable 13-year hit run with mostly ballad hits beginning in 1948 with "Ain't Mishavin'" and "West Side Baby." Idolizing Bessie Smith and Billie Holiday, "like Bessie, [Washington] could growl the blues or sing them full-throated and true; like Billie, she played dangerously with phrasing, purposely spitting out the end of the word, chopping it off with a constant attack that hung over the empty gap, and creating tension for the start of the next line which, by contrast, might be lazy or soft" (p. 148), wrote author Robyn Archer.

Notorious for her offstage behavior, the gun-toting Washington was a formidable, outspoken, assertive woman who terrified promoters, nightclub owners, and many fellow musicians with her temper. With her salty language, the quick-witted singer brought a bold sense of humor to her performances. Possessing a voracious appetite for husbands and lovers, once she physically attacked one of her nine husbands onstage.

Unlike her contemporaries, Washington recorded a number of cover versions of white pop hits, including "Wheel of Fortune" (1952), a hit for both Sunny Gale and Kay Starr; and "I Don't Hurt Anymore" (1953), originally a country hit for Hank Snow. Nonetheless, Mercury refused to market her records to pop audiences.

Under the guidance in the late 1950s of producer Clyde Otis, Washington jumped across genre lines, scoring a string of pop hits beginning with her blues-tinged signature ballad "What a Diff'rence a Day Makes" (1959). Although receiving no promotional support from her record company, her pop hit run continued with "Broken Hearted Melody" and a reprise of her earlier R&B hit "Unforgettable." Reluctantly teaming with R&B crooner Brook Benton, whom she constantly criticized in the studio, Washington landed a string of upbeat duet hits, including "Baby (You've Got What It Takes)" (1960) and "A Rockin' Good Way" (1960).

Squandering her earnings and always in need of cash, Washington was lured to Roulette Records in 1961 with a hefty advance. Although her hit run had ended, Washington continued to draw packed houses in the jazz and dinner theater circuit. By the 1960s, Washington also operated a booking agency, a civic welfare group, and a Detroit restaurant. A close friend of the Rev. C.L. Franklin, Washington mentored his daughter Aretha Franklin.

After years of abusing alcohol and diet pills, Washington died while watching television in 1963 at the age of 39. Accidentally overdosing on diet bills, she had wanted to lose weight before an important concert in Chicago. Three decades later, her life story was captured in the musical *Dinah Was*, with Yvette Freeman in the title role. Singer Patti Austin is Washington's goddaughter.

Bibliography

Archer, Robyn & Simmonds, Diana. (1986). *A Star is Torn*. New York: E.P. Dutton.
Bego, Mark. (1989). *Aretha Franklin: The Queen of Soul*. New York: St. Martin's Press.
Giddens, Gary. (1988, February 9). Dinah Washington: The once and future queen. *Village Voice*, p. 85.
Jones, Max. (1988). *Talking Jazz* (pp. 265-76). New York: W.W. Norton.
Saunders, Charles, L. (1964, March). Requiem for Queen Dinah. *Ebony*, p. 146.
Wilson, Evan. (1994, December 4). About the South. *Atlanta Journal and Constitution*, p. M2.

MUDDY WATERS. *(McKinley Morganfield; April 4, 1915 - April 30, 1983). Inducted in the Early Influence category in 1987*. Legendary American blues pioneer who influenced countless of rockers from the Rolling Stones and Beatles to Jimi Hendrix and Led Zeppelin, Muddy Waters played a crucial role in the rise of electrified Chicago blues. Born in Rolling Fork, Mississippi, Waters was sent to live with his maternal grandmother near Clarksdale in 1918, following his mother's death. Born McKinley Morganfield, he was nicknamed Muddy Waters by his grandmother for his penchant of playing in the muddy bank of a nearby creek.

At age 17, Waters built a homemade box guitar; a year later he formed a small blues group. In the mid-1930s, Waters acquired a store-bought instrument and stepped up to playing in a "bottleneck" style, influenced by blues greats Robert Johnson and Son House.

Waters was recorded in 1941 by musicologists Alan Lomax and John Work, near Clarksdale, Mississippi, for the Library of Congress folk music series. Bored with farming and convinced by Lomax to pursue a career in music, Waters left his family for Chicago in 1943.

Befriended by bluesman Big Bill Broonzy, Waters found steady club work. While backing Sonny Boy Williamson, Waters purchased an electric guitar in 1944 so as to be heard over loud, boisterous audiences.

Now a seasoned player, Waters recorded at Aristocrat Records in 1947. But the sessions were shelved for a year by label chiefs Leonard and Phil Chess who felt the tracks held no commercial potential. Finally released, Waters had gone against the urban-blues style of the day, scoring a local smash with "I Can't Be Satisfied," and a national hit with the Delta-styled "(I Feel Like) Going Home" (a reworked version of Son House's "Walking Blues"). With the latter song a huge smash, Waters single-handedly had re-popularized old, Delta-style blues.

As Aristocrat Records evolved into Chess records in 1950, Waters gave the label its first hit with "Rollin' Stone" (1950), a reworked version of Robert Petway's 1941 hit "Catfish Blues." Expanding his band, Waters was joined in the studio by a teenaged harmonica player, Little Walter, who employed a gospel-style call-and-response pattern; and by bassist Willie Dixon, who also provided Waters with many of his compositions. Waters' hits continued with "Louisiana Blues" (1950); "Long Distance Call" (1951); "Honey Bee" (1951); and, with Leonard Chess on drums, "She Moves Me" (1952).

In late 1953, Otis Spann joined Waters' band on piano, initially appearing on "Standing Around Crying." With Waters progressing from a trio to a blues orchestra, his hits continued with the voodoo-inspired Dixon composition "I'm Your Hoochie Coochie Man" (1954); "I Just Wanna Make Love to You" (1954); his last hit with Little Walter, "Mannish Boy" (1955); and "I Got My Mojo Workin'" (1956).

With his shouting vocals becoming the focus of his music, Waters experienced a chart slide. With the rise of rock and the decline of blues, Waters landed his final hit in 1958 with "Close to You."

But with blues resurging in the 1960s, Waters found a new generation of college-age fans. With the emergence of British, blues-based rock, Waters worked with his musical progeny, including the Yardbirds, Eric Burdon, Eric Clapton, and Jimmy Page. Initially a blues cover band, the Rolling Stones, took their moniker from Waters' 1950 hit "Rollin' Stone." Soon, budding American bluesmen like Mike Bloomfield and Paul Butterfield began journeying to South Side Chicago blues clubs in search of Waters, later joining their mentor on the album *FATHERS AND SONS*.

After sustaining serious injuries in a car crash in 1969, Waters was not expected to play again. But a year later, he was back on the concert trail. Waters would win his first Grammy Award in 1971 for the compilation album *THEY CALL ME MUDDY WATERS*.

Waters was joined in 1977 by Texas blues great Johnny Winter as the producer for a pair of retrospective albums *HARD AGAIN* and *I'M READY*. Touring together, Waters and Winter released a collaborative live album in 1979, *MUDDY MISSISSIPPI WATERS LIVE*. Winter also produced Waters' final album, *KING BEE* (1981). Waters died in 1983 of a heart attack.

Bibliography
Obrecht, Jas. (1990). Muddy Waters. In Jas Obrecht (Ed.), *Blues Guitar* (pp. 56-69). San Francisco: GPI.

Obrecht, Jas. (1994, March). Muddy Waters: The life and times of the hoochie coochie man. *Guitar Player*, p. 30.

Palmer, Robert. (1978, October 5). Muddy Waters: The Delta son never sets. *Rolling Stone*, p. 53.

Welding, Pete. (1994, February). Last king of the south side. *Down Beat*, p. 32.

JERRY WEXLER. *(January 10, 1917). Inducted in the Non-Performer category in 1987.* A driving force at Atlantic Records in the 1950s and Stax/Volt in the 1960s, Jerry Wexler discovered and produced the finest in R&B and soul. The son of an upper-class mother and a Polish-Jewish father who worked as a window washer, Wexler was raised in the New York City working-class neighborhoods of Washington Heights and the East Bronx. A rough, sport-loving youth, Wexler cared little for school, preferring to read fiction books. After barely graduating at age 15, Wexler attended college for two semesters during the Depression.

Directionless, Wexler drifted from job to job. Drawn to the big bands of the 1930s and becoming a record collector, he frequented Harlem nightclubs. Frequenting the legendary Savoy nightclub, he later applied what he saw in the recording studio.

Pushed by his strong-willed mother to earn a college degree, Wexler studied journalism at Kansas State in 1936. Whenever possible, Wexler journeyed east to Kansas City's bustling jazz and blues scene, and catch the likes of Big Joe Turner and Pete Johnson mastering their craft. Flunking out of college, Wexler returned to New York City, where he grudgingly joined his father in the window-cleaning business.

Marrying in 1942 to keep from getting drafted, Wexler managed only to delay a military stint. Though never seeing action, Wexler's life was turned around in the army's structured environment. Motivated and channeled, he returned to Kansas State, earning a journalism degree.

Hired in 1947 by BMI, an upstart royalty-collection service, Wexler made many contacts in the music industry. Applying his college degree, Wexler landed a $75-a-week writer's job at *Billboard* magazine, where he was mentored by a fellow jazz and blues fan, music editor Paul Ackerman.

At *Billboard*, Wexler's monumental achievement came in 1949, when the editors adopted his suggestion to change the title of their "Race" music chart to "Rhythm and Blues." Quitting his position in protest in 1951, Wexler had refused to write an incriminating, slanted piece about the left-leaning folk group the Weavers.

Hired as a promotional director for MGM's publishing branch, Big Three, Wexler's duties were to convince record companies, artists, and deejays to record and play his company's compositions. Here he learned the inner workings of the music business.

Wanting to work at a jazz or blues record company, Wexler approached the upsurging New York-based Atlantic Records. But when Wexler boldly demanded a full partnership, a bemused Ahmet Ertegun turned him down. But when Atlantic co-owner Herb Abramson was drafted, Ertegun relented, and Wexler bought his way into the company.

As an active producer, talent scout, and promoter, Wexler played a vital role in the label's success. In the next several years, Atlantic came to dominate the booming R&B industry. Aided by sound engineer Tom Dowd, Wexler produced hits for Ray Charles, LaVern Baker, Etta James, and, from his college days, Big Joe Turner.

When Atlantic Records entered into a distribution deal with the emerging Memphis-based Stax-Volt Records, Wexler took his production skills to the label. Utilizing a studio band built around Booker T. & the MG's, Wexler also produced Atlantic artists like soul singer Wilson Pickett.

Having succeeded at Stax, Wexler journeyed south to Rick Hall's Fame studio in Muscle Shoals, Alabama, first landing a hit with Percy Sledge's "When a Man Loves a Woman." At Muscle Shoals, Wexler bought out session guitarist Duane Allman's recording contract for $15,000, placing him on an Atlantic-distributed label, Capricorn Records.

With Atlantic Records venturing into rock music in the late 1960s, Wexler discovered Vanilla Fudge and Buffalo Springfield. Returning to his soul base, Wexler's biggest signing came in 1966 with Aretha Franklin. Joined by co-producer Arif Mardin, Wexler nurtured the career of the Queen of Soul, a relationship that lasted until 1974.

When Atlantic Records was sold to Warner Brothers/Seven Arts for $17.5 million, Wexler and the majority of Atlantic's staff were retained. Unhappy with Atlantic's hard-rock turn in the late 1960s, Wexler moved to Miami, where he found little success producing groups such as the Dixie Flyers.

Returning to the New York offices of Atlantic in the early 1970s, Wexler was shocked to see his former responsibilities taken over by others. His last major signing came in 1975, acquiring the Average White Band's contract for $10,000.

Working as A&R executive for Warner Brothers (Atlantic's parent label) beginning in 1977, Wexler signed rock acts such as Dire Straits and the B-52's. Though semiretired, Wexler remained active in the music.

Bibliography

Clark, Sue C. (1968, September 28). Wexler: A man of dedications. *Rolling Stone*, p. 8.
Goodman, Fred. (1993, November). Production without style—on purpose: Jerry Wexler. *Musician*, p. 56.
Harrington, Richard. (1985, December 22). The rock of Atlantic: Record czar Ahmet Ertegun, letting the music do the talking. *Washington Post*, p. H1.
Skelly, Richard. (1994, February 4). Jerry Wexler: Mr. Rhythm 'N' Blues. *Goldmine*, p. 36.
Wexler, Jerry & Ritz, David. (1993). *Rhythm and the Blues: A Life in American Music*. New York: Alfred A. Knopf.
White, Timothy. (1980, November 27). Jerry Wexler: The godfather of rhythm & blues. *Rolling Stone*, p. 49.

THE WHO. *Roger Daltrey (March 1, 1944); John Entwistle (John Alec Entwistle; October 9, 1944); Keith Moon (August, 23, 1947 - September 7, 1978); Pete Townshend (Peter Dennis Blandford Townshend; May 19, 1945). Inducted in 1990.* Archetypical mod-rockers, the Who emerged out of the British R&B movement in the early 1960s. Like his future bandmates in the Who, Pete Townshend grew up in a working-class section of London. Raised in a dysfunctional family, he destroyed his first guitar at a young age to anger his grandmother. Switching to the banjo at age 13, Townshend joined trumpet player John Entwistle in a Dixieland group.

Entwistle jumped from the trumpet to bass in 1960 as he joined the Detours, a rock group led by guitarist Roger Daltrey. A former school bully who worked at a steel factory, Daltrey transplanted his tough-guy veneer to the stage. With the departure of the Detours' second guitarist, Pete Townshend was brought in. With Townshend the superior guitarist, Daltrey took over the lead vocal duties.

Jumping on the "mod" bandwagon, the group was renamed the High Numbers (a popular mod expression), and convinced by manager Peter Meaden to cut their hair and don bright, mod clothing. With Meaden fearing the group's drummer was too old to relate to the group's teenage fans, 35-year-old drummer Doug Sandom was fired. When a drunken 17 year old drummer, Keith Moon, asked to practice with the group before a performance at the Oldfield Hotel in Greenford, he was instantly hired. Polished by Fontana Records, the High Numbers released an obscure single, "I'm the Face."

Their contract purchased by new managers, Chip Stamp and film director Kit Lambert, the renamed Who premiered their onstage ritual of smashing their instruments, when Townshend accidentally rammed his guitar into the ceiling at the Railway Hotel in Harrow. At an extended residency at London's famed Marquee club, the nightly destruction of Townshend's guitar drew crowds to the club. Out of economic necessity, Townshend soon began building replacement instruments from salvageable pieces.

Influenced by the Kinks' early work, the Who's forceful debut single, "I Can't Explain" (1965), featured guest guitarist Jimmy Page. A British hit, it originally fared poorly in the U.S., as did the follow-up, "My Generation" (1965). Both tracks appeared on *THE WHO SINGS MY GENERATION*, the album recorded in two days.

An integral part of the British Invasion, the Who landed their first U.S. top-40 hit in early 1967 with "Happy Jack." After earning U.S. exposure at the Monterey Pop Festival and as the opening act for Herman's Hermits, the Who scored their only top-10 pop hit with "I Can See For Miles" (1967) from the album *THE WHO SELL OUT*. The Who's hit run continued with "Call Me Lightning" (1968) and "Magic Bus" (1968).

With the release of the single "Pinball Wizard" in 1969, the Who predated the double-album *TOMMY*, much of which was debuted at their Woodstock performance. Composed primarily by the group's musical genius, Pete Townshend, as an autobiographical account of his tortured childhood, the Who's *TOMMY* was a serious attempt at elevating the stature of rock music. Centered around a deaf, dumb, and blind pinball player, the project spawned the hits "We're Not Gonna Take It," "See Me, Feel Me," and "I'm Free." Promoting *TOMMY* through worldwide performances, the production was eventually staged at the New York Metropolitan Opera House in June 1970, the Who becoming the first rock band to appear at the prestigious venue.

Meanwhile, drummer Keith Moon drew attention to the group with his eccentric antics. Acquiring a reputation for excessive alcohol and drug use, practical jokes, and violent tantrums, in 1970 he once accidentally drove over and killed his chauffeur while escaping from a group of skinheads.

Considered their finest album, *WHO'S NEXT?* (1971) emerged from the remnants of a failed thematic album project. Featuring Townshend's pioneering synthesizer work, the album was highlighted by the rock standards "Baba O'Riley," "Won't Get Fooled Again," and "Behind Blue Eyes." One of most durable rock acts of the 1970s, the Who churned out a series of hit albums, including a second rock opera, *QUADROPHENIA* (1973), highlighted by tracks "Love Reign O'er Me" and "The Real Me"; and *THE WHO BY NUMBERS* (1975), spawning a hit with the bawdy "Squeeze Box."

In 1975, director Ken Russell adapted *TOMMY* to film, starring Roger Daltrey and Ann-Margret, who earned a Best-Actress Oscar nomination. Also appearing in the film was Elton John, who scored a hit with a new recording of "Pinball Wizard."

With the Who experiencing a brief hiatus in the mid-1970s, all four members pursued various solo projects. Moon recorded a surf-styled album with guitarist Dick Dale; Entwistle released solo material and produced the Fabulous Poodles; Townshend joined Ronnie Lane of the Faces on the album *ROUGH MIX*. The most successful of the four, Daltrey scored a hit with his album *RIDE A ROCK HORSE*.

Tragedy struck the Who twice in the late 1970s. First, Keith Moon died at the age of 31 from an accidental drug overdose. The Who suffered another blow on December 3, 1979, when 11 fans were crushed to death at a concert at Cincinnati's Riverfront Stadium.

The Who released two more films: *The Kids Are Alright*, a documentary that combined interview clips and live performances; and based on their rock opera of the same name, *Quadrophenia*, which was set in the British mod movement of the mid-1960s, the film starring Phil Daniels and featuring the Police's Sting.

Pursuing solo projects in the 1980s, the drug-impaired Townshend released his best-seller *EMPTY GLASS* (with the hits "Let My Love Open the Door" and "Rough Boys"), while Daltrey's output was highlighted by the soundtrack to *McVicker*, and his tribute to Keith Moon, *UNDER A RAGING MOON*.

With Townshend beating his drug addiction, The Who enjoying a resurgence in the early 1980s. Leaving Decca/MCA for Warner Brothers, the Who released a pair of hard-rocking albums with *FACE DANCES* (highlighted by "You Better You Bet") and a project Daltrey abhorred, *IT'S HARD*, with its hits "Athena" and "Eminence Front."

Amicably disbanding at the end of 1982, the Who occasionally reunited in the 1980s. Regrouping for a 25th-anniversary tour in 1989 with Simon Phillips on drums, the Who added a horn section and three backup vocalists. Suffering from severe hearing loss, Townshend switched to an acoustic guitar for the tour.

In celebration of the 20th anniversary of the rock opera *Tommy*, The Who reunited for a performance at New York's Radio City Music. While recuperating from a shattered wrist in 1991, Townshend adapted *Tommy* into a Broadway show. Directed by Des McAnuff, the production won a Tony in 1993.

In 1996, the Who took a stage production of *Quadrophenia* on the road, the cast featuring Gary Glitter, Billy Idol, Zak Starkey, and Pete Townshend's younger brother,

Simon. Townshend's next project was to produce a Broadway version of his 1993 solo album, *PSYCHODERELICT*.

Bibliography

Castro, Peter. (1994, February 28). Jammin' with . . . Roger Daltrey: Turning 50, the Dorian Gray of rock discovers he's still a Who at heart. *People*, p. 84.

Flippo, Chet. (1980. January 24). Rock & roll tragedy. *Rolling Stone*, p. 1.

Harrington, Richard. (1993, July 4). Talkin' ' bout his regeneration: after the drugs, the tumult and the Who, Pete Townshend finds new life on Broadway. *Washington Post*, p. G1.

Sharp, Ken. (1994, July 8). Look who's talking: A conversation with Roger Daltrey. Goldmine, p. 16.

Sheff, David. (1994, February). Playboy interview: Pete Townshend. *Playboy*, p. 51.

Smith, Joe. (1988). *Off the Record* (pp. 217-19). New York: Warner.

Thompson, Dave. (1996, September). Quadrophenia—fourth time lucky. *Discoveries*, p. 38.

HANK WILLIAMS. *(Hiram Williams; September 17, 1923). Inducted in the Early Influence category in 1987.* Popularizing danceable, honky-tonk-styled country music, Hank Williams legitimized the genre. Hiram "Hank" Williams was raised during the Depression by his imposing church organist mother, Lillie, after his father was committed to the mental ward of a veterans' hospital.

Drawn to music and Southern religion, Williams was influenced by the moral themes offered by the preacher at his Baptist church. Spurning school at a young age, Williams received an informal musical education from a black, sidewalk, blues guitarist named Rufe "Tee-Tot" Payne.

Acquiring an acoustic guitar, 14-year-old Williams won a talent show, playing his own composition "WPA Blues." Forming the Drifting Cowboys during his teens, Williams was a rowdy and reckless, carrying a steel bar to protect himself during his many bar brawls.

Touring from Texas to Florida, Williams landed a 15-minute radio program at WSFA in Montgomery in 1942. Encouraged by his strong-willed wife, Audrey, Williams moved to the country music capital of Nashville in 1946. Signed as a songwriter by Fred Rose of the powerful Acuff-Rose publishing firm, Williams' early material was recorded by Molly O'Day.

Sensing talent, Acuff-Rose aided Williams in signing with the new MGM label, his first hit coming with the fast-driving "Move It On Over" (1947). A significant country hit, the record landed Williams a spot in the *Louisiana Hayride* radio show.

Like country pioneer Jimmie Rodgers, Williams employed a yodel on his first major hit, a countrified version of a 1922 Tin Pan Alley song, "Lovesick Blues" (1949). Leaving the *Louisiana Hayride* for the legendary Grand Ole Opry stage, Williams formed a new Drifting Cowboys lineup from studio musicians. Also landing his own radio show at WSM, Williams would close his show with the farewell, "If the Good Lord's willing and the creeks don't rise, we'll see you next time—I'm coming Bocephus!"

Becoming a country superstar, Williams sported a traditional, usually all-white western cowboy costume of boots, frayed shirt, and 10-gallon Stetson hat. A skinny man whose ears stuck out, Williams became an unlikely sex symbol. Combining folk, western swing, and country blues, Williams reinvented country music with songs that were meant for dancing and getting drunk. With his pained, wailing, mournful voice, which was drenched in a Dixie accent, Williams sang about heartbreak, womanizing, and hard times. Though not very literate, Williams had a strong grasp of human emotion, his lyrics coming from his personal relationships, including "You're Gonna Change or I'm Gonna Leave" and "Mind Your Business."

Not a big hit at the time, "I Saw the Light" was indicative of Williams' spiritual roots. A God-fearing man, he recorded Christian songs throughout his career, usually under the pseudonym Luke the Drifter.

Williams' country hits continued with "I'm So Lonesome I Could Cry" (1950); spawning a million-selling, breakthrough pop hit cover for Tony Bennett, "Cold, Cold Heart" (1951); and "Hey, Good Lookin'" (1951).

His drinking habit intensifying, Williams divorced his wife Audrey in 1952. Williams drank heavily primarily to ease the constant pain of a spinal injury suffered in a pair of horse-riding accidents. After missing dozens of concerts and radio performances, Williams was fired by the Opry. Writes biographer Jay Caress, "Though Hank's talent still shone through the bleary haze of his booze and drug habits, and though most audiences still loved him and forgave him, he was becoming hard to book" (p. 195).

Remarried, Williams returned to the smaller *Louisiana Hayride*, quitting after two months due to poor health. Scoring a Cajun-flavored hit with, "Jambalaya" Williams enjoyed pop success via several cover versions. Still bitter over his divorce, Williams wrote "Cold, Cold Heart" and the archetypical country song "Your Cheatin' Heart." At the same session, he recorded a novelty song about a cigar-store wooden Indian, "Kaw-Liga."

His body decimated by years of abuse, Williams died at age 29, New Year's Eve, 1953, in the back seat of a Cadillac en route to a concert in Canton, Ohio. His untimely death from hard drinking, womanizing, and drugs made Williams a prototype rock and roller. His rebellious, rough style of country was later embraced by black-hatted country-rock artists like Johnny Cash, Merle Haggard, Waylon Jennings, and Willie Nelson.

Hank Williams Jr. has carried on his father's legacy, even joining him in some electronically synchronized duets in 1965 and again in 1989 with "There's a Tear in my Beer" (which was accompanied by a simulated video). Featuring the vocals of Hank Williams III, the 1996 album *THREE HANKS* featured three generations of Williams singers. To the ire of Hank Jr., Williams' daughter, Cathy Dupree Adkinson (later taking the name Jett Williams), proved her parentage in court, winning a portion of her father's estate.

Bibliography
Blaser, Kent. (1985, Winter). Pictures from life's other side: Hank Williams, country music, and popular culture in America. *South Atlantic Quarterly*, p. 12.
Bull, Derek. (1990, January). Hank Williams. *Record Collector*, p. 79.

Jackie Wilson 329

Caress, Jay. (1979). *Hank Williams: Country Music's Tragic King*. New York: Stein and Day.
Escott, Colin. (1991, June 14). Hank Williams: Long gone lonesome blues. *Goldmine*, p. 8.
Frank, Jeffrey A. (1989, December 3). Her cheated heart. *Washington Post*, Magazine sect., p. 21.
Large, Alan. (1979, June). *Hank Williams*. Goldmine, p. 6.

JACKIE WILSON. *(Jack Leroy Wilson; June 9, 1934 - January 20, 1984)*. *Inducted in 1987*. An all-around entertainer, Jackie Wilson was an explosive force in soul music. Born and raised in Detroit, Wilson earned his musical education as a member of a Baptist church group, the Ever Ready Gospel Singers.

At 16, Wilson lied about his age and entered the boxing ring, soon quitting to appease his mother. An exaggerated Motown bio sheet claimed that Wilson won several championships.

Still using his boxing name, Sonny Wilson, he won a number of talent shows, and released a pair of singles at Dee Gee Record, including the traditional Irish ballad, "Danny Boy" (1952). Later in the year he briefly joined the Thrillers, the forerunners of the Royals/Midnighters. When King Records scout Johnny Otis came to a Detroit talent show, he was impressed by several of the acts. While the Royals had passed their audition, King Records-owner Syd Nathan rejected Wilson.

Determined, Johnny Otis aided Wilson in landing a spot in the Billy Ward-led, hit doo-wop group the Dominoes. Apprenticing under lead singer Clyde McPhatter, Wilson quickly mastered the group's vocal and dance routines. Consequently when McPhatter was abruptly fired in 1953, Wilson stepped up to the first tenor spot, singing lead on "You Can't Keep a Good Man Down" (1953), "Rags to Riches" (1954), and the crossover pop entry "St. Therese Of the Roses" (1956).

Quitting the Dominoes after a fistfight with Billy Ward, Jackie Wilson pursued a solo career. Hiring manager Al Green (not the 1970s singer), Wilson signed with the Decca subsidiary, Brunswick Records. Targeting the pop-crossover market, Brunswick's musical director, Dick Jacobs, teamed Wilson in the studio with white backup singers and a small orchestra.

Wilson landed his first hit with "Reet Petite," co-written with his cousin Billy Davis and boxing friend Berry Gordy Jr. Wilson penned several more compositions, giving Wilson the breakthrough pop hits "To Be Loved" (1958), "Lonely Teardrops" (1958), "That's Why (I Love You So)" (1959), and "I'll Be Satisfied" (1959). Gordy dissolved the writing partnership over a royalty dispute, and launched Motown Records.

Wilson's career was aided by powerful disc jockey Alan Freed. Appearing in Freed's rock flick *Go Johnny Go* (1959), Wilson scored the R&B hit "You Better Know It." An energetic dynamo who wowed audiences with his physical prowess, Wilson earned the nickname "Mr. Excitement." Defying the laws of gravity with his jumps, flips, and full splits, Wilson was later copied by Michael Jackson. Becoming a sex-symbol, Wilson was shot and nearly killed by an obsessive fan in 1961.

Scoring over two dozen chart hits in the 1960s with his searing falsetto, Wilson enjoyed crossover success with "Doggin' Around" (1960); the first of several songs co-written with Alonzo Tucker, "Baby Work Out" (1963); and a new recording of his 1952 release, "Danny Boy" (1965). Wilson also recorded with LaVern Baker, Linda Hopkins, and Count Basie.

Moving to Chicago in 1966, Wilson was teamed with producer Carl Davis, scoring hits with "(Your Love Keeps Lifting Me) Higher and Higher" (1967) and "I Get the Sweetest Feeling" (1968). Receiving few royalties and given substandard material, Wilson refused to record in the late 1960s. His life marred by tragedy, Wilson entered drug rehab in 1968; two years later his son was killed in a burglary attempt.

After joining Dick Clark's popular Las Vegas rock oldies show in 1974, Wilson enlisted in a subsequent touring revue. But on September 25, 1975, Wilson collapsed from a heart attack while performing at the Latin Casino nightclub in Camden, New Jersey. Striking his head on the concrete floor, he quit breathing and suffered permanent brain damage.

Institutionalized, Wilson was nearly forgotten at the time of his death in 1985. While the Spinners raised $60,000 for his medical care, much of the money went for litigation as Wilson's estranged wife, Harlean, battled son Tony over control of the singer's estate. With lawsuits raging, Wilson was buried in an unmarked grave, a fan later raising funds for a tombstone.

Rita Coolidge scored a top-ten cover hit in 1977 with Wilson's "(Your Love Has Lifted Me) Higher and Higher." In 1986, Wilson's "Reet Petite" hit number one in Britain and its follow-up, "I Get the Sweetest Feeling," went top-10. Wilson's goddaughter is singer Jody Watley.

Bibliography

Jacobs, Dick & Holmes, Tim. (1988, January). Jackie Wilson: A producer remembers "Mr. Excitement." *Musician*, p. 21.
James, Etta and Ritz, David. (1995). *The Etta James Story: Rage to Survive*. New York:
Newman, Ralph M. & Kaltman, Alan. (1977, September/October). *Time Barrier Express*, p. 29.
Nickols, Pete. (1984, April). Jackie Wilson. Record Collector, p. 15.
Pollak, Bill. (1978, August 14). Jackie Wilson's lonely tears. *Village Voice*, p. 1.
Pruter, Robert. (1991, November 1). Jackie Wilson: The most tragic figure in rhythm 'n' blues. *Goldmine*, p. 10.

STEVIE WONDER. *(Steveland Judkins Hardaway; May 13, 1950). Inducted in 1989*. A child prodigy, Stevie Wonder overcame adversity to emerge as a pop and soul superstar. Born in Saginaw, Michigan, Wonder moved to Detroit following his parent's divorce. Blinded shortly after birth due to a problem with his incubator, Wonder was later taken by his mother to a faith healer.

Given a harmonica and then a piano, Wonder quickly mastered both instruments. A playmate of a cousin of Miracles member Ronnie White, Wonder was granted an audition. Playing the harmonica, Wonder impressed White and songwriter Brian Holland.

Signed by Motown in 1960 at age 12, "Little" Stevie Wonder scored a pop-soul smash hit with his chart debut, "Fingertips, Part 2" (1963). Using his disability as an empowerment, Wonder told biographer Leonard Pitts Jr., "It's kind of a stereotype. Sometimes I do feel that with blindness, I am able to say things that, say, had another black person said, they would not necessarily get airplay" (p. 67). With Motown wanting crossover exposure, Wonder appeared in two beach films in 1964, *Muscle Beach Party* and *Bikini Party*.

Standing over six-feet-tall, and his voice maturing, 15-year-old Wonder first displayed his songwriting prowess on the album, *UPTIGHT*, co-penning the title track, "Uptight (Everything's Alright)" (1965). Enjoying a string of hits in the late 1960s, Wonder remained a crossover favorite with "I Was Made to Love Her" (1967); "For Once in My Life" (1968); a B-side hit, "My Cherie Amour" (1969); and a Johnny Bristol/Harvey Fuqua production "Yester-Me, Yester-You, Yesterday" (1969). Rush-released in 1970, "Sign, Sealed, Delivered I'm Yours" was actually the rough demo version.

Hurt over the loss of a number of Motown stars, label president Berry Gordy negotiated a lucrative contract with Wonder, who gained publishing rights and greater artistic control. With Motown discovering a market for black R&B LPS in the wake of a pair of Marvin Gaye's successes, Stevie Wonder embraced the format with a string of top-10 albums. Adopting a mature sound on *TALKING BOOK*, Wonder scored a pair of number-one hits with "Superstition" and "You Are the Sunshine of My Life."

Increasing his fan base after a 50-date tour as the opening act for the Rolling Stones, Wonder was soon headlining large arena concerts. His next album, *INNERVISIONS*, was highlighted by the urban-flavored "Living for the City" and the spiritually-themed "Higher Ground." Involved in a near-fatal, freak auto accident in 1973, Wonder miraculously recovered.

The following March, Wonder earned a then-record five Grammys (he won four the next year). Though divorcing his wife, former Motown secretary Syreeta Wright, he produced and co-wrote the tracks for her 1974 album, *STEVIE WONDER PRESENTS SYREETA*.

Considered his musical opus, the two-album set *SONGS IN THE KEY OF LIFE* spawned a pair of number-one singles, "I Wish" (1976) and a tribute to Duke Ellington, "Sir Duke" (1977). A non-single album track hit, "Isn't She Lovely," captured the first cry of his newborn daughter.

Taking three years to complete, the primarily instrumental album *JOURNEY THROUGH THE SECRET LIFE OF PLANTS* was intended as the soundtrack to an unreleased film documentary and managed only one top-40 hit, "Send One Your Love" (1979). Returning to top form in 1980, *HOTTER THAN JULY*, was highlighted by the reggae-influenced "Master Blaster (Jammin')."

Moving in a pop direction, Wonder teamed with Paul McCartney on the chart-topping smash "Ebony and Ivory" (1982). Providing music for the 1984 film *Woman in Red*, Wonder landed a pair of ballad hits with the heartfelt "I Just Called to Say I Loved You" and "Love Light in Flight" (1984). Released in 1985, the Grammy-winning album *IN SQUARE CIRCLE* spawned the hits "Part Time Lover" and "Go

Home."

Adopting an urban-contemporary sound in the late 1960s, Wonder lost crossover airplay and retail sales. Infusing rap into his music, Wonder earned critical acclaim with the soundtrack to the Spike Lee film *JUNGLE FEVER*, and the musically complex *CONVERSATION PIECE* (1995).

Bibliography

Breskin, David. (1984, February). Waiting for the man. *Musician*, p. 52.
Clark, Sue C. (1971, September 30). Stevie Wonder gets good and pissed. *Rolling Stone*, p. 12.
Fong-Torres, Ben. (1973, April 26). The formerly Little Stevie Wonder. *Rolling Stone*, p. 48.
Pitts, Leonard Jr. (1984). *Mr. Wonderful*. Cresskill, NJ: Sharon.
Robinson, Smokey & Ritz, David. (1989). *Smokey: Inside My Life*. New York: McGraw-Hill.
Taraborrelli, J. Randy. (1986). *Motown: Hot Wax, City Cool & Solid Gold* (pp. 182-88). New York: Dolphin/Doubleday.
White, Timothy. (1990). *Rock Lives: Profiles & Interviews* (pp. 204-9). New York: Henry Holt.

JIMMY YANCEY. *(James Edward Yancey; February 20, 1898 - September 18, 1951). Inducted in the Early Influence category in 1986.* The father of boogie-woogie piano, Jimmy Yancey remained relatively obscure during his lifetime, enjoying little fame and fortune. With its roots in ragtime, the boogie-woogie style was the precursor of the 1950s rock and roll of Jerry Lee Lewis and Little Richard.

Raised in Chicago, "Papa" Jimmy Yancey was the son of a vaudeville actor and musician. Joining his father in a local revue at age 5, Yancey toured across the Midwest and East Coast at age 10. At 15 he criss-crossed Europe, once entertaining King George V at Buckingham Palace. The Yancey family refused to perform in the Jim Crow South, never venturing past Louisville. With the decreasing interest in vaudeville, 16-year-old Yancey quit the stage and spent a year playing baseball in the Negro League.

With the help of his brother, Alonzo, Yancey learned to play the piano. Instrumental in popularizing boogie-woogie piano playing in Chicago, Yancey was a quiet, unassuming performer, playing a repeating, Latin-tinged bass line with his left hand, and an improvised, eight-bar, blues-based melody with his right. Finding receptive audiences in the Chicago "rent party" circuit with his blues-Latin hybrid style, he only occasionally performed in nightclubs.

Abandoning music as his primary source of income, Yancey took a groundskeeper position at Chicago's Comiskey Park, grooming the field for the likes of the White Sox Hall of Famer Luke Appling (later recalled in the song "White-Sox Stomp").

While Yancey did no recording until late in life, he spawned an entire generation of imitators. One of his compositions, "Yancey Special," was popularized by one of his students, Meade "Lux" Lewis, in 1936 and then Bob Crosby in 1938. Lewis and another Yancey student, Albert Ammons, joined Kansas City native Pete Johnson at a 1938 concert at Carnegie Hall, bringing respectability to boogie-woogie music.

With the country experiencing a boogie-woogie revival in the late 1930s, Yancey attracted the interest of numerous record companies. Finally garnering notoriety outside Chicago, Yancey recorded several tracks for the Don Qualey-owned Solo Art label, including "Jimmy's Stuff"/"The Fives". His star on the ascent, Yancey appeared on CBS radio later in the year.

Yancey landed at Victor-Bluebird Records, releasing his complex signature piece, "Yancey's Stomp." He followed up with "State Street Special" and "Tell 'Em about Me." At Columbia-Vocalion he recorded "Bear Trap Blues" and, with Faber Smith on vocals, "I Received a Letter." (Vocalion also had released the first boogie-woogie record in 1928, "Pine Top's Boogie Woogie," by Clarence "Pine Top" Smith.)

Coaxed back into the studio in 1943 by the tiny Session Record Company, Yancey was assisted on vocals by his wife, Estelle "Mama" Yancey, recording what are considered to be his best tracks, including "Death Letter Blues," "State Street Special," the definitive version of "Tell'em About Me."

Stricken with diabetes, Yancey suffered a stroke in the mid-1940s. Recovering in 1948, he returned to club work, frequently joined by his wife. Because of his grounds-keeping position, Yancey rarely left Chicago.

Joined by his wife, Yancey's last recording session came in 1951 for Atlantic Records, the tracks produced by Ahmet Ertegun. By year's end, Yancey died from a diabetes-related stroke. Mama Yancey continued her music career, later teaming with pianists Little Brother Montgomery and Art Hodes.

Bibliography

Harrington, Spencer. (1990, December). Blue Light Special. *Spin*, p. 90.

Russell, William. (1959). In Martin T. Williams (Ed.), *The Art of Jazz* (pp. 98-104). New York: Oxford University Press.

Silvester, Peter J. (1988). *A Left Hand Like God: A History of Boogie-Woogie Piano*. New York: Da Capo.

Yancey, Jimmy. (1953, August). House rent party. *Ebony*, p. 102.

THE YARDBIRDS. *Jeff Beck (June 24, 1944); Eric Clapton (Eric Clapp; March 30, 1945); Chris Dreja (November 11, 1946); Jim McCarty (July 25, 1943); Jimmy Page (James Patrick Page; January 9, 1944); Keith Relf (March 24, 1944 - May 14, 1976); Paul Samwell-Smith (May 8, 1943). Inducted in 1992.* The Yardbirds were responsible for nurturing some of finest British blues-rock musicians in the 1960s, many of whom went on to greater fame. In the burgeoning music scene of west London, members of what became the Yardbirds often crossed paths. Influenced by the English blues of pioneering bands led by Cyril Davies and Alexis Korner, a teenaged collector of American blues records, Keith Relf, formed the Metropolitan Blues Quartet.

Evolving into the Yardbirds, the group featured the asthmatic Relf on lead vocals and harmonica; rhythm guitarist Chris Dreja; drummer Jim McCarty; and joining lastly, bassist Paul Samwell-Smith. (McCarty and Samwell-Smith were previously bandmates in a top-40 group, the Country Gentlemen, playing Rick Nelson and Cliff Richard covers.) The Yardbirds' breakthrough came in 1963, when Relf convinced band leader Cyril Davies to allow the group to perform during breaks at the Eel Pie

Island club.

With guitarist Tony Topham leaving the Yardbirds when his parents demanded he return to college, Chris Dreja hired his former art school classmate as second guitarist, 18-year-old Eric Clapton. A spiffy dresser and extraordinary guitarist, Clapton had earned his "Slowhand" nickname for the leisurely pace at which he replaced his frequently broken guitar strings.

Landing a residency at the famed Crawdaddy Club as the replacement for the Rolling Stones, the Yardbirds entered into a management deal with the club's Russian-born owner. Backing American blues legend Sonny Boy Williamson on a series of London gigs, the collaboration was captured on the live album *WITH SONNY BOY WILLIAMSON*.

Signing with British EMI's Columbia label, the Yardbirds garnered their first chart hit with a cover of an obscure R&B song, "Good Morning Little Schoolgirl." Although constantly on the road or in the recording studio during the next several years, the group would earn little.

The Yardbirds' first American album release, *FOR YOUR LOVE*, spawned their first hit with the guitar-driven, psychedelic-styled title track, "For Your Love." Written by future 10cc member Graham Gouldman, the song typified the group's subsequent guitar-heavy releases.

Disillusioned by the Yardbirds' abandonment of traditional blues, Clapton left the group in March 1965 to join John Mayall's Bluesbreakers. As his replacement, the Yardbirds hired another guitar virtuoso Jeff Beck, whose intricate, feedback-driven guitar work predated that of Jimi Hendrix.

Garnering heavy exposure as the opening act for the Beatles, the Yardbirds enjoyed a U.S. hit run with the Gouldman-penned "Heart Full of Soul" (1965) and "Shapes of Things" (1966). During their first U.S. tour, the group stopped at the Sun studio in Memphis to recorded Tiny Bradshaw's rock standard, "Train Kept a-Rollin'," the session produced by Sam Phillips at his Sun studio in Memphis.

Far ahead of their time, the Yardbirds laid the groundwork for the progressive rock genre of the 1970s. The Yardbirds would parallel (some say, predate) the Beatles with their Eastern influences, and with the introduction of the Indian sitar as a rock instrument. Though continuing to record blues standards, the group began to rely on the compositions of Keith Relf.

With Samwell-Smith leaving the group in 1966, guitarist Jimmy Page was added. Dreja moving to bass to accommodate Beck's superior skills. Releasing their second studio album, *OVER, UNDER, SIDEWAYS, DOWN*, the group landed a hit with the psychedelic-flavored title track. Moving away from their blues roots, the Yardbirds experimented with Gregorian chants and Middle Eastern scales.

Unhappy with rigors of the road, Beck quit the Yardbirds after the second stop of a Dick Clark Caravan of Stars tour. Beck's last Yardbirds hit came with "Happenings Ten Years Time Ago" (1966). Hiring new manager Peter Grant, the group was finally able to earn a decent wage.

Joined by new producer, Mickie Most, the Yardbirds' hits continued with "Little Games" (1967) and a cover of a Manfred Mann song, "Ha Ha Said the Clown" (1967). In concert, Jimmy Page began performing "I'm Confused," the prototype of a future Led Zeppelin song, "Dazed and Confused." But disillusioned with Mickie Most's pop-oriented tinkerings, the Yardbirds disbanded in July of 1968.

With only Page (and for a while Dreja) remaining to fulfill scheduled tour dates, a replacement group was assembled. Calling themselves the New Yardbirds, they evolved into the blues-rock supergroup, Led Zeppelin. Keith Relf and Jim McCarty went on to launch the progressive rock group Renaissance, combining elements of folk-rock with classical music. Relf died in a freak electrical accident in 1976.

After a 1983 reunion gig at the Marquee Club's 25th anniversary, most of the Yardbirds regrouped the following year as Box of Frogs, with new vocalist John Fiddler. The group released a pair of albums beginning with the moderate seller *BACK WHERE I STARTED*.

Bibliography

Aldridge, W. Lynne. (1983, May-June). Five long years: An interview with the Yardbirds' Chris Dreja. *Blitz*, p. 8.

Doggett, Peter. (1992, April). The Yardbirds. *Record Collector*, p. 20.

Harrington, Richard. (1988, April 17). Eric Clapton's long and winding road. *Washington Post*, p. F1.

Heatley, Michael. (1992, June 12). One for all and all for one—founding members Chris and Jim McCarty remember the Yardbirds. *Goldmine*, p. 15.

Platt, John; Dreja, Chris & McCarty, Jim. (1983). *Yardbirds*. London: Sidgwick and Jackson.

Sharkey, John. (1974). Beck is back. *Rock Guitarists* (pp. 8-9). Saratoga, CA: Guitar Player Productions.

NEIL YOUNG. *November 12, 1945. Inducted in 1995*. With his nasally singing style, plaid shirts, and gritty-rock sound, Neil Young predated the grunge movement of the 1990s. Born in Toronto, Young suffered a permanent slight limp from a childhood bout with polio. After his parents' divorce, he was raised by his mother in Winnipeg.

Idolizing local guitarist Randy Bachman (later with BTO), 14-year-old Young formed a garage band called the Jades. Dropping out of high school in 1962, Young then formed an instrumental surf-rock band, the Squires. Touring through Ontario, the Squires once co-headlined a bill with the Company, a folk-rock band led by Stephen Stills.

After moving to Toronto in 1965, the bickering Squires soon disbanded. Joining the Detroit-based Mynah Birds, Young recorded some unreleased tracks for Motown. But after the arrest of leader Ricky James Matthews (later popular as Rick James), the group disbanded. Joined by bandmate Bruce Palmer, Young then drove his black hearse to Los Angeles, in search of Stephen Stills.

Miraculously running into Stills in a Los Angeles traffic jam, Young and Palmer joined Stills, Ritchie Furay, and others in forming a folk-rock group called the Herd. Renamed the Buffalo Springfield, the group landed its biggest hit with the anthemic "For What It's Worth" (1967), featuring Young on lead guitar. Quitting the group for four months in mid-1967, Young had refused to perform on *The Johnny Carson*

Show. Leaving for good in 1968 after three albums, Young pursued a solo career.

Befriended by Joni Mitchell's manager, Young signed with Warner-Reprise. Working with musical arranger Jack Nitzsche, Young fared poorly with his heavily produced, folk-flavored debut album, *NEIL YOUNG*. Switching to a hard-rock format, Young teamed with the talented backing group Crazy Horse. His breakthrough solo release, *EVERYBODY KNOWS THIS IS NOWHERE*, spawned the hits "Cinnamon Girl" and "Down By the River."

In 1969, Young rejoined Stephen Stills in the legendary folk-rock group Crosby, Stills, Nash & Young (CSN&Y), for a performance at Woodstock. In May 1970, Young wrote the antiwar lament "Ohio," following the National Guard confrontation with students at Kent State. Leaving CSN&Y after the release of the live album *4-WAY STREET*, Young occasionally rejoined the group.

Returning to a solo career, Young was aided by guest musicians Stephen Stills and 19-year-old Nils Lofgren on *AFTER THE GOLD RUSH* (1971). The album was highlighted by "Southern Man," an attack on Southern racism that also disparaged Southern-rock group Lynyrd Skynyrd. In response, Young was later mocked in Lynyrd Skynyrd's "Sweet Home Alabama."

Backed by a studio group called the Stray Gators, Young released his pinnacle album in 1972, *HARVEST*, highlighted by the biggest hits of his career, the country-toned "Heart of Gold" and "Old Man." But while Young continued to fill concert venues, his next few albums sold poorly.

During the middle of the recording sessions for a new CSN&Y album, Crosby and Nash left the group, their vocals removed from the final mix. The tracks were salvaged as a Young and Stills album, *LONG MAY YOU RUN* (1976). Young then left Stills during the middle of a supporting tour.

Returning a to folk and country sound, Young enjoyed a resurgence with "Like a Hurricane," from the album *AMERICAN STARS 'N' BARS* (1977). Following up in 1978 with his first top-10 album since 1972's *HARVEST*, the upbeat *COMES A TIME* featured Nicolette Larson and 22 session musicians. On his subsequent tour, Young employed giant props and hired members of Devo as theatrical performers.

Influenced by the electronic sound of Devo, Young reteamed with Crazy Horse on the album *RUST NEVER SLEEPS* (the title taken from the slogan of Rustoleum paint). A smash album, one side featured grinding punk rock, the other acoustic folk. A subsequent concert album, *LIVE RUST*, was certified platinum.

Moving to Geffen Records, Young experimented with synthesized vocals and flirted with New Wave, computer-driven sounds on the album *TRANS*. The project was inspired by Young's son, Ben, who suffers from severe cerebral palsy.

With Geffen rejecting Young's country-flavored album tentatively titled *ISLAND IN THE SUN*, an incensed Young retaliated with a 1950s doo-wop styled *EVERYBODY'S ROCKIN'*. Backed by the pompadour-wearing vocal trio, the Shocking Pinks, Young scored an MTV hit with the oddball track "Wonderin'."

Angered by Young's alleged foray into "uncommercial" music, Geffen sued the singer in 1983 for $3 million. Young responded by abandoning rock for country in 1985, releasing the fiddle-heavy album *OLD WAYS*. Hiring a new backing group, the

International Harvesters, Young toured with the likes of the Judds and Willie Nelson.

After settling with Geffen in 1987, Young signed with Reprise Records beginning with the album *THIS NOTE'S FOR YOU*. Hiring a new backing band, the Blue Notes, Young attacked the corporate sponsorship of rock music, lashing out at Eric Clapton, Michael Jackson, and others in his banned-by-MTV video *This Note's for You*. In 1988, Young regrouped with CSN&Y on the hit album *AMERICAN DREAM*.

Finally returning to his classic sound, Young released a series of critically hailed albums, *FREEDOM*; with by Crazy Horse, *RAGGED GLORY*; the live *WELD*; and, arranged by former associate, Jack Nitzsche, *HARVEST MOON*.

With his disheveled look, long unkempt hair, and plaid shirts, Young was at home with the grunge rock explosion, in 1991 touring with alternative rockers Sonic Youth. Teaming with Pearl Jam in 1993 for a sellout tour, Young also collaborated with the group on the 1995 album *MIRROR BALL*. But even with the Pearl Jam connection, Young landed little airplay on modern-rock stations. Returning to his roots, Young regrouped with Crazy Horse in 1996 for the hit album *BROKEN ARROW*.

Bibliography

Einarson, John. (1987, January). Neil Young: A rock legend talks about his early days. *Goldmine*, p. 8.

Fuentes, Jerry. (1987, February 13). Buffalo Springfield: A collector's retrospective. Goldmine, p. 8.

Kent, Nick. (1995, December). I build something up, I tear it right down: Neil Young at 50. *Mojo*, p 48.

Kitman, Marvin. (1988, August 1). Neil Young and MTV's video rule. *(New York) Newsday*, part II, p. 9.

Schoemer, Karen. (1992, November 25). At the deli with Neil Young: Still searching for a heart of gold. *New York Times*, p. C1.

Strauss, Neil. (1995, July 2). The predictably unpredictable Neil Young. *New York Times*, sect. 2, p. 26.

THE (YOUNG) RASCALS. *Eddie Brigati (October 22, 1946); Felix Cavaliere (November 29, 1944); Gene Cornish (May 14, 1945); Dino Danelli (July 23, 1945). Inducted in 1997.* A pioneering, blue-eyed soul group, the (Young) Rascals merged pounding rock and roll with gritty rhythm and blues. Reared on 1950s R&B, the group's driving force, Felix Cavaliere, frequented Greenwich Village nightclubs in the early 1960s with chums Neil Diamond and Carole King. After purchasing a Hammond B-3 organ, Cavaliere formed Felix and the Escorts with Mike Esposito (later with the Blues Magoos). Dropping out of a pre-med program at Syracuse University, Cavaliere became a full-time musician.

Landing a booking at New York's famed Peppermint Lounge, there Cavaliere met singer Eddie Brigati. Disbanding the Escorts, Cavaliere joined the club's house band, Joey Dee & the Starliters (of "Peppermint Twist" fame) for a European tour, crossing paths with the upstart Beatles.

After leaving Joey Dee for a profitable gig but unchallenging gig behind a Las Vegas cabaret singer, Cavaliere formed an R&B band with teenage jazz drummer

Dino Danelli. The group was expanded with two members from Joey Dee's Starliters, Canadian-born guitarist Gene Cornish and Cavaliere's old acquaintance, singer Eddie Brigati.

Costumed in Italian-styled knickers, the Rascals were named by comedian Soupy Sales. A huge draw around New York City, the group attracted black and white fans alike, wowing audiences with their soulful renditions of Wilson Pickett songs. Drawing the attention of local promoter Sid Bernstein (who had booked the Beatles at Shea Stadium), the Rascals signed a management deal.

Winning a bidding war, R&B powerhouse Atlantic Records signed the renamed Young Rascals as their first-ever rock group. Featuring Brigati on lead vocals, the group's debut release, "I Ain't Gonna Eat Out My Heart Anymore" (1965), was a radio hit in spite of its mediocre chart showing. With Cavaliere taking over lead vocal duties, the group reluctantly recorded a cover of the Olympics' 1965 R&B hit "Good Lovin'." Hating the song, the band members were astounded when it topped the pop charts in early 1966.

Beginning with the album *GOOD LOVIN'*, the group was writing most of its own material. With Brigati usually composing the lyrics, and Cavaliere the music, the group landed its first major self-penned hit with "Lonely Too Long." Now attired in paisley, Edwardian clothing, the renamed Rascals enjoyed sellout tours throughout 1967.

But tensions grew when Cavaliere began seeking spiritual guidance from the swami Satchinanda. Assuming the leadership role in the group, Cavaliere further alienated his formerly equal-footed bandmates.

Taking a stylistic turn, the Rascals's fourth album, *ONCE UPON A DREAM* (1968), was highlighted by the hit "It's Wonderful." In place of Cavaliere's trademark Hammond B-3 organ riffs, the Rascals were experimenting with Eastern-influenced sitars.

With the group's fortunes waning by 1969, Cavaliere told writer Edward Kiersh: "we were going so high up we lost control. Everything was happening too quickly. The notoriety overcomes you, the money, the wild parties, the women, the [fans] screaming, the constant pressure to produce. . . . It ruined us" (p. 154). Unhappy with his role as sideman, Brigati resigned from the Rascals in 1971, with Cornish following soon after.

Leaving Atlantic for Columbia Records, the Rascals experimented with jazz. Employing session players from the Crusaders and Paul Butterfield, the group's final album, *THE ISLAND OF REAL* (1972), bombed. Dropped by their record label, they disbanded.

Pursuing other projects, none of the former Rascals would match their previous success. Cornish and Danelli formed Bulldog (landing a minor hit in 1972 with the hit single, "No") and then Fotomaker with former Raspberries guitarist Wally Bryson. Cavaliere found only moderate success as a solo artist, his best effort coming with 1980's *CASTLES IN THE AIR* (highlighted by the hit single "Only a Lonely Heart Sees"). Brigati, in the mid-1970s, joined his brother, David, in a disco band. In the mid-1980s, Danelli joined Steven Van Zandt's band, the Disciples of Soul.

Following a reunion (minus Brigati) at the Atlantic Records 40th Anniversary concert at Madison Square Garden in May 1988, the Rascals regrouped for a summer tour. Disbanding after several months, the Rascals splintered over Cavaliere's legal ownership the group's name.

Returning to music in 1994, Cavaliere updated his classic Hammond B-3 organ sound on the Don Was co-produced solo album *DREAMS IN MOTION*. In 1995, Cavaliere joined the International Ringo Starr All Star Band, touring with Mark Farner, Billy Preston, and others.

Bibliography

Boehm, Mike. (1988, August 19). Rascals past and present tangle over reunion tour playing here. *The Los Angeles Times*, Calendar sect., p. 21.

Flans, Robyn. (1988, May 6). The Rascals: Groovin'. *Goldmine*, p. 7.

Kiersh, Edward. (1986). *Where Are You Now, Bo Diddley?* (pp. 152-60). Garden City, NY: Doubleday.

Lombardi, John. (1970, October 1). The blackest white group of them all. *Rolling Stone*, p. 27.

Vorda, Allan & Russo, Joe. (1991). *The (Young) Rascals: Groovin'*. Discoveries, p. 34.

FRANK ZAPPA. *(Frank Vincent Zappa Jr; December 21, 1940 - December 4, 1993). Inducted in 1995.* A groundbreaking avant-garde rock artist, Frank Zappa ignored the established boundaries between musical genres, borrowing from classical, jazz and rock. Born to Sicilian and Greek parents in Baltimore, Zappa was frequently uprooted, his family eventually settling in southern California. Frank Sr. was rarely at home, spending most of his time working in the defense industry.

Influenced by an obscure classical drummer named Edgar Varese, Zappa bought a drum set and began composing classical pieces. Discovering R&B and doo-wop during his mid-teens, Zappa reluctantly joined a rock band, the Ramblers, as a drummer. After switching to guitar in 1956, 15-year-old Zappa formed a racially integrated eight-piece R&B group, the Black-Outs, while a student at Antelope Valley High School.

After a taking a few college courses, Zappa relocated to the nearby artsy, Echo Park section of Los Angeles. Returning to school in 1959, Zappa pursued a music degree at Chaffee Junior College. Marrying a year later, he dropped out of school for good and took a job as a lounge musician. Determined to educate himself, Zappa spent countless hours in libraries researching music.

Paid little, in 1960 Zappa wrote and produced a classical music score for a low-budget, art film, *The World's Greatest Sinner*. Recording at the tiny Pal Studio, Zappa released a number of obscure singles, many of them in collaboration with Ray Collins. One of Zappa's early compositions, "Memories of El Monte," became a minor doo-wop hit for the Penguins.

After scoring the music for another low-budget film, *Run Home Slow*, Zappa took the profits and purchased a recording studio for $2,300. Assuming various pseudonyms including Mr. Clean and Baby Ray & the Ferns, Zappa released a long string of singles in the early 1960s. But when an undercover agent commissioned the recording of a "dirty" party tape of faked moaning, Zappa was arrested and convicted of indecency. Sentenced to 10 days in jail and three years of probation, Zappa was inspired to fight all forms of censorship.

Returning to Los Angeles, Zappa joined an R&B group, the Soul Giants, led by his former partner, Ray Collins. Playing an increasingly central role in the group, Zappa soon emerged as the leader of the renamed Mothers.

Discovered by Tom Wilson and signed to MGM's new Verve subsidiary, the Mothers were forced by the label to change their name to Mothers of Invention. Stretching the bounds of popular music on the group's debut 1966 album, *FREAK OUT!* (rock music's first double album), Zappa chronicled street life on songs "Hungry Freaks, Daddy" and "Who Are the Brain Police?"

Leaving Verve in 1969 for Warner/Reprise Records, Zappa formed a pair of production companies, Bizarre and Straight (later evolving into DiscReet). Dabbling in studio production, Zappa oversaw efforts by Lenny Bruce, Captain Beefheart, Tim Buckley, and the debut album of Alice Cooper.

Zappa's 1970 album, a combination of studio and live recordings, *BURNT WEENIE SANDWICH*, would be the last with the original Mothers, as paying a dozen or so salaries became cost prohibitive. Instead, Zappa would form various incarnations of the Mothers (now minus the "of Invention" suffix), with the likes of Jack Bruce, Dale Bozzio, Lowell George, Steve Vai, and former Turtles members Flo and Eddie (better known as Mark Volman and Howard Kaylan). Another highlight of a very productive year, Zappa released a free-form jazz album, *WEASELS RIPPED MY FLESH*, the cover featuring a man shaving his face with a rodent. Hardly a household name in the early 1970s, Zappa struggled to land airplay, much of his music banned due to its raw lyrics.

Zappa experienced several tragedies in 1971: all of his band's equipment was destroyed by fire in Switzerland; in London, a jealous fan pushed Zappa off the stage, breaking his leg and damaging his back and larynx. When Zappa was finally able to speak, his singing voice had dropped one-third of an octave.

Entertaining a brief commercial period, Zappa's debut DiscReet release, *OVER-NITE SENSATION*, featured a bawdy song he wrote while in high school, "Dinah-Moe Humm" (1973). His highest-charting solo album, *APOSTROPHE*, was highlighted by a rare radio hit, the comical "Don't Eat the Yellow Snow" (1974). Released in 1975 with guest vocalist Captain Beefheart, *BONGO FURY* would be the last album attributed to the Mothers.

After a lengthy lawsuit against Verve, Zappa was awarded the master tapes of his five albums at the label. Zappa subsequently sparred with his parent record label, Warner Brothers, over the lyrical content of the 1978 album *ZAPPA IN NEW YORK*.

Forming his own record company, Zappa Records, he earned his first Grammy nomination with the antidisco album *SHEIK YERBOUTI* (1979), featuring a rare pop hit, "Dancin' Fool." Another track "Jewish Princess," angered the Jewish community. Also released in 1979 was the first of three volumes of the rock opera, *JOE'S GARAGE*, the first edition highlighted by "Catholic Girls."

With PolyGram refusing to release the single "I Don't Wanna Get Drafted," Zappa dissolved his distribution deal with the label in 1981 and formed Barking Pumpkin

Records. In 1982, Zappa released the first of another three-volume set, *SHUT UP 'N PLAY YER GUITAR*. Also in 1982, Zappa would score the only top-40 hit of his career in a duet with his daughter, Moon Unit. A novelty song, "Valley Girl" parodied young girls who spoke in a trendy, California accent.

Zappa began to indulge his love of classical music with the projects *THE LONDON SYMPHONY ORCHESTRA: ZAPPA VOL. 1* (1983) and, with conductor Pierre Boulez, *BOULEZ CONDUCTS ZAPPA: THE PERFECT STRANGER* (1984). Zappa won his only Grammy Award for 1986's *JAZZ FROM HELL*.

In the 1980s, Zappa attacked music censorship, challenging the Tipper Gore-led Parents Music Resource Center. A critic of all forms of censorship, the suited Zappa addressed several congressional committees, with many in middle America getting their first taste of the opinionated musician. Zappa later chronicled the event on the track "Porn Wars," from the album *FRANK ZAPPA MEETS THE MOTHERS OF PREVENTION* (1985).

Wanting to reissue his early albums on CD, Zappa discovered that the master tapes had deteriorated. After releasing the original, damaged recordings on the box set *OLD MASTERS*, Zappa angered many fans by reissuing the individual albums with newly recorded bass and drum tracks. Striking back at bootleggers, Zappa also issued a pair of box sets, *BEAT THE BOOTS*, the material taken from actual bootleg records.

Continuing his prolific string of albums, in 1988 Zappa released the first of a six-volume series, *YOU CAN'T DO THAT ON STAGE ANYMORE*. After the fall of communism in Eastern Europe, Czechoslovakian president Vaclav Havel made international news when he invited Zappa to speak on politics and social issues.

Initially hiding his diagnosis of prostate cancer from the public, Zappa admitted to his illness in 1991. He died two years later. Zappa's final studio album, *CIVILIZATION PHAZE III*, was released in 1995.

Bibliography

Considine, J.D. (1995, July 9). Frank Zappa: Complex artist, musical snob. *Baltimore Sun*, p. 1J.

Dewitt, Howard A. (1994, Spring). Frank Zappa: Child of the 1950s. *Blue Suede News*, p. 6.

Forte, Dan. (1982, April). Zappa. *Musician*, p. 36.

Fricke, David. (1994, January 27). Frank Zappa: 1940-1993. *Rolling Stone*, p. 11.

Ruhlmann, William. (1994, December 9). Frank Zappa: The present day composer. *Goldmine*, p. 14.

Wheeler, Drew. (1993, December 18). Zappa: A man who knew no boundaries. *Billboard*, p. 131.

Chronological Listing of Inductees

Formed in 1983, the Rock and Roll Hall of Fame Foundation inducted its inaugural class in 1986. Recording artists are eligible for induction into the Hall of Fame 25 years after the release of their first recording.

Induction into the Rock and Roll Hall of Fame is a three step process. A small selection committee comprising of about 30 music historians, journalists, and record industry executives meet in New York City to select the nominees. A final ballot is then sent to several hundred members of the music industry, with the top vote-getters (who must receive at least 50-percent of the vote) elected into the Hall of Fame. Additionally, the selection committee unilaterally names inductees in the following three categories: Early Influence, Non-Performer, and Lifetime Achievement, with the latter two categories comprised of deejays, songwriters, record company owners, producers, and promoters.

1986 INDUCTEES

Chuck Berry
James Brown
Ray Charles
Sam Cooke
Fats Domino
The Everly Brothers
Buddy Holly
Jerry Lee Lewis
Little Richard
Elvis Presley

Early Influences

Robert Johnson
Jimmie Rodgers
Jimmy Yancey

Non-Performers

Alan Freed
Sam Phillips

Lifetime Achievement

John Hammond

Nominees Not Inducted

Johnny Ace
LaVern Baker
Hank Ballard
Bobby "Blue" Bland
Ruth Brown
Solomon Burke
The Coasters
Eddie Cochran
King Curtis
Bobby Darin
Duane Eddy
The Flamingos
Aretha Franklin
Marvin Gaye
Bill Haley
Little Willie John
B.B. King
Ben E. King
Gladys Knight
Frankie Lymon
Clyde McPhatter
Ricky Nelson
Roy Orbison
Carl Perkins
Esther Phillips
Gene Pitney
Lloyd Price
Jimmy Reed
Smokey Robinson
Del Shannon
The Supremes
Big Joe Turner
Tina Turner
Gene Vincent
Muddy Waters
Mary Wells
Chuck Willis
Jackie Wilson

1987 INDUCTEES

The Coasters
Eddie Cochran

Bo Diddley
Aretha Franklin
Marvin Gaye
Bill Haley
B.B. King
Clyde McPhatter
Ricky Nelson
Roy Orbison
Carl Perkins
Smokey Robinson
Big Joe Turner
Muddy Waters
Jackie Wilson

Early Influences

Louis Jordan
T-Bone Walker
Hank Williams

Non-Performers

Leonard Chess
Ahmet Ertegun
Jerry Leiber & Mike Stoller
Jerry Wexler

Nominees Not Inducted

Johnny Ace
LaVern Baker
Hank Ballard
Bobby "Blue" Bland
Ruth Brown
Solomon Burke
King Curtis
Bobby Darin
Dion
Duane Eddy
The Flamingos
Little Willie John
Ben E. King
Gladys Knight
Frankie Lymon

Esther Phillips
Gene Pitney
Lloyd Price
Jimmy Reed
Del Shannon
The Supremes
Tina Turner
Gene Vincent
Mary Wells
Chuck Willis

1988 INDUCTEES

The Beach Boys
The Beatles
The Drifters
Bob Dylan
The Supremes

Early Influences

Woody Guthrie
Leadbelly
Les Paul

Non-Performer

Berry Gordy Jr.

Nominees Not Inducted

LaVern Baker
Hank Ballard
Bobby "Blue" Bland
Booker T. and the MG's
Ruth Brown
King Curtis
Bobby Darin
Dion
Duane Eddy
The 4 Seasons
Little Willie John
Ben E. King
Frankie Lymon
The Platters

Lloyd Price
Jimmy Reed
Del Shannon
Gene Vincent
Chuck Willis

1989 INDUCTEES

Dion
Otis Redding
The Rolling Stones
The Temptations
Stevie Wonder

Early Influences

The Ink Spots
Bessie Smith
The Soul Stirrers

Non-Performer

Phil Spector

Nominees Not Inducted

LaVern Baker
Hank Ballard
Bobby "Blue" Bland
Booker T. & the MG's
Ruth Brown
Solomon Burke
King Curtis
Bobby Darin
Duane Eddy
The 4 Seasons
The Four Tops
The Impressions
Little Willie John
Carole King
Gladys Knight & the Pips
Frankie Lymon
Martha & the Vandellas
Wilson Pickett
The Platters

Lloyd Price
Jimmy Reed
Del Shannon
Ike & Tina Turner
Gene Vincent
Chuck Willis

1990 INDUCTEES

Hank Ballard
Bobby Darin
The 4 Seasons
The Four Tops
The Kinks
The Platters
Simon & Garfunkel
The Who

Early Influences

Louis Armstrong
Charlie Christian
Ma Rainey

Non-Performers

Gerry Goffin & Carole King
Holland, Dozier & Holland

Nominees Not Inducted

The Animals
LaVern Baker
Ruth Brown
Solomon Burke
Johnny Cash
King Curtis
Duane Eddy
The Impressions
Little Willie John
Gladys Knight
Brenda Lee
Frankie Lymon
Bob Marley
Wilson Pickett

Gene Pitney
Jimmy Reed
Del Shannon
The Shirelles
Ike & Tina Turner
Gene Vincent
Chuck Willis
The Yardbirds

1991 INDUCTEES

LaVern Baker
The Byrds
John Lee Hooker
The Impressions
Wilson Pickett
Jimmy Reed
Ike & Tina Turner

Early Influence

Howlin' Wolf

Non-Performers

Dave Bartholomew
Ralph Bass

Lifetime Achievement

Nesuhi Ertegun

Nominees Not Inducted

Bobby "Blue" Bland
Johnny Cash
Duane Eddy
Elmore James
Frankie Lymon & the Teenagers
The Moonglows
Gene Vincent
The Yardbirds

1992 INDUCTEES

Bobby "Blue" Bland
Booker T. & the MG's
Johnny Cash
Jimi Hendrix Experience
Isley Brothers
Sam & Dave
The Yardbirds

Early Influences

Elmore James
Professor Longhair

Non-Performers

Leo Fender
Bill Graham
Doc Pomus

Nominees Not Inducted

David Bowie
Buffalo Springfield
Cream
Duane Eddy
Etta James
Frankie Lymon & the Teenagers
Gene Pitney
The Velvet Underground

1993 INDUCTEES

Ruth Brown
Cream
Creedence Clearwater Revival
The Doors
Etta James
Frankie Lymon & the Teenagers
Van Morrison
Sly & the Family Stone

Early Influence

Dinah Washington

Non-Performers

Dick Clark
Milt Gabler

Nominees Not Inducted

The Animals
Buffalo Springfield
Grateful Dead
Little Willie John
Rod Stewart
Velvet Underground
The (Young) Rascals
Frank Zappa

1994 INDUCTEES

The Animals
The Band
Duane Eddy
Grateful Dead
Elton John
John Lennon
Bob Marley
Rod Stewart

Early Influence

Willie Dixon

Non-Performer

Johnny Otis

Nominees Not Inducted

Buffalo Springfield
The Jackson 5
Martha & the Vandellas
Joni Mitchell

The Moonglows
Pink Floyd
The Velvet Underground
The (Young) Rascals
Frank Zappa

1995 INDUCTEES

The Allman Brothers Band
Al Green
Janis Joplin
Led Zeppelin
Martha & the Vandellas
Neil Young
Frank Zappa

Early Influence

The Orioles

Non-Performer

Paul Ackerman

Nominees Not Inducted

The Jackson 5
The Jefferson Airplane
Little Willie John
Joni Mitchell
The Shirelles
Velvet Underground

1996 INDUCTEES

David Bowie
The Jefferson Airplane
Little Willie John
Gladys Knight & the Pips
Pink Floyd
The Shirelles
Velvet Underground

Early Influence

Pete Seeger

Non-Performer

Tom Donahue

Nominees Not Inducted

The Bee Gees
Solomon Burke
King Curtis
The Flamingos
The Jackson 5
The Moonglows
Parliament-Funkadelic
Lloyd Price
The (Young) Rascals

1997 INDUCTEES

The Bee Gees
Buffalo Springfield
Crosby, Stills & Nash
The Jackson 5
Joni Mitchell
Parliament-Funkadelic
The (Young) Rascals

Early Influence

Bill Monroe
Mahalia Jackson

Non-Performer

Syd Nathan

Nominees Not Inducted

Black Sabbath
Solomon Burke
The Dominoes
Lynyrd Skynyrd

The Mamas and the Papas
The Meters
The Moonglows
Gene Pitney
Lloyd Price
The Stooges

1998 INDUCTEES

The Eagles
Fleetwood Mac
The Mamas and The Papas
Lloyd Price
Santana
Gene Vincent

Early Influence

Jelly Roll Morton

Non-Performer

Allen Toussaint

Nominees Not Inducted

Solomon Burke
Earth, Wind & Fire
Billy Joel
The Moonglows
Gene Pitney
Del Shannon
Dusty Springfield
The Stooges
Joe Tex

Rock and Roll Hall of Fame Timeline

1938

Former pawnbroker Leo Mintz opens the Record Rendezvous store in Cleveland, Ohio, initially selling used jukebox records.

1945

Leaving classical music station WKBN in Youngstown, Alan Freed is hired by WAKR in Akron and is quickly promoted from sports announcer to deejay at the age of 24.

1951

July 11: Sponsored by Record Rendezvous owner Leo Mintz, Alan Freed launches a rhythm and blues program at WJW radio in Cleveland and soon becomes "the King of the Moondoggers." Mintz and Freed would soon popularize the term "rock and roll."

1952

March 21: The first-ever "rock and roll" concert is staged at the Cleveland Arena, a hockey venue. "The Moondog Coronation Ball" attracts 20,000 fans, who riot during the performance of opening act Paul "Hucklebuck" Williams. Promotor Alan Freed is nearly arrested.

1954

September 7: Alan Freed is lured to WINS in New York City and quickly dominates the market with his revolutionary rock and roll format.

1955

February: Hired by Cleveland deejays Bill Randle and Tommy Edwards, the unknown Elvis Presley makes his first appearances north of the Mason-Dixon line.

1957

May 28: The National Academy of Recording Arts & Sciences is established in reaction to the dominance of rock music. Its annual Grammy Awards ceremony ignores rock artists for a number of years.

1959

November 21: Targeted in the payola scandals, Alan Freed is fired from his deejay post at WABC in New York. A disgraced figure, his career is left in ruins.

1965

January 20: Alan Freed's death from uremia goes virtually unnoticed in the national press.

1983

Early discussions are held between Atlantic Records founder Ahmet Ertegun and lawyer Suzan Evans about a small hall of fame and museum honoring rock music's pioneers.

1984

The Rock and Roll Hall of Fame Foundation is established.

1985

July 18: Cleveland officials make their first bid to attract the proposed hall.

August 5: The Hall of Fame is established in New York City by Ahmet Ertegun. The hall's board of director includes 21 members from the music industry.

August 17: In attempt to lure the Hall of Fame, petitions are distributed around Cleveland. Within two months, 660,000 signatures are gathered (oddly, the city's population is only 536,000).

October 3: Rock Hall officials arrive to a jubilant public reception in Cleveland; then-mayor George Voinovich Rock and Roll Day.

November 12: From a list of 41 nominees, the Hall of Fame's premiere class of 10 members is announced.

December 4: The Rock and Roll Hall of Fame is officially incorporated. The organization employs only three full-time employees during the next eight years.

1986

January 21: Cleveland tallies 110,315 calls in a *USA Today* 1-900 poll; Memphis comes in a distant second with 7,268 votes.

January 23: The inaugural induction ceremony is held at New York City's Waldorf Astoria. Cleveland is the front-runner in the site selection, according to board member Jann Wenner.

February 3: Chicago launches an effort to grab the hall from front-leaning Cleveland.

February 14: Philadelphia mayor Wilson Good unveils a $45.7 million financial package to attract the hall.

February 24: Attempting to sway the selection committee, the Ohio General Assembly allocates $4 million for the proposed Rock Hall.

March: Cleveland native Eric Carmen releases the single "The Rock Stops Here" as a Rock Hall anthem.

March 21: In an effort to bring the Hall of Fame Museum to Cleveland, a massive citywide celebration commemorates the 34th anniversary of the original Moondog Coronation Ball. At 7:58 P.M., five television and nine radio stations simultaneously air Bill Haley's "Rock around the Clock."

April 6: The *Chicago Tribune* reports that Los Angeles has been selected as the site of the Hall of Fame.

May 5: Cleveland is officially selected as the site for the reported $20 million facility.

May 6: Joan Jett and Michael J. Fox shoot the rock film, *Light of Day* in Cleveland as part of a fictitious group called the Barbusters.

September 18: Fifty-five members of the Cleveland and New York business, civic and music communities are named to a Hall of Fame board.

November 4: The *Cleveland Plain Dealer* aids the fund-raising effort by offering for sale a single, "Heart of the City," by then-unknown local singer Marc Cohn. The song was originally an advertising jingle for the newspaper.

November 22: Rock Hall officials postpone the selection of a site in Cleveland until 1987.

1987

January 26: Members of the New York board arrive in Cleveland to inspect prospective sites, including the location of the now demolished Cleveland Arena.

March 9: The New York board selects a site next to the Tower City retail complex, on a bluff overlooking the Cuyahoga River. The hall's cost is estimated at $25 million.

June 3: The Cleveland Founders Club launches a $26 million fund-raising drive, mapping a strategy to raise $22 million from corporate sponsors and a $5 million endowment from the television rights of the induction ceremonies. The campaign is a flop.

November 2: Sore losers, the cities of San Francisco and Philadelphia announce plans for their own rock halls. Seattle later constructs its own rock museum.

November 27: Richard Kelso is named the production manager of the hall, in charge of construction.

November 29: Chinese-born architect I.M. Pei unveils the plans for a sloping, riverside museum.

December 4: The Rock Hall is now priced at $29 million, with opening scheduled for 1991.

1988

January 20: A model of the Rock and Roll Hall of Fame is unveiled in New York City. The price tag for the 95,000-square-foot hall jumps to $45 million.

September 1: The Rock Hall remains in Cleveland after securing a minimum $18 million demanded by New York board. The construction cost has been revised at $48 million.

October 12: Larry R. Thompson is named the director of the Hall of Fame.

1989

January 12: Director Larry Thompson promises groundbreaking by 1992.

May 22: The Cleveland and New York boards enter into separate operations. The New York-based foundation retains the legal rights to the museum's name and licensing and will exclusively oversee the nomination and selection process of the inductees.

May 25: Cleveland mayor George Voinovich unveils a plan to grant $15 million in property taxes to the hall.

June 12: Cleveland City Council president George Forbes threatens to withhold local tax dollars earmarked for the hall if the ceremonies are not brought to the city.

July 20: Art Modell, the majority owner of the Cleveland Browns and the lessee of the Cleveland Stadium, pledges free use of the stadium once a year for five years as a site for fund-raising concerts.

July 27: The New York-based Hall of Fame Foundation refuses to move the induction ceremony to Cleveland, citing inconvenience.

September 11: The Ohio General Assembly pitches in an additional $1 million to the rock museum's construction.

September 13: Cuyahoga County approves a $5 million bond issue for the Hall of Fame now estimated to cost almost $50 million.

October: Syndicated oldies radio deejay and Hall of Fame board member Norm N. Nite donates 50-percent of the royalties of his *Rock On Almanac* to the Rock Hall.

October 12: Cleveland's request for a $6.9 million urban grant for the Rock Hall is rejected by HUD chief Jack Kemp.

October 14: Cleveland officials are miffed when the New York board leaks the names of the new class of inductees hours before a scheduled Cleveland press conference.

November 15: Cleveland reaches a $40 million interim goal, under a threat of losing the hall. The only evidence of the museum is a weed-infested sign proclaiming CLEVELAND WELCOMES . . . FUTURE HOME OF ROCK AND ROLL HALL OF FAME.

1990

January 17: MTV broadcasts highlights of the fifth annual ceremony, the first time the event is shown on television.

March: The Burdick Group of San Francisco is chosen to design the rock museum's displays.

March 27: New York board members are upset by the opening of a Record Town store at Tower City, near the site of the planned hall, and demand a change in the hall's location.

July 19: Cleveland's hometown hero, Alan Freed, is honored in a plaque presentation.

December 18: The site of the Rock Hall has been moved from the Tower City Center retail complex to North Coast Harbor, near Cleveland Stadium. The hall is scheduled to open in 1994.

December 17: The Rock Hall acquires its first piece of rock memorabilia, paying $17,600 for Jimi Hendrix's handwritten lyrics to "Purple Haze" at a Sotheby's auction.

1991

January 6: The hall construction price is now tagged at $60 million.

January 13: William Hulett is hired as the Rock Hall's cochairman.

February: Larry Thompson announces groundbreaking for December 12; $44 million has been raised.

March 29: The Cleveland School Board objects to a plan to give $18 million in city tax money to the hall. The board later drops it opposition in return for a $200,000 annual payment from the hall and 50,000 free admission passes.

May 2: Rock Hall officials unveil plans for the museum's interior designs. A rejected proposal by Malibu-based designer Barry Howard called for moving sidewalks with visitors wearing radio-controlled headphones at all times. The cost of the hall is now estimated at between $60 to $70 million.

May 7: Bruce Harrah-Conforth is named the director of Curatorial and Educational Affairs.

June 14: Using slides and drawings, architect I.M. Pei unveils his redesigned plans for the museum, featuring a main tower surrounded by separate buildings, with the Hall of Fame on the top level. Local officials are unhappy with the modifications. The museum's cost is now tagged at $68 million.

June 25: Eager to show off its acquisitions, the Hall of Fame opens its first public exhibit of 150 items at the Cleveland's Western Reserve Historical Society museum. The opening of the "Are You Experienced" exhibition is attended by Jimi Hendrix's bassist, Noel Redding.

August: John Fogerty is the first outsider permitted at a nominating committee meeting. He is there to lobby for the induction of his musical idol, Duane Eddy.

September 20: Architect I.M. Pei offers a modified design for the museum for its new North Coast Harbor site. The pyramid shape resembles his previous buildings, the Kennedy Library and the Louvre addition.

October 23: Bruce Harrah-Conforth announces his first major acquisition: 300 Janis Joplin items.

December 11: The museum's unofficial groundbreaking occurs with utility workers rerouting transmission lines. I.M. Pei's contract is finalized, with the famed architect receiving $5.35 million for the expected $65 million project, down from June's $68 million estimate.

1992

January 15: At the seventh induction ceremony, hall officials bemoan the absence of major corporate sponsors.

February 28: K. Michael Benz succeeds Larry Thompson as executive director.

March 12: Cleveland radio station WMJI hosts the 40th anniversary Moondog Coronation ball. Returning from the original concert is Paul "Hucklebuck" Williams.

November: A plan to sell financing bonds that will be retired by corporate sponsors and local bed taxes is approved. The record industry also donates $5 million to the hall. A final tax plan is approved by state officials the following February.

1993

January 12: The annual induction ceremony moves to Los Angeles at Century Plaza, Staged with little fanfare, fewer than two dozen stargazing fans show up to catch a glimpse of rock's royalty.

April 6: K. Michael Benz announces his resignation as the hall's executive director.

June 7: To the music of the Rolling Stones' "Satisfaction," Chuck Berry, Pete Townshend, and Billy Joel turn over the inaugural shovels of dirt at the Hall of Fame groundbreaking ceremony. Townshend tells the jubilant lunchtime crowd of 5,000 that he hopes the hall "doesn't become a monolith to a bunch of dinosaurs."

August 11: Replacing Bruce Harrah-Conforth, controversial figure Dennis Barrie is named the director of the Rock Hall, signing a three-year contract.

December 8: James Henke is named chief curator of the Rock and Roll Hall of Fame and Museum.

1994

July 28: A topping-off ceremony marking the placement of the final beam is attended by 5,000. Rock Hall officials announce the museum's first major sponsor, Radio Shack, which enters into a five-year agreement worth $15 million. (Ford had donated $250,000 in 1989.)

December 6: Fashion designer Stephen Sprouse is named costume curator, in charge of the museum's 100 mannequins.

1995

April: Moody Blues fans deliver a 5,000 name petition to the nominating committee.

June 6: The concert for the Hall of Fame is announced; ticket prices range from $30 to $540.

August 21: The Rock Hall goes on line; its World Wide Web address is http://www.rockhall.com/

August 24: Cleveland radio station WMMS is the first to broadcast from the Rock Hall's working, state-of-the-art broadcast studio. The first out-of-state station to use the facility is WXRT of Chicago.

September 1: Attended by 30,000, the Rock Hall ribbon-cutting ceremony features Yoko Ono, Little Richard, and numerous other rock and political dignitaries. Costing $92 million, the museum was tagged at $15 million nine years earlier.

September 2: Escorted by the Supreme's Mary Wilson, James Brown cuts the red ribbon opening the museum's HMV record store. In its first year of operation, profits would surpass initial expectations by four fold.

September 2: The Concert for the Rock and Roll Hall of Fame is staged at the 65-year-old Cleveland Stadium to a crowd of 63,515. Broadcast on HBO, the $4 million dollar production is billed as "the concert of a lifetime," as musicians are paired in never-before combinations on a revolving stage. Acts include Chuck Berry, Al Green, the Kinks, Bruce Springsteen, and hometown singer Chrissie Hynde. The event is emceed by local deejay Len "Boom Boom" Goldberg and former WMMS deejay-turned-record-executive "Kid Leo" Travagliante.

September: Curator Jim Henke issues the much criticized list, "The 500 most influential songs in rock history."

September 16: Meat Loaf became the first artist to debut an album at the Rock Hall.

October 12: William N. Hulett is appointed the Rock Hall's chief executive officer.

November 13: Buckling to critics, the Rock Hall opens on Mondays for a seven-day-a week schedule.

1996

January: Following Cleveland's lead, neighboring Pittsburgh studies the feasibility of a jazz hall of fame while Cincinnati plans a classical music hall of fame.

January 1: The hall records 353,000 visitors in four months, with an average stay of 4 ½ hours.

January 18: A premature announcement by Ahmet Ertegun grants Cleveland the induction ceremonies in 1997. Executive director Suzan Evans and others initially dispute the report.

January 23: Museum director Dennis Barrie unexpectedly announces his resignation, effective March 1, amid rumors that he was forced out by the New York board.

February 20: Jim Henke delivers the first annual Curator's Lecture to the museum's platinum-level members.

April 12: The Rock Hall kicks off its "Hall of Fame Lecture Series," with Ray Davies of the Kinks. Other speakers will include the Allman Brothers Band, the Byrds' Roger McGuinn, Aretha Franklin, Little Richard, Ruth Brown, Leiber & Stoller and producer Jerry Wexler.

April 18: The hall announces a 22,500-square-foot expansion, prompted by the hall's unexpected success as a meeting hall, hosting corporate functions, weddings and high school proms. In July the figure is revised to 30,000 square-feet at a cost of $10 million.

May 8: A nationwide teachers teleconference, "The Kids Are Alright: Rock and Roll Culture, Education and Youth Culture," airs via PBS' Adult Learning Service. The event is hosted by the Rock Hall's education direction, Robert Santelli.

August 7: The first educational travel program takes Rock Hall members on a weeklong guided tour of Jamaica to learn about reggae.

August 14: Premiering at the Rock Hall, the documentary *Freebird: The Movie* is attended by several Lynyrd Skynyrd veterans. The film opens nationwide two days later.

August 23: The museum welcomes its 1 millionth visitor, Cathy McDonell, who is awarded a classic 1965 Mustang convertible and 200 Ohio lottery tickets.

August 27: Columbia Records releases the 2-CD set *CONCERT FOR THE ROCK AND ROLL HALL OF FAME*, capturing 28 of the 68 performances. Notably absent from the project are Eric Burdon, Sheryl Crow, Little Richard and Chuck Berry.

September 20: Three exhibits debut: "Hard Travelin': The Life and Legacy of Woody Guthrie"; "Bang Your Head: Three Decades of Hard Rock and Heavy Metal"; and "Voices: Rock and Roll's Invisible Instruments." The latter replaces Pink Floyd's "The Wall" exhibit, which sent to a museum in San Francisco.

September 20: The 660,000-name petition, which helped Cleveland land the Rock Hall, is included in a local time capsule, not be opened until Cleveland's tricentennial in 2096.

October 1: A new exhibit, "Stand By Me: The Songs of Leiber & Stoller," traces the songwriting team's accomplishments.

October 11: Melissa Etheridge performs at Cleveland's Gund Arena to benefit the Rock Hall on its first anniversary, filling just 5,000 seats of the 20,562-seat venue.

December 12: AT&T pledges $5 million to construct a replacement Hall of Fame chamber, which will be moved from the sixth to the third floor.

1997

January 1: Adult admission price is boosted from $10.90 to $12.95.

January 17: The hall launches a traveling exhibit, scheduled to hit 40 cities in 11 months. The exhibit debuts in Fort Worth, Texas.

January 24: A new exhibit "My Town" traces Cleveland's rock music history and features Michael Stanley, the O'Jays, Devo, the Raspberries, Pere Ubu, Nine Inch Nails, and Bone Thugs-N-Harmony.

February 17: A new exhibit "Draw the Line: The Art of the Album Cover" features the original rock artwork of John Kosh, Joel Berstein, Andy Warhol, and others.

March 12: The Hall of Fame reports a 40-percent drop in attendance from a year earlier.

May 5: William Hulett resigns as Hall of Fame CEO and cochairman.

May 6: The induction ceremony moves to Cleveland on a rotational city basis. Tickets to the event sell out in two weeks.

May 15: The unveiling of "I Want to Take You Higher: Rock and Roll in the Psychedelic Era" exhibit coincides with the 30th anniversary of San Francisco's Summer of Love. A portion of the hall has been closed since April 1 to accommodate construction.

July 4: The Hall of Fame launches a weekly, nine-installment syndicated radio show, "I Want to Take You Higher: The Psychedelic Era 1965 to 1969," heard on 73 stations.

September 15: Teaming with the Country Hall of Fame in Memphis, the Rock Hall stages a conference on country music pioneer Jimmie Rodgers.

November 17: The Democratic National Committee (DNC) holds a controversial fund-raising dinner at the Hall of Fame. Vice President Al Gore is the featured speaker.

November 20: A new exhibit "Whole Lotta Shakin' Goin' on" highlights early rockers Bobby Darin, Ritchie Valens, Ricky Nelson and others.

1998

January 9: Interim executive director David T. Abbott is named the executive director of the Rock and Roll Hall of Fame. Chief curator James Henke is given the additional title of deputy director.

January 12: The induction ceremony returns to New York. The annual jam session has been cut from the evening's festivities.

January 20: Freelance photographer Charles Gentile wins his lawsuit against the Hall of Fame which had charged that his posters of the museum were a trademark infringement. A federal appeals court judge rules that the taxpayer-funded building is a public site.

February: The Rock and Roll Hall of Fame teams up with *Rolling Stone* to present a 20 city traveling exhibition "The Rolling Stone Covers Tour," in celebration of the magazine's 30th anniversary.

February: An exhibit showcasing 1970s progressive rock opens.

April 2: The redesigned "Hall of Fame" portion of the museum opens.

August: A major Elvis Presley exhibit is unveiled. Many of the artifacts are on loan from Graceland and include his army uniform.

Selected Bibliography

Allan, Tony & Treadwell, Faye. (1993). *Save the Last Dance For Me: The Musical Legacy of the Drifters, 1953-1993*. Ann Arbor, MI: Popular Culture Ink.

Archer, Robyn & Simmonds, Diana. (1986). *A Star Is Torn*. New York: E.P. Dutton.

Bego, Mark. (1989). *Aretha Franklin: The Queen of Soul*. New York: St. Martin's Press.

Belz, Carl. (1969). *The Story of Rock*. New York: Oxford University Press.

Bernardin, Claude & Stanton, Tom. (1995). *Rocket Man: The Encyclopedia of Elton John*. Westport, CT: Greenwood Press.

Berry, Chuck. (1987). *Chuck Berry: The Autobiography*. New York: Harmony.

Blesh, Rudi. (1979). *Combo USA: Eight Lives in Jazz*. New York: Da Capo.

Boyer, Horace Clarence. (1995). *How Sweet the Sound: The Golden Age of Gospel*. Washington, DC: Elliott & Clark.

Britt, Stan. (1984). *The Jazz Guitarists*. Poole, England: Blanford.

Bronson, Fred. (1992). *The Billboard Book of Number One Hits*, (3rd ed.). New York: Billboard.

Broughton, Viv. (1985). *Black Gospel: An Illustrated History of the Gospel Sound*. Poole, England: Blanford.

Broven, John. (1978). *Rhythm & Blues in New Orleans*. Gretna, LA: Pelican.

Cantor, Louis. (1992). *Wheelin' on the Beale*. New York: Pharos.

Caress, Jay. (1979). *Hank Williams: Country Music's Tragic King*. New York: Stein and Day.

Charles, Ray & Ritz, David. (1978). *Brother Ray: Ray Charles' Own Story*. New York: Warner.

Chilton, John. (1994). *Let the Good Times Roll: The Story of Louis Jordan*. Ann Arbor: University of Michigan Press.

Clark, Dick & Robinson, Richard. (1976). *Rock, Roll & Remember*. New York: Crowell.

Collier, James Lincoln. (1989). *Benny Goodman and the Swing Era*. New York: Oxford University Press.

Collins, Ace. (1996). *The Stories Behind Country Music's All-Time Greatest 100 Songs*. New York: Boulevard.

Cott, Jonathan & Doudna, Christine (Eds.). (1982). *The Ballad of John and Yoko*. Garden City, NY: Rolling Stone.

Dance, Helen Oakley. (1987). *Stormy Monday: The T-Bone Walker Story*. Baton Rouge: Louisiana State University Press.

Davis, Sharon. (1988). *Motown: The History*. London: Guinness.

Davis, Stephen. (1986). *Hammer of the Gods*. New York: Ballantine.

Dawson, Jim & Propes, Steve. (1992). *What Was the First Rock 'N' Roll Record*. Boston: Faber and Faber.

DeWitt, Howard A. (1993). *Elvis, the Sun Years: The Story of Elvis Presley in the Fifties*. Ann Arbor, MI: Popular Culture Ink.

Dixon, Robert M.W. & Godrich, John. (1970). *Recording the Blues*. New York: Stein and Day.

Eliot, Marc. (1993). *Rockonomics: The Money Behind the Music*. New York: Citadel.

Eremo, Judie (Ed.). (1987). *Country Musicians*. Cupertino, CA: GPI.

Elson, Howard. (1982). *Early Rockers*. New York: Proteus.

Ewen, David. (1970). *Great Men of American Popular Song* (pp. 116-22). Englewood Cliffs, NJ: Prentice-Hall.

Flanagan, Bill. (1986). *Written in My Soul*. New York: Contemporary.

Friedland, Will. (1990). *Jazz Singing: America's Great Voices From Bessie Smith to Bebop and Beyond*. New York: Charles Scribner's Sons.

Gart, Galen. (1986). *First Pressings: Volume One*. Milford, NH: Big Nickel.

Giddens, Gary. (1981). *Riding on a Blue Note: Jazz and American Pop*. New York: Oxford.

Gillett, Charlie. (1974). *Making Tracks*. New York: E.P. Dutton.

Goldman, Vivian. (1981). *Bob Marley: Soul Rebel/Natural Mystic*. New York: St. Martin's.

Guralnick, Peter. (1989). *Searching for Robert Johnson*. New York: Obelisk-Dutton.

Haley, John W. & von Hoelle, John. (1990). *Sound and Glory*. Wilmington, DE: Dyne-American.

Hammond, John & Townsend, Irving. (1977). *John Hammond on Record: An Autobiography*. New York: Ridge/Summit.

Hampton, Wayne. (1986). *Guerrilla Minstrels*. Knoxville: The University of Tennessee Press.

Harris, Craig. (1991). *The New Folk Music*. Crown Point, IN: White Cliffs Media.

Handy, W.C. (1941). *Father of the Blues*. New York: Macmillan.

Heilbut, Anthony. (1985). *The Gospel Sound: Good News and Bad Times* (rev. ed.). Limelight: New York.

Herbst, Peter (Ed.). (1981). *The Rolling Stone Interviews*. New York: St. Martin's.

Heylin, Clinton. (1993). *From the Velvets to the Voidoids: A Pre-Punk History for a Post-Punk World*. New York: Penguin.

Hildebrand, Lee & O'Neal, Mary Lovelace. (1995). *Colors and Chords: The Art of Johnny Otis*. San Francisco: Pomegranate Art Books.

Hirshey, Gerri. (1984). *Nowhere to Run: The Story of Soul Music*. New York: Times Books.

Hopkins, Jerry. (1971). *Elvis*. New York: Simon & Schuster.

Jackson, John A. (1991). *Big Beat Heat: Alan Freed and the Early Years of Rock & Roll*. New York: Schirmer.

Jackson, Mahalia & Wylie, Evan McLeod. (1966). *Movin' On Up*. New York: Hawthorn.

James, Etta & Ritz, David. (1995). *The Etta James Story: Rage to Survive*. New York: Villard.

Jancik, Wayne. (1990). *The Billboard Book of One Hit Wonders*. New York: Billboard.

Jancik, Wayne & Lathrop, Tad. (1995). *Cult Rockers*. New York: Fireside.

John, Elton. (1991). *Two Rooms: Elton John & Bernie Taupin in their own Words*. London: Boxtree.

Jones, Hettie. (1995). *Big Star Fallin' Mama* (rev. ed). New York: Viking.

Jones, Max. (1988). *Talking Jazz*. New York: W.W. Norton.

Kiersh, Edward. (1986). *Where Are You Now, Bo Diddley?* Garden City, NY: Doubleday.

Krieger, Susan. (1979). *Hip Capitalism*. Beverly Hills, CA: Sage.

Lewis, Myra & Silver, Murray. (1982). *Great Balls of Fire: The Uncensored Story of Jerry Lee Lewis*. New York: St. Martin's.

Little Richard & White, Charles. (1984). *The Life and Times of Little Richard*. New York: Harmony.

Lydon, Michael. (1971). *Folk Rock*. New York: Citadel.

Martin, Linda & Segrave, Kerry. (1988). *Anti-Rock: The Opposition to Rock 'n' Roll*. New York: Da Capo.

McDonough, Jack. (1985). *San Francisco Rock*. San Francisco: Chronicle.

McKeen, William. (1993). *Bob Dylan: A Bio-Bibliography*. Westport, CT: Greenwood Press.

Millar, Bill. (1971). *The Drifters: The Rise and Fall of the Black Vocal Group*. New York: Macmillan.

Norman, Philip. (1984). *The Stones*. New York: Simon & Schuster.

O'Brien, Lucy. (1995). *She Bop: The Definitive History of Women in Rock, Pop and Soul*. New York: Penguin.

Oliver, Paul. (1959). *Bessie Smith*. New York: Perpetua.

O'Neil, Thomas. (1993). *The Grammys: For the Record*. New York: Penguin.

Otis, Johnny. (1968). *Listen to the Lambs*. New York: W.W. Norton.

Palmer, Robert. (1978). *Baby, That Was Rock & Roll: The Legendary Leiber & Stoller*. New York: Harcourt Brace Jovanovich.

Paris, Mike & Comber, Chris. (1981). *Jimmie the Kid: The Life of Jimmie Rodgers*. New York: Da Capo.

Passman, Arnold. (1971). *The Deejays*. New York: Macmillan.

Perkins, Carl & Rendleman, Ron. (1978). *Disciple in Blue Suede Shoes*. Grand Rapids, MI: Zondervan.

Phillips, John & Jerome, Jim. (1986). *Papa John*. Garden City, NY: Dolphin.

Phillips, Michelle. (1986). *California Dreamin': The True Story of the Mamas and the Papas*. New York: Warner.

Pitts, Leonard, Jr. (1984). *Mr. Wonderful*. Cresskill, NJ: Sharon.

Pollock, Bruce. (1981). *When Rock Was Young*. New York: Holt, Rineholt, and Winston.

Pomerance, Alan. (1988). *Repeal of the Blues: How Black Entertainers Influenced Civil Rights*. Secaucus, NJ: Citadel.

Pratt, Ray. (1990). *Rhythm and Resistance: Explorations in the Political Uses of Popular Music*. New York: Praeger.

Presley, Priscilla. (1985). *Elvis and Me*. New York: Putman.

Pruter, Robert. (1991). *Chicago Soul*. Urbana: University of Chicago Press.

Riedel, Johannnes. (1975). *Soul Music Black and White: The Influences of Black Music on the Churches*. Minneapolis: Augsburg.

Ritz, David. (1985). *Divided Soul: The Life of Marvin Gaye*. New York: McGraw-Hill.

Robinson, Smokey & Ritz, David. (1989). *Smokey: Inside My Life*. New York: McGraw-Hill.

Rock Guitarists. (1974). Saratoga, CA: Guitar Player Productions.

Roland, Tom. (1991). *The Billboard Book of Number One Country Hits*. New York: Billboard.

Schuller, Gunther. (1989). *The Swing Era: The Development of Jazz, 1930-1945*. New York: Oxford University Press.

Scott, Barry. (1994). *We Had Joy, We Had Fun: The "Lost" Recording Artists of the Seventies*. Boston: Faber and Faber.

Sculatti, Gene & Seay, Davin. (1985). *San Francisco Nights: The Psychedelic Music Trip,*

1965-1968. New York: St. Martin's.

Selvin, Joel. (1994). *Summer of Love*. New York: Dutton.

Shapiro, Harry & Glebbeek, Caesar. (1990). *Jimi Hendrix: Electric Gypsy*. New York: St. Martin's.

Shaw, Arnold. (1978). *Honkers and Shouters: The Golden Years of Rhythm and Blues*. New York: Collier.

Silvester, Peter J. (1988). *A Left Hand Like God: A History of Boogie-Woogie Piano*. New York: Da Capo.

Smith, Joe. (1988). *Off the Record*. New York: Warner.

Smith, John L. (comp.). (1985). *The Johnny Cash Discography*. Westport, CT: Greenwood Press.

Smith, Richard D. (1995). *Bluegrass: An Informal Guide*. Chicago: A Capella.

Swaggert, Jimmy & Lamb, Robert Paul. (1977). *To Cross a River*. Plainfield, NJ: Logos International.

Taraborrelli, Randy J. (1986). *Motown: Hot Wax, City Cool & Solid Gold*. Garden City, NY: Dolphin/Doubleday.

Taylor, Don & Henry, Mike. (1995). *Marley and Me: The Real Bob Marley Story*. New York: Barricade.

Thiele, Bob & Golden, Bob. (1995). *What a Wonderful World: A Lifetime of Recordings*. New York: Oxford University Press.

Tosches, Nick. (1982). *Hellfire: The Jerry Lee Lewis Story*. New York: Delacorte.

Tracy, Steven C. (1993). *Going to Cincinnati: A History of the Blues in the Queen City*. Urbana: University of Illinois Press.

Turner, Steve. (1993). *Van Morrison: Too Late to Stop Now*. New York: Viking.

Wade, Dorothy & Picardie, Justine. (1990). *Music Man: Ahmet Ertegun, Atlantic Records, and the Triumph of Rock 'n' Roll*. New York: Norton.

Watson, Deek & Stephenson, Lee. (1967). *The Story of the Ink Spots*. New York: Vantage.

Wexler, Jerry & Ritz, David. (1993). *Rhythm and the Blues: A Life in American Music*. New York: Alfred A. Knopf.

White, Adam & Bronson, Fred. (1993). *The Billboard Book of Number One Rhythm & Blues Hits*. New York: Billboard.

White, Mark. (1985). *You Must Remember This: Popular Songwriters 1900-1980*. New York: Charles Scribner's Sons.

White, Timothy. (1990). *Rock Lives: Profiles & Interviews*. New York: Henry Holt.

Williams, Martin T. (Ed.). (1962). *Jazz Panorama*. New York: Crowell-Collier.

Williams, Richard. (1972). *Out of His Head: The Sound of Phil Spector*. New York: Outbridge & Lazard.

Wolf, Daniel & Crain, S.R. (1995). *You Send Me: The Life and Times of Sam Cooke*. New York: William Morrow.

Wolfman Jack & Laursen, Byron. (1995). *Have Mercy*. New York: Warner.

Index